EU Electricity Trade Law

Petri Mäntysaari

EU Electricity Trade Law

The Legal Tools of Electricity Producers in the Internal Electricity Market

Springer

Petri Mäntysaari
Dept. of Accounting and Commercial Law
Hanken School of Economics
Vaasa
Finland

ISBN 978-3-319-16512-7 ISBN 978-3-319-16513-4 (eBook)
DOI 10.1007/978-3-319-16513-4

Library of Congress Control Number: 2015938910

Springer Cham Heidelberg New York Dordrecht London

Printed on acid-free paper

Springer International Publishing AG Switzerland is part of Springer Science+Business Media (www.springer.com)

Preface

The target for the completion of the internal electricity market was 2014. The NWE region leads the way in market integration.

The gradual emergence of an internal electricity market has changed the legal and commercial landscape for wholesale electricity market participants. The most important wholesale market participants are electricity producers.

This book has four principal aims. The first is to describe the characteristic objectives of electricity producers in electricity wholesale markets. The second is to find out what legal tools and practices electricity producers can use to reach their characteristic objectives in the NWE region. Third, the book describes the regulation of the internal electricity market at EU level from the perspective of wholesale electricity producers. Fourth, this book contributes to theory-building in commercial law. Commercial law research—and legal science in general—can give an alternative view of markets if it focuses on the study of actual market behaviour through the lense of market participants' legal tools and legal practices.

Vaasa, Finland Petri Mäntysaari

Abbreviations

ACER	Agency for the Cooperation of Energy Regulators
BaFin	Bundesanstalt für Finanzdienstleistungsaufsicht
BGB	Bürgerliches Gesetzbuch
BSC	Balancing and Settlement Code
CACM	Capacity Allocation and Congestion Management
CACM Regulation	Draft Commission Regulation (EU) No . . ./.. establishing a Guideline on Capacity Allocation and Congestion Management
CAISO	The California Independent System Operator
CASC	Capacity Allocation Service Company
CCS	Carbon capture and storage
CEER	Council of European Energy Regulators
CFTC	The Commodity Futures Trading Commission
CfD	Contract for Difference
CHP	Combined heat and power
CISG	Convention on the International Sale of Goods
CJEU	The Court of Justice of the European Union
CM	Clearing Member
Commission	European Commission
CRD IV	Directive 2013/36/EU of the European Parliament and of the Council of 26 June 2013 on access to the activity of credit institutions and the prudential supervision of credit institutions and investment firms, amending Directive 2002/87/EC and repealing Directives 2006/48/EC and 2006/49/EC
CRR	Regulation (EU) No 575/2013 of the European Parliament and of the Council of 26 June 2013 on prudential requirements for credit institutions and investment firms and amending Regulation (EU) No 648/2012
CWE	Central Western Europe
DCUSA	The Distribution Connection and Use of System Agreement

DCFR	Draft Common Frame of Reference
DG	European Commission, Directorate General
DSO	Distribution System Operator
ECC	European Commodity Clearing AG
ECR	European Court Reports
EEG	Gesetz für den Vorrang erneuerbarer Energien (Erneuerbare-Energien-Gesetz)
EEX	European Energy Exchange AG
EFET	European Federation of Energy Traders
EMCC	European Market Coupling Company GmbH
EMIR	Regulation (EU) No 648/2012 of the European Parliament and of the Council of 4 July 2012 on OTC derivatives, central counterparties and trade repositories
ENTSO-E	European Network of Transmission System Operators for Electricity
EnWG	Gesetz über die Elektrizitäts- und Gasversorgung (Energiewirtschaftsgesetz)
EPAD	Electricity Price Area Differential
ERGEG	European Regulators Group for Electricity and Gas
FCR	Frequency Containment Reserves
FERC	The Federal Energy Regulatory Commission
FRR	Frequency Restoration Reserves
FTR	Financial Transmission Right
GCM	General Clearing Member
ISDA	International Swaps and Derivatives Association, Inc.
ISO	Independent System Operator
ITVC	Interim Tight Volume Coupling
KWG	Kreditwesengesetz
LFCR	Load-Frequency Control and Reserves
MAD II	Directive 2014/57/EU of the European Parliament and of the Council of 16 April 2014 on criminal sanctions for market abuse (market abuse directive)
MAD, MAD I	Directive 2003/6/EC of the European Parliament and of the Council of 28 January 2003 on insider dealing and market manipulation (market abuse)
MAR	Regulation (EU) No 596/2014 of the European Parliament and of the Council of 16 April 2014 on market abuse (market abuse regulation) and repealing Directive 2003/6/EC of the European Parliament and of the Council and Commission Directives 2003/124/EC, 2003/125/EC and 2004/72/EC
MCO	Market Coupling Operator
MiFID II	Directive 2014/65/EU of the European Parliament and of the Council of 15 May 2014 on markets in financial instruments and amending Directive 2002/92/EC and Directive 2011/61/EU (recast)

MiFID, MiFID I	Directive 2004/39/EC of the European Parliament and of the Council of 21 April 2004 on markets in financial instruments amending Council Directives 85/611/EEC and 93/6/EEC and Directive 2000/12/EC of the European Parliament and of the Council and repealing Council Directive 93/22/EEC
MiFIR	Regulation (EU) No 600/2014 of the European Parliament and of the Council of 15 May 2014 on markets in financial instruments and amending Regulation (EU) No 648/2012
NC CACM	Network Code for Capacity Allocation and Congestion Management
NC FCA	Network Code on Forward Capacity Allocation
NC RfG	Network Code on Requirements for Grid Connection applicable to all Generators
NC	Network Code
NEMO	Nominated Electricity Market Operator
NordREG	Nordic Energy Regulators
NOU	Norges offentlige utredninger
NPS	Nord Pool Spot AS
NRA	National Regulatory Authority
NVE	Norges vassdrags- og energidirektorat
NWE	North-Western Europe
NYISO	The New York Independent System Operator
Ofgem	Office of Gas and Electricity Markets
OTC	Over-the-counter
Ot.prp.	Odelstingsproposisjon
PCR	Price Coupling of Regions
PSH	Pumped storage hydropower
PTR	Physical Transmission Right
REMIT	Regulation (EU) No 1227/2011 of the European Parliament and of the Council of 25 October 2011 on wholesale energy market integrity and transparency
RES-E	Electricity generated from renewable sources
RR	Restoration Reserves
RTO	Regional Transmission Organization
SEC	The Securities and Exchange Commission
SOU	Statens Offentliga Utredningar
SWE	South-Western Europe
TCC	Transmission Congestion Contract
TEU	The Treaty on European Union
TFEU	The Treaty on the Functioning of the European Union
TSO	Transmission System Operator
UCC, U.C.C.	Uniform Commercial Code

USC, U.S.C.	United States Code
UIOLI principle	The use-it-or-lose-it principle
UIOSI principle	The use-it-or-sell-it principle
ULIS	Convention relating to a Uniform Law on the International Sale of Goods

Contents

Part IV Financial Contracts

Chapter 1
Introduction

The basis of wholesale electricity markets is electricity trade at transmission grid level. The generation business is at the heart of wholesale electricity markets. There is no physical electricity to be supplied, consumed, transmitted, or traded, unless it is generated. Obviously, electricity producers matter.[1]

Electricity generation is one of the riskiest of industrial activities. It is capital intensive and requires large long-term investments in generation installations that tend to have no alternative uses (asset specificity).[2]

Investments in generation assets are influenced by wholesale electricity prices and electricity producers' risk exposure. Wholesale electricity prices are determined on electricity exchanges. They will play an increasingly important role in the future as more products will be exchange-traded because of market regulation.[3] If wholesale prices are distorted, investment in generation will be distorted as well.[4]

Electricity Producers Similar to all other firms and electricity market participants, electricity producers have their own interests. They are not identical with the interests of system operators[5] or with regulators' interests. For example, a firm is

[1] Electricity networks matter as well. In 2000, the National Academy of Engineering (US) selected and ranked the engineering achievements with the greatest impact on quality of life in the twentieth century. The top achievement was electrification—"the vast networks of electricity that power the developed world".

[2] Thomas S (2001), pp. 94–95; Bhattacharyya SC (2011), pp. 163–165.

[3] See, for example, Article 12(2) of Regulation 714/2009 on conditions for access to the network for cross-border exchanges in electricity.

[4] See, for example, Joskow PL (2008), pp. 161–162.

[5] For the interests of TSOs, see Supponen M (2011), p. 4.

P. Mäntysaari, *EU Electricity Trade Law*, DOI 10.1007/978-3-319-16513-4_1

not in the business of electricity production just to increase general welfare or consumer benefits,[6] but the invisible hand of competition between electricity producers can increase production efficiency and even benefit consumers in the long run. Neither is a firm in the business of electricity supply or distribution to sell at the lowest prices,[7] but prices can reflect the level of competition in the long run.

This book focuses on the legal tools and practices, which electricity producers use to reach their commercial objectives in the Nordic and Western Central European wholesale markets that are the core of the NWE area.

The topic is interesting from a wider perspective. Electricity markets are in the process of being liberalised.[8] European wholesale markets have been undergoing a major change because of ambitious EU-wide policy objectives. In February 2011, the European Council set the target of 2014 for the completion of the internal electricity market. The European Council summed up the required measures as follows: "This requires in particular that in cooperation with ACER national regulators and transmission systems operators step up their work on market coupling and guidelines and on network codes applicable across European networks".[9] To illustrate, EU electricity law now requires the use of market-based mechanisms, that is, implicit or explicit auctions for the allocation of cross-border or cross-zonal transmission capacity with continuous trading as an option for intraday trade.[10] EU electricity law also requires the preferential treatment of electricity generated from renewable sources (RES-E).

Whether the broad policy objectives will be reached depends on how market regulation affects electricity producers in the wholesale market.[11]

---

[6] Compare Hunt S and Shuttleworth G (1996), pp. 77 and xi. The authors chose the utility regulator's perspective rather than the firm's perspective in Part I of their book.

[7] Compare, however, Joined Cases T-80/06 and T-182/09 Budapesti Erőmű Zrt v Commission, ECLI:EU:T:2012:65, para 83: "... MVM's commercial objective, like that of any electricity wholesaler faced with the same obligations and market conditions as MVM, was to supply the regulated segment of the Hungarian retail market at the lowest prices ...".

[8] See OECD/IEA (2005), pp. 28–29 and 42–43. In the UK, a government white paper (Privatising Electricity, February 1988) was followed up with the Electricity Act 1989. See OECD/IEA (2005), p. 171. The Nordic market started in Norway in 1991 after the entry into force of the Energy Act 1990 (energiloven). The other Nordic countries joined during the second half of the 1990s. See OECD/IEA (2005), p. 171. For Europe generally, see Chicco G (2009).

[9] European Council, 4 February 2011, Conclusions.

[10] Point 2.1 of Annex I (Guidelines on the management and allocation of available transfer capacity of interconnections between national systems) to Regulation 714/2009 on conditions for access to the network for cross-border exchanges in electricity.

[11] See, for example, ACER/CEER (2013), p. 28: "In the long run, network access and wholesale market integration should cascade to retail markets, because integration at wholesale level contributes to serving total demand at least cost".

Physical and Financial Contracts The starting point in this book is the contract for the physical supply of electricity. It is the most important contract type for electricity producers and end consumers in electricity wholesale markets.[12] Other contracts, tools, and practices either facilitate the conclusion and performance of electricity supply contracts or are designed to complement them.

Physical electricity can be traded in various ways. Standardised contracts can be traded on an exchange. The majority of electricity trading occurs in the OTC market where trading is bilateral and contracts are not standardised. Structured contracts are bilateral and usually long-term contracts between an electricity producer and an end consumer or distributor.[13] Electricity producers use financial contracts to manage price risk and volumetric risk.

Objectives, Legal Tools and Practices The "liberalisation" of electricity markets has increased the number and diversity of market participants. Obviously, each participant has its own particular commercial objectives in the electricity market, and each participant uses its own combination of legal tools and practices to reach them.

However, there are patterns of behaviour shared by all market participants, which belong to the same class. These patterns of behaviour can be explained by the participants' similar high-level objectives and the particular characteristics of electricity and the electricity trade.

The behaviour of electricity producers as electricity market participants is studied here by studying their legal tools and practices. It should be possible to describe how electricity markets work and predict patterns of behaviour by using legal concepts rather than economic concepts or concepts borrowed from other social sciences.[14]

All Transactions At a higher level of generality, all firms work in similar ways. It is this general assumption that underlies management science and economics. For the purposes of commercial law, one could say that all firms share the same objectives in all transactions at a high level of generality.[15]

One may assume that there are firms—organisations—which try to survive in the long term. For this purpose, these firms manage: cash-flow and the exchange of goods and services; risk; principal-agency relationships; and information.

Moreover, all firms use a combination of five generic types of legal tools and practices, which are present in all transactions. They include: the choice of a business form; contracts, regulatory compliance and organisational measures;

---

[12] See, for example, OECD/IEA (2005), p. 100.

[13] See, for example, Ofgem (2009), paras 1.15–1.18.

[14] Mäntysaari P (2013). For Management-based Commercial Law (MBCL), see Mäntysaari P (2011, 2012). The "function-based legal design and analysis" (FULDA) method is a related approach. See Knops HPA (2007).

[15] Generally, see Mäntysaari P (2010, 2011, 2012).

generic ways to manage principal-agency relationships; and generic ways to manage information.

Context Depending on the commercial context, firms customarily manage particular characteristic issues in addition to the general issues managed in all transactions. For example, firms manage risks in all transactions, but they tend to manage particular risks depending on the context.

Electricity Trade In the context of electricity trade, parties must address particular issues because of physical laws and efficiency constraints (Sect. 2.5). The electricity producer thus manages not only generic issues such as cash flow and risk but even these particular issues. They include: (a) grid access, delivery point, and voltage level; (b) volume; (c) transmission and distribution capacity; (d) balance; (e) measurement; (f) separation of physical rights, service rights, and financial rights; and (g) price volatility. Distinguishing between general and particular issues helps to understand what is characteristic of electricity markets.

This distinction between general and particular issues has not been made in the past. For example, the risks that electricity market participants are exposed to have been classified in various ways: (a) According to Hunt S and Shuttleworth G (1996), an electricity producer is subject to: market price risk (market price may be higher or lower than expected); sales quantity risk (market conditions influence output); fuel price risk (fuel prices may rise and fall); and availability risk (a power plant may not always be available to run)[16]; (b) In addition to various kinds of market operation risks, an electricity producer is exposed to regulatory risks,[17] weather risks, and uncertainty according to Perrels A and Kemppi H (2003)[18]; (c) According to Spicker J (2010), the risks that an electricity market participant is exposed to in OTC trade include: price risks, volumetric risks, currency risks, open positions, estimation risks, transformation risks (relating to merchantability as wholesale products should be transformed into retail products), organisational risks, and credit risks.[19]

Some of these risks—such as credit risk and various forms of counterparty risk, including legal and regulatory risk—are general and managed in all transactions. Other risks may be particular risks managed in electricity transactions.

Business Models Each market participant uses a business model. Large industrial consumers, retail distributors, portfolio managers, brokers, electricity wholesalers, and electricity producers use different business models. This book focuses on the business models of the electricity producer. They include both generation and supply and trading.

[16] Hunt S and Shuttleworth G (1996), p. 121.

[17] For example, discrimination (preferential treatment of RES-E) and change of the regulatory framework (political and legal risk).

[18] Perrels A and Kemppi H (2003), p. 33, Table 4.1.

[19] Spicker J (2010), pp. 138–139, point 237.

Regulation, No Liberalisation of the Wholesale Market for Electricity Producers From a regulatory perspective, the key to achieving the benefits of competition is to introduce competition in as many parts of the value chain as possible—from generation to consumption.[20]

At the same time, electricity markets must be highly regulated for operational reasons. To illustrate, electricity producers would not gain access to electricity markets without a large regulatory framework.[21] Another example is the use of marginal pricing. According to this pricing and trading principle facilitated by market regulation, the last accepted bid sets the price for the whole market.[22]

The level of regulation depends on the choice of perspective. There is more central planning and more regulation where market regulation is designed to foster economic efficiency by maximising the global surplus of market agents.[23] There is less regulation where each market participant has discretion to act according to its own interests without any third party trying to estimate what the maximum global surplus should be.

Where central planning is replaced by the discretion of market participants, markets are liberalised. The discretion of market participants is limited, for instance, where the regulatory framework imposes a duty to deal,[24] where it provides for price controls, where the regulatory authorities have discretion to accept or refuse investment, and so forth.

In any case, there are ways to liberalise wholesale markets for electricity producers and ways to liberalise retail markets for end consumers. They are not the same thing. The EU seems to have focused on liberalising retail markets from a consumer perspective rather than physical wholesale markets from a producer perspective.

The regulation of physical wholesale markets at the EU level is largely from central planning with several contradictory objectives. The objectives are not limited to ensuring that competition is free and to increasing the liquidity[25] and

---

[20] OECD/IEA (2005), pp. 15 and 47.

[21] See Hunt S and Shuttleworth G (1996), pp. 3–4, citing Joskow PL and Schmalensee R (1983). Hunt and Shuttleworth mentioned: (1) a regional transmission-coordination system with interconnected generating plants; (2) a mechanism for dispatching generating plants that facilitates control but permits and encourages economic (least cost) dispatch; (3) a method for coordinating unit commitment and maintenance; (4) a method for ensuring that adequate generating capacity is built; (5) a method for ensuring minimum cost investment; and (6) a method for dealing with emergencies.

[22] OECD/IEA (2005), pp. 72–73.

[23] Pérez-Arriaga IJ and Smeers Y (2003), pp. 175–176: "Economic efficiency mandates that prices should be chosen to maximise the global surplus of the market agents, both in the operation of the power system (short-term), and in their investment decisions, including the choice of a location (long-term), by sending the appropriate network-related economic signals".

[24] Laying down a duty to deal belongs to the central regulatory tools in electricity markets. See Hermes (2002).

[25] Liquidity is reduced by vertical integration. DG Competition report on energy sector inquiry, SEC(2006) 1724, 10 January 2007, para 451. Indications of liquidity include the churn ratio (the

transparency of electricity wholesale markets.[26] They include even the operational efficiency of the electricity system and fostering the use of particular generation technologies that are not efficient (electricity generated from renewable sources, RES-E). In the physical wholesale market, the EU seems to have focused on aspects related to financial markets (such as clearing) and the trading of standardised contracts (in particular on exchanges) rather than the supply of electricity as such (under bilateral or other physical contracts).[27]

To liberalise wholesale markets, it would be necessary to focus on the perspective of the electricity producer. To illustrate, EU household electricity prices rose 4 % a year for the 5-year-period 2008–2012 and retail electricity prices for industry by approximately 3.5 % a year. In contrast, wholesale electricity prices fell by between 35 % and 45 % on the major European wholesale electricity benchmarks.[28] RES-E support schemes limited to certain production technologies are partly to blame for the increased price differences.[29] These schemes have also contributed to increased carbon emissions. From a producer perspective, the effect of RES-E support schemes is rather obvious. One should, therefore, replace the preferential treatment of RES-E with a regime that is neutral as far as production technology is concerned. This might reduce carbon emissions at a lower cost.[30]

Wholesale markets are not truly liberalised when the Member States are asked to discriminate against electricity producers on the basis of production technology and when the Member States do not have faith in the market mechanism.[31] In the long run, retail prices can be expected to remain higher than they could be unless a level playing field is created for electricity firms with greater reliance on the market mechanism and free competition at the producer level. Moreover, the various contradictory objectives of the regulation of physical wholesale markets are less likely to be achieved through central planning in relation to the market mechanism.[32]

Contents Chapter 2 discusses several general issues that set the scene for the EU electricity market. Chapter 3 provides an overview of the regulation of electricity

ratio of traded volume to generated volume is high in liquid markets), the total number of trades (high in liquid markets), the range of products available to market participants (large in liquid markets), the size of bid-offer spreads (small in liquid markets), the extent of forward trading, and the number of market participants. Ofgem (2009), paras 2.2–2.6.

[26] Recital 39 of Directive 2009/72/EC (Third Electricity Directive); Ofgem (2009), para 1.9.

[27] Point 19 of Article 2 of Directive 2009/72/EC (Third Electricity Directive): "'supply' means the sale, including resale, of electricity to customers". For the difference of trading and supply, see, for example, Fried J (2010), p. 165, point 263.

[28] Communication from the Commission, Energy prices and costs in Europe, COM(2014) 21 final. Generally, see Pollitt MG (2012).

[29] See, for example, ACER/CEER (2013), Sect. 2.2.2.

[30] Frank CR (2014) and Joskow PL (2011). For the effect of the preferential treatment of RES-E on the business of Vattenfall, see, for example, Mihm A (2014).

[31] Monopolkommission (2013), number 514.

[32] Generally, see von Hayek F (1944).

markets. Chapters 4–7 focus on various kinds of marketplaces (electricity exchanges, transmission marketplaces, marketplaces for emission rights, and market coupling). The related physical contracts are discussed in Chaps. 8–10 (supply contracts, balancing contracts, and transmission contracts) and the related financial contracts in Chaps. 11 and 12 (electricity derivatives and derivatives on transmission capacity). We can start with the characteristic issues of electricity trade law.

References

ACER/CEER (2013) Annual report on the results of monitoring the internal electricity and natural gas markets in 2012

Bhattacharyya SC (2011) Energy economics: concepts, issues, markets and governance. Springer, Heidelberg. doi:10.1007/978-0-85729-268-1

Chicco G (2009) Electricity market evolution in Europe. Sci Bull Electr Eng Fac 2009(2):13–22

Frank CR (2014) The net benefits of low and no-carbon electricity technologies. The Brookings Institution, Global Economy and Development Working Paper 73, May 2014

Fried J (2010) B. Rechtliche Bewältigung des OTC-Handels. In: Schwintowski HP (ed) Handbuch Energiehandel, 2nd edn. Erich Schmidt Verlag, Berlin, pp 153–336

Hermes G (2002) Die Regulierung der Energiewirtschaft zwischen öffentlichem und private Recht – Zugleich ein Beitrag zum Kontrahierungszwang. Zeitschrift für das gesamte Handelsrecht und Wirtschaftsrecht 166(4):433–463

Hunt S, Shuttleworth G (1996) Competition and choice in electricity. Wiley, Chichester

Joskow PL (2008) Capacity payments in imperfect electricity markets: need and design. Utilities Policy 16(3):161–162. doi:10.1016/j.jup.2007.10.003

Joskow PL (2011) Comparing the costs of intermittent and dispatchable electricity generating technologies. Am Econ Rev 101(3):238–241. doi:10.1257/aer.101.3.238

Joskow PL, Schmalensee R (1983) Markets for power: an analysis of electric utility deregulation. MIT Press, Cambridge, MA

Knops HPA (2007) Creating a functional model for the system to function. In: Bertram G (ed) The proceedings of the 30th conference of the international association for energy economics: from restructuring to sustainability: energy policies for the 21st century. IAEE, Wellington, pp 1–9

Mäntysaari P (2010) The law of corporate finance. General principles and EU law, vol I: Cash flow, risk, agency, information. Springer, Heidelberg

Mäntysaari P (2011) Handelsrättens teori: en teoretisk referensram för handelsrättslig forskning. Tidsskrift for rettsvitenskap 124(2):197–226

Mäntysaari P (2012) Organising the firm: theories of commercial law, corporate governance and corporate law. Springer, Heidelberg

Mäntysaari P (2013) Was sollte man tun? Ein Plädoyer für anwenderfreundliche Rechtswissenschaft. Rechtstheorie 44(2):189–207. doi:10.3790/rth.44.2.189

Mihm A (2014) Energieerzeuger stehen vor weiterer Talfahrt. Frankfurter Allgemeine Zeitung, 31 March 2014, p 24

Monopolkommission (2013) Sondergutachten 65. Energie 2013: Wettbewerb in Zeiten der Energiewende. Sondergutachten der Monopolkommission gemäß § 62 Abs. 1 EnWG. Bonn

OECD/IEA (2005) Lessons from Liberalised Electricity Markets. IEA, Paris

Ofgem (2009) Liquidity in the GB wholesale energy markets, 8 June 2009

Pérez-Arriaga IJ, Smeers Y (2003) Guidelines on tariff setting. In: Lévêque F (ed) Transport pricing of electricity networks. Kluwer, Boston, pp 175–203. doi:10.1007/978-1-4757-3756-1_7

Perrels A, Kemppi H (2003) Liberalised electricity markets: strengths and weaknesses in Finland and NordPool. VATT research reports 97. Government Institute for Economic Research, Helsinki

Pollitt MG (2012) The role of policy in energy transitions: lessons from the energy liberalisation era. Energy Policy 50(C):128–137. doi:10.1016/j.enpol.2012.03.004

Spicker J (2010) A. Formen des OTC-Handels. In: Schwintowski HP (ed) Handbuch Energiehandel, 2nd edn. Erich Schmidt Verlag, Berlin, pp 31–152

Supponen M (2011) The influence of national and company interests on european electricity transmission investments. Dissertation, Aalto University

Thomas S (2001) Corporate strategies in the British electricity supply industry. In: Midttun A (ed) European energy industry business strategies. Elsevier Global Energy Policy and Economics Series. Elsevier, the Netherlands, pp 75–150

von Hayek F (1944) The road to serfdom. The University of Chicago Press, Chicago

Part I
General Aspects

Chapter 2
Setting the Scene

2.1 General Remarks

The purpose of this chapter is to give a broad introduction to the structure and participants of electricity markets (Sect. 2.2), introduce the business models of electricity producers and related wholesale market participants (Sect. 2.3), give a brief introduction to the relevant physical laws (Sect. 2.4), introduce the characteristic issues that must be managed in physical electricity markets (Sect. 2.5), discuss the various competition models (Sect. 2.6), and explain how the supply of electricity and the transmission of electricity can be regarded as services (Sect. 2.7).

2.2 Electricity Markets

2.2.1 General Remarks

There are various kinds of electricity markets. First, there is a wholesale market and a retail market. This book focuses on wholesale markets. Second, one can distinguish between physical and financial wholesale markets. Third, electricity can be traded over-the-counter (OTC) or on an exchange (an organised trading venue). Fourth, there are markets for electricity, markets for transmission capacity, and markets for emission allowances. Fifth, electricity wholesale markets can generally be organised in different ways. The size of physical markets can be increased by market coupling. All these issues are discussed in this book in the context of wholesale markets.

P. Mäntysaari, *EU Electricity Trade Law*, DOI 10.1007/978-3-319-16513-4_2

2.2.2 The Wholesale Market

The existence of wholesale marketplaces and supply (retail) marketplaces can be explained by economic efficiency in combination with physical constraints (Sect. 2.4) and market regulation (Sect. 3.5).

Existence To begin with, there would be neither wholesale markets nor competition without high-voltage transmission. It is less costly to move electricity through high-voltage transmission lines. This is because of losses in transformation and distribution.[1] In the absence of high-voltage transmission, generation would have to be located very close to demand. The best economic option for electricity generation would be a regulated local monopoly.[2] High-voltage transmission allows a more favourable location of generators, and also allows the possibility of economies of scale in generation.

Generators can control their output voltage by adjusting their magnetic field. The voltage is lowered by resistance in electric lines (impedance). Transformers in the distribution system can adjust their output voltage and adjust for the drop in voltage caused by the line losses.

Electricity is supplied at a certain frequency. The system frequency is determined by the running speed of the generators. Where electricity demand exceeds the driving power of the generators, the rotational speed of the generators drops and the frequency of the voltage decreases. Moreover, the power capacity of a generator decreases when its rotational speed drops.[3]

Because of economies of scale in electricity production and transmission as well as the existence of transaction costs, electricity producers have an incentive to sell electricity to large customers with stable loads at the high-voltage level. Where electricity and transmission prices reflect costs, high-voltage customers pay less than low-voltage consumers. There should thus be a price difference between the wholesale level and the retail level. Charging the same price would mean that high-voltage consumers pay subventions to low-voltage consumers. From a legal perspective, this means that price differences between wholesale and retail markets are not discriminatory as such.[4]

Before the restructuring and unbundling of electricity markets, the participants in the wholesale market were mainly vertically integrated firms each of which had a local or regional monopoly. Electricity trade was thus trade between monopoly

[1] See Hogan WW (2010), p. 113.

[2] Pérez-Arriaga IJ and Smeers Y (2003), pp. 177–178.

[3] Hotakainen M and Klimstra J (2011), pp. 78–79.

[4] See, for example, British Oxygen Co Ltd v South of Scotland Electricity Board (No. 2) [1959] 2 All ER 225, 1959 SC (HL) 17, [1959] UKHL 4, 1959 SLT 181, [1959] 1 WLR 587. EU law distinguishes between different kinds of customers. See, for example, Article 3(3) of Directive 2009/72/EC (Third Electricity Directive); letter d of paragraph 1 of Annex I to Directive 2009/72/EC (Third Electricity Directive). See also Spence DB (2008), pp. 796–797.

firms and mainly consisted of long-term supply contracts.[5] After the restructuring of markets, more participants have been able to enter the wholesale market.

Function The wholesale market has many functions. (a) Generally, the wholesale marketplace provides information about the *price* of electricity. The spot market determines the reference price for day-ahead or intraday deliveries of electricity in the wholesale market. The financial market provides reference prices for the physical delivery of electricity in the future.[6] Changes in the prices of spot contracts, options, and futures in the wholesale market indicate that the prices charged from end consumers will change as well.[7] For this reason, electricity exchanges are important for all electricity consumers whether they participate in the wholesale market or not. (b) The wholesale marketplace provides a *distribution channel* for electricity producers and a *source of supply* for electricity suppliers and large electricity consumers such as industrial firms.[8] (c) Wholesale market products help system operators to ensure security of supply and maintain *system frequency* in real time. (d) The products traded in the wholesale market can enable an efficient *portfolio and risk management*.[9] This will also foster *investment* in electricity generation and transfer infrastructure and increase security of supply.[10]

Physical and Financial Settlement Electricity contracts are settled physically and/or financially in the wholesale market.

Contracts that are settled physically (physical contacts) can be short-term contracts (spot contracts) or long-term contracts (forwards or other long-term contracts). (a) The spot market is the market for exchange-traded short-term electricity contracts that are settled physically. The spot market can be used to achieve a transparent, competition-driven price for a short period of time in advance. The spot market reacts to short-term changes such as the weather or technical problems.[11] There is a day-ahead market for each hour of the following day. There is also an intraday market enabling market players to balance their positions ahead of physical delivery. The intraday market is becoming increasingly important because of increased use of intermittent sources of electricity (such as wind power with uncontrolled increases or decreases in output). (b) Long-term contracts can be

[5] Meller E and Walter B (2009), § 9, number 1.

[6] Meller E and Walter B (2009), § 9, numbers 11–12.

[7] Meller E and Walter B (2009), § 9, number 8.

[8] Meller E and Walter B (2009), § 9, number 8.

[9] Meller E and Walter B (2009), § 9, number 20.

[10] Recital 39 of Directive 2009/72/EC (Third electricity Directive). See also Meller E and Walter B (2009), § 9, number 22.

[11] Meller E and Walter B (2009), § 9, number 8.

relatively simple forwards or more complex long-term contracts such as total supply contracts, base-load contracts, delivery schedules,[12] peak-load contracts, or reserves.[13] They can also be contracts in which the price is linked to an index for electricity (the market price on an exchange) or fuel (such as oil, gas, or coal),[14] or structured contracts (Sect. 8.2). (c) The spot market is complemented by the balance market or market for control reserves (Sect. 4.10).

Financial contracts are settled financially (in cash or by the delivery of underlying physical contracts). The financial market (contract market) enables market participants to transfer the price risk. Alternatively, market participants may speculate against price developments in the future. Customary financial contracts include options, futures, and swaps.

In practice, contracts called futures are either contracts for difference and settled in cash, or contracts which lead to the physical delivery of electrical energy. The same can be said of forwards. (For the terminology and the difference between futures and forwards, see Sects. 8.2.3 and 11.2).[15]

Exchanges and OTC Markets Electricity is traded on electricity exchanges or over the counter (OTC). OTC trading of electricity means all wholesale trade outside electricity exchanges. While exchange-traded electricity contracts must always be standardised and many OTC-traded contracts are relatively standardised in practice, OTC contracts can also be negotiated individually between the parties.[16] Such individually-negotiated contracts are customarily long-term contracts made directly between the buyer (distributor or a large industrial customer) and the seller (a large energy generator) for large amounts of power (Chap. 8).

Cross-Border Trade Cross-border trade has an effect on electricity prices. Cross-border electricity flows make it easier to meet peak demand when there is not enough generation capacity, or to balance supply and demand when there is excess supply. Moreover, cross-border electricity flows help to optimise the use of different kinds of utilities, and to benefit from regional differences in the mix of primary sources of energy.[17] Cross-border trade is constrained by the availability of interconnector capacity.[18]

---

[12] For a definition, see Article 2(2) of ENTSO-E Network Code on Operational Planning and Scheduling (24 September 2013): "... Generation Schedule means a Schedule representing the Generation of electricity of a Power Generating Module or a group of Power Generating Modules;... Schedule means a reference set of values representing the Generation, consumption or exchange of electricity between actors for a given time period ..."

[13] Spicker J (2010), pp. 94–95, points 137–138.

[14] Spicker J (2010), p. 97, point 144.

[15] For oil, see Däuper O (2009), § 3, number 19.

[16] Meller E and Walter B (2009), § 9, number 7.

[17] Lokau B and Ritzau M (2009), § 5, number 15.

[18] For constraints, see Report from the Commission to the Council and the European Parliament – Progress in creating the Internal Gas and Electricity Market. Brussels, 15 April 2008, COM(2008) 192 final.

For example, interconnector capacity makes it possible to import electricity to Finland from Sweden, Russia, Estonia, or Norway when Finnish power demand exceeds generation.[19]

Most of the electricity generated in Norway is hydropower. With sufficient interconnector capacity, Norwegian hydropower could complement the increased use of intermittent generation technologies in other countries.

The variable production costs of hydropower are low. However, higher prices could be imported to Norway from other Nordic countries and from the European continent through interconnectors.[20] For the same reason, Swedish electricity prices are lower in the North and higher in the South.

Cross-border trade could be increased if there were storage capacity on the other side of the border. When the price of electricity is negative in Germany, an Austrian firm that has invested in pumped hydro storage (PHS) plants in the Alps could switch on the pumps and get paid for extracting electricity from the German grid. When German electricity prices are high, the firm could produce hydropower and get paid for supplying electricity to the German grid.

Prices and Liquidity Prices on electricity exchanges can function as reliable price indicators provided that there is enough liquidity. The prices are important not only for participants trading on the particular exchange but also for parties to bilateral contracts such as supply contracts between producers and industrial customers. The most liquid products are customarily derivative contracts traded on organised trading venues. They attract the broadest group of users and investors.

In the future, prices determined on electricity exchanges will become even more important because of unbundling, the increased integration of national electricity markets, market coupling, and the allocation of cross-border transmission capacity through auctions. Market coupling means that available day-ahead cross-border capacity is considered in determining the energy price (Chap. 6). In addition, market coupling enables cross-border price arbitrage.[21]

The vertically integrated market model tends to reduce liquidity. Unbundling tends to increase it. On the other hand, liquidity might also be increased by increasing interconnector capacity, the participation of large consumers and financial institutions in the wholesale market, higher utilisation of clearing and exchange-based trading, as well as reliable reference prices.[22] The collapse of Enron in 2001–2002 and the following exit of a number of active wholesale market participants reduced liquidity in the UK.[23]

The Balancing Market The system operator is responsible for maintaining balance in the grid. For this reason, it must estimate future generation and load. However,

[19] Imports to Finland from different countries in 2013 in GWh (Finnish Energy Industries): Sweden 12,373. Russia 4,713. Estonia 459. Norway 46.

[20] Godager K (2009) § 18, number 17. Article 2(1) of Regulation 714/2009 (on conditions for access to the network for cross-border exchanges in electricity): "… 'interconnector' means a transmission line which crosses or spans a border between Member States and which connects the national transmission systems of the Member States".

[21] Kindler J (2008).

[22] Ofgem (2009), para 2.29.

[23] Ofgem (2009), paras 2.26 and 2.28.

actual generation and actual consumption become known in real time. The system operator fills the gaps in the balancing market (Sect. 4.10).

The balancing market is facilitated by the TSO's contractual framework. (a) As a rule, a market participant has no access to the physical market without accepting the TSO's contractual framework. Acceptance of this framework is often called a "balance agreement". (b) In addition, there are particular contracts for the provision of market participants' "ancillary services" in the balancing market for the balancing of the system (Chap. 9). Since there are many different products for the balancing of the system, there are in fact many balancing markets.[24] (c) A new European regulatory framework facilitates the integration of balancing markets (Sect. 4.10).

The Transmission Marketplace The wholesale market for electricity is complemented by the market for transmission capacity (Chap. 5). The marketplace for transmission capacity resembles the electricity wholesale market in that there are both physical and financial markets for transmission capacity. There is no electricity trade without transmission capacity and no effective physical market without non-discriminatory network access.[25]

Scarce physical transmission capacity must be allocated. In an efficient electricity market, the available transmission capacity should be transparent for market participants and there should be an efficient method for allocating it. In the internal market, this requires the harmonisation of security, planning and operational standards.[26]

Physical transmission capacity can be allocated in various ways (Chap. 5). Generally, the method for capacity allocation goes hand in hand with the pricing method. The methods can be market-based or not market-based. (a) Market-based allocation methods mean implicit or explicit auctions. They are widely used in European electricity markets. (b) However, many methods are not market-based. They include, for instance, the reservation of transmission capacity under long-term bilateral contracts. In gas markets, it has been customary to use pro rata allocation and the first-come-first-serve method.[27]

[24] Lanz M et al. (2011), section 4.4.3, p. 128: "Es ist angebracht, nicht von einem Regelenergiemarkt, sondern von Regelenergiemärkten zu reden, da zur Bereitstellung der jeweiligen Regelenergiearten unterschiedliche Kraftwerke herangezogen werden, jeweils unterschiedliche Anbieter(zahlen) vorzufinden sind und vor allem da jeweils eigene Markt- und Preisbildungsmechanismen gelten".

[25] Meller E and Walter B (2009), § 9, number 3.

[26] See, for example, recitals 16 and 17 of Regulation 714/2009 on conditions for access to the network for cross-border exchanges in electricity. See also Meller E and Walter B (2009), § 9, number 3.

[27] Talus K (2010), p. 102.

The physical transmission market is complemented by the financial market. The availability of derivatives on electricity transmission capacity can improve access to transmission capacity and safeguard investment in transmission networks.

Cross-border flows require both internal and cross-border transmission capacity.[28] Although the volume of cross-border electricity trade was not large in the past,[29] cross-border electricity flows have become increasingly important.

> German transmission bottlenecks provide an example of the effect of internal congestion on cross-border flows. While wind power capacity and new conventional power plants are mainly located in the north, demand rises mostly in the south. There are similar issues in Sweden. While hydro reservoirs are concentrated in the north of Sweden, most of the consumption is in the south.[30]

Many Markets For many reasons, the electricity wholesale market thus consists of many markets. (a) Physical wholesale markets are national or regional. European markets used to be national, because the European market is mostly divided into the control areas of national TSOs with scarce cross-border interconnection capacity between the areas.[31] Market coupling projects have increased the geographical scope of markets. (b) Most physical electricity used to be traded OTC, but electricity exchanges are becoming increasingly important. In principle, the liberalised market model could consist of bilateral contracting complemented by an electricity exchange (for instance, the Nordic countries, Germany, and the Netherlands) or mandatory centralised auction in which all power, except industrial self-generation, is offered (for example, the UK and Spain).[32] (c) There are different markets for different physical products. One can distinguish between a market for long-term bilateral supply contracts, physical spot markets (day-ahead markets, intraday markets), and markets for balancing energy and reserves. (d) Physical markets for electricity are complemented by other markets. There is a market for transmission capacity. The method of allocating transmission capacity and the pricing method depend on the country.[33] There is also a market for emission rights. (e) In financial markets, products can again be traded OTC or on an exchange.

Products Table 2.1 shows what products customarily are traded in the physical electricity wholesale market.

---

[28] Teusch J et al. (2012), p. 5.

[29] For constraints, see Report from the Commission to the Council and the European Parliament – Progress in creating the Internal Gas and Electricity Market. 15 April 2008, COM(2008) 192 final.

[30] Teusch J et al. (2012), p. 23.

[31] See, for example, ERGEG, Draft Framework Guidelines on Capacity Allocation and Congestion Management for Electricity: Initial Impact Assessment. Ref: E10-ENM-20-04 (8 September 2010), pp. 9–10 and 36–38.

[32] Perrels A and Kemppi H (2003), p. 13.

[33] ENTSO-E (2013).

Table 2.1 Physical products

Long-term supply	OTC	Delivery schedules, forwards, structured contracts
	Exchange	Futures with physical settlement
Spot	OTC	Standardised products: day-ahead contracts
	Exchange	Day-ahead contracts, intraday contracts
Reserves	OTC	Long-term reserve capacity contracts, long-term demand response contracts
	Auctions	Frequency containment reserves, frequency restoration reserves, replacement reserves
Transmission	OTC	Reservation under long-term contracts
	Exchange	Implicit auctions, explicit auctions for physical transmission rights with or without the UIOLI or UIOSI principles, market coupling contracts

2.2.3 Participants in the Physical Wholesale Market

Participants in the physical wholesale market include electricity producers, wholesalers, distributors, and particular transmission and distribution system operators (TSOs and DSOs). These participants are electricity undertakings.[34] Even large end consumers (final customers)[35] can participate in the physical wholesale market. The relatively narrow range of participants can be explained by physical constraints and economic efficiency as well as legal regulation. Participation in physical electricity markets requires grid access and compliance with the legal framework that facilitates physical electricity trade.

In principle, a market participant can have one or more functions (roles). The various roles in physical electricity markets have been described and defined in The Harmonised Electricity Market Role Model, a document published by ebIX®, EFET, and ENTSO-E.

Electricity Producers Electrical energy is generated and sold in bulk by electricity producers.[36] The generation business is the heart of the electricity supply industry. Electricity generation used to be the largest component of an end consumer's electricity costs. Generation is also combined with a high level of risk for electricity producers.[37]

[34] Point 35 of Article 2 of Directive 2009/72/EC (Third Electricity Directive).

[35] Points 9 and 19 of Article 2 of Directive 2009/72/EC (Third Electricity Directive): "'final customer' means a customer purchasing electricity for his own use ... 'supply' means the sale, including resale, of electricity to customers".

[36] Points 1 and 2 of Article 2 of Directive 2009/72/EC (Third Electricity Directive): "'generation' means the production of electricity; 'producer' means a natural or legal person generating electricity".

[37] Thomas S (2001), pp. 94–95.

Suppliers There are two kinds of electricity suppliers: (a) electricity wholesalers supply electricity to other electricity firms[38] or large end consumers; and (b) electricity retailers supply electricity to end consumers.[39] Electricity retailers can also be called load-serving entities (LSE).

Electricity suppliers must either buy or generate the electricity that they intend to supply. One can distinguish between (a) vertically integrated firms that generated electricity and (b) pure electricity suppliers.

In the past, many electricity suppliers were vertically integrated utilities. There is more room for pure electricity suppliers in unbundled electricity markets.

The entry barriers are low. Unlike electricity generation, electricity supply is not capital intensive. An electricity supplier does not need to own any network facilities or power plants. It can outsource meter reading and billing. In other words, an electricity supplier needs little more than a telephone and a computer to operate a supply business. Electricity supply is a high turnover, but low capital and low margin business. Compared with electricity generation and transmission/distribution, electricity supply is the smallest component of an end consumer's electricity bill.[40] It includes metering and billing.

One could say that the supply company negotiates with the generation sector on behalf of end consumers. The supply company represents the electricity industry's main interface with end consumers.

End Consumers End consumers try to obtain adequate security of supply at low cost. There is a difference between large consumers and small consumers.

Large consumers tend to be commercial or industrial firms or public sector entities that can buy electrical energy at the high-voltage grid level. If they are directly connected to the transmission grid, they may be able to offer balancing services (demand response or demand side response[41]) to the system operator.

Small consumers customarily are residential (household) consumers or small firms.[42] They pay the local distribution system operator (DSO) for grid access and distribution capacity and buy electricity from a retailer. Their participation in the electricity market is usually limited to choosing the retailer and consuming electricity. In unbundled markets, the DSO is the retailer.

---

[38] Point 35 of Article 2 of Directive 2009/72/EC (Third Electricity Directive).

[39] Points 7–9 of Article 2 of Directive 2009/72/EC (Third Electricity Directive): "'customer' means a wholesale or final customer of electricity; 'wholesale customer' means a natural or legal person purchasing electricity for the purpose of resale inside or outside the system where he is established; 'final customer' means a customer purchasing electricity for his own use".

[40] Thomas S (2001), pp. 98–99.

[41] Article 2(2) of ENTSO-E Network Code on Demand Connection (21 December 2012): "... Demand Side Response (DSR) means demand offered for the purposes of, but not restricted to, providing Active or Reactive Power management, Voltage and Frequency regulation and System Reserve ..." "... Demand Aggregation means a set of Demand Facilities which can be operated as a single facility for the purposes of offering one or more Demand Side Response services ..."

[42] See recital 45 and Article 3(3) of Directive 2009/72/EC (Third Electricity Directive).

System Operators System operators provide a wide range of important services. Transmission rights must be defined and allocated to system users. Transfers may need to be rescheduled by a party responsible for dispatching to make them consistent with available transmission capacity. It is necessary to cover losses and balance the system in real time. It is necessary to meter energy flows and to arrange payments for imbalances and ancillary services.[43] The system operator must also be notified by system users in advance of scheduled electricity transfers.

Transmission and Distribution One can distinguish between commercial transmission and commercial distribution of electricity. Electrical energy is transmitted in bulk to wholesalers and large industrial customers at a high voltage level.[44] It is distributed in smaller quantities to retail customers at a lower voltage level.[45]

Transmission Firms One can also distinguish between transmission firms and transmission system operators. They have different functions: (1) A transmission firm owns transmission system assets such as lines, cables, transformers, and reactive compensation devices. For instance, a merchant line is a particular interconnector.[46] (2) The transmission system is operated according to the instructions of a transmission system operator (TSO). Generally, transmission planning is more difficult in liberalised markets.[47] (3) Whether a transmission firm or a transmission system operator may own electricity generation plants depends on regulation.

In the EU, the main rule is that the first and second of these three functions are combined and the third separated. Each undertaking that owns a transmission system *must* act as a transmission system operator. The transmission firm/transmission system operator *must not* perform any of the functions of generation or supply.[48]

There can also be independent system operators.[49] An independent system operator (ISO) is independent of the owner of transmission assets and owns computing and communication assets.

A Member State of the EU may designate an independent system operator under certain circumstances.[50] The terminology is different in the US (see Sect. 3.5.5).

---

[43] Hunt S and Shuttleworth G (1996), pp. 183–184.

[44] Point 3 of Article 2 of Directive 2009/72/EC (Third Electricity Directive): "'transmission' means the transport of electricity on the extra high-voltage and high-voltage interconnected system with a view to its delivery to final customers or to distributors, but does not include supply".

[45] Point 5 of Article 2 of Directive 2009/72/EC (Third Electricity Directive): "'distribution' means the transport of electricity on high-voltage, medium-voltage and low-voltage distribution systems with a view to its delivery to customers, but does not include supply".

[46] See Article 17(1)(c) of Regulation 714/2009.

[47] Pérez-Arriaga IJ and Smeers Y (2003), p. 182.

[48] Article 9(1) of Directive 2009/72/EC (Third Electricity Directive).

[49] Article 13(4) of 2009/72/EC (Third Electricity Directive).

[50] Article 13(1) of Directive 2009/72/EC (Third Electricity Directive): "Where the transmission system belongs to a vertically integrated undertaking on 3 September 2009, Member States may

Distribution System Operators A distribution system operator (DSO) owns and operates a distribution network.[51] Compared with electricity transmission, electricity distribution: has more customers; must adapt to larger variation in load; requires a larger investment for the same amount of supplied energy; can cause lower interruption costs; and requires less monitoring.

Each power distribution firm enjoys a monopoly for the distribution of electricity to retail customers in a given geographical area. For this reason, electricity distribution is a regulated business. The distribution firm can try to maximise the regulated profit. Competition can be increased, if the operation and development of the distribution network is separated from the supply of electrical energy to retail customers. In the EU, this is addressed by the unbundling regime.

Market Operators An organised market for electrical energy has a market operator. A market operator has two main functions. It runs the computer system that matches bids and offers submitted by buyers and sellers. In addition, it runs the market settlement system by monitoring the delivery of energy and transmitting payments from buyers to sellers. The market operator tries to run an efficient market to encourage trading.

Regulators Regulators are government bodies. They determine or approve market rules, investigate suspected abuses of market power, and set the prices for products and services provided by monopolies. The regulator tries to ensure: that the overall electricity sector operates in a fair and economically efficient manner; that the overall electricity sector operates in a reliable manner (adequacy and security); and the quality of supply.

2.2.4 The Financial Market and the Emission Allowances Market

The physical market provides the financial market with underlying commodities or contracts (Sect. 4.3). The financial electricity market attracts a wider range of participants, because participation is not constrained by grid access.

---

decide not to apply Article 9(1) and designate an independent system operator upon a proposal from the transmission system owner. Such designation shall be subject to approval by the Commission".

[51] Points 5 and 6 of Article 2 of Directive 2009/72/EC (Third Electricity Directive): "'distribution' means the transport of electricity on high-voltage, medium-voltage and low-voltage distribution systems with a view to its delivery to customers, but does not include supply; 'distribution system operator' means a natural or legal person responsible for operating, ensuring the maintenance of and, if necessary, developing the distribution system in a given area and, where applicable, its interconnections with other systems and for ensuring the long-term ability of the system to meet reasonable demands for the distribution of electricity".

The most common financial electricity contracts are based on electricity supply contracts (Chap. 11). The same entities that participate in the physical electricity market—electricity producers, distributors, utilities, and large end consumers—customarily manage risk in the financial electricity market. On the other hand, derivatives can also be used for arbitrage and speculation. This is of interest to banks, investment firms, and investment funds.

Banks can also act as market-makers for financial electricity derivatives. Whether banks are allowed to act as market-makers can depend on the scope of ring-fencing rules such as the Volcker Rule in the US or the Financial Services (Banking Reform) Act 2013 or the Trennbankengesetz in Europe.

The Volcker Rule,[52] a central provision in the Dodd-Frank Act, bans proprietary trading by banking entities[53] in the US. Proprietary trading means transacting in securities or derivatives for the purpose of benefitting from short-term price movements.[54] The Volcker Rule contains a market-making exemption.[55] As a result, US banking entities are still permitted to act as market-makers in financial electricity markets. There is a further exemption for risk-mitigating hedging transactions.[56] This means that banking entities that act as market-makers in financial electricity markets may trade in short-term derivatives for this purpose.

The Financial Services (Banking Reform) Act 2013 separates investment banking from retail activity in the UK. The ring fence is an internal one and applies to large banks. Unless trading or market-making in commodities or electricity derivatives are exempted (section 142D), it will influence financial electricity markets as well. If ring-fenced banks are not allowed to offer derivatives products to electricity market participants, their customers can move to smaller banks or foreign banks that are not subject to ring-fencing.

In Germany, ring-fencing is required by the Trennbankengesetz.[57] These provisions will become binding in 2016.

The financial market is not limited to contracts with electricity supply contracts as the underlying commodity. There is a market for financial transmission contracts (Chap. 12). The availability of derivatives on electricity transmission capacity can improve access to transmission capacity and foster investment in transmission networks. There is also a market for emission derivatives.

---

[52] 12 U.S.C. § 1851(a)(1).

[53] For the definition of "banking entity", see 12 U.S.C. § 1851(h)(1).

[54] See the definition of "proprietary trading", 12 U.S.C. § 1851(h)(4), and the definition of "trading account", 12 U.S.C. § 1851(h)(6).

[55] 12 U.S.C. § 1851(d)(1)(B): "The purchase, sale, acquisition, or disposition of securities and other instruments described in subsection (h)(4) in connection with underwriting or market-making-related activities, to the extent that any such activities permitted by this subparagraph are designed not to exceed the reasonably expected near term demands of clients, customers, or counterparties".

[56] 12 U.S.C. § 1851(d)(1)(C): "Risk-mitigating hedging activities in connection with and related to individual or aggregated positions, contracts, or other holdings of a banking entity that are designed to reduce the specific risks to the banking entity in connection with and related to such positions, contracts, or other holdings".

[57] Gesetz zur Abschirmung von Risiken und zur Planung der Sanierung und Abwicklung von Kreditinstituten und Finanzgruppen. For banks, see §§ 25, 47, and 48 KWG.

Electricity generation is one of the main sources of greenhouse emissions. Participants in the emissions allowances market include a wide range of firms that must comply with emissions rules as well as financial firms operating as intermediaries (Chap. 7).

2.3 Business Models

2.3.1 General Remarks

The most important wholesale electricity market participants are producers, suppliers, traders, and end consumers. Each market participant has its own business model. The business model depends on the role of the market participant. A market participant can combine two or more of the different roles. A supplier-trader can also be called an energy merchant. A producer-supplier is called an integrated firm.

There are also other market participants such as brokers and portfolio managers. We can have a look at the business models and start with large end consumers and retail suppliers. The business models of electricity producers will also be discussed in Sect. 8.2 in greater detail.

2.3.2 Large Consumers and Retailers

A large industrial consumer must purchase electricity to match its own electricity consumption profile (load). A retail supplier (a retailer) must purchase electricity to cover the future expected electricity consumption of a pool of customers. Compared with a monopoly firm, a retail supplier must find customers and has higher search costs (including marketing).[58]

For the purpose of matching generation and load, both use supply contracts (such as long-term contracts, spot contracts, and physically-settled derivatives)[59] as well as direct or indirect investments in generation facilities (for block-ownership and structured contracts, see Sect. 8.2).

Large industrial consumers and retailers use the portfolio of contracts in two main ways. First, they use it to hedge the load. The portfolio facilitates the supply of electricity in future time periods. Second, they use it to settle differences between fixed and variable prices. Both large industrial consumers and retail distributors try to minimise the costs for hedging the expected load at the acceptable risk level.[60]

---

[58] Booz & Company (2013), p. 21; Kwoka J and Pollitt M (2010).

[59] See, for example, Hunt S and Shuttleworth G (1996), p. 107.

[60] Huisman R et al. (2009), pp. 169–174.

End consumers and suppliers can do all this internally or use the services of portfolio managers.

2.3.3 Brokers and Portfolio Managers

Market participants can trade bilaterally or with a central counterparty. In addition, they can trade directly or indirectly, that is, through a broker. A broker can act on behalf of a market participant or on its own behalf. Market participants can also use portfolio managers.

Brokers A market participant may prefer to use a broker for various reasons.[61] First, trading on electricity exchanges is limited to members, and not all market participants are exchange members. Non-members can trade through a broker that is a member. Second, using brokers may reduce search costs (a component of transaction costs) in OTC markets, because brokers tend to be well-informed. They would not be able to match parties without a network of clients and information about their specific needs. Third, a market participant may prefer to remain anonymous. For instance, a market participant that needs to purchase or sell large quantities of electricity may want to keep its total trading quantities secret to avoid an adverse impact on price. Moreover, each market participant has internal limits for trading with other market participants, and small internal limits may prevent it from dealing with a market participant whose quota is full. Using a broker enables an electricity firm to divide its total supply or demand between various contract parties.

A broker that has an established analysis unit and a customer base may be in a position to move to portfolio management.[62]

Portfolio Managers The services of portfolio managers include: pure advisory services (the portfolio is managed by the customer); portfolio optimisation (the customer outsources the management of the whole portfolio but takes the decisions itself); portfolio management (the customer outsources the management of the whole portfolio); and load-serving total supply contracts (vertical integration).[63]

Portfolio management is a service that could be used by industrial consumers that have limited resources and cannot afford a separate analysis unit.[64] On the other hand, even large industrial consumers can outsource part of their work in this way. The same can be said of electricity suppliers.[65]

---

[61] See, for example, Midttun A et al. (2001), pp. 55–56.

[62] Midttun A et al. (2001), p. 57.

[63] Spicker J (2010), pp. 104–105, point 156.

[64] Midttun A et al. (2001), p. 56.

[65] Spicker J (2010), pp. 107–108, point 169.

2.3.4 Energy Merchants

In principle, energy merchants could play an important role in liberalised energy markets. Energy merchants can be described as integrated physical and financial market participants.

Energy merchants (Energiegroßhändler)[66] combine the physical supply of energy with financial risk management, trading, and arbitrage. On one hand, energy merchants act as suppliers, traders of energy contracts, and service providers. On the other, their business is based on the portfolio management approach. The portfolio management approach means that an energy merchant manages its own portfolio consisting of physical and financial resources as well as customers.

Different resources have different characteristics and mean different kinds of risk taking. As an illustration, power plants and distribution systems require plenty of capital and are natural long positions. Trading and arbitrage mean large volumes, low margins, and high volatility. They are a financial risk-taking strategy. Structured contracts can be designed as price neutral contracts with lower volumes and higher margins. However, they require in-depth knowledge.[67]

An energy merchant has a portfolio of upstream positions and downstream positions (wholesale contracts and retail contracts). The portfolio is diversified. An energy merchant hedges its positions.[68] Hedging and maintaining a diversified portfolio protects the energy merchant against price volatility, volumetric risks (supply shortages or overproduction), and other risks it prefers not to accept. Energy merchants can thus benefit from economics of scale.

Unlike electricity producers that rely on their electricity generation assets and high electricity prices for profits, energy merchants try to be price neutral. Energy merchants try to make a profit regardless of electricity prices being high or low.[69]

An energy merchant does not need to own any generation assets. Should it need generation assets, it can gain access to them through partnerships and contracts.[70]

---

[66] Spicker J (2010), pp. 120–122, points 196–199 as well as pp. 125–131, points 205–220.

[67] Spicker J (2010), p. 126, point 208.

[68] Deng SJ and Oren SS (2006), p. 945: "Electricity call and put options are the most effective tools available to merchant power plants and power marketers for hedging price risk because electricity generation capacities can be essentially viewed as call options on electricity, particularly when generation costs are fixed".

[69] Spicker J (2010), p. 125, point 206.

[70] Hunt S and Shuttleworth G (1996), pp. 128–129: "Generator companies can assemble a portfolio of generators so that responsibility for fulfilling one contract (and the associated risk) is spread over a number of different plants. It is sometimes thought that generator companies have to be large to assemble a portfolio of generating plants, which raises the spectre of market power. However, small companies can develop a portfolio of generators by taking part in a large number of joint ventures, or even just by owning shares in a wide range of generator companies. In the electricity markets of the future, the diversification of shareholdings may allow private investors to spread their risks over several companies, which would greatly reduce the need for generator companies to manage their risks internally".

Such outsourcing ("buy") is more flexible and less capital intensive than vertical integration ("make"). At the same time, an energy merchant uses owners of generation assets as a source of funding (and as what we can call "asset investors" rather than debt or equity investors from the perspective of the energy merchant).[71] It is easier to adjust the portfolio because of its inherent flexibility. An energy merchant can also obtain access to generation assets as a shareholder.[72]

An energy merchant buys and sells its positions and assets. Its decisions are influenced by expected market changes, the preferred shape of its portfolio, and the chance to make a profit. For instance, an energy merchant with plenty of generation assets in just one country could prefer to diversify its portfolio. It could raise funding for investments in other markets by selling the assets. Alternatively, it could swap the assets.

Electricity producers and energy merchants thus view generation assets in different ways. For an electricity producer, generation assets are the main source of income. For an energy merchant, its own generation assets are a call option on the energy price.[73] Generation assets (the power plant) with unsold capacity can be regarded as a long futures position or a long spark spread position (for spark spreads, see Sect. 11.4). Where the spark spread widens, the power plant becomes more profitable. Where it is reduced, the power plant becomes less profitable. Where it is too small, the power plant can lose money.[74] Spark spreads options can also be regarded as functional equivalents of owning generation assets.[75]

Energy merchants use structured contracts (Sect. 8.2). Structured contracts include, for instance, tolling contracts and load-serving contracts. An energy merchant deconstructs the complex individually negotiated structured contracts into their basic components that are relatively simple standard contracts with a market price.[76] It can thus use markets to price physical contracts and financial equivalents to provide liquidity to physical contracts.

Energy merchants can also offer more exotic products such as weather derivatives. Moreover, they can bundle commodity contracts with funding. To illustrate, an arrangement called production payments means that an energy merchant provides a project loan that is to be repaid by means of rights to the production of the project company. In addition, energy merchants could act as market makers.

There are various arbitrage opportunities for energy merchants. Energy merchants can use fuel source arbitrage, regional or geographic arbitrage, or time

---

[71] For "asset investors", see Mäntysaari P (2010), section 9.2.

[72] Hunt S and Shuttleworth G (1996), p. 129.

[73] Spicker J (2010), p. 126, point 207.

[74] Salomon Smith Barney (2002), p. 46.

[75] Maribu KM et al. (2007), p. 176: "The spark spread is the electricity price less the natural gas cost of generating a unit of electricity at given power plant efficiency … Buying a spark-spread option is equivalent to owning a power plant with operational flexibility if we disregard operational costs and operational constraints".

[76] Spicker J (2010), p. 128, point 212.

arbitrage. (a) Fuel source arbitrage means taking advantage of cost differences between different fuels. Power plants could be regarded as options to turn fuel inputs into power outputs with volatility measured as spark spreads. Cost differences between different fuels matter, because the price of electricity does not depend on the fuel (or would not depend on it in the absence of regulatory intervention such as the preferential treatment of RES-E). (b) Regional or geographic arbitrage takes advantage of electricity or fuel price differences in different regions.[77]

2.3.5 Electricity Producers and Integrated Firms

Electrical energy is produced and sold in bulk by electricity producers.[78] Electricity producers could adopt many aspects of the business model of energy merchants. However, there are fundamental differences.

Electricity Producers An electricity producer tries to make a profit from the supply of energy and the provision of ancillary services. An electricity producer owns and/or operates one or more plants. This can be a single plant, a portfolio of plants with the same technology, a portfolio of plants with different technologies, or a portfolio of plants with different locations. Different plant types are needed for different segments of electricity production.

Depending on the market segment, an electricity producer must choose between intermittent generation technologies (such as wind or solar) and dispatchable technologies (that will generate electricity during all hours of the year)[79]: (a) Base-load plants should have low fuel costs and be able to run 24 h/day at fixed load. The start-up time and the ramp-up rate are less relevant for base-load plants. Nuclear power is an example of base-load generation. (b) Intermediate load plants should be able to ramp up rapidly and deliver close to constant output during, say, 15 h. (c) Peaking plants should need relatively low investments (as they will be used rarely) and be able to run, for instance, less than 4 h with plenty of output variation. (d) Balancing and regulating plants must be flexible. For instance, hydropower is suitable for this purpose.[80] (e) Back-up capacity in smart grids

---

[77] Salomon Smith Barney (2002), p. 45: "For example, let us say that in [A], power can be bought from [B] three months from now at a certain futures price. Because of price differentials, it might be possible, however, to more cheaply transport natural gas from [B] to [C], convert it to power at an efficient plant there, and supply power from [C] to [A]. An Energy Merchant with active trading desks in gas and power for all three regions would likely detect this arbitrage. The Energy Merchant could sell power futures ... and then close its futures obligation ... "

[78] Points 1 and 2 of Article 2 of Directive 2009/72/EC (Third Electricity Directive). When an electricity producer coexists with a vertically integrated utility, it is often called an independent power producer (IPP).

[79] Joskow PL (2011), p. 240.

[80] Hotakainen M and Klimstra J (2011), pp. 135 and 142–143; Supponen M (2011), pp. 14–17.

should be provided by power generation that has seemingly conflicting characteristics: high fuel efficiency, quick starting, and a fast response to load steps.[81] This could be achieved, for instance, by cascading a number of parallel high-performance generating units[82] (that is, switching parallel generators on and off depending on power demand).[83]

The plant type is connected with the availability and liquidity of contracts. To illustrate, the absence of long-term supply contracts and liquid forward contract markets can reduce electricity producers' incentives to invest in capital intensive generation technologies and increase the popularity of less capital intensive technologies (such as combined-cycle gas turbines, CCGT). The availability of long-term supply contracts and the existence of a liquid forward contract market can make it easier for electricity producers to invest in capital intensive technologies.[84]

The plant types influence market prices. The lack of base-load plants, which customarily require a large capital investment, means that marginal prices are higher during a larger part of the year.[85] Moreover, the choice of the RES-E support mechanism will influence investment in different types of plants and therefore also market prices.[86]

Changes in market regulation have had an impact on the choice of technologies and investment trends as electricity producers' exposure to market and legal risk has increased. Electricity producers are less likely to invest in capital intensive technologies with long construction times. They are more likely to prefer technologies with short lead times that can be built in small incremental steps. To manage commercial risk and regulatory uncertainty, they may prefer to postpone investment decisions until risk can be replaced by information.[87] Moreover, the preferential treatment of RES-E has had a very large impact on investment.

Integrated Firms One can distinguish between pure electricity producers and so-called integrated firms. A pure electricity producer—for instance, a merchant power plant (Sect. 8.2.3)—sells its power in the wholesale market. An integrated firm is an electricity producer that supplies electricity to end consumers.

Firms become integrated firms because of commercial benefits. They could include, for instance, (a) reductions in transaction costs,[88] wholesale market volatility, operating costs, and counterparty risk,[89] and (b) increased business opportunities. However, it is important for many electricity producers to integrate into

---

[81] Hotakainen M and Klimstra J (2011), p. 166. See also pp. 158–159.

[82] Hotakainen M and Klimstra J (2011), p. 159.

[83] Hotakainen M and Klimstra J (2011), p. 163.

[84] de Hauteclocque A (2009).

[85] Green R (2006).

[86] For a comparison of feed-in tariffs, bidding, and exchangeable quotas, see Finon P and Perez Y (2007, 2008).

[87] OECD/IEA (2005), pp. 23 and 99–100.

[88] Coase RH (1937).

[89] Ofgem (2009), para 3.10.

electricity supply to end consumers to (c) secure off-take (customers and consumption). An electricity producer may need to secure its market. Electricity producers used to compete on price since there was hardly any room for product differentiation before the boom in "green" electricity. Electricity resellers and large end consumers are very price-sensitive. Smaller consumers are less price-sensitive and less likely to change their supplier when prices change. Vertical integration can reduce risk and make it easier for the electricity producer to invest in generation installations.

Other Forms of Integration Electricity firms can choose even other integration models. One can distinguish between vertical integration, horizontal integration, and integration across value chains.

Electricity producers integrate vertically in two directions and not just downstream. An electricity producer can integrate into power plant fuel supply. (a) Integrating a fuel supply and electricity generation business may provide a hedge against volatile fuel prices. To illustrate, a UK company with its own supply of gas can choose to sell the gas directly, export the gas to continental Europe, or use it to generate electricity, depending on what will offer the highest profits. Integration into coal supply is less attractive for electricity generators because of the lack of alternative markets for coal other than electricity generation.[90] (b) Fuel suppliers can integrate vertically and enter the generation market to ensure a market for their product and to obtain a better price. Industrial firms may enter into electricity generation to ensure security of supply and to reduce costs. They can sell surplus power or purchase additional power.[91]

Electricity producers can also choose horizontal integration. To illustrate, an electricity producer can offer new products to its customers by supplying complementary services.

The provision of distribution or transmission services is an example of integration across value chains. In complete vertical integration, there is one firm for the production of electricity and the operation of the transmission and the distribution system.

Suppliers Electricity producers are electricity suppliers as well. Electricity suppliers are electricity wholesalers or electricity retailers. (a) A wholesaler either generates or buys electricity to supply it to other electricity firms[92] or large end consumers. Electricity producers have an incentive to sell electricity to large industrial customers with stable loads. (b) A retailer that does not generate electricity must buy electricity on the wholesale market and resell it downstream to retail customers.[93] This enables it to earn a profit from the difference between wholesale and retail prices (buy low, sell high).

---

[90] Thomas S (2001), p. 96.

[91] *Ibid*, p. 96.

[92] Point 35 of Article 2 of Directive 2009/72/EC (Third Electricity Directive).

[93] Points 7–9 and 19 of Article 2 of Directive 2009/72/EC (Third Electricity Directive).

Trading in Physical Markets Both electricity producers and electricity suppliers need to trade in the wholesale market. (a) A pure electricity producer sells its generation in the wholesale market. (b) An integrated firm needs to trade when it is long or short. Where an integrated firm is long in generation (meaning that its generation output is greater than its own supply requirement), it needs to sell this surplus output. Where an integrated firm is short in generation, it needs to buy to fill the gap. (c) An integrated firm would often trade even where its total generation matched its supply requirements. The reasons can be summed up as:

- profile mismatch (generators often prefer to sell output further out compared to the period over which the suppliers generally purchase energy, the generation mix may prevent integrated companies from internalising significant volumes, there are imbalances because demand profiles are not entirely stable or predictable);
- reliability (forced outages force the firm to trade in the wholesale markets);
- market dynamics (parties respond to changes in market conditions and information)[94]; and
- small firm size (smaller firms are less flexible and less well-informed).[95]

Level of Intra-Firm Integration of Generation and Supply Large electricity producers that are integrated firms can choose the level of integration for their generation and supply activities. In other words, they can organise their business in different ways. Their choices are applications of the "make-or-buy" decision.[96] Vertical integration tends to reduce trading on the market.[97]

Generally, one can distinguish between three integration strategies or models: fusion; fission; and semi-integration.[98] The electricity producer can thus coordinate generation and supply activities in two main ways. It can: (a) coordinate them internally (the fusion model); or (b) let the generation unit and the supply unit trade on the market (the fission model).

The fusion model (internal coordination, "make") means that the firm's generation and supply units maximise internal transactions and minimise external trade. Contracts in external markets are only resorted to when there is excess capacity or demand. This can also mean the centralisation of trading competencies. Trading competencies can be accumulated in a single unit that serves the whole company and balances its portfolio on behalf of both the supply and the generation side.[99]

This can be illustrated with the business of fully integrated utilities according to DG Competition: "Typically, within fully integrated utilities, specialised affiliates are

---

[94] Ofgem (2009), para 3.18.

[95] *Ibid*, para 3.50.

[96] See already Coase RH (1937).

[97] See, for example, DG Competition Report on Energy Sector inquiry, 10 January 2007, SEC (2006) 1724, paras 449 and 451.

[98] Midttun A et al. (2001), p. 49.

[99] *Ibid*, pp. 50–51.

> dedicated to the different activities, such as generation, trading, supply and network operations. Usually, the entire output of the generation affiliate is sold under intra-firm arrangements to the affiliated trading entity which in turn manages the undertaking's overall portfolio i.e. sells electricity to the supply affiliate(s) and sells it to or buys it from third parties through bespoke bilateral contracts or traded wholesale markets. Integrated companies can produce more or less electricity than is required for their own customer portfolio. The larger integrated companies often generate more electricity than they need for their final customers".[100]

The fission model (market-based transactions, "buy") means that the firm's generation and supply units are allowed to trade freely in the open market, without any preference for internal trade. In this case, trading competencies are decentralised. Since the generation and supply units are not coordinated internally, the work of central management is more focused on financial matters.[101]

The semi-integrated model means that the firm has organised an internal market for preferential internal trading.[102]

Inter-Firm Integration Electricity producers and suppliers can also co-operate with similar firms to reduce costs and increase economies of scale. To illustrate, suppliers can form joint-purchasing organisations or co-operate in the supply of electricity to end consumers.[103] An electricity producer can also increase co-operation with a downstream electricity supplier. Rather than selling electricity to a downstream electricity supplier for resale to end consumers, the electricity producer could pay the downstream supplier a commission.[104]

Scale or Diversification An electricity producer can choose between scale (mergers in the same field of activity, vertical integration) or scope (integration across value chains). (a) Since product differentiation is difficult because of the physical characteristics of electricity and since there is transmission congestion on interconnectors, the introduction of liberalised and competitive markets could increase cross-border mergers that increase economies of scale and enable electricity producers to sell locally-generated electricity in more and more countries.[105] (b) The alternative is integration across value chains. To illustrate, an integrated electricity firm can take over a gas firm and invest in the production of heat as well. In this way, it can become an integrated energy and heat distribution company.[106] An integrated electricity firm can also prefer to take over a distribution system.

---

[100] DG Competition report on energy sector inquiry, 10 January 2007, SEC(2006) 1724, para 329.

[101] Midttun A et al. (2001), pp. 49–50.

[102] *Ibid*, pp. 51–52.

[103] *Ibid*, pp. 59–61.

[104] *Ibid*, p. 61.

[105] Arentsen MJ et al. (2001), p. 162: "Between 1985 and 1999, distributors continued enlarging the scale of business. These mergers started to respond to the 1985 efficiency push of the Dutch government". See also p. 186: "One of the striking points of the market developments over the last decade is the strong focus on business scale of companies, both in generation and distribution".

[106] *Ibid*, pp. 166–167: "With a strong position in energy sales (gas, electricity and heat) the larger companies started to develop strategies across value chains, extending their business orientation to other utilities".

Relevance The business models of electricity producers or integrated firms are important from a policy perspective. If these business models are made attractive, security of supply can be increased and retail prices reduced.

This is because of the nature of electricity producers' business. Electricity producers cannot make a profit unless their production costs are lower than the market price.[107] To increase their profits, electricity producers must produce larger volumes of electricity at a low cost. For this reason, they have incentives to invest in new generation installations and to reduce production costs in competitive markets.

From a policy perspective, there is a fundamental difference between electricity producers and energy merchants. Energy merchants try to be price neutral and make a profit regardless of whether electricity prices are high or low. Electricity producers need to invest in better generation installations. Lower market prices are more likely to be the result of long-term investments made by electricity producers than attributable to the trading and risk management activities of energy merchants.

As will be discussed in this book, the regulation of electricity markets has other goals than supporting the business models of electricity producers or integrated firms. (a) The preferential treatment of RES-E means that markets are not competitive and that investments are not allocated between different technologies based on the cost of production. As a result, electricity prices are higher than they could be. (b) Moreover, the regulation of electricity markets is not designed with the perspective of electricity producers in mind. It focuses more on end consumers, suppliers, transmission, financial markets, or the environment.

Integration of the Business Models of Electricity Producers and Energy Merchants One can see traces of the convergence of business models.

If electricity markets were fully liberalised in the EU, electricity producers would have incentives to adopt the business model of an energy merchant.[108] This is because generation installations are large long-term investments and it is important for electricity producers to manage their exposure to risk.

On the other hand, there are factors that provide incentives to move towards the business model of energy merchants even in the absence of fully liberalised and competitive markets in the EU. Such factors include: increased customer churn[109]; the fact that investments in generation are to a large extent driven by regulation; the preferential treatment of RES-E; and the high exposure to political and legal risk. The preferential treatment of RES-E fosters investment in RES-E, but laws may change. At the same time, the preferential treatment of RES-E hampers investment in other forms of generation. In other words, electricity producers have further incentives to look for business models that help them reduce the risk exposure of the firm.

---

[107] Power plants hardly generated any profits from "energy-only markets" under 2010 EEX prices. See Schröder A et al. (2013).

[108] Spicker J (2010), p. 131, point 220: "Der Trend geht … zu Unternehmen, die ihre Assets vermarkten".

[109] See, for example, Shaw DR et al. (2006).

The convergence of business models is not one-way traffic. There are incentives for energy merchants to move towards the business model of electricity producers in the EU. The unbundling regime means that electricity merchants cannot control both generation and transmission assets (as Enron did in the US gas markets). The preferential treatment of RES-E can mean that it is easier for many electricity producers to sell their production and to sell it at premium prices. Moreover, the business model of energy merchants is constrained by the regulation of capital markets. In particular, the MiFID regime with its authorisation and regulatory capital requirements for investment firms (Sect. 4.8) as well as increased requirements as to clearing and collateral (EMIR). As a result, the business of energy merchants has become more regulated and capital intensive. Part of the business model is constrained by the market abuse regime (REMIT) that limits the use of information for the purposes of arbitrage.

Both may need to move towards the generation of RES-E, vertical integration, distribution, and the provision of a broad range of complementary services.

In any case, electricity producers can use the same portfolio approach, the same structured contracts, and the same derivatives as energy merchants.

Trends The evolution of business models in the European electricity industry has been discussed in Midttun A (2001).[110] Recent business model trends can be illustrated with the cases of Vattenfall and DONG Energy, the effects of the preferential treatment of RES-E, and the case of E.ON. We can nevertheless start with the US case of Enron, the archetype of an energy merchant.

Enron The origins of Enron lie in the US natural gas industry. The well-known Enron case generally shows how the choice of different business models and contract types can be influenced by market changes. Similar mechanisms are relevant for electricity producers.

- First phase: regulated markets, complete vertical integration. Enron was the result of the merger of two pipeline companies when US gas markets were still heavily regulated. The logic behind the merger was that companies with the best pipeline networks would prevail.[111]

  The pipeline business was long-term business that was capital intensive and risk averse.[112] Natural gas used to be sold under long-term contracts between producers, pipeline companies, and local utilities. Pipeline companies undertook take-or-pay obligations to protect themselves against future shortages.[113]
- Second phase: spot markets, trading. In the late 1980s, however, some 75 % of gas was sold in the spot market.[114] This reduced the margins of pipeline

[110] Midttun A (2001).

[111] McLean B and Elkind P (2004), pp. 2 and 33.

[112] *Ibid*, p. 15.

[113] *Ibid*, p. 9.

[114] *Ibid*, p. 33.

companies, increased price volatility, and reduced security of supply.[115] Enron dealt with this problem in two ways.

First, Enron focused more on gas buyers' needs. While traditional pipeline companies were vertically integrated suppliers and movers of gas, Enron offered long-term contracts for the supply and delivery of gas even when it did not own the necessary pipelines. To achieve this, it had to ensure that it had enough gas to supply, and arrange for the necessary transportation capacity. As such deals were not constrained by the capacity of Enron's own pipeline network, Enron could promise security of supply even when the volumes were large. This increased deal size and the geographical market. Moreover, customers were prepared to pay a premium for the security of supply in long-term contracts.[116] This increased profits. In effect, Enron acted as a "physical gas bank" with suppliers of gas and transmission capacity on one side, gas buyers on the other side, and Enron taking a margin in the middle.

Second, Enron used more of the gas itself. Enron increased vertical integration by investing in power plants that used large amounts of natural gas as fuel.[117]

- Third phase: investments in production capacity. Increased sales created a new problem. While Enron could find long-term gas customers downstream, it could not find enough producers of natural gas prepared to sign long-term contracts at a fixed price upstream. Enron addressed this issue by paying a lump sum up front for long-term gas deliveries. In effect, Enron became a source of funding that enabled producers to develop new capacity and was perceived as a business partner.[118] For its contract parties, Enron was an alternative to bank funding. Had Enron not been subject to funding constraints itself, Enron could have offered better terms compared with the terms offered by banks, because Enron had better information about gas prices and the commercial viability of the project—it was Enron that bought the gas.

  Enron nevertheless had funding constraints, because its business model was very capital intensive and debt funding with the customary covenants and credit enhancements would have constrained its activities too much. Enron addressed this issue by starting to securitise the future gas deliveries that it had financed. This required the use of special-purpose entities.[119] The use of securitisation enabled Enron to turn to capital markets and reduce its reliance on lenders. Generally, Enron tried to keep debt off its balance sheet and put a minimal amount of Enron's own capital at risk.[120] Enron ended up using securitisation on a large scale.[121]

---

[115] *Ibid*, pp. 23–24.
[116] *Ibid*, pp. 34–35.
[117] *Ibid*, pp. 48–49.
[118] *Ibid*, pp. 35–36.
[119] *Ibid*, pp. 66–67.
[120] See, for example, *ibid*, p. 77.
[121] *Ibid*, p. 158.

- Fourth phase: financial instruments. Now, Enron had acted as a "physical gas bank". Enron was nevertheless exposed to a price risk, because long-term supply contracts could not be perfectly hedged by long-term purchase contracts. Enron mitigated this risk by becoming more like a "bank". For this purpose, it created a market for standardised contracts that could be traded, and a market for gas derivatives. Both enabled Enron to see its commitments as financial commitments and its portfolio as a portfolio of contracts rather than as a portfolio of physical assets.[122]
- Fifth phase: electricity market. In the 1990s, Enron's business model had to be revised for two reasons. First, gas producers had access to bank funding and did not need Enron as a source of funding. Second, large industrial consumers could use their own traders and did not need to sign long-term contracts with Enron. One of the attempted solutions was to enter the electricity market,[123] that is diversification or integration across value chains.

Vattenfall Vattenfall is an example of the move from complete vertical integration to unbundled markets and electricity generation from renewable sources combined with coal-powered generation. The Vattenfall case shows that the business models of electricity producers are heavily influenced by regulatory choices and the structure of the market. Vattenfall's evolution can be summarised as follows:

- Regulated markets, complete vertical integration. The origins of Vattenfall lie in Swedish hydropower. Vattenfall started as a state enterprise that built, owned, and operated large hydropower plants as well as transmission lines. In 1952, Vattenfall became the owner and operator of the entire Swedish high-voltage grid.
- Market integration. There were three major changes in the 1990s in anticipation of the unbundling of generation and transmission as well the integration of European electricity markets. First, Vattenfall was incorporated as Vattenfall AB, a Swedish limited-liability company (1992). Second, responsibility for the national grid was transferred to the newly formed state authority Svenska Kraftnät (1992). Third, Vattenfall's board chose a European expansion strategy. As a result, Vattenfall became Germany's third-largest electricity producer in 2002.
- Unbundling. Unbundling followed. The Swedish electricity grid operations were separated from electricity generation and sales in 1996. In 2010, Vattenfall sold 50Hertz Transmission GmbH, its high-voltage transmission grid in Germany.
- Renewable electricity generation, climate control. EU law and German law fostered electricity generation from renewable sources and gave an incentive not to invest in electricity generation from other sources. There was a trend of

[122] *Ibid*, p. 37.

[123] *Ibid*, pp. 105–106.

falling wholesale electricity prices.[124] Vattenfall invested more in wind power. In 2008, Vattenfall decided to be climate neutral by 2050.
- Divestment of nuclear power. The Energiewende of 2011 was a major policy change after Fukushima.[125] The German parliament decided to take all nuclear power plants in Germany out of operation. As a result, Vattenfall had to start focusing on its other core operations. Several divestments followed.
- Market overcapacities in electricity generation and low prices caused by the preferential treatment of RES-E forced Vattenfall to reduce investment in new generation installations, cut production costs, and increase the flexibility of its coal-burning installations.[126]

DONG Energy The case of DONG Energy is an example of a move from the business model of a diversified energy merchant to a less diversified and more generation-focused business model.

- DONG Energy is the result of the merger of DONG and five other Danish energy companies in 2006. DONG's origins lie in Dansk Naturgas A/S, a company founded by the Danish state in 1972. The name of Dansk Naturgas A/S was changed to Dansk Olie og Naturgas A/S in 1973 and to DONG in 2002.
- The activities of DONG Energy included: the exploration and production of oil and natural gas; the generation of electricity and RES-E; the distribution of natural gas and electricity; as well as sales, advisory services, and trading.
- DONG Energy expanded through organic growth and acquisitions both in Denmark and across Europe. In 2013, most of its electricity and heat was generated at central coal-fired, gas-fired, and biomass-fired CHP plants in Denmark as well as at new gas-fired power plants in Norway, the Netherlands, and the UK. DONG Energy had also built more offshore wind farms than any other company in the world. DONG Energy supplied energy to customers in the Danish, Swedish, German, Dutch, and UK markets and traded on European energy hubs and exchanges.
- After heavy losses, however, DONG Energy had to change its business model. On 27 February 2013, the company announced its intention to divest non-core activities and focus on financial value creation and transformation to green energy. The assets it divested already the same year included gas-fired power plants, on-shore wind farms, a stake in a hydropower company (Kraftgården AB), a stake in a utility company (Stadtwerke Lübeck GmbH), and electricity transmission assets. DONG Energy invested more in offshore wind projects and the production of gas.

[124] Mihm A (2014a): "Um Planungssicherheit zu haben, verkaufen viele Stromproduzenten große Teile ihrer Erzeugung auf Termin, also zu heutigen Konditionen, aber späterer Lieferung ... Pech nur, dass das Überangebot an Elektrizität für weiter fallende Preise sorgt".

[125] For a summary of Energiewende legislation, see, for example, Ortlieb B (2011).

[126] Mihm A (2014b).

- The result was a less diversified firm that was more focused on off-shore electricity generation as well the exploration and production of gas and oil. DONG Energy's corporate structure consisted of four business units: Exploration & Production, Wind Power, Thermal Power, and Customers & Markets.

Effect of Preferential Treatment of RES-E The preferential treatment of RES-E has increased the supply of zero-marginal cost electricity in the EU. On one hand, this can reduce average wholesale electricity prices and demand for conventional generation. On the other, conventional generation can provide reserve capacity if it can operate flexibly. It will need to start and stop more frequently and be used at different capacity levels.[127]

The preferential treatment of RES-E has also increased competition and the scope of services provided by market participants. To illustrate, one can identify four types of corporate wind power ownership: large utility companies and developers with a portfolio of generating capacity; independent wind farm developers; wind turbine manufacturers and companies involved in the supply of component parts; and companies providing specialist services.[128]

Moreover, the preferential treatment of RES-E has increased levels of microgeneration and self-generation by end consumers.

Electricity producers need to adapt their business model to market changes caused by the preferential treatment of RES-E.

First, depending on the market, electricity producers may try to choose between being remunerated for energy and ancillary services or compensated for their installed or available capacity.[129]

Second, electricity producers may need to invest in RES-E themselves or find themselves reduced to the role of providers of a residual service (that supply energy when other sources are not available) and suppliers of balance energy (that provide ancillary services to the system operator). Their incentives and the choice of generation technology depend on the RES-E support mechanism in each Member State.[130]

Third, electricity producers may also choose to provide services to microgenerators and self-generators.[131] Electricity firms can facilitate microgeneration and end consumers' own generation by means of virtual power plants (Sect. 8.2.3) or other structured contracts (Sect. 8.2.4) and by providing other services.

> There will be stronger incentives for end consumers to invest in their own generation capacity, because: the high costs of the preferential treatment of RES-E are allocated to end

---

[127] Baker PE et al. (2010), p. 7.

[128] Strachan PA et al. (2006), p. 5; Strachan PA et al. (2010), p. 5.

[129] Bushnell J (2010), p. 160.

[130] For a comparison of feed-in tariffs, bidding, and exchangeable quotas, see Finon D and Perez Y (2007).

[131] Green R (2010), p. 137.

consumers; own generation can reduce these costs[132]; own generation can enable consumers to sell surplus generation and benefit from the preferential treatment of RES-E; and the increased share of RES-E generation makes it necessary for large consumers to manage risk and increase security of supply.[133]

Fourth, electricity producers may need to increase vertical integration, do more business outside the EU, or diversify to other business areas.

Fifth, electricity producers may need to decide what to do with their traditional other activities.

E.ON The case of E.ON shows how a traditional integrated firm may need to take bold action to adapt to market changes caused by the preferential treatment of RES-E. In 2014, E.ON went further than Vattenfall and DONG Energy.

- E.ON AG was the result of the 2000 merger of VEBA and VIAG, two large German companies. In 2012, E.ON AG was reincorporated as E.ON SE.
- E.ON first chose to increase the share of RES-E, move further into electricity retailing, and to invest in emerging markets.[134]
- In 2014, E.ON decided to focus on renewables, distribution networks, and customer solutions. It decided to incorporate its conventional generation, global energy trading, and exploration and production businesses into a new company and spin the majority of shares in the new company to E.ON shareholders (subject to approval by the E.ON shareholders meeting in 2016).[135]

2.4 The Physical Characteristics of Electrical Energy

Electricity is a peculiar commodity. It is different from both money and other goods. One could say that an increase in the amount of most goods apart from money can increase welfare.[136] But unlike money and other goods, electricity cannot be stored in large quantities. Electricity is more like a *service* that is consumed the moment it is produced.

The physical characteristics of electricity influence the commercial objectives of market participants and the way they use legal tools and practices to reach them. Most of the particular characteristics of electricity supply contracts can be explained by the physical characteristics of electricity.

[132] For Germany, see § 61 EEG 2014.

[133] See, for example, Bardt H et al. (2014).

[134] See, for example, E.ON press releases, 3 May 2013 (2013 E.ON Annual Shareholders Meeting: building the new E.ON) and 13 November 2013 (E.ON stays on course in difficult environment).

[135] E.ON press release, 30 November 2014.

[136] Money is different, because its only function is to work as a medium of exchange. An increase in the amount of money is designed to reduce its value and redistribute wealth. These effects are also known as Cantillon effects.

Balance and Storage First, although energy can be stored, electrical energy cannot be stored as such in the wholesale market in quantities large enough to meet demand. For this reason, electrical energy must be generated by electricity producers the moment it is consumed by end consumers, and supply and demand must be balanced at all times. Demand—also known as the load—means the sum of (a) the amount of power consumers require at a particular time and (b) losses.[137] System demand is measured in megawatts.

Electricity is typically "stored" in the form of spare generating capacity and fuel inventories at power plants. As the load varies over time, a certain amount of generation capacity must always be held in reserve, and the cost of producing electrical energy changes with the load. Even electricity generation—in particular, generation from different sources—can vary over time. This makes it necessary to keep different forms of generation capacity in reserve. On the other hand, in unbundled and liberalised markets, the high cost of idle capacity discourages electricity producers from acquiring surplus capacity that would rarely operate.[138]

If electrical energy could be stored in large quantities, stored energy could be used for "peak shaving". Peak shaving would help to reduce the amount of investment in alternative reserve generation capacity. The storage of electrical energy could enable "time shifting" to address the characteristic problems inherent in hydro, wind, and solar power.

Whereas electricity cannot be stored as such in the wholesale market, it is technically possible to consume electricity to store energy in another form. There are some widely-used forms of bulk-energy storage. However, they are not commercially viable.[139] Some storage systems can help to smooth short-term variations in output from renewable sources.[140]

The problem with bulk-energy storage is that much of energy will be lost in the process and that typically they can only be used for a relatively short period of time.[141] (a) By far the most important form of bulk-energy storage is pumped storage hydropower (PSH) that uses two water reservoirs at different heights and gravity. In 2012, PSH may have accounted for more than 99 % of bulk storage capacity worldwide.[142] There are hundreds of PSH power plants in the world, in particular in countries such as Japan or the USA with favourable geographic conditions. However, the use of PSH is constrained by the availability of suitable locations in the mountains and their relatively small size.[143] (b) The "power-to-gas"

137 There are losses because of resistance. Materials typically have no resistance at temperatures approaching absolute zero (−273 °C).

138 U.S. Energy Information Administration (2002), Chapter 4.

139 See, for example, Hotakainen M and Klimstra J (2011), section 3.5.

140 Hotakainen M and Klimstra J (2011), section 3.5.

141 Monopolkommission (2013), number 327.

142 The Economist Technology Quarterly, Packing some power (3 March 2012), referring to the Electric Power Research Institute (EPRI), the research arm of America's power utilities.

143 Monopolkommission (2013), number 327.

method would be less efficient compared with PSH.[144] (c) On a smaller scale, one might be able to use batteries. There are hundreds of power plants with battery storage. However, their capacity is relatively small and the lifetime of batteries is short. Batteries are often used in the connection of wind parks. There are no batteries that could store and discharge electricity in large quantities for a long period in the wholesale market. (d) One can also name compressed-air energy storage (CAES), and pumped heat energy storage (PHES). However, they are not yet commercially viable.

The EU tries to foster the development of bulk-energy storage technologies.[145] Interestingly, the preferential treatment of RES-E has had a negative impact on bulk-energy storage in the EU. In the past, bulk-energy storage firms bought electricity at night when electricity consumption and electricity prices were lower and sold electricity when consumption and electricity prices were higher. Because of the preferential treatment of RES-E, spot prices can be low when consumption is high since solar power is available by day and the marginal production costs of wind power and solar power are low.

Transfer The second characteristic aspect relates to electricity transfer. Electrical energy cannot be transferred without a conducting material. Commercially, it cannot be transmitted and distributed without lines and the grid.

The grid consists of nodes (busses or busbars) connected by lines and/or transformers. To organise the market, groups of nodes are aggregated into areas. Transmission lines called interconnectors can be used to connect areas with other areas. One or more areas may form a zone controlled by a system operator.

Some electrical energy is lost as heat because of resistance when electricity is generated or transmitted.

In theory, superconducting cables could help. Superconducting cables can carry many times more current in the same unit area while reducing energy losses to a small fraction. However, superconducting cables are very expensive to make. In the long term, superconducting cables could bring benefits when electricity is transmitted over a very long distance (especially when wind or solar power is transmitted from remote places), or when electricity must be generated, transmitted, or transformed in very small space (in very crowded cities, in high-altitude wind turbines, in trains).

Flow Third, according to Kirchhoffs's laws, electricity that flows between two points—such as the generator and the customer—moves through *all lines* connecting the two. This can cause the problem of "loop flows".[146] System operators must carefully balance power inflows and outflows so that individual transmission and distribution wires are not overloaded. For the same reason, electricity transmission is not like the transportation of physical commodities.[147]

[144] *Ibid*, number 326.

[145] See Annex II (energy infrastructure categories) to Regulation 347/2013 on guidelines for trans European energy infrastructure.

[146] See, for example, Brown MH and Sedano RP (2004), p. 62.

[147] See, for example, Oren SS et al. (1995), p. 26; Hsu M (1997).

Spreading of Electric Charge Over a Conducting Surface Fourth, electric charge has a tendency to spread itself as evenly as possible over a conducting surface. Electricity flows over all paths made available to it and over the path of least resistance. This means that electrical energy transmitted in the grid is homogeneous in the physical sense regardless of how it is generated.

Unit The fifth characteristic aspect relates to the "unit" of electricity. The unit of electrical energy as a commodity should be conditioned on both *time and location*, and electrical energy can mean either the *flow* or the *accumulation* of power.

Electrical energy can thus mean one of two things as a commodity. (a) The flow of energy (the average power) during a particular interval of time at a particular location on the transmission grid can be described in the following way: "4 MW at bus K during hour H". (b) The accumulation of power (the total energy) during a particular time interval at a particular location on the transmission grid can be described in this way: "6 MWh at bus K during hour H".

2.5 Characteristic Issues

2.5.1 General Remarks

Contracts for the physical supply of electricity are complex contracts that must address several issues. The core terms of electricity supply contracts are thus not limited to the supplier's obligation to supply electricity and the buyer's obligation to pay the price.[148]

Because of *physical laws* and *efficiency constraints*, there are *characteristic issues* that must be managed by market participants. Moreover, they must manage both *physical flows* and *legal rights*.

The parties must address characteristic issues relating to: (a) grid access, delivery point, and voltage level; (b) volume; (c) transmission and distribution capacity; (d) balance; (e) measurement; (f) the separation of physical rights, service rights, and financial rights; and (g) price volatility.

The characteristic issues influence the contents of electricity supply contracts, the contents of electricity derivatives, and the structure of electricity markets.[149]

[148] Such terms may be important when the contract is classified as one of sale for the purposes of determining whether the contract falls within the scope of certain substantive provisions of contract law applicable to sale of goods. See, for example, Bydlinski F (1972), p. 33. Bydlinski defines the delivery of electricity for consideration as the primary performance. *Ibid*, p. 37.

[149] For the physical market, see, for example, DG Competition report on energy sector inquiry, SEC(2006) 1724, 10 January 2007, para 321: "The electricity industry chain involves five main activities: (1) the production or generation of electricity, (2) the transport of electricity on high voltage levels (transmission), (3) its transportation on low voltage levels (distribution), (4) the marketing of electricity to final customers (supply), and (5) the selling and buying of electricity on

This section will focus on the characteristic issues of electricity supply contracts. The terms of model contracts—in particular, certain terms of the EFET General Agreement Concerning the Delivery and Acceptance of Electricity—illustrate how the characteristic issues are addressed by a large number of market participants in Europe. The EFET General Agreement will be discussed in more detail in Chap. 8. The characteristic issues of electricity transmission contracts will be discussed in Chap. 10.

2.5.2 Grid Access, Delivery Point and Voltage Level

As electricity cannot be transmitted and distributed without wires, there must be transmission and distribution grids. Electricity producers and consumers need grid access. Access to the grid, the delivery point, and the voltage level belong to the characteristic issues that must be addressed by parties to physical electricity supply contracts in the wholesale market.

Delivery Point In the physical sense, electricity must always be supplied to the grid at a certain grid and voltage level at a certain point. The voltage and current at any point are determined by the behaviour of the system as a whole (that is, impedance) rather than by the actions of any two individual parties to a supply contract.[150] The same applies when electricity is extracted from the grid.

Even in the legal sense, physical settlement requires a place for the performance of the obligation to supply electricity. Electricity is "delivered" at a certain grid and voltage level at a certain delivery point and in accordance with the standards of the system operator.[151]

"Delivery" is a term customarily used in sale of goods. However, it could be slightly misleading to use it in the context of electricity supply contracts. There are two main differences between sale of goods and electricity trading in this respect. The first relates to place and the second to its legal relevance.

Place In sale of goods, the buyer is expected to receive exactly the same goods supplied by the seller. The goods cannot simultaneously be in more than one place, and there cannot be more than one place for the physical handling of the goods at a certain point in time. It is possible and meaningful to agree that the goods must

wholesale markets (trading). Sometimes services such as metering are mentioned as additional activity".

150 U.S. Energy Information Administration (2002), Chapter 4.

151 This is reflected in the EFET General Agreement (Version 2.1(a)), § 6.1: "Current/Frequency/ Voltages: Electricity shall be delivered in the current, frequency and voltage applicable at the relevant Delivery Point agreed in the Individual Contract and in accordance with the standards of the Network Operator responsible for the Delivery Point".

possess the required characteristics in a certain place, or attach the passing of risk to that place. This place is customarily called the place of delivery.[152]

In electricity markets, however, it is not possible to identify such a place for technical reasons. (a) It would be impossible to identify the location of goods that do not exist in the first place. In electricity markets, the main rule is that a particular electricity consumer does not really receive any physical "goods" supplied by any particular electricity producer. Electric charge spreads itself over a conducting surface and electrical energy transmitted in the grid is homogeneous in the physical sense. (b) Moreover, the place where electricity is supplied to the grid is not the place where electricity is extracted from the grid. There are entry points for electricity flows into the grid and exit points for electricity flows from the grid. There is a boundary point at which a plant or appliance is connected to the grid. Generators and end consumers do not share the same grid connection. Moreover, a central counterparty—the contract party in a very large number of trades—would not have a grid connection at all. It would not be meaningful to choose the point of the central counterparty's grid connection as the place of delivery in transactions with a central counterparty.

In practice, it is sufficient to identify the grid and the grid level, or—where buy and sell orders are matched on an exchange—the "bidding area". Matching bids must necessarily relate to electricity flows in the same grid and at the same grid level. Since grids traditionally have been regional or national, the points of entry and exit customarily are in the same country in electricity spot markets and the bidding area is located inside the borders of one country or a smaller region.[153] Market coupling makes it possible to choose entry and exit point in different zones.

The Legal Relevance of the Place of Delivery The second difference between sale of goods and electricity supply contracts relates to the legal relevance of the place of delivery. In sale of goods, the place of delivery is the place where: goods are handed over to the buyer or a carrier[154]; goods must comply with the agreed or implied specifications[155]; and risk passes to the buyer.[156] In electricity trading, however, the place of delivery does not have to be connected with such issues. Electricity cannot be "handed over" to the buyer, because electricity can neither be stored nor transferred without wires (or other conducting material). Moreover, a consumer that extracts electricity from the grid does not really consume electricity supplied to the grid by a certain electricity producer, because electric charge is

---

[152] See CISG Article 30.

[153] Nord Pool Spot Market, Trading Appendix 1, Definitions (27 November 2014): "Bidding Area means a sub area of the Electricity Exchange Area defined by the TSOs. The Electricity Exchange area is divided into bidding areas in order to handle transmission constraints. Participants must make Orders according to where their production or consumption is physically connected in the grid thus specifying the bidding area for each Order".

[154] CISG Articles 30 and 31.

[155] CISG Articles 35(1) and 36(1) as well as CISG Articles 41 and 42.

[156] CISG Article 67.

spread evenly and electricity is supplied to the grid and extracted from the grid at different points.

There are nevertheless actions or functions that can be connected to a place of delivery. First, electricity should be supplied to the grid. The place of delivery can be used as the point where the supplier supplies the agreed volumes to the grid for the purpose of matching the extraction of electricity by its contract party—a downstream distributor or end consumer, or the transmission or distribution system operator—somewhere else in the grid. Second, the place of delivery can be used to allocate responsibility for the availability of transmission capacity. Electricity cannot be transferred without grid connection and transmission capacity. Third, the place of delivery can be used to allocate the responsibility for costs and risks.

A delivery point is used in the EFET General Agreement: "In accordance with each Individual Contract, the Seller shall Schedule, sell and deliver, or cause to be delivered, and the Buyer shall Schedule, purchase and accept, or cause to be accepted, the Contract Quantity at the Delivery Point; and the Buyer shall pay to the Seller the relevant Contract Price".[157] The delivery point is used for risk allocation: "Seller shall bear all risks associated with, and shall be responsible for any costs or charges imposed on or associated with Scheduling, transmission and delivery of the Contract Quantity up to the Delivery Point. Buyer shall bear all risks associated with, and shall be responsible for any costs or charges imposed on or associated with acceptance and transmission of, the Contract Quantity at and from the Delivery Point".[158]

The function of the place of delivery can depend on the competition model (Sect. 2.6). In the vertically integrated market model with one electricity company responsible for the generation and distribution of electricity, the point of delivery can be used roughly in the same way as in sale of goods as the consumer has just one contract party.[159] In the liberalised (unbundled) market model, however, the electricity producer customarily does not control electricity flows in the grid.

The following term of the EFET General Agreement reflects the vertically integrated market model rather than the liberalised market model: "Delivery shall be effected by making available the Contract Quantity at the Contract Capacity at the Delivery Point. Delivery and receipt of the Contract Quantity . . . shall take place at the Delivery Point".[160]

The place of delivery can further influence the scope and application of other rules applicable to electricity markets. To illustrate, the prohibition of market abuse under REMIT (Sect. 4.7) does not apply unless there are "wholesale energy products" that fall within its scope, and the physical supply contracts that fall within its scope include: "contracts for the supply of electricity or natural gas where delivery is in the Union".[161] In this case, "delivery" can be given an autonomous interpretation in the light of the purpose of REMIT.

---

[157] EFET General Agreement (Version 2.1(a)), § 4.1.

[158] EFET General Agreement (Version 2.1(a)), § 6.7.

[159] See, for example, Bydlinski F (1972), pp. 46–47 for Austrian law.

[160] EFET General Agreement (Version 2.1(a)), § 6.3.

[161] Point 4 of Article 2 of Regulation 1227/2011 (REMIT).

2.5.3 Volume

The volume of electrical energy must be determined in a particular way. First, there are particular *units* for electricity (current, frequency, voltage) and electrical energy. Second, if the volume of electrical energy is determined in advance, the unit for electrical energy as a commodity must be conditioned on both *location and time*.

Let us assume that the location is a particular location on the transmission grid. Electrical energy can then mean two things as a commodity. It can mean the *flow* of energy (the average power) during a particular interval of time at that particular location (expressed in MW) or the *accumulation* of power (the total energy) during a particular time interval at that particular location (expressed in MWh).

> The EFET General Agreement distinguishes between contract capacity (MW) and contract quantity (MWh): "... 'Contract Capacity' means, in respect of an Individual Contract, the capacity agreed between the Parties, expressed in MW; ... 'Contract Quantity' means, in respect of an Individual Contract, the quantity agreed between the Parties, expressed in MWh ..."[162]
>
> The seller undertakes a duty to supply a certain total energy volume during a certain supply period at a certain location: "In accordance with each Individual Contract, the Seller shall Schedule, sell and deliver, or cause to be delivered, and the Buyer shall Schedule, purchase and accept, or cause to be accepted, the Contract Quantity at the Delivery Point; and the Buyer shall pay to the Seller the relevant Contract Price".[163]

2.5.4 Transmission and Distribution Capacity

It is not enough to agree on the volume to be supplied and grid access. Electricity producers, wholesalers, and retailers cannot supply electricity to end consumers or other customers without sufficient transmission and/or distribution capacity.[164]

Congestion Electricity flows are constrained by the available system capacity. When demand for transmission or distribution capacity exceeds the available capacity, there is congestion. Congestion can be caused by technical constraints or economic restrictions (such as priority feed-in rules or contract enforcement limits). An efficient system is sometimes congested, because the costs for building new system capacity can exceed the costs of congestion at the times of peak flows.[165]

---

[162] Annex 1 to the EFET General Agreement, Version 2.1(a).

[163] EFET General Agreement (Version 2.1(a)), § 4.1.

[164] For definitions of these terms, see Article 2 of Directive 2009/72/EC (Third Electricity Directive).

[165] Green R (2003), p. 137.

Loop Flows When managing transmission and distribution capacity and congestion, system operators must take into account loop flows. Loop flows make it more difficult to determine actual flow-based paths (parallel flows) when multiple users compete on the same transmission system.

Models for Capacity Allocation and Pricing Regulators and TSOs must choose a model for capacity allocation and pricing. There is a long list of models to choose from (Chap. 5).

In normal market conditions, the chosen model should preferably give such locational and temporal signals for electricity supply (feed-in) and extraction (load) that reflect the costs caused by grid users. The absence of such signals implies that costs are socialised and leads to an inefficient infrastructure use. The existence of proper signals contributes to a more efficient use of transmission infrastructure—in particular where the transmission system is well interconnected and has several alternative sources of supply.

Allocation of Responsibilities and Costs Regardless of the model for capacity allocation, somebody should be responsible for ensuring that the necessary transmission/distribution capacity is available. (a) The allocation of responsibility is clear in vertically integrated markets. In this case, one electricity firm controls both the supply of electricity and the grid. (b) In the liberalised and unbundled electricity markets of the EU, the parties must buy transmission/distribution capacity from a transmission/distribution system operator.

In principle, parties to a bilateral supply contract can freely allocate the responsibility for the availability of transmission/distribution capacity and its costs.[166]

> In the EFET General Agreement, the Delivery Point is used to allocate the responsibility for the availability of transmission/distribution capacity between the parties.[167] The main rule is that the responsibility for the availability of transmission/distribution capacity changes at the Delivery Point.[168]

2.5.5 Balance

Electricity generation must always be balanced with electricity consumption, and electricity consumption must always be balanced with electricity generation. Even minor imbalances can cause the system frequency to fall or rise to unacceptable levels. However, the volumes of energy actually generated and consumed tend to deviate from the quantities for which contracts have been made in advance. These

---

[166] In the gas market, shippers are typically interested in booking capacity from a specific source to a specific destination without being particularly interested in intermediate interconnections. See Ruester S et al. (2012), section 5.4.

[167] EFET General Agreement (Version 2.1(a)), § 4.1.

[168] EFET General Agreement (Version 2.1(a)), § 6.7.

imbalances can be created both by consumers and by generators. For instance, generators cause imbalances when they supply more than—or less than—the quantities they have scheduled in advance.

Different kinds of electricity firms can have different objectives as far as the balancing of electricity flows is concerned. (a) All electricity firms manage quantity risks (volumetric risks) in the physical market. (b) An end consumer, retailer, or wholesaler tries to ensure security of supply.[169] (c) An electricity producer, wholesaler, or retailer tries to ensure security of consumption (off-take) by finding electricity consumers for the electricity that it will generate or has purchased. (d) The system operator (TSO/DSO) must ensure that there is a balance of electricity fed into the system on one hand and electricity extracted from the system and losses on the other.

As a result, you could say that there is no such thing as "sale of electricity". In reality, what is often known as the "sale" of electricity means the provision of a particular service: the balancing of electricity consumption or extraction with electricity generation or supply at a certain point of the grid.

The language and concepts of sale of goods nevertheless tend to be used even where they do not reflect the physical world of electricity as well as they should. They can therefore be misleading.[170] The misleading language can partly depend on the broad scope of sale of goods laws. The relevance of the classification of electricity as sale of goods or the provision of a service will be discussed in Sect. 2.7 in greater detail.

Quantity Risks, Security of Supply, Security of Off-Take/Consumption Parties to an electricity supply contract can allocate quantity risks (volumetric risks) in many ways.

The agreed volumes can be fixed or variable. (a) When the quantities are fixed, security of off-take/consumption is increased for the supplier. For the consumer, security of supply is limited to the agreed minimum quantities. (b) When the volumes are variable, security of supply and security of consumption can depend on the level of discretion and its allocation between the parties. If the quantities extracted by the end consumer are left to its own discretion, security of supply is increased for the consumer. The volumetric risk is then transferred to the supplier.[171] It would be less common to leave the quantities to the discretion of the generator. There can be exceptions such as the right to sell RES-E to the DSO/TSO in Germany.

---

[169] The legislator can facilitate this in various ways. See Finon D and Pignon V (2008).

[170] See, for example, Nord Pool Spot Market, Trading Appendix 1, Definitions (27 November 2014): "Delivery means the electricity amount to be delivered upon settlement of Transactions as further provided for in Appendix 4". However, there cannot be any actual delivery of certain electrons from the generator to the end consumer. See, therefore, Nord Pool Spot Physical Markets, Trading Appendix 4, Clearing Rules (27 November 2014), section 4.1.4 (on cash settlement) and section 4.1.3 (on physical settlement).

[171] See also Bydlinski F (1972), p. 44. Bydlinski discusses the contract law nature of the buyers' discretion to extract electricity.

In unbundled electricity markets, even electricity wholesalers and retailers must manage quantity risks, because the quantities extracted by end consumers and the quantities fed into the grid by electricity producers vary. Both can nevertheless be estimated in advance to some extent. It is, therefore, possible for electricity retailers to match the estimated downstream load profile with a mix of upstream contracts that share the same profile.

To illustrate, where a retailer expects that its customers will consume 100 MWh during a certain hour of operation, it can purchase two contracts of 30 MWh and 70 MWh, respectively, before the hour of operation.

Where it can estimate its customers' consumption for several consecutive hours, it can make a block-order for a block of consecutive hours (for block-orders, see Sect. 4.5.4).[172]

Balance, Dispatching of Power Plants, Use of Interconnectors There must a party responsible for the operation and management of the transmission or distribution system as well as for balance management. In unbundled electricity markets, the system operator—customarily the TSO—is responsible for balancing the transmission system.[173]

System operators must balance power generation to load at any time during real-time operations. For this reason, they can also be made responsible for dispatching power plants and for the use of interconnectors.

The Third Electricity Directive provides that the TSO must use published criteria for this purpose. The criteria must be objective, applied in a non-discriminatory manner, and ensure the proper functioning of the internal market in electricity. The criteria must also be approved by the regulatory authority.[174]

Balancing Energy Market To be able to balance the system, the system operator must: meter the quantities produced and consumed by each party; compare these with the quantities covered by bilateral contracts; ensure that there is balancing energy (physical settlement); and provide financial settlement for the differences and balancing energy.

This can be illustrated with the following example. A retailer expects its customers to consume 100 MWh during a certain hour of operation. It purchases 100 MWh before the hour of operation and pays its suppliers for 100 MWh. However, it turns out that the retailer's customers have only used 85 MWh during this hour of operation. There must be a trade that creates a balance between the retailer's total trading and its customers' consumption. There must be a balancing trade even where the retailer's customers use 110 MWh or 10 MWh more than the retailer bought before the hour of operation.

System operators and market participants use a balancing energy or real-time market after the closure of the spot market. While individual trades may be voluntary on this market, participation may be mandatory for some market participants. A party may not get access to the transmission grid or a spot exchange

[172] Spicker J (2010), p. 98, point 148.

[173] Article 15(1) of Directive 2009/72/EC (Third Electricity Directive).

[174] Article 15(2) of Directive 2009/72/EC (Third Electricity Directive).

without a contract on balancing arrangements (see Sects. 4.4.4 and 4.4.5 on clearing and settlement and Sect. 9.2 on balance responsibility).

In the EU, this requirement is also based on the Third Electricity Directive. A TSO must adopt rules for balancing the electricity system[175] and even a DSO may have to adopt such rules.[176] A supplier must follow the applicable trading and balancing rules.[177] The provision of balancing services is controlled by the regulatory authority that also approves their terms.[178]

The requirement on balancing arrangements can also be illustrated with the regulatory practices in the Nordic spot market (Nord Pool Spot), the continental European spot market (EPEX Spot) and the market for England and Wales. (a) Nord Pool Spot. Each Participant and Client must in its own name or through another company have entered into an agreement on balance responsibility with the relevant balance responsible party or TSO.[179] (b) EPEX Spot. An Exchange Member can be a party that has entered into a Balance Responsible Agreement with a Balance Responsible,[180] or the Balance Responsible that has concluded an agreement with a TSO on balance responsibility.[181] (c) BSC. In England, the National Grid Company (NGC) must apply the Balancing and Settlement Code (BSC) according to the terms of its own licence. The BSC provides for a balancing mechanism that enables the NGC as the system operator to buy or sell additional energy and to deal with operational constraints of the transmission system. Neither electricity producers not suppliers will be granted a Generation and Supply Licence unless they sign the BSC Framework Agreement (which gives contractual force to the BSC).[182]

Both the TSO and market participants may need to pay for balancing energy. The TSO pays for balancing energy both (a) when it needs up-regulating energy and (b) when it needs down-regulating energy. Competitive market mechanisms are increasingly sought for market participants' balancing services (also known as the ancillary services of market participants).[183]

---

[175] See Articles 12(d), 15(1) and 15(7) of Directive 2009/72/EC (Third Electricity Directive).

[176] See Articles 25(1), 25(5) and 25(6) of Directive 2009/72/EC (Third Electricity Directive).

[177] Article 3(4) of Directive 2009/72/EC (Third Electricity Directive).

[178] See Articles 37(6), 37(7) and 37(8) of Directive 2009/72/EC (Third Electricity Directive). See also recital 35 of Directive 2009/72/EC (Third Electricity Directive).

[179] Nord Pool Spot's Physical Markets, General Terms, Trading Rules (1 February 2015), section 3.1.4. The relevant TSO is one of the following: Energinet.dk (Denmark); Statnett SF (Norway); Svenska Kraftnät (Sweden); Fingrid Oyj (Finland); Elering OÜ (Estonia); Litgrid (Lithuania); and Augstsprieguma tīkls (AST, Latvia).

[180] EPEX Spot Exchange Rules (13 May 2014), Article 2.23: "EPEX Spot can, for the maintenance of a proper Spot Trading in power, indicate a specific TSO area for the fulfilment of the electricity delivery obligations. If an Exchange Member is not in possession of Balance Responsible Agreement with a balance area Responsible, and if therefore an admission requirement with ECC is missing, the Exchange Member can be suspended from Trading for the period of the non-fulfilment of the admission requirement".

[181] EPEX Spot Rules & Regulations, Appendix, Definitions (28 November 2014): "Balance Responsible. Legal entity obligated to pay a TSO for the after-the-fact Imbalances of a grid-user coming within the Balance Responsible's Perimeter".

[182] See ELEXON, Overview of the Balancing and Settlement Code (BSC) Arrangements (December 2011. Version 2.0).

[183] Madlener R and Kaufmann M (2002), section 2.6.3.

After the closure of the spot market, participants can submit bids in the balancing energy market. The bids specify, for a specific volume and for immediate performance, the prices market participants require or offer to (a) increase their generation or decrease their consumption (up-regulating energy), or (b) decrease their generation or increase their consumption (down-regulating energy). The up-regulating price is customarily higher than the day-ahead exchange price for the particular hour (the market price), and the down-regulating price is customarily lower than the market price.

The TSO sells balancing energy to traders whose purchases and sales are imbalanced. A trader must ensure that it is buying and selling the same amount of energy during each hour. If there is an imbalance, the trader must settle balancing energy with the TSO.

The TSO also sells balancing energy to market participants whose customers consume more than planned and to market participants that produce less electricity than planned. (a) Where the customers of a retailer have used more energy than the quantities that the retailer bought before the hour of operation, the retailer has to buy additional quantities from the TSO and the TSO will invoice the retailer for the additional quantities. (b) A supplier may also need to buy balancing energy when it does not have the electricity it has sold because of a technical failure or otherwise. Where the supplier is an electricity producer whose plant breaks down just before the hour of operation starts, it cannot buy electricity from another supplier. As its customers extract electricity from the grid anyway, the supplier must buy balancing energy from the TSO. The supplier's customers must pay the supplier. The supplier must pay the TSO for balancing energy.

Curtailment While the balancing energy market is partly based on voluntary transactions, curtailment is not. An electricity producer connected to the grid may be curtailed by the system operator during emergency situations to ensure system reliability and operational security (Sects. 5.5 and 10.7.3).[184]

Parties to a supply contract will therefore have to regulate the effect that curtailment or the system operator's other actions will have on their mutual obligations. For instance, curtailment could be defined as a force majeure event in the contract.

The EFET General Agreement makes the actions of a network operator a force majeure event.[185] As a result, a party is relieved from liability under the EFET General Agreement even in situations in which a party would not be relieved from liability under the CISG in sale of goods law.[186]

In the US, curtailment is defined as a force majeure event in the Pro Forma Open Access Transmission Tariff.[187]

---

[184] First subparagraph of Article 16(2) of Regulation 714/2009 on conditions for access to the network for cross-border exchanges in electricity.

[185] EFET General Agreement (Version 2.1(a)), § 7.1.

[186] CISG Article 79.

[187] FERC Order No. 888, Pro Forma Open Access Transmission Tariff, Appendix D, Section 10.1 Force Majeure.

Curtailment is not mentioned as a force majeure event in ACER's CACM Framework Guidelines and the CACM Regulation.[188] On the contrary, there is a distinction between force majeure and curtailment, because the force majeure provisions have been drafted with the TSO's obligations in mind.[189] One may ask whether curtailment can be regarded as an "unforeseeable" event for others (see Sects. 10.7.2 and 10.7.3).

Remedies for Breach of Contract Because of the balance requirement, the performance of physical delivery or off-take obligations may not be a feasible remedy in the event of their breach. While payment delays or delays in the furnishing of collateral do not change these obligations as such,[190] delays in the performance of obligations relations to physical electricity flows may change the obligations.

2.5.6 Measurement

The next characteristic issue that participants must manage in physical electricity markets is measurement. Measurement is made more difficult by loop flows. Loop flows can also make it more difficult to forecast the use of the system.

Measurement is nevertheless vital because of the balance requirement and the fact that the transmission of electricity is not possible without available transmission capacity. It is necessary to (a) estimate electricity generation and consumption in advance and (b) measure actual deliveries and receipts.[191] In addition, measurement is necessary to (c) determine the price payable by the parties for electricity extraction (or supply) and to (d) determine the price payable for the use of transmission capacity. The question of measurement must thus be regulated in many contexts, in particular in electricity supply contracts, in the context of clearing and settlement, and in transmission contracts.

Parties that supply electricity by feeding electricity into the grid and parties that extract electricity from the grid must agree on the measurement of electricity deliveries and receipts unless measurement is regulated by the system operator.

The EFET General Agreement contains terms on measurement: "Each Party is responsible for ensuring that electricity deliveries and receipts are measured or verified by means that can be reasonably evidenced in accordance with the Network Operator's procedures governing the relevant Delivery Point".[192]

The measurement term is connected with a term on the documentation of deliveries and receipts: "Upon reasonable request, a Party shall: (a) provide to the other Party documentation in its possession or control that evidences Schedules, quantities, deliveries and

[188] ACER, Framework Guidelines on Capacity Allocation and Congestion Management for Electricity (29 July 2011), section 6.2; point 45 of Article 2 of Commission Regulation …/.. (CACM Regulation).

[189] See Article 72(1) of Commission Regulation …/.. (CACM Regulation).

[190] See Härle PA (2010), pp. 438–439, points 891–892.

[191] Bydlinski F (1972), pp. 45–46.

[192] EFET General Agreement (Version 2.1(a)), § 6.4.

receipts of electricity for the purposes of determining the cause of any deviations between the terms of an Individual Contract and actual deliveries and receipts of electricity; and (b) use its reasonable and diligent efforts to request and acquire from the Network Operator, and shall share with the requesting Party, any additional documentation necessary to reconcile inconsistencies between Scheduled and actual flows of electricity".[193]

2.5.7 *The Separation of Physical Rights, Service Rights and Financial Rights*

General Remarks

A further issue characteristic of electricity trade is the separation of physical rights, service rights, and financial rights. Market participants end up managing legal rights belonging to these three categories because of (a) physical laws and (b) the existence of imbalances between contract volumes and the actual generation or consumption volumes.[194]

Physical Rights

"Physical rights" to electrical current can here be defined as property rights or title to electrical current as such. One could say that there cannot be any physical rights to electrical current. The reason is its physical nature.

While generation, transmission, and distribution assets are owned by somebody and can be sold or used as collateral, it is more difficult to determine how the concepts of property rights or ownership could be applied to electrical current that is simultaneously generated, supplied, transmitted, distributed, and consumed.

Electrical current is a natural force rather than a thing that can be owned by somebody. Electrical current consists of electrons that: travel at the speed of light; are spread evenly over the conducting surface; and flow through all lines connecting two points. Because of these physical laws, it is impossible to separate electricity generated by one power plant from electricity generated by another power plant in the grid.

Moreover, participants to physical electricity markets provide various kinds of services. While it is customary to apply the concept of ownership to corporeal goods that are capable of being in the physical possession of a person, it would be more difficult to apply it to a natural force that does its work when a service provider provides the service. To illustrate, a hired tree-feller benefits from the existence of gravity but does not own the particles that cause the gravitational force that makes the tree fall.

[193] EFET General Agreement (Version 2.1(a)), § 6.5.

[194] For mismatches, see, for example, Hunt S and Shuttleworth G (1996), p. 137.

In Germany, electrical current is not regarded as a "thing" (Sache). Only corporeal assets that can be controlled can be regarded as things. This definition excludes natural forces, energy, and electrical current.[195] Depending on the context, electricity can nevertheless be regarded as goods ("Waren").[196]

In the EU, the Draft Common Frame of Reference (DCFR) excludes electricity from the Book that applies to the acquisition and loss of ownership of goods.[197] The DCFR defines "goods" as corporeal movables.[198] It is also assumed that "goods" are capable of being in the possession of a person in the sense that a person has direct physical control or indirect physical control over the goods.[199]

This does not prevent the parties from addressing the question of property rights in the contract when they wish to do so. It may be in the parties' interests to do so as part of the management of legal risk. Just in case, they may need to align the wording of the contract to the regulation of property rights under the governing law.

The EFET General Agreement provides an example: "Delivery and receipt of the Contract Quantity, and the transfer from Seller to Buyer of all rights to title free and clear of any adverse claims thereto, shall take place at the Delivery Point".[200]

Service Rights

Although the concepts of property rights and ownership cannot be applied to electrical current, it is customary to apply these concepts to contractual rights. There are various contractual rights relating to electricity. One can distinguish between "service rights" and "financial rights". Service rights can be defined as rights to receive a service provided by a service provider. There are many service contracts in the electricity market. What the service is can depend on the customer.

Electricity Supply Contracts Electricity supply contracts[201] can here be defined as contracts for the balancing of the agreed electricity extraction (supply or end consumption) with the agreed electricity inputs according to the agreed schedule.

---

[195] § 90 BGB. See Larenz K (1989), § 16 II. The Greek CC art. 947 par. 2 adds: "Natural forces or energies, especially electrical current and warmth, also constitute things so far as they are restricted to a specific space and can be controlled". See von Bar C and Drobnig U (2004), p. 317, number 468.

[196] See, for example, BaFin (2011), II.1.b: "Strom ist eine Ware im Sinne des § 1 Abs. 11 KWG".

[197] DCFR VIII. –1:101(1) and DCFR VIII. –1:101(4): "This Book does not apply to: ... (b) electricity".

[198] DCFR VIII. –1:201.

[199] DCFR VIII. –1:205(1): "Possession, in relation to goods, means having direct physical control or indirect physical control over the goods".

[200] EFET General Agreement (Version 2.1(a)), § 6.3.

[201] For definitions, see points 19 and 32 of Article 2 of Directive 2009/72/EC (Third Electricity Directive).

They are contracts to achieve a result (Werkvertrag) rather than contracts to provide work and use skill and care (Dienstvertrag).[202]

This distinction must influence the core obligations of the supplier under the governing law in two ways. First, the supplier undertakes a duty to take all physical steps necessary for the balancing of extraction with the agreed inputs. There is no duty to supply electricity from a certain power plant. In fact, there is no duty to actually generate the balancing energy in the first place.[203] Second, the duty to supply electricity is not a personal duty. It is sufficient for the supplier to procure that the agreed volumes are fed into the grid.

On the other hand, the freedom of contract applies and the parties may choose to regulate the use of power plants, energy sources, the energy mix, and other things in detail.

The end consumer may need to ensure that its consumption is balanced with electricity generated from renewable resources or otherwise in a certain way. Many end consumers choose between different suppliers based on the generation technology or fuel. Such practices are fostered by labelling rules[204] and green certificates (Sect. 7.2).

Electricity Transmission or Distribution Contracts Electricity transmission contracts[205] and electricity distribution contracts[206] are contracts that facilitate, in various ways, the balancing of electricity extraction and electricity inputs. (a) First, they—or particular contracts on grid connection—provide a connection to wires that connect the point of electricity inputs with the point of electricity outputs. (b) Second, they make transmission or distribution capacity available. (c) Third, they facilitate the provision of grid management services and other ancillary services required to ensure the smooth functioning and reliability of the system.[207]

For example, these grid management services can include "energy imbalance services, spinning or non-spinning reserve capacity, supplemental reserve capacity, reactive power supply and voltage control services, and voltage regulation and frequency response services".[208] System users[209] can have rights to receive such a service as parties supplying electricity to the transmission or distribution system, or as parties being supplied by the system.

Perspective What the service is depends on the customer (see Sect. 2.5.8). From the perspective of the end consumer,[210] both electricity transmission

[202] Bydlinski F (1972), p. 38.

[203] *Ibid*, p. 37.

[204] First subparagraph of Article 3(9) of Directive 2009/72/EC (Third Electricity Directive). See also Note of DG Energy & Transport on Directives 2003/54 and 2003/55 on the Internal Market in Electricity and Natural Gas: Labelling provision in Directive 2003/54/EC.

[205] Point 3 of Article 2 of Directive 2009/72/EC (Third Electricity Directive).

[206] Point 5 of Article 2 of Directive 2009/72/EC (Third Electricity Directive).

[207] Points 4, 6 and 17 of Article 2 of Directive 2009/72/EC (Third Electricity Directive).

[208] U.S. Energy Information Administration (2002), Chapter 4.

[209] Point 18 of Article 2 of Directive 2009/72/EC (Third Electricity Directive).

[210] Points 9 and 19 of Article 2 of Directive 2009/72/EC (Third Electricity Directive).

(or distribution) contracts and electricity supply contracts facilitate the use of electrical appliances. An electricity transmission (distribution) contract is a contract that facilitates access to the system and makes transmission (distribution) capacity available. An electricity supply contract is a contract for the balancing of electricity consumption with electricity supplied to the grid.

Market participants provide even ancillary services in addition to the core services. For example, it is necessary to maintain balance between supply and demand during each operational hour (Sects. 4.6 and 9.3). These ancillary services could, in principle, be provided by the system operator or grid users. (a) In the US, related ancillary services are defined as services "that are necessary to support the transmission of capacity and energy from resources to loads while maintaining reliable operation of the Transmission Provider's Transmission System in accordance with Good Utility Practice".[211] The transmission service provider is required to provide these ancillary services and the transmission customer is required to purchase them from the transmission provider.[212] (b) Even the TSO can be a customer and purchase these ancillary services from electricity producers and end consumers. In the EU, the TSO has a duty to monitor the availability of these ancillary services and purchase them.[213]

Core Services and Take-or-Pay Clauses The fact that the core service in electricity supply contracts relates to balancing rather than the actual supply or off-take of electrical energy makes it easier to understand why take-or-pay clauses are so often used in electricity wholesale markets. A take-or-pay clause means that the buyer pays the price even in the absence of off-take. It is connected with the core balancing services as it allocates the risk of imbalances on the buyer's side between the contract parties. Therefore, it may have a material effect on the pricing of the supplier's core service (Sect. 8.5.3).

Assignment of Rights to Be Supplied Electricity While a party may assign its rights under general contract law principles, the assignment of physical service rights in the wholesale market is constrained by the fact that the rights cannot be separated from the assignor's obligations to the system operator.

First, electricity can neither be supplied nor transmitted without grid connection, and there is no grid connection without an agreement with the system operator.

---

[211] FERC Order No. 888, Pro Forma Open Access Transmission Tariff, Appendix D, Section 1.1.

[212] FERC Order No. 888, Pro Forma Open Access Transmission Tariff, Appendix D, Section 3. Ancillary Services: "Ancillary Services are needed with transmission service to maintain reliability within and among the Control Areas affected by the transmission service. The Transmission Provider is required to provide (or offer to arrange with the local Control Area operator . . .), and the Transmission Customer is required to purchase, the following Ancillary Services (i) Scheduling, System Control and Dispatch, and (ii) Reactive Supply and Voltage Control from Generation Sources".

[213] Article 50(1) of ENTSO-E Network Code on Operational Planning and Scheduling (24 September 2013).

Second, electricity cannot be supplied without rights to transmission capacity, and rights to transmission capacity again require an agreement with the system operator.

Third, service rights in the wholesale market can be mirrored by the party's obligations to use them. A party has a contractual duty to make the scheduled flows happen.

Fourth, the system operator would be affected if the assignment of physical service rights were permitted. (a) The reserved flows might not be relevant for the assignee. The assignee might need to change the specifications set out in the agreement with the system operator. For example, it would need to change the agreed grid points for electricity supply or extraction.[214] (b) Actual flows depend on the holder of the physical rights. The system operator will take actual flows into account when managing system flows. If the assignment of physical service rights were permitted, one might ask whether the reserved flows would take place regardless of the load characteristics of potential assignors and, if this is not necessarily the case, whether the system operator can allocate this risk to another party.

For these reasons, it is customary that the assignor is prevented from assigning its service rights without the consent of the system operator, and the assignee of service rights would not be able to enforce the assigned rights without the consent of the system operator. Generally, assignment is not possible unless the assignee is party to the contractual framework governing the service right in question.

This can be illustrated with an example. (a) In the physical markets of Nord Pool Spot, the rights of a market participant under the Trading Rules are not assignable or otherwise transferable without the prior written consent of NPS.[215] Moreover, the members are under an obligation to deliver or off-take the agreed volumes[216] and cash settlement is based on the transactions recorded with NPS regardless of actual non-delivery or non-off-take.[217] (b) Generally, exchange-traded physical contracts can only be traded between market participants that are parties to the system operator's legal framework (Sect. 4.5.3).

Assignment of Transmission Rights Electricity supply and transmission have been regulated in different ways in this respect. Market-based mechanisms for the allocation of transmission capacity can require the transferability of rights to

[214] See FERC Order No. 888, Pro Forma Open Access Transmission Tariff, Appendix D, Section 23.2 Limitations on Assignment or Transfer of Service.

[215] Nord Pool Spot's Physical Markets, General Terms, Trading Rules (1 February 2015), section 17.1: "Save as set out in Section 1.1.6, the rights of a Participant under the Trading Rules are not assignable or otherwise transferable without the prior written consent of NPS". Section 1.1.6: "All Transactions entered into on the Physical Markets will be automatically and mandatory subject to Clearing, whereby Members will become Counterparties to NPS acting as central counterparty in all Transactions as further set out in the Clearing Rules".

[216] Nord Pool Spot Physical Markets, Trading Appendix 4, Clearing Rules (27 November 2014), section 4.1.3.

[217] Nord Pool Spot Physical Markets, Trading Appendix 4, Clearing Rules (27 November 2014), section 4.1.4.

transmission capacity. In practice, the transferability of transmission capacity rights is facilitated by the firmness of those rights (Sect. 10.8).

For example, the FERC allows the assignment of firm transmission rights to another eligible customer according to the Pro Forma Open Access Transmission Tariff in the US.[218] Firm point-to-point customers can reassign and resell unused portions of their reserved firm capacity to third parties. As a result, the transmission provider must make firm point-to-point transmission capacity available to the customer regardless of its load characteristics or use.[219]

Financial Rights

"Financial rights" can be defined as a service provider's rights to collect payments for its services from the users of services. Service users include both end consumers and various kinds of electricity undertakings.[220] These financial rights are transferable. One may ask whether financial rights are influenced by the particular characteristics of electricity trade.

In contract law, the traditional starting points are freedom of contract (parties are free to agree when they want, what they want, and with whom they want) and privity of contract (only contract parties may rely on the contract), and it would be unusual for a party to undertake contractual obligations for free. Contracts are voluntary exchanges of goods and services customarily against a remuneration. While the existence of remuneration is not a legal requirement in civil law countries,[221] it is a requirement as to form in common law countries.

There are nevertheless exceptions to core contract law principles in electricity markets. They relate to the imperfect alignment of contracts and payments and to public service requirements.

Contracts and Payments First, because of the physical nature of electricity and the fact that there will always be smaller or larger mismatches between agreed volumes and actual production or consumption,[222] payments might not be perfectly allocated to the electricity undertaking that actually provides the service.

This can be illustrated with a simple supply contract. An electricity producer (A) and an end consumer (B) agree that a certain quantity of electricity consumed by B is balanced with electricity fed into the grid by B. However, it turns out that A's power plant is not available. The fact that A fails to feed any electricity into the grid does not prevent B from consuming the agreed quantity. B nevertheless has a

[218] FERC Order No. 888, Pro Forma Open Access Transmission Tariff, Appendix D, Section 23.1 Procedures for Assignment or Transfer of Service.

[219] FERC, Order No. 888, pp. 301–304.

[220] For the definition, see point 35 of Article 2 of Directive 2009/72/EC (Third Electricity Directive).

[221] See, for example, CISG Articles 11 and 29(1).

[222] Hunt S and Shuttleworth G (1996), p. 137.

contractual obligation to make payments to A and no contractual obligation to make payments to other electricity producers. Other electricity undertakings must be remunerated for their services in other ways.[223]

Transmission capacity provides another example. Sometimes the financial rights of the owner or operator of wires are not perfectly matched by system users' obligations to pay for the use of transmission services. There are three reasons for this: (a) Electricity does not flow over the contractual path. It flows over multiple parallel paths. (b) System users' payment obligations depend on the model for the allocation of transmission capacity, because the payment model goes hand in hand with that model (Chap. 5). (c) Moreover, the tariffs or the method of calculating them are fixed or approved by the regulatory authority.[224] In principle, the owners of lines should be given proper incentives and sufficient financial rights to ensure the operation of the transmission system and to foster investment in electricity transmission capacity.[225] In practice, however, there can be political or other constraints that prevent the regulatory authority from acting in this way. Different countries can apply different principles.[226]

Public Service Requirements The second exception to core contract law principles in electricity markets relates to public service obligations. Electricity firms can have public service obligations that restrict the freedom of contract. Public service obligations customarily are motivated by: the fact that modern life is based on the extensive use of electrical appliances; the impact of the availability and cost of electricity on social cohesion; and the impact of electricity generation and transmission on society and the environment.

In the EU, public service requirements are based on the Third Electricity Directive. One of its objectives is to ensure that all EU citizens can enjoy universal service obligations and other public service obligations.[227]

According to the Third Electricity Directive, public service requirements may relate to security of supply, regularity, quality, and price of supplies, among other things.[228] However, Member States have plenty of discretion. They may define the public service requirements at national level, taking into account national circumstances.[229]

Public service obligations include even "universal service obligations".[230] The most important universal service obligations relate to supply and network access. (a) First, household customers and, where the Member State deems it appropriate, small enterprises have a right to be supplied with electricity at reasonable and non-discriminatory prices.[231]

---

[223] For the management of the availability risk, see Hunt S and Shuttleworth G (1996), pp. 128–129.

[224] Article 37(1)(a) of Directive 2009/72/EC (Third Electricity Directive).

[225] Articles 36 and 37(8) of Directive 2009/72/EC (Third Electricity Directive).

[226] Bundesnetzagentur (2006), pp. 108–122.

[227] Recital 50 of Directive 2009/72/EC (Third Electricity Directive).

[228] Article 3(2) of Directive 2009/72/EC (Third Electricity Directive).

[229] Recital 50 of Directive 2009/72/EC (Third Electricity Directive).

[230] Article 1 of Directive 2009/72/EC (Third Electricity Directive).

[231] Article 3(3) of Directive 2009/72/EC (Third Electricity Directive).

To ensure the provision of universal service, Member States may appoint a supplier of last resort.[232] (b) Second, distribution companies have an obligation to connect customers to their network.[233] (c) Third, Member States must take appropriate measures to protect final customers. In particular, they must ensure that there are adequate safeguards to protect vulnerable customers.[234]

The right to be supplied electricity at reasonable prices[235] can open the door for litigation when prices are increased.[236]

2.5.8 *Core and Ancillary Services from the Perspective of an End Consumer or a Retailer*

A service can be only be identified from the perspective of its consumer. From a consumer perspective, the service can consist of core services and ancillary services. Since we are discussing the practices of electricity producers in this book, the characteristic consumers include final customers (end consumers), retailers, and system operators. They purchase partly similar, partly different core and ancillary services. For example, the so-called "ancillary services" that a system operator purchases from market participants (Sect. 4.10) could really be defined as a core service from the system operator's perspective. We can have a look at these services from the perspective of an end consumer and a retailer.

End Consumer It is easy to see the service nature of electricity supply from the perspective of an electricity end consumer in the wholesale market. There are striking similarities between the characteristics of services and electricity supply and striking differences between electricity supply and manufacturing.[237] The main reasons why electricity supply is akin to a service include the following:

- Time: The product is produced and consumed at the same time (simultaneous generation and consumption).
- Storage: Electricity cannot be stored in the wholesale market (at least not in large quantities).
- Demonstration in advance: The product cannot be demonstrated in advance because of simultaneous generation and consumption (it does not exist before it is produced).

---

[232] Article 3(3) of Directive 2009/72/EC (Third Electricity Directive). See also recital 47.

[233] Article 3(3) of Directive 2009/72/EC (Third Electricity Directive). See also Article 37(6).

[234] Article 3(7) of Directive 2009/72/EC (Third Electricity Directive).

[235] Article 3(3) of Directive 2009/72/EC (Third Electricity Directive).

[236] For German law, see Metzger A (2008). For the application of § 315 BGB when the price of gas is increased, see BGH, 13 June 2007—VIII ZR 36/06.

[237] For differences between manufacturing and service industries, see Normann R (1991), p. 15. The characteristics of services have also been described by Grönroos C (1983). Both represent the Nordic School of Services. See Grönroos C (1991).

- Resale: Electricity cannot be resold as such, because it cannot be stored and because it is simultaneously generated and consumed. Only physical and financial rights can be sold.
- Customer participation in production: Because of the balance requirement, the customer participates in the generation of electricity by consuming electricity.

From the perspective of an electricity end consumer, the service consists of two core services and various ancillary services. (Ancillary services have a different meaning depending on the perspective, see Sect. 4.10)

Core service: facilitating the use of electrical appliances. One core service is facilitating the use of electrical appliances. The end consumer pays for services that enable him to use electrical appliances.

From a legal perspective, it is important to understand whether the provider of this service has information about the nature of the end consumer's use and electrical appliances.

Service providers customarily do not know what electrical appliances an individual end consumer chooses to use. There is a wide range of electrical appliances and service providers cannot read anybody's mind. Service providers do have statistical information about past consumption and demand patterns.[238] However, they tend to lack information about the intentions of individual end consumers for the future. There are some exceptions.

First, service providers customarily obtain information about the intentions of the end consumer when the contract is an individually negotiated b-to-b contract for the supply and/or transmission of large quantities.

Second, there can be service providers that supply electricity just for one purpose. For example, there can be car battery recharging points designed just for cars.

Example: car battery recharging. The energy storage of a car battery is finite. Once discharged, it must be disposed of or recharged. (a) In the technical sense, a car equipped with an electric engine can be refuelled by recharging its existing battery or by changing the battery. The car's owner can recharge the battery at home by using her own domestic supply or at a recharging point designed for this particular purpose. The battery could be changed at a particular car-charging and battery-swapping station (a petrol station). (b) Again in the technical sense, all ways of refuelling the car have the same result: the car will have fully charged batteries. All forms of ensuring that the car has fully charged batteries resemble the provision of a service. (c) However, there is a difference between the consumer's own domestic supply and other methods. Whereas the supplier of electricity for domestic use cannot know in what ways the consumer uses electricity, the supplier or service provider is very much aware of the customer's intentions when the parties choose a method designed just for the recharging of car batteries.

Third, past consumption patterns may enable service providers not only to estimate future consumption but even to understand what electrical appliances an individual end consumer uses. For example, the consumption pattern can show that

[238] Demand patterns differ from country to country. See, for example, Hotakainen M and Klimstra J (2011), Chapter 3.

the end customer likes to watch a popular TV series or cook food according to a certain schedule.

Core service: facilitating access to electrical energy. The second core service is facilitating access to electrical energy. The end consumer also pays for access to electrical energy. As electrical appliances cannot be used without access to wires, the provision of access to wires and transmission/distribution capacity is a core service.

Ancillary services. There can also be various kinds of ancillary services. The end consumer can pay for: the easiness of use of electrical energy (advice, technical work, the choice of the same service provider as end consumers that belong to the same group or network); the security of electricity supply (risk management); or emotional content.

Emotional content plays a growing role in electricity markets. While electricity that flows in the grid is homogeneous regardless of how it is generated, emotional content may help electricity suppliers to differentiate their services. For example, a customer can sponsor a certain form of power generation rather than another (this is made easier by labelling provisions in the EU)[239] or choose a certain service provider because of the mere strength of its brand. Physically homogeneous electricity can thus be marketed as "green", "yellow",[240] or "culture-friendly".[241]

One may ask whether power generation is an ancillary service. From the perspective of the end consumer, power generation as such is not what the end consumer pays for. It is, therefore, neither a core service nor an ancillary service. It is true that electricity has to be generated at the same time as it is consumed. But because an electric charge has a tendency to spread itself as evenly as possible over the conducting surface, electrical energy consumed by a certain end consumer is not really electrical energy generated by a certain electricity producer, unless there is only one electricity producer in the grid. In most cases, billing the end consumer for power generation is just a way to allocate costs for maintaining the required voltage and frequency and to pass them on to the end consumer.

On the other hand, power generation can be an ancillary service from the perspective of the end consumer because of the perceived emotional content linked to power generation that the end consumer wants to pay for.

Retailer A retailer must balance the load in wholesale markets. From the perspective of the retailer, the core service is thus balancing the load. In other words, the core of wholesale electricity trading consists of services.[242]

[239] Article 3(9) of Directive 2009/72/EC (Third Electricity Directive).

[240] Yello Strom GmbH, a subsidiary of EnBW Energie Baden-Württemberg AG, markets yellow electricity.

[241] Kraft & Kultur AB, a subsidiary of Troms Kraft AS, sells green electricity and books.

[242] EFET (2012), p. 3: "... wholesale energy trading resemblances services such as rail transport, stevedoring, post and telecommunications services, which cannot be provided on truly competitive terms unless enterprises that do not own the relevant essential infrastructure are allowed access on equal terms and conditions to the facilities of those that do".

2.5.9 Price Volatility

The last issue characteristic of physical electricity contracts relates to price volatility. Spot prices are volatile because of the physical characteristics of electricity. As wholesale electricity is non-storable and electricity generation must always be balanced with electricity consumption, electricity prices can change radically when there is an imbalance in consumption and generation.

When electricity consumption is scarce, the price of electricity can fall radically. In extreme cases, consumers get paid for consuming more electricity. As a result, electricity consumers can benefit if they purchase electricity as late as possible, but electricity producers try to safeguard electricity deliveries as early as possible.

When electricity generation is scarce, the price of electricity can increase radically. In extreme cases, many electricity-consuming industries must curtail their own production. Electricity consumers could try to purchase electricity or secure the price as early as possible, but electricity producers can benefit if they conclude contracts as late as possible.

The volatility of prices is influenced by the high cost of idle electricity production and transmission capacity. High costs can discourage investment. Suppliers may be prevented from importing cheaper electricity from other regions because of the limited size of interconnector capacity, and demand may have to be met by running cheaper generators to their limits and by dispatching more expensive generators. The traditional inelasticity of consumer demand increases price volatility even more.[243]

The high volatility of electricity prices means that it is important for all wholesale market participants to manage price risks. The collapse of California's electricity market in 2000 provides horror examples of what can happen when demand exceeds supply and a distributor has been unable to transfer the price risk.[244]

2.6 Competition Models in the Physical Market

2.6.1 General Remarks

Regulators may choose between different competition models. There are alternative competition models for the electricity market. They are influenced by the characteristics of electrical energy.

To begin with, there is no physical supply of electricity in large quantities without lines: transmission lines in the wholesale market, distribution lines in the retail market, interconnectors, or direct lines.[245] The transmission and distribution

---

[243] U.S. Energy Information Administration (2002), Chapter 4.

[244] See, for example, Ferrey S (2004), pp. 1845–1848 and 1852–1853.

[245] For definitions, see Article 2(1) of Regulation 714/2009 (on conditions for access to the network for cross-border exchanges in electricity); point 15 of Article 2 of Directive 2009/72/

of electricity are natural monopolies, because it would be highly inefficient to run several parallel transmission or distribution lines.[246]

These natural monopolies could lead to complete vertical integration. However, the generation, purchase, and sale of electricity are not natural monopolies. For this reason, there are alternative competition models.

2.6.2 Choice of a Competition Model

Legislators and market regulators must choose a competition model. Market participants will need to adapt to the model and comply with its regulatory framework.

The choice of a competition model for a particular market is a question of economic efficiency. When choosing the competition model, four aspects provide the starting point. First, transmission and distribution are *natural monopolies*. There is nevertheless a difference between transmission and distribution on one hand and generation and sales on the other. There can be competition at the level of power generation and the supply of electricity to wholesalers and retail consumers. Second, there are *economies of scale*. It is cheaper to generate electrical energy on a large scale. The third aspect relates to *price sensitivity*. It is characteristic of the electricity market that demand for electrical energy is not very sensitive to price fluctuations. Unlike most services, the transmission, distribution, and supply of electrical energy are vital for the functioning of modern society.[247] Fourth, electricity has its own *technical characteristics* that influence the electricity market.[248]

Complete Vertical Integration Complete vertical integration is "a model of technical organization involving central control over a synchronised network".[249]

It used to be the regulator's market structure of choice.[250] The existence of local or regional monopolies was expected to increase long-term investment in the electricity infrastructure and to prevent investments in parallel transmission and distribution networks.[251] Doing things internally was also expected to reduce

EC (Third Electricity Directive). See also Articles 26(2)(c) and 34 of Directive 2009/72/EC (Third Electricity Directive).

[246] To illustrate, each system must comply with complex technical rules that ensure safety and interoperability. See Article 5 of Directive 2009/72/EC (Third Electricity Directive).

[247] Cameron PD (2007), p. 7 para 1.10 distinguishes the following characteristics of electricity and gas industries: there are natural monopolies, they provide essential services, these sectors are strategic, they are capital intensive, there are requirements as to reliability, and energy sub-sectors are integrated.

[248] See, for example, Cameron PD (2007), pp. 22–23 para 1.63.

[249] Cameron PD (2007), p. 8 para 1.12.

[250] See, for example, Perrels A and Kemppi H (2003), p. 12, Table 2.1.

[251] Lokau B and Ritzau M (2009), § 5 number 4.

electricity firms' transaction costs.[252] Complete vertical integration was complemented by price regulation.[253]

On the other hand, complete vertical integration means combining sectors that are natural monopolies (transmission and distribution) and sectors that are not natural monopolies (generation and supply). As a result, complete vertical integration does not foster economic efficiency.

Problems If left unregulated, monopoly suppliers would produce less at a higher price.[254] Vertically integrated utilities must, therefore, be subject to price controls and the regulation of conditions of service. Conditions of service must be regulated, because price controls would not be sufficient. Customarily, vertically integrated utilities are allowed what is perceived as a fair return on investment. If they are allowed to operate under regulated rates designed to cover costs and normal profit, they have no incentive to operate efficiently. Their operation costs tend to be higher than they could be. They pay no penalty for planning mistakes, because costs of unnecessary or poorly considered investments are passed along to consumers.

It would not be sufficient to require the incorporation of the divisions of a vertically integrated firm. Three kinds of problems arise where the transmission system operator is a legal entity within an integrated company.[255]

First, the transmission system operator may treat its affiliated companies better than competing third parties. Vertically integrated companies may use network assets to increase entry barriers for competitors. This inherent conflict of interest is almost impossible to control by regulatory means.

Second, non-discriminatory access to information cannot be guaranteed as there is no effective means of preventing transmission system operators releasing market sensitive information to the generation or supply branch of the integrated company.

Third, investment incentives within an integrated firm are not aligned with total economic welfare. The network investment decisions made by vertically integrated firms tend to be biased to the needs of its own supply affiliates. Vertically integrated network operators have an inherent interest to limit new investment that would benefit competitors.

Introducing Competition Introducing competition can bring many benefits from a regulatory perspective. Competition can facilitate the allocation of investments in more efficient power generation, transmission, and distribution. If the efficiency of power generation, transmission, and distribution is increased, end consumers end up paying less for electricity.

---

[252] Ofgem (2009), para 3.10.

[253] Lokau B and Ritzau M (2009), § 5 number 5. Vertically integrated wholesalers (or those with long-term contracts) may have less incentive to raise wholesale prices when retail prices are determined in advance. Bushnell JB et al. (2008).

[254] See, for example, Spence DB (2008), pp. 767 768.

[255] Proposal for a Directive amending Directive 2003/54/EC, SEC(2007) 1179, SEC(2007) 1180, COM/2007/0528 final, COD 2007/0195, Explanatory memorandum, 1.1.

The first step of increasing competition requires restructuring. Restructuring means the breaking up of vertically integrated utilities through unbundling (Sect. 3.5.5).

Unbundling Unbundling means the separation of the "wire business" (transmission and distribution) from the "energy business" (generation and supply). If vertically integrated utilities are broken up, barriers of entry are reduced as it becomes more difficult to prevent competitors from entering the market. As a result, the energy business can become part of a competitive market. There can be competition both at the wholesale level and at the retail level).

This can be illustrated with retail competition. (a) Many retailers used to be local vertically integrated utilities that owned local distribution assets. The previous structures can still limit competition at the retail level.[256] Retail competition is restricted even more if contracts are long term.[257] (b) On the other hand, the number of potential retailers has been increased by unbundling. In unbundled markets, electricity retailers do not need to own large physical assets, and the customers of any one retailer can be spread over multiple distinct distribution networks.

One can distinguish between: full structural separation by law (such as ownership and control unbundling); functional separation (such as management unbundling); and separation for accounting purposes (such as ring-fencing the accounts of different types of businesses).[258]

The wire business must remain regulated and a public good. The grid must be regulated to ensure open access for all potential users and to facilitate wholesale and retail competition. The management of the transmission and distribution networks should be independent of the trading of electricity. For example, a market participant should not be able to keep others from competing for energy trades by inducing congestion that prevents power inflow.

Market Coupling Various trading and balancing mechanisms can be used to facilitate a more competition-driven market. However, local or regional markets cannot be changed into European markets without market coupling (Chap. 6).

Producer Perspective From a producer perspective, there are even other ways to increase competition. The "limited supplier competition model" (Sect. 2.6.3) could be replaced by a "supplier competition model" or "full producer competition".

---

[256] Communication from the Commission – Inquiry pursuant to Article 17 of Regulation (EC) No 1/2003 into the European gas and electricity sectors (Final Report), SEC(2006) 1724, COM(2006) 0851 final, paras 14 and 16.

[257] *Ibid*, paras 16 and 31–32.

[258] Cameron PD (2007), p. 32, para 1.85.

2.6.3 Classification of Competition Models

Competition models can range from the dominance of vertically integrated utilities to unbundled and competitive electricity systems. Competition models can be classified in different ways. The starting point could be the perspective of the customer, the level of regulation, transition from one model to the other, or the perspective of the producer.

Customer Perspective Hunt S and Shuttleworth G (1996) seem to have chosen the perspective of the customer. They distinguish between four types of models by the degree of competition: (1) no competition; (2) a single buyer or purchasing agency; (3) distributors may choose their supplier; and (4) customers may choose their supplier.[259]

Alternatively, these models could be divided into six types: (1) the monopoly model with complete vertical integration; (2) the monopoly model with distribution handled by one or more separate distribution companies; (3) the integrated purchasing agency model; (4) the disaggregated purchasing agency model; (5) the wholesale competition model; and (6) the retail competition model.[260]

The monopoly models mean that the market is dominated by vertically integrated utilities. In complete vertical integration, each vertically integrated utility has operational control over generation, transmission, and distribution in its own area, subject to regulatory oversight. Alternatively, distribution can be handled by one or more separate distribution companies.

Under the purchasing agency model, competition is added to power generation. Independent electricity producers supply electricity to a utility (purchasing agency) that is responsible for transmission, distribution, and the retail market. This was how the US Public Utilities Regulatory Policy Act (PURPA, 1978) introduced competition in generation.[261] One can distinguish between an integrated purchasing agency and a disaggregated purchasing agency. Under the integrated purchasing agency model, the wholesale purchasing agency can be responsible for distribution and participate in electricity generation. Under the disaggregated purchasing agency model, independent power producers are responsible for electricity generation and distribution companies for distribution.

An unbundled and competitive electricity system is characterised by the existence of many categories of market participants with different roles under the wholesale competition model or the retail competition model.

Level of Regulation On the other hand, the existence of many electricity producers and retail customers does not mean that markets are free. Electricity markets can never be totally "free", because they would not work without extensive regulation.

---

[259] Hunt S and Shuttleworth G (1996), p. 12.

[260] Hunt S and Shuttleworth G (1996); Kirschen DS and Strbac G (2004).

[261] See Hunt S and Shuttleworth G (1996), p. 4.

Table 2.2 Classification of regulation models

	Generation	Sales to wholesale customers	Sales to retail customers
Full producer comp.	Competitive	Competitive	Competitive
Supplier competition	Not competitive[a]	Competitive	Competitive
Limited supplier comp.	Not competitive	Competitive	To some extent competitive[b]
Trading competition	Not competitive	Competitive	Not competitive
Compl. vert. integration	Not competitive	Not competitive	Not competitive

Producer perspective
[a]Regulation of investment, operation, and dispatching for policy reasons other than technical or economic necessity
[b]Regulation of prices, demand by end consumers, and long-term contracts

There can nevertheless be some room for bilateral contracting or the use of market-based mechanisms. One should take into account the scope and level of regulation.

Green R (2010) distinguishes between various models of regulation.[262] They include: retail competition; wholesale competition; the single buyer model; and integrated firms. He distinguishes between the functions of generation transmission/distribution, and retail.

Transitional Models Some models are intermediate arrangements for moving from one model to the other. Because of path dependency, an intermediate structure applied during a transition period should be compatible with the final structure.[263]

Regulation Model from a Producer Perspective However, an electricity producer would see a different competition or regulatory landscape in the EU. For example, the building of new generation installations is subject to regulatory constraints that depend on policy preferences. There is a large regulatory regime with conflicting policy objectives for wholesale markets. Retail pricing is not free.

The four competition models based on the consumer perspective (Hunt S and Shuttleworth G 1996) or the four related models of regulation (Green R 2010) can thus be complemented by further models from the producer perspective.

Table 2.2 shows the classification of regulation models from a producer perspective. In unbundled markets, one can nowadays distinguish between: full producer competition; supplier competition; limited supplier competition; and trading competition. (1) Under the full producer competition model, electricity producers have a level playing field regardless of their production technology. They can sell to end consumers in the retail market or to wholesale market participants. Their success depends on low production costs. (2) Under the supplier competition

[262] Green R (2010), pp. 139–141; Bhattacharyya SC (2011), p. 699.

[263] See Bhattacharyya SC (2011), pp. 704–707.

Table 2.3 Classification of regulation models

	Transmission	Distribution	Provision of complementary services to customers	Provision of balancing services to TSO/DSO
Full producer competition	Unbundling, not permitted	Unbundling, not permitted	Competitive	Competitive
Supplier competition	Unbundling, not permitted	Unbundling, not permitted	Competitive	Not fully competitive[a]
Limited supplier competition	Unbundling, not permitted	Fairly free with or without unbundling	Not fully competitive[b]	Not fully competitive
Trading competition[c]	Fairly free with or without unbundling	Permitted, not competitive[d]	Not competitive	Not competitive
Compl. vert. integr.	Monopoly	Monopoly	Not competitive	Not competitive

Producer perspective in the light of permitted intra-firm integration
[a]On one hand, the provision of balancing services is not fully competitive if generation is not competitive. On the other, it is possible to distinguish between the provision of balancing services to the TSO and the supply of electricity to suppliers or end consumers
[b]The provision of complementary services to customers cannot be fully competitive without effective unbundling
[c]Limited supplier competition is a transitional model from trading competition to supplier competition
[d]The unbundling regime has a narrow scope in this case

model, suppliers have a level playing field but electricity generation (investment, operation, dispatching) is regulated rather than competitive because of policy reasons other than technical or economic necessity. (3) The limited supplier competition model means that even consumer behaviour is regulated rather than free. Under this model, the use of long-term supply contracts can also be limited. (4) Trading competition means that wholesale traders are the only market participants that are free to buy and sell electricity in a competitive market. If long-term bilateral supply contracts are banned, liquidity on spot and forward markets is increased.

The characteristic model of regulation applied by the EU could, therefore, be described as limited supplier competition.

Regulation and Intra-Firm Integration The regulation model can also be combined with an intra-firm integration model. Intra-firm integration means the replacement of market mechanisms with authority (Coase). An electricity producer may choose vertical integration, horizontal integration, and integration over value chains. Integration is constrained by the unbundling regime. Table 2.3 shows the classification of regulation models in the light of permitted intra-firm integration.

2.7 Classification of Electricity Supply Contracts

2.7.1 General Remarks

Electrical energy is not supplied like customary commodities. Because of the characteristics of electrical energy, the supply of electrical energy to end consumers resembles the provision of a *service*. Whether electricity supply contracts can be regarded as contracts for the provision of services not only in fact but even in law is a question of *classification*.

The *purpose* of classification is important, because the contents of the legal framework depend on the applicable rules and the applicable rules depend on the classification of the issue. For example, the classification of electricity or electricity supply contracts can determine the contractual rights and duties of the parties, the statute of limitations,[264] product liability,[265] vertical integration by means of business-to-consumer distance contracts, and tax treatment.[266]

As a rule, the meaning of a concept depends on the *context*. In principle, the classification of electricity or electricity supply contracts for one legal purpose in a certain jurisdiction does not have to influence classification for another legal purpose or in another jurisdiction as the same word does not necessarily have the same meaning in different legal contexts.[267]

The traditional question seems to be whether electricity supply contracts should fall within the scope of the regulation of *sale of goods*. For example, this was one of the core preliminary questions in the flood of litigation that followed the collapse of California's electricity market in 2000.[268]

[264] See, for example, Helvey v. Wabash County REMC, 278 N.E.2d 608, 610 (Ind. Ct. App. 1972). Mr. Helvey's 110-V household appliances were damaged by an electrical current in excess of 135 V. The electricity provider argued that it provided a good or product that was subject to the 4-year statute of limitations set out in UCC § 2-725. Helvey argued that electricity is a service and invoked a 6-year common law statute of limitations. See also Cincinnati Gas & Electric Co. v. Goebel, 502 N.E.2d 713 (Ohio Mun. 1986) in which the plaintiff failed to commence its action within 4 years as required by the UCC in Ohio.

[265] See, for example, Pierce v. Pacific Gas & Electric Co., 212 Cal. Rptr. 283, 288 n.4 (Ct. App. 1985).

[266] See Ferrey S (2004), p. 1874.

[267] In Pierce v. Pacific Gas & Electric Co., 212 Cal. Rptr. 283, 288 n.4 (Ct. App. 1985), the California court did not apply this principle. The court found that electricity is a "product" for the purposes of strict liability. In the light of this finding, the court assumed that electricity is a "good" for the purposes of the UCC. See Ferrey S (2004), p. 1881.

[268] See Ferrey S (2004), p. 1860.

2.7.2 Classification as Provision of Services or Sale of Goods in Contract Law

General Remarks

This book focuses on the legal tools and practices of electricity producers. Contracts belong to the most basic and widely used legal tools. The contractual relationship does not consist of the express terms of the contract alone. It is complemented by mandatory and dispositive law. Now, different contract types tend to be governed by different dispositive or mandatory provisions of law. The classification of electricity supply contracts can thus influence the legal framework and influence the position of the parties especially in liberalised markets.[269]

Traditional contract law rules have not been designed with electricity supply contracts in mind. In particular, they have not been designed for: the provision of access to the grid; the operation of a grid from which some parties extract electricity and to which other parties feed electricity; the balancing of electricity consumption with electricity generation; and the charging of a price for the balancing of electricity consumption with electricity generation. As a result, it can be difficult to fit electricity supply contracts in the traditional typology of contracts.

The classification of electricity supply contracts can also depend on the characterisation of electricity. On the other hand, the legal relevance of the characterisation of electricity can depend on the area of law.

For example, competition law can apply to all kinds of transactions between undertakings and even to unilateral acts. The scope of competition law is therefore not dependent on the nature of electricity. In EU law, the scope of rules on each of the four freedoms depends on the classification of the issue as one of goods, services, establishment, or people. In *Almelo*, the CJEU defined electricity as "goods" for the purposes of the free movement of goods.[270]

In contrast, one of the basic questions in contract law is whether electricity supply contracts fall within the scope of rules applicable to the "sale of goods".

---

[269] Ferrey S (2004), p. 1865: "In a deregulated power market, individual contracts will need to address a variety of factors: how primary and back-up power resources will be supplied; the allowable loss, disruption, or variation in the quality and quantity of electricity supplied; the remedies and damages for failure to supply; specific force majeure provisions to relieve supply obligations, general allocation of risk among various suppliers, transporters, intermediaries, and users of power; insurance provisions to support power supply obligations; and agreement on the standard of provision of electric power".

[270] Case C-393/92 Gemeente Almelo v Energiebedrijf IJsselmij NV [1994] ECR I-1477, para 28: "In Community law, and indeed in the national laws of the Member States, it is accepted that electricity constitutes a good within the meaning of Article 30 of the Treaty. Electricity is thus regarded as a good under the Community's tariff nomenclature (code CN 27.16). Furthermore, in its judgment in Case 6/64 Costa v ENEL [1964] ECR 1141 the Court accepted that electricity may fall within the scope of Article 37 of the Treaty". See also Case 7/68 Commission/Italy [1968] ECR 1968 p. 423: "... products which can be valued in money and which are capable, as such, of forming the subject of commercial transactions".

Typically, the applicability of sale of goods laws depends on what is being bought and sold. Electricity supply contracts can be regarded as contracts for the sale of goods if electricity is regarded as "movable goods".

How should electricity supply contracts then be classified? Are they contracts for the sale of movable goods, are they contracts for the provision of a service, or should they be regarded as a particular contract type?

There are differences depending on the jurisdiction and the contract law framework. They can be illustrated by: the CISG; Nordic laws; German, Austrian, and Swiss law; US law; and the DCFR. It is interesting to study even the position of US law because of great variation in the case-law of different states.

The CISG

Electrical energy is treated as an extraordinary commodity in the CISG. According to the Secretariat Commentary on the 1978 Draft of the CISG, international sales of electricity present "unique problems" that are different from those presented by the usual international sale of goods.[271] For this reason, the CISG does not apply to sales of electricity.[272]

Many of the "unique problems" are obviously caused by the physical characteristics of electrical energy. Specific electrons cannot be identified and delivered to the buyer.[273] In liberalised markets, there is no "sale" and "delivery" of electricity in any meaningful sense.[274] From the perspective of the end consumer, different electricity companies provide different services.

> The distribution company provides access to wires and determines many of the required technical characteristics of the electricity flows.[275] The supplier of electricity procures that electricity extracted by the end customer is balanced with electricity fed into the distribution system.
>
> The end consumer does not consume electricity produced by the supplier or electricity produced just by the supplier. Rather, the end customer extracts electricity produced by all electricity producers that feed electricity into the grid at the moment when the customer uses electrical appliances.
>
> The "supply" of electricity is not necessarily connected to the actual generation of electricity. The "supplier" just charges a price for the balancing of electricity extraction with electricity generation. The "supplier" cannot balance the two unless it either generates

---

[271] Official Records, p. 16.

[272] CISG Article 2(f).

[273] See also Ferrey S (2004), p. 1863.

[274] See already Bydlinski F (1972), p. 41: "Wieso sollen das kaufvertragliche Pflichten sein, da doch von der Leistung einer Kaufsache auch im weitesten Sinn keine Rede sein kann?"

[275] See, for example, EPEX Spot Operational Rules (28 November 2014), Article 1.2, Main contracts specifications, Underlying: "Electrical power transiting over a Transmission System managed by a TSO, which defines the voltage, frequency, cosine φ (displacement factor) and cut-off frequencies, in compliance with the contractual obligations of the prevailing concession agreement for the general power grid".

electricity or pays another electricity company for feeding electricity into the grid. In some cases, prices are negative and the price is charged by the end consumer rather than the "supplier".[276]

Negative wholesale prices can occur when a producer wants to avoid closing down a plant because of high costs of ramping up and down, when a subsidy is an important part of the producer's income, or when reducing production increases costs.[277] Negative wholesale prices have become more common as European countries turn to renewables.[278]

A distinction should nevertheless be made between the supply of electrical energy as such and the sale of physical goods used for the purpose of storing electrical energy. (a) The scope of the CISG is limited by excluding certain categories of international sales contracts. Electricity is mentioned in one of the exclusions.[279] There was a similar exclusion in the ULIS that preceded the CISG.[280] The sales of different commodities and different manufactured goods can always pose different and "unique" problems,[281] but there are fundamental differences between the sale of electrical energy and sales of energy commodities such as gas and crude oil or sales of manufactured goods.[282] The exclusion of sales of electrical energy from the scope of the CISG can be explained by the fact that the supply of electrical energy is more akin to the provision of a service.[283] (b) On the other hand, the sale of physical goods used for the purpose of storing electrical energy raises the same questions as the sale of other physical goods. For example, the sale of batteries does fall within the scope of the CISG.

Nordic Laws

The Nordic Sale of Goods Acts are—with the exception of the Danish Sale of Goods Act—based on Nordic legislative cooperation in the 1980s which explains why they are fairly similar. There is also a close connection between the Nordic Sale of Goods Acts, the ULIS, and the CISG.

Main Rule Most Nordic Sale of Goods Acts do not apply to the sale of electricity.[284] Electricity is regarded as a peculiar commodity with its own characteristics.

---

[276] See, for example, EPEX Spot Operational Rules (28 November 2014), Article 1.2, Main contracts specifications, Negative Prices: "Negative prices are authorised where specified below ... When a contract is traded with a negative price, it is legally analysed as a supply of service (removal service) by the recipient of power to the delivering party and not anymore as a supply of goods by the party delivering the power".

[277] OECD/IEA (2005), pp. 74–75.

[278] See, for example, The Economist, Charlemagne, when the wind blows (7 September 2013).

[279] CISG Article 2(f).

[280] The electricity exemption can found in ULIS Article 5(1).

[281] See, for example, Ferraria F (2005), footnote 84, citing Winship P (1984).

[282] See, for example, Fried J (2010), p. 166, point 266; Winship (1990).

[283] For the opposite views, see Ferraria F (2005).

[284] See, for example, Stridbeck U (1994), p. 49.

On the other hand, there is no general codification of the general principles of contract law in the Nordic countries. The provisions of the Sale of Goods Acts can therefore be applied to other kinds of contracts in a flexible way by analogy as expressions of the general principles of contract law.

Norwegian Law For example, the Norwegian Sale of Goods Act (lov om kjøp, kjøpsloven) governs sales[285] but neither the provision of services[286] nor, according to its preliminary works, the supply of electricity. The Sale of Goods Act can nevertheless be applied by analogy as evidence of general contract law principles.[287] This has been recognised in case law as well.[288]

The Norwegian Consumer Sale of Goods Act (lov om forbrukerkjøp, forbrukerkjøpsloven) was adopted after the entry into force of the Norwegian Sale of Goods Act. There was again discussion about whether to apply sale of goods law to electricity supply contracts and there were again different opinions.[289] It was decided not to apply the Consumer Sale of Goods Act to the supply of electrical energy.[290] Consumers were protected in other ways.[291]

Norwegian law is important, because it has been chosen as the law that governs derivatives transactions and clearing in the Nordic market. The application of the CISG is expressly excluded.[292] On Elspot and Elbas, matters relating to the physical delivery of electricity are governed by "the local law of the delivery country".[293]

Danish Law Danish law is the exception to the main rule in the Nordic countries as Denmark did not participate in the harmonisation of the Nordic Sale of Goods Acts

[285] Kjøpsloven, § 1(1): "Loven gjelder kjøp for så vidt ikke annet er fastsatt i lov. For forbrukerkjøp gjelder forbrukerkjøpsloven. For kjøp av fast eiendom gjelder avhendingslova".

[286] Kjøpsloven, § 2(2): "Loven gjelder ikke avtale som pålegger den part som skal levere tingen, også å utføre arbeid eller annen tjeneste, og dette utgjør den overveiende del av hans forpliktelser".

[287] Ot.prp. nr. 80 (1986–1987), p. 48.

[288] For example, Rt 2000.632: "... kjøpslovens erstatningsregler må kunne anvendes analogisk på mislighold av den type vi har med å gjøre i denne sak, og som ikke går inn under loven ... men jeg antar at alminnelige kontraktsrettslige prinsipper langt på vei vil gi de samme erstatningsrettslige konsekvenser ..."

[289] Ot.prp. nr. 44 (2001–2002), section 3.8.7.

[290] Forbrukerkjøpsloven, § 2: "Loven gjelder ikke for ... c) avtale med en kraftleverandør om levering av elektrisk energi. Kapittel 5 om forsinkelse gjelder likevel ved forsinket oppstart av levering av elektrisk energi. Bestemmelsene i § 61 a om nemndsbehandling av visse tvister gjelder også for slike avtaler ..."

[291] See NOU 2004:4, Lovregulering av strømavtaler sluttet med forbrukere.

[292] NASDAQ OMX Oslo ASA, General Terms, Trading Rules, Commodity Derivatives (7 April 2014), section 14.1; NASDAQ OMX Clearing AB, General Terms, Clearing Rules, Commodity Derivatives (9 June 2014), section 18.1.

[293] Nord Pool Spot, General Terms, Trading Rules, Nord Pool Spot's Physical Markets (effective from NWE/PCR Go-live 2013), section 18.1.1: "These Trading Rules, all Transactions, Settlement and Clearing effected under them, and all non-contractual obligations arising out of or in connection with them, shall be governed by and construed in accordance with Norwegian law, except for matters relating to physical delivery of electricity where the local law of the delivery country shall apply".

in the 1980s. The Danish Sale of Goods Act applies to all sales apart from the sale of immovable goods.[294] This might partly be explained by Denmark's proximity to Germany.

German, Austrian and Swiss Law

In Germany, Austria, and Switzerland, electricity supply contracts fall within the scope of sale of goods laws, because (a) electricity falls within the general definition of goods or (b) the supply of electricity falls within the general definition of sale of goods. As a result, sale of goods laws provide the default contract law framework for electricity supply contracts.

Austrian Law In Austria, electricity falls within the very broad definition of goods under the ABGB.[295] Electricity is regarded as intangible rather than tangible goods, because all goods that are not defined as tangible are defined as intangible.[296] Moreover, an electricity supply contract is regarded as a long-term sales contract (Dauerkauf) combined with a right to extract electricity (Bezugsrecht).[297] Electricity supply contracts between undertakings are regarded as commercial sales contracts (Handelskauf).[298]

This is the firmly established mainstream view.[299] The minority view is that the physical characteristics of electricity should be considered.[300] However, the physical characteristics of electricity are not relevant as far as the classification of electricity is concerned.[301]

Although the supply of electricity is governed by provisions applicable to sale of goods, they can only be applied with some modifications. (a) According to the mainstream view, the core obligation of the supplier is to enable the extraction of electricity by the buyer.[302] This reflects complete vertical integration rather than the present market structure. (b) An electricity supply contract is always a contract for a

---

294 Købeloven, § 1a: "Loven gælder for alle køb, bortset fra køb af fast ejendom".

295 § 285 ABGB. Energy is defined as goods also in Austrian consumer law. See § 15(1) KSchG.

296 § 292 ABGB: "Körperliche Sachen sind diejenigen, welche in die Sinne fallen; sonst heißen sie unkörperliche; z. B. das Recht zu jagen, zu fischen und alle andere Rechte".

297 Bydlinski F (1972), p. 46: "Ein Dauerkauf, verbunden mit höchst eigenartig ausgestaltetem Bezugsrecht als Wahl- und Optionsrecht liegt vor".

298 Bydlinski F (1972), p. 39.

299 *Ibid.* See also Eccher B (2010), § 285 Rz 4 and § 292 Rz 1.

300 See already Mahler F (1931).

301 See Bydlinski F (1972), p. 35: "Einen extremeren Standpunkt formuliert in der österreichischen Literatur MAHLER, der es aus physikalischen Gründen schlechtweg für unmöglich erklärt, die Energie mit der Sache gleichzustellen. Soweit er darüber hinaus Rechtsausführungen macht, sind diese erstaunlich".

302 Bydlinski F (1972), p. 37: "Die Lieferung, und zwar die jederzeit abrufbare Lieferung, ist ... die Hauptleistung des Lieferanten ..."

certain period of time. The contract cannot be rescinded for past deliveries as electricity is supplied and consumed simultaneously.[303] (c) The contract will not expire just because a certain volume of electricity has been supplied.[304] The volume is at the discretion of the buyer. The buyer is free to extract electricity whenever it wants and as much it wants.[305] Again, this seems to reflect complete vertical integration.

German Law In Germany, electricity supply contracts are regarded as contracts for the sale of goods, because electricity falls within the definition of movable goods.[306] Electricity supply contracts fall within the scope of the regulation of sale of goods ("Warenkauf", § 433 BGB rather than § 311(1) BGB) directly or by analogy.[307] Electricity futures/forwards that are settled physically are thus regarded as sales contracts. They are sales contracts even when they are settled by an offsetting transaction rather than physically. Whether they can be regarded as sales contracts when they are settled financially is more problematic. The majority view seems to be that they can.[308] In addition, electricity supply contracts are regarded as long-term contracts (Dauerschuldverhältnis).[309] Most electricity supply contracts must comply with mandatory provisions of law governing standard contract terms.[310] They do not apply to individually negotiated terms.[311] There are also modifications for electricity supply contracts regarding the manner of incorporation.[312]

The EFET General Agreement is governed by German law.[313] German law governs clearing on ECC (and the clearing of EPEX Spot products)[314] while the EPEX Spot Trading Agreement is governed by French law[315] and the "execution of the physical settlement of transactions" is governed by the "material law of the place at which physical fulfilment is

---

[303] § 918(2) ABGB.

[304] Bydlinski F (1972), p. 40.

[305] Bydlinski F (1972), p. 44: "Der Vertrag bestimmt, daß ein Vertragspartner, der Bezieher, die entsprechende Bestimmung nach seinem Belieben treffen und laufend ergänzen kann".

[306] § 90 BGB, § 433(1) BGB, and § 453(1) BGB. See Neveling S and Schönrock KP (2009), § 29 number 7.

[307] RGZ 56, 403, 404; RGZ 67, 229, 232; BGH, judgment of 2 July 1969—VIII ZR 172/68. Fried J (2010), p. 154, point 265.

[308] Fried J (2010), pp. 280–281, point 491: "Hiernach sind Forwards allgemein als Kaufverträge i. S. v. § 433 BGB zu qualifizieren".

[309] Neveling S and Schönrock KP (2009), § 29 number 7.

[310] §§ 305–310 BGB. See, in particular, § 307 BGB. Neveling S and Schönrock KP (2009), § 29 number 9.

[311] § 305(1) BGB.

[312] §§ 305a and 310(2) BGB.

[313] EFET General Agreement (Version 2.1(a)), § 22.1.

[314] ECC Clearing Conditions (0022a, 30 April 2014), section 6.4(1).

[315] EPEX Spot Trading Agreement (Version 2.2), Article 7. EPEX Spot Operational Rules (28 November 2014) are vague about the governing law. See Article 2.6 that lays down a regulatory compliance obligation without choosing the governing law.

actually provided" and/or "the material law applicable to the transmission system operator ... within whose transmission system delivery is effected".[316]

Swiss Law In Switzerland, the Swiss Federal Court (Schweizerisches Bundesgericht) and the majority view regard electricity supply contracts as contracts for the sale of goods and instalment contracts (Sukzessivlieferungsvertrag), where the seller has only undertaken to supply electricity.[317] However, electricity supply contracts can only be regarded as contracts sui generis as it would be difficult to apply traditional sale of goods rules on place of delivery, time of delivery, non-compliance, and remedies in the event of breach of contracts. Under an electricity supply contract, the buyer may extract electricity against the payment of the purchase price. The volume can be fixed ex ante by the parties or left open. The volumes are metered. The purchase price is payable after the supplier has fulfilled its obligations.[318]

Summary Compared with the CISG and the laws of most Nordic countries, the laws of countries belonging to the German legal family represent the opposite approach. The physical characteristics of electricity play no major role in German, Austrian, and Swiss law, because the classification of electricity supply contracts is regarded as a "purely legal" exercise.[319] However, the mainstream view seems to reflect complete vertical integration, that is, the competition model of the past.

US Law

In the US, the classification of electricity supply contracts depends on the state and the court. There is plenty of variation.

UCC or Common Law The basic contract law question is whether power supply contracts are governed by Article 2 of the Uniform Commercial Code (UCC) that applies to sale of goods, or by traditional common law. In tort law, the question is whether electricity is a product for product liability purposes.

The scope of the UCC can be important, because Article 2 of the UCC is designed for the sale of physical goods, and because common law differs from the UCC in many states. The choice between Article 2 of the UCC and traditional common law can alter the outcome of a legal dispute.[320]

---

[316] ECC Clearing Conditions (0022a, 30 April 2014), section 6.4(1).

[317] Art. 713 ZGR, Art. 187(1) OR, and BGE 76 II 107: "Der Vertrag über die Lieferung elektrischer Energie gilt nach der Rechtsprechung des Bundesgerichtes als Kaufvertrag, wenn das Elektrizitätswerk lediglich den Strom zur Verfügung zu stellen hat; besteht seine vertragliche Leistung dagegen in der Herbeiführung eines bestimmten Erfolges, so charakterisiert sich das Verhältnis als Werkvertrag (BGE 48 II 370 f.)". For instalment contracts, see also CISG Article 73.

[318] See Balthasar M (2007), p. 61.

[319] For Austrian law, see Bydlinski F (1972), p. 35.

[320] Ferrey S (2004), pp. 1861–1863 and 1929–1955 (Appendix).

However, electricity is treated in confusing ways in the courts. For example, different decisions in California hold that: electricity is personal property (1913); electricity is a product (for product liability) and may also be a good (1985); electricity is a service until it is metered (1991); and electricity is an intangible or service (2002).[321]

The wording of the UCC leaves room for interpretation. Article 2 of the UCC applies to "transactions in goods".[322] The UCC defines "goods" as "all things ... which are movable at the time of identification to the contract for sale".[323] Even "future goods" are goods provided that they are identifiable.[324] There are different views on whether electricity falls within the definition of goods under the UCC.

Electricity as a Service Many courts regard the provision of electricity as a service rather than a good.[325] Some courts consider electricity a service even in commercial contract litigation.[326] Some courts have come to the same conclusion on grounds that it would not be desirable to apply the UCC's warranty remedies to electricity supply contracts.[327]

> Several courts have followed the reasoning in *Bowen v. Niagra Mohwak Power Corp.*[328]: "[T]he provision of electricity is a service, not the sale of a product ... Electricity is the flow of electrically charged particles along a conductor. The utility does not 'manufacture' electrically charged particles, 'but rather, sets in motion the necessary elements that allow the flow of electricity.' ... The consumer pays for electricity by kilowatt hour, that is, the length of time electricity flows through the system. There is no individual product. Instead, the consumer pays for use of the electricity".[329]

Electricity as a Good The opposite view is that electricity is a good. The courts have found that electricity falls within the definition of goods in the UCC on grounds that it is a movable thing.

> In *Baldwin-Lima-Hamilton Corp. v. Superior Court*,[330] the court noted that "[e]lectricity is a commodity which, like other goods, can be manufactured, transported and sold". In *Puget*

[321] *Ibid*, p. 1864, citing Hill v. Pac. Gas & Elec. Co., 136 P. 492 (Cal. Ct. App. 1913); Pierce v. Pac. Gas & Elec. Co., 166 Cal. App. 3d 68 (1985); Mancuso v. S. Cal. Edison Co., 232 Cal. App. 3d 88 (1991); and California State Board of Equalization, Appeal of PacifiCorp, No. 90027, September 12, 2002.

[322] UCC § 2–102.

[323] UCC § 2–103(1)(k).

[324] UCC § 2–105(1): "Goods must be both existing and identified before any interest in them may pass. Goods that are not both existing and identified are 'future' goods. A purported present sale of future goods or of any interest therein operates as a contract to sell".

[325] See Ferrey S (2004), pp. 1871–1873.

[326] See Norcon Power Partners, L.P. v. Niagara Mohawk Power Corp., 705 N.E.2d 656 (N.Y. Ct. App. 1998).

[327] See New Balance Ath. Shoe v. Boston Edison Co., 1996 Mass. Super. LEXIS 496 (Mass. Super. 1996).

[328] Ferrey S (2004).

[329] Citing Otte v Dayton Power & Light Co., 37 Ohio St 3d 33, 523 N.E.2d 835.

[330] Baldwin-Lima-Hamilton Corp. v. Superior Court, 208 Cal. App. 2d 803, 819 (1962).

Sound Energy, Inc. v. Pacific Gas & Electric Co.,[331] electricity was regarded as a good under the UCC. The court argued: "Simply put, electricity in this instance is a thing movable at the time of identification to the contract for sale. That is clearly demonstrated by the fact that the Agreement calls for the shipment of specific quantities of electricity. The electricity is moved through the power lines and the amounts are metered and therefore identifiable. The court will apply the U.C.C." Other notable cases include *In re Pac. Gas And Elec. Co.*,[332] in which the court regarded the transport of a quantity of electricity as a movable good within the meaning of the UCC, and *Enron Power Marketing, Inc. v. Nevada Power Co.*,[333] in which the US District Court for the Southern District of New York found electricity to be a good under the UCC.

However, the courts have not defined all electricity as a good under the UCC. Some courts have distinguished between "raw" and "metered" electricity.[334]

Electricity and Metering The third alternative used by some courts is to take into account metering. They regard electricity as a good when it passes the metering point. For example, electricity is not a good when it flows in transmission lines and is still "raw"; it is a good when the customer extracts it and its flow is metered.

In *Hedges v. Public Service Co. of Indiana*,[335] the plaintiffs sought remedies under the UCC's warranty provisions, but failed as the court refused to apply the UCC: "The high-voltage electricity with which the [plaintiffs] came into contact was not the good [the utility] was intending to sell or the [plaintiffs] were intending to buy ..." In *Cincinnati Gas & Electric Co. v. Goebel*,[336] the court distinguished "electricity in its raw state from metered amounts passing through utility-owned conduits and into the homes of consumers". The court regarded only the latter as 'goods' as defined in the UCC. In *Schriner v. Pennsylvania Power & Light Co.*,[337] the court developed this further: "... while still in the distribution system, electricity is a service, not a product; electricity only becomes a product, for purposes of strict liability, once it passes through the customer's meter and into the stream of commerce".

Draft Common Frame of Reference

Unlike the CISG, the Draft Common Frame of Reference (DCFR) has addressed the problem of sales of electrical energy in a confusing way. The DCFR reflects a legalistic approach that resembles the laws of German-speaking countries. This

[331] Puget Sound Energy, Inc. v. Pacific Gas & Electric Co., 271 B.R. 626, 640 (N.D. Cal. 2002).

[332] In re Pac. Gas And Elec. Co., 2004 U.S. Dist. LEXIS 22023 (September 30, 2004).

[333] Enron Power Marketing, Inc. v. Nevada Power Co., 2004 U.S. Dist. LEXIS 20351 (S.D.N.Y. October 12, 2004).

[334] In Helvey v. Wabash County REMC, 278 N.E.2d 608, 610 (Ind. Ct. App. 1972), the court held that electricity was a good after having passed the consumer's meter.

[335] Hedges v. Public Service Co. of Indiana, 396 N.E.2d 933, 936 (Ind. Ct. App. 1979).

[336] Cincinnati Gas & Electric Co. v. Goebel, 502 N.E.2d 713 (Hamilton County Mun. Ct., 1986).

[337] Schriner v. Pennsylvania Power & Light Co., 501 A.2d 1128, 1134 (Pa. Super. 1985).

means that the physical characteristics of electricity are not as relevant compared with the CISG, the laws of most Nordic countries, and the case-law of some US courts.

Book IV of the DCFR contains both a part applicable to sale of goods (Part A) and a part applicable to contracts for the supply of a service (Part C). The part applicable to contracts for the supply of a service does not apply to electricity sales.[338] Instead, the sale of goods part of the DCFR applies to contracts for the sale of electricity "with appropriate adaptations".[339]

The application of the sale of goods part of the DCFR to the sales of electrical energy "with appropriate adaptations" does not seem justified to the extent that sales of electrical energy in reality resemble the provision of a service rather than the sale of goods. The application of the provisions governing the sale of goods might be easier to explain in the case of markets with complete vertical integration, all-inclusive contracts, or pure contracts for the balancing of electricity extraction with electricity generation. In such cases, the supplier could more easily be deemed to have undertaken a duty to achieve a result by providing electricity according to certain terms (Werkvertrag) rather than a duty to provide work and use skill and care (Dienstvertrag).

The chosen path of the EU is unbundling, the opposite of complete vertical integration. As a result, the DCFR does not properly reflect existing EU law.

2.7.3 *Result or Work, Supply for a Particular Purpose*

General Remarks

There are contracts to achieve a result (Werkvertrag) and contracts to provide work (Dienstvertrag). Sales contracts are contracts to achieve a result. Contracts for the provision of services can belong to both categories. Whether electricity supply contracts are contracts to achieve a result or contracts to provide work is a matter of interpretation. It depends on the classification of the contracts as sale of goods or the provision of services (Sect. 2.7.2). One may also ask whether an electricity supply contract can be regarded as a contract to supply electricity for a particular purpose. This could, again, be a matter of interpretation.[340]

The answer can depend on the relationship. Because of technical and commercial reasons, one should distinguish between (a) the relationship between the electricity producer and the end consumer on one hand and (b) the relationship between the electricity producer and the transmission/distribution system operator

---

[338] It applies, in particular, to "contracts for construction, processing, storage, design, information or advice, and treatment". DCFR IV.C.–7:101(2).

[339] DCFR IV.A.–1:101(2)(a).

[340] Compare CISG Article 35(2)(b) and 36(2).

on the other. Moreover, one should distinguish between (c) different forms of electricity supply.

Electricity Producer, End Consumer

Particular Purpose The main rule must be that electricity is not supplied for any particular purpose. In the relationship between the electricity producer and the end consumer, this can be explained by information-related and technical reasons.

Electricity is homogeneous in the grid. Electricity producers that supply electricity to the grid do not supply the electricity actually consumed by the end consumer (unless the market model is vertical integration in which electricity producers also act as electricity suppliers), and electricity supplied to the grid (at a higher voltage level) customarily is not the same kind of electricity that is consumed by the end consumer (at a lower voltage level).[341] Electricity supplied to the grid must comply with certain technical requirements, and electricity distributed to the end consumer in a form that can be consumed by the end consumer must comply with other technical requirements.

Electricity producers do not need to know by whom electricity is consumed when it is consumed by the end consumer. It is sufficient that consumption is attributable to a contract party.[342]

Electricity producers customarily have statistical information about the past behaviour of a large number of end consumers. Statistical information can be used to predict end consumers' behaviour in the future. However, electricity producers customarily do not possess information about the intentions of an individual end consumer.

Result or Work Done In the relationship between the electricity producer and the end consumer, the main rule in unbundled electricity markets must be that the obligations of an electricity producer under an electricity supply contract are obligations to provide work rather than to achieve a result.[343]

In unbundled or "liberalised" electricity markets, the question seems to be one of the allocation of risk rather than functions. There must be a contract for the purchase of electricity before electricity may be extracted from the grid, but the ability of the end consumer to extract electricity from the grid does not depend on whether or not its contract party or a particular electricity producer has supplied electricity to the grid. It is the duty of the TSO/DSO to keep electricity flows in balance in the grid. It is difficult to see why electricity producers generally should be responsible for the result of the system operator's work.

[341] See also Ferrey S (2004), p. 1888.

[342] See also Bydlinski F (1972), pp. 44–45.

[343] Compare Bydlinski F (1972), p. 38 arguing that an electricity supply contract is regarded as a contract for the sale of goods under Austrian law, but a contract to provide heating or light is regarded as a contract to achieve a result (Werkvertrag).

On the other hand, a supply contract can be interpreted otherwise in whole or in part because of its wording or other circumstances. The circumstances can vary. For example, an electricity supply contract can provide for ancillary services the performance of which cannot be ensured by the TSO/DSO.

System Operator, End Consumer

The relationship between the system operator and the end consumer is different. Unlike electricity generation as such, the provision of grid access as well as transmission/distribution capacity is a core service from the end consumer's perspective. The purpose of this service is clear in advance. In principle, it would be possible to make the system operator responsible for the result.

Such obligations can be based on many sources. (a) They can be based on electricity law. (b) System operators have duties in contract, but it is customary for system operators to limit their contractual liability to customers to the extent permitted by the governing law.[344] (c) System operators can also be liable in tort to third parties. It is customary to complement general tort rules with legislation that provides for strict liability.

System Operator, Electricity Producer

Similar questions arise in the relationship between system operators and electricity producers. In this case, the parties have agreed on the volumes that the electricity producer shall supply to the grid.

2.7.4 *Product Liability*

General Remarks

Electricity supply contracts and electricity must be classified even for the purposes of product liability. The role of classification has been discussed in numerous cases in the US and is well understood in that country. In the EU, however, it does not seem to have been discussed in detail. US law can thus help to understand these issues better.

The US

In the US, product liability can be based on several causes of action including negligence, breach of contract, and strict liability. The underlying question is whether the electricity firm should be made liable or not, and the classification of

---

[344] See Philippe & Partners (2010).

electricity for product liability purposes may be driven or at least influenced by the desired outcome.

As negligence can be hard to prove,[345] some courts will impose strict liability on utilities for public policy reasons.[346] A plaintiff bringing a strict products liability action faces a lower burden of proof. Such a plaintiff does not need to prove negligence, recklessness, or intention to harm by the manufacturer or distributor of the product. There are also other public policy considerations.[347]

Strict liability can apply where injury is caused by a product (or good) placed in the stream of commerce. A strict liability claim thus requires the existence of a "product".[348] Because of the lower burden of proof, injured plaintiffs who sue an electricity company in tort will ask the court to characterise electricity as a product or good. As courts do not impose strict product liability on services, the defendant electricity company will try to avoid strict liability by arguing that electricity constitutes a service.[349]

The majority of state courts have held that electricity is a product that can be manufactured, transported, and sold. Only a minority of state courts regard electricity as a service.[350] However, most of the court opinions do not address the physical characteristics of electricity.[351]

In *Ransome v. Wis. Elec. Power Co.*,[352] a leading Wisconsin case, the Supreme Court of Wisconsin stated that it need not be concerned with the accurate technical descriptions of electricity. The court construed electricity as a product because the court believed the ordinary user contemplated electricity as one.

In *Pierce v. Pac. Gas & Elec. Co.*,[353] public policy reasons prevailed over technical arguments. The court held that public policy reasons support the imposition of strict product liability. They were as follows: (1) to provide a shortcut to liability where negligence may be present but is difficult to prove; (2) to provide an economics incentive for improved product safety; (3) to induce the reallocation of resources toward safer products; and (4) to spread the risk of loss among all who use the products.[354]

In *Otte v. Dayton Power & Light Co.*,[355] however, the Supreme Court of Ohio held that electricity is not a product for strict liability purposes. According to the court, public policy considerations lack legitimacy in a highly regulated environment.

---

[345] See, for example, Singer Co., Link Simulation Sys. Div. v. Bait. Gas & Elec. Co., 558 A.2d 419 (Md. Ct. Spec. App. 1989).

[346] Ferrey S (2004), pp. 1878–1879.

[347] See Pierce v. Pac. Gas & Elec. Co., 212 Cal. Rptr. 283 (Ct. App. 1985); Ferrey S (2004), p. 1883.

[348] Section 402A of the Restatement (Second) of Torts. See Ferrey S (2004), p. 1877.

[349] Ferrey S (2004), p. 1879.

[350] See Ferrey S (2004), pp. 1877 and 1882.

[351] Ferrey S (2004), p. 1878.

[352] Ransome v. Wis. Elec. Power Co., 275 N.W.2d 641, 643 (Wis. 1979).

[353] Pierce v. Pac. Gas & Elec. Co., 212 Cal. Rptr. 283 (Ct. App. 1985).

[354] Ferrey S (2004), p. 1883.

[355] Otte v. Dayton Power & Light Co., 523 N.E.2d 835 (Ohio 1988). See also Bowen v. Niagara Mohawk Power Corp., 183 A.D.2d 293 (N.Y. App. Div. 1992).

The courts customarily hold that high-voltage electricity does not constitute a product for product liability purposes. It is "not the refined product that the customer intends to buy".[356] On the other hand, electricity can be regarded as a product if it is the kind of electricity that the customer can use. Many courts refuse to impose strict product liability to injuries occurring upstream of the retail meter. They regard electricity as a product for product liability purposes when two things apply: (1) electricity has passed through a meter and (2) it is suitable for ordinary use.[357] In reality, a change in voltage of the electricity occurs at the point of transformation, not at metering.[358]

Characterising electricity as a service rather than a good does not mean that the electricity company is completely free of liability as a service provider. It means that different rules apply instead of the strict product liability or implied warranties under the UCC.[359]

The EU

In the EU, the Product Liability Directive applies to "products".[360] It is clear from the wording of the Directive that electricity is a product that falls within the scope of the Directive.[361]

However, there are problems. In practice, the particular physical characteristics of electricity mean that the Product Liability Directive can hardly be applied to electricity without major modifications.

First, the Directive is designed with a view to products that can be "put into circulation",[362] but electricity cannot be in "circulation" in any meaningful sense as it is generated and consumed at the same time.

Second, it is difficult to find a "producer" in any meaningful sense. (a) According to the wording of the Product Liability Directive, "producer" means "the manufacturer of a finished product, the producer of any raw material or the manufacturer of a component part and any person who, by putting his name, trade mark or other distinguishing feature on the product presents himself as its producer".[363] However,

---

[356] G & K Dairy v. Princeton Elec. Plant Bd., 781 F. Supp. 485,490 (W.D. Ky. 1991). See Ferrey S (2004), p. 1870.

[357] See Ferrey S (2004), p. 1885.

[358] Ferrey S (2004), p. 1889.

[359] See G & K Dairy v, Princeton Elec. Plant Bd., 781 F. Supp. 485,491 (W.D. Ky. 1991); Ferrey S (2004), p. 1876.

[360] For Directive 85/374/EEC (Product Liability Directive) generally, see Schaub R (2011).

[361] Article 2 of Directive 85/374/EEC (Product Liability Directive) (as amended by Directive 1999/34/EC): "For the purpose of this Directive 'product' means all movables even if incorporated into another movable or into an immovable. 'Product' includes electricity".

[362] Recital 3 of Directive 85/374/EEC (Product Liability Directive) as well as Articles 6(1)(c), 6 (2), 7, 11, and 17.

[363] Article 3(1) of Directive 85/374/EEC (Product Liability Directive).

electricity consumed by an end consumer is not the same kind of electricity that the electricity producer has supplied to the grid. For example, it is in most cases supplied at a different voltage level. (b) In addition, electricity flowing in the grid is homogeneous. It is created by all electricity producers that supply electricity to the grid at a particular moment. It is impossible to put the name of a certain electricity producer on electricity that flows in the grid when there are two or more generators supplying electricity to the grid, which is usual. It is of course impossible to attach the name of any party on electricity that flows at the speed of light and is generated and consumed at the same time for all practical purposes. (c) The Product Liability Directive also provides that "any person who imports into the Community a product for sale, hire, leasing or any form of distribution in the course of his business shall be deemed to be a producer within the meaning of this Directive and shall be responsible as a producer".[364] However, electricity markets are regional or national to a very large extent, and there is very little electricity imported to the EU from third countries. The use of interconnectors does not change the physical characteristics of electricity.

Third, an electricity producer cannot influence the "safety" of electricity flowing in the grid and extracted by an end consumer in any way.[365] The quality of electricity that flows in the grid is managed by the transmission or distribution system operator responsible for the grid rather than any particular electricity producer.

Fourth, it is difficult to find a meaningful connection between a "producer" and the "product". According to the wording of the Product Liability Directive, "[t]he producer shall be liable for damage caused by a defect in his product".[366] In restructured and unbundled markets, however, the electricity flowing in the grid is homogeneous. Although it is created by all electricity producers that supply electricity to the grid at a particular moment, its quality is not managed by them. An electricity producer cannot control the existence or non-existence of "defects" in the electricity that flows in the grid or is extracted by end consumers. There is hardly any causal relationship between the behaviour of an electricity producer and "defects" in electricity extracted from the grid.

[364] Article 3(2) of Directive 85/374/EEC (Product Liability Directive).

[365] Article 6(1) of Directive 85/374/EEC (Product Liability Directive): "A product is defective when it does not provide the safety which a person is entitled to expect, taking all circumstances into account, including: (a) the presentation of the product; (b) the use to which it could reasonably be expected that the product would be put; (c) the time when the product was put into circulation".

[366] Article 1 of Directive 85/374/EEC (Product Liability Directive).

2.7.5 *Distance Contracts*

In unbundled energy markets, the regulation of distance contracts can be important for electricity producers as distance contracts can enable vertical integration and business-to-consumer sales. In the EU, consumer distance contracts are governed by the Directive on consumer rights[367] (and, to some extent, by the Directive on electronic commerce).[368]

The Consumer Rights Directive applies to "contracts concluded between consumers and traders".[369] It applies both to contracts for the sale of goods and to service contracts. (a) In some cases, electricity is regarded as "goods". According to the wording of the Consumer Rights Directive, electricity is considered as goods where it is "put up for sale in a limited volume or a set quantity".[370] (b) Electricity supply contracts can fall within the scope of the Consumer Rights Directive even where electricity is not regarded as goods.[371] Electricity supply contracts can then be regarded as service contracts governed by the Directive.[372] Moreover, the Directive applies to "distance contracts". Distance contracts are not limited to sales contracts or contracts for the provision of a service.[373] (c) Electricity is expressly mentioned in the Directive.[374] The Directive also contains particular provisions on electricity contracts.[375]

The rights of consumers under the Consumer Rights Directive and the Third Electricity Directive are cumulative.[376] In contrast, the Electronic Commerce Directive is without prejudice to consumer rights and does not apply to consumer contracts.[377]

---

[367] Directive 2011/83/EU on consumer rights. See also paragraph 1 of Annex I to Directive 2009/72/EC (Third Electricity Directive): "Without prejudice to Community rules on consumer protection . . . the measures referred to in Article 3 are to ensure that . . .".

[368] Directive 2000/31/EC (Directive on electronic commerce).

[369] Article 1 of Directive 2011/83/EU on consumer rights.

[370] Points 3 and 5 of Article 2 of Directive 2011/83/EU on consumer rights.

[371] Recitals 19 and 25 of Directive 2011/83/EU on consumer rights.

[372] Point 6 of Article 2 of Directive 2011/83/EU on consumer rights.

[373] Point 7 of Article 2 of Directive 2011/83/EU on consumer rights.

[374] Article 3(1) of Directive 2011/83/EU on consumer rights.

[375] Directive 2011/83/EU on consumer rights, Article 6(2) (information requirements for distance and off-premises contracts), Article 7(3) (formal requirements for off-premises contracts), Article 8(8) (formal requirements for distance contracts), Article 9(2)(c) (right of withdrawal), Article 14(4) (obligations of the consumer in the event of withdrawal), Article 17 (scope). Annex I to Directive 2011/83/EU on consumer rights, A.6.

[376] Recital 11 of Directive 2011/83/EU on consumer rights; paragraph 1 of Annex 1 to Directive 2009/72/EC (Third Electricity Directive).

[377] Recital 11 of Directive 2000/31/EC (Directive on electronic commerce) and Annex to the Directive. See, for example, Mäntysaari P (2003).

References

Arentsen MJ, Fabius JW, Künneke RW (2001) Dutch business strategies under regime transition. In: Midttun A (ed) European energy industry business strategies. Elsevier Global Energy Policy and Economics Series. Elsevier, the Netherlands, pp 151–194

BaFin (2011) Merkblatt – Hinweise zur Erlaubnispflicht von Geschäften im Zusammenhang mit Stromhandelsaktivitäten. June

Baker PE, Mitchell C, Woodman B (2010) Electricity market design for a low-carbon future. The UK Energy Research Centre, London

Balthasar M (2007) Elektrizitätslieferungsverträge im Hinblick auf die Strommarktöffnung unter besonderer Berücksichtigung des schweizerischen und europäischen Wettbewerbsrechts. Schulthess, Zürich

Bardt H, Chrischilles E, Growitsch C et al (2014) Gutachten. Eigenerzeugung und Selbstverbrauch von Strom. Stand, Potentiale und Trends. Im Auftrag des BDEW Bundesverband der Energie- und Wasserwirtschaft e. V. Institut der deutschen Wirtschaft Köln (IW), Energiewirtschaftliches Institut an der Universität zu Köln (EWI), Cologne, 4 April

Bhattacharyya SC (2011) Energy economics: concepts, issues, markets and governance. Springer, Heidelberg. doi:10.1007/978-0-85729-268-1

Booz & Company (2013) Benefits of an integrated European energy market: revised final report. Prepared for European Commission Directorate-General – Energy. 20 July

Brown MH, Sedano RP (2004) Electricity transmission: a primer. National Council on Electricity Policy, Washington DC

Bundesnetzagentur (2006) Bericht der Bundesnetzagentur nach § 112a EnWG zur Einführung der Anreizregulierung nach § 21a EnWG. 30 June

Bushnell J (2010) Building blocks: investment in renewable and nonrenewable technologies. In: Moselle B, Padilla J, Schmalensee R (eds) Harnessing renewable energy in electric power systems: theory, practice, policy. Earthscan, Washington, pp 113–136

Bushnell JB, Mansur ET, Saravia C (2008) Vertical arrangements, market structure, and competition: An analysis of restructured US electricity markets. Am Econ Rev 98(1):237–266

Bydlinski F (1972) Energielieferung und Kaufrecht. In: Wünsch H (ed) Festschrift für Hermann Hämmerle. Leykam Verlag, Graz, pp 31–53

Cameron PD (2007) Competition in energy markets: law and regulation in the European Union, 2nd edn. Oxford University Press, Oxford

Coase RH (1937) The nature of the firm. Economica (New Series) 4(16):386–405

Commission of the European Communities, Communication from the Commission – Inquiry pursuant to Article 17 of Regulation (EC) No 1/2003 into the European gas and electricity sectors (Final Report), SEC(2006) 1724, COM(2006/) 0851 final

Commission of the European Communities, Report from the Commission to the Council and the European Parliament – Progress in creating the internal gas and electricity market, 15 April 2008, COM(2008) 192 final

Däuper O (2009) The oil market (empirical analysis). In: Zenke I, Schäfer R (eds) Energiehandel in Europa. Öl, Gas, Strom, Derivate, Zertifikate, 2nd edn. C.H. Beck, München, § 3

de Hauteclocque A (2009) Efficiency, competition and long term contracts in electricity markets. Summary and conclusions. Presented at the workshop organized by the Loyola de Palacio Program of the European University Institute and Gis Larsen, Florence, 15–16 January 2009

Deng SJ, Oren SS (2006) Electricity derivatives and risk management. Energy 31(6–7):940–953. doi:10.1016/j.energy.2005.02.015

DCFR (2009) See Study Group on a European Civil Code. http://ec.europa.eu/justice/policies/civil/docs/dcfr_outline_edition_en.pdf

DG Competition Report on Energy Sector inquiry, 10 January 2007, SEC(2006) 1724

Eccher B (2010) In: Koziol H, Bydlinski P, Bollenberger R (eds) Kurzkommentar zum ABGB. Springer, New York

EFET (2012) Towards a single European energy market. EFET website http://www.efet.org/

ENTSO-E (2013) Overview of transmission tariffs in Europe: synthesis, June 2013
Ferraria F (2005) What sources of law for contracts for the international sale of goods? Why one has to look beyond the CISG. Int Rev Law Econ 25:314–341. doi:10.1016/j.irle.2006.02.002
Ferrey S (2004) Inverting choice of law in the wired universe: thermodynamics, mass, and energy. William Mary Law Rev 45:1839–1955
Finon D, Perez Y (2007) The social efficiency of instruments of promotion of renewable energies: a transaction-cost perspective. Ecol Econ 62(1):77–92. doi:10.1016/j.ecolecon.2006.05.011
Finon D, Perez Y (2008) Investment risk allocation in restructured electricity markets. The need of vertical arrangements. LARSEN Working Paper no. 12
Finon D, Pignon V (2008) Electricity and long-term capacity adequacy: the quest for regulatory mechanism compatible with electricity market. Utilities Policy 16(3):143–158. doi:10.1016/j.jup.2008.01.002
Fried J (2010) B. Rechtliche Bewältigung des OTC-Handels. In: Schwintowski HP (ed) Handbuch Energiehandel, 2nd edn. Erich Schmidt Verlag, Berlin, pp 153–336
Godager K (2009) Impacts of MiFID on the Nordic electricity derivatives market. In: Zenke I, Schäfer R (eds) Energiehandel in Europa. Öl, Gas, Strom, Derivate, Zertifikate, 2nd edn. C.H. Beck, München, § 18
Green R (2003) Cost recovery and the efficient development of the grid. In: Lévêque F (ed) Transport pricing of electricity networks. Kluwer, Boston, pp 137–153. doi:10.1007/978-1-4757-3756-1_5
Green R (2006) Investment and generation capacity. In: Lévêque F (ed) Competitive electricity markets and sustainability. Edward Elgar, Cheltenham, pp 21–53. doi:10.4337/9781847204356.00011
Green R (2010) Energy regulation in a low-carbon world. In: Moselle B, Padilla J, Schmalensee R (eds) Harnessing renewable energy in electric power systems: theory, practice, policy. Earthscan, Washington, pp 137–158
Grönroos C (1983) Marknadsföring i tjänsteföretag. Liber Ekonomi, Malmö
Grönroos C (1991) Scandinavian management and the Nordic School of Services – contributions to service management and quality. Int J Serv Industry Manag 2(3):17–25
Härle PA (2010) B. Rechtliche Bewältigung es Handels an der EEX. In: Schwintowski HP (ed) Handbuch Energiehandel, 2nd edn. Erich Schmidt Verlag, Berlin, pp 399–456
Hogan WW (2010) Electricity wholesale market design in a low carbon future. In: Moselle B, Padilla J, Schmalensee R (eds) Harnessing renewable energy in electric power systems: theory, practice, policy. Earthscan, Washington, pp 113–136
Hotakainen M, Klimstra J (2011) Smart power generation, 4th improved edn. Avain, Helsinki
Hsu M (1997) An introduction to the pricing of electric power transmission. Utilities Policy 6 (3):257–270. doi:10.1016/S0957-1787(97)00013-1
Huisman R, Mahieu R, Schlichter F (2009) Electricity portfolio management: optimal peak/off-peak allocations. Energy Econ 31(1):169–174. doi:10.1016/j.eneco.2008.08.003
Hunt S, Shuttleworth G (1996) Competition and choice in electricity. Wiley, Chichester
Joskow PL (2011) Comparing the costs of intermittent and dispatchable electricity generating technologies. Am Econ Rev 101(3):238–241. doi:10.1257/aer.101.3.238
Kindler J (2008) The future role of power exchanges: a regulator's view. Energy Viewpoints 14:12–13
Kirschen DS, Strbac G (2004) Fundamentals of power system economics. Wiley, Chichester
Kwoka J, Pollitt M (2010) Do mergers improve efficiency? Evidence from restructuring the US electric power sector. Int J Ind Organ 28(6):645–656. doi:10.1016/j.ijindorg.2010.03.001
Lanz M, Fricke B, Anthrakidis A et al (2011) CO2-Emissionsminderung durch Ausbau, informationstechnische Vernetzung und Netzoptimierung von Anlagen dezentraler, fluktuierender und erneuerbarer Energienutzung in Deutschland. Umweltbundesamt, Climate Change 20/2011
Larenz K (1989) Allgemeiner Teil des deutschen Bürgerlichen Rechts. Ein Lehrbuch, 7th edn. C.H. Beck, München

Lokau B, Ritzau M (2009) Der Markt für Strom (empirische Darstellung). In: Zenke I, Schäfer R (eds) Energiehandel in Europa. Öl, Gas, Strom, Derivate, Zertifikate, 2nd edn. C.H. Beck, München, § 5
Madlener R, Kaufmann M (2002) Power exchange spot market trading in Europe: theoretical considerations and empirical evidence. OSCOGEN, Discussion Paper No. 5, March
Mahler F (1931) Der Sachbegriff im modernen Elektrizitätsrecht. Juristische Blätter 60:93–94
Mäntysaari P (2003) The Electronic Commerce Directive and the conflict of laws: the case of investment services. Tidskrift utgiven av Juridiska föreningen i Finland 139(3):338–380
Mäntysaari P (2010) The law of corporate finance. General principles and EU law, vol I: Cash flow, risk, agency, information. Springer, Heidelberg
Maribu KM, Galli A, Armstrong M (2007) Valuation of spark-spread options with mean reversion and stochastic volatility. Int J Electr Bus Manag 5(3):173–181
McLean B, Elkind P (2004) The smartest guys in the room. The amazing rise and scandalous fall of Enron. Penguin, The United States of America (updated paperback edn)
Meller E, Walter B (2009) Die Bedeutung des Energiehandels für die Energieversorgung. In: Zenke I, Schäfer R (eds) Energiehandel in Europa. Öl, Gas, Strom, Derivate, Zertifikate, 2nd edn. C.H. Beck, München, § 9
Metzger A (2008) Energiepreise auf dem Prüfstand: Zur Entgeltkontrolle nach Energie-, Kartell- und Vertragsrecht. Zeitschrift für das gesamte Handelsrecht und Wirtschaftsrecht 172 (4):458–477
Midttun A (ed) (2001) European energy industry business strategies. Elsevier Global Energy Policy and Economics Series. Elsevier, the Netherlands
Midttun A, Handeland J, Henriksen JT et al (2001) Nordic business strategies. In: Midttun A (ed) European energy industry business strategies. Elsevier Global Energy Policy and Economics Series. Elsevier, the Netherlands, pp 23–74
Mihm A (2014a) Energieerzeuger stehen vor weiterer Talfahrt. Frankfurter Allgemeine Zeitung, 31 March 2014, p 24
Mihm A (2014b) Vattenfall will aus deutscher Braunkohle aussteigen. Frankfurter Allgemeine Zeitung, 30 October 2014
Monopolkommission (2013) Sondergutachten 65. Energie 2013: Wettbewerb in Zeiten der Energiewende. Sondergutachten der Monopolkommission gemäß § 62 Abs. 1 EnWG. Bonn
Neveling S, Schönrock KP (2009) Nicht standardisierte Liefer- und Handelsverträge sowie vertragliche Voraussetzungen auf der Netzzugangsseite. In: Zenke I, Schäfer R (eds) Energiehandel in Europa. Öl, Gas, Strom, Derivate, Zertifikate, 2nd edn. C.H. Beck, München, § 29
Normann R (1991) Service management. Strategy and leadership in service business, 2nd edn. Wiley, Chichester
OECD/IEA (2005) Lessons from liberalised electricity markets. IEA, Paris
Ofgem (2009) Liquidity in the GB wholesale energy markets, 8 June 2009
Oren SS, Spiller PT, Varaiya P, Wu F (1995) Nodal prices and transmission rights: a critical appraisal. Electr J 8(3):24–35. doi:10.1016/1040-6190(95)90198-1
Ortlieb B (2011) Das Gesetzespaket zur Energiewende – Zusammenfassender Überblick über die wesentlichen Inhalte der acht am 8. Juli 2011 endgültig verabschiedeten, mittlerweile im Bundesgesetzblatt veröffentlichten (und zum größten Teil auch bereits in Kraft getretenen) Gesetze. EWeRK 11(4):151–156
Philippe & Partners (2010) Final report on liability of electricity transmission system operators for supply failure, Brussels, 26 July
Pérez-Arriaga IJ, Smeers Y (2003) Guidelines on tariff setting. In: Lévêque F (ed) Transport pricing of electricity networks. Kluwer, Boston, pp 175–203. doi:10.1007/978-1-4757-3756-1_7
Perrels A, Kemppi H (2003) Liberalised electricity markets: strengths and weaknesses in Finland and NordPool. VATT research reports 97. Government Institute for Economic Research, Helsinki

Ruester S, von Hirschhausen C, Marcantonini C et al (2012) Topic 6. EU Involvement in electricity and natural gas transmission grid tarification. Final Report. European University Institute. doi:10.2870/35676
Salomon Smith Barney (2002) Merchant Energy Primer, 22 January
Schaub R (2011) Europäische Produkthaftung: Wie weit reicht die Harmonisierung heute? ZEuP 19(1):41–64
Schröder A, Kunz F, Meiss J et al (2013) Current and prospective costs of electricity generation until 2050. Deutsches Institut für Wirtschaftsforschung, Data Documentation 68
Shaw DR, Holland CP, Kawalek P et al (2006) Electronic commerce strategy in the U.K. electricity industry: the case of Electric Co and Dataflow Software. Int J Technol Hum Interact 2(3):38–60
Spence DB (2008) Can law manage competitive energy markets? Cornell Law Rev 93:765–818
Spicker J (2010) A. Formen des OTC-Handels. In: Schwintowski HP (ed) Handbuch Energiehandel, 2nd edn. Erich Schmidt Verlag, Berlin, pp 31–152
Strachan PA, Lal D, von Malmborg F (2006) The evolving UK wind energy industry: critical policy and management aspects of the emerging research agenda. Eur Environ 16(1):1–18. doi:10.1002/eet.400
Strachan PA, Toke D, Lal D (2010) Assessing national patterns of wind ownership. In: Strachan PA, Toke D, Lal D (eds) Wind power and power politics: international perspectives. Routledge studies in science, technology, and society 9. Routledge, New York, pp 1–17
Stridbeck U (1994) Att lägga förhållandena till rätta: konsumenträttsliga krav på livsnödvändigheter speciellt med tanke på elektricitet, vatten och telefon. TemaNord 1994:633. Nordiska Ministerrådet, København
Supponen M (2011) The influence of national and company interests on european electricity transmission investments. Dissertation, Aalto University
Talus K (2010) Vertical natural gas transportation capacity, upstream commodity contracts and EU competition law. Dissertation, University of Helsinki
Teusch J, Behrens A, Egenhofer C (2012) The benefits of investing in electricity transmission: lessons from Northern Europe. CEPS Special Report, January
Thomas S (2001) Corporate strategies in the British electricity supply industry. In: Midttun A (ed) European energy industry business strategies. Elsevier Global Energy Policy and Economics Series. Elsevier, the Netherlands, pp 75–150
U.S. Energy Information Administration (2002) Derivatives and risk management in the petroleum, natural gas, and electricity industries, October
von Bar C, Drobnig U (2004) The interaction of contract law and tort and property law in Europe. A comparative study. Sellier, München
Winship P (1984) The scope of the Vienna convention on international sales contracts. In: Galston NM, Smit H (eds) International sales. The United Nations convention on contracts for the international sale of goods. Matthew Bender, New York
Winship P (1990) Energy contracts and the United Nations sales convention. Tex Int Law J 25:365–379

Chapter 3
Introduction to the Regulation of Electricity Markets

3.1 General Remarks

This chapter gives an introduction to some fundamental aspects of the regulation of electricity markets in EU law.

The regulatory regime for electricity markets consists of many components: the regulation of electricity markets; the regulation of financial markets; the regulation of energy efficiency and greenhouse gas emissions; and competition law. Electricity markets are "affected with the public interest"[1] in various ways and different components of the regulatory regime are designed to further different policy objectives.

The regulation of electricity markets is regarded as important for many reasons. (a) The first is simply that energy issues have attracted plenty of political interest. Energy issues have become a large battlefield for politicians with conflicting preferences. (b) The second is the size and growth of the electricity market. While the energy industry is a large and important sector of the European economy, the production and consumption of electricity grow faster than the overall energy market. To illustrate, the attainment of the EU's 2020 climate-change target requires more electricity, more transmission capacity, and smarter grids.[2] The 2030 targets require more effort. (c) The third is security of supply. An effective EU-wide electricity market could increase the security of energy supply and help to reduce the EU's reliance on imported gas. (d) Fourth, the regulation of the electricity market could help to sustain the competitiveness of European industry. While a lower price of electricity contributes to higher economic growth, higher

[1] In Munn v. Illinois 94 U.S. 113 (1876), the US Supreme Court recognised that an economic activity may become a proper subject for regulation when it becomes "affected with the public interest". For the development of US regulation, see Spence DB and Prentice R (2012).

[2] Smart grids are not a legal concept in EU law. See Pront-van Bommel S (2011).

P. Mäntysaari, *EU Electricity Trade Law*, DOI 10.1007/978-3-319-16513-4_3

tariffs hamper growth. (e) Fifth, it would not be possible to develop an effectively functioning emissions trading mechanism without a competitive electricity market.

We begin with an overview of liberalisation (Sect. 3.2), the several regulatory sectors (Sect. 3.3), and a brief history of electricity regulation (Sect. 3.4). There is an introduction to the most important electricity directives and network codes (Sect. 3.5). In addition, it is necessary to discuss competition law (Sect. 3.6), environmental regulation (Sect. 3.7), as well as the regulation of marketplaces and financial markets (Sect. 3.8) to the extent that they can be relevant for electricity producers.

3.2 Liberalisation

Liberalising the internal electricity market would be a big task, because it is not possible to liberalise European electricity markets without extensive regulation.

There are examples of how things can go wrong. In California, the goal was a competitive market for the buying and selling of power. While markets were deregulated at the wholesale level, price caps were used at the retail level. This led to the Western Energy Crisis (the Californian electricity crisis).[3] The German electricity market shows how the preferential treatment of electricity generated from renewable sources (RES-E) can increase greenhouse gas emissions, increase retail electricity prices, limit investment, and reduce security of supply.

There are also better examples of liberalisation. The more mature liberalised European markets can be found in the Nordic countries for electricity and in Britain for electricity and gas. There is a new, north-west and central European power-trading zone with Germany in the middle (the NWE region).[4]

Obviously, electricity producers would benefit from a fully liberalised internal electricity market. It would help electricity firms to scale up[5] and even to increase the number of market participants. Unbundling that restricts some forms of vertical integration is bound to increase other forms of vertical integration by facilitating access to end consumers and to give incentives for horizontal integration.[6]

However, year 2014 did not bring about a fully liberalised internal electricity market. The new legislation was not intended to liberalise markets—at least not from the perspective of electricity producers. The regulatory regime facilitating the internal electricity market has other objectives. What explains the low level of liberalisation?

[3] ISDA (2003), p. 8.

[4] EFET (2005), section 2.2.

[5] Midttun A (2001), p. 1.

[6] For horizontal and vertical integration in value chains, see Midttun A (2001), p. 11.

Objectives of Regulation To begin with, the "liberalisation" of electricity markets does not mean deregulation.[7] The efficiency of electricity markets can only be facilitated by extensive regulation. In the EU, energy markets are governed by a regulatory regime that is both detailed and large in scope.

The regulatory regime is partly necessary because of the nature of electricity markets. For instance, the functioning of physical electricity markets requires detailed standardisation for technical reasons.

There are reasons that increase the scope of the EU regulatory regime and its level of detail. First, the regulatory regime is designed to further many different and sometimes conflicting public policy objectives. For instance, one of the present-day goals of the EU is to foster energy efficiency and energy saving, but this is not the only objective of EU energy policy. It should also: ensure security of energy supply; ensure the functioning of the energy market; foster the interconnection of energy networks; and foster the development of new and renewable forms of energy.[8] Second, in some policy areas (such as financial markets and competition), the objectives of the EU have resulted in extensive harmonisation of Member States' national regulatory regimes.

It would be just as misleading to talk about deregulation in the US. FERC's regulation of RTO/ISOs has been described as "pervasive".

Unlike the SEC and the CFTC, FERC is a "rate regulator" with a mandate grounded in the Federal Power Act of 1935. It has an obligation to ensure that prices in wholesale electricity markets, and the terms and conditions of the various products and services used to establish prices in these markets, are "just and reasonable". RTOs and ISOs cannot establish unilaterally their rules of operation. Instead, RTOs/ISOs are subject to a FERC administered program comprehensively regulating their planning of the transmission grid, their dispatch of generation operation of the grid, their compliance with reliability standards, and their administration of the markets they operate. Every material action taken by an RTO/ISO in performing these functions must be authorised by a rule. Every rule must be embodied in a tariff. Every tariff provision must be filed with and adjudicated by the FERC to meet the requirements of the Federal Power Act.[9]

The collapse of Enron increased the regulation of financial electricity markets first in the US.[10] It has increased the regulation of financial markets in the EU as well.

Market-Based Mechanisms Rather than deregulation, the liberalisation of electricity markets means the adoption of new legislation designed to: increase access to the market (open up the market); facilitate increased use of market-based mechanisms; and facilitate the coupling of markets.

---

[7] See, for example, Cameron PD (2007), p. 30, para 1.76.

[8] Article 194 TFEU. See also Commission Green Paper, A European Strategy for Sustainable, Competitive and Secure Energy, 8 March 2006, COM(2006) 105 final. For German law, see § 1 (1) EnWG: "Zweck des Gesetzes ist eine möglichst sichere, preisgünstige, verbraucherfreundliche, effiziente und umweltverträgliche leitungsgebundene Versorgung der Allgemeinheit mit Elektrizität und Gas".

[9] US Senate Committee on Energy and Natural Resources (2010), statement of Vincent P. Duane.

[10] ISDA (2003) and Brunet A and Shafe M (2007).

The use of market-based mechanisms means: (a) the introduction of electricity exchanges for the trading of spot electricity, electricity forwards, and electricity derivatives in a similar manner as securities and commodities are traded in the financial market; (b) the introduction of auctions for balance energy; (c) the introduction of auctions for the allocation of transmission capacity; and (d) a secondary market for transmission capacity.

Not the Same Thing as Creating a Single Market Liberalisation is not the same thing as creating a single (or internal) market for electricity (whether liberalised or not). An internal market relates to the absence of barriers to cross-border trade.

Creating the internal market for electricity is not uncomplicated, because the markets traditionally have been national. The integration of electricity markets requires breaking up vertically integrated utilities, investments in new interconnectors between national grids, effective cooperation between transmission system operators, and a clear and stable regulatory framework to foster investment in generation and transmission capacity.

Creating the internal electricity market requires large investments in electricity infrastructure, and it can only be created in stages. The first stage was creating electricity markets that were regional rather than national. The Commission planned seven regional markets for electricity. The second stage is to integrate the regional markets.[11]

No Liberalisation of the Wholesale Market for Electricity Producers In any case, there are ways to liberalise wholesale markets for electricity producers and ways to liberalise retail markets for end consumers. They are not the same thing.

As regards wholesale markets, it would not be enough to liberalise just one market or national electricity markets. There are many wholesale electricity markets in the EU and the markets are connected in various ways.[12]

The EU seems to have focused on liberalising retail markets from a consumer perspective rather than physical wholesale markets from a producer perspective. (a) The regulation of physical wholesale markets at the EU level is largely based on central planning with several contradictory objectives. The objectives include the operational efficiency of the electricity system, fostering the use of particular generation technologies that are not efficient (RES-E), fostering investment in RES-E even in the most isolated Member States and regions, ensuring that consumers can purchase energy at affordable prices, ensuring nevertheless that competition is free, ensuring security of supply, and increasing the liquidity and transparency of electricity wholesale markets.[13] (b) In the physical wholesale

[11] Meller E and Walter B (2009), § 9, numbers 23 and 25.

[12] See, for example, Meeus L et al. (2005).

[13] Recital 6 of Directive 2009/72/EC (Third Electricity Directive) and recitals 1–3 of draft Commission Regulation …/.. (CACM Regulation). For liquidity, see recital 39 of Directive 2009/72/EC (Third Electricity Directive) and also Ofgem (2009b), para 1.9. Indications of liquidity include the churn ratio (the ratio of traded volume to generated volume is high in liquid markets), the total number of trades (high in liquid markets), the range of products available to

market, the EU seems to have focused on aspects related to financial markets (such as clearing) and the trading of standardised contracts (in particular on exchanges) rather than the supply of electricity as such (under bilateral or other physical contracts).[14]

Wholesale markets are not truly liberalised when the Member States are asked to discriminate against electricity producers depending on their production technology and when the Member States do not have faith in the market mechanism.[15]

The prevailing competition model in the EU is limited supplier competition (see Sect. 2.6.3). The low level of liberalisation and the preferential treatment of RES-E have: increased investment in RES-E installations; led to overcapacities in generation; reduced wholesale prices and increased retail prices; reduced investment in new generation installations other than RES-E generation installations; made old coal-burning installations more competitive; contributed little to a reduction of greenhouse gas emissions; and made the business of electricity producers more difficult.[16] The low level of liberalisation and the preferential treatment of RES-E also mean higher exposure to legal and regulatory risk as well as problems caused by the lower level of liquidity.[17]

3.3 Regulatory Sectors

The regulatory regime for electricity markets serves various potentially conflicting policy objectives, because EU law has conflicting objectives and the regulatory regime is based both on the four freedoms and sectoral legislation in many overlapping areas (competition law, financial regulation, environmental law, and energy law).

Competition Law The EC Treaty that preceded the TFEU made it clear that it was not enough to apply the four freedoms in the internal market. It was just as important to ensure that competition is free.[18] The TFEU requires the EU and the Member States to conduct their economic policies in accordance with the principle

market participants (large in liquid markets), the size of bid-offer spreads (small in liquid markets), the extent of forward trading, and the number of market participants. Ofgem (2009b), paras 2.2–2.6.

[14] For definitions, see point 19 of Article 2 of Directive 2009/72/EC (Third Electricity Directive). For trading, see, for example, Fried J (2010), p. 165, point 263.

[15] Monopolkommission (2013), number 514.

[16] See, for example, Mihm A (2014a): "Grund für die historisch niedrigen Börsenpreise sind gewaltige Überkapazitäten in der Stromerzeugung. Die machen heute schon den Betrieb vor allem von teuren Gas- und Steinkohlekraftwerken unrentabel . . ."

[17] Ofgem (2009b), para 1.10.

[18] Article 4(1) of the Treaty establishing the European Community (EC Treaty): ". . . the adoption of an economic policy . . . conducted in accordance with the principle of an open market economy with free competition".

of an open market economy with free competition.[19] Since *Almelo*, it has been clear that EU competition law applies to the electricity sector.[20]

EU competition law has played an important role in the regulation of the electricity markets even for three other general reasons. On one hand, there is no single European energy regulator to control the markets and Member States may be slow to open their markets as this could be to the detriment of their own national champions or state-owned utilities. On the other, there is a well-developed body of competition law in the EU because market behaviour is constrained by EU competition law (Articles 101, 102, and 107 TFEU), national competition laws (such as the GWB and UWG[21]), or both.[22] Moreover, the Commission has both wide powers to enforce competition law and an opportunity to do so in the light of the existence of monopolies and the use of long-term contracts in electricity markets.[23]

Financial Regulation The regulation of energy markets resembles financial regulation in many respects and is partly governed by the same regulatory framework. After the restructuring and unbundling of electricity markets and the growth of physical and financial electricity exchanges as well as OTC-trading, the regulatory regime for financial markets has replaced competition law as the most important regulatory regime complementing the sectoral regulation of energy. Much of this book focuses on the financial regulation of electricity markets.

The most important EU legislation in this area consists of MiFID II/MiFIR,[24] EMIR,[25] MAR/MAD II,[26] REMIT,[27] CRD IV/CRR,[28] as well as the Financial Collateral Directive[29] and the Settlement Finality Directive.[30] Electricity markets are influenced even by other sectoral directives such as insurance directives[31] and the UCITS Directive that regulate the use of derivative contracts for some potential market participants.[32]

---

[19] Articles 119(1) and 120 TFEU.

[20] Case C-393/92 Gemeente Almelo v Energiebedrijf IJsselmij NV [1994] ECR I-1477.

[21] Gesetz gegen Wettbewerbsbeschränkungen (GWB), Gesetz gegen den unlauteren Wettbewerb (UWG).

[22] For the relationship between Articles 101 and 102 the Treaty and national competition laws, see Article 3 of Regulation 1/2003.

[23] Spence DB (2008), pp. 782–785.

[24] Directive 2014/65/EU (MiFID II); Regulation 600/2014 (MiFIR).

[25] Regulation 648/2012 (EMIR).

[26] Regulation 596/2014 (MAR); Directive 2014/57/EU (MAD II).

[27] Regulation 1227/2011 (REMIT).

[28] Directive 2013/36/EU (CRD IV); Regulation 575/2013 (CRR).

[29] Directive 2002/47/EC (Directive on financial collateral arrangements).

[30] Directive 98/26/EC (Directive on settlement finality).

[31] See, for example, Directive 2002/83/EC (Directive on life assurance).

[32] Article 50(1) of Directive 2009/65/EC (UCITS Directive): "The investments of a UCITS shall comprise only one or more of the following . . ." For limits, see Article 51(3) and Article 52(1) of

Environmental Law The 20/20/20 targets adopted by the European Council in March 2007 have had a major impact on the electricity industry. Their impact is not limited to the introduction of greenhouse emission permits for installations[33] and a market-based mechanism for emissions trading under Directive 2003/87/EC (as amended).[34] In practice, the environmental law regime makes investment in electricity generation and transmission installations largely regulation-driven and subject to regulatory permits (Sect. 3.7.7). As the market mechanism is replaced by central planning, the costs of meeting the 20/20/20 targets are likely to be much higher than they could be.

The 20/20/20 targets are part of the Europe 2020 strategy.[35] Of the three targets, a 20 % reduction in greenhouse gas emissions when compared to 1990 levels and raising the share of energy consumption produced from renewable resources to 20 % are nationally binding targets implemented by The climate and energy package.[36] The third of the targets is a 20 % improvement in the EU's energy-efficiency compared to 1990 levels.

The Europe 2020 strategy is complemented by the 2030 Framework proposed by the Commission in January 2014[37] and agreed on by the European Council in October 2014. The main objectives set out in the 2030 Framework are: a reduction in greenhouse gas emissions by 40 % relative to the 1990 level; an EU-wide binding target for renewable energy of at least 27 %; renewed ambitions for energy efficiency policies; and a new governance system and a set of new indicators to ensure a competitive and secure energy system.

Particular Treaty Provisions on Energy Markets The regulation of electricity markets is based on the provisions of the Treaty on European Union (TEU) and the TFEU. The Treaties contain particular provisions on energy markets. Some of these provisions regulate the division of competence between the bodies of the EU and the Member States. Others regulate how and for what purpose these competences may be exercised.

The competences may be exercised for certain purposes. To begin with, the TEU defines the general objectives of the EU. In addition to establishing an internal market and various other objectives, the EU shall "work for the sustainable development of Europe based on balanced economic growth and price stability, a highly competitive social market economy, aiming at full employment and social progress,

---

Directive 2009/65/EC (UCITS Directive). See also recitals 43 and 45–46 of Directive 2009/65/EC (UCITS Directive) and Directive 2010/43/EU (implementing the UCITS Directive).

[33] Article 4 of Directive 2003/87/EC (Emissions Trading Scheme Directive).

[34] See, for example, Poncelet C (2011) and Nield K and Pereira R (2011).

[35] Communication from the Commission, EUROPE 2020 A strategy for smart, sustainable and inclusive growth. COM(2010) 2020 final, 3 March 2010.

[36] Decision 406/2009/EC of the European Parliament and of the Council; Directive 2009/28/EC (RES Directive).

[37] Communication from the Commission – A policy framework for climate and energy in the period from 2020 to 2030. COM(2014) 15 final, 22 January 2014.

and a high level of protection and improvement of the quality of the environment" as well as "promote scientific and technological advance".[38]

The TFEU lays down two broad objectives for the EU's energy policy in an effort to clarify the relative weight of the various general objectives of the EU set out in the TEU. The two broad objectives include, first, the establishment and functioning of the *internal market* and, second, the preservation and improvement of the *environment*.

To attain these broad objectives, the EU's energy policy has more specific goals. It aims to: (a) ensure the functioning of the EU's energy market; (b) ensure security of energy supply in the EU; (c) promote energy efficiency and energy saving and the development of new and renewable forms of energy; and (d) promote the interconnection of energy networks.[39] According to the TFEU, the setting-up of an area without internal frontiers requires even trans-European energy infrastructures.[40] The EU's energy policy is also influenced by its environmental policy and legislation. The fact that environmental policy can influence energy sources and the structure of a Member State's energy supply has been considered in the decision-making process.[41]

3.4 Brief History of Electricity Regulation

The regulation of energy markets has long roots in the EU.[42] In fact, the origins of the EU lie in the regulation of the energy industry.

Treaties The European Coal and Steel Community, which was established by the Treaty of Paris in 1951, created a common market for coal and steel between France, Germany, Italy, Belgium, Luxembourg, and the Netherlands. The ECSC Treaty was in force from 23 July 1952 to 23 July 2002. The European Atomic Energy Community was established by the 1957 Euratom Treaty, one of the two Treaties of Rome.

Energy is nowadays mentioned in the Treaty on the Functioning of the EU (TFEU). In addition, energy markets fall within the scope of the four freedoms and EU competition law.

Liberalisation The process of liberalising the European electricity market started in the 1990s when the Community decided to open up gas and electricity markets to competition and to create an integrated European energy market. The Community's

---

[38] Article 3(3) TEU.

[39] Article 194(1) TFEU.

[40] Article 170(1) TFEU.

[41] Article 192(2) TFEU.

[42] See Talus K (2013).

energy markets policy has been implemented through sector-specific legislation and by means of EU competition law.[43]

> In the US, the Public Utility regulatory Policy Act of 1978 (PURPA) is regarded as the first step towards creating more competitive power markets. Section 210 of PURPA encouraged non-utility generators to build power plants using principally non-fossil energy sources. PURPA was followed by the Energy Policy Act of 1992 (EPA). According to EPA, an "exempt wholesale generator" could own a generation facility and sell power exclusively into the wholesale power market. In 1996, the FERC issued Order No. 888 designed to unbundle all the services offered by existing public utilities into their various components so that the new participants would also have access to those services and a chance to compete against such utilities on a level playing field. By Order No. 2000, the FERC directed that "all transmission owning entities in the Nation, including non-public utility entities, place their transmission facilities under the control of appropriate regional transmission institutions (RTOs)".[44]
>
> FERC is a federal agency created in 1977 to regulate, among other things, interstate wholesale sales and transportation of gas and electricity at "just and reasonable" rates.[45]

Directives, Three Legislative Packages The EU electricity markets have been restructured gradually on a piece-meal basis. The first step was to adopt two directives in 1990 to improve price transparency and the use of the grid for electricity transit.

According to the Price Transparency Directive, undertakings that supply gas or electricity to industrial end-users must disclose the prices and terms and the price systems in use.[46] The Electricity Transit Directive facilitated transit of electricity between high-voltage grids. The Member States were given a duty to take the necessary measures.[47] Transit contracts were to be negotiated between the entities responsible for the grids concerned rather than between a supplier/consumer and the operator of each grid.[48] The Electricity Transit Directive also laid down the general standards for the conditions of transit such as non-discrimination, fairness, and no endangering of security of supply and quality of service.[49]

The EU's ambitious restructuring and integration process started a few years later when the first of three legislative packages was adopted.[50] The first legislative package consisted of the First Electricity Directive[51] (Sect. 3.5.1) and a similar

---

[43] For Germany, see Lokau B and Ritzau M (2009), § 5, number 6.

[44] ISDA (2003), pp. 5–6.

[45] U.S. Energy Information Administration (2002), Chapter 1; OECD/IEA (2005), p. 58.

[46] Article 1 of Directive 90/377/EEC (Price Transparency Directive).

[47] Article 1 of Directive 90/547/EEC (Directive on the transit of electricity through transmission grids).

[48] Article 3(1) of Directive 90/547/EEC (Directive on the transit of electricity through transmission grids).

[49] Article 3(2) of Directive 90/547/EEC (Directive on the transit of electricity through transmission grids).

[50] For the integration of electricity markets generally, see Creti A et al. (2010).

[51] Directive 96/92/EC (First Electricity Directive).

Directive for the natural gas market in 1996. According to the First Electricity Directive, the internal market in electricity needs to be established gradually.[52]

The process was reinforced by the second legislative package and the Second Electricity Directive (Sect. 3.5.2)[53] in 2003 as well as the third legislative package and the Third Electricity Directive (Sect. 3.5.4)[54] in 2009.

The Third Electricity Directive is the directive that requires the effective unbundling of generation and network assets. In addition, conditions for access to the network for cross-border exchanges in electricity were introduced by Regulation 714/2009 to encourage cross-border competition.[55]

The European Council set the target of 2014 for the completion of a fully liberalised internal electricity market. Its cornerstone is the Third Electricity Directive.[56] ACER (Agency for the Cooperation of Energy Regulators)[57] and ENTSO-E (European Network of Transmission System Operators for Electricity) were created to improve the legislatory process.

Target Model In addition to the general 2014 target, there is also a target model. In 2008, a Project Coordination Group of experts was given the task of developing an EU-wide target model for the integration of regional electricity markets. According to this target model, a single price-coupling mechanism (implicit auction) should be implemented across all European countries (Sect. 5.2).[58] Regulation 714/2009 is in line with this target model.[59]

The electricity market target model is a developing set of proposals. It is based on two broad principles: "energy only" regional markets (electricity producers' revenues should primarily depend on the price for each marginal unit of energy supplied); and market coupling.[60] The target model is set out in the Framework

52 Recital 5 of Directive 96/92/EC (First Electricity Directive).

53 Directive 2003/54/EC (Second Electricity Directive).

54 Directive 2009/72/EC (Third Electricity Directive).

55 Regulation 714/2009 (on conditions for access to the network for cross-border exchanges in electricity).

56 Directive 2009/72/EC (Third Electricity Directive).

57 ACER was established by Regulation 713/2009.

58 ERGEG, Draft Framework Guidelines on Capacity Allocation and Congestion Management for Electricity: Initial Impact Assessment. Ref: E10-ENM-20-04 (8 September 2010), p. 43 and Annex 4, p. 73; Creti A et al. (2010).

59 Point 2.1 of Annex I to Regulation 714/2009: "Congestion-management methods shall be market-based in order to facilitate efficient cross-border trade. For that purpose, capacity shall be allocated only by means of explicit (capacity) or implicit (capacity and energy) auctions. Both methods may coexist on the same interconnection. For intra-day trade continuous trading may be used". Point 2.8 of Annex I: "In regions where forward financial electricity markets are well developed and have shown their efficiency, all interconnection capacity may be allocated through implicit auctioning".

60 Keay M (2013).

Guidelines on Capacity Allocation and Congestion Management for Electricity published by ACER in July 2011 (Sect. 5.1).[61]

Deeper Harmonisation The 2014 target for the completion of the internal electricity market does not prevent the Member States from taking action to increase market integration.

The Nordic regulators (NordREG) have taken steps to create, by 2015, a common harmonised market with a supplier-centric model as its cornerstone. The long-term vision is a fully integrated market.

NordREG has defined these goals as follows[62]: (a) A common harmonised market means "a market where the most critical barriers for suppliers to establishing business in another Nordic country are eliminated. In the common harmonised market legislation regarding key issues such as responsibilities in the customer interface, billing, risk management, tax collection, number of contracts, making and ending contracts, universal service (supplier of last resort and default supplier), supplier switching, moving, information exchange, data format, regulation regarding DSO neutrality, balance settlement, access to data and metering, may or will be subject to changes". (b) A supplier centric model "is characterised by the defined customer interface, where a majority of the customer contacts will be handled by the supplier. However, the DSO will still have ultimate responsibility towards customers regarding strictly network related issues".[63] (c) A fully integrated market "is the long term vision of a market where all relevant legislation and processes are harmonised to the extent that they are almost identical". However, this does not include the harmonisation of business legislation of general application such as tax laws.

3.5 The Electricity Directives

3.5.1 The First Electricity Directive: Construction of Generation Capacity

The present market structure is the result of the adoption of three energy packages. We can study the three electricity directives in more detail to the extent that they are relevant for electricity producers. The restructuring of the European electricity markets started with the First Electricity Directive.

Construction of New Generation Capacity The First Directive made it easier to construct new generation capacity. For this purpose, Member States could choose an authorisation procedure and/or a tendering procedure. Both must be conducted in

---

[61] ACER, Framework Guidelines on Capacity Allocation and Congestion Management for Electricity (29 July 2011); European Commission, Public consultation on the governance framework for the European day-ahead market coupling, D(2011) 1176339 (28 November 2011).

[62] NordREG (2013), p. 5.

[63] See also Bjørnebye H and Alvik I (2012).

accordance with objective, transparent and non-discriminatory criteria.[64] The Directive listed the permitted criteria.[65]

Unbundling The First Directive did not prohibit complete vertical integration. Integrated electricity firms could still own transmission or distribution assets. However, the First Directive required the separation of functions. Member States were required to designate operators for the transmission and distribution systems.[66] The TSO had to be "independent at least in management terms from other activities not relating to the transmission system".[67]

Retail Competition The First Directive made an attempt to increase retail competition by giving eligible customers—distribution companies and large consumers—a right to choose the supplier.[68]

Access to the Network Moreover, TSOs and DSOs were required to grant non-discriminatory access to the network under negotiated third party access (nTPA), regulated third party access (rTPA), or the "single buyer" option. (a) Germany was the only Member State to opt for *negotiated* third-party access (nTPA).[69] Under negotiated access, generators and retail suppliers were required to negotiate with the system operators for access to the network. An indicative range of prices had to be published. (b) All other Member States opted for *regulated* third-party access (rTPA). Under regulated access, generators and retail suppliers were allowed access at published tariffs. (c) Under the *single buyer* option, a Member State could designate a "single buyer" responsible for purchasing the country's (or a smaller region's) electricity needs. The single buyer would determine which plants were used.[70]

Effect The First Electricity Directive did not go very far. First, it did not require a wholesale market to be set up. Even if companies were free to build new power plants, they did not necessarily have the means to bring their power to market.[71] Second, the unbundling requirements did not guarantee independence of access to

---

[64] Article 4 of Directive 96/92/EC (First Electricity Directive).

[65] Article 5(1) of Directive 96/92/EC (First Electricity Directive): "Where they opt for the authorization procedure, Member States shall lay down the criteria for the grant of authorizations for the construction of generating capacity in their territory. These criteria may relate to: (a) the safety and security of the electricity system, installations and associated equipment; (b) protection of the environment; (c) land use and siting; (d) use of public ground; (e) energy efficiency; (f) the nature of the primary sources; (g) characteristics particular to the applicant, such as technical, economic and financial capabilities; (h) the provisions of Article 3".

[66] Articles 7(1) and 10(2) of Directive 96/92/EC (First Electricity Directive).

[67] Article 7(6) of Directive 96/92/EC (First Electricity Directive).

[68] Article 19(3) of Directive 96/92/EC (First Electricity Directive).

[69] See VV II Strom, Verbändevereinbarung über Kriterien zur Bestimmung von Netznutzungsentgelte für elektrische Energie.

[70] Articles 16, 17(1), 17(4) and 18(1) of Directive 96/92/EC (First Electricity Directive).

[71] For German law, see Lokau B and Ritzau M (2009), § 5, number 10.

the network. Third, retail competition was restricted, with no more than a few thousand consumers able to choose by 2003 even in the largest countries. Fourth, it did not require an independent sector regulator.[72]

3.5.2 *The Second Electricity Directive: Retail Competition*

In practice, most countries went much further than was required to meet the terms of the First Directive.[73] This encouraged the Commission to introduce new proposals to close loopholes. The First Electricity Directive was replaced by the Second Electricity Directive designed to cure some of its shortcomings.[74]

The Second Electricity Directive placed more stringent requirements on Member States to de-integrate their electricity industries and introduce competition in power generation and the retail market. The Second Directive placed requirements in the same four areas covered by the First Directive but went further. Moreover, it required the designation of an independent sector regulator.

Construction of New Generating Capacity The rules on the construction of new capacity built on the provisions of the First Directive. But while the First Directive permitted the Member States to choose an authorisation procedure and/or a tendering procedure for the construction of new capacity,[75] the Second Directive made the authorisation procedure the main rule.[76] Tendering may only be used if the authorisation procedure fails to produce sufficient capacity to ensure supply security.[77] The authorisation procedure was the method preferred by the Member States.[78]

Retail Competition The Second Directive went much further than the First Directive in fostering retail competition. The Second Directive opened up the market first for all non-household customers and then for all customers. Since July 2007, all customers have been allowed to choose their retail electricity supplier.[79]

---

[72] Thomas S (2004).

[73] Lokau B and Ritzau M (2009), § 5, number 10.

[74] Recital 2 of Directive 2003/54/EC (Second Electricity Directive). See also recital 5: "The main obstacles in arriving at a fully operational and competitive internal market relate amongst other things to issues of access to the network, tarification issues and different degrees of market opening between Member States".

[75] Articles 4 and 5(1) of Directive 96/92/EC (First Electricity Directive).

[76] Article 6(1) of Directive 2003/54/EC (Second Electricity Directive). For the criteria, see Article 6(2) of Directive 2003/54/EC (Second Electricity Directive).

[77] Article 7(1) of Directive 2003/54/EC (Second Electricity Directive).

[78] Recital 22 of Directive 2003/54/EC (Second Electricity Directive).

[79] See point 12 of Article 2 in combination with Article 21(1) of Directive 2003/54/EC (Second Electricity Directive): "Member States shall ensure that the eligible customers are: ... (c) from 1 July 2007, all customers".

Unbundling The Second Directive did not prohibit complete vertical integration. Like the First Directive, the Second Directive distinguished between ownership and operation of a TSO or DSO that is part of a vertically integrated undertaking.

Unbundling requirements relating to the firm's *operation* were complemented by requirements relating to the firm's *legal structure*. In other words, the TSO or DSO must be independent not only functionally but even organisationally. The TSO or DSO must comply with forms of independence: independence in terms of legal form, independence of organisation, and independence of decision-making from other activities not relating to transmission distribution.[80]

However, there were no unbundling requirements relating to corporate *ownership*. The TSOs or DSOs could be under the same corporate ownership as a company active in generation and/or retail provided that they were legally distinct companies.[81]

Network Access The Second Directive simplified third party access (TPA). The negotiated access and the "single buyer" option were withdrawn. The regulated TPA became mandatory.[82]

Regulatory Authorities While the First Directive did not address the question of effective monitoring, the Second Directive required the designation of independent regulatory authorities. They were to be responsible for "ensuring non-discrimination, effective competition and the efficient functioning of the market".[83]

Effect The Second Electricity Directive did not yet create an internal market in electricity. It did not create a "fully open market" that would have enabled "all consumers freely to choose their suppliers and all suppliers freely to deliver to their customers".[84] Neither did it open the electricity sector fully to competition. First, there was no specific requirement to introduce a wholesale electricity market. Second, the company operating the network could still be owned by a company active in a generation or retail business.[85] Third, there were no specific measures to break up dominant companies ("national champions"). Fourth, the Second Directive did not regulate the question of security of supply in detail. Monitoring was increased for this purpose.[86]

---

[80] Articles 10 and 15 of Directive 2003/54/EC (Second Electricity Directive).

[81] Recital 8 and Articles 10(1) and 15(1) of Directive 2003/54/EC (Second Electricity Directive).

[82] Article 20(1) of Directive 2003/54/EC (Second Electricity Directive).

[83] Article 23(1) of Directive 2003/54/EC (Second Electricity Directive). See also recital 15.

[84] Recital 3 of Directive 2009/72/EC (Third Electricity Directive).

[85] Recital 10 of Directive 2009/72/EC (Third Electricity Directive).

[86] See recital 23 of Directive 2003/54/EC (Second Electricity Directive).

3.5.3 *The Directive on Security of Supply*

After the Commission's 2000 green paper on supply security[87] and the 2003 power blackouts in Europe and the USA, voices were raised for more regulation. This led to the adoption of the Directive on security of supply[88] that required greater government involvement.

The purpose of the Directive was to ensure: an adequate level of generation capacity; an adequate balance between supply and demand; and an appropriate level of interconnection between Member States for the development of the internal market.[89]

The nature of the duties laid down by the Directive is fairly general.[90] Member States must: ensure a high level of *security of supply*[91]; establish a regulatory framework that fosters *network investment*[92]; take appropriate measures to maintain a *balance* between supply and demand[93]; and ensure that transmission system operators set the minimum operational rules and obligations on *network security*.[94] The Directive on security of supply paved the way for the third legislative package.

3.5.4 *The Third Electricity Directive: Effective Unbundling*

Core Rules

The third legislative package was adopted by the Commission in 2009. The Third Electricity Directive[95] was designed to cure the failings of the Second Electricity Directive.[96] The Third Directive introduced more effective unbundling rules[97] designed to break up dominant companies,[98] gave large non-household customers

[87] Green Paper – Towards a European strategy for the security of energy supply, 29 November 2000, COM(2000) 769 final.

[88] Directive 2005/89/EC (on security of supply).

[89] Article 1 of Directive 2005/89/EC (on security of supply).

[90] The direct effect of a directive depends on whether its provisions directive appear, so far as their subject-matter is concerned, to be unconditional and sufficiently precise. See, for example, Joined Cases C-397/01 to C-403/01 Pfeiffer and Others [2004] ECR I-8835, para 103.

[91] Article 3(1) of Directive 2005/89/EC (on security of supply).

[92] Article 6 of Directive 2005/89/EC (on security of supply).

[93] Article 5 of Directive 2005/89/EC (on security of supply). See also recital 23 of Directive 2003/54/EC (Second Electricity Directive).

[94] Article 4 of Directive 2005/89/EC (on security of supply).

[95] Directive 2009/72/EC (Third Electricity Directive).

[96] Recital 7 of Directive 2009/72/EC (Third Electricity Directive).

[97] Recitals 4, 11 and 13 of Directive 2009/72/EC (Third Electricity Directive).

[98] Recital 14 of Directive 2009/72/EC (Third Electricity Directive).

the right to choose several suppliers,[99] and fostered energy production from renewable sources.[100] Moreover, the third legislative package created a European Network of Transmission System Operators (ENTSO) for electricity (ENTSO-E) and gas,[101] and an Agency for the Cooperation of Energy Regulators (ACER).[102]

Construction of New Generating Capacity The Third Electricity Directive gave new incentives to invest in new power generation capacity. There were two main changes.

While the Second Directive recognised "the nature of the primary sources" as part of the permitted criteria for the grant of authorisations for the construction of generating capacity,[103] the third Directive went much further in fostering investment in energy from *renewable sources* and the reduction of emissions.[104] In addition, the Third Directive was designed to foster investment in *decentralised* electricity generation.[105]

Retail and Wholesale Competition The Second Directive gave all customers the right to choose their suppliers. The Third Directive increased competition in both the retail and the wholesale market by giving large non-household customers a right to enter into contracts with *several* suppliers to secure their electricity requirements. Such customers were thus protected against exclusivity clauses.[106]

Network Access, TPA Rights One of the main goals of the Third Electricity Directive was to achieve non-discriminatory network access.[107] Non-discriminatory grid access at the transmission level determines downstream

[99] Recital 20 of Directive 2009/72/EC (Third Electricity Directive).

[100] Recital 6 of Directive 2009/72/EC (Third Electricity Directive).

[101] ENTSO was established by Regulation 714/2009. See recital 7 and Article 4 of Regulation 714/2009 on conditions for access to the network for cross-border exchanges in electricity.

[102] The Agency was established by Regulation 713/2009. See also Article 39(1) of Directive 2009/72/EC (Third Electricity Directive).

[103] Articles 6(2) and 6(3) of Directive 2003/54/EC (Second Electricity Directive).

[104] Article 7(2) of Directive 2009/72/EC (Third Electricity Directive): ". . . In determining appropriate criteria, Member States shall consider: . . . (c) the protection of the environment; . . . (f) energy efficiency; (g) the nature of the primary sources; . . . (j) the contribution of the generating capacity to meeting the overall Community target of at least a 20 % share of energy from renewable sources in the Community's gross final consumption of energy in 2020 referred to in Article 3(1) of Directive 2009/28/EC of the European Parliament and of the Council of 23 April 2009 on the promotion of the use of energy from renewable sources; and (k) the contribution of generating capacity to reducing emissions". See also recital 6.

[105] Article 6(3) of Directive 2003/54/EC (Second Electricity Directive) and first subparagraph of Article 7(3) of Directive 2009/72/EC (Third Electricity Directive).

[106] Recital 20 and Article 41 of Directive 2009/72/EC (Third Electricity Directive). For definitions, see points 7, 11 and 12 of Article 2 of Directive 2009/72/EC (Third Electricity Directive).

[107] Recital 4 of Directive 2009/72/EC (Third Electricity Directive).

access to customers at the retail level.[108] Competition can be increased further by cross-border grid access for new suppliers of electricity.[109]

Creating the internal electricity market would not have been possible without particular third-party access rights (TPA rights) for electricity firms.[110] The European Commission based the legislative reforms that lead to TPA rights on three foundations. The first was that the technique of an imposed competition based on obligatory access was already part of EU competition law.[111] The second was that the energy sector was subject to an extensive regulatory framework in the Member States.[112] Competition law would not have been enough to open markets.[113] The third was the prevailing view that the provision of energy is a public service.[114]

This is reflected in the Third Electricity Directive. According to the Directive, the Member States may impose on undertakings operating in the electricity sector, in the general economic interest, *public service* obligations.[115] There must also be a system of *third party access* to the transmission and distribution systems. It must be based on published tariffs, applicable to all eligible customers, and applied objectively and without discrimination between system users.[116] The transmission or distribution system operator may not refuse access unless it lacks the necessary capacity.[117] The Member States may also take measures to ensure a *level playing field*.[118] Such measures must be proportionate, non-discriminatory and transparent.[119]

On the other hand, there are limitations to third party access rights.

First, the corresponding duties to grant third party access apply to transmission or distribution system operators. They do not apply to electricity firms that cannot be regarded as TSOs or DSOs. In *citiworks*, the CJEU noted that voltage is the sole distinguishing

[108] Recital 26 of Directive 2009/72/EC (Third Electricity Directive).

[109] Recitals 8 and 57 of Directive 2009/72/EC (Third Electricity Directive).

[110] Kotlowski A (2009).

[111] Kotlowski A (2009).

[112] See recital 7 of Directive 2009/72/EC (Third Electricity Directive).

[113] Communication from the Commission – Inquiry pursuant to Article 17 of Regulation (EC) No 1/2003 into the European gas and electricity sectors (Final Report), SEC(2006) 1724, COM(2006) 0851 final, para 40.

[114] Kotlowski A (2009).

[115] Article 3(2) of Directive 2009/72/EC (Third Electricity Directive). Compensation is possible provided that the obligations are public service obligations and compensation cannot be regarded as prohibited state aid. Joined Cases T-80/06 and T-182/09 Budapesti Erőmű Zrt v Commission, ECLI:EU:T:2012:65, paras 90–92; Case C-280/00 Altmark Trans and Regierungspräsidium Magdeburg [2003] ECR I-7747.

[116] Article 32(1) of Directive 2009/72/EC (Third Electricity Directive). For refusal of access, see Article 32(2).

[117] Article 32(2) of Directive 2009/72/EC (Third Electricity Directive).

[118] Article 43(1) of Directive 2009/72/EC (Third Electricity Directive).

[119] Article 43(2) of Directive 2009/72/EC (Third Electricity Directive).

criterion between transmission and distribution.[120] Particular transmission or distribution systems were not excluded from the scope of the Second Electricity Directive by reason of their size or consumption of electricity. There were particular rules for "small isolated systems" and "micro isolated systems".[121]

Second, third party access rights do not include the right to be connected to the grid. In *Sabatauskas*,[122] the question was whether a party is free to choose the system (a transmission system or a distribution system) to which it wishes to connect and whether the system operator must permit connection to the system.[123] According to the CJEU, the terms "access" and "connection" mean different things. The term "access" is linked to the supply of electricity. The term "connection" is used in a technical context and relates to physical connection to the system. Therefore, third party access rights under the Second Electricity Directive did not include connection to the system.[124]

Third, refusal to permit a grid connection or access to the grid does not always amount to abuse of a dominant position (Article 102 TFEU, see Sect. 3.7).

Effective Unbundling While the Second Electricity Directive required legal and functional/operational unbundling but not ownership unbundling, the Third Directive requires "effective unbundling". Effective unbundling means the "effective separation of networks from activities of generation and supply".[125]

US wholesale markets and interstate transmission are regulated by the Federal Energy Regulatory Commission (FERC). In 1996, the FERC ordered utilities to unbundle their generation, transmission, and distribution functions and provide non-discriminatory access to the national electricity grid (FERC Order 888).[126]

Security of Supply According to the Third Electricity Directive, security of supply is fostered in three main ways. (a) The first is the independence of system operators facilitated by unbundling.[127] (b) The second is investment in electricity generation. Investments are made easier by unbundling and pricing signals.[128] (c) The third is the development of interconnections.

There can be no internal market for electricity without cross-border interconnections. Without cross-border interconnections, it would be difficult to reach the Directive's objectives relating to security of supply and competitive prices.[129] For this reason, the Third Electricity Directive requires the Member States to provide adequate economic incentives for the maintenance and construction of

---

[120] Case C-439/06 citiworks [2008] ECR I-03913, para 48.

[121] Case C-439/06 citiworks [2008] ECR I-03913, paras 48–49 and 61–62.

[122] Case C-239/07 Sabatauskas [2008] ECR I-07523.

[123] Case C-239/07 Sabatauskas [2008] ECR I-07523, para 21.

[124] Case C-239/07 Sabatauskas [2008] ECR I-07523, paras 40–42.

[125] See recitals 9–10 of Directive 2009/72/EC (Third Electricity Directive).

[126] FERC Order 888, Final Rule, 18 CFR Part 35 and 385 (April 24, 1996). A new price discovery mechanism for transmission tariffs was created by FERC Order 889, Final Rule, 18 CFR Part 37 (April 24, 1996). See U.S. Energy Information Administration (2002), Chapter 4.

[127] Recitals 25 and 11 of Directive 2009/72/EC (Third Electricity Directive).

[128] Recitals 11 and 60 of Directive 2009/72/EC (Third Electricity Directive).

[129] Recital 5 of Directive 2009/72/EC (Third Electricity Directive). For definitions, see points 13–14 of Article 2.

interconnection capacity and to enable an adequate level of interconnection capacity even in other ways.[130]

Regulatory Authority

The Third Electricity Directive provides that each Member State must designate a single national regulatory authority at national level.[131] There are limited exceptions for regional regulatory authorities.[132] The exception could be relevant for Member States that are federal states.[133]

The regulatory authority must be independent. Its independence is safeguarded through organisational measures and constraints on the authority's decision-making.[134] Its staff and the persons responsible for its management must act independently from any market interests and must neither seek nor take direct instructions when carrying out the regulatory tasks.

The regulatory authority has a very broad range of duties.[135] It fixes or approves transmission or distribution tariffs or their methodologies,[136] ensures that electricity undertakings comply with their obligations under Community legislation, and has a large number of monitoring duties and information rights.

The regulatory authority can: issue binding decisions on electricity undertakings; require transmission and distribution system operators to modify terms and conditions to ensure that they are proportionate and applied in a non-discriminatory manner; and "decide upon and impose any necessary and proportionate measures to promote effective competition and ensure the proper functioning of the market".

It can also "impose effective, proportionate and dissuasive penalties on electricity undertakings not complying with their obligations", or propose that a competent court impose such penalties. This includes the power to "impose or propose the imposition of penalties of up to 10 % of the annual turnover".[137]

[130] See Articles 3(10), 15(5) and 38(2) of Directive 2009/72/EC (Third Electricity Directive).

[131] Article 35(1) of Directive 2009/72/EC (Third Electricity Directive).

[132] Article 35(2) of Directive 2009/72/EC (Third Electricity Directive): "Paragraph 1 of this Article shall be without prejudice to the designation of other regulatory authorities at regional level within Member States, provided that there is one senior representative for representation and contact purposes at Community level within the Board of Regulators of the Agency in accordance with Article 14(1) of Regulation (EC) No 713/2009". See also Article 35(3).

[133] Raschauer N and Haumer V (2010), p. 492.

[134] Articles 35(4) and 35(5) of Directive 2009/72/EC (Third Electricity Directive). For effects on Austrian law, see Raschauer N and Haumer V (2010), p. 493.

[135] Article 37 of Directive 2009/72/EC (Third Electricity Directive).

[136] See also Article 37(8) of Directive 2009/72/EC (Third Electricity Directive).

[137] Article 37(4) of Directive 2009/72/EC (Third Electricity Directive).

The regulatory authority acts as a complaints and dispute settlement authority. Its decisions are binding. There may nevertheless be rights of appeal. In this case the decision has binding effect unless and until overruled on appeal.[138]

Decisions taken by the regulatory authority must be "fully reasoned and justified to allow for judicial review".[139] There must be "suitable mechanisms" at national level under which a party affected by a decision of a regulatory authority has a right of appeal to a body independent of the parties involved and of any government.[140]

Liberalisation and the Four Freedoms

One of the broad objectives of the three electricity packages was to contribute to an internal electricity market in which the so-called four freedoms apply.[141] In practice, the four freedoms have been applied to foster the interests of retail consumers rather than the interests of electricity producers.

Benefits for Consumers The electricity directives recognise that the free movement of goods, the freedom of establishment, and the freedom to provide services are rights guaranteed by the TFEU to EU citizens.[142] It is assumed that these rights are achievable only in a "fully open market". A fully open electricity market is a market that enables "all consumers freely to choose their suppliers and all suppliers freely to deliver to their customers".[143]

> This reflects the case-law of the CJEU according to which measures which hinder access to the market fall within the scope of the free movement of goods regardless of whether they are discriminatory or not.[144]

In addition to guaranteeing the four freedoms to EU citizens, the purpose of the internal market in electricity is to reduce costs, improve standards of service, and reduce risk. In particular, it tries to "achieve efficiency gains, competitive prices, and higher standards of service, and to contribute to security of supply and sustainability".[145]

---

[138] Articles 37(11), 37(12) and 37(15) of Directive 2009/72/EC (Third Electricity Directive).

[139] Article 37(16) of Directive 2009/72/EC (Third Electricity Directive).

[140] Article 37(17) of Directive 2009/72/EC (Third Electricity Directive). See Eifert M (2010).

[141] Article 4(1) of the Treaty establishing the European Community (EC Treaty); recital 4 of Directive 2003/54/EC (Second Electricity Directive); recital 3 of Directive 2009/72/EC (Third Electricity Directive).

[142] Article 20(2) TFEU: "Citizens of the Union shall enjoy the rights and be subject to the duties provided for in the Treaties . . ."

[143] Recital 4 of Directive 2003/54/EC (Second Electricity Directive); recital 3 of Directive 2009/72/EC (Third Electricity Directive).

[144] Case C-142/05 Mickelsson [2009] ECR I-4273, para 26. See also C-110/05 Commission v. Italy (motorcycle trailers) [2009] ECR I-519, para 56.

[145] Recital 1 of Regulation 714/2009 on conditions for access to the network for cross-border exchanges in electricity; recital 1 of Directive 2009/72/EC (Third Electricity Directive).

The benefits are to be achieved when electricity consumers and electricity firms use the freedoms guaranteed to them. The four freedoms are expected to result in "real choice" given to all electricity consumers, new business opportunities, and an increase in cross-border trade.[146]

No Producer Perspective However, the focus is on the retail market and the consumer perspective rather than the wholesale market and the perspective of electricity producers. This is regardless of the fact that the role of the wholesale market is recognised[147] and there are third-party access rights (TPA rights). There is no "fully open market" for producers. (a) While the electricity directives regulate "security of supply" for consumers, they fail to regulate security of consumption/ off-take for electricity producers or suppliers. (b) The electricity directives do not ensure a level playing field for electricity producers. Different technologies are treated differently. Because of the preferential treatment of RES-E, the regulation of electricity markets makes it more difficult for electricity producers to find consumers depending on the Member State and the fuel or technology. These kinds of differences are likely to affect electricity trade between the Member States. (c) Pricing is regulated rather than free. The underlying assumption is that prices can "impair competition and proper functioning of the market".[148] The electricity directives are designed to limit prices paid by end consumers[149] and not designed to enable wholesale market participants to profit from the market mechanism. Tampering with the market mechanism can have an adverse effect on investment in generation installations and increase electricity prices in the long run contrary to the stated objectives of the electricity directives.[150] One of the proposed ways to address this problem is tampering with clearing prices in the day-ahead and intraday markets or "the introduction of harmonized maximum and minimum clearing prices that contribute to the strengthening of investment conditions".[151] (d) The broad scope of unbundling provisions can increase entry barriers (Sect. 3.5.6).

---

[146] Recital 1 of Regulation 714/2009 and recital 1 of Directive 2009/72/EC.

[147] Recital 3 of Regulation 1228/2003 on conditions for access to the network for cross-border exchanges in electricity: "The creation of a real internal electricity market should be promoted through an intensification of trade in electricity, which is currently underdeveloped compared with other sectors of the economy".

[148] Recital 61 of Directive 2009/72/EC (Third Electricity Directive).

[149] Recital 1 of Directive 2009/72/EC (Third Electricity Directive): "competitive prices". Recital 5: "the most competitive prices to consumers and industry". Recital 8: "the most competitive price". Recital 45: "... household customers ... enjoy the right to be supplied with electricity ... at ... reasonable prices ..." Recital 50: "fair prices", "reasonable prices".

[150] Recital 56 of Directive 2009/72/EC (Third Electricity Directive): "Market prices should give the right incentives for the development of the network and for investing in new electricity generation". Recital 60: "Securing common rules for a true internal market and a broad supply of electricity accessible to all should also be one of the main goals of this Directive. To that end, undistorted market prices would provide an incentive for cross-border interconnections and for investments in new power generation while leading, in the long term, to price convergence".

[151] Recital 29 of draft Commission Regulation .../.. (CACM Regulation). See Article 54.

In principle, EU law should guarantee a level playing field in the internal market even for electricity producers by the prohibition of quantitative restrictions and measures having equivalent effect,[152] by the regulation of state monopolies (such as state-owned TSOs),[153] by the prohibition of state aid,[154] and in other ways.

3.5.5 *Effective Unbundling*

General Remarks

The Third Electricity Directive requires "effective unbundling". Effective unbundling means the "effective separation of networks from activities of generation and supply".[155] The effective unbundling regime applies to transmission. The unbundling regime applies even to distribution but not with its full force.[156]

The effective unbundling regime can hamper the business of a large electricity producer (or consumer) that has the financial means to invest in new transmission infrastructure. To illustrate, a large electricity producer could benefit from a new merchant interconnector as it could help to increase exports and influence prices in the price zones that the interconnector is connecting.[157]

Model

Effective unbundling should be *effective* in two respects according to the Directive. First, to "create incentives for the necessary investments" and "guarantee the access of new market entrants under a transparent and efficient regulatory regime", it should be "effective in removing any conflict of interests between producers, suppliers and transmission system operators". Second, it "should not create an overly onerous regulatory regime for national regulatory authorities".[158]

The Third Electricity Directive provides for *four forms* of effective unbundling: ownership unbundling[159]; control unbundling; management unbundling; and the appointment of an independent operator. Moreover, Member States may choose

---

[152] Article 34 TFEU. Electricity is regarded as a good for these purposes. Case C-393/92 Almelo [1994] ECR I-1477, para 28.

[153] Article 37 TFEU.

[154] Article 107(1) TFEU.

[155] Recital 10 of Directive 2009/72/EC (Third Electricity Directive). See also recital 9.

[156] Article 29 of Directive 2009/72/EC (Third Electricity Directive).

[157] Supponen M (2011), p. 40.

[158] Recital 12 of Directive 2009/72/EC (Third Electricity Directive).

[159] See recital 15 of Directive 2009/72/EC (Third Electricity Directive).

between *three unbundling regimes*: Full Ownership Unbundling,[160] Independent System Operator (ISO), and Independent Transmission Operator (ITO). (a) The standard model is Full Ownership Unbundling.[161] It was nevertheless diluted[162] due to resistance from France and Germany and because of an alleged conflict with the proportionality principle and the right to property.[163] (b) The ISO is the alternative.[164] Under the ISO model, a vertically integrated undertaking can retain ownership of the transmission network assets, provided that the operation of the network is assigned to a third party operator. At the same time, it loses most of its entrepreneurial rights.[165] (c) The ITO is the second alternative.[166]

Distribution The unbundling regime does not apply to distribution systems with its full force. There can be various categories of DSOs in this respect: DSOs that fall or do not fall within the scope of the unbundling regime; DSOs subject or not subject to ownership unbundling requirements; and DSOs subject or not subject to requirements as to the independence of organisation and decision-making.[167] (a) A Member State may decide not to apply the regime to "integrated electricity undertakings serving less than 100,000 connected customers, or serving small isolated systems".[168] (b) There is no mandatory ownership unbundling for distribution assets under the Third Electricity Directive.[169] (c) Where the distribution system operator is part of a vertically integrated undertaking, it must be "independent in terms of its

[160] Recital 21 of Directive 2009/72/EC (Third Electricity Directive). See also recital 18.

[161] Article 9 of Directive 2009/72/EC (Third Electricity Directive).

[162] Recital 17 of Directive 2009/72/EC (Third Electricity Directive): "Where, on 3 September 2009, an undertaking owning a transmission system is part of a vertically integrated undertaking, Member States should therefore be given a choice between ownership unbundling and setting up a system operator or transmission operator which is independent from supply and generation interests". See also recital 19.

[163] See Talus K (2013), pp. 81–82; Pielow JC et al. (2009).

[164] Chapter V of Directive 2009/72/EC (Third Electricity Directive).

[165] Scholz U and Purps S (2010), pp. 38–39.

[166] Articles 9(8) and 9(9) of Directive 2009/72/EC (Third Electricity Directive). Scholz U and Purps S (2010), pp. 38–39: "The inclusion of the ITO as an alternative model was prompted by a joint proposal of eight Member States which sought to maintain existing ownership structures and, at the same time, guarantee the factual independence of the transmission business".

[167] See, for example, Energy Market Authority, Finland (2014), pp. 6–7: "In July 2014 a total of 52 distribution system operators of 80 operators were legally unbundled in Finland. The requirement for separate management for the electricity network company is limited to legally unbundled system operators with 50,000 customers or more and at the end of 2013 it covered 18 distribution system operators in Finland. The requirements for professional interests and compliance programmes are limited to legally unbundled electricity system operators with 50,000 customers or more and it covers 18 distribution system operators in Finland. The threshold of 100,000 customers was set into 50,000 customers by the Electricity Market Act updated in September 2013".

[168] Article 26(4) of Directive 2009/72/EC (Third Electricity Directive).

[169] Articles 26(1) and 29 of Directive 2009/72/EC (Third Electricity Directive).

organisation and decision-making from the other activities not related to distribution".[170]

One may ask what happens when a vertically integrated public utility is divided into a generation entity and a distribution entity. Can the separated entities both be public utilities? Would it mean that these entities are part of the same legal entity? In the context of transmission, the public bodies exercising control over the two entities would have to be separate public bodies in order not to be regarded as the same person.[171] This question may not always have been properly understood in the past.[172]

Third Countries There is a stricter regime for transmission system owners or operators controlled by a person from a third country. The third country clause is also known as the Gazprom clause. The Member State will refuse authorisation unless it is demonstrated that the entity complies with the unbundling requirements and that "granting certification will not put at risk the security of energy supply of the Member State and the Community".[173]

Ownership Unbundling

Unlike the management of the system, ownership unbundling would not be necessary for technical or operational reasons.[174] It has other objectives. Ownership unbundling is regarded as necessary to remove "the incentive for vertically integrated undertakings to discriminate against competitors as regards network access and investment".[175]

Ownership unbundling works in three ways. First, each undertaking which owns a transmission system must also act as a transmission system operator. Second, there are restrictions on that undertaking's right to own a business that performs any of the functions of generation or supply.[176] Third, there are similar restrictions on the rights of a firm that performs any of the functions of generation or supply to own

[170] Article 26(1) of Directive 2009/72/EC (Third Electricity Directive). For the minimum criteria, see Article 26(2).

[171] Article 9(6) of Directive 2009/72/EC (Third Electricity Directive). See also OECD/IEA (2005), pp. 51–52.

[172] Compare Energy Market Authority, Finland (2013), p. 20: "The legally unbundled distribution system operators are not required to be structured any special legal form. The only limitation is that the separated companies cannot both be public utilities because then these companies would be part of the same legal entity".

[173] Article 11 of Directive 2009/72/EC (Third Electricity Directive).

[174] Pérez-Arriaga IJ and Smeers Y (2003), p. 181.

[175] Recital 11 of Directive 2009/72/EC (Third Electricity Directive).

[176] Article 9(1)(a) of Directive 2009/72/EC (Third Electricity Directive). For joint ventures, see Article 9(5) of Directive 2009/72/EC (Third Electricity Directive).

a transmission business. (Control unbundling and borderline cases are discussed later in this section.)[177]

In other words, ownership unbundling implies "the appointment of the network owner as the system operator and its independence from any supply and production interests".

In the US, the entities responsible for operating the transmission system are Independent System Operators (ISOs). While transmission system operations in the EU are managed by entities that own the transmission assets (TSOs), ISOs do not own transmission assets in the US.[178]

Control Unbundling

The control unbundling provisions of the Third Electricity Directive use the concepts of *persons* (that can be natural persons, public bodies,[179] or undertakings[180]) and *control* (taken from the EC Merger Regulation[181]) and distinguish between two categories of *undertakings*: (1) the TSO/DSO or transmission/distribution system undertaking; and (2) the generation or supply undertaking. The unbundling provisions of the Third Directive seek to prevent relationships in which *persons* that exercise *control* over an *undertaking* belonging to one category exercise *control* or *any right* over an undertaking belonging to the other category.[182]

According to the wording of the Third Directive, one can distinguish between the exercising of control and the exercising of any right.[183] For instance, the Member States are required to ensure that the same persons are not entitled to exercise *control* over a generation undertaking and, at the same time, exercise *any right* over a transmission system. Conversely, *control* over a transmission system operator should preclude the possibility of exercising *control* over a supply undertaking.

Control While these rights have been defined in the Third Electricity Directive,[184] the exercising of control has not been defined therein. The exercising of control is a broad concept.

---

[177] Articles 9(1)(b) and 9(2) of Directive 2009/72/EC (Third Electricity Directive).

[178] See, for example, US Senate Committee on Energy and Natural Resources (2010), statement of Vincent P. Duane.

[179] Article 9(6) of Directive 2009/72/EC (Third Electricity Directive). Two separate public bodies are not regarded as the same person.

[180] Article 9(12) of Directive 2009/72/EC (Third Electricity Directive).

[181] Recital 13 of Directive 2009/72/EC (Third Electricity Directive). See Article 3(2) and Article 3 (3) of Regulation 139/2004 (EC Merger Regulation).

[182] Recital 11 and Article 9(12) of Directive 2009/72/EC (Third Electricity Directive).

[183] Article 9(1)(b) of Directive 2009/72/EC (Third Electricity Directive).

[184] Article 9(2) of Directive 2009/72/EC (Third Electricity Directive).

Regardless of the recitals of the Third Electricity Directive,[185] it is possible that control is not limited to the types of control mentioned in the EC Merger Regulation. There are two reasons for this. First, the definition of the term "any right" under the Third Electricity Directive resembles the definition of control under the EC Merger Regulation.[186] This leaves the term control. The term control under the Third Directive should be given a meaning that makes it effective. Second, the EC Merger Regulation applies to the "concentration" of previously independent firms; concentration means change of control on a lasting basis.[187] For the purposes of the Third Electricity Directive, however, it should not be relevant whether control is exercised on a lasting basis. For instance, structured contracts can provide control over generation or transmission assets for a limited period of time (Sect. 8.2).

In the absence of any other party exercising control, an undertaking is de facto controlled by its *management*.[188] A *block of shares* can also provide control. The size of the block depends on the firm. In practice, even a relatively small block of shares can provide control in large firms with a dispersed share ownership structure. There can thus be a controlling minority shareholding in many cases.[189] On the other hand, a minority shareholding is not prohibited as such as it does not always provide control.[190]

In Finland, two generating companies (Fortum and Pohjolan Voima) were shareholders of the TSO (Fingrid). The regulator took steps to implement the new unbundling requirements. Fortum and Pohjolan Voima therefore divested their holding in Fingrid to the State of Finland and Ilmarinen, a mutual pension insurance company, in April 2011. After the transaction, Fingrid's shares were held by the State of Finland and institutional investors.[191]

Rights The rights mean here (a) voting rights; (b) the power to appoint members of the supervisory board, the administrative board, or bodies legally representing the undertaking; or (c) rights attached to a majority share.[192] For instance, a person can hold a minority block of shares in an undertaking that belongs to the other category (provided that the person does not control that undertaking in other ways).

The wording of the Directive implies that the provisions on ownership unbundling do not prevent an undertaking belonging to one category (rather than

185 Recital 13 of Directive 2009/72/EC (Third Electricity Directive).

186 Article 9(2) of Directive 2009/72/EC (Third Electricity Directive); Articles 3(2) and 3(3) of Regulation 139/2004 (EC Merger Regulation).

187 Article 3(1) of Regulation 139/2004 (EC Merger Regulation.

188 The classic text on the separation of ownership and management in large listed corporations is Berle AA and Means GC (1932).

189 See Mäntysaari P (2010), sections 9.4 and 9.5.

190 Recital 11 of Directive 2009/72/EC (Third Electricity Directive): "... a generation or supply undertaking should be able to have a minority shareholding in a transmission system operator or transmission system". See also recital 18.

191 Energy Market Authority, Finland (2014), p. 6.

192 Article 9(2) of Directive 2009/72/EC (Third Electricity Directive).

a party controlling it) from having a non-controlling minority shareholding in an undertaking belonging to the other category.[193]

Borderline cases of ownership and control unbundling

Borderline cases can be illustrated with various customary sources of funding and the case of merchant lines.

Financial Investors One of the objectives of effective unbundling is to "create incentives for the necessary investments".[194] Investments must be funded in one way or another. Obviously, it would be contrary to the stated purpose of effective unbundling to hamper infrastructure investments by restricting system operators' access to funding.

Now, infrastructure investments are customarily funded by specialised and institutional investors that are likely to have invested in other energy projects as well. Whether they are permitted to provide the necessary funding can depend on the interpretation of the unbundling provisions.

Block of Shares How small should a block of shares be before it does not provide "control"? The question is relevant, because an institutional investor may have invested in the shares of an electricity producer in, say, Sweden and may want to subscribe for shares in a system operator in, say, Germany. Infrastructure investment will be hampered, if the threshold of "control" is low.

The Commission has clarified its practice in a staff working document.[195] Generally, the Commission does not want to refuse certification of a TSO "in cases where it can be clearly demonstrated that there is no *incentive* for a shareholder in a TSO to influence the TSO's decision making to favour his generation, production and/or supply interest to the detriment of other network users".

The Commission identified two main forms. The first was geographic separation of activities. In certain situations, "it was evident from the facts of the concrete case that the simultaneous participation in transmission activities on the one hand, and in generation, production and/or supply activities on the other hand, did not give rise to any potential conflict of interest or incentive to exploit it, and as a consequence did not in any way risk to impact negatively on the independent management of the TSO. This was for instance the case where a shareholder had a participation in a transmission network in the EU, as well as a participation in generation activities in the United States or in Australia, with no connection or interface between the energy systems concerned".

[193] Recitals 11 and 18 of Directive 2009/72/EC (Third Electricity Directive).

[194] Recital 12 of Directive 2009/72/EC (Third Electricity Directive).

[195] Commission Staff Working Document, Ownership Unbundling: The Commission's Practice in Assessing the Presence of Conflict of Interest Including in Case of Financial Investors (8 May 2013) SWD(2013) 177 final. See also Van Vyve C (2014).

The second related to the circumstances of financial investors: "For financial investors, ownership unbundled TSOs form an important class of potential investment opportunities, taking into account that investments in transmission infrastructure with regulated network tariffs offer stable, low risk returns that fit well with their investment profile. Cooperation with financial investors may enable ownership unbundled TSOs to raise the necessary funds for the capital expenditure that is needed to realise the investments in the EU energy network infrastructure. In situations as referred to above, where it can be clearly demonstrated that even though one or more of the circumstances referred to in Article 9(1)(b), (c) and/or (d) appear to be present, there is clearly no incentive for a shareholder in a TSO to influence the decision making in this TSO with the intention to favour its generation, production and/or supply interests to the detriment of other network users, the Commission has taken the view that a refusal to certify such a TSO given the fact that such participation in generation, production and/or supply activities does not lead to a situation which the unbundling rules seek to prevent".

Leasing Can other forms of funding provide control? One of the ways for a firm to finance its activities is to use somebody else's assets. To illustrate, the system operator does not have to raise other external funding to the extent that it can use assets owned by somebody else under a leasing agreement.[196] The question is when the ownership of transmission assets can be regarded as ownership of a transmission "system" and to what extent the ownership of a transmission system requires the ownership of transmission assets.

> For instance, there are no requirements for ownership unbundling of DSOs in Finland. At the end of 2012, 9 DSOs operated a distribution network leased from their parent company. Other DSOs used some network assets such as substations under a lease contract.[197]

Merchant Lines Ownership unbundling raises even some questions relating to merchant lines. Investment in merchant lines could increase transmission capacity. However, the Third Electricity Directive does not recognise operators of merchant lines as such. This can hamper investment.

The Directive applies to "electricity undertakings". This broad category includes even owners or operators of merchant lines regardless of how merchant lines are defined.[198] According to the terminology of the Directive, the functional equivalent of a merchant line could be an "interconnector", that is, equipment used to link electricity systems[199] (rather than a "direct line"[200]).

However, the owner of transmission assets such as interconnectors should be a TSO. This seems reasonable in the light of the fact that an interconnector is similar to a simple transmission network in the physical sense. On the other hand, the

[196] For "asset investors", see Mäntysaari P (2010), section 9.2.

[197] Energy Market Authority, Finland (2013), p. 20.

[198] Point 35 of Article 2 of Directive 2009/72/EC (Third Electricity Directive).

[199] Point 13 of Article 2 of Directive 2009/72/EC (Third Electricity Directive).

[200] Point 15 of Article 2 of Directive 2009/72/EC (Third Electricity Directive).

function of an interconnector may also be close to a generation facility[201] and a TSO has more functions compared with the necessary functions of the operator of a merchant line.[202]

Neither Regulation 1228/2003 nor Regulation 714/2009 mentions merchant lines. There can be interconnectors that are owned by a natural or legal person separate from the system operators in whose systems the interconnector is built.[203] That person can be a system operator.[204]

Management Unbundling

The provisions on ownership and control unbundling are complemented by provisions on management unbundling. The same person should (a) neither be a *member* of the managing boards of undertakings belonging to different categories (b) nor be entitled to *appoint* members of the managing boards of an undertaking belonging to one category and exercise control or any right over an undertaking belonging to the other category[205] (or such a firm in the gas market[206]). (c) Moreover, *staff* of a transmission system operator which was part of a vertically integrated undertaking must not be transferred to undertakings performing any of the functions of generation and supply.[207] (d) It is also prohibited to transfer commercially sensitive *information* from a transmission system operator to a generation or supply undertaking.[208] On the other hand, the latter are bound to transfer such information to the TSO in the course of normal operations.

The Appointment of an Independent Operator

The main form of effective unbundling is complemented by one or two exceptions. The Third Electricity Directive does not necessarily force vertically integrated undertakings to sell their transmission networks. An undertaking that was a vertically integrated undertaking on 3 September 2009 could maintain its ownership of a transmission network provided that the undertaking set up an *independent transmission operator* which is independent from the supply and generation interests of

[201] For competition law aspects, see Talus K and Wälde T (2006).

[202] For the tasks of a transmission system operator, see Article 12 of Directive 2009/72/EC (Third Electricity Directive).

[203] See Article 17(1)(c) of Regulation 714/2009/EC and Article 7(1)(c) of Regulation 1228/2003.

[204] Point 4 of Article 2 of Directive 2009/72/EC (Third Electricity Directive).

[205] Recital 15 and Article 9(1)(b)–(d) of Directive 2009/72/EC (Third Electricity Directive).

[206] Article 9(3) of Directive 2009/72/EC (Third Electricity Directive).

[207] Article 9(7) of Directive 2009/72/EC (Third Electricity Directive).

[208] Article 9(7) of Directive 2009/72/EC (Third Electricity Directive).

the vertically integrated undertaking.[209] The appointment of an independent operator requires a proposal by the vertically integrated undertaking, approval by the Member State's regulatory authority, and approval by the Commission.[210] An independent operator must be monitored even by the Member State's competition authorities.[211] The Third Electricity Directive lays down a detailed framework for the operation of independent system operators.[212]

Alternatively, the Member States may use methods that are more effective in guaranteeing the independence of the transmission system operator.[213] However, this can only be a rare exception in the light of the stringent requirements that independent system operators must fulfil.

Unbundling and Extraterritorial Effect

In principle, the unbundling provisions of the Third Electricity Directive do not have extraterritorial effect. One may nevertheless ask whether the scope of unbundling provisions is limited to the same Member State in which the transmission system operator operates or whether the regulatory authority of a Member State must take into account activities in other Member States or third countries as well. For instance, may an electricity company operate a transmission system in one Member State and generate electricity in another Member State or a third country?

In practice, the unbundling provisions of the Third Electricity Directive do have extraterritorial effect. The scope of the unbundling provisions is not limited to activities in the same Member State. The operation or control of a transmission system located in a Member State is a restricted activity and reserved only for persons that fulfil the unbundling requirements—regardless of whether these persons are EU companies, citizens of the EU, or from third countries.[214] One could say that "fully effective separation of network activities from supply and generation activities should apply throughout the Community to both Community and non-Community undertakings".[215]

The broad scope of unbundling provisions could raise some legal concerns. First, the broad scope of unbundling provisions could make it more difficult for electricity companies from other Member States or third countries to enter the market contrary to the main objectives of the electricity directives—and the four freedoms. Second, neither the Third Electricity Directive nor the national provisions of Member States' laws may restrict freedom of establishment for firms established in a

[209] Article 9(8) of Directive 2009/72/EC (Third Electricity Directive).

[210] Article 13 of Directive 2009/72/EC (Third Electricity Directive). See also Recitals 16–17.

[211] Article 13(6) of Directive 2009/72/EC (Third Electricity Directive).

[212] Chapter V of Directive 2009/72/EC (Third Electricity Directive).

[213] Articles 9(9) and 9(10) of Directive 2009/72/EC (Third Electricity Directive).

[214] Recital 25 of Directive 2009/72/EC (Third Electricity Directive).

[215] Recital 24 of Directive 2009/72/EC (Third Electricity Directive).

Member State. Third, the broad scope unbundling provisions could increase entry barriers for electricity companies from third countries, and the Community may have international obligations relating to market entry.[216]

For this reason, the Commission may give an opinion on certification in relation to a transmission system owner or a transmission system operator which is controlled by a person or persons from a third country or third countries.[217]

3.5.6 Network Codes

Network codes play a very important role in structuring electricity markets. Each electricity network must operate according to certain common rules because of technical reasons and network security. In the past, there was a different set of rules for each country. The internal electricity market requires common rules for many countries.

The need for common rules was addressed by Regulation 714/2009 that lays down a mechanism to adopt network codes for transactions with a cross-border impact.[218] A network code has the same status as a European Regulation and is directly applicable in all EU Member States. A network code takes precedence over domestic law. Network codes can be preceded by ACER's framework guidelines that set out principles for developing them.[219]

Common network codes are developed for cross-border network issues and market integration issues. They are without prejudice to the Member States' right to establish national network codes which do not affect cross-border trade.[220] National network codes will continue to exist.[221]

The CACM Regulation is the first of the ten EU network codes developed in accordance with the Third Energy Package. Member States voted to adopt the CACM Regulation on 5 December 2014. It was preceded by ENTSO-E Network Code for Capacity Allocation and Congestion Management (final draft of 27 September 2012) that was based on ACER Framework Guidelines.[222] The Commission chose to call the CACM Regulation a guideline regulation instead of

[216] Recitals 24–25 of Directive 2009/72/EC (Third Electricity Directive).

[217] Article 11 of Directive 2009/72/EC (Third Electricity Directive).

[218] Article 6 of Regulation 714/2009 on conditions for access to the network for cross-border exchanges in electricity.

[219] Recital 6 and Article 6(2) of Regulation 714/2009.

[220] Article 8(7) of Regulation 714/2009.

[221] See, for example, ERGEG, Draft Framework Guidelines on Capacity Allocation and Congestion Management for Electricity: Initial Impact Assessment. Ref: E10-ENM-20-04 (8 September 2010), p. 16.

[222] ACER, Framework Guidelines on Capacity Allocation and Congestion Management for Electricity (29 July 2011).

a network code. ENTSO-E began to use the term "guideline" or "binding guideline" for this network code after the 20–21 May 2014 Florence Forum.[223]

After CACM, the Network Code for Requirements for Generators (NC RfG) became the second network code to enter Comitology, the process by which they will become law.

Obviously, implementing ten new network codes (or guideline regulations) increases the complexity of the regulatory framework and market participants' exposure to legal risk.

3.6 Competition Law

3.6.1 General Remarks

After the electricity directives, the second area of sectoral legislation that will be discussed here is competition law. Competition law has a role to play in electricity markets due to the existence of natural monopolies, national champions, other large electricity producers that used to be vertically integrated firms, and long-term contracts.[224] In addition, EU competition law has played an important role in the regulation of the electricity markets, because it has been easier for the Commission to apply competition law than sectoral regulation. The role of competition law has diminished with the increasing size of the sector-specific regulatory regime and the growing use of electricity exchanges and auctions.

The Market, Structural Remedies Electricity wholesale markets are, to a large extent, national or regional. Electricity flows between different Member States are limited by congestion on cross-border interconnectors. While the existence of price differences between different markets can be explained by congestion, cross-border electricity flows cannot be explained by the existence of price differences between markets.[225]

After the second legislative package, the European Commission launched sector inquiries into the functioning of the European electricity markets (and gas markets). The Commission's sector inquiry is a point of reference for many legislative developments in the energy sector and some national competition authorities have launched their own sector inquiries.[226] The Commission's 2007 final report on the sector inquiry identified the essential features of the European electricity markets:

[223] 26th meeting of the European Electricity Regulatory Forum, Florence, 20–21 May 2014.

[224] For the nature of restrictions on competition in the German electricity market, see also BGH, judgment of 11 November 2008, KVR 60/07 as well as Monopolkommission (2009, 2013).

[225] Lanz M et al. (2011), section 4.1.2, pp. 76–77.

[226] See Scholz U and Purps S (2010), pp. 44–47. For Germany, see Bundeskartellamt (2011). For the UK, see Ofgem (2008, 2009a).

- Transport activities remain regulated, because they are a natural monopoly. Generation, wholesale trading, and retail supply have been progressively opened to competition.[227]
- Third party access to the network is essential.[228]
- The price elasticity of electricity demand is very low over the short term.[229]
- The use of different fuels results in different cost structures. This influences price formation on short term electricity markets as the price is based on short-term marginal costs.[230]
- Balancing markets tend to be more concentrated than the underlying wholesale markets, because balancing requires additional technical characteristics of plants.[231]
- There are various market structures and various business models in the EU. Business strategies are more diverse in areas that were liberalised earlier. Vertically integrated companies, or very strong ownership and/or contractual links between generators and suppliers, are predominant in more recently liberalised Member States.[232]
- Electricity markets are vulnerable to the exercise of market power.[233]

The Commission's 2007 final report on the sector inquiry also identified the following deficiencies:

- market concentration was high at the wholesale level[234];
- there were high barriers to entry (such as the foreclosure of downstream markets, an insufficient level of unbundling, insufficient cross-border capacities, and balancing regimes that favoured incumbents);
- existing network capacities were largely controlled by incumbent companies (as a result, there were information asymmetries between incumbents and market entrants, and incumbents had an incentive not to expand network capacities for the benefit of market entrants);
- there was foreclosure of downstream markets (caused by an insufficient level of unbundling, long contract durations, the lack of competitive offers from non-incumbent suppliers, and restrictive practices in relation to the operation of supply contracts);
- there was a lack of efficient and transparent price formation; and

---

227 DG Competition report on energy sector inquiry, SEC(2006) 1724, 10 January 2007, para 322.

228 *Ibid*, para 323.

229 *Ibid*, para 324.

230 *Ibid*, para 325.

231 *Ibid*, para 327.

232 *Ibid*, para 328: "In the UK, as well as the larger integrated companies, a number of independent generators with their own business strategies exist. On the Nordic market(s) consisting of Norway, Sweden, Finland and Denmark independent suppliers are relatively important".

233 *Ibid*, para 326.

234 *Ibid*, para 393.

- balancing regimes were often found to favour incumbents.

While some of these deficiencies can be addressed by competition law, others require regulatory and structural measures. The Commission acknowledged that regulatory and structural measures were necessary for tackling the insufficient unbundling of networks, gaps in the regulatory environment regarding cross-border trade, the lack of liquidity in electricity wholesale markets, and the general lack of transparency in market operations.

This contributed to the adoption of the third legislative package in 2009. In other words, sector-specific regulation was recognised as the most important tool.

However, the Commission would have preferred clearer unbundling rules than the complicated rules adopted in the Third Electricity Directive. Because the Third Electricity Directive does not prevent the Commission from applying EU competition law, the Commission has an incentive to use general competition law to achieve the intended result.

Lower Threshold to Use EU Competition Law It is easier for the Commission to use general competition law than sector-specific regulation.

To begin with, the sector-specific regulation of electricity markets is secondary EU law primarily applied by national energy regulators. The Commission's powers in the energy markets are limited to its general powers.[235] There is no single European energy regulator to control the markets. Unlike the sector-specific regulation of electricity markets, EU competition law is *Treaty law* that can be applied by the Commission (in addition to national competition authorities and courts[236] that apply even national competition law[237]). The Commission is the regulatory authority by virtue of the TFEU.[238]

> The Commission does act as the regulatory authority in many cases[239] and the Agency for the Cooperation of Energy Regulators (ACER) in some cases[240] under the Third Electricity Directive. However, one may ask whether the Commission's enforcement powers fall within the scope of the TEU and the TFEU in the light of the wording of the Treaties. The Third Electricity Directive was based on Treaty provisions on the mutual recognition of qualifications, freedom to provide services, and the approximation of laws. None of the Treaty provisions referred to in the Third Electricity Directive can be used as a basis for

---

235 Article 17(1) TEU. For the objectives of the EU in the area of energy, see Article 194(1) TFEU.

236 Article 105(1) TFEU, Article 104 TFEU, points (d) and (e) of Article 103(2) TFEU, Article 105 (3) TFEU.

237 In Germany, the provisions of Gesetz gegen Wettbewerbsbeschränkungen (GWB). See § 1 GWB (prohibition of restrictions of competition), § 19 GWB (prohibition of abuse of a dominant position), and § 20 GWB (prohibition of discriminatory practices).

238 Article 105(1) TFEU. See also points (d) and (e) of Article 103(2) TFEU and Article 105 (3) TFEU.

239 See the following provisions of Directive 2009/72/EC (Third Electricity Directive): Article 9 (10), Article 10(4), Article 10(6), Article 10(7), Article 11(6), Article 11(10), Article 13(1), Article 14(3), Article 33(2)(b), Article 37(1)(d), Article 38(5), Article 39(6), Article 39(9), Article 40(4), Article 42, Article 43(1), Article 43(2), Article 44(1), and Article 45.

240 Articles 39(1) and 6(4) of Directive 2009/72/EC (Third Electricity Directive).

making the Commission a regulatory authority that exercises powers in relation to individual market participants ex ante.[241] The administrative powers that the TFEU vests in the Commission are powers exercised in relation to Member States ex post.[242]

The Commission also has an *incentive* to resort to competition law. On one hand, there is no single European energy regulator to control energy markets. On the other, the Commission has wide powers to enforce competition law, the Commission has an opportunity to do so in the light of the existence of monopolies and long-term contracts in electricity markets,[243] the assessment of market power depends on how the Commission defines the market,[244] and there is a well-developed body of competition law in the EU.

One of the drawbacks with the application of competition law is that the best way to tackle the issues may not be ex-post investigations. The application of competition law is combined with a high level of uncertainty and legal risk. It can be time-consuming and difficult to assess the positive and negative effects of contract practices.[245]

Complementary Regime Competition law does not reduce the Commission's other powers, and the scope of EU competition law is not limited by the scope of sector-specific regulation. EU competition law and sector-specific regulation are *complementary* rather than mutually exclusive. The Commission can assess the case from a competition law perspective even where the issue is governed by sector-specific regulation.

In *Deutsche Telekom*, the Court of First Instance found that that the scope of Article 102 TFEU is not affected by the scope of sector-specific regulation applied by Member States' national authorities.[246]

There is a difference between EU competition aw and US antitrust law. While EU competition law has a very broad scope, the scope of the application of US antitrust law is constrained by sector-specific legislation according to the ruling of the US Supreme Court in *Verizon v. Trinko*.[247]

The *Trinko* ruling suggests that sector-specific remedies are the primary remedies where they are available. Moreover, it marks the recognition of a "pre-emption" or "exhaustion" principle in the field of antitrust. Where a sector-specific remedy exists, private claims on the basis of antitrust rules should be exhausted. The US Supreme Court's reasoning is based

---

[241] Directive 2009/72/EC (Third Electricity Directive): "Having regard to the Treaty establishing the European Community, and in particular Article 47(2) and Articles 55 and 95 thereof, . . ."

[242] Article 258 TFEU: ". . . If the State concerned does not comply with the opinion within the period laid down by the Commission, the latter may bring the matter before the Court of Justice of the European Union". See also Talus K (2010), pp. 86–87.

[243] Spence DB (2008), pp. 782–785.

[244] For a critical view, see Kaplow L (2010).

[245] Bellantuono G (2008).

[246] Case T-271/03 Deutsche Telekom v Commission [2008] ECR II-477, para 120. See Geradin D and O'Donoghue R (2005); Talus K (2010), pp. 86–87.

[247] Verizon v. Trinko, 540 U.S. 398 (2004). See Petit N (2004) and Monti G (2008).

on costs/benefits arguments. When a regulatory structure has been set up to reduce and remedy the risks of a competitive harm, the additional benefits from antitrust enforcement are likely to be limited according to the court.[248]

Constraints There are constraints on the application of EU competition law. The constraints relate to the subjective scope of the prohibitions (the addressees of the rules) and proportionality.

EU competition law can only prohibit behaviour for which one or more *undertakings* are responsible (*EDP*, *Deutsche Telekom*).[249] As EU competition law applies to undertakings but sector-specific regulation is addressed to Member States, the relevant issue is who is responsible for the anti-competitive behaviour. EU competition law cannot prohibit undertakings from taking action necessary for the purpose of complying with sector-specific regulation, and it cannot prohibit acts for which the regulator is responsible. The fact that EU competition law and sector-specific regulation are not addressed to the same parties can, in effect, act as a constraint on the application of EU competition law without limiting its scope as such.

In *EDP*, the Court of First Instance considered the relationship between the EC Merger Regulation and the Second Gas Directive. In some cases, the creation or strengthening of a dominant position may in itself have the consequence that competition is significantly impeded, in which case a concentration cannot be permitted.[250] In *EDP*, however, the absence of effective competition was caused by national and Community legislation. According to the Court of First Instance, "[u]ndertakings cannot be criticised for significantly impeding effective competition where that competition does not exist as a result of national and Community legislation".[251]

In *Deutsche Telekom*, a case on the abuse of a dominant position, the relevant issue was who was responsible for pricing. The charges were approved in advance by the regulatory authority.[252] On the other hand, an undertaking in a dominant position may have a special responsibility to submit applications for adjustment of its charges.[253] The question was thus who was responsible for the anti-competitive behaviour.[254]

In addition, the application of competition law is constrained by the general principle of *proportionality*. Measures adopted by Community institutions must not exceed what is appropriate and necessary for attaining the objective pursued. Where

[248] See Petit N (2004).

[249] Case T-87/05 EDP v Commission [2005] ECR II-3745; Case T-271/03 Deutsche Telekom v Commission [2008] ECR II-477.

[250] Case T-87/05 EDP v Commission [2005] ECR II-3745, paras 45–47.

[251] Case T-87/05 EDP v Commission [2005] ECR II-3745, para 126.

[252] Case T-271/03 Deutsche Telekom v Commission [2008] ECR II-477, paras 7–9.

[253] Case T-271/03 Deutsche Telekom v Commission [2008] ECR II-477, para 122.

[254] Case T-271/03 Deutsche Telekom v Commission [2008] ECR II-477, para 121.

there is a choice between several appropriate measures, the least onerous measure must be used.[255] There are even other constraints such as constraints relating to the use of structural remedies.

3.6.2 *Structural Remedies*

The main rule is that EU competition law provides for behavioural rather than structural remedies. Article 101 TFEU prohibits restrictive agreements and similar practices between undertakings rather than the existence of market structures that are not effective. Article 102 prohibits the abuse of a dominant position rather than its mere existence. Structural remedies can nevertheless be based on the EC Merger Regulation, Regulation 1/2003, and the case-law of the CJEU.

The EC Merger Regulation The EC Merger Regulation applies to concentrations defined as qualified changes of control.[256] It applies to significant and lasting structural changes—such as mergers and acquisitions and joint ventures—with a Community dimension.[257] It does not apply to the mere existence of market structures even where the market structures impede effective competition.[258] In change of control situations, however, the Commission has plenty of discretion to apply structural remedies ex ante and ex post.

There is a duty to notify concentrations before they are implemented.[259] Whether a concentration that falls within the scope of the EC Merger Regulation is permitted or not depends on whether the concentration is "compatible with the common market".[260] The participating undertakings may enter into commitments vis-à-vis the Commission to make the concentration "compatible with the common market", and the Commission may attach to its decision conditions and obligations intended to ensure that the undertakings comply with the commitments.[261]

---

[255] Case 15/83 Denkavit Nederlandv Hoofdproduktschap voor Akkerbouwprodukten [1984] ECR 2171, para 25; Case 265/87, Schräder [1989] ECR 2237, para 21; Case T-260/94 Air Inter v Commission [1997] ECR II-997, para 147; Case T-65/98, Van den Bergh Foods v Commission [2003] ECR II-4653, para 201. See also Commitments Decision in Case COMP/39.315—ENI, para 85.

[256] Article 3(1) of Regulation 139/2004 (the EC Merger Regulation). For US law, see U.S. Department of Justice and the Federal Trade Commission, Horizontal Merger Guidelines (issued: August 19, 2010).

[257] For Community dimension, see Article 1 of Regulation 139/2004 (the EC Merger Regulation). See also recitals 8 and 20.

[258] See Articles 2(2) and 2(3) of Regulation 139/2004 (the EC Merger Regulation).

[259] Article 4(1) of Regulation 139/2004 (the EC Merger Regulation).

[260] Article 2(1) of Regulation 139/2004 (the EC Merger Regulation).

[261] Article 2(1) and subparagraph 2 of Article 8(2) of Regulation 139/2004 (the EC Merger Regulation).

The Commission may take structural measures even where a concentration has been implemented without the Commission's consent or the commitments are not complied with.[262] Where a concentration has not been notified in advance, the Commission may analyse it and declare it incompatible with the common market if it does not fulfill the statutory criteria.[263] Subject to the principle of proportionality,[264] the Commission may order any appropriate measure to ensure that the undertakings concerned dissolve the concentration or take other restorative measures as required in its decision.[265] It is expressly stated in the Regulation that the Commission may order the dissolution of the merger or the disposal of all the shares or assets acquired to restore the situation prevailing prior to the implementation of the concentration.

The Commission has applied structural remedies in a number of electricity market cases under Article 8 of the Merger Regulation.[266]

In *EDP/ENI/GDP*, the Commission declared a concentration incompatible with the common market.[267]

In *EDF/EnBW*,[268] the Commission declared a concentration compatible with the common market subject to compliance with extensive commitments. To illustrate, EnBW (Energie Baden-Württemberg AG) agreed to divest its shareholding in WATT AG (an electricity company in Switzerland), in which it held 24.5 % of the voting stock.

Structural remedies were used also in *Gaz de France/Suez*. To illustrate, Gaz de France agreed to divest its stake in SPE (a company that is present in the Belgian electricity and natural gas markets and provides energy services).[269]

The threshold of "control" is rather low according to the practice of the Commission. Even a minority holding may suffice. A low threshold of control increases the number of concentrations that fall within the scope of the EC Merger Regulation[270] and makes EU merger control more restrictive.

In *Gaz de France/Suez*, a supply company (Suez) held 27.45 % of the shares in a Belgian electricity TSO (Elia).[271] The Commission was of the opinion that the supply company

[262] Subparagraph 1 of Article 8(4) of Regulation 139/2004 (the EC Merger Regulation).

[263] Article 2(1) of Regulation 139/2004 (the EC Merger Regulation).

[264] See recital 30 of Regulation 139/2004 (the EC Merger Regulation). See also Case T-102/96 Gencor v Commission [1999] ECR II-879, para 319; Case T-170/06 Alrosa v Commission [2007] ECR II-2601, para 92; Case T-170/06 Alrosa v Commission [2007] ECR II-2601, paras 88–89; Case T-260/94, Air Inter v Commission [1997] ECR II-997, para 144; Case C-174/05 Zuid-Hollandse Milieufederatie and Natuur en Milieu [2006] ECR I-2443, para 28.

[265] Subparagraph 1 of Article 8(4) of Regulation 139/2004 (the EC Merger Regulation).

[266] For instance, COMP/M.4180—Gaz de France/Suez, COMP/M.3868—DONG/Elsam/Energi E2, COMP/M.3696—E.ON—MOL and COMP/M.931—Neste—IVO. See, for example, Talus K (2010), pp. 179–180.

[267] Commission decision in Case COMP/M.3440—EDP/ENI/GDP, para 914.

[268] Case COMP/M.1853—EDF/EnBW.

[269] Commission decision in Case COMP/M.4180—Gaz de France/Suez, paras 1223–1224.

[270] Articles 1(1) and 3(1) of Regulation 139/2004 (the EC Merger Regulation).

[271] Commission decision in Case COMP/M.4180—Gaz de France/Suez, para 6.

could exercise control or significant influence over the transmission company in the circumstances of the case.[272]

Regulation 1/2003 The use of general competition law for unbundling purposes is made easier by Regulation 1/2003 that empowers the Commission to apply not only behavioural but even structural remedies.[273]

While the EC Merger Regulation has a limited scope (it applies to transactions that bring about lasting changes of control and have a Community dimension), the scope of Regulation 1/2003 is much wider. Regulation 1/2003 covers other situations that fall within the scope of general EU competition law.

While it is easiest for the Commission to apply structural remedies when undertakings offer commitments, the Commission does not have unlimited discretion. The commitments accepted by the Commission must be *necessary* and *sufficient* to address the concerns identified by the Commission and *not disproportionate*.[274]

Most competition law commitments are behavioural rather than structural. For policy reasons,[275] structural commitments were used in some energy cases—*E.ON*, *RWE*, *ENI*—in which the Commission forced energy firms to unbundle ownership.

In two *E.ON* cases,[276] the Commission made structural commitments binding on an undertaking in the German electricity wholesale market and the balancing market. In the first case, the Commission had concerns that E.ON might have withdrawn available generation capacity from the German wholesale electricity markets to raise prices, and deterred investments in energy generation by competitors. In the second case, the Commission had concerns that the transmission subsidiary of E.ON might have favoured its production affiliate for providing balancing services, while passing the resulting costs on to final consumers, and prevented power producers from other Member States from exporting balancing energy into its transmission zone. E.ON offered to divest around 5,000 MW of its generation capacity to address the concerns regarding the wholesale market. E.ON also

[272] Commission decision in Case COMP/M.4180—Gaz de France/Suez, paras 633 and 631.

[273] Article 7(1) of Regulation 1/2003 (on the implementation of the rules on competition laid down in Articles 81 and 82 of the EC Treaty).

[274] Case 15/83 Denkavit Nederland v Hoofdproduktschap voor Akkerbouwprodukten [1984] ECR 2171, para 25; Case 265/87, Schräder [1989] ECR 2237, para 21; Case T-260/94 Air Inter v Commission [1997] ECR II-997, para 147; Case T-65/98, Van den Bergh Foods v Commission [2003] ECR II-4653, para 201. See also Commitments Decision in Case COMP/39.315—ENI, para 85.

[275] Commission staff working paper accompanying the Communication from the Commission to the European Parliament and Council – Report on the functioning of Regulation 1/2003, COM (2009)206 final, SEC/2009/0574 final, para 97: "In sectors where a number of infringements derive from the very complex nature of business decisions (e.g. decisions taken on an hourly or finer basis for a large portfolio of assets and/or using a large number of non-programmable parameters) and from the structure (e.g. vertical integration) of the operators, structural measures may indeed be necessary".

[276] Cases COMP/B-1/39.388—German Electricity Wholesale Market and COMP/B-1/39.389—German Electricity Balancing Market.

committed to divest its extra-high voltage network to meet the concerns on the electricity balancing market.[277]

In *RWE*,[278] the Commission applied structural commitments in the German natural gas market. The Commission had concerns that RWE might have abused its dominant position on the gas transmission market. To address these concerns, RWE committed to divest its existing Western German high-pressure transmission network to an independent purchaser, the acquisition by whom would not give rise to prima facie competition concerns.[279]

In the *ENI* case,[280] the Commission believed that ENI infringed Article 102 TFEU when it managed and operated its natural gas transmission pipelines. ENI committed to divest its transmission business. According to the Commission, the commitments were necessary and sufficient to address the concerns identified by the Commission and not disproportionate.[281]

In practice, the Commission has plenty of discretion to determine whether the commitments are proportionate or not.[282]

3.6.3 *Foreclosure*

General Remarks

Many electricity cases relate to foreclosure. The Commission's 2007 final report on the sector inquiry identified foreclosure as one of the deficiencies of European electricity markets. Generally, one can distinguish between horizontal and vertical foreclosure. Both can consist of other than price-based exclusion and price-based exclusion.[283]

Horizontal Foreclosure Horizontal foreclosure looks different in the context of electricity markets because of the physical characteristics of electricity. There are four important causes of foreclosure here: restriction of access to transmission networks (Chap. 5); vertical integration of network and supply activities (such as complete vertical integration or the integration of generation and distribution, Sect. 2.3.5); vertical integration of generation and retail (so-called integrated firms, Sect.

---

277 Commission staff working paper – Report on the functioning of Regulation 1/2003, COM (2009)206 final, SEC(2009) 0574 final, para 98.

278 Case COMP/39.402—RWE Gas Foreclosure.

279 Commission staff working paper accompanying the Communication from the Commission to the European Parliament and Council – Report on the functioning of Regulation 1/2003, COM (2009) 206 final, SEC(2009) 0574 final, para 98.

280 Case COMP/39.315—ENI.

281 Commitments Decision in Case COMP/39.315—ENI, para 85.

282 Case C-441/07 P Commission v Alrosa [2010] ECR I-05945, paras 41 and 42: "Judicial review for its part relates solely to whether the Commission's assessment is manifestly incorrect". See also Commitments Decision in Case COMP/39.315—ENI, para 86.

283 DG Competition discussion paper on the application of Article 82 of the Treaty to exclusionary abuses, December 2005, para 73.

2.3.5); and exclusive long-term contracts (Chap. 8). They give rise to two forms of foreclosure: infrastructure foreclosure and market foreclosure.

Infrastructure Foreclosure Infrastructure foreclosure means the lack of access to electricity networks on transparent and non-discriminatory conditions. Restriction of access to transmission networks is a form of infrastructure foreclosure. Vertical integration of network and supply activities (complete vertical integration) increases the risk of infrastructure foreclosure. As European electricity markets cannot be opened up without network access, infrastructure foreclosure is something that the Commission and national competition authorities have focused on.

Market Foreclosure There are two forms of market foreclosure: vertical integration of generation and retail; and exclusive long-term contracts.

The Commission has investigated market foreclosure as alleged breaches of Article 102 TFEU. The investigated cases include: the limitation of transport capacities through refusal to deal or underinvestment; and market foreclosure through long-term supply or transmission capacity contracts.

In practice, it could be difficult to apply Article 101 TFEU to market foreclosure. Market foreclosure is often caused by the existence of market structures that are not effective, but Article 101 TFEU does not prohibit the existence of any particular market structure as such (for Article 102 TFEU, see Sect. 3.7.2).

Restriction of Access to Transmission Networks There are three main forms of restricting access to transmission networks.

First, a TSO may have an incentive to abuse its natural monopoly.[284]

In *Svenska Kraftnät*, the issue was whether the Swedish electricity TSO had curtailed export transmission capacity on Swedish interconnectors to neighbouring countries. The curtailment of export transmission capacity means that domestically generated or imported electricity is reserved for domestic consumption contrary to the objective of creating an internal market for electricity.[285] Svenska Kraftnät offered commitments that enabled it to manage congestion in the Swedish transmission system without limiting trading capacity on interconnectors, and commitments designed to reduce congestion.[286]

Second, a vertically integrated undertaking may have an incentive to restrict access to its transmission network to use the transmission capacity itself. The Commission has investigated such situations in the light of Article 102 TFEU in both gas[287] and electricity markets.[288]

---

[284] See the examples mentioned in Article 102 TFEU.

[285] Summary of Commission Decision in Case COMP/39.351—Swedish Interconnectors, para 3.

[286] Summary of Commission Decision in Case COMP/39.351—Swedish Interconnectors, para 4.

[287] Case COMP/39.402—RWE gas foreclosure; Case COMP/M.4180—Gaz de France/Suez; Case COMP/39.315—ENI.

[288] Cases COMP/B-1/39.388—German Electricity Wholesale Market and COMP/B-1/39.389—German Electricity Balancing Market.

Third, the existence of long-term contracts for the use of transmission capacity can lead to infrastructure foreclosure (this issue is discussed in the context of market foreclosure through long-term contracts).

Vertical Integration of Network and Supply Activities

Vertical integration of network and supply activities (complete vertical integration) increases the risk of infrastructure foreclosure. Preventing competitors from having access to infrastructure necessary for competing in upstream or downstream markets may amount to abuse of a dominant position (Article 102 TFEU).

Essential Facilities The Commission has applied principles developed under the concept of essential facilities. The first time the Commission used this concept explicitly was in *Sea Containers/Stena Sealink*.[289]

> The essential facilities doctrine was imported to the EU from the US as a legal transplant. It first appeared in the US[290] as a limitation to the main competition law rule that businesses may choose their contract parties (the Colgate doctrine).[291] The essential facilities doctrine is used to impose on owners of essential facilities a duty to deal with competitors. However, the essential facilities doctrine is nowadays regarded as a flawed means of deciding whether a unilateral, unconditional refusal to deal harms competition in the US.[292] The relevance of the essential facilities doctrine was reduced by the *Trinko* case.[293]
>
> In *Trinko*, the Supreme Court declined to find a duty to deal. The Supreme Court argued: "Firms may acquire monopoly power by establishing an infrastructure that renders them uniquely suited to serve their customers. Compelling such firms to share the source of their advantage is in some tension with the underlying purpose of antitrust law, since it may lessen the incentive for the monopolist, the rival, or both to invest in those economically beneficial facilities. Enforced sharing also requires antitrust courts to act as central planners, identifying the proper price, quantity, and other terms of dealing—a role for which they are ill suited. Moreover, compelling negotiation between competitors may facilitate the supreme evil of antitrust: collusion. Thus, as a general matter, the Sherman Act 'does not restrict the long recognized right of [a] trader or manufacturer engaged in an entirely

---

289 Commission Decision in Case IV/34689—Sea Containers/Stena Sealink—Interim measures, para 66. Commitments Decision in Case COMP/39.315—ENI, para 39. See also DG Competition discussion paper on the application of Article 82 of the Treaty to exclusionary abuses (December 2005).

290 United States v. Terminal Railroad Association of St. Louis, 224 U.S. (1912). See also Areeda P (1989–1990); Lipsky A and Sidak JG (1999); Pitofski R et al. (2002); Waller SW (2008). The essential facilities doctrine is connected with the common law common carrier doctrine. For an application of the common carrier doctrine, see, for example, Speta JB (2002).

291 United States v Colgate & Co, 250 US 300, 39 S. Ct. 465 (1919): "In the absence of any purpose to create or maintain a monopoly, the [Sherman Act] does not restrict the long recognized right of trader or manufacturer engaged in an entirely private business, freely to exercise his own independent discretion as to parties with whom he will deal".

292 U.S. Dep't of Justice, Competition and Monopoly: Single-Firm Conduct Under Section 2 of the Sherman Act (2008). See also Areeda P (1989–1990).

293 Verizon v. Trinko, 540 U.S. 398 (2004). See, for example, Petit N (2004).

private business, freely to exercise his own independent discretion as to parties with whom he will deal'".[294]

On the other hand, the Supreme Court stated that the right to refuse to deal with rivals is not "unqualified". The Court reserved the possibility that a refusal to cooperate with rivals can constitute anticompetitive conduct and violate §2 of the Sherman Act "[u]nder certain circumstances".[295]

The European Court of Justice has dealt with refusals to deal in various cases after *Commercial Solvents*.[296] Unlike the European Commission, however, the CJEU has not used the term "essential facilities". In *Bronner*, the plaintiff argued that the essential facilities doctrine was established under the case-law of the CJEU,[297] but the CJEU refused to use the concept of essential facilities. In addition, the CJEU restricted the scope of the duty to deal.[298]

In *Bronner*, it was not sufficient that the undertaking had a dominant position. The wording of Article 102 TFEU does not prohibit a dominant undertaking from doing things internally as a vertically integrated firm. An undertaking has a right to provide a service or refuse to do so even when it has a dominant position—subject to general competition law constraints such as the rule that a dominant undertaking may not use "methods different from those that condition normal competition" (*Hoffmann-La Roche*).[299]

The exercise of this right by a dominant undertaking may, in exceptional circumstances, constitute an abuse.[300] According to judgment of the CJEU in *Bronner*, there are such exceptional circumstances where: (1) the service in itself is "indispensable" to carrying on the other party's business because there is "no actual or potential substitute in existence" for the requested service; (2) the refusal to provide the service would be "likely to eliminate all competition" in the market on the part of the person requesting the service; and (3) the refusal would be "incapable of being objectively justified".[301] In effect, the test laid down

[294] Verizon v. Trinko, 540 U.S. 398 (2004), pp. 407–408 (quoting United States v. Colgate & Co., 250 U.S. 300, 307 (1919)).

[295] Verizon v. Trinko, 540 U.S. 398 (2004), p. 408. In the US, Section 2 of the Sherman Act prohibits monopolisation: "Every person who shall monopolize, or attempt to monopolize, or combine or conspire with any other person or persons, to monopolize any part of the trade or commerce among the several States, or with foreign nations, shall be deemed guilty of a felony, and, on conviction thereof, shall be punished by fine not exceeding $100,000,000 if a corporation, or, if any other person, $1,000,000, or by imprisonment not exceeding 10 years, or by both said punishments, in the discretion of the court".

[296] Refusal to deal was first dealt with in Joined Cases 6/73 and 7/73 Istituto Chemioterapico Italiano S.p.A. and Commercial Solvents Corporation v Commission [1974] ECR 223, para 25.

[297] Case C-7/97 Oscar Bronner GmbH & Co. KG v Mediaprint Zeitungs- und Zeitschriftenverlag GmbH & Co. KG [1998] ECR I-7791, para 24.

[298] For economic arguments restricting the duty to deal, see Bergman MA (2000, 2005).

[299] Case 85/76 Hoffmann-La Roche v Commission [1979] ECR 461, para 91. Article 102 TFEU contains examples of such prohibited methods. See also Case 6/72 Europemballage and Continental Can v Commission [1973] ECR 215, paras 26–27.

[300] Case C-7/97 Oscar Bronner GmbH & Co. KG v Mediaprint Zeitungs- und Zeitschriftenverlag GmbH & Co. KG [1998] ECR I-7791, paras 38–39.

[301] *Ibid*, paras 40–41.

by the CJEU in *Bronner* prohibits the monopolisation of the market in a way that resembles §2 of the Sherman Act after *Trinko* but has a broader scope. Because the test is an objective one, it is not necessary to consider intent in the EU.[302]

Strategic Underinvestment An alternative approach could be the doctrine of strategic underinvestment.[303] The prevailing view is that a dominant undertaking may have a duty to deal under the essential facilities doctrine under some circumstances, but no duty under Article 102 TFEU to expand existing facilities or construct new ones to improve market entry. The Commission seemed to share this view in its 2009 Guidance on Article 82 of the EC Treaty (now Article 102 TFEU).[304] In *ENI*, however, the Commission indicated that there could be such an obligation, and investment commitments were used in *Gaz de France/Suez*.[305]

In *ENI*, the Commission discussed the relationship between the essential facilities doctrine and strategic underinvestment. If the holder of an essential facility has a dominant position and its capacities are fully used, it has, according to the Commission, an obligation to "take all possible measures to remove the constraints imposed by the lack of capacity and to organise its business in a manner that makes a maximum amount of capacity of the essential facility available".[306] The Commission identified the strategic limitation of investment as one of the competitive concerns of ENI's alleged refusal to supply strategy.[307] As the concerns were cleared when ENI divested its essential facility (transport business),[308] it was not necessary for ENI to offer any investment commitments.

Gaz de France/Suez was a merger control case. A study by the CREG (Belgium's Commission for Electricity and Gas Regulation) found a persistent state of (contractual) congestion on the Belgian gas transmission network caused by inadequate investment.[309] According to the Commission, the proposed merger would have discouraged investment.[310] The parties undertook to make a series of investments to increase Belgian and French gas infrastructure capacity.[311]

---

[302] The concept of abuse is an objective one. Case 85/76 Hoffmann-La Roche v Commission [1979] ECR 461, para 91.

[303] Summary of Commission Decision in Case COMP/39.315—ENI, para 6; Summary of Commission Decision in Case COMP/39.316—GDF, para 3.

[304] Communication from the Commission—Guidance on the Commission's enforcement priorities in applying Article 82 of the EC Treaty to abusive exclusionary conduct by dominant undertakings, OJ C 45, 24.2.2009, pp. 7–20, para 75: "The existence of such an obligation – even for a fair remuneration – may undermine undertakings' incentives to invest and innovate and, thereby, possibly harm consumers. The knowledge that they may have a duty to supply against their will may lead dominant undertakings – or undertakings who anticipate that they may become dominant – not to invest, or to invest less, in the activity in question. Also, competitors may be tempted to free ride on investments made by the dominant undertaking instead of investing themselves. Neither of these consequences would, in the long run, be in the interest of consumers".

[305] Case COMP/39.315—ENI; Case COMP/M.4180—Gaz de France/Suez.

[306] Commitments Decision in Case COMP/39.315—ENI, footnote 43.

[307] Commitments Decision in Case COMP/39.315—ENI, paras 59–61.

[308] Commitments Decision in Case COMP/39.315—ENI, para 93.

[309] Commission Decision in Case COMP/M.4180—Gaz de France/Suez, para 237.

[310] Commission Decision in Case COMP/M.4180—Gaz de France/Suez, paras 248 and 447.

[311] Commission Decision in Case COMP/M.4180—Gaz de France/Suez, paras 1204–1207.

The power to establish and enforce investment obligations would be problematic. One may ask whether Article 102 TFEU should vest such powers in competition authorities.[312] First, the interpretation of Article 102 is constrained not only by the principle of proportionality[313] but also by the right to property and the freedom to conduct a business.[314] Second, it would be very difficult for outsiders such as judges or competition authorities to take rational investment decisions on behalf of the undertakings concerned. The perceived quality of investment decisions depends on very subjective preferences on what should be done (strategy), cash flow (return), and risk, and on the quality of available information. Judges or competition authorities are not better equipped to take investment decisions. For instance, this explains the business judgment rule in company law.[315] Third, the obligation to invest would be likely to cement the dominant position.

Vertical Integration of Generation and Retail

Vertical integration of generation and retail reduces the need to trade on wholesale markets. For the vertically integrated firm, this may bring benefits.[316]

The vertical integration of generation and retail is not prohibited by the electricity directives. The purpose of the Third Electricity Directive is, among other things, to make retail activities easier for electricity producers. The electricity directives should, according to their stated objectives, reduce obstacles to the sale of electricity to wholesale and retail customers,[317] facilitate the right to choose the supplier,[318] and increase price competition between suppliers.[319] The vertical integration of generation and retail is thus assumed to increase competition between producers.

---

312 Temple Lang J (1994), p. 496: "The owner of an essential facility cannot be obliged to invest in new capacity to provide facilities for more competitors". See also Scholz U and Purps S (2010), pp. 47–48.

313 Articles 5 TEU and 296 TFEU.

314 Article 16 of the Charter of Fundamental Rights of the European Union: "The freedom to conduct a business in accordance with Union law and national laws and practices is recognised". Article 17(1) of the Charter of Fundamental Rights of the European Union: "Everyone has the right to own, use, dispose of and bequeath his or her lawfully acquired possessions. No one may be deprived of his or her possessions, except in the public interest and in the cases and under the conditions provided for by law, subject to fair compensation being paid in good time for their loss. The use of property may be regulated by law in so far as is necessary for the general interest".

315 See, for example, Smith v. Van Gorkom, 488 A.2d 858 (Del. 1985) in the US and § 93(1) AktG in Germany.

316 For transaction costs, see Coase RH (1937); Williamson OE (1985). For transaction costs in electricity markets, see Erdmann G (2009).

317 Recital 4 of Directive 2009/72/EC (Third Electricity Directive).

318 Recital 20 of Directive 2009/72/EC (Third Electricity Directive).

319 Recital 8 of Directive 2009/72/EC (Third Electricity Directive).

However, vertical integration reduces the liquidity of wholesale markets.[320] If all electricity producers had their own retail businesses, there would be hardly any room for independent suppliers whose business does not include generation, because independent suppliers would have limited access to uncommitted generation. As a result of the absence of independent suppliers, it would be more difficult for independent electricity producers to supply electricity directly to the wholesale market.[321] Moreover, unlike the various distribution channels in sale of goods, electricity distribution is a natural monopoly.

The Third Electricity Directive addresses this issue in two ways. (a) Effective unbundling is designed to ensure that independent electricity producers can supply electricity to end consumers who may choose their suppliers.[322] (b) From 1 July 2007, all customers have been regarded as "eligible customers" who may choose their own suppliers.[323] The supplier may be a local one or established in any Member State of the EU,[324] and distribution system operators must not discriminate between system users.[325]

However, the Third Electricity Directive requires the effective unbundling of generation and transmission rather than the separation of generation and distribution activities.[326] The unbundling rules apply to distribution in a diluted form because the rules do not require ownership unbundling.[327] Moreover, while the Third Directive facilitates "non-discriminatory network access", it does not facilitate a level playing field for electricity producers regardless of their generation technology (Sect. 3.7.7).

Exclusive Long-Term Contracts

Exclusive long-term contracts can lead to market foreclosure, because a party that commits to deal exclusively with its contract party has no need to deal with anyone else. Contracts that have vertical foreclosure as their purpose or effect can infringe Articles 101 or 102 TFEU.

Exclusive Long-Term Supply Contracts In principle, long-term supply contracts could be the cause of vertical foreclosure as their effects can be similar to vertical

[320] DG Competition report on energy sector inquiry, SEC(2006) 1724, 10 January 2007, para 451.

[321] See DG Competition report on energy sector inquiry, SEC(2006) 1724, 10 January 2007, paras 449 and 451 on how vertical integration reduces wholesale trading.

[322] Articles 9(1) and 26(1) of Directive 2009/72/EC (Third Electricity Directive).

[323] Point 12 of Article 2 of Directive 2009/72/EC (Third Electricity Directive); Article 33(1) of Directive 2009/72/EC (Third Electricity Directive).

[324] Article 3(4) of Directive 2009/72/EC (Third Electricity Directive).

[325] Article 25(2) of Directive 2009/72/EC (Third Electricity Directive).

[326] Article 9(1) of Directive 2009/72/EC (Third Electricity Directive). For definitions, see points 19–21 of Article 2.

[327] Article 26(1) of Directive 2009/72/EC (Third Electricity Directive).

integration.[328] The Third Electricity Directive provides that the Member States should encourage the use of interruptible supply contracts.[329]

In practice, however, Article 101 TFEU is not applied to vertical agreements to the extent that they do not contain prohibited clauses.[330] Moreover, long contract duration can often be regarded as compatible with competition law because of its benefits. It is particularly interesting that long-term contracts can increase infrastructure investments by reducing investment risk and by making it easier to raise funding. The benefits of long-term contracts have been recognised in EU competition law.

They were recognised by the Commission in *Scottish Nuclear* in which a long contract term was permitted on the following grounds: "The agreement, which was originally to apply for a period equivalent to the remaining lifetime of the nuclear power stations, i.e. 30 years, has, at the Commission's request, been limited to 15 years. This period of validity provides the stability and guarantee necessary for long-term planning and allows the necessary adjustments to be made to the new situation after a reasonable start-up period. However, this period seems necessary to allow Scottish Nuclear to attain full profitability and become competitive".[331]

Some long-term obligations have been addressed by the Vertical Block Exemption Regulation. The scope of the block exemption for vertical agreements depends on the market power of the parties,[332] the nature of the contract, and the duration of the contract.[333] Supply contracts contain non-compete obligations when the buyer has an obligation to purchase more than 80 % of its total purchases from the supplier.[334] There is a 5-year-limit for such non-compete obligations.[335] If the share of total purchases is lower, the limit does not apply. However, a party will not benefit from the block exemption where its market share is too large. There is 30 % threshold for the market share of a party.[336]

In the *E.ON Ruhrgas* case, the German Bundeskartellamt imposed a fixed maximum contract duration depending on the supplier's share of the customer's total purchases

[328] DG Competition report on energy sector inquiry, SEC(2006) 1724, 10 January 2007, para 450.

[329] Recital 41 and Article 5(2) of Directive 72/2009/EC (Third Electricity Directive). See also Article 2(29) of Directive 2009/72/EC (Third Electricity Directive).

[330] Article 2(1) of Regulation 330/2010 (Vertical Block Exemption Regulation).

[331] Commission Decision in Case IV/33.473—Scottish Nuclear, para 40.

[332] Recitals 7–9 of Regulation 330/2010 (Vertical Block Exemption Regulation).

[333] See recital 11 of Regulation 330/2010 (Vertical Block Exemption Regulation).

[334] Article 1(1)(d) of Regulation 330/2010 (Vertical Block Exemption Regulation).

[335] Article 5(1) of Regulation 330/2010 (Vertical Block Exemption Regulation). The market threshold and the 5-year limit were mentioned in Bundeskartellamt Decision of 10 February 2009, B 8—113/03 E.ON Ruhrgas.

[336] Article 3(1) of Regulation 330/2010 (Vertical Block Exemption Regulation): "The exemption provided for in Article 2 shall apply on condition that the market share held by the supplier does not exceed 30 % of the relevant market on which it sells the contract goods or services and the market share held by the buyer does not exceed 30 % of the relevant market on which it purchases the contract goods or services".

according to these principles. A big market share and a big share of purchases reduce the permitted duration of the contract.[337]

One may ask how Article 102 TFEU can be applied to long-term supply contracts. In *Distrigaz*, the Commission identified five elements to be considered when determining whether long-term supply contracts infringe Article 102 TFEU: the market position of the supplier; the share of the customers' demand tied under the contracts; the duration of the contracts; the overall share of the market covered by contracts containing such ties; and efficiencies.[338] The Commission introduced a model according to which a certain part of the overall demand in the market concerned is subject to competition. The model required more than limiting contract durations.

Prior to the liberalisation of the gas sector,[339] Distrigaz had the exclusive right to transport and store gas underground in Belgium and was the only supplier of gas to large customers. After the liberalisation, Distrigaz remained the largest gas importer and supplier in Belgium. The Commission took the preliminary view that Distrigaz held a dominant position in the Belgian market for the sale of high calorific gas to large customers.

Distrigaz had entered into long-term gas supply agreements. According to the Commission, Distrigaz covered the total demand of its customers in most cases. The customers of Distrigaz were customarily required to offtake a certain minimum amount from Distrigaz.

The Commission expressed concerns that the long-term gas supply contracts would foreclose other gas suppliers' access to the market by preventing customers from switching the supplier. On the other hand, the Commission acknowledged that long-term contracts may be justified if they generate efficiencies that outweigh their negative effects.

Distrigaz offered and the Commission accepted various commitments. First, on average a minimum of 70 % of the gas volumes supplied by Distrigaz to industrial users and electricity producers in Belgium must return to the market each year. Second, contracts with industrial users and electricity producers must not be longer than 5 years (contracts relating to new power plants with a capacity exceeding 10 MW were not subject to the commitments). Third, Distrigaz undertook not to conclude any gas supply agreements with resellers with duration of over 2 years. Fourth, Distrigaz confirmed that it would not introduce use restrictions into its supply contracts.[340]

The criteria developed in the *Distrigaz* case were applied by the Commission in the *EdF* case on the French electricity market and in the *Electrabel* case on the Belgian electricity market (Sect. 8.2.5).[341]

[337] In the E.ON Ruhrgas case, the German Bundeskartellamt imposed a fixed maximum contract duration depending on the supplier's share of the customer's total purchases. Bundeskartellamt Decision of 10 February 2009, B 8—113/03 E.ON Ruhrgas (upheld by the Bundesgerichtshof, Decision of 10 February 2009, KVR 67/07).

[338] Commission, Antitrust: Commission increases competition in the Belgian gas market—frequently asked questions, MEMO/07/407, 11 October 2007.

[339] As a result of the implementation of Directive 98/30/EC (First Gas Directive).

[340] Summary of Commission Decision in Case COMP/B-1/37.966—Distrigaz, para 3.

[341] Case COMP/39.386—Long-term electricity contracts in France; Case COMP/39.387—Long-term electricity contracts in Belgium.

Exclusive Long-Term Transmission Capacity Contracts It is open whether the *Distrigaz* model can be applied to long-term transmission capacity contracts.

Unlike supply contracts, transmission capacity contracts are subject to sector-specific regulation under the Third Electricity Directive. As a result, the behaviour of TSOs and DSOs is at least partly determined by mandatory provisions of law. Whether their behaviour infringes EU competition law in a regulated environment can depend on the extent of the regulation and the scope of discretion left to the parties.[342]

Long-term transmission capacity contracts do not infringe EU competition law as such.[343] Sometimes they do. In *Gaz de France*, the Commission's starting point was that the foreclosure of long-term transmission capacity could infringe Article 102 TFEU.[344] These concerns were remedied by the commitments offered by GDF Sucz.[345]

3.7 Environmental Aspects and the Preferential Treatment of RES-E

3.7.1 General Remarks

The third regulatory sector discussed here relates to the environment. No form of energy is free from negative environmental impacts caused by generation, trans port, waste management, and other things. Environmental aspects play an important role in the regulation of the electricity sector[346] and must be considered by electricity producers. Investments in new generation installations are, to a large extent, driven or constrained by EU environmental laws, in particular by: the preferential treatment of RES-E (which reduces incentives to invest in other energy production); the allocation of network investment costs to the TSO or the socialisation of these costs (which increase incentives to invest in decentralised power generation in remote places); and regulatory permits (which enable micro-management by the regulatory authorities).

Environmental legislation can generally protect both local and global interests. (a) Electricity infrastructure projects may have local impacts such as impacts on water quality, bird and wildlife, noise, and property values. Such interests are protected by planning laws, nature conservation laws, and environmental protection

[342] Case T-271/03 Deutsche Telekom AG v Commission [2008] ECR II-477, paras 85–90.

[343] See, for example, Case COMP/37.966—Distrigaz.

[344] Summary of Commission Decision in Case COMP/39.316—GDF, para 3.

[345] Summary of Commission Decision in Case COMP/39.316—GDF, para 4.

[346] Article 11 TFEU: "Environmental protection requirements must be integrated into the definition and implementation of the Union's policies and activities, in particular with a view to promoting sustainable development".

laws. Neighbour interests can be protected by neighbour law or nuisance law.[347] (b) Global interests can be protected by the regulation of energy sources, emissions, and nuclear power.

EU law addresses both local and global environmental issues. Local issues are addressed by directives on environmental assessment[348] as well as the protection of bird and wild life. Global issues are addressed by the regulation of: generation and transmission[349]; greenhouse gas emissions and trading in emission allowances[350]; and nuclear safety.[351]

The goal is not total harmonisation.[352] The EU nevertheless aims at a high level of protection.[353] Environmental directives customarily do not prevent Member States from introducing stricter protective measures.[354]

The preferential treatment of RES-E has so far meant tampering with the market mechanism. It has had a very large impact on the business of electricity producers.

3.7.2 *Environmental Assessment*

EU law or Member States' national laws can require an environmental assessment of infrastructure investments. Environmental assessment is a procedure that ensures that environmental implications are considered before the decisions are made.

In the EU, environmental assessment is based on two directives. Environmental assessment can be required for public plans or programmes under the SEA

[347] Egelund Olsen B (2010), p. 241. The decisive criterion is usually whether an activity results in unreasonable interference.

[348] Directive 2001/42/EC (SEA Directive); Directive 85/337/EEC (EIA Directive).

[349] Directive 2009/72/EC (Third Electricity Directive).

[350] Directive 2003/87/EC establishes a scheme for greenhouse gas emission allowance trading within the Community. Directive 2014/65/EU (MiFID II) includes in the list of financial instruments certain commodity derivatives, contracts relating to emission allowances, and emission allowances. See Annex I, Section C.

[351] Directive 2009/71/Euratom of 25 June 2009 establishing a Community framework for the nuclear safety of nuclear installations; Directive 96/29/Euratom of 13 May 1996 laying down basic safety standards for the protection of the health of workers and the general public against the dangers arising from ionising radiation; Directive 2006/117/Euratom of 20 November 2006 on the supervision and control of shipments of radioactive waste and spent fuel.

[352] Case C-2/10 Azienda Agro-Zootecnica Franchini Sarl, Eolica di Altamura Srl v Regione Puglia [2011] ECR I-6561, para 48: "... European Union rules do not seek to effect complete harmonisation in the area of the environment (see, inter alia, Case C-318/98 Fornasar and Others [2000] ECR I-4785, paragraph 46, and Case C-6/03 Deponiezweckverband Eiterköpfe [2005] ECR I-2753, paragraph 27)".

[353] Article 191(2) TFEU.

[354] Article 193 TFEU. Case C-2/10 Azienda Agro-Zootecnica Franchini Sarl, Eolica di Altamura Srl v Regione Puglia [2011] ECR I-6561, para 50; Case C-6/03 Deponiezweckverband Eiterköpfe v Land Rheinland-Pfalz [2005] ECR I-2777, para 58.

Directive[355] (Strategic Environmental Assessment) and for individual projects under the EIA Directive[356] (Environmental Impact Assessment). The two directives share the principle that plans, programmes and projects likely to have significant effects on the environment must be made subject to an environmental assessment prior to their approval or authorisation.[357]

The two key features of environmental assessment are the preparation of an environmental report[358] and consultation with the public.[359] The report and the opinions must be considered during the process.[360] As the directives lay down obligations of a procedural nature,[361] they do not say how exactly the report and the opinions should be considered. The main way to protect the environment under these two directives is through disclosure of environmental effects.[362] The directives do not regulate the contents of the final planning or investment decisions.

Energy ventures can fall within the scope of both directives.[363] The EIA Directive distinguishes between different kinds of energy projects. Some must be made subject to an assessment in all Member States (Annex I).[364] Whether other projects are made subject to an assessment depends on the Member State (Annex II).[365]

Most industrial installations for the production of electricity belong to Annex II. Nuclear power stations and large thermal power stations fall within the scope of Annex I. Even

[355] Point (a) of Article 2 of Directive 2001/42/EC (SEA Directive): "'plans and programmes' shall mean plans and programmes, including those co-financed by the European Community, as well as any modifications to them: – which are subject to preparation and/or adoption by an authority at national, regional or local level or which are prepared by an authority for adoption, through a legislative procedure by Parliament or Government, and – which are required by legislative, regulatory or administrative provisions".

[356] Article 2(1) of Directive 85/337/EEC (EIA Directive): "... 'project' means: – the execution of construction works or of other installations or schemes, – other interventions in the natural surroundings and landscape including those involving the extraction of mineral resources ..."

[357] Article 2(1) of Directive 85/337/EEC (EIA Directive). See also Article 1 of Directive 2001/42/EC (SEA Directive): "... a high level of protection of the environment ..."

[358] Article 5 of Directive 2001/42/EC (SEA Directive).

[359] Articles 2(b) and 6(2) of Directive 2001/42/EC (SEA Directive).

[360] Articles 8 and 9(1) of Directive 2001/42/EC (SEA Directive).

[361] Recital 9 and Article 1 of Directive 2001/42/EC (SEA Directive).

[362] See Annex I and Annex II of Directive 2001/42/EC (SEA Directive).

[363] Article 3(2) of Directive 2001/42/EC (SEA Directive): "Subject to paragraph 3, an environmental assessment shall be carried out for all plans and programmes, (a) which are prepared for ... energy, industry, ... waste management, water management, ... town and country planning or land use and which set the framework for future development consent of projects listed in Annexes I and II to Directive 85/337/EEC, or (b) which, in view of the likely effect on sites, have been determined to require an assessment pursuant to Article 6 or 7 of Directive 92/43/EEC".

[364] Article 4(1) of Directive 85/337/EEC (EIA Directive): "Subject to Article 2 (3), projects of the classes listed in Annex I shall be made subject to an assessment in accordance with Articles 5 to 10".

[365] Article 4(2) of Directive 85/337/EEC (EIA Directive).

waste-disposal installations for the incineration of toxic and dangerous wastes fall within the scope of Annex I. In *Commission v Italian Republic*, the CJEU held that an establishment, which generates electricity from the incineration of biomass and combustible materials derived from waste, falls within the category of disposal installations in Annex I. An environmental impact assessment procedure is compulsory for the project.[366]

3.7.3 Prohibitions

Energy investments can be constrained by sector-specific prohibitions intended to protect the environment as well as Member States' national laws.[367] These prohibitions fall outside the scope of this book.

3.7.4 Authorisations and Permits

The construction of electricity installations may require authorisations and permits on several environmental grounds. The Third Electricity Directive regulates authorisation criteria for new generation capacity.[368] Particular environmental directives or the national provisions of Member States' laws may also require authorisations for installations.

New Generation Capacity, Third Electricity Directive Environmental aspects are considered in the authorisation procedure for new generation capacity. The authorisation criteria must contain criteria that address not only safety and zoning issues[369] and the characteristics of the applicant,[370] but also environmental issues

[366] C-486/04 Commission v Italian Republic [2006] ECR I-11025, para 45.

[367] Case C-2/10 Azienda Agro-Zootecnica Franchini Sarl, Eolica di Altamura Srl v Regione Puglia [2011] ECR I-6561.

[368] Article 7(1) of Directive 2009/72/EC (Third Electricity Directive).

[369] Article 7(2) of Directive 2009/72/EC (Third Electricity Directive): "... Member States shall consider: (a) the safety and security of the electricity system, installations and associated equipment; (b) the protection of public health and safety; ... (d) land use and siting; (e) the use of public ground; (f) energy efficiency; ..."

[370] Article 7(2) of Directive 2009/72/EC (Third Electricity Directive): "... Member States shall consider: ... (h) the characteristics particular to the applicant, such as technical, economic and financial capabilities; (i) compliance with measures adopted pursuant to Article 3; ..."

such as energy efficiency,[371] the protection of the environment, the nature of the primary sources, the contribution of the generating capacity to meeting the EU's overall 20/20 target for the use of energy from renewable sources, and the contribution of generating capacity to reducing emissions.[372] The Member States may also take into account environmental aspects when they use a tendering procedure for new capacity.[373]

The Third Electricity Directive restricts the use of complementary authorisation requirements as the Directive requires an authorisation procedure[374] and lists the criteria that may be considered by the Member State.[375]

> There is a particular provision on land use. A Member State must include the construction of new generation capacity within the scope of land use permit procedures, where it has established particular land use permit procedures that apply to major new infrastructure projects.[376]

Transmission Capacity, Third Electricity Directive The authorisation procedure for grid infrastructure has not been harmonised.[377] The Third Electricity Directive requires the designation and certification of transmission system operators[378] rather than the authorisation of new transmission capacity.[379] Moreover, the Third Directive regulates TSOs' responsibilities (Sect. 3.7.5).

---

[371] Point 29 of Article 2 of Directive 2009/72/EC (Third Electricity Directive): "'energy efficiency/demand-side management' means a global or integrated approach aimed at influencing the amount and timing of electricity consumption in order to reduce primary energy consumption and peak loads by giving precedence to investments in energy efficiency measures, or other measures, such as interruptible supply contracts, over investments to increase generation capacity, if the former are the most effective and economical option, taking into account the positive environmental impact of reduced energy consumption and the security of supply and distribution cost aspects related to it".

[372] Article 7(2) of Directive 2009/72/EC (Third Electricity Directive): "... Member States shall consider: ... (c) the protection of the environment; ... (f) energy efficiency; (g) the nature of the primary sources; ... (j) the contribution of the generating capacity to meeting the overall Community target of at least a 20 % share of energy from renewable sources in the Community's gross final consumption of energy in 2020 referred to in Article 3(1) of Directive 2009/28/EC ...; and (k) the contribution of generating capacity to reducing emissions".

[373] Article 8(1) and recital 43 of Directive 2009/72/EC (Third Electricity Directive).

[374] Article 7(1) of Directive 2009/72/EC (Third Electricity Directive).

[375] Article 7(2) of Directive 2009/72/EC (Third Electricity Directive).

[376] Article 7(3) of Directive 2009/72/EC (Third Electricity Directive).

[377] See Article 16(1) of Directive 2009/28/EC (RES Directive).

[378] Article 10(1) of Directive 2009/72/EC (Third Electricity Directive).

[379] See Article 22 of Directive 2009/72/EC (Third Electricity Directive).

Emissions Directive 2003/87/EC requires the operator of an installation[380] to have a greenhouse gas emissions permit before it undertakes an activity resulting in regulated greenhouse gas emissions (Sect. 3.7.6).[381]

3.7.5 TSO's Responsibilities

A TSO has a duty to act with "due regard to the environment" in many ways.[382] These duties relate to the following issues:

- grid access (a duty to grant electricity produced from renewable energy sources priority or guaranteed access to the grid)[383];
- transmission and distribution (a duty to guarantee the transmission or distribution of electricity produced from renewable energy sources)[384];
- dispatching (a duty to give priority to generating installations using renewable energy sources when the TSO is responsible for dispatching the generating installations in its area)[385] (in so far as the secure operation of the national electricity system permits it)[386];
- combined heat and power (a Member State may require TSOs to give priority to generating installations producing combined heat and power when the they dispatch generating installations)[387]; and
- tariffs (there is a particular duty not to charge discriminatory tariffs for the transmission or distribution of electricity from renewable energy sources).[388]

[380] Article 3 of Directive 2003/87/EC (Emissions Trading Scheme Directive): "... (e) 'installation' means a stationary technical unit where one or more activities listed in Annex I are carried out and any other directly associated activities which have a technical connection with the activities carried out on that site and which could have an effect on emissions and pollution; (f) 'operator' means any person who operates or controls an installation or, where this is provided for in national legislation, to whom decisive economic power over the technical functioning of the installation has been delegated; ..."

[381] Article 4 of Directive 2003/87/EC (Emissions Trading Scheme Directive).

[382] Article 12(a) of Directive 2009/72/EC (Third Electricity Directive).

[383] Point (b) of Article 16(2) of Directive 2009/28/EC (RES Directive).

[384] Point (a) of Article 16(2) of Directive 2009/28/EC (RES Directive).

[385] Article 15(1) of Directive 2009/72/EC (Third Electricity Directive).

[386] Point (c) of Article 16(2) of Directive 2009/28/EC (RES Directive).

[387] Article 15(3) of Directive 2009/72/EC (Third Electricity Directive). See also Article 16(11) of Directive 2009/28/EC (RES Directive).

[388] Article 16(7) of Directive 2009/28/EC (RES Directive): "... including in particular electricity from renewable energy sources produced in peripheral regions, such as island regions, and in regions of low population density ..." Article 16(8) of Directive 2009/28/EC: "Member States shall ensure that tariffs charged by transmission system operators and distribution system operators for the transmission and distribution of electricity from plants using renewable energy sources reflect realisable cost benefits resulting from the plant's connection to the network. Such cost benefits could arise from the direct use of the low-voltage grid".

3.7.6 Emissions

The regulation of carbon dioxide and other greenhouse gas emissions[389] and the regulation of emissions trading[390] play an important role in the electricity markets for three reasons. First, the EU and some US States have adopted aggressive targets for reducing greenhouse gas emissions.[391] Much of the reduction has to come from the electricity industry, because the electricity industry emits substantial volumes of carbon dioxide. Second, the polluter pays principle means that the emitter must now pay for emissions. Emission rights are closely associated with electricity generation. Third, the EU has also set a target for 2020 of producing 20 % of its energy from renewable sources.[392]

Targets European businesses entered a carbon-constrained economic environment on 1 January 2005 when the Kyoto Protocol entered into force.

The general objectives of the EU's environmental policy and the choice of a high level protection are laid down in Article 191 TFEU. The greenhouse gas emission targets are heavily influenced by an international framework. In 1993, the European Community ratified the 1992 United Nations Framework Convention on Climate Change (Framework Convention, UNFCCC).[393] The Framework Convention was followed by the Kyoto Protocol. The Kyoto Protocol was ratified by the EU in 2002.[394]

The Kyoto Protocol contains the undertakings entered into by the industrialised countries to reduce their emissions of six greenhouse gases which are responsible for global warming.[395] The total emissions of the developed countries are to be reduced by at least 5 % over the period 2008–2012 compared with 1990 levels. The first Kyoto Commitment Period thus commenced on 1 January 2008.

---

[389] Point 1 of Article 2 of Decision 406/2009/EC of the European Parliament and of the Council: "'Greenhouse gas emissions' means the emission of carbon dioxide (CO_2), methane (CH_4), nitrous oxide (N_2O), hydrofluorocarbons (HFCs), perfluorocarbons (PFCs) and sulphur hexafluoride (SF_6) from the categories listed in Annex I, expressed in terms of tonnes of carbon dioxide equivalent, as determined pursuant to Decision No 280/2004/EC, excluding greenhouse gases emissions covered under Directive 2003/87/EC . . ."

[390] Directive 2003/87/EC (Emissions Trading Scheme Directive).

[391] For the Commission's plans, see Communication from the Commission, A European Strategic Energy Technology Plan: Towards a low carbon future, COM(2007) 723 final, 22 November 2007. See also Kramer L (2010).

[392] See, for example, Kramer L (2010).

[393] Council Decision 94/69/EC of 15 December 1993. The Framework Convention entered into force on 21 March 1994.

[394] Council Decision 2002/358/EC of 25 April 2002 concerning the approval, on behalf of the European Community, of the Kyoto Protocol to the United Nations Framework Convention on Climate Change and the joint fulfilment of commitments thereunder.

[395] The greenhouse gases are carbon dioxide (CO_2), methane (CH_4), nitrous oxide (N_2O), hydrofluorocarbons (HFCs), perfluorocarbons (PFCs), and sulphur hexafluoride (SF_6).

The EU and its Member States undertook to fulfil their reduction commitments jointly.[396] Each Member State was allocated a quota.[397]

The EU's own targets were outlined in the 2006 Action Plan for Energy Efficiency published in a Commission Communication.[398] The action plan described a framework of policies and measures that could help the EU to realise savings of 20 % in annual primary energy consumption by 2020.[399]

The European Council built on this in March 2007 when it adopted the EU's action plan (Energy Policy for Europe, EPE) and the so-called 20/20/20 targets to be met by 2020. They relate to:

- energy use (a 20 % reduction in primary energy use compared with projected levels, to be achieved by improving energy efficiency)[400];
- greenhouse gas emissions (the European Council accepted "a firm independent commitment" to achieve at least a 20 % reduction of greenhouse gas emissions by 2020 compared to 1990 levels)[401]; and
- renewable resources (20 % of EU energy consumption coming from renewable resources).

Originally, the 20/20/20 target seems to have been binding in the political sense rather than in the legal sense. At the time they were first accepted by the European Council, the European Council was not yet an institution of the EU.[402] The 20/20/20 target was nevertheless confirmed in a legally binding 2009 decision[403] laying down the minimum contribution of Member States to meeting the greenhouse gas emission reduction commitment of the Community for the period from 2013 to 2020.[404]

---

[396] Article 2 of Council Decision 2002/358/CE.

[397] Articles 2 and 3 of Council Decision 2002/358/CE.

[398] Communication from the Commission, Action Plan for Energy Efficiency: Realising the Potential, COM(2006)545 final, 19 October 2006.

[399] Action Plan for Energy Efficiency: Realising the Potential, COM(2006)545 final, p. 4: "This Action Plan outlines a framework of policies and measures with a view to intensify the process of realising the over 20 % estimated savings potential in EU annual primary energy consumption by 2020. The Plan lists a range of cost-effective measures, proposing priority actions to be initiated immediately, and others to be initiated gradually over the Plan's six-year period. Further action will subsequently be required to reach the full potential by 2020".

[400] Paragraph 6 of Annex I to Presidency Conclusions of the Brussels European Council (8/9 March 2007).

[401] Presidency Conclusions of the Brussels European Council (8/9 March 2007), para 32. See also recital 2 of Decision 406/2009/EC of the European Parliament and of the Council.

[402] The European Council acquired a formal status in the 1992 Treaty of Maastricht, but it did not become an institution of the EU until 1 December 2009 with the entry into force of the Treaty of Lisbon. See also Kramer L (2010), p. 314.

[403] Decision 406/2009/EC of the European Parliament and of the Council on the effort of Member States to reduce their greenhouse gas emissions to meet the Community's greenhouse gas emission reduction commitments up to 2020.

[404] Article 1 of Decision 406/2009/EC of the European Parliament and of the Council.

In January 2014, the Commission presented a new EU framework on climate and energy for 2030.[405] The framework extends the 2020 targets and requires Member States to reduce their greenhouse gas emissions by 40 % from 1990 levels by 2030. The renewables target for 2030 is 27 %. The Communication setting out the 2030 framework is accompanied by a Report on energy prices and costs.

Permits Directive 2003/87/EC provides that the operator of an installation[406] must have a greenhouse gas emissions permit before it undertakes an activity resulting in regulated greenhouse gas emissions.[407] The competent authority must issue the permit if it is satisfied that the operator is capable of monitoring and reporting emissions.[408] The scope of this scheme has gradually been increased to cover larger parts of the economy.

> Aviation has been included in the allowance trading scheme.[409] In *Air Transport Association of America*,[410] the CJEU held that the inclusion of aviation in the allowance trading scheme did not breach the obligations of the EU under international law (the Chicago Convention).

Allowances There is a mechanism for the allocation of emission allowances[411] by the Member States. Emission allowances are allocated according to the terms of the permit. When allocating allowances, the Member States should, nevertheless, "have regard … to the potential for industrial process activities to reduce emissions".[412]

The operator of an installation has a duty to return allowances to the competent authority according to the terms of the emission permit.[413] This duty is complemented by sanctions that punish non-compliance.[414] The sanctions must include at least the payment of an excess emissions penalty (which does not release

[405] Communication from the Commission, A policy framework for climate and energy in the period from 2020 to 2030, COM(2014) 15 final (22 January 2014).

[406] For definitions, see points (e) and (f) of Article 3 of Directive 2003/87/EC (Emissions Trading Scheme Directive).

[407] Article 4 of Directive 2003/87/EC (Emissions Trading Scheme Directive).

[408] Article 6(1) of Directive 2003/87/EC (Emissions Trading Scheme Directive).

[409] See Article 3a of Directive 2003/87/EC (Emissions Trading Scheme Directive), inserted by Article 1(4) of Directive 2008/101/EC.

[410] Case C-366/10 Air Transport Association of America and Others v Secretary of State for Energy and Climate Change [2011] ECR I-13755.

[411] Article 3 of Directive 2003/87/EC (Emissions Trading Scheme Directive): "… (a) 'allowance' means an allowance to emit one tonne of carbon dioxide equivalent during a specified period, which shall be valid only for the purposes of meeting the requirements of this Directive and shall be transferable in accordance with the provisions of this Directive; … (j) 'tonne of carbon dioxide equivalent' means one metric tonne of carbon dioxide (CO2) or an amount of any other greenhouse gas listed in Annex II with an equivalent global-warming potential".

[412] Recital 8 of Directive 2003/87/EC (Emissions Trading Scheme Directive).

[413] Point (e) of Article 6(2) of Directive 2003/87/EC (Emissions Trading Scheme Directive).

[414] Article 16(1) of Directive 2003/87/EC (Emissions Trading Scheme Directive).

the operator from the obligation to surrender an amount of allowances equal to the excess emissions)[415] and the publication of the operator's name.[416]

Trading The EU introduced its own trading system for greenhouse gas emission allowances on 1 January 2005. The system is established by Directive 2003/87/EC.[417] As a rule, these allowances are transferable[418] and recognised by the competent authorities of other Member States.[419]

The allowances are transferable in the EU between "persons within the Community"[420] but to some extent even across the EU's border "between persons within the Community and persons in third countries" under international agreements.[421] International trading is organised by the UN through the Green Development Mechanism.

There is a connection between trading in emission allowances, international emissions trading, and Member States' emission targets.[422] Emission credits are recognised even where a Member State purchases them from another country.[423]

Market-based emissions trading has been hampered by the regulatory regime that fosters investment in energy generation from renewable resources.[424] Emissions trading is discussed in Chap. 7.[425]

Carbon Capture and Storage There are plenty of legal, policy and regulatory issues surrounding the potential application of carbon capture and storage (CCS) in the EU.[426] A major concern is the risk of leakage and environmental liability.[427] In practice, however, CCS technology is not yet available. It is regarded as a

---

[415] Article 16(3) of Directive 2003/87/EC (Emissions Trading Scheme Directive).

[416] Article 16(2) of Directive 2003/87/EC (Emissions Trading Scheme Directive).

[417] Directive 2003/87/EC (Emissions Trading Scheme Directive). In Germany, the ETS Directive has been implemented by Gesetz über den Handel mit Berechtigungen zur Emission von Treibhausgasen (Treibhausgas-Emissionshandelsgesetz, TEHG).

[418] Article 12(1) of Directive 2003/87/EC (Emissions Trading Scheme Directive).

[419] Article 12(2) of Directive 2003/87/EC (Emissions Trading Scheme Directive).

[420] Article 12(1)(a) of Directive 2003/87/EC (Emissions Trading Scheme Directive).

[421] Article 12(1)(b) of Directive 2003/87/EC (Emissions Trading Scheme Directive). For mutual recognition, see Articles 25(1) and 25(2) of Directive 2003/87/EC (Emissions Trading Scheme Directive).

[422] Article 30(3) of Decision 406/2009/EC of the European Parliament and of the Council on the effort of Member States to reduce their greenhouse gas emissions to meet the Community's greenhouse gas emission reduction commitments up to 2020: "Linking the project-based mechanisms, including Joint Implementation (JI) and the Clean Development Mechanism (CDM), with the Community scheme is desirable and important to achieve the goals of both reducing global greenhouse gas emissions and increasing the cost-effective functioning of the Community scheme . . ."

[423] Article 5 of Decision 406/2009/EC.

[424] Bundesministerium für Wirtschaft und Technologie (BMWi) (2012).

[425] See, for example, Roberts R and Staples C (2008).

[426] For the regulation of CCS in the EU, see Schlacke S and Much S (2010).

[427] Tscherning R (2011), Bergsten M (2011) and Adelman DE and Duncan IJ (2011).

"bridging technology".[428] The Rotterdam Climate Initiative (RCI) is the only CCS project left in the EU. RCI wants to store carbon dioxide in underground locations, especially under the North Sea.

Nuclear Safety Member States are free under EU law to decide whether they rely on nuclear energy or not, but they have a duty to improve nuclear safety and the management of radioactive waste. There is a framework of European safety standards for nuclear power.[429]

3.7.7 RES-E and Conflicts Between Different Policy Objectives

There are obvious conflicts between the various policy objectives. As a result, there is no level playing field for electricity producers according to the present state of EU law. Electricity investments are regulation-driven (and combined with a high exposure to political and legal risk[430]) rather than market-driven. Investments and wholesale prices are influenced by state aid (Sect. 3.7.8). Laws designed to reduce carbon emissions may actually increase carbon emissions—in any case, the cost-benefit ratio of the 20/20/20 package has been rather poor.[431] At the core of these problems is the preferential treatment of electricity generated from renewable sources (RES-E).[432]

Regulation Rather Than Market Mechanisms Investments in the generation of energy from renewable sources have been increased by many legislative reforms[433] and there are various promotion strategies for renewables (see Sect. 7.2).[434]

The regulatory drivers that make investments in RES-E regulation-driven rather than market-driven include: authorisations; feed-in tariffs and alternative systems; priority access and dispatching; allocation of costs for grid connection; duties of the TSO/DSO; net metering; and guarantees of origin.

---

[428] Recital 4 of Directive 2009/31/EC (Directive on the geological storage of carbon dioxide).

[429] Directive 2009/71/Euratom of 25 June 2009 establishing a Community framework for the nuclear safety of nuclear installations; Directive 96/29/Euratom of 13 May 1996 laying down basic safety standards for the protection of the health of workers and the general public against the dangers arising from ionising radiation; Directive 2006/117/Euratom of 20 November 2006 on the supervision and control of shipments of radioactive waste and spent fuel.

[430] For example, laws may change, and EU environmental law is subject to high interpretation risk. See Beijen BA (2011).

[431] Tol RJS (2012). See also Lomborg B (2013).

[432] Generally, see also Helm D (2012).

[433] See Haas R et al. (2011); Kitzing L et al. (2012); Jones C (2010); Green R and Yatchew A (2012), pp. 83–98; Ollikka K (2013).

[434] Haas R et al. (2011), section 5.1.

The combined effect of priority authorisation, grid access, dispatching, and feed-in tariffs is to: reduce the market price for electricity; reduce incentives to invest in electricity generation from non-renewable sources; reduce the scope of the free electricity market that works on a competitive basis; and increase subventions. At the same time, dependence on the current favourable regulation and high levels of future subventions is combined with increased exposure to political and legal risk.

Components of the Preferential Treatment of RES-E The main components of the preferential treatment of RES-E include the following (see Sect. 7.2 for details):

- Authorisations. The 20 % target influences the *authorisation procedure* for the construction of new generating capacity.[435]
- Guarantees of origin. Guarantees of origin are designed to *increase demand* for electricity from renewable sources or from high-efficiency cogeneration plants. Guarantees of origin are regulated by the Directive on the promotion of the use of energy from renewable sources (RES Directive) (energy from renewable sources),[436] the Directive on the promotion of cogeneration, and the Energy Efficiency Directive (electricity produced from high-efficiency cogeneration plants).[437]
- Feed-in tariffs and alternative systems. Feed-in tariffs—in combination with priority access to the grid and priority dispatching—are the main mechanism for Member States of the EU give support to generators of electricity from renewable sources. Feed-in tariffs attract plenty of investment where they are set above the generation level and sufficiently generous.
- The choice between feed-in tariffs and alternative systems such as government tendering systems and quota-based trading systems has a major impact on investment. The Member States of the EU use many different feed-in tariff systems.[438]
- Priority access, dispatching. Preferential feed-in tariffs are complemented with priority access to the grid (subject to some security of supply constraints[439]). Member States must ensure that TSOs and DSOs (a) guarantee the transmission and distribution of electricity produced from renewable energy sources; and (b) provide for either priority access or guaranteed access to the grid-system of electricity produced from renewable energy sources. What applies to electricity from renewable sources applies to (c) electricity produced from waste or the production of combined heat and power (CHP).[440]

---

[435] Article 7(2) of Directive 2009/72/EC (Third Electricity Directive). See points c, f, g, j, and k.

[436] Article 15 of Directive 2009/28/EC (RES Directive).

[437] Recital 39 and Article 14(10) of Directive 2012/27/EU (Energy Efficiency Directive).

[438] Kitzing L et al. (2012); Jones C (2010); Haas R et al. (2011), section 6; Ollikka K (2013).

[439] Article 16(2)(c) of Directive 2009/28/EC (RES Directive).

[440] Article 16(2) of Directive 2009/28/EC (RES Directive). See also Articles 15(3) and 25(4) of Directive 2009/72/EC (Third Electricity Directive). For the basics of CHP, see, for example, Lanz M et al. (2011), section 3.3.

- Other investment incentives. Member States provide various investment incentives and investment-based tax incentives for electricity generation from renewable sources.[441]
- Allocation of costs for grid connection. As major grid investments are necessary, incentives to invest in generation installations can also depend on the allocation of costs for connecting the installation to the grid. There will be: costs for connecting the installation to the grid connection point; and costs for upgrades in the distribution network and regional network. The position of EU law is to allocate most costs to the system operators and to socialise them. The TSO is responsible for the transmission grid[442] and the DSO is responsible for the connection of microgenerators to the distribution grid.[443]
- The duties of the TSO/DSO. The duties of the system operator are designed to *increase the supply* of electricity produced from renewable sources. A system operator has a general duty to act with due regard to the environment.[444] System operators have particular RES-E duties relating to: grid access[445]; transmission and distribution[446]; dispatching[447]; combined heat and power (CHP)[448]; and tariffs.[449]
- Net metering. The introduction of net metering and net billing is designed to *increase supply*. Net metering and net billing tend to increase microgeneration that is distributed generation and often generation from renewable sources (Sect. 7.2.1).
- Signalling the use of RES-E. Firms can signal their use of RES-E in many ways. The main options are procuring certificates, procuring RES-E, power purchase agreements, and ownership of RES-E generation assets.[450]

There are thus various promotion strategies for renewables and various legislative projects designed to increase RES-E. Preferential feed-in tariffs seem to have had the biggest impact in the EU.

---

[441] See Haas R et al. (2011), sections 6.4 and 6.5.

[442] Article 12 of Directive 2009/72/EC (Third Electricity Directive).

[443] Articles 3(3) and 25 of Directive 2009/72/EC (Third Electricity Directive).

[444] Point a of Article 12 of Directive 2009/72/EC (Third Electricity Directive).

[445] Point b of Article 16(2) of Directive 2009/28/EC (RES Directive).

[446] Point a of Article 16(2) of Directive 2009/28/EC (RES Directive).

[447] In so far as the secure operation of the national electricity system permits. Point c of Article 16 (2) of Directive 2009/28/EC (RES Directive). Article 15(1) of Directive 2009/72/EC (Third Electricity Directive).

[448] Article 15(3) of Directive 2009/72/EC (Third Electricity Directive). See also Article 16(11) of Directive 2009/28/EC (RES Directive).

[449] Articles 16(7) and 16(8) of Directive 2009/28/EC (RES Directive).

[450] Global Corporate Renewable Index (CREX) 2012, section 2.2.

3.7.8 State Aid

One may ask whether the various forms of preferential treatment can be aligned with the prohibition of state aid under Article 107(1) TFEU.[451] In certain cases, state aid may be compatible with the internal market under Articles 107(2) and (3) of the Treaty.

To begin with, environmental support measures are treated in the same way as any other measures. An environmental support measure qualifies as state aid if it fulfils all the following four criteria: financing through state resources; advantage for the undertaking; selectivity; and distortion to competition and effect on trade between Member States.[452] State aid must be notified to the Commission in advance.[453]

After the entry into force of the First Electricity Directive, the Commission adopted a particular stranded costs approach[454] as state aid was not covered by the transitional provisions of the Directive.[455] The Commission permitted state aid "designed to facilitate the transition for electricity undertakings to a competitive electricity market". In particular, the Commission allowed Member States, for a certain period of time, to grant state aid "designed to compensate for the cost of commitments or guarantees that it might no longer be possible to honour on account of Directive 96/92/EC" where the stranded costs would significantly have affected the competitiveness of the undertaking concerned.

As regards preferential feed-in tariffs, the answer has depended on how the monetary flows have been organised. Are they "granted by a Member State or through State resources"?

The CJEU has discussed the distinction between state and non-state resources in the *Stardust Marine* case.[456]

[451] Article 107(1) TFEU: "Save as otherwise provided in the Treaties, any aid granted by a Member State or through State resources in any form whatsoever which distorts or threatens to distort competition by favouring certain undertakings or the production of certain goods shall, in so far as it affects trade between Member States, be incompatible with the internal market".

[452] Report from the Commission, State Aid Scoreboard – Spring 2008 Update – COM(2008), 304 final, pp. 11–12.

[453] Article 108(3) TFEU.

[454] Commission Communication relating to the methodology for analysing State aid linked to stranded costs, Commission letter SG (2001) D/290869, 6 August 2001. See also OECD/IEA (2005), pp. 44–45.

[455] Article 24 of Directive 96/92/EC (First Electricity Directive).

[456] Case C-482/99 France v Commission [2002] ECR I-04397.

It is clear that tax exemptions for RES-E are financed through state resources. They can also be regarded as selective measures as was the case in *Adria-Wien Pipeline GmbH*.[457]

In *PreussenElektra v Schleswag*,[458] private electricity distributors had a statutory duty to pay higher feed-in tariffs for RES-E. However, the CJEU refused to prohibit the use of these guaranteed and higher feed-in tariffs as there was no transfer of state resources.[459]

On the other hand, the CJEU banned a statutory surcharge to the electricity transmission rate in *Essent Netwerk*,[460] a case about the reimbursement of stranded costs. A fixed component of the electricity tariff designed to cover stranded costs was deemed unlawful also in *Iride*.[461]

Feed-in tariffs and many other aid measures are addressed by the Commission's new guidelines on public support for environmental protection and energy.[462] The Commission has identified several environmental and energy measures for which state aid under certain conditions may be compatible with the internal market under Article 107(3)(c) TFEU.[463] Schemes that were approved under the previous rules will not be affected.

The new guidelines both support Member States in reaching their 2020 climate targets and address the market distortions that may result from subsidies granted to renewable energy sources. The guidelines are designed to foster a gradual move to market-based support for renewable energy. Preferential feed-in tariffs will gradually be replaced by feed-in premiums, which expose renewable energy sources to market signals. There is a pilot phase in 2015 and 2016 to test competitive bidding procedures. There is also a special regime for small installations.

Measures that can be compatible with the internal market include, for instance: aid for energy from renewable sources; aid for energy efficiency measures, including cogeneration and district heating and district cooling; aid for generation adequacy measures; aid in the form of tradable permits; and aid in the form of reductions in or exemptions from environmental taxes.[464]

---

[457] Case C-143/99 Adria-Wien Pipeline GmbH and Wietersdorfer & Peggauer Zementwerke GmbH v Finanzlandesdirektion für Kärnten [2001] ECR I-08365. In Wienstrom, the Commission decided to raise no objections. N 317/B/2006, decision C(2006) 2964 final of 4 July 2006 (OJ 2006 C 221, p. 9). Neither did the Court find any conflict with the regulation of state aid. Case C-384/07 Wienstrom GmbH v Bundesminister für Wirtschaft und Arbeit [2008] ECR I-10393. See also paras 8–10.

[458] Case C-379/98 PreussenElektra v Schleswag [2001] ECR I-2099, paras 54, 58, and 59.

[459] See also Report from the Commission, State Aid Scoreboard – Spring 2008 Update – COM (2008), 304 final, p. 12.

[460] Case C-206/06 Essent Netwerk Noord BV and Others [2008] ECR I-05497.

[461] Case T-25/07 Iride and Iride Energia v Commission [2009] ECR II-00245. The Court distinguished the case from PreussenElektra in para 27. Appeal dismissed in C-150/09 P Iride and Iride Energia v Commission [2010] ECR I-00005.

[462] Communication from the Commission – Guidelines on State aid for environmental protection and energy 2014-2020 (2014/C 200/01).

[463] Paragraph 18 of Guidelines on State aid 2014–2020.

[464] Paragraph 18 of Guidelines on State aid 2014–2020.

There is no notification requirement if the aid either (a) does not exceed certain thresholds or (b) is granted on the basis of a competitive bidding process. For example, there is a generation capacity threshold of 250 MW for plants that generate of RES-E[465] and/or CHP and a cogeneration electricity capacity threshold of 300 MW for cogeneration installations.[466]

The Commission will consider state aid for environmental protection and energy objectives compatible with the internal market if "it leads to an increased contribution to the Union environmental or energy objectives without adversely affecting trading conditions to an extent contrary to the common interest" on the basis of "common assessment principles".[467]

New rules for operating aid schemes for RES-E will be implemented gradually in three steps. (1) In a transitional phase covering the years 2015 and 2016, the Commission wants aid for at least 5 % of the planned new RES-E capacity to be granted in a competitive bidding process on the basis of clear, transparent and non-discriminatory criteria.[468] (2) New conditions apply from 1 January 2016 to installations that are not small.[469] The conditions are designed to ensure that beneficiaries sell their electricity directly in the market and are subject to market obligations. The conditions are as follows: (a) "aid is granted as a premium in addition to the market price (premium) whereby the generators sell its electricity directly in the market"; (b) "beneficiaries are subject to standard balancing responsibilities, unless no liquid intra-day markets exist"; and (c) "measures are put in place to ensure that generators have no incentive to generate electricity under negative prices".[470] (3) From 1 January 2017, the main rule is that aid may only be granted "in a competitive bidding process on the basis of clear, transparent and non-discriminatory criteria",[471] unless the installation is a small one.[472]

Support for renewable energy sources may be granted by using market mechanisms such as green certificates that allow all renewable energy producers to benefit indirectly from guaranteed demand for their energy.[473] There can also be tradable permit schemes.[474]

---

[465] Paragraph 20(a) of Guidelines on State aid 2014–2020.

[466] Paragraph 20(d) of Guidelines on State aid 2014–2020.

[467] Paragraph 23 of Guidelines on State aid 2014–2020.

[468] Paragraph 126 of Guidelines on State aid 2014–2020.

[469] Paragraph 125 of Guidelines on State aid 2014–2020: "The conditions established in paragraph (124) do not apply to installations with an installed electricity capacity of less than 500 kW or demonstration projects, except for electricity from wind energy where an installed electricity capacity of 3 MW or 3 generation units applies".

[470] Paragraph 124 of Guidelines on State aid 2014–2020.

[471] Paragraph 126 of Guidelines on State aid 2014–2020.

[472] Paragraph 126 of Guidelines on State aid 2014–2020.

[473] Paragraph 135 of Guidelines on State aid 2014–2020.

[474] Paragraph 234 of Guidelines on State aid 2014–2020.

There is a General Block Exemption Regulation for certain categories of aid.[475] It is about to be revised.

The new Guidelines were applied by the Commission when it assessed the compatibility of the draft EEG 2014 in Germany. (a) According to EEG 2014, small installations will continue to benefit from feed-in tariffs (Einspeisevergütung) and do not have to sell on the market.[476] This part of the scheme was approved for 10 years. (b) Other producers of RES-E are supported by market premiums (Marktprämie) paid on top of the market price.[477] Until 31 December 2016, the market premiums will be determined by reference to administratively set reference values. The support to RES-E is approved until 31 December 2016. (c) Tenders will be introduced by new legislation that will apply from 1 January 2017. The tenders to be organised under EEG 2014 will be opened for up to 5 % of the tendered capacity to installations located in Member States which have concluded a cooperation agreement with Germany.[478] (d) A pilot tender will be organised for solar installations on the ground. The pilot tender will determine the level of the premiums and allocation of the aid between participants to the tender. (e) The support system under EEG 2014 is financed from the EEG surcharge (EEG-Umlage) that is to be paid to the TSO by: suppliers when electricity is supplied to end consumers in Germany[479]; and by auto-generators (Eigenversorger, electricity producers for self-consumption).[480] (f) There are reductions from the EEG-surcharge. First, reductions are provided for energy-intensive users in certain sectors because the Guidelines allow reductions on competitiveness grounds in sectors that are both electro-intensive and exposed to international trade.[481] Second, there are reductions granted to certain auto-generators: auto-generators using small installations (de minimis threshold); auto-generators using renewable energy sources; and auto-generators which are energy-intensive. Reductions granted to other types of installations will be reviewed.[482]

[475] Regulation 800/2008 (General block exemption Regulation).

[476] § 37(2) EEG 2014.

[477] § 34(1) EEG 2014.

[478] § 2 EEG 2014.

[479] § 60(1) EEG 2014.

[480] § 61 EEG 2014.

[481] See § 64 EEG 2014 and Annex 4 to EEG 2014.

[482] §§ 61(2) and 61(3) EEG 2014.

3.8 The Regulation of Marketplaces and Financial Markets

3.8.1 General Remarks

The regulation of marketplaces and financial markets is now at the core of the regulation of electricity market. The unbundling of electricity markets was designed to increase electricity trading. Larger quantities of electricity can now be traded on exchanges. Transmission capacity is increasingly allocated by means of market-based mechanisms (auctions).

The nature of the regulatory regime depends on the products, the marketplace, and the market participant. There are various kinds of traded products, marketplaces, and market participants in electricity markets. The applicable regulatory regime can thus vary depending on the context.

One can distinguish between contracts for electrical energy, transmission capacity, or emission rights. The contracts can be physical contracts, that is, contracts that are settled physically, or financial instruments such as derivatives that are settled in cash.

Electricity trading can be direct (bilateral) or centralised (exchanges and other organised marketplaces). The marketplace can be a regulated market, multilateral trading facility, or organised trading facility, and contracts can also be traded over-the-counter.

The contract is concluded between the parties, with a central counterparty, or through a middleman. In physical trade that results in the physical supply of electricity, participants range from electricity producers to end consumers. In trade that does not result in physical settlement, the number of participants can be much larger, because financial instruments can be issued and traded by many financial institutions. Moreover, many entities—the exchange operator, a clearing house—contribute to the operation of an organised marketplace. In physical markets, the TSO plays an important role.

To some extent, EU electricity markets fall within the scope of the regulatory regime for financial markets. Even when this is not the case, there are similarities between the regulatory regimes for each market.

We can have a brief look at the similarities and differences (Sect. 3.8.2) between the regulation of financial and electricity markets as well as the regulation of different marketplaces (Sect. 3.8.3). These questions are discussed in Chap. 4 in detail.

3.8.2 Similarities and Differences Between Financial Regulation and Electricity Regulation

Although electricity is a peculiar commodity, EU electricity markets and financial markets are partly governed by the same regulatory framework and there are similarities between the regulatory regimes for each market.[483]

[483] Generally, see Zenke I and Schäfer R (2009), § 1.

Similarities First, there are authorisation, concession, licence, or registration requirements. (a) An electricity wholesale market participant must register with one national regulatory authority in the EU.[484] It is characteristic of physical electricity markets that many activities require a permit. A licence may be required for: the exploitation of natural resources (the Hydrocarbons Licensing Directive,[485] the EU Emissions Trading Scheme Directive[486]); the building or operation of installations (the Third Electricity Directive,[487] for gas the Third Gas Directive[488]); and the use of land areas (zoning laws). Various permits may be necessary during the course of a construction project. There can be standard design certifications, early site permits, construction permits, and operating licenses. (b) Doing business as an investment firm can require other licenses (MiFID II[489]) and compliance with minimum capital requirements (CRD IV/CRR[490]).

Second, market participants must comply with prudential rules that regulate market conduct as well as transparency and disclosure obligations (Sect. 4.7). The rules on market conduct customarily belong to the same regulatory regime that requires an authorisation for market participants (MiFID II,[491] the Third Electricity Directive,[492] the Third Gas Directive[493]). There are similar regimes for market abuse (MAR/MAD II,[494] REMIT[495]). Moreover, the operators of regulated marketplaces or transmission systems have an obligation to adopt their own market conduct rules complementing the statutory rules.

Third, market participants that need an authorisation must comply with organisational requirements (the Third Electricity Directive,[496] the Third Gas Directive,[497] or MiFID II[498]). There are extensive regulatory compliance and risk management requirements both in the market for the physical delivery of energy

484 Second subparagraph of Article 9(1) of Regulation 1227/2011 (REMIT).

485 Directive 94/22/EC (Hydrocarbons Licensing Directive).

486 Directive 2003/87/EC (Emissions Trading Scheme Directive).

487 Directive 2009/72/EC (Third Electricity Directive). See also Communication from the Commission to the Council and the European Parliament: "Nuclear Illustrative Programme"—COM/2007/565-1, OF 4.10.2007. Licensing can include standard design certifications, early site permits, construction permits, operating licenses, or combined licenses.

488 Directive 2009/73/EC (Third Gas Directive).

489 Directive 2014/65/EU (MiFID II).

490 Directive 2013/36/EU (CRD IV); Regulation 575/2013 (CRR).

491 Directive 2014/65/EU (MiFID II).

492 Articles 12 and 25 of Directive 2009/72/EC (Third Electricity Directive).

493 Articles 3, 13, 16, 17, 25, and 27 of Directive 2009/73/EC (Third Gas Directive).

494 Regulation 596/2014 (MAR); Directive 2014/57/EU (MAD II).

495 Regulation 1227/2011 (REMIT).

496 See, for example, Articles 9, 14, 18, 19, 20, and 26 of Directive 2009/72/EC (Third Electricity Directive).

497 See, for example, Articles 9, 15, 18, 19, 20, and 26 of Directive 2009/73/EC (Third Gas Directive).

498 Directive 2014/65/EU (MiFID II).

(the Third Electricity Directive,[499] the Third Gas Directive[500]) and in financial markets (MiFID II[501]).

Fourth, the sector-specific regulation of energy markets and financial markets is complemented by general EU law. While competition law plays a particular role in energy markets, even other areas of EU law can be relevant depending on the context. State influence in national energy champions can be constrained by EU company law (and case-law on golden shares) and rules restricting state aid. Rules on state aid can further limit the preferential treatment of electricity generated from renewable sources (RES-E). The purchase of energy by public sector entities is constrained by rules on public procurement. In unbundled energy markets, the regulation of distance contracts is important in business-to-consumer sales (Sect. 2.7.5). Even other areas can be important depending on the case.[502]

Differences While electricity markets are partly governed by the same or at least a similar regulatory framework as financial markets, there are some important differences.

First, while financial markets are not constrained by physical laws, there are physical constraints on the supply of electricity. Contracts cannot be settled physically without a physical infrastructure.[503] Moreover, the system operator must maintain balance in the system. As a result, participation in physical markets is not possible without a detailed legal framework for physical clearing and settlement as well as transmission/distribution capacity, and the cost of physical products depends on the availability and cost of transmission/distribution capacity.

Second, it is relatively easy to participate in trading in financial markets, but there are high barriers to entry into physical wholesale markets. The regulation of network access and mechanisms designed to lower barriers of entry play an important role in the regulation of energy markets.

Third, while financial markets are becoming increasingly global, electricity markets are largely national or regional. The lack of cross-border transmission capacity can restrict electricity trade. For this reason, the regulation of energy markets focuses on cross-border trade and interconnectors.

Fourth, financial markets are not constrained by environmental concerns. The production of energy may cause harm to humans or the nature in the form of CO_2 emissions, hazardous substances, or otherwise. The cost of energy production can depend on emission and waste controls and the cost of emission rights. The regulation of energy markets therefore focuses on environmental aspects.

[499] Articles 6(4), 14(2), 21, and 26(2) of Directive 2009/72/EC (Third Electricity Directive).

[500] Article 21 of Directive 2009/73/EC (Third Gas Directive).

[501] Directive 2014/65/EU (MiFID II).

[502] Talus K (2010), p. 82.

[503] Generally, see Erdmann G (2009).

3.8.3 The Regulation of Marketplaces

There are differences in the regulation of marketplaces depending on the product. Where electricity supply contracts are settled physically, it is necessary to ensure that the legal framework of the marketplace is aligned with the legal framework of the TSO in addition to the regulation of energy markets. Where the contracts are settled financially, the physical constraints are less relevant and it is easier to apply the regulation of financial markets.

Financial Instruments In 2011, few electricity exchanges were regulated markets under MiFID that governed financial markets.[504] The MiFID regime has recently been modernised. MiFID has partly been recast as MiFID II[505] and partly replaced by MiFIR.[506] The central aim was to create a level playing field and ensure that all organised trading is conducted on regulated trading venues.[507]

All organised trading in financial instruments must be conducted on regulated markets, multilateral trading facilities (MTFs), or organised trading facilities (OTFs). OTFs are a new type of trading platform.[508]

Electricity contracts that must be settled physically do not fall within the scope of the MiFID II/MiFIR regime. Generally, the regulation of securities markets customarily does not apply to supply contracts. The Directive on market abuse (MAD), which regulated insider trading and market manipulation, did not apply to OTC-trading in electricity contracts or the trading of physically-settled electricity contracts (spot contracts) on an electricity exchange, because such contracts were

[504] Article 47 of Directive 2004/39/EC (MiFID); Annotated presentation of regulated markets, OJ 2011/C 209/13, 15.7.2011. For the definition of regulated markets, see Article 4(1)(14) of Directive 2004/39/EC (MiFID) and Article 4(1)(21) of Directive 2014/65/EU (MiFID II): "'regulated market' means a multilateral system operated and/or managed by a market operator, which brings together or facilitates the bringing together of multiple third-party buying and selling interests in financial instruments – in the system and in accordance with its non-discretionary rules – in a way that results in a contract, in respect of the financial instruments admitted to trading under its rules and/or systems, and which is authorised and functions regularly and in accordance with Title III of this Directive".

[505] Proposal for a Directive on markets in financial instruments, COM(2011) 656 final; Directive 2014/65/EU (MiFID II).

[506] Proposal for a Regulation on markets in financial instruments, COM(2011) 652 final; Regulation 600/2014 (MiFIR).

[507] Section 3.4.1 of the Explanatory Memorandum, COM(2011) 656 final.

[508] Article 4(1)(23) of Directive 2014/65/EU (MiFID II): "'organised trading facility' or 'OTF' means a multilateral system which is not a regulated market or an MTF and in which multiple third-party buying and selling interests in bonds, structured finance products, emission allowances or derivatives are able to interact in the system in a way that results in a contract in accordance with Title II of this Directive". See also section 3.4.1 of the Explanatory Memorandum, COM(2011) 656 final.

neither financial instruments nor admitted to trading on a regulated market.[509] The Market Abuse Regulation (MAR) that replaced MAD I refers to MiFID II definitions.[510] The Prospectus Directive does not apply to such electricity contracts as they are not regarded as securities.[511]

Physical Products Marketplaces for physical products do not fall within the scope of the MiFID II/MiFIR regime. Neither have wholesale electricity marketplaces been regulated in the Third Electricity Directive directly. The main rule is that the Third Electricity Directive permits the existence of various kinds of market organisation.[512]

In some cases, sectoral legislation nevertheless requires the use of market-based methods (auctions). Market-based methods should be used for the maintenance of reserve generation capacity,[513] balancing mechanisms,[514] the allocation of cross-border transmission capacity,[515] congestion management,[516] and the auctioning of emission allowances.[517]

The common rules for the trading of electricity in auctions and in continuous trading pave the way for a common institutional framework for power exchanges. Single day-ahead and intraday coupling is fostered by common requirements for the designation of nominated electricity market operators (NEMOs) and for their

[509] Point 3 of Article 1 of Directive 2003/6/EC (Directive on market abuse): "'Financial instrument' shall mean: ... – derivatives on commodities, – any other instrument admitted to trading on a regulated market in a Member State or for which a request for admission to trading on such a market has been made".

[510] Point 1 of Article 3(1) of Regulation 596/2014 (MAR).

[511] Recital 12 of Directive 2003/71/EC (Prospectus Directive).

[512] Recital 22 of Directive 2009/72/EC (Third Electricity Directive).

[513] Article 15(6) of Directive 2009/72/EC (Third Electricity Directive). See also recital 10 of Directive 2005/89/EC (on security of supply): "Measures which may be used to ensure that appropriate levels of generation reserve capacity are maintained should be market-based and non-discriminatory and could include measures such as contractual guarantees and arrangements, capacity options or capacity obligations. These measures could also be supplemented by other non-discriminatory instruments such as capacity payments".

[514] Article 15(6) of Directive 2009/72/EC (Third Electricity Directive). See also recital 35.

[515] Article 12(2) Regulation 714/2009 (on conditions for access to the network for cross-border exchanges in electricity). See also Article 12(6).

[516] Point 2.1 of Annex I to Regulation 714/2009: "Congestion-management methods shall be market-based in order to facilitate efficient cross-border trade. For that purpose, capacity shall be allocated only by means of explicit (capacity) or implicit (capacity and energy) auctions. Both methods may coexist on the same interconnection. For intra-day trade continuous trading may be used".

[517] Regulation 1031/2010 (Auctioning Regulation).

tasks.[518] TSOs and NEMOs will develop more detailed common terms and conditions approved by the regulatory authorities.[519]

The scope of the regulatory regime for trading in financial instruments is, in effect, enlarged by the Regulation on OTC derivatives, central counterparties and trade repositories (EMIR). EMIR has a wide scope and may concern even many electricity producers. EMIR lays down uniform requirements covering financial counterparties, non-financial counterparties (exceeding certain thresholds) and all categories of OTC derivative contracts.[520] For example, central counterparties that provide clearing services must obtain an EMIR authorisation.[521] Moreover, the market abuse regime for securities trading (MAR/MAD II)[522] is complemented by REMIT (Regulation on wholesale energy market integrity and transparency)[523] that applies to certain "wholesale energy products" such as "contracts for the supply of electricity or natural gas where delivery is in the Union".[524]

The G-20 Leaders' Pittsburgh Agreement In the past, central counterparties were not customarily used for OTC derivative instruments. The obligation to clear OTC derivatives and the increased use of central counterparties have their roots in the G-20 leaders' Pittsburgh agreement of 2009.[525]

They reached the following agreement: "All standardised OTC derivative contracts should be traded on exchanges or electronic trading platforms, where appropriate, and cleared through central counterparties by end-2012 at the latest. OTC derivative contracts should be reported to trade repositories. Non-centrally cleared contracts should be subject to higher capital requirements".

In the US, the Pittsburgh agreement was implemented by the Dodd-Frank Act.[526] On one hand, the Act requires the reporting of OTC derivative contracts

---

[518] Recitals 19 and 27 of Commission Regulation .../.. (CACM Regulation). Point 23 of Article 2 of Commission Regulation .../.. (CACM Regulation): "'nominated electricity market operator (NEMO)' means an entity designated by the competent authority to perform tasks related to single day-ahead or single intraday coupling".

[519] Recital 30 of Commission Regulation .../.. (CACM Regulation).

[520] Article 1(1) of Regulation 648/2012 (EMIR): "This Regulation lays down clearing and bilateral risk-management requirements for over-the-counter ('OTC') derivative contracts, reporting requirements for derivative contracts and uniform requirements for the performance of activities of central counterparties ('CCPs') and trade repositories". Article 1(2): "This Regulation shall apply to CCPs and their clearing members, to financial counterparties and to trade repositories. It shall apply to non-financial counterparties and trading venues where so provided".

[521] Article 14(1) of Regulation 648/2012 (EMIR): "Where a legal person established in the Union intends to provide clearing services as a CCP, it shall apply for authorisation to the competent authority of the Member State where it is established (the CCP's competent authority), in accordance with the procedure set out in Article 17".

[522] Directive 2003/6/EC (Market Abuse Directive).

[523] Regulation 1227/2011 (REMIT).

[524] Point 4 of Article 2 of Regulation 1227/2011 (REMIT).

[525] Recital 5 of Regulation 648/2012 (EMIR).

[526] Dodd-Frank Wall Street Reform and Consumer Protection Act.

and the clearing of eligible contracts. On the other, it puts in place strict capital and collateral requirements for OTC derivatives that remain bilaterally cleared. In addition, it puts in place a regulatory framework for trade repositories and upgrades the existing regulatory framework for CCPs.

In the EU, the Pittsburgh agreement was implemented by EMIR.[527] EMIR provides for: a reporting obligation for OTC derivatives; a clearing obligation for eligible OTC derivatives; measures to reduce counterparty credit risk and operational risk for bilaterally cleared OTC derivatives; common rules for central counterparties and for trade repositories[528]; and rules on the establishment of interoperability between central counterparties.

References

Adelman DE, Duncan IJ (2011) The limits of liability in promoting safe geologic sequestration of CO_2. Duke Environ Law Policy Forum 22(1):1–66. doi:10.2139/ssrn.1788350

Areeda P (1989—1990) Essential facilities: an epithet in need of limiting principles. Antitrust L J 58(3):841—853

Beijen BA (2011) The implementation of European environmental directives: are problems caused by the quality of the directives? Eur Energy Environ Law Rev 20(4):150–163

Bellantuono G (2008) Long term contracts in US and EU: where are we going? EU Energy Policy Blog

Bergman MA (2000) The Bronner case: a turning-point for the essential facilities doctrine. ECLR 21(2):59–63

Bergman MA (2005) When should an incumbent be obliged to share its infrastructure with an entrant under the general competition rules? J Ind Competition Trade 5(1):5–26

Bergsten M (2011) Environmental liability regarding carbon capture and storage (CCS) operations in the EU. Eur Energy Environ Law Rev 20(3):108–115

Berle AA, Means GC (1932) The modern corporation and private property. The Macmillan Company, New York

Bjørnebye H, Alvik I (2012) Legal analysis of contract models in a common Nordic electricity retail market: legal advantages and disadvantages with different contract approaches under a supplier centric model. A report commissioned by Nordic Energy Research

Brunet A, Shafe M (2007) Beyond Enron: regulation in energy derivatives trading. Northwestern J Int Law Bus 27(3):665–706

Bundeskartellamt (2011) Sektoruntersuchung Stromerzeugung Stromgroßhandel: Bericht gemäß § 32e Abs. 3 GWB

Bundesministerium für Wirtschaft und Technologie (BMWi) (2012) Wege zu einer wirksamen Klimapolitik. Gutachten des Wissenschaftlichen Beirats beim Bundesministerium für Wirtschaft und Technologie, Februar

Cameron PD (2007) Competition in energy markets: law and regulation in the European Union, 2nd edn. Oxford University Press, Oxford

[527] Recital 5 of Regulation 648/2012 (EMIR).

[528] Points 1–2 of Article 2 of Regulation 648/2012 (EMIR): "'CCP' means a legal person that interposes itself between the counterparties to the contracts traded on one or more financial markets, becoming the buyer to every seller and the seller to every buyer; 'trade repository' means a legal person that centrally collects and maintains the records of derivatives".

Coase RH (1937) The nature of the firm. Economica (New Series) 4(16):386–405
Commission Green Paper, Towards a European strategy for the security of energy supply, COM (2000) 769 final, 29 November 2000
Commission Green Paper, A European Strategy for Sustainable, Competitive and Secure Energy. COM(2006) 105 final, 8 March 2006
Commission Staff Working Document, Ownership Unbundling: The Commission's Practice in Assessing the Presence of Conflict of Interest Including in Case of Financial Investors, SWD (2013) 177 final, 8 May 2013
Commission staff working paper accompanying the Communication from the Commission to the European Parliament and Council – Report on the functioning of Regulation 1/2003, COM (2009) 206 final, SEC(2009) 0574 final
Commission, Antitrust: Commission increases competition in the Belgian gas market – frequently asked questions, MEMO/07/407, 11 October 2007
Commission, Public consultation on the governance framework for the European day-ahead market coupling, D(2011) 1176339, 28 November 2011
Committee on Energy and Natural Resources (2010) Financial Derivatives on Energy Markets. Senate Hearing 111-752. The U.S. Government Printing Office, Washington
Communication from the Commission, Guidance on the Commission's enforcement priorities in applying Article 82 of the EC Treaty to abusive exclusionary conduct by dominant undertakings, OJ C 45, 24.2.2009, pp 7–20
Communication from the Commission, Nuclear Illustrative Programme. COM(2007) 0565 final
Communication from the Commission, A European Strategic Energy Technology Plan: Towards a low carbon future, COM(2007) 723 final, 22 November 2007
Communication from the Commission, A policy framework for climate and energy in the period from 2020 to 2030, COM(2014) 15 final, 22 January 2014
Communication from the Commission, Inquiry pursuant to Article 17 of Regulation (EC) No 1/2003 into the European gas and electricity sectors (Final Report), SEC(2006) 1724, COM/2006/0851 final
Communication from the Commission, Action Plan for Energy Efficiency: Realising the Potential, COM(2006) 545 final, 19 October 2006
Creti A, Fumagalli E, Fumagalli E (2010) Integration of electricity markets in Europe: relevant issues for Italy. Energy Policy 38(11):6966–6976. doi:10.1016/j.enpol.2010.07.013
DG Competition (2005) DG Competition discussion paper on the application of Article 82 of the Treaty to exclusionary abuses, December
DG Competition report on energy sector inquiry, SEC(2006) 1724, 10 January 2007
EFET (2005) The past and future of European energy trading. EFET website, June
Egelund Olsen B (2010) Wind energy and local acceptance: how to get beyond the Nimby effect. Eur Energy Environ Law Rev 19(5):239–251
Eifert M (2010) Die gerichtliche Kontrolle der Entscheidungen der Bundesnetzagentur. Zeitschrift für das gesamte Handelsrecht und Wirtschaftsrecht 174(6):449–485
Energy Market Authority, Finland (2013) National Report 2013 to the Agency for the Cooperation of Energy Regulators and to the European Commission, 12 July
Energy Market Authority, Finland (2014) National report 2014 to the agency for the Cooperation of Energy Regulators and to the European Commission, 10 July
Erdmann G (2009) Grundlagen des Handels mit leitungsgebundenen Energieträgern – Existenzberechtigung herstellerunabhängiger Energiehändler. In: Zenke I, Schäfer R (eds) Energiehandel in Europa. Öl, Gas, Strom, Derivate, Zertifikate, 2nd edn. C.H. Beck, München, § 2
ERGEG (2010) Draft framework guidelines on capacity allocation and congestion management for electricity: initial impact assessment. Ref: E10-ENM-20-04, 8 September
Fried J (2010) B. Rechtliche Bewältigung des OTC-Handels. In: Schwintowski HP (ed) Handbuch Energiehandel, 2nd edn. Erich Schmidt Verlag, Berlin, pp 153–336

Geradin D, O'Donoghue R (2005) The concurrent application of competition law and regulation: the case of margin squeeze abuses in the telecommunications sector. J Comp Law Econ 1 (2):355–425. doi:10.1093/joclec/nhi009
Global Corporate Renewable Index (CREX). See Bloomberg New Energy Finance, Vestas Wind Systems A/S (2012)
Green R, Yatchew A (2012) Support schemes for renewable energy: an economic analysis. Econ Energy Environ Policy 1:83–98
Haas R, Panzer C, Resch G et al (2011) A historical review of promotion strategies for electricity from renewable energy sources in EU countries. Renewable Sustainable Energy Rev 15 (2):1003–1034. doi:10.1016/j.rser.2010.11.015
Helm D (2012) The carbon crunch: how we're getting climate change wrong – and how to fix it. Yale University Press, New Haven
ISDA (2003) Restoring confidence in U.S. energy trading markets. ISDA website, April
Jones C (2010) The European Union's policy on the development of renewable energy. In: Moselle B, Padilla J, Schmalensee R (eds) Harnessing renewable energy in electric power systems: theory, practice, policy. Earthscan, Washington, pp 233–252
Kaplow L (2010) Why (ever) define markets? Harv Law Rev 124:438–517
Keay M (2013) The EU "Target Model" for electricity markets: fit for purpose? Oxford Energy Comment. The Oxford Institute for Energy Studies website, May
Kitzing L, Mitchell C, Morthorst PE (2012) Renewable energy policies in Europe: converging or diverging? Energy Policy 51:192–201. doi:10.1016/j.enpol.2012.08.064
Kotlowski A (2009) Access rights to European energy networks – a construction site revisited. In: Delvaux B, Hunt M, Talus K (eds) EU energy law and policy issues – ELRF collection, 2nd edn. Euroconfidentiel, Brussels, pp 1–39
Kramer L (2010) Klimaschutzrecht der Europäischen Union. SZIER/RSDIE 20(3):311–337
Lanz M, Fricke B, Anthrakidis A et al (2011) CO_2-Emissionsminderung durch Ausbau, informationstechnische Vernetzung und Netzoptimierung von Anlagen dezentraler, fluktuierender und erneuerbarer Energienutzung in Deutschland. Umweltbundesamt, Climate Change 20/2011
Lipsky A, Sidak JG (1999) Essential facilities. Stanford Law Rev 51(5):1187–1249
Lokau B, Ritzau M (2009) Der Markt für Strom (empirische Darstellung). In: Zenke I, Schäfer R (eds) Energiehandel in Europa. Öl, Gas, Strom, Derivate, Zertifikate, 2nd edn. C.H. Beck, München, § 5
Lomborg B (2013) Extrem viel Geld für wenig Klimaeffekt. Frankfurter Allgemeine Zeitung, 7 October, p 18
Mäntysaari P (2010) The law of corporate finance. General principles and EU law, vol I: Cash flow, risk, agency, information. Springer, Heidelberg
Meeus L, Purchala K, Belmans R (2005) Development of the internal electricity market in Europe. Electr J 18(6):25–35. doi:10.1016/j.tej.2005.06.008
Meller E, Walter B (2009) Die Bedeutung des Energiehandels für die Energieversorgung. In: Zenke I, Schäfer R (eds) Energiehandel in Europa. Öl, Gas, Strom, Derivate, Zertifikate, 2nd edn. C.H. Beck, München, § 9
Midttun A (2001) Perspectives on commercial positioning in the deregulated European electricity markets. In: Midttun A (ed) European energy industry business strategies. Elsevier Global Energy Policy and Economics Series. Elsevier, the Netherlands, pp 1–22
Mihm A (2014a) Energieerzeuger stehen vor weiterer Talfahrt. Frankfurter Allgemeine Zeitung, 31 March, p 24
Monopolkommission (2009) Sondergutachten 54. Strom und Gas 2009: Energiemärkte im Spannungsfeld von Politik und Wettbewerb. Sondergutachten der Monopolkommission gemäß § 62 Abs. 1 EnWG
Monopolkommission (2013) Sondergutachten 65. Energie 2013: Wettbewerb in Zeiten der Energiewende. Sondergutachten der Monopolkommission gemäß § 62 Abs. 1 EnWG

Monti G (2008) Managing the intersection of utilities regulation and EC competition law. Comp Law Rev 4(2):123–145

Nield K, Pereira R (2011) Fraud on the European Union emissions trading scheme: effects, vulnerabilities and regulatory reform. Eur Energy Environ Law Rev 20(6):255–287

NordREG (2013) Road map towards a common harmonised Nordic end-user market. NordREG Report 5/2013

OECD/IEA (2005) Lessons from liberalised electricity markets. IEA, Paris

Ofgem (2008) Energy supply probe – initial findings report. Consultation, 140/08, 6 October

Ofgem (2009a) Addressing market power concerns in the electricity wholesale sector – initial policy proposals. Consultation, 30/09, 30 March

Ofgem (2009b) Liquidity in the GB wholesale energy markets, 8 June

Ollikka K (2013) Uusiutuvien energiamuotojen tukeminen. Kansantaloudellinen aikakauskirja 109(3):289–310

Pérez-Arriaga IJ, Smeers Y (2003) Guidelines on tariff setting. In: Lévêque F (ed) Transport pricing of electricity networks. Kluwer, Boston, pp 175–203. doi:10.1007/978-1-4757-3756-1_7

Petit N (2004) Circumscribing the scope of EC competition law in network industries? A comparative approach to the US Supreme Court ruling in the Trinko case. Utilities Law Rev 13(6):185–191

Pielow JC, Brunekreeft G, Ehlers E (2009) Legal and economic aspects of ownership unbundling in the EU. J World Energy Law Bus 2(2):96–116. doi:10.1093/jwelb/jwp001

Pitofski R, Patterson D, Hooks J (2002) The essential facilities doctrine under U.S. antitrust law. Antitrust Law J 70:443–462

Poncelet C (2011) The emission trading scheme directive: analysis of some contentious points. Eur Energy Environ Law Rev 20(6):245–254

Pront-van Bommel S (2011) Smart energy grids within the framework of the third energy package. Eur Energy Environ Law Rev 20(2):32–44

Raschauer N, Haumer V (2010) Energiemarktreform und Energieregulierung – Die Auswirkungen des Dritten Liberalisierungspakets auf die österreichische Regulierungsorganisation. Wirtschaftsrechtliche Blätter 24(10):489–498. doi:10.1007/s00718-010-1699-x

Report from the Commission, State Aid Scoreboard – Spring 2008 Update – COM(2008) 304 final

Roberts R, Staples C (2008) Emissions trading in the European Union. Capital Mark Law J 3 (1):5–17. doi:10.1093/cmlj/kmm036

Schlacke S, Much S (2010) Rechtsprobleme der CO_2–Sequestrierung. SZIER/RSDIE 20 (3):287–309

Scholz U, Purps S (2010) The application of EC competition law in the energy sector. J Eur Competition Law Pract 1(1):37–51. doi:10.1093/jeclap/lpp007

Spence DB (2008) Can law manage competitive energy markets? Cornell Law Rev 93:765–818

Spence DB, Prentice R (2012) The transformation of American energy markets and the problem of market power. B C Law Rev 53(1):131–202

Speta JB (2002) A common carrier approach to internet interconnection. Fed Commun Law J 54:225–279

Supponen M (2011) The influence of national and company interests on European electricity transmission investments. Dissertation, Aalto University

Talus K (2010) Vertical natural gas transportation capacity, upstream commodity contracts and EU competition law. Dissertation, University of Helsinki

Talus K (2013) EU energy law and policy. Oxford University Press, Oxford

Talus K, Wälde T (2006) Electricity interconnectors: a serious challenge for EC competition law. Competition Regul Netw Ind 7(3):355–391

Temple Lang J (1994) Defining legitimate competition: companies' duties to supply competitors and access to essential facilities. Fordham Int Law J 18:437–524

Thomas S (2004) Electricity industry reforms in smaller EU countries: EXPERIENCE from the Nordic region. University of Greenwich, Public Services International Research Unit (PSIRU). PSIRU website

Tol RJS (2012) A cost–benefit analysis of the EU 20/20/2020 package. Energy Policy 49:288–295. doi:10.1016/j.enpol.2012.06.018

Tscherning R (2011) The EU ETS rules on carbon leakage and energy intensive industry in the Federal Republic of Germany. Eur Energy Environ Law Rev 20(1):2–16

U.S. Energy Information Administration (2002) Derivatives and risk management in the petroleum, natural gas, and electricity industries, October

U.S. Dep't of Justice (2008) Competition and Monopoly: Single-Firm Conduct Under Section 2 of the Sherman Act

Van Vyve C (2014) Financial investors and the unbundling provisions for TSOs. Eur Energy Environ Law Rev 23(2):63–71

Waller SW (2008) Areeda, epithets, and essential facilities. Wisconsin Law Rev 3(2):359–386

Williamson OE (1985) The economic institutions of capitalism. Free Press, New York

Zenke I, Schäfer R (2009) Einleitung: Der Großhandel von Energie und Energieträgern in Europa. In: Zenke I, Schäfer R (eds) Energiehandel in Europa. Öl, Gas, Strom, Derivate, Zertifikate, 2nd edn. C.H. Beck, München, § 1

Part II
Marketplaces

Chapter 4
Electricity Marketplaces

4.1 General Remarks

Competitive electricity markets can be structured in two basic ways. Electricity trading can be direct (bilateral) or centralised (exchanges and other organised marketplaces).[1] This chapter focuses on the latter. OTC contracts are discussed later in this book.

Centralised trading on exchanges is a good thing to start with when you want to study electricity supply contracts, because exchange-traded contracts are standardised and relatively simple. While the contracts may be uncomplicated, trading is governed by market rules and a large legal framework that is much like the one applied in securities markets. Most of this chapter discusses issues that are regulated even in securities markets. In contrast, individually negotiated bilateral contracts are complex contracts not governed by exchange rules (Sect. 8.1). In both cases, the system operator's rules influence product specifications and physical settlement.

In this chapter, we will focus on the core NWE area. After a brief introduction to European electricity exchanges (Sect. 4.2) and the reasons causing their variation (Sect. 4.3), we will study the organisation of some financial (Sect. 4.4) and spot (Sect. 4.5) exchanges. Special attention will be paid to the reduction of counterparty risk and systemic risk through collateral requirements, margining, daily settlement, and netting (Sect. 4.6), because these questions influence the cash flow of market participants. The spot market, that is, the day-ahead and intraday market, is complemented by the balancing market, that is, the market for control reserves (Sect. 4.10). We will also study the regulation of market conduct, market abuse, and money laundering (Sect. 4.7), particular obligations under the EMIR and MiFID II/MiFIR regimes (Sect. 4.8), and market surveillance (Sect. 4.9).

---

[1] Krause T (2003), p. 4.

P. Mäntysaari, *EU Electricity Trade Law*, DOI 10.1007/978-3-319-16513-4_4

This chapter is complemented by Chap. 5 that focuses on the transmission marketplace, Chap. 6 that discusses the coupling of markets, and Chap. 7 that gives a brief introduction to the allocation of emission allowances.

4.2 Introduction to European Electricity Exchanges

The role of electricity exchanges depends on the market model. While there is no room for electricity exchanges in complete vertical integration, they play an important role in liberalised energy markets.

Electricity exchanges have many functions in liberalised energy markets. (1) They provide a distribution channel for electricity producers. (2) They increase security of supply for electricity wholesalers, retailers, and large end consumers. (3) They can also provide a marketplace for transmission capacity (Chap. 5). (4) They provide a pricing mechanism for both electricity and transmission capacity. The lack of an electricity exchange would not prevent wholesale trade, but it would mean the absence of a reliable price index. (5) Electricity exchanges facilitate the transfer and management of risk. (6) Moreover, they increase the liquidity and transparency necessary for the efficient functioning of electricity markets.[2]

European electricity exchanges emerged earlier in countries like England and Wales and the Nordic countries that were the first to liberalise their electricity markets.[3] The three most important early exchanges were ICE Futures Europe (the UK),[4] Nord Pool (the Nordic countries), and European Energy Exchange (EEX, Germany).[5]

Electricity exchanges are undergoing a process of restructuring. This requires plenty of planning and coordination between the exchanges.

In the Nordic area, Nord Pool is now divided into two exchanges. (a) Nord Pool Spot, the physical market, is operated by Nord Pool Spot AS, a company owned by the Nordic and Baltic transmission system operators. (b) The derivatives exchange is operated by NASDAQ OMX Oslo ASA that is part of the NASDAQ OMX group. The brand name for the group's commodity related activities was changed to Nasdaq Commodities in 2014. (c) Nord Pool Spot and Nasdaq Commodities used to operate N2EX in the UK market jointly. Since 1 October 2014, Nord Pool Spot is the sole operator of the short-term physical market of N2EX. Nasdaq Commodities

---

[2] Meller E and Walter B (2009), § 9, number 8.

[3] See Midttun A et al. (2001), p. 23; Thomas S (2001), p. 76.

[4] Formerly known as the International Petroleum Exchange (IPE), its name was changed after it was taken over by IntercontinentalExchange, Inc. (ICE). See, for example, Däuper O (2009), § 3, number 23.

[5] For an introduction to EEX, see, for example, CFTC letter No. 04-33 dated 25 October 2004 (in response to a no-action request).

remains the operator of the financial power market of N2EX. The transfer aims to replicate in the UK the Nordic wholesale power market model with Nasdaq Commodities operating the derivatives markets and Nord Pool Spot the short-term physical market.

There are similar structures in continental Europe. (a) EPEX Spot SE operates EPEX Spot, the spot market for Germany, France, Austria, and Switzerland. EPEX Spot SE, a French company based in Paris, is controlled by European Energy Exchange AG (EEX) directly and via Powernext SA (Powernext) with HGRT as a minority shareholder. EEX has thus assigned its power spot markets for Germany/ Austria and Switzerland to EPEX Spot.[6] (b) The derivatives market for Germany and France is operated by EEX Power Derivatives GmbH, a German company based in Leipzig and a subsidiary of EEX (80 %) with Powernext (20 %) owning the remaining shares. (c) APX-ENDEX in the Netherlands and Belgium is now divided into the spot exchange APX and the derivatives exchange ICE Endex.

Other European electricity exchanges include OMIE (the Iberian market, previously OMEL in Spain and OMIP in Portugal), POLPX (Eastern Europe), EXAA (Austria), and IPEX (Italy, also known as GME).[7]

Coordination is constrained by competition laws. For instance, Nord Pool Spot and EPEX Spot are expected to act like competitors. It is prohibited to agree on market sharing. In March 2014, the Commission fined Nord Pool Spot and EPEX Spot € 5.9 million in a cartel settlement for their non-competition agreement.[8]

On the other hand, existing market operators are also expected to co-operate as NEMOs "[f]or efficiency reasons and in order to implement single day-ahead and intraday market coupling as soon as possible",[9] but co-operation between NEMOs is "strictly limited to what is necessary for the efficient and secure design, implementation and operation of single day-ahead and intraday coupling".[10]

4.3 Variation of Electricity Marketplaces

There are many markets for wholesale electricity trade. While all open and competitive markets are constituted by a similar set of rules at a general level (Ostrom),[11] there are differences between electricity exchanges and securities exchanges, and between physical and financial electricity exchanges.

[6] EEX Exchange Rules (0031b, 22 November 2014), section 2(2).

[7] See, for example, Hünerwadel A (2007), p. 53; Karas J and Sulamaa P (2013), chapter 2.

[8] Case COMP/AT.39952—Power Exchanges, C(2014) 1204 final.

[9] Recital 14 of Commission Regulation .../.. (CACM Regulation). See also recitals 20 and 25–26.

[10] Article 7(4) of Commission Regulation .../.. (CACM Regulation).

[11] Ostrom E (2005), p. 835. The set of rules consists of position rules, boundary rules, authority rules, scope rules, aggregation rules, information rules, and payoff rules.

Obviously, there can be more marketplaces, (a) because contracts can relate to different services and rights (electricity supply, transmission capacity, or greenhouse emission rights), (b) because electricity markets are local, national, or regional, (c) because marketplaces and market participants can be regulated in different ways (as financial or physical markets under legal rules implementing EU law or national regulation), and (d) because of the benefits of specialisation and economies of scale.

Moreover, like all marketplaces, electricity wholesale markets and electricity exchanges can be organised in many ways.[12] There are many exchanges in the European electricity market with different institutional designs and traded products and sometimes overlapping market areas.[13]

Physical Supply Contracts Traded on Electricity Exchanges Few contract types that are settled physically can be traded on an electricity exchange. It would not be possible to settle contracts physically without the simultaneous availability of transmission capacity and the simultaneous generation and consumption of electricity.

Long-term contracts for the physical supply of electricity are not traded on electricity exchanges (Sect. 8.1). In practice, they require closer technical co-operation and more detailed management of the contractual (principal-agency) relationship between the parties. They are always negotiated individually.

Physical contracts can be traded on an electricity exchange provided that they are standardised short-term contracts. They are traded in the spot market or in the intraday market.

Physical Characteristics of Electricity The variety of marketplaces is partly caused by the physical characteristics of electricity.

The number of exchanges has been increased by the fact that the physical characteristics of electricity have kept electricity markets national or regional. The transmission of electricity requires lines and transmission capacity. Because of cross-border and cross-zonal congestion, there may be a weak connection between pricing on different electricity exchanges.[14]

Because of the physical characteristics of electricity, access to trading on a physical exchange must be limited. Trading on a physical exchange results not only in financial clearing and settlement but even in physical clearing and settlement. The electricity pool that can be used for supply purposes is limited, because market participants trading on the exchange must have access to the transmission grid.

The balance requirement influences the matching of bids. While the auction mechanisms are relatively uncomplicated in securities markets, a wider range of mechanisms can be used in electricity markets. Different trades can be settled at

---

[12] See Sioshansi FP (2008). See also Hogan WW (2010); Green R (2010); Hogan WW (2009).

[13] Kindler J (2008).

[14] U.S. Energy Information Administration (2002), Chapter 4.

different prices like in securities markets, or a system price may be used for different trades (Sect. 4.4.4). Because of physical constraints, market pricing must depend on a large and complex set of calculations.[15]

Because of the balance requirement, the auction mechanism and physical matching are different things. The TSO must always be responsible for the physical real-time matching of supply with demand.[16]

The balancing requirement makes it necessary to define the electricity pool that can be used for balancing purposes. This is achieved by the TSO's balancing rules. In the EU, a supplier may not obtain access to the transmission grid or a spot exchange without a contract on balancing arrangements. The supplier must comply with the TSO's balancing rules and the applicable trading rules.[17]

Real-time balancing requirements act as a constraint on the physical settlement of contracts and complicate both the settlement process and the legal framework. For instance, some electricity market transactions occur before the system constraints are fully known or the price is calculated. In extreme cases, the settlement price may be readjusted up to several months later.[18]

Financial Electricity Exchanges Similar aspects must be considered even by financial electricity exchanges. First, the underlying commodity is a contract for the physical supply of electricity. The characteristics of the market in the underlying commodity influence the characteristics of the derivates market.[19] The quality of the financial electricity market depends on the quality of the underlying physical electricity market: "Until the market for the underlying commodity is working well, it is hard for a robust derivatives market to develop".[20] Second, some of the financial contracts can be settled either in cash or physically.

However, financial electricity exchanges can attract a wider range of participants. While the physical electricity wholesale market is reserved for parties connected to the grid, there is no such requirement for financial electricity products.

[15] Hunt S and Shuttleworth G (1996), p. 156.

[16] Point (d) of Article 12 of Directive 2009/72/EC (Third Electricity Directive). See also Article 15 (1) on dispatching the generating installations and Article 15(7) on rules for balancing the electricity system.

[17] See, for example, Article 3(4) of Directive 2009/72/EC (Third Electricity Directive).

[18] *Ibid.*

[19] U.S. Energy Information Administration (2002), Chapter 4: "Barriers to the development of the electricity derivatives market are numerous: * The physical supply system is still encumbered by a 50-year-old legacy of vertical integration. * Electricity markets are subject to Federal and State regulations that are still evolving. * As a commodity, electricity has many unique aspects, including instantaneous delivery, non-storability, an interactive delivery system, and extreme price volatility. * The complexity of electricity spot markets is not conducive to common futures transactions. * There are also substantial problems with price transparency, modeling of derivative instruments, effective arbitrage, credit risk, and default risk".

[20] U.S. Energy Information Administration (2002), Chapter 4.

Financial derivatives can be used for arbitrage and speculation by banks, investment firms, and investment funds.[21]

For the same reason, there can be a larger variety of contract types traded on electricity exchanges.

Regulation The variation of marketplaces is increased by the fact that marketplaces are subject to different regulatory regimes.

The applicable regulatory regime tends to be a mix of three main components: the regulatory regime for the electricity sector (physical markets); the regulatory regime for the financial sector (financial markets and derivatives); and environmental law (greenhouse gas emission rights, Chap. 7). Each of these three main components can regulate a marketplace, market participants, products to be traded, and the market participants' activities, and they can be combined in different ways.

Moreover, market participants are regulated differently depending on their home country, the location of their activities, and how their activities fall within the scope of the relevant regulatory regimes.

Market Design Globally, differences between exchanges can partly be explained by differences in wholesale market design. They can be caused by the following factors:

- Stage and nature of liberalisation. All markets are not liberalised and the liberalised markets are not liberalised in the same way. The market design can reflect complete vertical integration or a certain type of liberalised market model.
- Independent system operator. The use of an independent system operator (TSO or ISO) is mandatory in the EU with liberalised electricity markets, but globally the use of independent system operators may depend on the country.
- Trading structure. A three-tiered trading structure consisting of a "day-ahead" market, an "hour-ahead" market, and a "real-time" market is customary in the EU, but there are countries outside the EU that have chosen another structure.[22]
- Centralisation. There can be differences relating to the level of centralisation worldwide. The two opposites are a compulsory centralised market (a gross pool) and a system where bilateral physical trading is allowed.
- Settlement price. There can be differences relating to the settlement price. Short-term trades can be settled at a uniform price or with discriminatory pricing.
- Transmission effects. Moreover, transmission effects can be treated in different ways. Whereas markets in Europe try to minimise the effect of transmission constraints on the price, markets in the US treat them explicitly.

---

[21] Godager K (2009), § 18, number 4: "Based on the market share of the groups of participants at Nord Pool it seems that approximately 1/3 of the market participants are producers, 1/3 are retailers and 1/3 are institutions without natural connection to the physical electricity business".

[22] U.S. Energy Information Administration (2002), Chapter 4.

4.4 The Organisation of Financial Electricity Exchanges in the EU

4.4.1 General Remarks

The most important electricity derivatives exchanges in the EU include Nasdaq Commodities (the Nordic countries), the EEX Power Derivatives Market (Germany and France), ICE Futures Europe (a large marketplace with most of its action in the US); and ICE Endex (Belgium and the Netherlands). It is characteristic of derivatives exchanges that they can offer competing products with underlying electricity contracts in the same countries. For example, Nasdaq Commodities offers products even for the German, UK (N2EX), and Dutch power markets.

Somebody must be responsible for the exchange. To function properly, modern exchanges need a market operator that coordinates all activities and acts as the licence-holder, if the holding of a licence is a legal requirement. Moreover, somebody must provide matching, clearing, and settlement services. There could also be a party that holds collateral, money, and other assets belonging to market participants. There can also be brokers.

It is easier to organise and regulate financial electricity exchanges than physical electricity exchanges. The absence of physical settlement reduces transaction costs and increases liquidity.[23]

The MiFID II Regime All electricity exchanges operate in a highly regulated environment. As a rule, derivative contracts that are settled financially fall within the regulatory regime for financial markets. Contracts for the physical supply of electricity do not fall within the regulatory regime for financial markets—provided that the contracts can only be settled physically. However, complicated questions of interpretation may arise where contracts for the physical supply of electricity can be settled both physically and financially.[24]

From a regulatory perspective, there are three main categories of financial electricity exchanges in the EU: venues that fall within the scope of the MiFID/MiFID II regime, venues that fall within the scope of the EMIR regime, and other venues. The scope of the MiFID II regime is very important for parties that wish to do business on an exchange.

Trading venues. Trading venues that fall within the scope of the MiFID II regime are "regulated markets", "multilateral trading facilities" (MTFs), or "organised trading facilities" (OTFs).[25] OTC markets do not fall within the scope of the

[23] Godager K (2009), § 18, number 25.

[24] See, for example, Hünerwadel A (2007), p. 58.

[25] For definitions, see point 24 (trading venue), point 21 (regulated market), point 22 (MTF) and point 23 (OTF) of Article 4(1) of Directive 2014/65/EU (MiFID II).

MiFID II regime, unless the OTC marketplace is a "multilateral system",[26] that is, an organised exchange.[27]

Contracts. In addition to trading venues, the nature of contracts is important. The scope of the MiFID II regime depends on the contracts traded on the exchange. The regime customarily applies to contracts that are settled financially. The regime can thus apply to financial electricity exchanges. Sometimes the regime applies regardless of how contracts end up being settled.[28]

Moreover, certain derivatives must be traded on trading venues that are governed by the MiFID II/MiFIR regime. There is an obligation to trade on a regulated market, MTF, or OTF where derivatives belong to a class of derivatives that has been declared subject to the trading obligation.[29] There are particular rules on trading on third country trading venues[30] or with third country financial institutions.[31]

There are similar obligations in the US under the Commodity Exchange Act (CEA) that restricts trading in futures.[32] According to the CEA, the CFTC has jurisdiction over futures contracts, that is, "contracts of sale of a commodity for future delivery". The CEA was amended by the Commodity Futures Modernization Act of 2000 (CFMA). The enactment of the CFMA brought about a 'three-tiered' layering of commodities and derivatives regulation. The greatest degree of regulation takes place on the designated contract markets, where retail futures trading occurs.[33] Futures must not be traded other than on boards of trade designated or registered as a contract market or derivatives transaction execution facility by the CFTC (subject to certain exemptions).[34] Swaps subject to mandatory clearing must also be traded through a board of trade designated as a contract market or on a registered or exempt swap execution facility.[35] However, many swap agreements are exempt transactions.[36]

---

[26] Point 19 of Article 4(1) of Directive 2014/65/EU (MiFID II).

[27] For US law, see 7 U.S.C. § 1a(37).

[28] Section C of Annex to Directive 2014/65/EU (MiFID II): "... (4) ... derivative contracts ... which may be settled physically or in cash; (5) derivative contracts ... that must be settled in cash or may be settled in cash at the option of one of the parties ... (6) derivative contracts ... that can be physically settled provided that they are traded on a regulated market, a MTF, or an OTF, except for wholesale energy products traded on an OTF that must be physically settled; (7) ... derivative contracts relating to commodities, that can be physically settled not otherwise mentioned in point 6 of this Section and not being for commercial purposes, which have the characteristics of other derivative financial instruments; ... (11) Emission allowances consisting of any units recognised for compliance with the requirements of Directive 2003/87/EC (Emissions Trading Scheme)".

[29] Article 28(1) of Regulation 600/2014 (MiFIR).

[30] Article 28(1)(d) of Regulation 600/2014 (MiFIR).

[31] Article 28(2) of Regulation 600/2014 (MiFIR).

[32] 7 USC § 6(a).

[33] duPont JC (2009), p. 865.

[34] 7 USC § 6(a).

[35] 7 USC §2(h)(8). See also 15 USC §78c-3(h) on clearing for security-based swaps.

[36] 17 CFR § 35.2 exempts swap agreements from regulation under the CEA provided they are entered into by eligible swap participants, are customized agreements, the creditworthiness of a party subject to the contract was a material consideration in determining the terms of the agreement, and the agreement was not entered into and traded on or through a multilateral transaction facility.

EMIR and Mandatory Clearing The MiFID II regime is complemented by EMIR that lays down mandatory clearing obligations for some OTC derivatives.[37] Consequently, there must be clearing members and other market participants that deal through clearing members.[38]

In the US, futures trading is a regulated activity.[39] Clearing is required for any swap which the CFTC or SEC has decided should be required to be cleared.[40] The requirement was inserted into the Commodity Exchange Act by the Dodd-Frank Act.[41] The Commodity Exchange Act sets out five factors to be considered by the Commission in reviewing a swap or class of swaps for mandatory clearing.[42] There is a connection between mandatory clearing and the requirement that swaps subject to mandatory clearing must be traded on a designated contract market or swap execution facility.[43]

The distinction between clearing members and other members or clients makes it easier for electricity producers to trade. The distinction is also important for credit institutions that can play two kinds of roles in electricity derivatives markets. First, credit institutions may fulfil margin requirements and provide guarantees on behalf of market participants and act as lenders to them. Second, they can act as general clearing members responsible for the settlement of market participants' duties. In the latter case, credit institutions assume the counterparty risk.[44]

This may bring benefits, because a credit institution tends to have information about its customers' total financial position and ability to settle the transactions, and because a credit institution that acts as a general clearing member for several customers and may be able to net some of the positions in the margin payment process.

Credit institutions in the EU customarily act as general clearing members in the electricity derivatives market.[45] When they do, they must comply with capital requirements for their positions. They must also comply with rules on large exposures. These rules can raise concerns for credit institutions, because some energy firms are very large and have large exposures.[46]

In the following, we can briefly study the regulation of the most important service providers in the light of the practices of major electricity derivatives exchanges. Similar and related issues are discussed in detail in the context of spot markets (Sect. 4.5).

[37] Article 4(1) of Regulation 648/2012 (EMIR).

[38] Recital 33 and points 14–15 of Article 2 of Regulation 648/2012 (EMIR).

[39] 7 USC § 6(a).

[40] 7 USC §2(h)(1)(A) and 7 USC §2(h)(2)(A)(i).

[41] Section 723(a)(3) of the Dodd-Frank Act.

[42] 7 USC § 2(h)(1)(D)(ii).

[43] 7 USC § 2(h)(8)(A).

[44] Godager K (2009), § 18, number 29.

[45] Godager K (2009), § 18, number 28.

[46] Godager K (2009), § 18, number 30.

4.4.2 The Operator

A financial electricity exchange has an operator that coordinates the exchange's activities. The operator makes the rules and decides on access to trading. In the legal sense, one could distinguish between the exchange/market/system/firm, a person that actually manages it, and the business form/legal person.[47] Depending on the context, the operator could thus be the exchange/market/system itself, the legal person that the exchange/market/system belongs to, or a person that actually operates the exchange/market/system.[48] If the exchange needs an authorisation, the authorisation is given to the system, but both the system and the operator must comply with the requirements[49] (for the scope of the MiFID II regime, see Sects. 4.8.2 and 4.9). The regulation of authorisation under MiFID II can be complex.[50]

An operator can operate (a) one or more markets (b) in one or more countries (c) on its own or in cooperation with another entity or entities. The most important electricity derivatives exchanges in the EU are regulated in different ways and monitored by different regulatory authorities.

Nasdaq Commodities Nasdaq Commodities is the Nordic marketplace operated by NASDAQ OMX Oslo ASA, a Norwegian company authorised as a commodity derivatives exchange in Norway under the Norwegian Act on Exchanges.[51] It is a regulated market under MiFID[52] and supervised by Finanstilsynet (the Financial Supervisory Authority of Norway).[53] In addition, Nasdaq Commodities is a

[47] In German law, it is traditionally distinguished between the firm (das Unternehmen) and the legal entity as its carrier (Unternehmensträger).

[48] This is reflected in EU law as well. Point 18 of Article 4(1) of Directive 2014/65/EU (MiFID II): "'market operator' means a person or persons who manages and/or operates the business of a regulated market and may be the regulated market itself".

[49] Article 5(1) of Directive 2014/65/EU (MiFID II). Section A of Annex I to Directive 2014/65/EU (MiFID II): "Investment services and activities . . . (8) Operation of an MTF; (9) Operation of an OTF". Article 5(2) of Directive 2014/65/EU (MiFID II): "By way of derogation from paragraph 1, Member States shall authorise any market operator to operate an MTF or an OTF, subject to the prior verification of their compliance with this Chapter". For regulated markets, see Article 44 of Directive 2014/65/EU (MiFID II).

[50] For German law, see § 4(1) BörsG: "Die Errichtung einer Börse bedarf der schriftlichen Erlaubnis der Börsenaufsichtsbehörde. "For the nature of an exchange, see § 2(1), § 5(1) and § 2(5) BörsG.

[51] § 33(1) of lov om regulerte markeder (børsloven, Act on Exchanges), § 33(1): "Virksomhet som børs kan bare drives av foretak som har tillatelse til dette fra departementet. Foretak som ikke har tillatelse som børs etter denne lov, kan ikke benytte betegnelsen børs i eller som tillegg til sitt navn, eller ved omtale av sin virksomhet, dersom bruken er egnet til å gi inntrykk av at foretaket har tillatelse etter denne loven".

[52] Annotated presentation of regulated markets and national provisions implementing relevant requirements of MiFID (Directive 2004/39/EC of the European Parliament and of the Council), OJ C 209, 15.7.2011, pp. 21–28.

[53] § 1 of lov om tilsynet med finansinstitusjoner mv. (finanstilsynsloven).

marketplace for NASDAQ OMX UK Power Futures. The central counterparty and clearing house is NASDAQ OMX Clearing AB.[54]

N2EX There is a connection between the Nordic marketplace and N2EX. N2EX used to be a joint venture. In 2010, the Futures & Options Association (FOA) chose the market operated by NASDAQ OMX Commodities Europe (now known as Nasdaq Commodities) and Nord Pool Spot as the preferred marketplace for the trading of UK electricity contracts. On 1 October 2014, Nord Pool Spot took over the physical markets of N2EX. Nasdaq Commodities continued to operate the financial markets of N2EX.

Before the takeover on 1 October 2014, the party acting as clearing house and central counterparty on N2EX was NASDAQ OMX Clearing AB (NOMX Clearing).

Formerly known as NASDAQ OMX Stockholm AB, the company was renamed in September 2013. Its exchange-related operations were moved to a separate company that assumed the name NASDAQ OMX Stockholm AB. The reason was compliance with EMIR.[55] NASDAQ OMX Clearing AB is authorised in Sweden and in Norway where it is acting through its Norwegian branch NASDAQ OMX Oslo NUF.[56] It was the first clearing house in Europe to submit an application for a re-authorisation of the clearing house under EMIR.[57]

NASDAQ OMX Clearing AB operates within the scope of an exemption from the need for UK authorisation. It applied for Recognised Overseas Clearing House (ROCH) status in the UK in 2011 when it was still known as NASDAQ OMX Stockholm AB.[58] ROCH status would have given it more flexibility and regulatory certainty in the way it conducted its business related to UK. However, an EMIR authorisation is effective for the entire territory of the EU.[59]

On 1 October 2014, the clearing and central counterparty functions relating to the physical markets of N2EX were transferred to Nord Pool Spot AS.

The EEX Power Derivatives Market EEX is a regulated market under MiFID and a licenced exchange under the German Exchange Act (BörsG).[60] Its operating entity

[54] NASDAQ OMX Clearing AB, General Terms, Clearing Rules, Commodity Derivatives (9 June 2014), section 1.2; NASDAQ OMX Oslo ASA and NASDAQ OMX Clearing AB, Trading Appendix 1/Clearing Appendix 1, Definitions, Commodity Derivatives (7 April 2014).

[55] NASDAQ OMX, press release of 21 August 2013.

[56] NASDAQ OMX, Trading Appendix 1/Clearing Appendix 1, Definitions, Commodity Derivatives (7 April 2014): "Clearinghouse means NASDAQ OMX Clearing AB, a Swedish company with reg. no 556383-9058 in the Swedish company register, acting through its Norwegian branch NASDAQ OMX Oslo NUF with reg. no 994 583 352 in the Norwegian company register".

[57] Article 14(1) of Regulation 648/2012 (EMIR): "Where a legal person established in the Union intends to provide clearing services as a CCP, it shall apply for authorisation to the competent authority of the Member State where it is established (the CCP's competent authority), in accordance with the procedure set out in Article 17".

[58] Under sections 288 and 292 of the Financial Services and Markets Act 2000 (FSMA).

[59] Article 14(2) of Regulation 648/2012 (EMIR). Article 14(5) of Regulation 648/2012 (EMIR): "Authorisation referred to in paragraph 1 shall not prevent Member States from adopting or continuing to apply, in respect of CCPs established in their territory, additional requirements including certain requirements for authorisation under Directive 2006/48/EC".

[60] § 2 BörsG.

European Energy Exchange AG is regulated under the German Exchange Act. In 2011, Eurex Group acquired a majority stake in European Energy Exchange AG. The sole shareholder of Eurex is Deutsche Börse Group.

EEX consists of several sub-markets. A sub-market of EEX, the EEX Power Derivatives Market is the electricity derivatives market for Germany and France. The EEX Power Derivatives Market is jointly operated by European Energy Exchange AG through its subsidiary EEX Power Derivatives GmbH in Leipzig.[61]

The competent supervisory authority for the exchange is Sächsisches Staatsministerium für Wirtschaft und Arbeit (the Saxon Ministry for Economic Affairs and Labour) in Dresden.[62] BaFin (Bundesanstalt für Finanzdienstleistungsaufsicht, the Federal Financial Supervisory Authority) is responsible for its share of supervision under the German Securities Trading Act (WpHG). In particular, BaFin is responsible for supervising the prohibition of insider trading and market manipulation.[63]

The central counterparty and clearing house is European Commodity Clearing AG (ECC) in Leipzig.[64] It is authorised as a central counterparty under German law.[65] At the national level it is supervised by BaFin and the Bundesbank.

---

[61] EEX Exchange Rules (0031b, 22 November 2014), § 2(1): "EEX AG is operating the exchange. EEX AG operates the EEX Power Derivatives Market through EEX Power Derivatives GmbH, EEX Gas Market through EGEX European Gas Exchange GmbH and EEX Emission Market through Global Environmental Exchange GmbH. EEX AG itself is operating EEX Coal Market". See also § 1(1): "These Exchange Rules govern the organisation of the Spot and Commodity Derivatives Exchange, the European Energy Exchange (EEX) with the following lines of business: – Sub-market of EEX Power Derivatives Market for derivatives trading in Power, – Sub-market of EEX Gas Market for spot and derivatives trading in natural gas, – Sub-market of EEX Emission Market for spot and derivatives trading in emission rights, – Sub-market of EEX Coal Market for derivatives trading in Coal".

[62] § 3(1) BörsG; Annotated presentation of regulated markets and national provisions implementing relevant requirements of MiFID (Directive 2004/39/EC of the European Parliament and of the Council), OJ C 209, 15.7.2011, pp. 21–28.

[63] § 14 WpHG (insider trading) and § 20a WpHG (market manipulation).

[64] EPEX Spot Exchange Rules (13 May 2014), Article 1.5: "European Commodity Clearing AG has been designated by EPEX Spot SE as the Clearing House of the Exchange. As the Clearing House it acts as the Central Counterparty for Payment and Delivery of the contracts traded or registered at the Exchange. The rules and proceedings of ECC are stated in the ECC Clearing Conditions in its current version.
Clearing Houses are credit institutions that handle the clearing of Contracts traded on EPEX Spot, in accordance with the specific procedures for each type of Product. In a given Market Segment, the Clearing House operates under the terms of an agreement signed with the Clearing Members designated by the Exchange Members".

[65] § 1(1) of the Banking Act (KWG, Kreditwesengesetz): "Kreditinstitute sind Unternehmen, die Bankgeschäfte gewerbsmäßig oder in einem Umfang betreiben, der einen in kaufmännischer Weise eingerichteten Geschäftsbetrieb erfordert. Bankgeschäfte sind ... 12. die Tätigkeit als zentraler Kontrahent im Sinne von Absatz 31". § 1(31) KWG: "Ein zentraler Kontrahent ist ein Unternehmen, das bei Kaufverträgen innerhalb eines oder mehrerer Finanzmärkte zwischen den Käufer und den Verkäufer geschaltet wird, um als Vertragspartner für jeden der beiden zu dienen, und dessen Forderungen aus Kontrahentenausfallrisiken gegenüber allen Teilnehmern an seinen Systemen auf Tagesbasis hinreichend besichert sind".

Eurex Clearing AG (ECAG) provides clearing services for transactions in certain markets and in certain products (co-operation products) as a central counterparty (Sub-CCP) based on a separate agreement (CCP-Sub-CCP Agreement).

ICE Futures Europe UK electricity futures can also be traded on ICE Futures Europe in London. ICE Futures Europe is operated and owned by Intercontinenta-lExchange, Inc., a Delaware company (ICE).

The status of ICE Futures Europe is particularly interesting, because ICE Futures Europe has connections to many regulatory regimes. First, it is a regulated market under MiFID.[66] Second, it is a Recognised Investment Exchange (RIE) and a Recognised Auction Platform (RAP) supervised by the Financial Conduct Authority (FCA) in the UK.[67] Recognition as a Recognised Investment Exchange under the Financial Services and Markets Act 2000 gives an exemption from the need to be authorised to carry on a regulated activities in the UK. As an RIP, ICE is permitted to operate an auction platform for the purposes of auctioning primary emission allowances under Phase III of the EU Emissions Trading Scheme. Third, ICE is an Exempt Commercial Market (ECM) in the US.

Unlike ICE Futures Europe, ICE's US competitor NYMEX is a Designated Contract Market (DCM) and Self-Regulatory Organization (SRO). It is therefore subject to full oversight by the Commodity Futures Trading Commission (CFTC) in the US. ICE is subject to less US regulation, in particular because it trades its energy futures overseas through ICE Futures Europe.[68]

ICE Endex Futures Exchange and APX-ENDEX The roots of ICE Endex lie in APX-ENDEX. APX-ENDEX Holding B.V. was a holding company that owned operators of spot markets and derivatives markets in the Netherlands, Belgium, and the UK. It was behind APX-ENDEX Derivatives and APX Power UK.

APX-ENDEX Derivatives was the electricity derivatives market for the Netherlands and Belgium. It was a regulated market operated by APX-ENDEX Derivatives B.V., a Dutch company.[69] APX-ENDEX Derivatives B.V. was supervised by the Netherlands Authority for the Financial Markets and by the Dutch Central Bank. APX Power UK was a market operated by APX Commodities Limited, a company authorised by the UK Financial Services Authority (FSA) to act as a Multilateral Trading Facility (MTF).

ICE Endex Futures Exchange was established in March 2013 after the split of APX-ENDEX into a derivatives exchange and an exchange for physical products.

It is a regulated market operated by ICE Endex Derivatives B.V., a Dutch company. The company's majority shareholder is ICE with N.V. Nederlandse Gasunie as a minority shareholder. ICE Clear Europe Limited, a company registered in England & Wales, acts

---

[66] *Ibid.*

[67] The Financial Services Authority (FSA) used to be the sole body responsible for financial services regulation in the UK. On 1 April 2013, a new system came into effect. The FSA was replaced by two new regulators: the Financial Conduct Authority (FCA); and the Prudential Regulation Authority (PRA).

[68] Murray JV (2009), pp. 320–322; Markham JW and Harty DJ (2008), p. 921; Diaz-Rainey I et al. (2011).

[69] Annotated presentation of regulated markets and national provisions implementing relevant requirements of MiFID (Directive 2004/39/EC of the European Parliament and of the Council), OJ C 209, 15.7.2011, pp. 21–28.

as the central counterparty and clearing house. ICE Clear Europe is a recognised clearing house under section 288 of the Financial Services and Markets Act 2000 supervised by the Bank of England.

Phase III Auction Platforms Most emission allowances are auctioned in Phase III of the EU ETS (Sect. 7.2). The procedure is based on the Auctioning Regulation[70] that also lays down the selection procedure for auction platforms.[71] There are several auction platforms. (a) There is a common auction platform.[72] The Commission has appointed European Energy Exchange AG (EEX) as the first common platform. (b) However, a Member State may decide not to participate in the joint action.[73] Germany, Poland, and the UK have decided to opt out of the common platform and to appoint their own auction platforms. EEX has been selected by Germany as its opt-out auction platform. The UK has appointed ICE Futures Europe as its opt-out auction platform.

4.4.3 Access to Trading

General Remarks

Electricity producers can have access to trading as members, non-members, or clients. They do not necessarily have to become exchange members that trade for their own behalf. Access to trading on a financial electricity exchange is limited in four main ways. First, there is sectoral legislation on access to trading and access to clearing. Second, there is sectoral legislation on authorisations. Third, financial electricity exchanges have their own trading rules. Fourth, there may be legal restrictions on the power of an entity to use derivative instruments.

Non-discrimination As regards access to trading on a regulated market, the main rule is non-discrimination. Markets governed by the MiFID II regime must have "transparent and non-discriminatory rules, based on objective criteria, governing access to or membership of the regulated market".[74]

[70] Regulation 1031/2010 (Auctioning Regulation).

[71] Recital 34 of Regulation 1031/2010 (Auctioning Regulation).

[72] Recital 7 and Article 26 of Regulation 1031/2010 (Auctioning Regulation).

[73] Article 30 of Regulation 1031/2010 (Auctioning Regulation).

[74] Article 53(1) of Directive 2014/65/EU (MiFID II). See also Article 53(2) of Directive 2014/65/EU (MiFID II): "The rules referred to in paragraph 1 shall specify any obligations for the members or participants arising from: (a) the constitution and administration of the regulated market; (b) rules relating to transactions on the market; (c) professional standards imposed on the staff of the investment firms or credit institutions that are operating on the market; (d) the conditions established, for members or participants other than investment firms and credit institutions, under paragraph 3; (e) the rules and procedures for the clearing and settlement of transactions concluded on the regulated market".

Direct and Indirect Access Member States must also ensure that the rules on access to or membership of the regulated market provide for the "direct or remote participation of investment firms and credit institutions".[75] The rules on access to the regulated market are complemented by rules on "direct and indirect access to CCP, clearing and settlement systems".[76]

Access can thus be direct or indirect. (a) Financial electricity exchanges distinguish between exchange members (clearing members or non-clearing members) that have direct access to trading and non-members that may not trade directly. Exchange members must comply with margin and collateral requirements and accept netting (Sect. 4.4.5). (b) On the other hand, non-members may be able to trade indirectly, that is, bilaterally with exchange members. While clearing members are contract parties of the central counterparty, a non-member or a non-clearing member has a clearing member as its own contract party. The same margining, clearing, settlement, and netting requirements apply either directly or indirectly.

Entities There are some restrictions on who may be admitted as member or participant. Regulated markets and MTFs are subject to similar requirements.[77] They may admit as members or participants "persons who: (a) are of sufficient good repute; (b) have a sufficient level of trading ability, competence and experience; (c) have, where applicable, adequate organisational arrangements; (d) have sufficient resources for the role they are to perform, taking into account the different financial arrangements that the regulated market [or MTF] may have established in order to guarantee the adequate settlement of transactions".[78]

Authorisation Some market participants that trade in derivatives need an authorisation under the MiFID II regime (Sect. 4.10). There is thus a difference between access to financial electricity markets and access to electricity spot markets. Access to electricity spot markets does not depend on whether or not the firm has an authorisation under the MiFID II regime.

However, exemptions from the authorisation requirements play an important role in commodities derivatives markets. There is no requirement to apply to any regulatory authority for an exemption under the MiFID II regime (or EMIR). Their scope has been reduced.

There are stricter authorisation requirements in Switzerland. According to Swiss law, only securities traders (Effektenhändler) may have access to an exchange. These securities traders are authorised and monitored by FINMA. A Swiss company cannot trade on financial electricity exchanges in the EU without having obtained a Swiss authorisation as a securities trader (Effektenhändler). There is no difference between financial and physical settlement. The financial electricity exchanges that permit remote access to

---

[75] Article 53(5) of Directive 2014/65/EU (MiFID II).

[76] Article 37 of Directive 2014/65/EU (MiFID II).

[77] See recital 14 and Article 19(2) of Directive 2014/65/EU (MiFID II).

[78] Article 53(3) of Directive 2014/65/EU (MiFID II).

Swiss market participants are regarded as foreign exchanges that need an authorisation under Swiss law.[79]

There are registrations requirements in the US under the Commodity Exchange Act (7 USC Chapter 1).[80] It is unlawful for any person to act as a swap/SBS dealer (swap/ "security-based swap" dealer), a futures commission merchant, or an MSP/MSBSP ("major swap participant"/"major security-based swap participant") unless registered as one.[81] There are nevertheless exemptions from the registration requirement. For instance, certain financing affiliates of commercial end-users may be excluded from the definition of MSPs.[82]

Where an entity needs an authorisation under the MiFID II regime, the entity must also comply with prudential requirements. They consist of capital adequacy requirements and large exposure restrictions (Sect. 4.10), including rules on the protection of client assets. The MiFID II regime is complemented by EMIR that imposes prudential requirements on central counterparties. Moreover, where an entity subject to EMIR enters into an uncleared OTC derivative contract, the entity is required to ensure that appropriate risk mitigation arrangements are in place, including "accurate and appropriate exchange of collateral".

In the US, swap/SBS dealers and MSPs/MSBSPs are subject to prudential requirements set by the CFTC/SEC (or, if applicable, the relevant prudential regulator related to capital, margin, and other prudential requirements). Dealers and MSPs/MSBSPs are also subject to rules related to segregation and risk management.[83]

Transactions There can be restrictions on the entity's power to enter into derivative contracts. While some restrictions are more closely related to the person or entity using derivatives, others are more closely related to the instruments. Both types of restrictions can be general or sector-specific.

Some restrictions apply to certain types of entities only. For example, the capacity and power of a limited-liability company to enter into transactions is limited,[84] and insurance firms must comply with investment restrictions.[85]

There are also restrictions that are more closely related to the instruments. For instance, the prohibition of market manipulation applies to certain instruments (Sect. 4.7).

[79] For Swiss law, see Hünerwadel A (2007), p. 59. See Art. 37 BEHG and Art. 14 BEHV (authorisation for foreign exchanges). Art. 2 letter B and Art. 7 BEHG (regulated access to trading).

[80] See, for example, 7 USC § 6d(f)(1) on the registration requirement for dealing in swaps.

[81] 7 U.S.C. §§6d(f) and 6 s(a) and 15 U.S.C. §§ 78c-5(a) and 78o-8(a).

[82] 7 U.S.C. §1a and 15 U.S.C. §78c.

[83] 7 U.S.C. §6 s and 15 U.S.C. §78o-8.

[84] For counterparty corporate risk, see Mäntysaari P (2010b), section 6.2.

[85] Article 132(1) and second subparagraph of Article 132(4) of Directive 2009/138/EC (Solvency II) (recast).

One might also ask whether the Regulation on short selling, which restricts uncovered short sales in shares and in sovereign debt[86] and lays down transparency obligations,[87] applies to the short selling of commodity derivatives.[88] The better alternative would seem to be no.[89] Commodity derivatives fall within the scope of MiFIR rather than the Regulation on short selling.[90] MiFIR confers intervention powers on the ESMA and Member States' competent authorities.[91]

In the US, there are more restrictions on how certain entities may enter into derivatives contracts. The Commodity Exchange Act provides that a market participant must be an "eligible contract participant"[92] unless the transaction is entered into on, or subject to the rules of, a contract market or a SBS transaction effected on a registered national securities exchange.

Exchange Members and Non-members

Exchange Members Exchange members may trade on the exchange in various ways depending on the exchange. On one hand, a member can trade directly or through a clearing member. On the other, a member can trade in its own name for its own account, for the account of other members, or for the account of a third party.

Exchange members include electricity producers, distributors, utilities, large consumers (often in energy-intensive industries), brokers, financial institutions, investment firms, funds, and banks that have been accepted as exchange members. Many of them are thus regulated investment firms that must comply with the MiFID

[86] Articles 12 and 13 of Regulation 236/2012 (on short selling and certain aspects of credit default swaps).

[87] See recital 10 of Regulation 236/2012 (on short selling and certain aspects of credit default swaps).

[88] Article 1(1) of Regulation 236/2012 (on short selling and certain aspects of credit default swaps): "This Regulation shall apply to the following: (a) financial instruments ... (b) derivatives ... that relate to a financial instrument ..." Article 1(2) of Regulation 236/2012 (on short selling and certain aspects of credit default swaps): "Articles 18, 20 and 23 to 30 shall apply to all financial instruments within the meaning of point (a) of Article 2(1)". Article 2(1) of Regulation 236/2012 (on short selling and certain aspects of credit default swaps): "For the purpose of this Regulation, the following definitions apply: (a) 'financial instrument' means an instrument listed in Section C of Annex I to Directive 2004/39/EC; ..."

[89] See, for example, IMF (2013), Chapter 2: "Finally, as regards policy, the results do not justify the recent ban imposed in Europe on uncovered purchases of SCDS, as it may result in unintended consequences that could negatively affect market liquidity and cause dislocations in other markets. The regulatory reforms underway for over-the-counter (OTC) derivatives generally represent a better avenue to countering any deleterious effects of SCDS markets".

[90] See Article 2(1)(b) of Regulation 236/2012 (on short selling and certain aspects of credit default swaps).

[91] Article 1(1) of Regulation 600/2014 (MiFIR): "This Regulation establishes uniform requirements in relation to the following: ... (e) product intervention powers of competent authorities, ESMA and EBA and powers of ESMA on position management controls and position limits; ..."

[92] 7 USC § 1a(18).

II regime. In contrast, it would be unusual for a firm active in the physical supply of energy to be a regulated investment firm.[93]

> Physical and financial electricity markets share some market participants, but it is a rule of thumb that an electricity producer cannot have trading in financial markets as its core activity. The reasons are both commercial and legal. The Enron case is an example of the commercial reasons.[94]

Clearing Members A clearing member is the contract party for both the CCP and non-clearing members. In other words, clearing members are members that assume responsibility for ensuring the performance of contracts entered into by other market participants and the responsibility for discharging the financial obligations arising from that participation.[95] While the CCP's exposure to counterparty risk is limited to clearing members, clearing members are exposed to counterparty risk in their dealings with non-clearing members and non-members. Consequently, clearing members bear much of the counterparty risk.[96]

Clearing members need an authorisation as regulated investment firms. Clearing firms are investment firms, because (a) clearing members provide investment services relating to financial instruments[97] and (b) the wording of MiFID II, MiFIR, and EMIR distinguishes between clearing members (that are investment firms) and their clients (that may or may not be investment firms).[98] Many of the duties of clearing members have been set out in a Commission Delegated Regulation supplementing EMIR.[99]

---

[93] CESR and ERGEG advice to the European Commission in the context of the Third Energy Package: Responses to the fact-finding questions of the mandate C.1–C.3 and E.12–E.17 (CESR/08–527) (July 2008), C.1: "... The majority of countries (22) indicated that there are no undertakings which are active in supply of electricity and at the same time have a license of an investment firm. In case that there are such companies the numbers are relatively low ..."

[94] ISDA (2003), p. 9: "A large proportion of Enron's losses were the result of trying to reconcile two conflicting strategies: one was to invest in energy, telecommunications, and other technology businesses, which required substantial debt; the second was to grow into a major dealer in swaps, which required substantial creditworthiness".

[95] For definitions, see points 1 (CCP), 14 (clearing member) and 15 (client) of Article 2 of Regulation 648/2012 (EMIR).

[96] Pilgram T (2010), p. 379, point 697.

[97] Section A of Annex I to Directive 2014/65/EU (MiFID II): "(1) Reception and transmission of orders in relation to one or more financial instruments; (2) Execution of orders on behalf of clients; (3) Dealing on own account ..."

[98] See, for example, recital 33 and Articles 1(2), 4(3), 2(14), and 2(15) of Regulation 648/2012 (EMIR); Articles 29(2) and 30(1) of Regulation 600/2014 (MiFIR); Article 17(6) of Directive 2014/65/EU (MiFID II).

[99] Commission Delegated Regulation (EU) No 149/2013 of 19 December 2012 supplementing Regulation (EU) No 648/2012 of the European Parliament and of the Council with regard to regulatory technical standards on indirect clearing arrangements, the clearing obligation, the public register, access to a trading venue, non-financial counterparties, and risk mitigation techniques for OTC derivatives contracts not cleared by a CCP.

To obtain an authorisation, clearing members must fulfil the MiFID II requirements (Sect. 4.8). For instance, the main rule is that an investment firm must be incorporated in a Member State of the EU, a Member State of the EES, or Switzerland.[100]

Clearing members have an obligation to make margin payments to the central counterparty and even other contributions (Sect. 4.4.5). Daily margin calls are the norm. In the EU, it is a legal requirement under EMIR that applies to organised OTC trading and imposes prudential requirements on central counterparties. The prudential requirements include exposure management, margins, a default fund, and even other funds such as a clearing fund.[101] In OTC markets, a central counterparty collects margins on an intraday basis.[102]

Clearing members not only make margin payments. To reduce their own capital needs and risk exposure, clearing members collect similar payments from their clients.

Market-Makers Market-makers are an alternative way to match bids in financial electricity markets. A market-maker is a party that has a duty to supply bid and ask quotes and to enter into transactions on such a basis.

> This can be illustrated with EEX. The exchange rules of EEX facilitate the business of market-makers.[103] The Board of Management of EEX may decide that market-making will be used for the trading of certain products. An exchange participant may then apply for admission as a market-maker for one or several products. The market-maker assumes the obligation to simultaneously enter limited bid and ask orders (quotes) into the EEX trading system at any time during trading hours and to do business based on such quotes.[104]

Non-clearing Members While clearing members are investment firms on financial electricity exchanges, exchange members that deal through clearing members are regarded as clients.[105] Clients are not investment firms under the MiFID II in their capacity as clients.[106]

In the past, exchange members could trade for the account of other members without being regarded as investment firms, provided that a clearing member was

[100] Article 5(1) of Directive 2014/65/EU (MiFID II) and recital 28 of Directive 2004/39/EC (MiFID).

[101] Articles 41(1), 42 and 43(1) of Regulation 648/2012 (EMIR). See also recital 65.

[102] Article 41(3) of Regulation 648/2012 (EMIR). See, for example, NASDAQ OMX, General Terms, Clearing Rules, Commodity Derivatives (7 April 2014), section 5.1.1: "The Clearinghouse determines the Margin Requirement(s) for each Account Holder on each Bank Day ..."

[103] EEX Exchange Rules (0031b, 22 November 2014), section 4.3. See also Härle PA (2010), p. 406, points 747–748.

[104] EEX Exchange Rules (0031b, 22 November 2014), § 30(1).

[105] Point 15 of Article 2 of Regulation 648/2012 (EMIR).

[106] Point 9 of Article 4(1) of 2014/65/EU Directive 2014/65/EU (MiFID II): "'Client' means any natural or legal person to whom an investment firm provides investment or ancillary services".

responsible for ensuring the performance of the contract as a contract party or by means of a guarantee.[107]

Exchange members can still benefit from related exemptions under MiFID II. However, there is no general exemption for dealing on own account in commodity derivatives when executing client orders.[108] The exemptions are limited to the following services or entities:

- Intra-group investment services. MiFID II does not apply to "persons providing investment services exclusively for their parent undertakings, for their subsidiaries or for other subsidiaries of their parent undertakings".[109]
- Local energy utilities. Depending on the Member State, there is an optional exemption for entities that only hedge the commercial risks of local electricity undertakings (or natural gas undertakings) and are exclusively (100 %) owned or controlled by them.[110]
- Operators of industrial installations. Depending on the Member State, there is a related optional exemption for the benefit of entities owned by operators of industrial installations. This exemption is limited to entities that "provide investment services exclusively in emission allowances and/or derivatives thereof for the sole purpose of hedging the commercial risks of their clients".[111]
- No client funds. There is an optional exemption, under very limited circumstances, for persons who "are not allowed to hold client funds or client securities and which for that reason are not allowed at any time to place themselves in debit with their clients".[112]

Non-members A non-member may not trade on the exchange in its own name. It may enter into contracts in other ways. (a) It may deal as a client through a clearing member. (b) An alternative contract structure is that the client deals through an

[107] Article 2(1) of Directive 2004/39/EC (MiFID): "This Directive shall not apply to: . . . (l) firms which provide investment services and/or perform investment activities consisting exclusively in dealing on own account on markets in financial futures or options or other derivatives and on cash markets for the sole purpose of hedging positions on derivatives markets or which deal for the accounts of other members of those markets or make prices for them *and which are guaranteed by clearing members* of the same markets, where responsibility for ensuring the performance of contracts entered into by such firms *is assumed by clearing members* of the same markets; . . ."

[108] Point (j)(i) of Article 2(1) of Directive 2014/65/EU (MiFID II).

[109] Point (b) of Article 2(1) of Directive 2014/65/EU (MiFID II).

[110] Point (d) of Article 3(1) of Directive 2014/65/EU (MiFID II). See also recital 29 of Directive 2014/65/EU (MiFID II).

[111] Point (e) of Article 3(1) of Directive 2014/65/EU (MiFID II). See also recital 29 of Directive 2014/65/EU (MiFID II).

[112] Point (a) of Article 3(1) of Directive 2014/65/EU (MiFID II).

intermediary broker. Whether the broker is regarded as an investment firm under MiFID II depends on its activities.[113]

This can be illustrated with Exchange-for-Physical (EFP) transactions. (a) An EFP means the swapping of an OTC derivative for an exchange-traded derivative. It is thus a combination of an OTC transaction and an exchange transaction. (b) First, the parties decide to enter into an OTC transaction for a futures position. They negotiate either directly or through a broker. (c) Second, the parties negotiate with exchange members. An exchange transaction can only be registered by an exchange member. An EFP transaction cannot take place unless the OTC transaction and the exchange traded derivatives are substantially similar. (d) Third, the result of the EFP transaction is that the OTC position is transferred from the OTC market to the futures market. (e) The same mechanism can be used to transfer a futures position to the OTC market.[114]

4.4.4 The Central Counterparty, Clearing and Settlement

General Remarks

The organisation of a financial electricity exchange consists of various service providers in addition to the operator that holds the licence and exchange members that participate in trading. There is a party that acts as a central counterparty, a party that provides clearing services, and a party that provides settlement services.

Trades must be cleared and settled. If trades between market participants were bilateral and transactions were settled directly between the parties, transaction costs and exposure to counterparty risk would be increased and liquidity reduced. To reduce counterparty risk and increase liquidity when contracts are traded on an exchange, it is customary to use a central counterparty (an entity that becomes the buyer to every seller and the seller to every buyer) and clear transactions through a clearing house.[115] A trade repository can be used to centrally collect and maintain the records of derivatives.[116]

Centralised services can be used even in OTC markets (and in some cases must be used according to EMIR). On the other hand, the use of a central counterparty

---

[113] Section A of Annex I to Directive 2014/65/EU (MiFID II): "(1) Reception and transmission of orders in relation to one or more financial instruments; (2) Execution of orders on behalf of clients; (3) Dealing on own account . . ."

[114] Pilgram T (2010), pp. 384–385, points 706–707.

[115] Ofgem (2009), para 3.75: "It has been suggested that it can take up to 18 months for sufficient GTMAs to be negotiated with enough counterparties to allow a new entrant into the market to start trading. Conversely, where liquid forward and futures markets exist a non-physical player will only need to sign effectively one GTMA to participate on the exchange and can therefore enter and start trading almost immediately".

[116] Point 2 of Regulation 648/2012 (EMIR).

and centralised clearing can be more capital intensive for market participants if they are required to post significant amounts of initial and variation margins.[117]

The clearing houses of EEX, Nasdaq Commodities, and ICE Endex (ECC AG, NASDAQ OMX Clearing AB, and ICE Clear Europe Limited) provide clearing for exchange-traded standardised contracts, including standardised contracts traded in the over-the-counter (OTC) market. They can thus work as interfaces for the clearing of OTC transactions.[118]

Clearing and Settlement Clearing and settlement basically mean different things. While clearing means the calculation of positions, settlement means the discharging of obligations. In practice, the terms clearing and settlement are often used to describe overlapping functions.

EMIR defines clearing as "the process of establishing settlement positions, including the calculation of net positions, and the process of checking that financial instruments, cash or both are available to secure the exposures arising from a transaction". The central counterparty is responsible for the operation of the clearing system.[119]

According to the Auctioning Regulation, the term clearing can mean various processes before settlement, and it can include margining, netting, novation, or other services. The term "settlement system" means an infrastructure that can provide settlement services, which may include clearing, netting, management of collateral, or other services.[120]

The ECC Clearing Conditions define the term clearing as "financial and physical settlement of transactions as well as collateralisation of transactions".[121]

The NASDAQ OMX definition of settlement focuses on the fulfilment of obligations. Clearing is a broad concept that includes even settlement.[122]

Unbundling of Services These centralised functions do not necessarily have to be in the hands of one and the same party, that is, the operator of the market. While the operator coordinates activities on the exchange, many activities can be allocated to other parties.

There is a commercial trend towards unbundling driven by the benefits of specialisation, economies of scale, and management of systemic risk. According to the voluntary European Code of Conduct for Clearing and Settlement, the services of trading venues, central counterparties, and central securities depositories should be unbundled from each other, and central securities depositories should unbundle various services such as: account provision; clearing and settlement; and collateral management.[123]

---

[117] Ofgem (2009), paras 3.90 and 3.92.

[118] See, for example, Meller E and Walter B (2009), § 9, number 19.

[119] Points 1 and 3 of Article 2 of Regulation 648/2012 (EMIR).

[120] Points 32 and 36 of Article 3 of Regulation 1031/2010 (Auctioning Regulation). See also 7 USC § 1a(15)(A).

[121] ECC Clearing Conditions (0022a, 30 April 2014), 1 Definition of Terms.

[122] NASDAQ OMX, Trading Appendix 1/Clearing Appendix 1, Definitions, Commodity Derivatives (7 April 2014).

[123] European Code of Conduct for Clearing and Settlement (7 November 2006), para 39: "Organisations shall unbundle prices and services at least as follows (i) The services of trading venues, CCPs and CSDs will be unbundled from each other. (ii) Each CSD will unbundle the following

The regulatory trend is to make the use of a central counterparty and clearing mandatory for more market participants. EMIR makes the central counterparty responsible for the operation of the clearing system.[124] Some central counterparties thus act as clearing houses.

Clearing is mandatory under EMIR[125] that applies to OTC derivative contracts, central counterparties, and clearing members. In the US, the main rule under the Commodity Exchange Act is that commodity derivatives are traded on an "organized exchange".[126] An "eligible contract participant"[127] has more discretion in the US.

The Contractual Relationships As activities can be unbundled and allocated to different parties, it is possible to distinguish between different contractual relationships such as: the exchange membership (which is necessary for market access); the trading relationship (the contractual relationship between buyer and seller or the trader and the central counterparty); the clearing relationship (the contractual relationship between a party to a trade and the party that is responsible for the process of establishing positions and ensuring that financial instruments, cash, or both, are available to secure the exposures arising from those positions)[128]; the settlement relationship (the relationship between a party to a trade and the party that organises the payment of sums due by market participants); and the custodian and settlement bank relationship (assets that belong to market participants are kept safe by a custodian bank).

Nasdaq Commodities is operated by NASDAQ OMX Oslo ASA. There is an exchange membership contract between the operator and the member.[129] NASDAQ OMX Stockholm AB is used as the central counterparty, clearing house and settlement provider. NASDAQ OMX Clearing AB is a Swedish company acting through its Norwegian branch NASDAQ OMX Oslo NUF. Clearing and settlement are facilitated by a large number of contracts.[130]

In the EEX Power Derivatives Market, the operating entity is European Energy Exchange AG. European Commodity Clearing AG (ECC) acts as the central counterparty and provides clearing and settlement services.

---

services each from the other: a. Account provision, establishing securities in book entry form, and asset servicing; b. Clearing and settlement (including verification); c. Credit provision; d. Securities lending and borrowing; and e. Collateral management".

[124] Points 1 and 3 of Article 2 of Regulation 648/2012 (EMIR).

[125] Article 4(1) of Regulation 648/2012 (EMIR).

[126] 7 USC § 1a(37).

[127] 7 USC § 1a(18).

[128] Point 3 of Article 2 of Regulation 648/2012 (EMIR).

[129] See NASDAQ OMX Oslo ASA, Exchange Membership Agreement, Commodity Derivatives (December 2010), section 1.

[130] The clearing-related agreements included the following agreements in June 2012: General Clearing Membership Agreement; Clearing Membership Agreement; Clearing Client Agreement; EUR Settlement Bank Agreement; EUR Security collateral Agreement; EUR Bank Guarantee; GBP Collateral Security Deed; GBP Letter of Credit; GBP Bank Guarantee; GBP Settlement Account Instructions; Broker Agreement.

Governing Law The contractual framework can be governed by the laws of different countries depending on the relationship.

The exchange operator and clearing house will choose the governing law in their rules. They are likely to prefer the law of their own country. However, because physical settlement is to a large extent regulated by the TSO, it is feasible to agree that physical settlement is governed by the laws of the country to which physical delivery is more closely connected.

Norwegian law is the law that governs transactions and clearing in the Nordic market.[131] On Elspot and Elbas, matters relating to the physical delivery of electricity are governed by "the local law of the delivery country".[132]

German law governs clearing by ECC.[133] On EPEX Spot, "the execution of the physical settlement of transactions" is governed by "the material law of the place at which physical fulfilment is actually provided and/or, in the case of grid-bound products, the material law applicable to the transmission system operator or the hub operator within whose transmission system delivery is effected".[134] EEX has its closest connection to Germany.[135]

Clearing

Trades are cleared by the clearing house. The central counterparty customarily acts as the clearing house in organised markets.[136] Sometimes it is not the clearing house. For instance, there may be two or more counterparties, or a third party may act as the clearing house.

In the EEX Power Derivatives Market, ECC AG acts as the central counterparty and the party responsible for clearing and settlement.[137] Spot transactions are concluded even with ECC Lux. PXE spot transactions are concluded with EnCC.[138]

---

[131] NASDAQ OMX Oslo ASA, General Terms, Trading Rules, Commodity Derivatives (7 April 2014), section 14.1; NASDAQ OMX Clearing AB, General Terms, Clearing Rules, Commodity Derivatives (9 June 2014), section 18.1.

[132] Nord Pool Spot, General Terms, Trading Rules, Nord Pool Spot's Physical Markets (effective from NWE/PCR Go-live 2013), section 18.1.1.

[133] ECC Clearing Conditions (0022a, 30 April 2014), section 6.4(1).

[134] ECC Clearing Conditions (0022a, 30 April 2014), section 6.4(1).

[135] EEX Exchange Rules (0031b, 22 November 2014).

[136] Point 1 of Article 2 of Regulation 648/2012 (EMIR). In the US, any clearing agency that clears or settles securities transactions is required to register with the SEC under section 17A of the Securities Exchange Act of 1934.

[137] EEX Trading Conditions (0038a, 22 November 2014), § 7(2).

[138] ECC Clearing Conditions (0024a, 1 August 2014), § 3.3.1(2): "According to the more detailed definition provided in section 3.3.3, spot market transactions on the markets are concluded between ECC and ECC Lux and between ECC Lux and the Trading Participant at the same time. In deviation of the above neither ECC nor ECC Lux becomes a contractual party to the PXE spot market transactions. These transactions are being concluded between the Trading Participants and a counterparty (Energy Clearing Company a.s. – EnCC) commissioned by PXE. EnCC is a Clearing Entity according to section 2.6". ECC Clearing Conditions (0024a, 1 August 2014), section 1: "PXE. Power Exchange Central Europe a.s. is a market on which derivatives market

In practice, only some market participants get access to clearing by the central counterparty/clearing house. Marketplaces customarily distinguish between clearing members and other members, and between direct clearing and indirect clearing.

The trades of clearing members are cleared by the central counterparty. Other members or third parties may trade through clearing members. Direct clearing means that a client deals through a clearing member. When indirect clearing is used, the client deals through an intermediary broker, that is, a broker that is not a clearing member. The intermediary broker passes the client's trade onto the clearing member for clearing.

The intermediary broker can do this in two main ways. It can act as agent on behalf of the client (non-member broker model). Alternatively, it can act on its own behalf, in which case there is a chain of contracts from the original client to the central counterparty (CCP–CM; CM–client 1/intermediary broker; client 1/intermediary broker–client 2).

In the EEX Power Derivatives Market, there are two or three types of membership representing two levels of access. (a) Clearing members hold either a general clearing license or a direct clearing license based on the contractual framework. They are thus General Clearing Members or Direct Clearing Members. (b) Non-clearing members are trading participants.

Nasdaq Commodities distinguishes even between market participants that are members and market participants that are not members. (a) A clearing member is an entity that has been approved by the clearing house for clearing of principal transactions. A non-clearing member just has direct access to exchange trading. A general clearing member is an entity that has been approved by the clearing house for clearing of principal transactions and client transactions on behalf of non-clearing members. (b) In addition, there are clients representatives and clearing clients. A clearing client is not a member of the exchange. A clearing client trades through a client representative. The trades are registered in a clearing account where the clearing client is account holder. A client representative is a clearing member that represents a clearing client in respect of clearing.

Reason for the Existence of Members and Clearing Members The existence of two or more member classes can be explained by commercial and regulatory reasons.

The commercial reasons relate to various forms of transaction costs (operational costs, legal costs, costs for the management of risk and information) and the liquidity of the market.

- Operational costs: Generally, the central counterparty's costs can be reduced where the number of members that it has to deal with directly is reduced and where functions are delegated to members.
- Legal costs: The central counterparty's legal costs can be reduced if the number of members who have direct access to clearing is reduced, because it is expensive to put in place the necessary contractual framework and monitor compliance.
- Risk and information management: Information costs form a large part of transaction costs. A party responsible for a relatively small group may be able

transactions are traded or registered. Spot market transactions of PXE Trading Participants are traded on the common day-ahead market of PXE and OTE ('PXE Spot Market Transactions')".

to assess the quality of members better compared with a central counterparty that is less proximate to them.

- Liquidity and marketing: There can be more trading and more liquidity if some of the members (clearing members) are given an incentive to attract new members (non-clearing members).

There are also regulatory reasons. In regulated markets, MiFID II provides for indirect or remote membership or participation,[139] including direct or indirect access to CCP, clearing, and settlement systems.[140] In OTC markets, EMIR provides that market participants that are subject to a clearing obligation should be able to become a central counterparty's clearing members or access central counterparties as clients or indirect clients.[141] The duties of providers of indirect clearing services have been set out in a Commission Delegated Regulation.[142] Only authorised credit institutions or investment firms that are clients of a clearing member may provide indirect clearing services,[143] and a clearing member that offers to facilitate indirect clearing services must do so "on reasonable commercial terms".[144]

Settlement

Payment and delivery obligations are discharged when trades are settled.[145] They can be settled either by the parties themselves, which is possible in bilateral trading, or in an organised way after clearing, which is the rule in organised markets. An organised settlement system[146] is used for reducing transaction costs and counterparty risk.

In practice, the party responsible for settlement can be the clearing house or a third party. Where settlement is both daily and automatic, it is feasible to allocate both functions to the same party.

Nasdaq OMX Clearing AB is the clearing house, central counterparty, and settlement provider. Acting through its branch Nasdaq OMX Oslo NUF, it has a licence from

[139] Article 53(5) of 2014/65/EU (MiFID II). See Article 42(5) of Directive 2004/39/EC (MiFID).

[140] Article 37(1) of Directive 2014/65/EU (MiFID II).

[141] Recital 33 of Regulation 648/2012 (EMIR). See Article 4(3) of Regulation 648/2012 (EMIR). See also ISDA (2011).

[142] Articles 2–5 of Regulation 149/2013 (supplementing Regulation 648/2012).

[143] Article 2(1) of Regulation 149/2013 (supplementing Regulation 648/2012).

[144] Article 4(1) of Regulation 149/2013 (supplementing Regulation 648/2012).

[145] NASDAQ OMX, Trading Appendix 1/Clearing Appendix 1, Definitions, Commodity Derivatives (7 April 2014): "Settlement means that cash payment is made and received between the Counterparties, against Delivery and receipt of the relevant asset where applicable, in fulfilment of the Counterparties' respective obligations pursuant to one or more Clearing Transactions".

[146] For a definition, see points 36 and 37 of Article 3 of Regulation 1031/2010 (Auctioning Regulation).

Finanstilsynet (that supervises it under the Financial Supervision Act[147]) to engage in clearing. The licence is limited to the clearing of derivative trades only. However, the term clearing means even settlement according to Norwegian law.[148] Daily settlement is automatic and connected with clearing. Members are connected to the settlement system through several multinational settlement banks.

In the EEX Power Derivatives Market, ECC AG acts as the central counterparty and the party responsible for clearing and settlement. However, the ECC AG is not necessarily the only counterparty for traders. Non-clearing members trade through clearing members.[149]

4.4.5 Margining, Daily Settlement and Netting

In addition to the general use of a clearing system and a settlement system, counterparty and systemic risk can be reduced by: the use of margin payments; the choice between the settlement of trades at the expiry of the contract or daily; and the use of netting.[150] Apart from margining, these and other modalities of clearing and settlement are largely unregulated at Community level. There is a voluntary European Code of Conduct[151] containing very general recommendations (in addition to the EFET Code of Conduct for EFET's own members).

Margining Margining means the organised process by which collateral is furnished by market participants to cover financial positions. In the EU, margining is a legal requirement under EMIR[152] and the Auctioning Regulation.[153]

Margining is used both for exchange and for OTC trades. Margins are customarily required even in bilateral OTC trade. In exchange trade, the required collateral is posted directly with the clearing house. If a margin is posted in bilateral OTC trade, it can either be posted with the counterparty directly (which is customary) or through a clearing house.[154]

The amount of the required margins increases with higher price volatility. An increase in the volatility of spot market prices increases the amount of required margins in the derivatives market more.[155]

In principle, there can be cash collateral and non-cash collateral. (a) There is a distinction between highly liquid collateral and bank guarantees. According to

[147] Lov om tilsynet med finansinstitusjoner mv. (finanstilsynsloven), § 1.

[148] Lov om verdipapirhandel (verdipapirhandelloven), § 2–6 (section 2–6 of the Securities Trading Act).

[149] EEX Trading Conditions (0038a, 22 November 2014), § 7(2).

[150] See points 31 and 36 of Article 3 of Regulation 1031/2010 (Auctioning Regulation).

[151] European Code of Conduct for Clearing and Settlement (7 November 2006).

[152] Article 41 of Regulation 648/2012 (EMIR).

[153] For a definition, see point 33 of Article 3 of Regulation 1031/2010 (Auctioning Regulation).

[154] Ofgem (2009), para 3.88.

[155] Godager K (2009), § 18, numbers 18 and 20.

EMIR, a central counterparty may only accept "highly liquid collateral with minimal credit and market risk". For non-financial counterparties, it may accept bank guarantees that are demand guarantees. Where "appropriate and sufficiently prudent", it may accept the underlying of the derivative contract.[156] (b) A Commission Delegated Regulation specifies the applicable standards.[157] Cash, financial instruments, bank guarantees, and gold are regarded as "highly liquid collateral".[158] Collateral must usually be marked-to-market "on a near to real time basis".[159] There must be "prudent haircuts".[160] Moreover, collateral must remain "sufficiently diversified to allow its liquidation within a defined holding period without a significant market impact". There are thus concentration limits.[161]

Commission Delegated Regulation 153/2013 limits the use of financial instruments as highly liquid collateral. Only certain kinds of financial instruments, transferable securities and money market instruments are considered as highly liquid collateral according to Annex I.

Moreover, Annex I limits the use of bank guarantees as collateral. A commercial bank guarantee is not accepted unless it fulfils the following and other conditions: (1) it is a demand guarantee; (2) it is issued to guarantee a non-financial clearing member; (3) it is irrevocable and unconditional; and (4) the CCP can demonstrate to the competent authority that the issuer has low credit risk; (5) it is not issued by an entity that is part of the same group as the non-financial clearing member covered by the guarantee; and (6) it is "fully backed by collateral" that meets further conditions.

The wording of Annex I is problematic. Asking non-financial counterparties such as electricity producers, suppliers, and end consumers to pay for demand guarantees and back them fully by collateral has effects that are contrary to the stated purposes of EMIR.[162]

The effect of the rule that bank guarantees must be "fully backed by collateral" is that it becomes more difficult for electricity producers to use derivatives that are subject to the mandatory clearing obligation. Obviously, the collateral will need to be provided by the bank's customer which in most cases is an electricity producer, a supplier, or a large end consumer. This increases costs without reducing systemic risk. It cannot be assumed that both the issuer of the guarantee (a bank) and the customer (a participant active in electricity generation, supply, or consumption) would default at the same time, and the obligations of

[156] Article 46(1) and recital 66 of Regulation 648/2012 (EMIR).

[157] First subparagraph of Article 46(3) of Regulation 648/2012 (EMIR); Conditions applicable to financial instruments, bank guarantees and gold considered as highly liquid collateral, Annex I to Regulation 153/2013 (supplementing Regulation 648/2012).

[158] Articles 38 and 39 of Regulation 153/2013 (supplementing Regulation 648/2012). See also recital 66 of Regulation 648/2012 (EMIR).

[159] Article 40 of Regulation 153/2013 (supplementing Regulation 648/2012).

[160] Article 40 of Regulation 153/2013 (supplementing Regulation 648/2012).

[161] Article 42 of Regulation 153/2013 (supplementing Regulation 648/2012).

[162] Recital 4 of Regulation 648/2012 (EMIR).

non-financial counterparties customarily are backed by non-financial and other assets. Because it is very important for electricity producers, suppliers, and end consumers to use derivatives for hedging purposes, the rule that guarantees must be "fully backed by collateral" in a qualified way gives an incentive to use derivatives that are not subject to the clearing obligation. Consequently, transaction costs could be increased, transparency and liquidity reduced, and risks increased. The Delegated Regulation provides for a transitional period of 3 years ending in March 2016[163] because of other unwanted effects.[164] However, the main problem remains. From the perspective of all market participants, it would have been better to make the transitional exemption permanent.

Daily Settlement Counterparty risk is reduced if the settlement period is short. While there have been differences between markets in the past,[165] it is customary to use daily settlement of positions in financial electricity markets.

Nasdaq Commodities uses Daily Market Settlement and Expiry Market Settlement. In both cases, trades are settled on each bank day in cash. Only the net sum of the payable amounts will be paid to the clearing house.[166] Daily settlement is used also in the EEX Power Derivatives Market.

Netting Gross settlement would require more capital than the netting of payments. Netting belongs to the customary ways to reduce capital needs and manage counterparty risk.[167]

Netting should be facilitated by a contractual framework to make it enforceable and binding. It is customary to use the ISDA Master Agreement or a similar legal framework (Sect. 11.6). Legal risks relating to clearing and settlement are reduced in the EU by the Settlement Finality Directive[168] and the Collateral Directive.[169]

---

[163] Article 62 of Regulation 153/2013 (supplementing Regulation 648/2012).

[164] Recital 43 of Regulation 153/2013 (supplementing Regulation 648/2012).

[165] See Godager K (2009), § 18, number 25 for differences between markets in 2009: "Settlement period. In European electricity derivatives markets outside the Nordic area the settlement period from actual delivery to final settlement may be long. With financial settlement this is no big issue, but if some of the participants pay for the positions in the electricity derivatives markets with income from sold physical electricity in the electricity spot market then the participants may become short of liquidity. In Norway the settlement period of the physical spot contracts is normally a couple of days, but for instance in Germany the settlement period may be up to several weeks. With physical delivery this means that the CCP must include the settlement period risk as a part of the settlement risk for the financial instruments".

[166] NASDAQ OMX Clearing AB, General Terms, Clearing Rules, Commodity Derivatives (9 June 2014), section 6.2.1.

[167] See, for example, Godager K (2009), § 18, numbers 20, 23, and 24.

[168] Directive 98/26/EC (Directive on settlement finality).

[169] Directive 2002/47/EC (Directive on financial collateral arrangements).

4.5 The Organisation of Spot Exchanges in the EU

4.5.1 General Remarks

The organisation of spot exchanges must facilitate both financial and physical electricity flows. Spot exchanges are thus more complex compared with financial electricity exchanges.

On one hand, spot exchange operators may have more legal discretion. This is because spot markets and other physical markets for the physical supply of electricity do not fall within the scope of the MiFID regime.

On the other, they must consider physical constraints. Access to trading must be limited to market participants that have access to the grid and transmission capacity. Matching bids must necessarily relate to electricity flows in the same grid and at the same grid level.[170]

A spot exchange has a day-ahead market and an intraday market. The products traded on day-ahead markets are hourly power contracts for physical delivery in the next day's 24-h period. Day-ahead markets are complemented by an intraday market and a balance adjustment market. We will focus on day-ahead markets in this section. Intraday and balance adjustment markets are discussed in Sect. 4.10.

Electricity Pool, Auction Mechanism, Physical Matching A spot market needs an electricity pool, an auction mechanism, and physical matching.

Bids are matched by the operator of the exchange or the clearing house. There are bids to supply and bids to purchase electrical energy. For every hourly (or sometimes half-hourly) period of the following day, bids to supply are ranked in ascending order of price. Offers to purchase are ranked in descending order of price. The point where supply and demand intersects is the system (marginal) price for the entire geographic region covered by the electricity pool.

Physical real-time matching of supply and demand is done by the system operator that has to monitor the frequency of the power system and call up a producer (a balance provider) to increase or decrease electricity generation to keep the frequency within narrow bounds.

EPEX Spot The two most important Northern European spot markets are Nord Pool Spot (the Nordic and Baltic area and the UK) and EPEX Spot (Western Central Europe).

EPEX Spot is defined as "a fully electronic exchange offering spot trading in power by closed auction and continuous trading with expiries day ahead and intra-

[170] See, for example, Nord Pool Spot Market, Trading Appendix 1, Definitions (27 November 2014): "Bidding Area means a sub area of the Electricity Exchange Area defined by the TSOs. The Electricity Exchange area is divided into bidding areas in order to handle transmission constraints. Participants must make Orders according to where their production or consumption is physically connected in the grid thus specifying the bidding area for each Order".

day for the market areas Austria, France, Germany, and Switzerland".[171] One or more market segments are associated with each market area.

Nord Pool Spot Nord Pool Spot is the largest power market in Europe.[172] It is the physical wholesale marketplace for Denmark, Norway, Sweden, Finland, Estonia (since 2010), Lithuania (since 2011), and Latvia (since June 2013).[173] Because of market integration, there are no separate national wholesale electricity markets in this region. In 2013, the share of electricity traded on Nord Pool Spot was 84 % of the region's consumption (up from 76 % in 2011).[174]

Because of grid bottlenecks, the Nordic and Baltic area is divided into a number of bidding areas. For each country, the local TSO decides which bidding areas the country is divided into. The Nordic market used to be split into six price areas: Finland, Sweden, West Denmark (Jutland), East Denmark (Zealand), South Norway (Oslo), and North Norway (Tromsø). In 2010, Norway was split into five price areas. Sweden was split into four price areas in 2011. Each of Estonia, Latvia, and Lithuania is a price area.[175]

Nord Pool Spot has provided a model for the organisation of other sport markets in the EU[176] and it has activities even outside its core geographical area. Nord Pool Spot consists of Elspot, Elbas, and N2EX. N2EX is the physical market for the UK. The Elbas market covers even Germany.

Elspot Elspot is the common Nordic and Baltic market for trading physical electricity contracts with next-day supply. On Elspot, hourly power contracts are traded daily for physical delivery in the next day's 24-h period.

Elbas Elbas is a physical balance adjustment market for the Nordic and Baltic region including Germany.

Both the Elspot and Elbas market used to include even the KONTEK area in Germany. The German bidding area KONTEK in Nord Pool Spot's Elspot market

---

171 EPEX Spot Exchange Rules (13 May 2014), Article 1.1.

172 Nord Pool Spot, Exchange information, No. 02/2014, 16 January 2014:" Nord Pool Spot has secured its position as Europe's largest power market with the announcement of new volume and market share records in 2013. The year saw 493 TWh of power traded, compared to 432 TWh in 2012. Nord Pool Spot's traded power volumes include the Nordic and Baltic day-ahead auction Elspot (348.9 TWh), the Nordic, Baltic and German intraday market Elbas (4.2 TWh) and day-ahead auction volume in the UK power market N2EX (139.4 TWh). At the same time Nord Pool Spot's Nordic/Baltic market share reached an all-time high of 84 %".

173 Iceland is the only Nordic country that does not belong to the Nord Pool Spot area. The distance between Iceland and Norway/Denmark is long. See nevertheless Nord Pool Spot, Annual Review 2007, p. 8: "Iceland. Nord Pool Spot is supporting Landsnet in the establishment of a market place for electricity trading in Iceland. The market will be based on continuous trading and use of the Elbas system".

174 Energy Market Authority, Finland (2013), pp. 35–39; Energy Market Authority, Finland (2014), p. 8.

175 Energy Market Authority, Finland (2013), p. 31.

176 Pilgram T (2010), p. 343, point 632.

was closed down in November 2009 because of the launch of the EMCC market coupling between Denmark and Germany. However, the Elbas market covers Germany as well.

In June 2010, APX-ENDEX, Belpex and Nord Pool Spot agreed to create a cross-border intraday electricity market based on Nord Pool Spot's Elbas technology.

An improved version of the Elbas trading system was launched on 25 November 2014. The launch of Elbas 4 that replaced Elbas 3.2 (the previous intraday trading system) enabled trade across multiple markets. The transition was identical in all ten countries using Elbas: the Nordic countries, the Baltic countries, Germany, the Netherlands, and Belgium. Elbas 4 improved trading opportunities in all ten countries but even more in Germany.[177]

In May 2014, the power exchanges APX, Belpex, EPEX SPOT, Nord Pool Spot, and OMIE (including sixteen TSOs) agreed on the core building blocks of the future European Cross Border Intraday Solution. The future Intraday Solution will enable continuous cross-border trading across the whole of Europe with intraday adjustments to trades concluded in the day-ahead market.[178]

On Elbas, the trading hours are the coming 10–38 h. For the Nordic and Baltic areas, contracts are opened for trading the same day as the Elspot prices are set, normally at 14:00 CET. Trading is closed 1 h before delivery commences.

The German market is different. Before the launch of Elbas 4, trading was open from 08:00 until 13:45 CET and from 15:00 until 30 min before the commencement of delivery.[179] With Elbas 4 both 15-min and 30-min products were introduced initially only for trading in the German market area. To further improve trading opportunities within Germany, Germany is handled as four bidding areas. The four bidding areas are identical to the four TSO areas 50HZ, TTG, AMP and TBW.[180]

N2EX N2EX commenced its operations in 2010 after NASDAQ OMX Commodities and Nord Pool Spot had been selected by The Futures & Options Association (FOA) to provide market and clearing services for the UK wholesale power market. Since October 2014, N2EX is Nord Pool Spot's physical power market in the UK.

---

[177] Nord Pool Spot, Exchange information, No. 44/2014, 4 November 2014.

[178] Nord Pool Spot, Exchange information, No. 24/2014, 19 May 2014.

[179] Nord Pool Spot Physical Markets, Trading Appendix 3, Product Specifications (1 July 2014), section 3.1. For the reason of the difference between the markets, see Nord Pool Spot, Exchange information, No 23/2014, 15 May 2014: "This is because TSOs need to reach a comprehensive overview of planning for the next day after nomination deadline for day-ahead trading. Order series for delivery the following day will thus be closed for trading in Elbas in this time interval".

[180] Nord Pool Spot, Exchange information, No. 44/2014, 4 November 2014. Nord Pool Spot Physical Markets, Trading Appendix 3, Product Specifications (launch of Elbas4), section 3.1.

4.5.2 The Operator

A spot exchange must have an operator that coordinates its activities. A spot exchange can be operated by various kinds of entities.

Whether the operator requires an authorisation depends on the applicable national regulatory framework. A spot exchange operator does not need a MiFID II authorisation in this capacity, because the operation of a spot exchange is not an investment service and the operator of a spot exchange is not regarded as an investment firm under MiFID II.[181]

In any case, it is not necessary for the operator of a spot exchange to be an entity incorporated in the country in which the physical flows are located. Such a requirement (a) would not be feasible in the technical sense, because the location of physical flows depends on the actual use of the grid and the use of interconnectors, and (b) would not be permitted, because the freedom of establishment, the freedom to provide services, and the prohibition of discrimination based on nationality enable EU firms to operate electricity spot markets in any Member State.

EPEX Spot is operated by EPEX Spot SE, a European company incorporated in France.[182] There is no authorisation requirement for the operation of electricity spot markets in France.[183] EPEX Spot SE used to be a 50/50 joint-venture of European Energy Exchange AG (Germany) and Powernext SA (France).[184] On 1 January 2015, EEX sold part of its shares to the holding HGRT of European Transmission System Operators Elia (Belgium), RTE (France) and Tennet (Netherlands). In exchange, EEX Group got the 53 % stake of HGRT in Powernext. After these transactions, EEX is indirectly the majority shareholder of EPEX Spot. EEX holds 13.3 % of the shares directly. It is the majority shareholder in Powernext that holds 50 %. The remaining 36.7 % share in EPEX SPOT belongs to the holding HGRT.

Nord Pool Spot consists of Nord Pool Spot AS, a limited-liability company incorporated in Norway, and of its subsidiaries. Its shareholders are the Nordic transmission system operators (Statnett SF, Svenska Kraftnät, Fingrid Oyj, and Energinet.dk) and the Baltic transmission system operators (Elering, Litgrid, and Augstsprieguma tikls (AST)).

The physical markets of Nord Pool Spot are operated by Nord Pool Spot AS. Nord Pool Spot AS has two licences because of national regulatory requirements in its home country.

---

[181] First subparagraph of Article 4(1) of Directive 2014/65/EU (MiFID II): "The following definitions shall also apply: (1) 'investment firm' means any legal person whose regular occupation or business is the provision of one or more investment services to third parties and/or the performance of one or more investment activities on a professional basis". See also Section A of Annex I relating to any of the instruments listed in Section C of Annex I: "... (8) Operation of an MTF; (9) Operation of an OTF".

[182] EPEX Spot Exchange Rules (13 May 2014), Articles 1.2 and 1.20.

[183] Powernext SA, which owns 50 % of shares in EPEX Spot SE, is supervised by the Autorité des Marchés Financiers (AMF) and the Commission de Régulation de l'Energie (CRE) in addition to Direction Générale de l'Energie et du Climat (DGEC) and Banque de France and Commission Bancaire.

[184] Powernext SA is the operator of Powernext in the French market. Powernext is approved as a multilateral trading facility and is cleared by the ECC.

First, it has a licence for the organisation of a marketplace under the Norwegian Energy Act.[185] The competent regulatory authority is the Norwegian Water Resources and Energy Directorate (NVE). Second, the Norwegian Ministry of Petroleum and Energy (OED) allows Nord Pool Spot AS to organise the physical exchange of power with neighbouring countries.[186] Even the physical market of N2EX is operated by Nord Pool Spot AS.[187] The competent authority is again NVE.[188]

4.5.3 Access to Trading

An electricity producer needs access to the spot exchange to trade. Market participants' access to the spot exchange is regulated in several ways. There are (1) rules on the admission of market participants, (2) rules on the representation of market participants acting on their own behalf (such as rules on internal trading responsibles authorised to act as the market participant),[189] and (3) rules on the representation of market participants by a third party (such as rules on external client representatives authorised to act on behalf of the market participant).[190]

The parties that participate in the organisation and operation of electricity spot exchanges—exchange operators, clearing houses, and central counterparties—customarily organise financial electricity exchanges as well. Consequently, access to electricity spot markets is basically regulated in the same way as access to financial electricity exchanges. However, there are differences caused by the physical settlement of transactions.

Physical Settlement A condition for the approval of a trading participant is that the applicant can participate in the physical settlement of transactions. The exchange operator and the clearing house require evidence of the applicant's capability for physical settlement. The TSO's contractual framework therefore has to be in place for the applicant.

Participants in the N2EX physical market must be parties to the BSC and fulfil all applicable criteria for being ECV Transferees under the Clearing Rules, the ECV Transferee Agreement, and the BSC.[191]

---

[185] Sections 4–1 and 4–5 of energiloven (the Energy Act, Act nr 50 of 29 June 1990).

[186] Sections 4–2 (export and import) and 2–1 (authorisation requirement) of energiloven.

[187] N2EX Physical Market, General Trading Terms, Trading Rules (1 October 2014), Section 1.1: "NPS operates the N2EX Physical Market, which is a market place for Trading of electricity contracts with physical delivery". Section 1.2: "The Physical Market comprises the Prompt Market, the Auction Market and the Spot Market . . ."

[188] Sections 4–1 and 4–5 of energiloven (the Energy Act).

[189] See, for example, Nord Pool Spot's Physical Markets, General Terms, Trading Rules (1 February 2015), section 3.3.

[190] See, for example, Nord Pool Spot Physical Markets, Trading Appendix 4, Clearing Rules (27 November 2014), section 5.1.

[191] N2EX Physical Market, General Clearing Terms, Clearing Rules (27 November 2014), section 5.2.3.

Participants in the other physical markets of Nord Pool Spot must have in place all necessary agreements to enable them to trade in the physical markets and to perform their obligations[192], and they must have entered into an agreement on balance responsibility with the relevant balance responsible party or the TSO.[193]

Participants in trading on EPEX Spot must also have secured the orderly settlement of transactions.[194] According to the EPEX Spot Exchange Rules, the approval of an applicant as a trading participant requires the necessary declarations and evidence of the capability for physical settlement of transactions. The Exchange Rules focus more on financial settlement (in addition to technical facilities and personnel).[195]

This does not exclude the use of middlemen such as trading agents that act on behalf of one or more admitted participants.[196]

On EEX, Approved Trading Agents are entitled to effect the conclusion of transactions on behalf and for the account of trading participants. These Trading Agents do not have to be trading participants themselves.[197]

Clearing In addition to financial and physical settlement, the applicant must be able to participate in clearing. The applicant firm may do it directly (by being the central counterparty's counterparty in clearing transactions) or indirectly (by being a clearing member's client). The firm is not eligible as an exchange member unless it is eligible as a counterparty in clearing transactions under the applicable clearing rules.

On Elspot and Elbas, a member must fulfil the following conditions to be eligible as a counterparty to clearing transactions. It must: "a. have appointed a clearing responsible; b. have established one or more Trading Portfolio(s); c. have established one or more Cash Account(s) for settlement purposes to be either a Pledged or Non-pledged Cash Account; d. have established one or more Clearing Account(s); e. have established Collateral as a Pledged Cash Account or a On-Demand Guarantee, and have met its Collateral Call; and f. not have its access to Clearing suspended or terminated in accordance with the Trading Rules".[198] The member must at all times be able to document that it fulfils the criteria.[199]

On EPEX Spot, exchange members must take part in clearing on ECC. A clearing member must have concluded a Clearing Agreement with European Commodity Clearing AG, and a non-clearing member with a clearing member.[200]

---

[192] Nord Pool Spot's Physical Markets, General Terms, Trading Rules (1 February 2015), section 3.1.3.

[193] Nord Pool Spot's Physical Markets, General Terms, Trading Rules (1 February 2015), section 3.1.4.

[194] EPEX Spot Exchange Rules (28 November 2014), Article 2.5.

[195] EPEX Spot Exchange Rules (28 November 2014), Article 2.11. See also ECC Clearing Conditions (0022a, 30 April 2014), section 2.3.1(1)(c) and section 5.2.3(3).

[196] See also Härle PA (2010), p. 406, points 749–750.

[197] EEX Exchange Rules (0031b, 22 November 2014), § 15(3).

[198] Nord Pool Spot Physical Markets, Trading Appendix 4, Clearing Rules (27 November 2014), section 2.2.1.

[199] Nord Pool Spot Physical Markets, Trading Appendix 4, Clearing Rules (27 November 2014), section 2.2.2.

[200] EPEX Spot Exchange Rules (28 November 2014), Article 2.11. See also ECC Clearing Conditions (0022a, 30 April 2014), section 2.3.1(1)(c) and section 5.2.3(3).

Listing and Delisting In addition to rules on access to trading, the exchange operator adopts rules on the listing and delisting of contracts and decides on the admission of contracts to trading.

Nord Pool Spot AS (NPS) decides which instrument series will be listed on Elspot. NPS also decides on the removal (delisting) of a listed instrument series.[201]

In the physical market of N2EX, NPS decides which products will be listed and on their removal (delisting). However, delisting may not be effected for physical products which have an open Interest with the clearing house other than zero (0).[202]

In the EPEX Spot market, EPEX Spot SE decides on admission to trading, suspension, and delisting.[203] Suspension and delisting are possible for an important reason, such as where orderly exchange trading is jeopardized.[204] In both cases, the decision requires approval by the Exchange Council of EPEX Spot SE.[205]

4.5.4 The Matching of Bids

Somebody must match the bids in physical electricity markets. It would technically be possible to allocate this task either to the operator of the spot exchange or to another party.[206]

The operator of the spot exchange matches the bids in the three markets studied here. Bids on EPEX Spot are matched by EPEX Spot SE.[207] Nord Pool Spot AS matches the bids in the physical market of N2EX[208] (where its function was limited to that of the exchange operator until 1 October 2014) and in the Elspot market of Nord Pool Spot[209] (where it also acts as the clearing house and central counterparty).

Depending on the rules of the exchange, there can be even market-makers. Market-makers would need to be approved by the operator. In a market-maker agreement, the operator and the market-maker would agree on the period of day during which the market-maker is required to quote orders, the minimum volume to be quoted, and the maximum quotable net difference between bids and offers.

---

201 Nord Pool Spot's Physical Markets, General Terms, Trading Rules (1 February 2015), section 7.1.1.

202 N2EX Physical Market, General Trading Terms, Trading Rules (1 October 2014), section 6.

203 EPEX Spot Exchange Rules (28 November 2014), Article 5.4 and Article 5.6.

204 EPEX Spot Exchange Rules (28 November 2014), Article 5.7.

205 EPEX Spot Exchange Rules (28 November 2014), Article 5.4.

206 Hunt S and Shuttleworth G (1996), pp. 139–140.

207 EPEX Spot Exchange Rules (28 November 2014), Article 1.7; EPEX Spot Operational Rules (28 November 2014), Article 1.8.

208 N2EX Physical Market, General Trading Terms, Trading Rules (1 October 2014), section 7.1.2.

209 Nord Pool Spot's Physical Markets, General Terms, Trading Rules (1 February 2015), section 8.1.2.

On Nord Pool Spot, the rights and obligations of market-makers are set out in the individual market-maker agreement. The operator and the market-maker agree on the Market Maker Hours, the Market Maker Volume, and the Market Maker Spread.[210]

Bids are not necessarily matched in the same way as in securities markets. In securities markets, bids are matched when the submitted prices are equal, and different trades can be settled at different prices. There is more variation in electricity spot markets. Different trades can be settled at different prices in continuous trading. They can be matched by auction and a system price or area price[211] may be used for different trades. Bids can be matched to ensure the maximisation of economic surplus.[212] The merit order principle can be used for the ranking of bids. The matching of bids is also subject to transmission capacity constraints.

Continuous Trading Different trades are settled at different prices when bids on the spot exchange are matched continuously like in securities markets.

N2EX. The N2EX Prompt Market (with delivery taking place up to 7 days ahead)[213] and the N2EX Spot Market (with delivery normally taking place within the next 48 h period)[214] are markets for continuous trading. Transactions are matched automatically when concurring orders are registered in the market operator's system for electronic trading (ETS). Transactions resulting from orders being matched in the ETS are automatically and mandatory registered for clearing. The Auction Market is not a market for continuous trading.[215]

Elbas. Elbas is a market for continuous trading. Trading takes place every day around the clock until one hour before delivery. Concurring orders—the highest buy price and the lowers sell price are matched on a first-come, first-served basis.

EPEX Spot. Transactions on EPEX Spot are effected by matching bids either continuously (meaning that bids are entered into the order book for immediate execution) or by auction (meaning that there is an accumulation period during which bids are entered in the order book but not executed).[216] Continuous trading is used in intraday markets (in addition

[210] For definitions, see Nord Pool Spot Market, Trading Appendix 1, Definitions (27 November 2014).

[211] See, for example, NASDAQ OMX, Trading Appendix 2/Clearing Appendix 2, Contract Specifications, Commodity Derivatives (24 November 2014), Part B, section 1.2.1: "... Area Price means, for the applicable time of reference, the price of one (1) MWh of electric power for the applicable Electricity Area". "Electricity Area means a geographical area in which Nord Pool Spot AS organises electricity power trading with physical delivery and which is allocated a separate bidding area in the Nordic 'Elspot' market ..."

[212] See, for example, point 20 of Article 2 of Commission Regulation .../.. (CACM Regulation).

[213] N2EX Physical Market, Trading Appendix 3/Clearing Appendix 2, Product Specifications (27 November 2014), section 2.4.

[214] N2EX Physical Market, Trading Appendix 3/Clearing Appendix 2, Product Specifications (27 November 2014), section 3.4.

[215] N2EX Physical Market, General Trading Terms, Trading Rules (1 October 2014), section 1.2; N2EX Physical Market, Trading Appendix 3/Clearing Appendix 2, Product Specifications (27 November 2014), section 4.1.

[216] EPEX Spot Exchange Rules (28 November 2014), Article 6.4.

to intraday auctions for the German market area).[217] During the trading session, orders are then executed "at the best price available in the system": the best orders in the order book are matched automatically with same-priced orders entered in the order book.[218]

Auction The opposite of continuous trading is the matching of bids by auction. In this case, bids are accumulated in the order book during an accumulation period. Different bids are then matched at the same price.[219]

Single Contract Orders, Block Orders and Other Qualified Orders There can be various kinds of orders (bids) in auctions depending on the trading rules of the exchange. Orders can thus be qualified.

First, one can distinguish between single contract orders and block orders. The basic form is the single contract order that is limited to electricity supply during a certain hour. Block orders are aggregate bids for several hours, with a fixed price and volume throughout these hours.

For instance, a block of consecutive hours might allow an electricity producer to spread out the start-up costs and also to offer lower prices. An industrial firm as the end consumer might prefer to submit a block order for the start-up of an energy-intensive production process.[220]

One can also distinguish between various kinds of order types based on how an order is executed.

There are various order categories in continuous trading on EPEX Spot. Buy or sell orders can be "limit orders" (that carry a price limit and can only be executed at this price or at a better price) or "market sweep orders" (that are matched with several contracts).[221]

Moreover, EPEX Spot allows parties to use the following execution restrictions in continuous trading: "immediate-or-cancel" (IOC, market sweep orders are restricted in this way); "fill-or-kill" (FOK); "linked fill-or-kill" (LFOK); and "all-or-none" (AON). Orders can also be entered with the following validity restrictions: "good for session"; "good till date"; and "iceberg" or hidden-quantity. There are restrictions on how these restrictions may be combined.[222]

On Elspot, orders are hourly orders, flexible hourly offers, block orders, or linked block orders.[223] Block orders cover a minimum of three consecutive hours subject to the block

[217] EPEX Spot Exchange Rules (28 November 2014), Article 5.10. EPEX Spot Operational Rules (28 November 2014), Article 1.3.2.2, Continuous Trading: EPEX Spot French intraday; EPEX Spot German intraday; EPEX Spot Austrian intraday; EPEX Spot Swiss intraday. See also EPEX Spot Operational Rules (28 November 2014), Article 1.4 on market coupling contracts with daily auction.

[218] EPEX Spot Operational Rules (28 November 2014), Article 2.3.5.

[219] EPEX Spot Exchange Rules (28 November 2014), Article 6.4. See, for example, EPEX Spot Operational Rules (28 November 2014), Article 1.3.1: EPEX Spot Austrian/German day-ahead auction; EPEX Spot French day-ahead auction; EPEX Spot Swiss day-ahead auction.

[220] Creti A et al. (2010), citing Meeus L (2006).

[221] EPEX Spot Operational Rules (28 November 2014), Article 2.2.1.

[222] EPEX Spot Operational Rules (28 November 2014), Article 2.2.2.

[223] Nord Pool Spot Physical Markets, Trading Appendix 3, Product Specifications (launch of Elbas4). See also Nord Pool Spot Market, Trading Appendix 1, Definitions (27 November 2014).

order volume limit. In the Elspot market, block orders are "all-or-nothing orders" but can also be "linked blocked orders".[224]

In the Elbas market, the launch of the Elbas 4 trading system in November 2014 increased the number of order types. The previous rules provided for "block orders" and "fill orders". A block order was an "all-or-nothing order" covering one or more consecutive hours. The volume could also be limited in various ways.[225] A "fill order" meant an order that may be matched for the full volume or part of the volume. Both order types are still available. The launch of Elbas 4 made it possible for Nord Pool Spot to introduce three new order types: "Immediate-or-Cancel" (that resembles "Fill-and-Kill"), "Fill-or-Kill" and "Iceberg".[226]

There is some variation in the N2EX market depending on the product.[227] For the Prompt Market and the Spot Market with continuous trading, the order types are "Fill", "Fill-and-Kill" (that resembles "Immediate-or-Cancel"),[228] "Fill-or-Kill", "Stop Order",[229] and "All-or-Nothing". For the Auction Market, the order types are "Hourly Orders", "Flexible Orders", "Block Orders", and "Exclusive Groups".[230]

Second, exchange rules may even provide for other types of qualified orders to increase a closer alignment of orders with market participants' technical or commercial requirements.

---

[224] Nord Pool Spot Market, Trading Appendix 1, Definitions (27 November 2014); Nord Pool Spot, Elspot Market Regulations (1 July 2014), section 4.2.4.

[225] Nord Pool Spot Market, Trading Appendix 1, Definitions (NWE/PCR go-live 2014): "Block Order Volume Limit means the volume limit placed on each Block Order, as specified from time to time in the Product Specifications". "Energy Volume Limit means the maximum Energy Volume applicable to an Order where such designation is applicable". "Fill Order means an Order in Elbas that may be matched for the full volume or part of the volume".

[226] Nord Pool Spot, Exchange information, No. 44/2014, 4 November 2014. Nord Pool Spot Market, Trading Appendix 1, Definitions (27 November 2014): "Fill-or-Kill Order means an Order that shall be immediately matched for the whole order volume or cancelled". "Iceberg Order means an Order in the Elbas Market that has a partly hidden overall volume. Each part of the Iceberg Order is called a Clip. When the Order has been submitted, other Participants will only see the first Clip as a part of the total volume when the Order is submitted. When the first Clip is matched, the next Clip receives a new order number and time stamp". "Immediate-or-Cancel means an Order that shall be immediately matched for as much of the order volume as possible and then cancelled".

[227] N2EX Physical Market, Trading Appendix 3/Clearing Appendix 2, Product Specifications (27 November 2014), section 2.1 (Prompt Market), section 3.1 (Spot Market), and section 4.1 (Auction Market). See also N2EX Physical Market, Trading Appendix 2B, Auction Market Regulations (1 October 2014).

[228] N2EX Physical Market, Trading Appendix 1/Clearing Appendix 1, Definitions (27 November 2014): "Fill-and-Kill Order means an Order that shall be immediately matched for as much of the order volume as possible and then cancelled".

[229] N2EX Physical Market, Trading Appendix 1/Clearing Appendix 1, Definitions (27 November 2014): "Stop Order means a conditional Order that shall only be executed when a specific price level is reached, as further specified in the individual Stop Order through the input parameters of the ETS".

[230] N2EX Physical Market, Trading Appendix 1/Clearing Appendix 1, Definitions (27 November 2014): "Exclusive Group means a set of Block Orders nominated as an Exclusive Group by the Participant that submits such Block Orders which shall be subject to the following conditions . . ."

It is possible to use price steps to combine prices and volumes on Elspot.[231] Consequently, there can be hourly orders[232] and flexible hourly offers. A flexible hourly offer is defined as an "offer in the Elspot Market specifying which volume of electricity a participant would be willing to sell at a specified price in any Delivery Hour within the relevant Delivery Day".[233]

Third, exchange rules may facilitate gross bidding. When they do, a member may sell its full production volume on the exchange and purchase the full outbound sales volume on the exchange without the internal netting of volumes.

For a member, cross bidding is partly a "make or buy" question (Sect. 2.3.5). The member could choose to buy or sell net volumes and use internal invoicing for intra-firm transactions. If the member chooses cross bidding, the need for internal invoicing is reduced and it becomes easier for the member to benefit from the flexibilities of generation and sales.[234] On the other hand, there are fees for trading.

Cross bidding can be facilitated by lower fees for amounts that net to zero. The operator of the exchange may offer lower fees for gross bidding as it increases traded volumes and contributes to the liquidity and transparency of the power market.

Nord Pool Spot used to make its gross bidding service available for members in the Participant category only. From 1 February 2015, the gross bidding service was expanded to include the Client member category.[235]

The Gross Bidding Agreement includes additional provisions regarding Trading in Elspot by Participants with both sales portfolios and purchase portfolios. The agreement applies only to the area of one TSO.[236] The Participant undertakes to carry out gross bidding for all sales portfolios and purchase portfolios and to refrain from internal netting/matching of purchase interests in the purchase portfolio(s) with sales interest in the sales portfolio(s).[237] The Participant is entitled to a reduced fee. A reduced fee is paid for the

---

[231] Nord Pool Spot Market, Trading Appendix 1, Definitions (27 November 2014): "Price Step means a pair of Order Price and Energy Volume values on an Order curve in the Elspot Market between (and including) the upper and lower Order Price Limits of the Order".

[232] Nord Pool Spot Market, Trading Appendix 1, Definitions (27 November 2014): "Hourly Order means an Order in the Elspot Market where a Participant states volumes to buy or sell at different price levels in a set of Price Steps defined for a specific Delivery Hour. Each pair of price and volume is handled as a point on an Order Curve with linear interpolation between each pair".

[233] Nord Pool Spot Market, Trading Appendix 1, Definitions (27 November 2014): "Flexible Hourly Offer means an Offer in the Elspot Market specifying which volume of electricity a Participant would be willing to sell at a specified price in any Delivery Hour within the relevant Delivery Day".

[234] Nord Pool Spot, Exchange Information No. 3/2015—Gross Bidding service offered to Clients from 1 February 2015 (15 January 2015).

[235] Nord Pool Spot's Physical Markets, General Terms, Trading Rules (1 February 2015), section 6.1.1.

[236] Nord Pool Spot, Trading Agreement 3, Gross Bidding Agreement (27 October 2014), sections 1.2 and 1.3.

[237] Nord Pool Spot, Trading Agreement 3, Gross Bidding Agreement (27 October 2014), section 3.2.

amount of purchase and sales volumes that nets to zero. Standard fees are paid for the remaining volume.[238]

The Gross Bidding Agreement—Clients contains similar provisions for the Client member category.[239]

System Price The choice of the auction method can be combined with a system price. In the day-ahead market, bids to supply are ranked in ascending order of price for every hourly (or sometimes half-hourly) period of the following day. Offers to purchase are then ranked in descending order of price. The point where supply and demand intersects is the system (marginal) price for the entire geographic region covered by the electricity pool.

Trading on Elspot is based on a system price and area prices. There are general rules on the matching of hourly orders at the point of intersection between the aggregated offer and bid curves[240] and particular rules on the procedure to be applied in the event that a point of intersection between the purchase and sales curves is not achieved.[241]

After market participants have submitted bids indicating the amount of power they want to buy or sell at different price levels and the gate is closed,[242] Nord Pool Spot draws demand and supply curves for each hour based on the submitted prices and volumes.[243] All trades are settled at the price for the point where these curves meet (the intersection point, the system price). The results are subject to final confirmation in accordance with the applicable NWE Price Coupling procedures.[244]

This is nevertheless just the simplified main rule. Price calculation is made more difficult by the permission to submit various kinds of orders—hourly orders, flexible hourly offers, block orders, linked block orders, and convertible block offers[245]—and by transmission capacity constraints. The existence of transmission capacity constraints may require market splitting and area prices (Sect. 5.2).[246] Moreover, where a point of intersection is not achieved ("non-matching"), various actions will become necessary.[247]

---

[238] Nord Pool Spot, Trading Agreement 3, Gross Bidding Agreement (27 October 2014), section 2.1(b).

[239] Nord Pool Spot, Trading Agreement 3 A, Gross Bidding Agreement—Clients (1 February 2015).

[240] Nord Pool Spot Physical Market, Trading Appendix 2a, Elspot Market Regulations (18 November 2014), section 4.1.1 and section 4.1.2.

[241] Nord Pool Spot Physical Market, Trading Appendix 2a, Elspot Market Regulations (18 November 2014), section 4.3.

[242] Nord Pool Spot Physical Market, Trading Appendix 2a, Elspot Market Regulations (18 November 2014), section 2.4.1 and section 1.1.3.

[243] Nord Pool Spot Physical Market, Trading Appendix 2a, Elspot Market Regulations (18 November 2014), section 4.1.1.

[244] Nord Pool Spot Physical Market, Trading Appendix 2a, Elspot Market Regulations (18 November 2014), section 6.1.1.

[245] Nord Pool Spot Physical Market, Trading Appendix 2a, Elspot Market Regulations (18 November 2014), section 3.1.1 (hourly orders), section 3.2.1 (flexible hourly offers); section 3.3.1 (block orders); section 3.3.2 (linked block orders); section 3.4.1 (block offers that can be converted to hourly offers).

[246] Nord Pool Spot Physical Market, Trading Appendix 2a, Elspot Market Regulations (18 November 2014), section 1.1.5.

[247] Nord Pool Spot Physical Market, Trading Appendix 2a, Elspot Market Regulations (18 November 2014), section 4.3.1.

When bids on EPEX Spot are matched by auction (rather than continuously), supply and demand orders are matched after an accumulation period during which orders are entered in the order book.[248] The orders sent to EPEX Spot SE by exchange members remain in the order book unless they are executed, modified, or cancelled.[249] Once the order book is closed, orders may not be modified or cancelled and are irrevocable.[250] The auction takes place after the order book has closed.

The price determination algorithm aims at optimising "total welfare, i.e. the Seller Surplus, the Buyer Surplus and the Congestion Rent including tariff rates on interconnectors".[251] The price determined by the algorithm at the time of auction is the price at which all trades will be executed.[252] The price is the price at the intersection point of the supply and demand curves, that is, the aggregate supply and demand curves of exchange members' single orders and block orders for each contract. The existence of conditional bids makes it a bit more complicated to determine the intersection of the supply and demand curves.[253]

The particular provisions on volume market coupling on the German/Austrian auction segment are no longer necessary as EMCC has been replaced by NWE price coupling.[254]

Merit Order The merit order principle means two things. First, all trades are settled at the same clearing price. Second, bids are matched in the order of merit.

The merit order is the order in which generation capacity is utilised. In practice, the merit order ranking of a certain utility depends on its variable costs. Combined with competition in the electricity markets, the merit order principle could lead to the most efficient use of generation resources. Electricity with the lowest variable generation costs is used first (wind power, hydropower, nuclear power). Installations with higher variable costs are not used until required by demand.

Merit order rankings can be determined in different ways. (a) There could be a centralised way to determine them based on each utility's variable costs.

[248] EPEX Spot Exchange Rules (28 November 2014), Article 6.4.

[249] EPEX Spot Operational Rules (28 November 2014), Article 1.5.5.

[250] EPEX Spot Operational Rules (28 November 2014), Article 1.6.3.

[251] EPEX Spot Operational Rules (28 November 2014), Article 1.6.4.

[252] EPEX Spot Operational Rules (28 November 2014), Article 1.6.4.

[253] EPEX Spot Operational Rules (28 November 2014), Article 1.6.4: ". . . For Price determination purposes, the Member's interest is assumed to be linear between two price/quantity combinations . . ."

[254] Compare EPEX Spot Operational Rules (6 June 2013), Article 1.6.6: "In the framework of the execution of the single hour auction on the German/Austrian segment volume market coupling is carried out by EMCC acting as an auction office. Under this process EMCC receives the aggregated and anonymised purchase and sale curves including the list of anonymised block bids of EPEX Spot on the German/Austrian segment after the end of the submission of Orders and before pricing.
The Auction Office calculates the volume Orders (price-independent buy and sell Orders) for the respective single hours, which are required for the optimisation of capacity utilisation, on the basis of the available purchase and sale curves and the list of anonymised block bids and under consideration of available transmission rights on the cross-border transfer points. The auction office exclusively submits price-independent buy and sell Orders to the single hour auctions of the markets involved . . . The volume Orders by the auction office have to total zero across all the spot markets involved".

(b) Alternatively, the merit order could be determined based on the buy or sell orders submitted by rational market participants. This is the method used by Nord Pool Spot and one of the two methods used by EPEX Spot. (c) The ranking of utilities can also be manipulated by legislation.

The manipulation of merit order rankings by legislation would influence the use of generation resources and the allocation of investment in generation resources. The scope of the market that is based on the merit order principle can also be reduced by increased use of other mechanisms. The merit order principle benefits intermittent generation technologies with low (zero) variable costs. Merit order rankings could be manipulated, for instance, to increase investment in electricity produced from waste or the production of CHP. On the other hand, the scope of the market that is based on the merit order principle is partly reduced by the preferential treatment of RES-E.

Member States of the EU have a duty to ensure that TSOs and DSOs (a) guarantee the transmission and distribution of RES-E and (b) provide for its priority access or guaranteed access to the grid. What applies to RES-E applies to electricity produced from waste or the production of CHP.[255] Feed-in tariffs are manipulated under EU law and Member States' national laws.

In Germany, the biggest market in Europe, preferential treatment is facilitated by EEG 2014.[256] (a) EEG 2012[257] required TSOs to purchase renewable power at fixed feed-in tariffs.[258] They were compensated by electricity undertakings further down the chain.[259] Final consumers ended up paying the difference between market prices and the fixed feed-in tariffs.[260] (b) According to EEG 2014, small installations continue to benefit from fixed feed-in tariffs (Einspeisevergütung) and do not have to sell on the market.[261] Other producers of RES-E are supported by market premiums (Marktprämie) paid on top of the market price.[262] The TSO still has a duty to purchase RES-E.[263]

Contract The rules of the exchange can set out: at what point in time the matching of bids results in a binding contract; how long bids remain binding; whether bids are revocable[264]; and whether trades may be cancelled. There can also be different

---

[255] Article 16(2) of Directive 2009/28/EC (RES Directive); Articles 15(3) and 25(4) of Directive 2009/72/EC (Third Electricity Directive).

[256] For an introduction to EEG 2014, see Monopolkommission (2014), p. 74, point 68.

[257] For an introduction to EEG 2012, see Monopolkommission (2013), section 3.3.1.

[258] § 2 and § 5(1) EEG 2012.

[259] §§ 34–37 EEG 2012.

[260] § 34 EEG 2012.

[261] § 37(2) EEG 2014. The capacity thresholds are 500 kW (for installations taken into use before 1 January 2016) and 100 kW (for installations taken into use after 31 December 2015).

[262] § 34(1) EEG 2014.

[263] § 11(1) EEG 2014.

[264] See EPEX Spot Operational Rules (28 November 2014), Article 1.5.5: "The Orders sent to EPEX Spot SE by Exchange Members remain in the Order Book until: – the Order is cancelled by the Member that placed it, or, – the Member modifies the Order, or, – the Order is executed". Article 1.6.3: ". . . Once the Order Book is closed, Orders may not be modified or cancelled and are binding and irrevocable".

kinds of bids (order types) depending on the matching method (how an order is executed).

Limitation of Liability The matching of bids in the spot market is more difficult compared with the matching of bids in securities markets. To mitigate its own risk exposure, the operator of the exchange may want to increase its discretion to refuse orders and reduce its liability to bidders.

In Nord Pool Spot's physical markets, the exchange operator reserves a limited right to "reject, cancel or refuse to display or match" orders that are not in compliance with the Trading Rules or the applicable law.[265] In the physical market of N2EX, the exchange operator reserves a limited right to refuse orders.[266] There are usual limitation of liability clauses and a force majeure clause for both markets.[267]

On EPEX Spot, the operator is only subject to a best-efforts obligation and liable only for damage caused by wilful acts or through gross negligence. There is a cap for liability.[268]

4.5.5 Excursion: Unbundled or Integrated Post-trading Systems

Trades must be cleared and settled. Clearing and settlement systems belong to "post-trading" systems.[269] There is a difference between post-trading systems designed for securities and electricity spot markets.

Securities Markets It is customary to distinguish between flow-related activities and securities-related activities in securities markets. *Flow-related* activities start after the matching of bids and end with the transfer of securities, cash, or both between final market participants. *Securities-related* activities are independent of the completion of transactions. For example, they include establishing securities in book-entry form, deposit, account providing, and asset servicing.[270]

Spot Markets While similar flow-related activities are used in electricity spot markets, one can distinguish between activities relating to financial flows and physical flows. (a) Clearing activities relating to *physical flows* play an important role in electricity spot markets. Such electricity-related clearing activities relate to the maintenance of balance in the grid. The fact that there are electricity-related clearing activities influences the organisation of clearing and settlement.

---

265 Nord Pool Spot's Physical Markets, General Terms, Trading Rules (1 February 2015), section 8.5.1.

266 N2EX Physical Market, General Trading Terms, Trading Rules (1 October 2014), section 7.5.1.

267 Nord Pool Spot's Physical Markets, General Terms, Trading Rules (1 February 2015), section 12; N2EX Physical Market, General Trading Terms, Trading Rules (1 October 2014), section 11.

268 EPEX Spot Operational Rules (28 November 2014), Article 2.16 and Article 2.19.

269 Commission, Draft Working Document on Post-trading (2006), p. 6.

270 Commission, Draft Working Document on Post-trading (2006), pp. 6–7.

(b) Clearing activities relating to *financial flows* can be defined as the process of establishing settlement positions, including the calculation of net positions, and the process of checking that the necessary electricity, collateral, and cash are available.[271] (c) In electricity spot markets, securities-related activities are limited to collateral and can thus be called *collateral-related* activities.

Integration or Unbundling The various post-trading functions can be integrated or unbundled. This leads to questions about the market participant's counterparty. Should the clearing house be the central counterparty? Can the clearing house be the central counterparty regarding physical flows?

EMIR provides that the central counterparty is responsible for the operation of the clearing system.[272] The voluntary European Code of Conduct for Clearing and Settlement is based on the assumption that the functions of central counterparty and clearing house should be combined. However, the Code recommends the unbundling of the functions of trading venue (exchange operator) and central counterparty.[273]

The integration of the functions of clearing house and central counterparty, and the separation of the functions of exchange operator and clearing house, might be explained by issues relating to the management of risk, information, and costs. There are nevertheless differences between financial flows and physical flows.

Financial Flows There are issues for and against combining the roles of clearing house, central counterparty, and provider of settlement services for financial flows.

On one hand, combining the roles can reduce systemic risk and transaction costs by increasing access to information. As an information hub, the clearing house receives and produces information. Access to this information enables it to assess counterparty risk and its own risk exposure as central counterparty. One of the basic ways to manage systemic risk is to collect sufficient collateral from market participants in the form of margins and otherwise. Information costs (transaction costs) can be reduced if the same entity acts as a central counterparty, clearing house, settlement agent, and collateral agent.

On the other hand, it may be easier to manage systemic risk, if the clearing house is separate from the exchange operator. The separation of functions makes it necessary to exchange information. If the clearing house is not the exchange operator responsible for the access of market participants and the matching of bids, the operator and the clearing house should exchange information about:

[271] Compare Commission, Draft Working Document on Post-trading (2006), p. 7.

[272] Points 1 and 3 of Article 2 of Regulation 648/2012 (EMIR).

[273] European Code of Conduct for Clearing and Settlement (7 November 2006), para 39: "Organisations shall unbundle prices and services at least as follows (i) The services of trading venues, CCPs and CSDs will be unbundled from each other. (ii) Each CSD will unbundle the following services each from the other: a. Account provision, establishing securities in book entry form, and asset servicing; b. Clearing and settlement (including verification); c. Credit provision; d. Securities lending and borrowing; and e. Collateral management".

compliance with the terms of market access[274]; and matching bids.[275] The separation of functions can facilitate mutual monitoring. The exchange of information and mutual monitoring can increase transparency.

Physical Flows While the clearing house is often the party that acts as central counterparty for financial flows, it can neither supply nor extract electricity in its capacity as clearing house. The same can be said of the exchange operator. It does not matter whether the operator or the clearing house has a contractual obligation to supply or extract electricity. Neither the operator nor the clearing house can direct physical electricity flows. Physical flows must be managed by the TSO.

If the central counterparty for financial flows nevertheless acts as the central counterparty for physical electricity flows, it is exposed to the risk that the agreed flows will not happen because of the TSO's actions. This risk is addressed in the trading rules and clearing rules (Sect. 4.5.6).

4.5.6 The Central Counterparty

There is more work for central counterparties and parties responsible for clearing and settlement in spot electricity markets than on financial electricity exchanges. In both cases, the parties must regulate legal rights, especially financial rights. In spot markets, the parties must also regulate physical flows and service (supply or off-take) rights (Sect. 2.5.7). One can therefore ask whether the central counterparty is the central counterparty for financial or service rights or both, whether the clearing house is the clearing house for financial or physical flows or both, and whether the settlement provider is the settlement provider for financial or physical flows or both.

Central Counterparty for Financial Flows As regards the central counterparty for financial flows, EMIR provides that the central counterparty is responsible for the operation of the clearing system.[276] The voluntary European Code of Conduct for Clearing and Settlement recommends the unbundling of the functions of trading venue (exchange operator) and central counterparty.[277]

The spot exchanges studied here have designated the clearing house as the central counterparty, but the party designated as the clearing house/central counterparty can be either the exchange operator (Nord Pool Spot) or a third party (EPEX Spot and N2EX in the past).

---

[274] For instance, ECC AG must notify EPEX Spot SE of the approval of a Trading Participant. EPEX Spot Exchange Rules (28 November 2014), Article 2.11.

[275] For instance, EPEX Spot SE must notify ECC AG of transactions concluded by trading participants. EPEX Spot Exchange Rules (28 November 2014), Article 7.2.

[276] Points 1 and 3 of Article 2 of Regulation 648/2012 (EMIR).

[277] European Code of Conduct for Clearing and Settlement (7 November 2006), para 39.

EPEX Spot SE (a French company) has designated European Commodity Clearing AG (a company with its seat in Leipzig) as the clearing house. The clearing house acts as the central counterparty for payment and delivery of the contracts traded or registered at the exchange.[278]

The physical markets of Nord Pool Spot share the same operator, Nord Pool Spot AS (a Norwegian company). Nord Pool Spot AS is the counterparty for trading in the Elspot market and (since 1 January 2011) in the Elbas market (after replacing its subsidiary Nord Pool Finland Oy as the counterparty at Elbas).[279]

In the past, Nord Pool Spot AS was neither the clearing house nor the central counterparty for trading on N2EX. The clearing house and central counterparty was NASDAQ OMX Stockholm AB (a Swedish company).[280] Since 1 October 2014, Nord Pool Spot AS is the central counterparty and clearing house in the physical market of N2EX.[281]

If there is a central counterparty, there must also a contractual mechanism to ensure that once the bids are matched into a trade, the trade gives rise to two contracts with the central counterparty as there is no bilateral contract between the two market participants. If the exchange operator is the central counterparty (Nord Pool Spot), information flows are easier to manage. If the exchange operator is not the central counterparty (EPEX Spot), information flows must be regulated in more detail. To reduce risk in the latter case, clearing must be initiated by the exchange operator that matches the bids, and it must be initiated automatically.

The mechanism is relatively simple on Elspot, because Nord Pool Spot AS is both the exchange operator and the central counterparty/clearing house: "Clearing is initiated by NPS entering into a Transaction as central counterparty and registering the Transaction on the Clearing Accounts of the Account Holders involved".[282]

More regulation was needed in N2EX when Nord Pool Spot AS acted as the exchange operator and NASDAQ OMX Stockholm AB was the central counterparty/clearing

[278] EPEX Spot Exchange Rules (28 November 2014), Article 1.5.

[279] Nord Pool Spot Market, Trading Appendix 1, Definitions (27 November 2014): "Counterparty means the Participant and Clearing Customer entering into a Transaction, and NPS acting as central counterparty in all Transactions". "Nord Pool Spot or NPS means Nord Pool Spot AS, a Norwegian company with reg. no 984 058 098 in the Norwegian Company Register". Nord Pool Spot Physical Markets, Trading Appendix 4, Clearing Rules (27 November 2014), section 1.1.1: "These Clearing Rules apply to the Clearing of Products in the Physical Markets". Section 1.1.2: "Clearing is initiated by NPS entering into a Transaction as central counterparty and registering the Transaction on the Clearing Accounts of the Account Holders involved".

[280] N2EX Market, Trading Appendix 1/Clearing Appendix 1, Definitions (DRAFT NWE/PCR implementation): "Counterparty means the Account Holder(s) entering into a Clearing Transaction, and NOMX acting as counterparty in all Clearing Transactions". "NASDAQ OMX Stockholm AB or NOMX means NASDAQ OMX Stockholm AB, a Swedish company with reg. no 556420-8394 in the Swedish company register, in its capacity as a counterparty to all Clearing Transactions on the N2EX Market". "Clearing Transaction means a Transaction that is registered with and approved by NOMX for Clearing".

[281] N2EX Physical Market, Trading Appendix 1/Clearing Appendix 1, Definitions (1 October 2014).

[282] Nord Pool Spot Physical Markets, Trading Appendix 4, Clearing Rules (27 November 2014), section 1.1.2.

house.[283] Transactions concluded on the trading system are now automatically subject to clearing.[284]

On the derivatives market of EPEX Spot, contracts are deemed to have been concluded between European Commodity Clearing AG (ECC) as the central counterparty and each of the trading participants when corresponding orders are matched.[285] Spot market transactions are deemed to have been concluded both between ECC and ECC Lux (European Commodity Clearing Luxembourg S.a.r.l.) and between ECC Lux and the trading participant in the same way.[286] The clearing conditions of the central counterparty and clearing house focus on financial flows.[287]

Central Counterparty for Physical Flows One may ask whether the central counterparty for financial flows can act as the central counterparty also regarding physical electricity flows. Physical flows must be managed by the TSO. If the central counterparty for financial flows acts as the central counterparty for physical electricity flows, it is exposed to the risk that the agreed flows will not happen because of actions by the TSO.

There are various complementary ways to mitigate risk and agency costs in the relationship between the central counterparty and the TSO. They include, among others: information management; the alignment of interests; and risk management through contracts: (a) One can improve the TSO's chances to do its job properly by improving the quality of information and by making even market participants responsible for balancing and coordination. (b) Generally, agency costs between the central counterparty and the TSO could can be reduced where their interests are aligned through contracts, share ownership, or otherwise. (c) The central counterparty's risk exposure can be mitigated through contracts. First, the central counterparty's risk exposure can be mitigated by limiting or excluding its liability to trading participants in various ways: the responsibility for the physical settlement of trades can be allocated to a third party; the central counterparty can assume best

[283] N2EX Market, General Terms, Clearing Rules (3 September 2013), section 6.2.2: "Upon the conclusion of a Transaction on a Trading System and allocation of the Transaction to a Trading Portfolio, the Transaction will be immediately replicated (mirrored) to the Clearing Portfolio associated with the applicable Trading Portfolio, and Clearing Transactions are created and allocated to the applicable Clearing Accounts in accordance with Section 6.1". Section 6.2.3: "The Transaction Confirmation from the Market Operator also serves as Clearing Confirmation from NOMX in respect of the corresponding Clearing Transactions created".

[284] N2EX Physical Market, General Clearing Terms, Clearing Rules (27 November 2014), section 6.2.1.

[285] ECC Clearing Conditions (0022a, 30 April 2014), section 3.4.1(1).

[286] ECC Clearing Conditions (0022a, 30 April 2014), section 3.4.1(2): "According to the more detailed definition provided in section 3.4.3, spot market transactions on the markets are concluded between ECC and ECC Lux and between ECC Lux and the Trading Participant at the same time. In deviation of the above neither ECC nor ECC Lux becomes a contractual party to the PXE spot market transactions. These transactions are being concluded between the Trading Participants and a counterparty (Energy Clearing Company a.s. – EnCC) commissioned by PXE. EnCC is a Clearing Entity according to section 2.6".

[287] ECC Clearing Conditions (0022a, 30 April 2014), section 3.4.3(1): "Clearing Members are obliged to settle all obligations arising from matching of orders or registered OTC transactions which they have entered into the system on a market".

efforts obligations instead of obligations to achieve a result; or the liability of the central counterparty for loss or damage relating to physical settlement or actions attributable to the TSO can be limited or excluded. Second, the TSO can be made party to a three-party or multi-party contract relationship.

There are many examples of such practices in the spot markets studied here.

In the physical markets of Nord Pool Spot, all shares of the operator (Nord Pool Spot AS) are owned by the Nordic and Baltic TSOs. The operator acts as the clearing house and central counterparty. The TSOs' interests are therefore aligned with those of the clearing house and central counterparty.

However, there is no share ownership between the operator (Nord Pool Spot AS) and the relevant TSOs in the physical market of N2EX. Neither does the operator function as the central counterparty and clearing house. This requires a more detailed contractual framework that market participants must comply with.

Like the physical market of N2EX, the EPEX Spot market requires a detailed contractual framework with the TSOs. (a) There are multi-party agreements called balance agreements between the TSO, trading participants, the central counterparty/clearing house, and the party responsible for settlement.[288] Moreover, some participants in the EPEX Spot market are balance responsible parties responsible for balance groups.[289] (b) The liability of the central counterparty (European Commodity Clearing AG, ECC) is limited in various ways. First, the central counterparty (ECC) is not responsible for the physical fulfilment of trades. It only guarantees fulfilment. Second, its subsidiary (European Commodity Clearing Luxembourg S.a.r.l., ECC Lux) has assumed responsibility for the physical settlement of trades. Third, clearing members have a duty to settle all obligations arising from the matching of orders or registered OTC transactions[290] (and each clearing member is liable as a guarantor towards ECC Lux for non-clearing members' financial liabilities).[291] Fourth, ECC and ECC Lux exclude their liability for the actions of the TSO, and for their own actions to the extent that they are based on the TSO's actions.[292]

4.5.7 *Clearing*

General Remarks

The core of clearing is the calculation of net positions.[293] This core function can be complemented by various actions that reduce counterparty risk and make settlement

---

[288] ECC Clearing Conditions (0022a, 30 April 2014), 1 Definition of Terms: "Balance agreement: All contractual agreements between the transmission system operator or hub operator and the Trading Participant as well as between the transmission system operator/hub operator and ECC and ECC Lux regarding the settlement of power and natural gas deliveries".

[289] For the definition of balance responsible, see EPEX Spot Rules & Regulations, Appendix, Definitions (28 November 2014).

[290] ECC Clearing Conditions (0022a, 30 April 2014), section 3.4.3(1).

[291] ECC Clearing Conditions (0022a, 30 April 2014), section 3.4.3(2).

[292] ECC Clearing Conditions (0022a, 30 April 2014), section 5.2.5(4).

[293] See already point (e) of Article 2 of Directive 98/26/EC (Directive on settlement finality): "'clearing house' shall mean an entity responsible for the calculation of the net positions of institutions, a possible central counterparty and/or a possible settlement agent".

easier. It can also be complemented by the operation of settlement. One can distinguish between the clearing of financial flows and physical flows.

Clearing of Financial Flows

The clearing of financial flows can be combined with different functions. In the Nord Pool Spot and EPEX Spot markets, the clearing house is the central counterparty, holds collateral, and takes care of financial settlement. In the Nord Pool Spot market, the clearing house is the exchange operator. On EPEX Spot, the clearing house is a separate entity (ECC).

Clearing of Physical Flows

In practice, the most important electricity-related clearing and settlement activities belong to the responsibilities of the TSO. The contractual framework of the TSO dictates much of the contractual framework that regulates physical electricity flows.[294] The operator of the spot exchange and the clearing house must align their rules and actions with the TSO's regulatory framework and actions.

Allocation of Liability and Regulation This influences the contractual framework and the allocation of liability.

There can be differences between physical and financial flows and the legal path of electricity. (a) As a rule, financial flows are aligned with the legal path of electricity. (b) However, because of the physical characteristics of electricity, electricity flows do not necessarily follow the legal path. Electricity that a spot market buyer extracts from the grid is not really the same package of electricity that the electricity producer supplies to the grid. (c) Moreover, the TSO must maintain balance in the grid and has the regulatory framework for doing so. Balancing influences physical flows and financial flows.

Physical electricity flows do not have to be perfectly aligned with financial flows between market participants. On the other hand, contractual sanctions can be triggered where a party fails to fulfil its physical supply or off-take obligations. The TSO will take the necessary measures to maintain the physical balance and can also enforce contractual remedies against the defaulting party. Contractual remedies can also be enforced by the central counterparty, clearing house, or exchange operator. Liability can be allocated to a trading party or even to the central counterparty or the clearing house.

The allocation of liability is a question of proper management of agency relationships. Sanctions for non-compliance can increase incentives to comply

---

[294] EPEX Spot Exchange Rules (28 November 2014), Article 1.7: "... The Transmission System Operator (TSO) for a given Market Area provides the actual Delivery of the Contracts traded on EPEX Spot".

with contractual obligations, reduce counterparty and systemic risk, reduce transaction costs, increase liquidity, and increase the effectiveness of the marketplace.

It is possible for the exchange operator, clearing house, and central counterparty to take contractual measures to hold themselves harmless from actions by the seller, the buyer, and the TSO relating to physical electricity flows.

This is reflected in the contractual framework of the spot exchange in three main ways. First, the contractual framework of the spot exchange does not have to regulate electricity-related clearing in detail. Second, it requires the parties to agree on grid access, transmission capacity, and communications with the TSO. The contractual framework applied between market participants and the TSO is often called the balance agreement (Sect. 4.10). Third, the operator of the spot exchange, the clearing house, and the central counterparty exclude their liability for things caused by the TSO's actions and for non-fulfilment of physical supply or off-take obligations. Fourth, balance responsibility can be allocated to a balance responsible party.

Balance Agreement with the TSO The legal framework for the clearing of financial flows can thus be simplified when market participants are required to enter into a balance agreement either with the TSO or with a balance responsible party that has entered into a balance agreement with the TSO.

The trading rules of Nord Pool Spot require market participants and clients to have entered into an agreement on balance responsibility with a balance responsible party or the TSO.[295]

On N2EX, the deliverable electricity contract volumes are delivered in accordance with the terms of the BSC (including the terms of each clearing transaction or ECV Transfer and the clearing rules).[296] For this reason, the clearing house's counterparties must have established access to an energy account.[297]

On EPEX Spot, the physical delivery of spot market transactions must be effected according to the clearing conditions and the balance agreements.[298] Trading on EPEX Spot is not possible without a balance agreement or a balance responsible agreement.[299] The balance agreement means "all contractual agreements between the transmission system operator ... and the Trading Participant as well as between the transmission system operator ... and ECC and ECC Lux regarding the settlement of power ... deliveries".[300]

Communications to the TSO The parties' supply and off-take obligations must be communicated to the relevant TSO in an organised and timely way.[301]

---

[295] Nord Pool Spot's Physical Markets, General Terms, Trading Rules (1 February 2015), section 3.1.4.

[296] N2EX Physical Market, General Clearing Terms, Clearing Rules (27 November 2014), section 11.1.1.

[297] N2EX Physical Market, General Clearing Terms, Clearing Rules (27 November 2014), sections 3.2.2 and 5.2.

[298] ECC Clearing Conditions (0022a, 30 April 2014), section 5.2.3(1).

[299] EPEX Spot Exchange Rules (28 November 2014), Article 2.23.

[300] ECC Clearing Conditions (0022a, 30 April 2014), section 1.

[301] EPEX Spot Exchange Rules (28 November 2014), Article 1.7: "... The Transmission System Operator (TSO) for a given Market Area provides the actual Delivery of the Contracts traded on EPEX Spot".

In principle, the party responsible for these communications could be the exchange operator, the clearing house, the central counterparty, the relevant clearing member, or a non-clearing market participant. However, market participants cannot obtain information about the matching of bids and the existence of a contract with the central counterparty unless information is communicated to them.

Information should thus be communicated to market participants. To reduce risks inherent in communications, information about the matching of bids can be communicated automatically by the exchange operator to the clearing house, and the clearing house can communicate information about the contents of the supply and extraction obligations to the market participants (and the central counterparty, if the clearing house is not the central counterparty). Both communications can also be made simultaneously.

The operator of EPEX Spot sends contract information to the clearing house/central counterparty once orders have been matched.[302] The clearing house/central counterparty sends information to the trading participants, or it is provided within the system of the market.[303]

In the physical market of N2EX, communications are automatic. The exchange operator's transaction confirmation also serves as confirmation by the clearing house of the creation of the corresponding clearing transactions.[304]

Communications are simple on Elspot, because the same entity acts as the operator of the exchange, the clearing house, and the central counterparty. NPS can allocate information about matching bids and transactions to the relevant clearing accounts.[305]

Information should also be communicated to the TSO. (a) Generally, the operator of the exchange and the clearing house can decide on the scope and contents of the regulatory regime for the operator-clearing house-TSO interface. For instance, they can decide whether to regulate this issue in detail or leave it unregulated. (b) The scope and contents of the regime nevertheless depend on the number of TSOs as the exchange operator and the clearing house must adapt to the regulatory regime of the relevant TSO or TSOs.

The regime can be larger in scope and more detailed where the number of TSOs is one. In this case, it is easier to adapt the regulatory regime of the exchange operator and the clearing house to the regulatory regime of the TSO.

Where the number of potential TSOs is large, it would not be feasible to regulate the interface in detail for each and every TSO. Leaving the issue of communications to the TSO unregulated by the exchange operator and the clearing house would mean that communications to the TSO are regulated (1) by the TSO's legal framework for grid access and transmission capacity and (2) between each market participant and the TSO. In this case, the contractual framework of the spot

[302] EPEX Spot Exchange Rules (28 November 2014), Article 7.2.

[303] ECC Clearing Conditions (0022a, 30 April 2014), section 5.2.2(2).

[304] N2EX Physical Market, General Clearing Terms, Clearing Rules (27 November 2014), section 6.2.

[305] Nord Pool Spot Physical Markets, Trading Appendix 4, Clearing Rules (27 November 2014), section 4.1.2.

exchange would merely refer to contracts between TSO and the market participant (balance agreements). Another market participant can also act as a "balance responsible party" coordinating the activities of a group of market participants.

As the number of potential TSOs can influence the regulatory regime, there is a fundamental difference between Elspot or EPEX Spot on one hand and N2EX on the other. Whereas activities on Elspot and EPEX Spot must be adapted to the regulatory frameworks of many national TSOs, the only TSO relevant for the N2EX market is National Grid.

Communications relating to physical electricity flows are largely regulated by the TSO in the Elspot market of Nord Pool Spot and EPEX Spot.

Nord Pool Spot AS (NPS), the exchange operator/clearing house/central counterparty of Elspot requires market participants to have agreed on balance responsibility either with the TSO or a balance responsible party.[306] After clearing, exchange members must fulfil their physical supply or off-take obligations. Although NPS is the central counterparty, it excludes its own liability for non-fulfilment of these obligations: "Non-delivery or non-off-take is to be settled with the relevant Balance Responsible Party or Transmission System Operator in accordance with applicable rules, with no liability for NPS".[307] Instead, NPS has chosen to regulate cash flows based on cleared transactions.[308]

The same regulatory technique is used in the EPEX Spot market. Communications to the TSO are regulated by the relevant TSO rather than the exchange operator or the clearing house. The exchange operator (EPEX Spot SE) sends a confirmation to the parties[309] and information to the clearing house/central counterparty (ECC) once orders have been matched. After this, the exchange operator is not concerned about communications to the TSO. Following registration by ECC, the payment and delivery obligations arising from transactions are governed by the clearing conditions of ECC.[310] ECC communicates reports regarding transactions to the trading participants.[311] The physical delivery of the spot market transactions is "effected" directly by the trading participant towards ECC Lux,[312] and the delivery obligations are "executed" by nominating the purchases or sales to the relevant TSO (after which electricity is supplied to the grid and extracted from the grid).[313] Where a trading participant fails to fulfil its delivery or acceptance of delivery obligation, sanctions may be enforced by ECC (even on behalf of ECC Lux) under the clearing conditions and by the TSO under the balance agreement.[314]

---

306 Nord Pool Spot's Physical Markets, General Terms, Trading Rules (1 February 2015), section 3.1.4.

307 Nord Pool Spot Physical Markets, Trading Appendix 4, Clearing Rules (27 November 2014), section 4.1.3.

308 Nord Pool Spot Physical Markets, Trading Appendix 4, Clearing Rules (27 November 2014), sections 4.1.1 and 4.1.2. See also section 4.1.4: "Cash Settlement will be based on the Transactions recorded with NPS only, and will not reflect non-delivery or non-off-take".

309 EPEX Spot Operational Rules (28 November 2014), Article 1.8 (on auction trading).

310 EPEX Spot Exchange Rules (28 November 2014), Article 7.2.

311 ECC Clearing Conditions (0022a, 30 April 2014), section 5.2.2(2).

312 ECC Clearing Conditions, (0022a, 30 April 2014), section 5.2.3(1): "Physical delivery and acceptance of delivery of power is effected directly by the Trading Participant towards ECC Lux and at the same time between ECC Lux and ECC subject to the provisions specified in these Clearing Conditions and the respectively valid balance agreements. The delivery is effected by submitting a nomination or schedule in accordance with the requirements of the respective Balancing Agreement, which comprises the underlying delivery transaction as well as the binding confirmation of the nomination or schedule by the respective transmission system operator".

313 EPEX Spot Exchange Rules (28 November 2014), Article 5.2.

314 ECC Clearing Conditions (0022a, 30 April 2014), section 5.2.3(3).

4.5.8 Excursion: Clearing of Physical Flows in the N2EX Market

We can study the clearing of physical flows in more detail in the light of the N2EX market. In the N2EX market, communications to the TSO are regulated more explicitly compared with Elspot and EPEX Spot. The rules of the N2EX market can thus provide more information about the necessary mechanisms.

There are three major issues contributing to the more detailed regulation on N2EX. (a) The first is the existence of just one TSO (National Grid) for the market. (b) Moreover, the regulatory regime applied in the UK market is influenced by the contract and regulatory style characteristic of common law countries. In common law countries, contracts tend to be larger in scope and more detailed than in civil law countries.[315] (c) In addition, participants in the UK physical market must comply with the Balancing and Settlement Code (BSC) in the UK.

BSC is a legal document that sets out the rules and governance for the balancing mechanism and imbalance settlement process in the UK. BSC is delivered by the Balancing and Settlement Code Company (BSCCo). ELEXON is the BSCCo. The sole shareholder of ELEXON is National Grid.

Now, National Grid has, according to the terms of its own licence, a duty to establish statements and guidelines.[316] National Grid must have the BSC in force to comply with its own licence requirements. This is reflected in the licences of installations. It is a condition of a Generation and Supply Licence that licensees are bound by the BSC; they must become BSC Parties by signing and/or acceding to the BSC Framework Agreement which gives contractual force to the BSC.[317]

The BSC sets out in what capacities a party may act, that is, the available categories of BSC parties. Parties to the BSC are essentially entities that are parties to the Framework Agreement.[318] Each party may act in one or more participation capacities under the BSC. For example, a party can be: a Trading Party (a party that holds Energy Accounts); or a Supplier (a Party that holds a Supply Licence and has metering systems registered in Supplier Volume Allocation (SVA).[319]

Some entities have Energy Accounts. Energy Accounts are allocated to the following Parties: (a) Parties who are responsible for imports and exports of

---

[315] See, for example, Mäntysaari P (2010b), section 2.2.3.

[316] Special Condition C16 of the Statements of the Transmission Licence.

[317] ELEXON, Overview of the Balancing and Settlement Code (BSC) Arrangements.

[318] BSC, Section A, para 1.2. Parties include: (a) ELEXON; (b) the National Grid Company; (c) Licensees; and (d) others that voluntarily choose to become Parties.

[319] BSC, Section A, para 1.3. Each Party may have one or more different participation capacities under the BSC: (a) the Transmission Company (currently National Grid as Transmission Licensee); (b) a Distribution System Operator (i.e. those holding a Distribution Licence); (c) a Trading Party (a party that holds Energy Accounts); (d) a Supplier (a Party that holds a Supply Licence and has metering systems registered in Supplier Volume Allocation (SVA); (e) an Interconnector Error Administrator (IEA), or an Interconnector Administrator (IA) (see Section K).

electricity (typically generators and suppliers); (b) Interconnector Error Administrators (IEAs); (c) other Parties wishing to trade; and (d) National Grid (as the TSO).[320] A Party has only two energy accounts: a Production Energy Account; and a Consumption Energy Account.[321]

The operator of N2EX (Nord Pool Spot AS) and the market's central counterparty/clearing house (earlier Nasdax OMX Stockholm AB, since 1 October 2014 Nord Pool Spot AS) must adapt to the legal framework of the TSO (National Grid) including, in particular, the Balance and Settlement Code of the BSCCo (ELEXON).

As OTC markets must comply with the same requirements, the EFET General Agreement Concerning the Delivery and Acceptance of Electricity (Sect. 8.3) has been complemented by a GTMA Appendix. GTMA (the Grid Trade Master Agreement) is the standard set of terms under which the majority of electricity forward trades take place in the UK.[322] The EFET GTMA Appendix applies to individual contracts which must be notified and considered for settlement purposes under the Balancing and Settlement Code.[323]

Such compliance requirements are reflected in the clearing rules for the N2EX market. They can only be understood in the context of the BSC.

The clearing transactions are created automatically. The transaction confirmation from the market operator (Nord Pool Spot AS) also serves as a clearing confirmation from the clearing house.[324]

However, electricity contract volumes (ECVs) that are deliverable under a clearing transaction or any ECV transfer must be delivered in accordance with the terms of the BSC in addition to the terms of each clearing transaction or ECV transfer and the clearing house's clearing rules.[325]

Each clearing account holder must, therefore, maintain an energy account,[326] and each "energy contract volume transferee" (ECV transferee) must also be party to the BSC.[327] Clearing transactions registered to a clearing account will be notified to its associated energy account.[328]

Whenever a clearing transaction is registered to a clearing account that is associated with an energy account of an ECV transferee, a corresponding ECV

[320] BSC, Section A, para 1.4.

[321] BSC, Section A, para 1.4.2: "Subject to paragraph 1.4.3, no Party shall hold more than one Production Energy Account and more than one Consumption Energy Account and, accordingly, a Party which falls within more than one of the descriptions in paragraph 1.4.1(a), (b) or (c) shall hold one Production Energy Account and one Consumption Energy Account for all such activities".

[322] Ofgem (2009), para 3.74.

[323] § 1.1 of the EFET GTMA Appendix.

[324] N2EX Physical Market, General Clearing Terms, Clearing Rules (27 November 2014), section 6.2.3.

[325] *Ibid*, section 11.1.

[326] *Ibid*, section 5.2.1 and section 5.2.2.

[327] *Ibid*, section 5.2.3.

[328] *Ibid*, section 11.2.1.

Transfer will be deemed to be created and executed automatically between the relevant account holder and the ECV transferee.[329]

Notifications are important for the proper functioning of the exchange and for the management of physical electricity flows in the grid. Breaches of notification rules under the BSC can amount to a default on obligations under the clearing rules (cross-default).[330]

All notifications go via the clearing house. The clearing house (or its nominee) receives notifications and makes them on behalf of all counterparties.[331] In order for the notifications and procedures to have legal relevance and trigger physical electricity flows, the clearing house must follow the BSC.[332]

The clearing house cannot take care of notifications in respect of transfers to energy accounts, unless the clearing account holder appoints the clearing house as ECV Notification Agent according to the BSC.[333] This requires a particular contract (ECV Transferee Agreement) between the clearing house and the account holder,[334] and the account holder must party to the BSC.[335]

Although the clearing house takes care of notifications of energy contract volume transfers to energy accounts, such ECV transfers are separate from clearing transactions and do not influence clearing transactions as such.[336] ECV transfers do not create clearing transactions according to the legal framework applied by the clearing house/central counterparty. The clearing house has just an obligation to act as ECV Notification Agent. It is neither party to the ECV transfer nor a fiduciary. The clearing house has stated this both in the particular ECV Transferee Agreement[337] and in its clearing rules for the N2EX market.[338]

However, the clearing house is responsible for notification failures. Where the clearing house breaches its notification obligations, it is liable to indemnify the account holder for delivery failure costs.[339] Where the notification failure is the result of the failure of the account holder or its ECV transferee to comply with its own obligations under the clearing rules or under the BSC, the account holder must

---

[329] *Ibid*, section 11.3.1.

[330] *Ibid*, section 11.3.4.

[331] *Ibid*, section 11.2.2.

[332] *Ibid*, section 11.2.5.

[333] *Ibid*, section 11.1.3 and section 11.1.4.

[334] N2EX Physical Market, Clearing Agreement F, ECV Transferee Agreement (1 October 2014), section 3.1 and section 3.3.

[335] N2EX Physical Market, Clearing Agreement F, ECV Transferee Agreement (1 October 2014), section 1.2 and section 1.3.

[336] N2EX Physical Market, Clearing Agreement F, ECV Transferee Agreement (1 October 2014), section 4.2.

[337] N2EX Physical Market, Clearing Agreement F, ECV Transferee Agreement (1 October 2014), section 4.

[338] N2EX Physical Market, General Clearing Terms, Clearing Rules (27 November 2014), section 11.3.3.

[339] *Ibid*, section 11.4.

indemnify the clearing house in respect of any delivery failure costs directly attributable to that notification failure.[340]

4.5.9 Settlement

Clearing is followed by settlement. One can again distinguish between the settlement of financial flows and physical flows. In the spot market, the financial settlement of transactions means the payment of the purchase price for the bought volumes.[341] Table 4.1 shows the settlement of physical and financial flows in Nord Pool Spot.

Settlement of Financial Flows

Like financial clearing, financial settlement is regulated by the clearing rules of the clearing house.[342] EMIR requires central counterparties to use central bank money to settle their transactions, where practical and available,[343] and to use Zug-um-Zug mechanisms (delivery against payment).[344]

The clearing house is more focused on the settlement of financial flows than physical flows. In the EPEX Spot market, the exchange operator (EPEX Spot SE) defines "settlement" as the payment of transactions executed on EPEX Spot and handled by the clearing house.[345] The clearing conditions of the clearing house (ECC) regulate payments in detail.[346] On Elspot, the clearing rules of the central counterparty/clearing house regulate cash settlement[347] but not really physical settlement.[348]

Financial settlement can be governed by the law chosen by the clearing house. The clearing house would probably choose the law of its own country as the governing law. The choice would be limited to financial settlement and would not cover physical settlement that is to a large extent regulated by the TSO and governed by the laws of a country to which physical delivery is more closely connected.

---

[340] *Ibid*, section 11.4.5.

[341] Hünerwadel A (2007), p. 56.

[342] EPEX Spot Exchange Rules (28 November 2014), Article 2.11: "The orderly settlement of Transactions on EPEX Spot is deemed to be secured when all of the following requirements are fulfilled: – The Exchange Member has to take part in clearing on ECC AG in accordance with the respectively valid Clearing Conditions of European Commodity Clearing AG (ECC AG); ..."

[343] Article 50(1) of Regulation 648/2012 (EMIR).

[344] Article 50(3) of Regulation 648/2012 (EMIR).

[345] EPEX Spot Rules & Regulations, Appendix, Definitions (28 November 2014).

[346] Clearing Conditions of European Commodity Clearing AG (0022a, 30 April 2014).

[347] Nord Pool Spot Physical Markets, Trading Appendix 4, Clearing Rules (27 November 2014), section 4.2.

[348] Nord Pool Spot Physical Markets, Trading Appendix 4, Clearing Rules (27 November 2014), section 4.1.4.

Table 4.1 NPS settlement of physical and financial flows

Physical settlement[a]	TSO		
	Balance Responsible Party[b]		
Parties	Client[c]	Participant	NPS
Financial settlement[d]	Settlement Bank[e]	Settlement Bank	Settlement Bank

[a]Nord Pool Spot Physical Markets, Trading Appendix 4, Clearing Rules (27 November 2014), section 4.1.3: "... Non-delivery or non-off-take is to be settled with the relevant Balance Responsible Party or Transmission System Operator in accordance with applicable rules, with no liability for NPS"

[b]Nord Pool Spot's Physical Markets, General Terms, Trading Rules (1 February 2015), section 3.1.4

[c]Nord Pool Spot Physical Markets, Trading Appendix 4, Clearing Rules (27 November 2014), section 2.1.3: "NPS recognises the following membership categories: a. Participant b. Client Representative c. Client"

[d]Nord Pool Spot Market, Trading Appendix 1, Definitions (27 November 2014): "Settlement means the process which by trades in the Markets are handled through cash transactions". Nord Pool Spot Physical Markets, Trading Appendix 4, Clearing Rules (27 November 2014), section 4.1.4: "Cash Settlement will be based on the Transactions recorded with NPS only, and will not reflect non-delivery or non-off-take"

[e]Nord Pool Spot Physical Markets, Trading Appendix 4, Clearing Rules (27 November 2014), section 3.3.1: "Each Member must at its own cost establish and maintain at least one Cash Account in an NPS approved settlement bank and in a currency approved by NPS". Nord Pool Spot Market, Trading Appendix 1, Definitions (27 November 2014)

> On Elspot and Elbas, transactions are governed by Norwegian law. However, matters relating to the physical delivery of electricity are governed by "the local law of the delivery country".[349]
>
> On EPEX Spot, the clearing conditions are governed by German law. However, "the execution of the physical settlement of transactions" is governed by "the material law of the place at which physical fulfilment is actually provided and/or, in the case of grid-bound products, the material law applicable to the transmission system operator or the hub operator within whose transmission system delivery is effected".[350] Moreover, Leipzig has been chosen as the place of performance and venue.[351]

A market participant needs an account for the financial clearing and settlement of transactions.[352] Where the account is held depends on the nature of the market participant.

---

[349] Nord Pool Spot's Physical Markets, General Terms, Trading Rules (1 February 2015), section 18.1.1.

[350] ECC Clearing Conditions (0022a, 30 April 2014), section 6.4(1).

[351] ECC Clearing Conditions (0022a, 30 April 2014), section 6.4(2): "Leipzig shall be the exclusive legal venue for all conflicts arising in connection with these Clearing Conditions and Leipzig shall be the place of performance".

[352] ECC Clearing Conditions (0022a, 30 April 2014), 1 Definition of Terms: "Clearing account. Accounts of the Clearing Members, the Sub-CCP and ECC, which are kept by ECC or a third party on behalf of ECC and to which payments are credited or from which such are debited in batch processing during settlement of the transactions in accordance with these Clearing Conditions".

On Elspot, only members are eligible as counterparties to NPS in clearing transactions. To be eligible as a counterparty, the member must, in addition to other things, have established: one or more trading portfolios; one or more clearing accounts; and one or more cash accounts for settlement purposes.[353] The cash account or accounts must be maintained in an NPS approved settlement bank and in a currency approved by NPS.[354]

On EPEX Spot, each clearing member and the central counterparty must have a settlement account at the central bank.[355] There is no such requirement for non-clearing members and trading participants.[356]

Exposure to counterparty risk and systemic risk depends on how often trades are settled financially. To reduce counterparty risk and systemic risk, trades are settled daily.

Trades are settled daily on each business day on Nord Pool Spot's Elspot, Elbas,[357] and N2EX[358] markets including EPEX Spot.[359]

The clearing house issues invoices to trading participants. In practice, the payment time must depend on who takes the necessary actions. Payments can be made on the trading day when they are debited from the trading participant's account by the clearing house. Where the making of payments requires actions by trading participants, they cannot be made before the trading participant is notified of the amount due, and the trading participant must be given some time to organise payment. To reduce payment time, automated payments can be used.

On EPEX Spot, payments are made on the trading day.[360]

On N2EX, all invoices are due on the same banking day as they are issued.[361] This is combined with automated cash settlements. The bank is instructed and authorised to debit the account and make payments to the clearinghouse upon the clearinghouse's instructions.[362]

[353] Nord Pool Spot Physical Markets, Trading Appendix 4, Clearing Rules (27 November 2014), section 2.2.1.

[354] Nord Pool Spot Physical Markets, Trading Appendix 4, Clearing Rules (27 November 2014), section 3.3.1.

[355] ECC Clearing Conditions (0022a, 30 April 2014), section 2.1.2(5).

[356] ECC Clearing Conditions (0022a, 30 April 2014), section 2.2.1 and section 2.3.1.

[357] Nord Pool Spot Physical Markets, Trading Appendix 4, Clearing Rules (4 February 2014), section 4.2.2.

[358] N2EX Physical Market, General Clearing Terms, Clearing Rules (27 November 2014), section 10.1.1.

[359] ECC Clearing Conditions (0022a, 30 April 2014), section 3.6.6(1).

[360] ECC Clearing Conditions (0022a, 30 April 2014), section 5.2.2(3): "All payments including the taxes applicable as per the relevant laws are credited to the clearing account of the Clearing Member or debited from it during batch processing on the trading day or, if this day is not an Business Day, on the next Business Day".

[361] N2EX Physical Market, General Clearing Terms, Clearing Rules (27 November 2014), section 10.1.1.

[362] N2EX Physical Market, Clearing Agreement G, Cash Settlement Instructions (1 October 2014).

On Elspot, invoices fall due on the first clearing day following the invoice day.[363] The invoice due date is the same as the Elspot market's power contract delivery date (for all banking days).[364]

The clearing house issues self-billing invoices to itself, where the clearing house is the central counterparty. Where the clearing house issues self-billing invoices, it would have an incentive to delay its own payments to reduce its working capital.

On Elspot, the clearing house issues invoices to members and self-billing invoices to itself as the central counterparty.[365] An invoice falls due on the first clearing day following the invoice day.[366] The value date of a self-billing invoice is the second clearing day following invoice day.[367] Penalty interest is payable on overdue payment.[368]

Self-billing invoices are used on N2EX as well. All invoices are due on the same banking day as they are issued (and at such time as set out in the clearing schedule).[369]

Because of its function, a clearing member must undertake a duty to fulfil all payment obligations from transactions by its affiliated non-clearing members. A clearing member is thus not a mere agent. Sanctions will be triggered in the event of default on these payment obligations.

On EPEX Spot, the clearing rules provide that a clearing member must fulfil all payment obligations from transactions by its affiliated non-clearing members.[370] There are sanctions in the event of default.[371] One can distinguish between financial payment obligations and physical delivery obligations. (a) The liability of the clearing member for the fulfilment of the trading participant's obligations covers even physical delivery. Physical delivery obligations are fulfilled towards ECC Lux, a subsidiary of ECC.[372] This is because ECC

---

363 Nord Pool Spot Physical Markets, Trading Appendix 4, Clearing Rules (4 February 2014), section 4.2.5.

364 However, self-billing invoices are paid one day later. In the Elbas market, invoices are settled two days after the agreed delivery date and self-billing invoices are paid three days later.

365 Nord Pool Spot Physical Markets, Trading Appendix 4, Clearing Rules (27 November 2014), section 4.2.4.

366 Nord Pool Spot Physical Markets, Trading Appendix 4, Clearing Rules (27 November 2014), section 4.2.5.

367 Nord Pool Spot Physical Markets, Trading Appendix 4, Clearing Rules (27 November 2014), section 4.2.6.

368 Nord Pool Spot Physical Markets, Trading Appendix 4, Clearing Rules (27 November 2014), section 4.2.7: "In the event of overdue payment, the Parties may claim default interest pursuant to the Norwegian act of 17 December 1976 no. 100 regarding interest accrued in connection with late payment, as amended from time to time".

369 N2EX Physical Market, General Clearing Terms, Clearing Rules (27 November 2014), section 10.1.1.

370 ECC Clearing Conditions (0022a, 30 April 2014), section 3.1.1(2).

371 ECC Clearing Conditions (0022a, 30 April 2014), section 3.1.1(6).

372 ECC Clearing Conditions (0022a, 30 April 2014), section 3.4.5(1): "Physical delivery of transactions with regard to which ECC has assumed clearing is exclusively provided through its subsidiary – ECC Lux – with the effect that Trading Participants exclusively fulfil their delivery or acceptance of delivery obligations arising from derivatives market transactions and spot market transactions which are fulfilled physically according to their respective contract specifications towards ECC Lux. ECC guarantees the Trading Participants the fulfilment of these transactions by ECC Lux in accordance with the contract".

and the clearing member assign the claims to delivery and/or acceptance of delivery to ECC Lux.[373] ECC guarantees the fulfilment of physical delivery transactions by ECC Lux to the trading participants.[374] The clearing member can nevertheless only pay money to ECC Lux or ECC. Their duties are limited accordingly.[375] (b) In the derivatives market, the liability of a clearing member is limited to payment obligations.

Where a client trades through a client representative on Elspot, the client's counterparty is the central counterparty.[376] The client representative is not a counterparty, but it must ensure that its clients post collateral.[377] In the past, the central counterparty used any collateral posted by the client representative where the client representative failed to post missing collateral.[378] This rule was deleted in the 2014 Clearing Rules.

There are similar rules in the N2EX market. Interestingly, the client representative must immediately post the missing collateral where a clearing client fails to post collateral. If it does not post the missing collateral, the central counterparty applies collateral that the client representative has posted for principal trading.[379]

Financial settlement is based on cleared transactions, that is, transactions recorded with the clearing house. It does not reflect actual electricity flows, that is, supply or failure to supply electricity, or off-take or failure to off-take electricity. Actual electricity flows and the failure to comply with obligations to supply or off-take electricity are regulated by the TSO.[380]

Objections

The fact that financial settlement is separate from physical settlement also means that one must distinguish between objections against trade confirmations and objections against invoices. (a) Because of the balance requirement, objections against trade confirmations are more urgent. This should preferably be reflected in the market rules. Objections against trade confirmations should be made promptly

---

[373] ECC Clearing Conditions (0022a, 30 April 2014), section 3.4.5(2) and section 3.4.5(3).

[374] ECC Clearing Conditions (0022a, 30 April 2014), section 3.4.5(1).

[375] ECC Clearing Conditions (0022a, 30 April 2014), section 3.4.3(1), section 3.4.3(2) and section 3.4.5(3)(c).

[376] Nord Pool Spot Physical Markets, Trading Appendix 4, Clearing Rules (27 November 2014), section 5.1.1(c).

[377] Nord Pool Spot Physical Markets, Trading Appendix 4, Clearing Rules (27 November 2014), section 5.1.2(a).

[378] Nord Pool Spot Physical Markets, Trading Appendix 4, Clearing Rules (1 January 2012), section 5.1.2: "The Client Representative is responsible for the following with respect to Client Transactions: ... c. If the Client Representative does not post missing Collateral in accordance with section 4.3, the Collateral that a Client Representative has posted for Trading and any outstanding Settlement will be credited and applied by NPS to cover Collateral Calls made on Clients represented by the Clients Representative. When calculating Collateral Calls for a Client Representative, NPS will add uncovered Collateral Calls of the Client Representative's Clients".

[379] N2EX Physical Market, General Clearing Terms, Clearing Rules (27 November 2014), section 7.2.2.

[380] Nord Pool Spot Physical Markets, Trading Appendix 4, Clearing Rules (27 November 2014), section 4.1.3 and section 4.1.4.

and trade confirmations should be considered approved in the absence of such notifications. (b) Where objections are raised against invoices, the notice period could be longer.

On EPEX Spot, objections against trade confirmations must be raised immediately after receipt and no later than by 12:00 am on the next business day. Objections against invoices or credit notes by ECC or ECC Lux must be raised "forthwith, however, at the latest within a period of 10 ECC business days after receipt" of the invoice.[381]

On Elspot, a market participant must notify NPS of errors immediately after becoming aware of them.[382] The distinction between errors caused by NPS and other errors has been deleted.[383] The liability of NPS is limited. First, the trading rules of the Elspot market contain a no-waiver clause. Failure to exercise any right under the trading rules does not operate as a waiver of the party's rights or remedies.[384] Second, Nord Pool Spot has reserved the unilateral right to reject, cancel or refuse any order—on the other hand, it has such a right only where it deems that the order is not in compliance with the trading rules or the applicable law.[385]

In the N2EX market, market rules distinguish between trading errors, errors involving clearing transactions, and cash settlement errors. (a) Like on Elspot, the market operator (Nord Pool Spot AS) has a limited right to refuse orders in the event of trading errors. Any change or cancellation triggers a corresponding change or cancellation to the corresponding clearing transactions. An account holder may not raise any other objections against the clearing house (in the past NASDAQ OMX Stockholm AB, since 1 October 2014 Nord Pool Spot AS) in respect of trading errors.[386] (b) The clearing house may correct substantial errors involving registered clearing transactions.[387] (c) Where a cash settlement has been carried out incorrectly, the account holder must notify the clearing house as soon as possible and not later than five (5) banking days after the cash settlement took place.[388] However, the clearing house may carry out a corrected settlement in the event of certain

[381] ECC Clearing Conditions (0022a, 30 April 2014), sections 3.4.9(1) and 3.4.9(2).

[382] Nord Pool Spot Physical Market, Trading Appendix 2a, Elspot Market Regulations (18 November 2014), sections 7.1.1 and 7.1.2.

[383] For previous regulation, see Nord Pool Spot Physical Market, Trading Appendix 2a, Elspot Market Regulations (1 January 2011), section 7.1.1: "If a Participant wishes to claim errors caused by NPS, the Participant must notify NPS immediately, and in any event no later than 14:00 CET on the day of the relevant Auction". Section 7.1.4: "Inadequate or late complaints will bar the Participant from raising the complaint against NPS. If a valid complaint has not been received by the end of the complaint period as set out in Section 7.1.1, the Price Report transmitted will be regarded as final and binding for the quantities specified in the Price Report, notwithstanding any error". Section 7.2.1: "If the Participant becomes aware of errors in Order(s) which are not caused by NPS, the Participant shall notify NPS immediately of such errors".

[384] Nord Pool Spot's Physical Markets, General Terms, Trading Rules (1 February 2015), section 17.3.

[385] Nord Pool Spot's Physical Markets, General Terms, Trading Rules (1 February 2015), section 8.5.1.

[386] N2EX Physical Market, General Clearing Terms, Clearing Rules (27 November 2014), section 6.3.1.

[387] N2EX Physical Market, General Clearing Terms, Clearing Rules (27 November 2014), section 6.3.2.

[388] N2EX Physical Market, General Clearing Terms, Clearing Rules (27 November 2014), section 10.3.1 and section 10.3.2.

substantial errors.[389] (d) The clearing house is not liable to any account holder for any exercise or non-exercise of these powers provided that it acts in good faith.[390] (e) There is a no-waiver clause.[391]

Settlement of Physical Flows

The clearing of financial and physical flows and the settlement of financial flows is complemented by the settlement of physical flows. Cash settlement and physical delivery are the two main forms of contract settlement in commodity markets in general. However, electricity spot markets have their own characteristics.

In traditional commodity markets, a contract party has an obligation to deliver the commodity at maturity (where the party has a short position in the contract) or an obligation to take delivery of the commodity (where the party has a long position in the contract). The commodity is then delivered as specified in the delivery conditions of the contract. Most contracts for the delivery of a commodity set out the modalities of delivery, including, for instance, time of delivery, place of delivery, payment of transportation fees, quality, and possible quality substitutions. Furthermore, most commodities can be in the possession of somebody, and it would be possible for the central counterparty to hold title to the commodities to be delivered.

In electricity spot markets, however, there are constraints on the physical settlement of contracts. Because it is not yet technically and commercially possible to store electricity in large quantities for the purposes of trading, and because the transmission of electricity requires wires and transmission capacity, electricity is physically supplied to the grid and extracted from the same grid by the market participants themselves. Balance in the grid is managed by the TSO. The central counterparty is not in a position to supply or extract electricity.

The particular characteristics of physical electricity markets influence: (a) the regulation of access to the marketplace; (b) the obligations and liability of the central counterparty; (c) the scope of the TSO's contractual regime; and (d) the modalities of physical settlement.

Access To ensure that bidders are able to fulfil their obligations, the exchange operator must require evidence of the capability for the physical settlement of transactions before it can accept a market participant. This requires, in particular, evidence of: a clearing agreement; participation in the contractual framework of the TSO; and the necessary organisation (personnel and technical facilities).[392]

---

[389] N2EX Physical Market, General Clearing Terms, Clearing Rules (27 November 2014), section 10.3.3.

[390] N2EX Physical Market, General Clearing Terms, Clearing Rules (27 November 2014), section 10.3.4 and section 18.4.

[391] N2EX Physical Market, General Clearing Terms, Clearing Rules (27 November 2014), section 18.5.

[392] EPEX Spot Exchange Rules (28 November 2014), Article 2.11.

Liability of Central Counterparty The central counterparty has reduced its risk exposure by allocating the responsibility for the physical settlement of trades to a third party and by excluding or limiting its liability for non-performance.

In the EPEX Spot market, European Commodity Clearing Luxembourg S.a.r.l. (ECC Lux) has assumed responsibility for the physical settlement of all transactions for which European Commodity Clearing AG (ECC) has assumed clearing as the clearing house and central counterparty. ECC Lux is a subsidiary of ECC.[393] The central counterparty is not responsible for the physical fulfilment of trades. It only guarantees fulfilment.[394]

Where a trading participant has defaulted on its delivery or acceptance of delivery obligations, ECC is entitled to take all the required measures to safeguard the performance or reduction of the damage.[395] However, the most important consequences in the event of default are regulated in the legal framework applied by the TSO (the "balance agreement").[396]

Both ECC and ECC Lux (the central counterparties) have excluded all liability for measures by the TSO and their own measures based on the TSO's measures.[397] Where the TSO has taken measures, the changed volumes form the basis of settlement.[398]

There is a difference between EPEX Spot and the physical markets of Nord Pool Spot. In this case, rights are not assigned and the original central counterparty remains the central counterparty also for physical flows. Cash settlement is based on agreed flows. The central counterparty is not responsible for problems with physical flows. Actual electricity flows and obligations triggered by failure to comply with obligations to supply or off-take electricity are regulated by the TSO.[399]

TSO's Regime The modalities of settlement and delivery depend on the legal framework of the TSO. The exchange operator's and the clearing house's rules can regulate the settlement of payments and leave the settlement of electricity flows to be regulated by the TSO and effected by the buyer and seller.

This can be illustrated by the way EPEX Spot Operational Rules define the underlying electricity and delivery of EPEX Spot physical power contracts: "Electrical power transiting over a Transmission System managed by a TSO, which defines the voltage, frequency, cosine φ (displacement factor) and cut-off frequencies, in compliance with the contractual obligations of the prevailing concession agreement for the general power grid . . . Delivery at any Injection or Withdrawal point on the relevant Transmission System".[400]

---

[393] ECC Clearing Conditions (0022a, 30 April 2014), Preamble.

[394] ECC Clearing Conditions (0022a, 30 April 2014), section 3.4.5(1).

[395] ECC Clearing Conditions (0022a, 30 April 2014), section 5.2.3(3).

[396] ECC Clearing Conditions (0022a, 30 April 2014), section 5.2.3(3): ". . . Further consequences might arise from the provisions contained in the respective balance agreement". ECC Clearing Conditions (0022a, 30 April 2014), section 5.2.3(1): "Physical delivery of the spot market transactions is effected directly by the Trading Participant towards ECC Lux subject to the provisions specified in these Clearing Conditions and the respectively valid balance agreements . . ."

[397] ECC Clearing Conditions (0022a, 30 April 2014), section 5.2.5(4).

[398] ECC Clearing Conditions (0022a, 30 April 2014), section 5.2.5.

[399] Nord Pool Spot Physical Markets, Trading Appendix 4, Clearing Rules (27 November 2014), section 4.1.4 and section 4.1.3.

[400] EPEX Spot Operational Rules (28 November 2014), Article 1.2.

The exchange operator (EPEX Spot SE) defines "settlement" as the payment of transactions executed on EPEX Spot and handled by the clearing house.[401] The exchange operator thus focuses on payments. Moreover, the exchange rules refer to the clearing conditions of the clearing house (ECC)[402] that regulate payments but leave the modalities of physical electricity flows to be regulated by the TSO in what is known as "balance agreements".[403]

Evidence of the capability for physical settlement of transaction is a "precondition for approval as a Trading Participant" under the ECC Clearing Conditions.[404]

A trading participant has a legal obligation to fulfil its delivery obligations and/or acceptance of delivery obligations to ECC Lux.[405] ECC guarantees the trading participants the fulfilment of these transactions by ECC Lux in accordance with the contract.[406]

The clearing member is liable as a guarantor to the extent that ECC Lux can demand the payment of money instead of the delivery or the acceptance of delivery from the clearing member (in particular in the event of default).

Consequently, there are rather complicated multi-party relationships (trading participant—clearing member—central counterparty/ECC—central counterparty for physical deliveries/ECC Lux) that need to be regulated in ECC Clearing Conditions in detail and depending on the context (spot transactions,[407] derivatives transactions[408]).

Cascading is used for physical delivery where the delivery period of futures exceeds 1 calendar month.[409]

Modalities of Physical Settlement Electricity must always be supplied at a certain grid and voltage level at a certain delivery point. Moreover, electricity must be supplied in the current, frequency and voltage applicable at the relevant delivery point in accordance with the standards of the TSO and the contract terms.[410]

The contract must determine an entry point for electricity flows into the grid and an exit point for electricity flows from the grid. In practice, it is sufficient to identify the grid and the grid level, or the "bidding area".[411] A bidder must make bids in the area where the bidder's production or consumption is physically connected to the grid.[412] If there are many TSOs,[413] the area must be the area of the relevant grid operator.

---

[401] EPEX Spot Rules & Regulations, Appendix, Definitions (28 November 2014).

[402] EPEX Spot Exchange Rules (28 November 2014), Article 2.11.

[403] ECC Clearing Conditions (0022a, 30 April 2014), section 5.2.3(1).

[404] ECC Clearing Conditions (0022a, 30 April 2014), section 2.3.1(1)(c). See also ECC Clearing Conditions, (0022a, 30 April 2014), section 5.2.3(3).

[405] ECC Clearing Conditions (0022a, 30 April 2014), section 3.1.7(2).

[406] ECC Clearing Conditions (0022a, 30 April 2014), section 3.4.5(1).

[407] ECC Clearing Conditions (0022a, 30 April 2014), section 3.4.3 and section 3.4.5(1).

[408] ECC Clearing Conditions (0022a, 30 April 2014), section 3.4.5.

[409] ECC Clearing Conditions (0022a, 30 April 2014), section 4.2.2.1(3).

[410] See, for example. EFET General Agreement (Version 2.1(a)), § 6.1.

[411] See, for example, Nord Pool Spot Market, Trading Appendix 1, Definitions (27 November 2014).

[412] See, for example, Nord Pool Spot Physical Market, Trading Appendix 2a, Elspot Market Regulations (18 November 2014), section 2.2.4.

[413] See, for example, EPEX Spot Exchange Rules (28 November 2014), Article 5.10.

The points of entry and exit are customarily in the same country, because grids or bidding areas have traditionally been regional or national.

For technical reasons, it is not necessary to specify the place of the performance of the obligation to "deliver" electricity. If there is a "delivery point" for legal reasons, it could be any injection or withdrawal point on the relevant transmission system.[414]

The N2EX Trading Rules and Clearing Rules do not define the place of performance of the delivery obligation as such.[415] Neither does the Balancing and Settlement Code.

Physical settlement is effected by nominating purchases or sales to the relevant TSO.[416] A market participant cannot nominate them without a prior contractual framework with the TSO. The existence of a contractual framework that facilitates settlement belongs to the customary conditions for exchange membership. There can nevertheless be clearing members and non-clearing members with different obligations.[417] Where the market participant cannot fulfil its supply or off-take obligations itself, it should find a party that can.

On EPEX Spot, trade information is transmitted by the exchange operator (EPEX Spot SE) to the central counterparty and clearing house (ECC). The delivery procedure means nomination of the contract by ECC and the balance responsible members to the TSO.[418] In case of market coupling contracts, a contract is nominated to the TSOs on the electrical borders by the designated shipping agent.[419]

4.6 Reduction of Counterparty Risk and Systemic Risk

4.6.1 General Remarks

Counterparty risk and systemic risk are mitigated in various ways in both financial and physical electricity markets. First, there are collateral calls and margin requirements. Second, set-off and netting are used to reduce net exposure. Third, there is daily financial settlement. These techniques influence the cash flow of market

---

[414] EPEX Spot Operational Rules (28 November 2014), Article 1.2.

[415] N2EX Physical Market, General Clearing Terms, Clearing Rules (27 November 2014), section 11.1.1 and section 11.1.2.

[416] See, for example, EPEX Spot Exchange Rules (28 November 2014), Article 5.2. For a definition for the purposes of REMIT, see point 8 of second subparagraph of Article 2 of Commission Implementing Regulation 1348/2014: "'nomination' means, – for electricity: the notification of the use of cross zonal capacity by a physical transmission rights holder and its counterparty to the respective transmission system operator(s)(TSOs) . . ."

[417] See EPEX Spot Exchange Rules (28 November 2014), Article 2.11 on the requirements for the settlement of exchange transactions.

[418] EPEX Spot Operational Rules (13 May 2014), Articles 1.3.1 and 1.3.2.

[419] EPEX Spot Operational Rules (13 May 2014), Article 1.4.

participants. They can either give incentives to participate in organised trading or incentives to use bilaterally negotiated OTC contracts.

4.6.2 Collateral Calls and Margin Requirements

Market participants are required to furnish collateral to reduce the central counterparty's risk exposure and systemic risk. Collateral requirements limit the market participants access to the marketplace and trading (in addition to explicit trading limits[420]). Margins furnished by market participants are the most important form of collateral.[421]

Exposure to counterparty credit risk and the required amount of collateral can depend on the traded contract. (a) There is a difference between "one-sided" and "two-sided" exposure to credit risk. Financially-settled options lead to one-sided exposure because one counterparty has already fulfilled its own obligations after paying the premium. Exposure to counterparty credit risk is two-sided in forward-type contracts that are settled physically and in swaps. (b) Moreover, because a derivative contract derives its value from the underlying asset, its value changes during its life, creating difficulty and complexity in collateral arrangements as collateral is posted and reposted throughout the life of the contract.[422]

Collateral must be furnished by clearing members.[423] Depending on the exchange, non-clearing members may be required to furnish collateral to the relevant clearing member or the clearing house.

All members—participants or clearing customers—must furnish collateral in the Elspot market of Nord Pool Spot. Even clients must furnish collateral when trading through their client representatives.[424]

In the physical market of N2EX, each account holder is subject to collateral calls.[425]

---

[420] Nord Pool Spot Market, Trading Appendix 1, Definitions (27 November 2014): "Intraday Trading Limit means a trading limit that may be set by NPS for a Participant, based on the Account balance and the Collateral Posted".

[421] See also Articles 24–28 of Regulation 153/2013 (supplementing Regulation 648/2012).

[422] duPont JC (2009), p. 851.

[423] Article 46(1) of Regulation 648/2012 (EMIR). See also Article 46(3) of Regulation 648/2012 (EMIR) on regulatory technical standards.

[424] Nord Pool Spot Market, Trading Appendix 1, Definitions (27 November 2014): "Collateral Call means NPS's call for Collateral from a Participant or Clearing Customer in accordance with the Clearing Rules". Nord Pool Spot Physical Markets, Trading Appendix 4, Clearing Rules (27 November 2014), section 2.2.1 (on eligibility as a counterparty). Nord Pool Spot Physical Markets, Trading Appendix 4, Clearing Rules (27 November 2014), section 4.3.1: "Each Member must at its own cost establish and maintain Collateral in accordance with the Clearing Rules, and ensure that the value of its Collateral posted at all times meets the applicable Collateral Calls". For the client representative's obligations, see also Nord Pool Spot Physical Markets, Trading Appendix 4, Clearing Rules (27 November 2014), section 5.1.2.

[425] N2EX Physical Market, General Clearing Terms, Clearing Rules (27 November 2014), section 5.4.1.

As regards Nasdaq Commodities, each account holder must provide collateral under the clearing rules.[426]

Each exchange participant must deposit the required margins and the daily settlement payments on EEX.[427]

In the EPEX Spot market, each clearing member must deposit margins.[428] A non-clearing member must deposit margins at its clearing member.[429]

In principle, collateral should be furnished to the clearing house for the security of compliance with obligations owed to the central counterparty. In practice, however, the same entity often acts as the clearing house and the central counterparty. The rules of the market can therefore be vague about the beneficiary of the collateral and the obligations secured by the collateral.

In the physical markets of Nord Pool Spot, the beneficiary is Nord Pool Spot.[430] On EPEX Spot, the beneficiary is ECC and the obligations are the obligations of the clearing member towards ECC "for its participation in clearing at ECC". The margins furnished by a clearing member are intended to "secure risks from its own transactions or transactions guaranteed by it".[431]

Form of Collateral There are many potential forms of collateral and other credit enhancements.[432] In principle, there can be cash collateral and non-cash collateral. The quality of collateral is regulated by EMIR[433] and a Commission Delegated Regulation laying down the main rules.[434] (These requirements are discussed in Sect. 4.4.5). Within such limits, market participants may be given some discretion to choose the form of collateral. The level of discretion depends even on the exchange. For operational reasons and for the sake of liquidity and transparency,

---

[426] NASDAQ OMX Clearing AB, General Terms, Clearing Rules, Commodity Derivatives (9 June 2014), section 3.6.1.

[427] EEX Exchange Rules (0031b, 22 November 2014), § 51(1).

[428] ECC Clearing Conditions (0022a, 30 April 2014), section 3.5.1(1) and section 3.5.1(2).

[429] ECC Clearing Conditions (0022a, 30 April 2014), section 3.5.2(2).

[430] Nord Pool Spot Physical Markets, Trading Appendix 4, Clearing Rules (4 February 2014), section 7.1.1; Nord Pool Spot Market, Trading Appendix 1, Definitions (27 November 2014): "Base Collateral Call means NPS call for Collateral from a Participant or Clearing Customer in accordance with Section 8.2 of the General Terms of the Clearing Rules". "Pledged Cash Account means a pledged account established by a Participant in a Deposit Bank approved by NPS and which shall be applied in connection with cash Settlements and cash collateral deposits towards NPS".

[431] ECC Clearing Conditions (0022a, 30 April 2014), section 3.5.1(1) and section 3.5.1(2).

[432] See, for example, Mäntysaari P (2010b), Chapter 11.

[433] Article 46(1) and recital 66 of Regulation 648/2012 (EMIR).

[434] First subparagraph of Article 46(3) of Regulation 648/2012 (EMIR): "In order to ensure consistent application of this Article, ESMA shall, after consulting EBA, the ESRB and the ESCB, develop draft regulatory technical standards specifying: (a) the type of collateral that could be considered highly liquid, such as cash, gold, government and high-quality corporate bonds and covered bonds; (b) the haircuts referred to in paragraph 1; and (c) the conditions under which commercial bank guarantees may be accepted as collateral under paragraph 1". Conditions applicable to financial instruments, bank guarantees and gold considered as highly liquid collateral, Annex I to Regulation 153/2013 (supplementing Regulation 648/2012).

central counterparties prefer to limit collateral to cash deposits and/or on-demand guarantees. There is nevertheless variation between exchanges.

On Nord Pool Spot, members (that is, participants, client representatives, and clients)[435] must provide collateral through any one, or a combination, of the permitted forms of collateral.[436] The permitted forms of collateral are pledged cash accounts or demand guarantees.[437] A member must have one or more cash accounts for settlement purposes. A cash account is either a pledged or a non-pledged cash account.[438] A member may also provide as collateral "any security instrument accepted by NPS under an Aggregated Collateral Arrangement with the Member".[439]

These Aggregated Collateral Arrangements allow members who trade in both Elspot and N2EX markets to have their collateral requirements calculated on an aggregate basis and enable them to provide a single aggregated pool of collateral as security for their total exposure to Nord Pool Spot. This reduces their overall collateral costs and working capital requirements.

In the N2EX market, each account holder is subject to collateral calls.[440] Collateral can consist of cash, a letter of credit or bank guarantee, or of other collateral.[441] For instance, collateral for daily margin calls must be furnished in the form of cash or otherwise.[442] The value of cash collateral and bank guarantees has been defined in advance. The value of other acceptable collateral is determined by the clearing house.[443]

In the EPEX Spot market, each clearing member must deposit margins "in cash or in securities or stock loan rights accepted by ECC",[444] and a non-clearing member must deposit margins at its clearing member.[445] On EPEX Spot, the clearing house thus specifies the kind and amount of collateral that must be deposited by a clearing member.[446] ECC also determines their collateral value.[447]

[435] Nord Pool Spot Market, Trading Appendix 1, Definitions (27 November 2014); Nord Pool Spot Physical Markets, Trading Appendix 4, Clearing Rules (27 November 2014), section 2.1.3.

[436] Nord Pool Spot Physical Markets, Trading Appendix 4, Clearing Rules (27 November 2014), section 4.3.2.

[437] Nord Pool Spot Market, Trading Appendix 1, Definitions (27 November 2014).

[438] Nord Pool Spot Physical Markets, Trading Appendix 4, Clearing Rules (27 November 2014), section 2.2.1: "Only Members are eligible as Counterparties to NPS in Clearing Transactions. To be eligible as a Counterparty to Clearing Transactions, the Member must at the time that each Clearing Transaction is registered: … c. have established one or more Cash Account(s) for settlement purposes to be either a Pledged or Non-pledged Cash Account; … e. have established Collateral as a Pledged Cash Account or a On-Demand Guarantee, and have met its Collateral Call …"

[439] Nord Pool Spot Market, Trading Appendix 1, Definitions (27 November 2014).

[440] N2EX Physical Market, General Clearing Terms, Clearing Rules (27 November 2014), section 5.4.1.

[441] See N2EX Physical Market, General Clearing Terms, Clearing Rules (27 November 2014), section 8.1.2.

[442] N2EX Physical Market, General Clearing Terms, Clearing Rules (27 November 2014), section 8.3.6.

[443] N2EX Physical Market, General Clearing Terms, Clearing Rules (27 November 2014), section 8.1.2.

[444] ECC Clearing Conditions (0022a, 30 April 2014), section 3.5.1.

[445] ECC Clearing Conditions (0022a, 30 April 2014), section 3.5.2(2).

[446] ECC Clearing Conditions (0022a, 30 April 2014), section 3.5.1.

[447] ECC Clearing Conditions (0022a, 30 April 2014), section 3.5.5(1) and section 3.5.5(2).

Each exchange participant must deposit the required margins and the daily settlement payments in the EEX Power Derivatives Market.[448] A clearing member must deposit collateral in cash, securities, or book-entry security. Emission rights are not regarded as securities or book-entry security.[449] However, even they will be pledged by a trading participant.[450]

Nasdaq Commodities defines collateral as "assets in the form of cash in the eligible currencies and/or the eligible securities and/or Bank Guarantees, as specified in the Collateral List from time to time".[451] The Collateral List[452] sets out what collateral is eligible and how eligible collateral is valued. To illustrate, securities cannot be accepted as collateral unless they have daily prices available via Reuters. Market participants that are non-financial counterparties under EMIR are permitted to provide as collateral a demand guarantee issued by a bank.

The Auctioning Regulation distinguishes between futures and forwards based on margining. Futures are subject to cash variation margining. Forwards are variation margined through non-cash collateral.[453]

Margin Calls and Payments to the Default Fund There are various kinds of margin calls (or collateral calls). The customary forms are (a) initial or basic margin (collateral) calls and (b) variation margin (collateral) calls. In addition, (c) cross-margining and collateral groups can be used.

EMIR provides that the central counterparty must collect margins "on an intraday basis, at least when predefined thresholds are exceeded".[454] Regulated margins include initial margins and variation margins.[455]

---

[448] EEX Exchange Rules (0031b, 22 November 2014), § 51(1).

[449] ECC Clearing Conditions (0022a, 30 April 2014), section 3.5.1(4).

[450] ECC Clearing Conditions (0022a, 30 April 2014), section 3.5.9.

[451] NASDAQ OMX, Trading Appendix 1/Clearing Appendix 1, Definitions, Commodity Derivatives (7 April 2014).

[452] NASDAQ OMX, Clearing Appendix 10, Collateral List, Commodity Derivatives (12 June 2014). NASDAQ OMX Clearing AB, General Terms, Clearing Rules, Commodity Derivatives (9 June 2014), section 3.6.2.

[453] Recital 16 and point 1 of Article 3 of Regulation 1031/2010 (Auctioning Regulation): "'futures' means allowances auctioned as financial instruments, pursuant to Article 38(3) of Commission Regulation (EC) No 1287/2006, for delivery at an agreed future date at the auction clearing price determined pursuant to Article 7(2) of this Regulation and upon which variation margin calls to reflect price movements are payable in cash". Point 2: "'forwards' means allowances auctioned as financial instruments, pursuant to Article 38(3) of Regulation (EC) No 1287/2006, for delivery at an agreed forward date at the auction clearing price determined pursuant to Article 7(2) of this Regulation and upon which variation margin calls to reflect price movements may be secured, either through non-cash collateral or by means of an agreed government guarantee, at the option of the central counterparty".

[454] Article 41(3) of Regulation 648/2012 (EMIR). See, for example, also NASDAQ OMX Clearing AB, General Terms, Clearing Rules, Commodity Derivatives (9 June 2014), section 5.1.1: "The Clearinghouse determines the Margin Requirement(s) for each Account Holder on each Bank Day. Each Margin Requirement shall be calculated in accordance with the model applied by the Clearinghouse from time to time. Upon request, the Clearinghouse shall provide free of charge a description of the relevant model and the calculation method".

[455] Article 1 of Regulation 153/2013 (supplementing Regulation 648/2012): "... (4) 'margins' means margins as referred to in Article 41 of Regulation (EU) No 648/2012 which may include

EMIR also requires payments to a default fund to cover losses arising from the default of one or more clearing members when they exceed the losses to be covered by margin requirements.[456] The central counterparty decides on the size of the contributions.[457]

Initial or Basic Margin The purpose of initial margins (often referred to as base or basic margins) is to cover within-day price volatility and is payable at the time the contract is concluded.[458] Whenever a position is opened, a trading participant thus has to deposit this margin with its clearing member and the clearing member in turn has to deposit this margin with the clearing house. The more volatile the contract is, the greater is the initial margin requirement.[459]

The clearing house of Nasdaq Commodities (NASDAQ OMX Clearing AB) will set the base collateral requirement for each clearing account when the account is initially established. The clearing house will take into consideration the account holder's financial soundness, expected volume of transactions, the default fund requirement, and other factors which the clearing house deems relevant.[460]

Nord Pool Spot requires minimum collateral from all members. The minimum collateral call can be adjusted at NPS's discretion. It can also be set individually. The minimum collateral must be established prior to the commencement of trading.[461]

On N2EX, the clearing house determines the base collateral call for each clearing account when clearing accounts are initially established.[462]

ECC Clearing Conditions lay down the method for the calculation of the different margin requirements for derivatives market transactions (EEX) and for spot market transactions (EPEX Spot).[463]

On EEX, a SPAN® Initial Margin must be furnished for the costs of closing out net positions in futures and options.[464] On EPEX Spot, a Spot Initial Margin must be furnished

initial margins and variation margins; (5) 'initial margin' means margins collected by the CCP to cover potential future exposure to clearing members providing the margin and, where relevant, interoperable CCPs in the interval between the last margin collection and the liquidation of positions following a default of a clearing member or of an interoperable CCP default; (6) 'variation margin' means margins collected or paid out to reflect current exposures resulting from actual changes in market price . . ."

456 First subparagraph of Article 42(1) of Regulation 648/2012 (EMIR).

457 Article 42(2) of Regulation 648/2012 (EMIR).

458 Ofgem (2009), para 3.8: ". . . The Initial Margin is intended to cover within-day price volatility and is payable at the time the contract is entered into. Clearing Houses typically set this margin in the region of 8–10 % of the contract value (as measured by the current forward curve) . . ."

459 Pilgram T (2010), p. 380, point 699.

460 NASDAQ OMX Clearing AB, General Terms, Clearing Rules, Commodity Derivatives (9 June 2014), section 5.2.1.

461 Nord Pool Spot Physical Markets, Trading Appendix 4, Clearing Rules (27 November 2014), section 4.3.4.

462 N2EX Physical Market, General Clearing Terms, Clearing Rules (27 November 2014), section 8.2.1.

463 ECC Clearing Conditions (0022a, 30 April 2014), section 3.5.2(1).

464 ECC Clearing Conditions (0022a, 30 April 2014), section 4.1(1): "A margin (collateral) for the costs of closing-out (SPAN® Initial Margin) shall be furnished for net positions in futures and options".

Premium Margin is required for open short positions in options (and not required for open long options). It resembles the Additional Margin for futures.[492] The Delivery Margin is used for gas contracts rather than electricity contracts.[493]

Cross-Margining, Collateral Groups The use of cross-margining or collateral groups depends on the exchange.

Cross-margining means that margin requirements are applied over the lines of different kinds of products or entities. According to MiFIR, it fosters "non-discriminatory and transparent access to CCPs" and "effective competition between trading venues for derivatives".[494] EMIR permits "portfolio margining".[495]

ECC uses collateral groups. Collateral is divided into different groups based on the obligations that the collateral is designed to secure in the event of a clearing member's default.[496]

Calculation of Margin Requirements There must be a calculation method for margins. The question is addressed by the EMIR framework.[497] However, to ensure that central counterparties duly manage the risk they face, it does not specify the approach which they should take.[498] Various methods can thus be used to protect the "resilience" of the central counterparty depending on the exchange.[499]

NASDAQ OMX Clearing AB ("NOMX Clearing") uses various models. It uses a Nordic SPAN model for commodities.[500] Many of the features of its SPAN model differ from the original SPAN design.[501]

In the physical markets of Nord Pool Spot, the clearing house/central counterparty has discretion to determine the required amount of collateral.[502]

---

[492] Pilgram T (2010), p. 381, point 700.

[493] Pilgram T (2010), p. 381, point 701.

[494] See recital 28 of Regulation 600/2014 (MiFIR).

[495] Recital 24 and Article 27(1) of Regulation 153/2013 (supplementing Regulation 648/2012): "A CCP may allow offsets or reductions in the required margin across the financial instruments that it clears if the price risk of one financial instrument or a set of financial instruments is significantly and reliably correlated, or based on equivalent statistical parameter of dependence, with the price risk of other financial instruments". See also Article 27(4) of Regulation 153/2013 (supplementing Regulation 648/2012): "Where portfolio margining covers multiple instruments, the amount of margin reductions shall be no greater than 80 % of the difference between the sum of the margins for each product calculated on an individual basis and the margin calculated based on a combined estimation of the exposure for the combined portfolio. Where the CCP is not exposed to any potential risk from the margin reduction, it may apply a reduction of up to 100 % of that difference".

[496] ECC Clearing Conditions (0022a, 30 April 2014), section 3.9.3(4).

[497] Articles 24–28 of Regulation 153/2013 (supplementing Regulation 648/2012).

[498] Recital 24 of Regulation 153/2013 (supplementing Regulation 648/2012).

[499] See, for example, first subparagraph of Article 25(1), Article 28(1) and recital 26 of Regulation 153/2013 (supplementing Regulation 648/2012).

[500] SPAN® is a registered trademark of Chicago Mercantile Exchange Inc., used by NOMX Clearing under a license.

[501] Pilgram T (2010), p. 382, point 702.

[502] Nord Pool Spot Physical Markets, Trading Appendix 4, Clearing Rules (27 November 2014), section 4.3.

In the N2EX market, there are base collateral calls, daily margin calls, and extraordinary margin calls. (a) The amount of base collateral is in the discretion of the clearing house/ central counterparty (Nord Pool Spot AS) that considers "relevant factors".[503] (b) Moreover, account holders must on each clearing day provide collateral for any daily margin calls.[504] The clearing rules define how intraday and end-of-day margin calls are calculated.[505] The clearing house considers several components when calculating a daily margin call.[506] However, the relative weight of the calculation parameters is in the discretion of the clearing house.[507]

On EPEX Spot, the amount of margins is specified by the clearing house/central counterparty.[508] Margins are deposited to secure the contract obligations guaranteed by ECC.[509] ECC must use a method for the calculation of the margin.[510] The amount of the margin is based on the default risk of a clearing member and of its non-clearing Members.[511] A non-clearing Member must deposit margins at its clearing member at least to the amount established based on the calculation method of ECC.[512]

In principle, the required amount of collateral could reflect the bargaining position of the parties. Where the amount of collateral is in the discretion of the clearing house, the interests of the clearing house or the reduction of systemic risk have a higher relative weight. Where the amount of collateral is low or set out in advance and limited, or where its quality is low, the interests of electricity producers, buyers, or other market participants have a higher relative weight.

Because of the benefits of holding collateral, the holding of collateral signals a stronger position than not holding it. Possession of collateral reduces risk exposure, increases the efficiency of the use of capital (as the party does not furnish collateral itself or, if it does, may recollateralise collateral that is in its possession), and may even increase income (as assets used as collateral are re-invested).[513] For the same reasons, there can be an incentive to hoard collateral.

The fact that collateral is furnished to the clearing house signals that the reduction of systemic risk has a higher relative weight. Where collateral is furnished to clearing members, one can assume that the interests of clearing members have a higher relative weight.

---

[503] N2EX Physical Market, General Clearing Terms, Clearing Rules (27 November 2014), section 8.2.1.

[504] *Ibid*, section 8.3.1.

[505] *Ibid*, section 8.3.3.

[506] *Ibid*, section 8.3.4.

[507] *Ibid*, section 8.3.5.

[508] ECC Clearing Conditions (0022a, 30 April 2014), section 3.5.1(1).

[509] ECC Clearing Conditions (0022a, 30 April 2014), section 3.5.1(1).

[510] ECC Clearing Conditions (0022a, 30 April 2014), section 3.5.2(1): "The method for the calculation of the different margin requirements to be furnished shall be established by ECC. The bases for the determination of the margins are laid down in section 4.1 for Derivatives Market transactions and in section 5.1 for Spot Market transactions ..."

[511] ECC Clearing Conditions (0022a, 30 April 2014), section 3.5.2(1).

[512] ECC Clearing Conditions (0022a, 30 April 2014), section 3.5.2(2).

[513] Article 47 of Regulation 648/2012 (EMIR).

In the physical markets of Nord Pool Spot, members and clients provide collateral to the clearing house/central counterparty.[514]

On EPEX Spot, a clearing member furnishes collateral to the central counterparty/ clearing house (European Commodity Clearing AG)[515] and a non-clearing member to its clearing member.[516]

Extraordinary Margin Calls Systemic risk can rise to unacceptable levels where the amount of collateral held by the central counterparty is too low because of a change in circumstances or otherwise. For this reason, the clearing house/central counterparty must have discretion to make extraordinary margin calls.

In the physical markets of Nord Pool Spot, NPS may call for extraordinary and immediate posting of collateral. The collateral call can be set individually, according to member category, or for all members. NPS also has discretion to "apply any other risk calculation procedure that the NPS considers appropriate under the relevant circumstances".[517]

On N2EX, NPS may issue an extraordinary margin call to an account holder if it decides that extraordinary circumstances so require. Extraordinary circumstances are matters that indicate a higher credit risk in respect of the account holder.[518]

On EPEX Spot, ECC has the right to demand a supplementary margin at any time on account of the risk assessment which it carries out.[519]

4.6.3 Set-Off and Netting

The commercial purpose of set-off and netting is to reduce counterparty risk, systemic risk, and operational costs by replacing multiple payment (or delivery) obligations with one net payment (or delivery) obligation. Netting is easier where parties trade with a central counterparty.[520] In the EU, it is regulated by the Settlement Finality Directive[521] and the Collateral Directive.[522] Set-off and netting should be regulated carefully in the clearing rules to achieve their commercial purpose.

---

514 Nord Pool Spot Physical Markets, Trading Appendix 4, Clearing Rules (27 November 2014), section 4.3.4 and section 5.1.2. N2EX Physical Market, General Clearing Terms, Clearing Rules (27 November 2014), section 8.2.1 on the Base Collateral Call; section 8.3.1 on the Daily Margin Call; section 8.4.1 on the Extraordinary Margin Call.

515 ECC Clearing Conditions (0022a, 30 April 2014), section 3.5.1(1).

516 ECC Clearing Conditions (0022a, 30 April 2014), section 3.5.2(2).

517 Nord Pool Spot Physical Markets, Trading Appendix 4, Clearing Rules (27 November 2014), section 4.3.12.

518 N2EX Physical Market, General Clearing Terms, Clearing Rules (27 November 2014), section 8.4.1.

519 ECC Clearing Conditions (0022a, 30 April 2014), section 3.5.3(1), section 3.5.3(2) and section 3.5.1(3). EPEX Spot Exchange Rules (28 November 2014), Article 2.21 (suspension of admission of a member).

520 Pilgram T (2010), pp. 388–390, points 715–716.

521 Directive 98/26/EC (Directive on settlement finality).

522 Directive 2002/47/EC (Directive on financial collateral arrangements).

Terms When employed on electricity exchanges, the content of set-off and netting tends to be influenced by: the nature of the contractual obligations; the nature of the relationship between market participants; the event; and the bargaining power of the parties.

First, there are various kinds of contractual obligations. On physical electricity exchanges, contracts are settled both physically and financially, and there are payment obligations due to collateral calls. To achieve the purpose of set-off and netting, it is necessary for the operator of the exchange and the central counterparty to regulate all three aspects—physical, financial, and collateral-related aspects—of set-off and netting.

Second, there are different kinds of relationships between market participants. To begin with, there are different kinds of market participants. For instance, trading participants range from clearing and non-clearing members to clients, and each trading participant may belong to a group of companies. The functions of a central counterparty can be allocated to one entity or divided between a central counterparty and a sub-CCP. Moreover, the obligations of a party can be owed to one or more different market participants. For instance, there are obligations owed to the TSO, the CCP, and trading participants. It is therefore necessary to regulate payments in different kinds of party relationships.

Third, situations vary. One can distinguish between: normal business relationships; default; and insolvency.

Fourth, set-off and netting rules can reflect the bargaining power of the parties. There are differences between financial flows and physical flows.

As regards financial flows, the central counterparty would prefer to net at least all accounts receivable and accounts payable towards any clearing member. However, it would be customary for the central counterparty to ensure that the obligation to provide collateral cannot be set off against the central counterparty's payment obligations. The central counterparty and the TSO tend to reserve a unilateral set-off right in the event of a party's default, and they use close-out netting in the event of insolvency.

As regards physical flows, whether physical off-take or supply obligations can be netted depends on the rules of the TSO. This can be illustrated with the practices of Elspot, N2EX, and EPEX Spot.

Example: Elspot In the Elspot market of Nord Pool Spot, the previous trading rules setting out the central counterparty's right to set off obligations[523] have been replaced with netting rules. The older provisions on the central counterparty's right to set off obligations continue to apply in Nord Pool's physical gas market.[524]

[523] Nord Pool Spot AS, Rulebook for the Physical Markets, section 7.3.3: "NPS may set-off any and all claims and receivables between NPS and the respective Participant or Clearing Customer. NPS may also set-off delivery obligations".

[524] Nord Pool Spot, Clearing Rules, Gaspoint Nordic Physical Market, Issued by Nord Pool Spot AS, Version 1.1 (January 2014), section 7.6.5: "NPS may set-off any and all claims and receivables between NPS and the respective Member".

According to the new rules, cash settlement amounts are netted cash amounts and the open balance in each product series is a netted value, either a purchase position (a positive value) or a sales position (a negative value).[525] Collateral requirements are determined on a net basis for the whole group of companies.[526]

The central counterparty/clearing house may instruct a client representative to close out and net positions and set off obligations in the event of a client's non-compliance event.[527]

Example: N2EX The N2EX market shows the complex nature of set-off and netting rules. In the N2EX market, one must distinguish (a) between the legal framework of the TSO on one hand and the legal framework of the central counterparty/clearing house on the other, and (b) between payment obligations on one hand and the physical supply or off-take obligations on the other.

Physical supply and off-take obligations will be netted. Only the net position will be reported by the clearing house.[528]

Also payments cleared by the clearing house will be netted,[529] and the amount of daily margin calls is partly based on net positions.[530]

However, collateral calls and cash settlement amounts will be calculated separately. They will not be set off or netted against each other.[531]

Upon the occurrence of a material default event, the clearing house may close out and net the position of the account holder.[532]

Similar netting and set-off rules are applied to payments to or payable by the BSC Clearer. They will be netted "and replaced by a single obligation upon the Party or the BSC Clearer (as the case may be) who would have had to pay the larger aggregate amount to pay the net amount (if any) to the other".[533] However, while each party waives set off rights in relation to the BSC Clearer,[534] the BSC Clearer does not waive its own rights in the event of a party's default. In the event of a

[525] Nord Pool Spot Market, Trading Appendix 1, Definitions (27 November 2014). See also Nord Pool Spot Physical Markets, Trading Appendix 4, Clearing Rules (27 November 2014), section 4.2.2.

[526] Nord Pool Spot AS, Trading Agreement 9, Netting of Collateral Call Agreement, section 3.1 and section 2.1(a).

[527] Nord Pool Spot's Physical Markets, General Terms, Trading Rules (1 February 2015), section 11.1.3.

[528] N2EX Physical Market, General Clearing Terms, Clearing Rules (27 November 2014), section 11.2.3, section 11.2.4, section 11.3.2(d), section 11.3.4.

[529] *Ibid*, section 6.1.6.

[530] *Ibid*, section 8.3.3.

[531] *Ibid*, section 5.1.5.

[532] *Ibid*, section 12.2.2.

[533] The Balance and Settlement Code, Section N: Clearing, Invoicing & Payment, Version 13.0 (3 June 2010), section 2.4.1 on payment netting.

[534] The Balance and Settlement Code, Section N: Clearing, Invoicing & Payment, Version 13.0 (3 June 2010), section 4.6.7.

party's default, the amount owing by the BSC Clearer will be set off against the amount(s) in default.[535]

Example: EPEX Spot In the EPEX Spot market, the clearing house will net accounts receivable and accounts payable from spot market transactions. There are rules on netting: (a) by the clearing house/central counterparty (ECC) in relation to any clearing member and the Sub-CCP[536]; (b) by ECC Lux in relation to a trading participant[537]; and (c) by ECC Lux in relation to ECC.[538]

In the event of a clearing member's default, the clearing house/central counterparty may close out and net the clearing member's positions.[539]

There are close-out netting provisions applicable in the event of the insolvency of a clearing member. Clearing members may conclude similar close-out netting agreements with their non-clearing members.[540]

4.7 Market Conduct, Market Abuse and Money Laundering

4.7.1 General Remarks

In the EU, market participants must comply with an extensive market conduct regime on both financial and physical electricity exchanges. The regime reflects a piece-meal approach and consists of four broad areas: open ethical standards; specific rules on market integrity; specific rules on transparency and disclosures; and specific rules on money laundering. The regime is complemented by exchange rules and EFET's Principles of Good Conduct for energy trading.

You need both open ethical standards and specific rules. Open ethical standards foster compliance with the more specific business conduct obligations.[541] The standards are open in the sense that their exact contents can only be determined after the fact. Specific rules focus on the most important issues and are more precise.

Compliance Market participants need to comply with the market conduct regime. They also need to organise compliance to ensure that their representatives comply

---

535 The Balance and Settlement Code, Section N: Clearing, Invoicing & Payment, Version 13.0 (3 June 2010), section 2.6.1.

536 ECC Clearing Conditions (0022a, 30 April 2014), section 3.4.7(1).

537 ECC Clearing Conditions (0022a, 30 April 2014), section 3.4.7(3).

538 ECC Clearing Conditions (0022a, 30 April 2014), section 3.4.7(4).

539 ECC Clearing Conditions (0022a, 30 April 2014), section 3.9.3.

540 ECC Clearing Conditions (0022a, 30 April 2014), section 3.10.

541 For the role of ethics in the management of agency relationships, see, for example, Mäntysaari P (2010a), section 6.2.

with the applicable rules.[542] Particular compliance programmes help the firm to manage legal risk in advance.

Sources Because of the piece-meal approach, the market conduct regime that market participants must comply with has many sources. It has four main components. (a) One of them is the market conduct and market abuse regime of the governing law. (b) The provisions of the governing law must implement the EU market conduct regime. (c) In addition, the exchange operator may have adopted ethical guidelines and market conduct rules. (d) EFET's Principles of Good Conduct for energy trading can help to determine what behaviour is acceptable market practice.

EU Law and Convergence The limited scope of the EU market conduct regime has obviously contributed to the limited scope of mandatory legal regulation in the past. However, the fact that a sector or market is unregulated at EU level does not mean that it would be totally unregulated. There is industry self-regulation. Many aspects have been regulated by the operator of the electricity exchange and through contracts. For example, the prohibition of insider trading, the prohibition of market manipulation, and market conduct obligations, may also have been based on electricity exchanges' codes of conduct in the absence of mandatory regulation.[543]

The EU market conduct regime is nevertheless more important than its limited scope would imply. There is a spill-over effect. EU law influences the regulation of market conduct either directly or indirectly. On one hand, EU law can regulate the activities of market participants (such as investment firms, operators of regulated markets, central counterparties, or electricity firms) directly. On the other, sectoral regulation can influence behaviour outside its original scope.

Exchange operators and firms are often active in regulated sectors or markets and sectors or markets still unregulated at EU level.[544] (a) It is possible that part of the business of the operator of a power exchange falls within the scope of MiFID II (as the operation of a financial derivatives exchange[545] or an exchange for trading in emission rights fall within the MiFID II regime[546]). For instance, many marketplaces have fallen within the scope of the MiFID regime because the MiFID regime applies to various kinds of marketplaces that have rules (regulated markets and multilateral trading facilities are defined as marketplaces operated in accordance

542 For legal compliance programmes generally, see Mäntysaari P (2010a), section 4.3.

543 See EEX Code of Conduct (24 June 2010); Godager K (2009), § 18, number 1.

544 See, for example, Case C-248/11 Criminal proceedings against Rareş Doralin Nilaş and others, ECLI:EU:C:2012:166, paras 44–46.

545 Article 1(1) of Directive 2014/65/EU (MiFID II): "This Directive shall apply to investment firms, market operators ..." Section A of Annex I to Directive 2014/65/EU (MiFID II): "... (8) Operation of an MTF; (9) Operation of an OTF". For regulated markets, see Article 44 of Directive 2014/65/EU (MiFID II) and points (5)-(7) of section C of Annex I to MiFID II.

546 Points (4) and (11) of Section C of Annex I to Directive 2014/65/EU (MiFID II). See also recital 45 of Regulation 600/2014 (MiFIR).

with non-discretionary rules).[547] (b) Exchange operators have adopted particular market conduct rules as part of organisational requirements under MiFID[548] and MiFID II[549] and monitor compliance with them.[550] (c) On the other hand, part of the business may remain outside of the directive's scope (as intraday or day-ahead spot electricity contracts for the physical supply of electricity and balancing contracts are not financial instruments,[551] the operation of a spot exchange for electricity contracts that must be settled physically is not an investment service,[552] and the operator of such a spot exchange is not regarded as an investment firm under MiFID II[553]). (d) It would not be practicable for a market participant to adopt different internal compliance programmes and different ethical guidelines and market conduct rules for similar activities depending on whether an activity falls within the regulated or the unregulated area. If an exchange operator has to comply with the MiFID regime or a similar national regime anyway, the operator may require compliance with the same standards in a spot marketplace that does not fall within those regimes as such. (e) Moreover, to use EU law as a model or "platform" can help to reduce transaction costs where market participants are active in both regulated and unregulated areas and have a legal duty to comply with both regulatory regimes.

Consequently, the ethical guidelines and market conduct rules of the exchange operator are bound to be aligned with the rules and principles of the EU legal regime even in markets that do not fall within its scope.[554] There is convergence of the regulation of market conduct. Convergence is not driven by the bodies of the EU or Member States alone, or just by financial regulators in the US, the EU, or the Member States of the EU. It is also driven by exchange operators and market participants that voluntarily comply with regulation.

The harmonisation of regulation and the convergence of rules can bring several benefits according to ISDA[555]:

---

[547] Article 4(1)(21) of Directive 2014/65/EU (MiFID II); Article 4(1)(22) of Directive 2014/65/EU (MiFID II).

[548] Articles 39 and 42 of Directive 2004/39/EC (MiFID).

[549] Points (d) and (e) of Article 47(1) of Directive 2014/65/EU (MiFID II) and Article 53 of Directive 2014/65/EU (MiFID II).

[550] Article 54 of Directive 2014/65/EU (MiFID II).

[551] Points 6 and 7 of Section C of Annex I to Directive 2014/65/EU (MiFID II). See also recital 20 of Regulation 596/2014 (MAR).

[552] Point 19 of Section A of Annex I to Directive 2014/65/EU (MiFID II): "'multilateral system' means any system or facility in which multiple third-party buying and selling trading interests in financial instruments are able to interact in the system".

[553] Article 1(1) of Directive 2014/65/EU (MiFID II).

[554] EPEX Spot Code of Conduct (9 July 2012), section 1(2). "According to European Regulation n° 1227/2011 on wholesale energy market integrity and transparency (REMIT), the EPEX SPOT Code of Conduct establishes rules prohibiting abusive practices affecting wholesale energy markets".

[555] ISDA (2011).

- a reduction in market participants' costs for managing risks;
- an increase in cross-border business, customer choice, and competition;
- a reduction in distortions of competition as market participants can select their counterparties for trading based on economic rather than regulatory factors;
- a reduction in the risks to financial stability, because it becomes easier for firms to apply integrated risk management policies and easier for the competent authorities to monitor the more organised markets;
- an increase in the ability of financial firms to centralise booking and risk management of OTC derivatives in single entities;
- a reduction in compliance costs for firms no more subject to supervision and inspection by multiple regulators or no more subject to different requirements depending on the regulator; and
- a reduction in the relocation of businesses for regulatory rather than economic reasons.

The EU Legal Regime The EU legal regime for the regulation of market conduct consists of several components: MiFIR/MiFID II (replacing MiFID); REMIT (Regulation on wholesale energy market integrity and transparency)[556]; MAR (Regulation on insider dealing and market manipulation)/MAD II (Directive on criminal sanctions for insider dealing and market manipulation)[557] (both replacing MAD)[558]; and the Money Laundering Directive.[559]

Electricity exchanges fall within the scope of the MiFID II/MiFIR regime because of the definition of regulated markets, multilateral trading facilities, and organised trading facilities[560] (in combination with the definition of multilateral systems[561] and financial instruments). The operator of an electricity exchange must adopt particular market conduct rules as part of organisational requirements under MiFID II[562] and monitor compliance.[563]

Specific abusive practices affecting wholesale energy markets are prohibited in three main ways: through general financial markets legislation; through prohibitions of specific abusive practices in wholesale energy markets; and through competition law. (1) The general market integrity and disclosure regime for finan-

[556] Regulation 1227/2011 (REMIT).

[557] Regulation 596/2014 (MAR) and Directive 2014/57/EU (MAD II).

[558] Directive 2003/6/EC (Market Abuse Directive, MAD).

[559] Directive 91/308/EEC (Money Laundering Directive), as amended by Directive 2001/97/EEC.

[560] Article 4(1) of Directive 2014/65/EU (MiFID II).

[561] Point 19 of Article 4(1) of Directive 2014/65/EU (MiFID II): "'multilateral system' means any system or facility in which multiple third-party buying and selling trading interests in financial instruments are able to interact in the system".

[562] Articles 47 and 53 of Directive 2014/65/EU (MiFID II).

[563] Article 54 of Directive 2014/65/EU (MiFID II).

cial markets applies to investment firms (MiFIR[564]), issuers (MAR, the Prospectus Directive[565]), and a large group of other persons (MAR). The scope of this regime depends on the field of activity of the firm, the nature of contracts, to whom they are offered, and other things. (2) Specific abusive practices in wholesale energy markets are addressed by REMIT. The rules laid down by REMIT are aligned with those applicable in financial markets but consider the specific characteristics of wholesale energy markets.[566] In the future, similar rules may be adopted for carbon markets.[567] (3) REMIT is without prejudice to MAR/MAD II and MiFIR/MiFID II, including the application of European competition law.[568] The third alternative is thus competition law.

REMIT was adopted in 2011, because the earlier regulatory regime for financial markets did not properly address market integrity issues for electricity markets. Behaviour that undermined the integrity of electricity markets was not clearly prohibited.[569] The scope of the regime for financial markets was too limited as it only applied to financial instruments. Neither did it consider the electricity market's sector-specific conditions, in particular the connection between the derivatives markets and the underlying physical market.[570]

While few electricity producers have an obligation to comply with the MiFIR/MiFID II regime, many must comply with provisions implementing MAR, and all electricity wholesale market participants must now comply with REMIT.

EFET's Principles of Good Conduct for Energy Trading Laws are complemented by industry self-regulation such as the EFET Principles of Good Conduct. All new

---

[564] Point 1 of Article 2(1) of Regulation 600/2014 (MiFIR); point 1 of Article 4(1) of Directive 2014/65/EU (MiFID II): "'investment firm' means any legal person whose regular occupation or business is the provision of one or more investment services to third parties and/or the performance of one or more investment activities on a professional basis".

[565] Point (a) of Article 2(1) of Directive 2003/71/EC (Prospectus Directive): "'securities' means transferable securities as defined by Article 1(4) of Directive 93/22/EEC with the exception of money market instruments as defined by Article 1(5) of Directive 93/22/EEC, having a maturity of less than 12 months". For disclosure obligations, see Articles 3(1) and 7.

[566] Article 1(1) of Regulation 1227/2011 (REMIT).

[567] Recital 10 of Regulation 1227/2011 (REMIT).

[568] Article 1(2) of Regulation 1227/2011 (REMIT).

[569] Recitals 3 and 7 of Regulation 1227/2011 (REMIT).

[570] For the sector-specific conditions, see also Article 6(2) of Regulation 1227/2011 (REMIT): "The delegated acts referred to in paragraph 1 shall take into account at least: (a) the specific functioning of wholesale energy markets, including the specificities of electricity and gas markets, and the interaction between commodity markets and derivative markets; (b) the potential for manipulation across borders, between electricity and gas markets and across commodity markets and derivative markets; (c) the potential impact on wholesale energy market prices of actual or planned production, consumption, use of transmission, or use of storage capacity; and (d) network codes and framework guidelines adopted in accordance with Regulations (EC) No 714/2009 and (EC) No 715/2009". See also Godager K (2009), § 18, number 39.

EFET member companies have to sign up to ten principles before their membership application can be accepted.[571]

Compliance Market participants need to organise compliance to ensure that their personnel comply with the market conduct regime.[572] Particular compliance programmes help the firm to manage legal risk in advance by reducing bad practices. The firm can also try to mitigate or avoid risk by means of safe harbours (Sects. 4.7.4 and 4.7.5). In electricity markets, REMIT influences the organisation of compliance. MAR lays down similar requirements.[573]

REMIT requires "persons professionally arranging transactions" to take action against inside trading and market manipulation. Such persons include at least trading venues like energy exchanges and brokers.[574] First, they must "establish and maintain effective arrangements and procedures to identify breaches" of the two prohibitions. Second, "any person professionally arranging transactions in wholesale energy products" who "reasonably suspects" that a transaction might breach the prohibition of inside trading or the prohibition of market manipulation must notify it to the national regulatory authority without further delay.[575]

Therefore, these persons should pay attention to transactions that look suspicious.[576] ACER has given guidance on suspicious-looking transactions.[577]

> The Market Surveillance of North Pool Spot must report (1) any suspected cases of market manipulation and insider trading to the national regulatory authority under the REMIT and (2) any suspected breaches of other laws and regulations affecting the North Pool Spot market according to the terms of the market place licence from NVE.
>
> In practice, most actual breaches relate to disclosure obligations and cases of market manipulation and insider trading are relatively rare.[578]

4.7.2 Open Ethical Standards, Good Business Conduct, Fairness

Open ethical standards can be based on legal or non-legal sources. For electricity markets, the most important legal sources of open ethical standards include the

[571] The Principles are contained in EFET (2012). See also Spicker J (2010), pp. 141–142, numbers 240–241.

[572] For legal compliance programmes generally, see Mäntysaari P (2010a), section 4.3.

[573] Article 16 of Regulation 596/2014 (MAR).

[574] ACER, Guidance on the application of the definitions set out in Article 2 of Regulation (EU) No 1227/2011 (20 December 2011), section 4.2.

[575] Article 15 of Regulation 1227/2011 (REMIT).

[576] See also Ledgerwood S and Harris D (2012), p. 35.

[577] ACER, Guidance on the application of the definitions set out in Article 2 of Regulation (EU) No 1227/2011 (20 December 2011), section 4.4.

[578] North Pool Spot, Quarterly report for Market Surveillance: 1 January to 31 March 2014.

MiFID II/MiFIR regime, the regulation of electricity markets, rules adopted by spot market operators, and the governing law. The most general ethical standard characteristic of electricity markets is "fairness". We can focus on the MiFID II/MiFIR regime, the regulation of fairness, the EFET Principles, and exchange rules.

The MiFID II/MiFIR Regime MiFID II lays down open standards the operators of regulated markets, multilateral trading facilities, and organised trading facilities, and for investment firms dealing with customers.

The MiFID II/MiFIR regime requires, directly or in effect, because of the spill-over effect or after the adoption of its rules as legal transplants, exchange operators to apply the following rules:

- transparent and non-discretionary rules and procedures for *fair and orderly trading*[579];
- rules on the *disclosure* of sufficient publicly available information to enable users to form an investment judgement[580];
- the *prohibition* of disorderly trading conditions, conduct that may involve market abuse, and breaches of the rules;
- rules laying down an obligation to observe *fairness in dealings with clients*[581] regardless of the nature of the client or the client classification system[582]; and
- rules on regular *monitoring* of compliance with the rules.[583]

There is a similar regime in the US. The Commodity Exchange Act lays down business conduct standards for swap dealers.[584]

Fairness The MiFID II/MiFIR regime is not the only regulatory regime that lays down fairness requirements. Fairness requirements can be found in other parts of financial markets regulation and the regulation of electricity markets.

In the electricity sector, fairness requirements are particularly important because of the existence of natural monopolies,[585] the high volatility of spot prices, and the system's reliance on the integrity of market participants.

The question of fairness has been addressed in three main ways in EU electricity markets law. First, the regulator should determine or approve rules for the electricity sector according to the Third Electricity Directive. When doing so, it should try to ensure that the electricity sector operates in a fair and economically efficient

[579] Articles 18(1) and 51(1) of Directive 2014/65/EU (MiFID II).

[580] Second subparagraph of Article 18(2) of Directive 2014/65/EU (MiFID II).

[581] Article 24(1) of Directive 2014/65/EU (MiFID II) and second subparagraph of Article 30(1) of Directive 2014/65/EU (MiFID II).

[582] DG Internal Market and Services, Public Consultation, Review of the Markets in Financial Instruments Directive (MIFID) (8 December 2010), section 7.2.5.

[583] Article 31(1) of Directive 2014/65/EU (MiFID II). First subparagraph of Article 31(2) of Directive 2014/65/EU (MiFID II). Article 31(3) of Directive 2014/65/EU (MiFID II).

[584] 7 USC § 6 s(h)(1). See also 15 USC § 78o-8(h).

[585] See, for example, recital 57 of Directive 2009/72/EC (Third Electricity Directive).

manner.[586] Second, wholesale market participants must comply with the provisions of REMIT. REMIT is based on the general notion of fairness in dealings with other market participants and clients.[587] As regards financial markets, MiFID II focuses on fairness to clients and the adoption of rules for fair trading.[588] One can also note that an earlier proposal for EMIR contained a fairness obligation for central counterparties.[589] Third, the growing regulation of market coupling addresses fairness in many respects.[590]

Obviously, Member States' laws may lay down fairness obligations applied in contract or in tort. Civil liability of general application complements the specific obligations based on sectoral regulation. There is plenty of variation depending on the Member State.[591]

EFET's Principles of Good Conduct for Energy Trading The EFET Principles of Good Conduct are designed to reflect the following values: integrity of action; respect for others; open communication; professionalism; and observing the spirit of a truly open and sustainable wholesale marketplace. According to the wording of the ten principles, EFET member companies have a contractual duty to:

1. respect free and fair competition as the basis for trading energy;
2. engage in no activities that would amount to market abuse, market manipulation or fraud, and to relay no information known or strongly suspected to be false or misleading;
3. deal with each other in accordance with established market practices and the standards expected of professional market counterparties;
4. deal with customers fairly and with integrity and manage any conflicts of interest that may arise appropriately;
5. organise their energy trading business effectively, respecting appropriate segregation of staff duties, and exercise diligent control over trading functions;
6. establish effective risk management policies and control procedures governing the key risks managed by their energy trading functions;

[586] See, for example, Articles 15(2), 37(6) and 37(8) of Directive 2009/72/EC (Third Electricity Directive).

[587] Recitals 1–2 of Regulation 1227/2011 (REMIT).

[588] Recital 86 and Article 24 of Directive 2014/65/EU (MiFID II). Articles 18(1) and 47(1) of Directive 2014/65/EU (MiFID II).

[589] Proposal for a Regulation of the European parliament and of the Council on OTC derivatives, central counterparties and trade repositories, 2010/0250 (COD), Article 34(1): "When providing services to its clearing members, and where relevant, to their clients, a CCP shall act fairly and professionally in accordance with the best interests of the clearing members and clients and sound risk management".

[590] Article 3 of Commission Regulation . . ./.. (CACM Regulation).

[591] DG Internal Market and Services, Public Consultation, Review of the Markets in Financial Instruments Directive (MIFID) (8 December 2010), section 7.2.6.

7. establish compliance policies setting out the company's procedures for fulfilling all legal and regulatory obligations and any related corporate governance rules relating to their energy trading functions;
8. ensure that their traders are suitably qualified and properly supervised to carry out their duties, including where appropriate to have taken relevant industry examinations;
9. prohibit their employees from giving or receiving bribes and from indulging in other corrupt behaviour in all circumstances; and establish policies governing gifts and hospitality, highlighting acceptable and unacceptable practices; and
10. maintain accounts related to trading transactions and risk books in accordance with relevant accounting standards and respecting normal audit practices.

Exchange Rules All these issues on open ethical standards, good business conduct, and fairness have even been addressed in rules adopted by the operators of electricity exchanges. There can be a difference between physical markets and financial markets. While physical electricity exchanges need rules that ensure the operation of physical electricity markets, financial electricity exchanges need rules on conduct in relation to clients. This can again be illustrated with the physical markets of EPEX Spot and Nord Pool Spot, and the financial markets of Nasdaq Commodities and EEX.

EPEX Spot The operator of EPEX Spot (EPEX Spot SE) has adopted a Code of Conduct. The Code applies not only to exchange members but also to the operator itself.[592]

Exchange members must comply with the Code when doing business in the market. The Code reflects REMIT[593] but is not limited to matters governed by it. All instructions and rules of the relevant supervisory authorities, including EPEX SPOT SE are part of the Code.[594]

Generally, an exchange member must not take actions that "are detrimental to the orderly operation of the market". Failure to comply with the prohibitions of the Code is punished by a warning, a suspension, or the withdrawal of exchange membership.[595] The sanctions are cumulative.[596] The operator of the market may also seek compensation for damage.[597]

[592] EPEX Spot Code of Conduct (9 July 2012), Section 1(1).

[593] EPEX Spot Code of Conduct (9 July 2012), section 1(2).

[594] EPEX Spot Code of Conduct (9 July 2012), section 6.1.1.

[595] EPEX Spot Exchange Rules (28 November 2014), Article 3.2. See also EPEX Spot Code of Conduct (9 July 2012), sections 6.1.2 and 6.3.1.

[596] EPEX Spot Code of Conduct (9 July 2012), section 6.3.2.

[597] EPEX Spot Exchange Rules (28 November 2014), Article 3.2.

EEX Like the EPEX Spot Code of Conduct, the EEX Code of Conduct is focused on market abuse and transparency.[598] In addition, it regulates the way to treat clients.

Nord Pool Spot Nord Pool Spot has adopted ethical guidelines (that are no longer in force after a major change in October 2014)[599] and market conduct rules (that are in force).[600] Before Nord Pool Spot took over the N2EX market in the UK, the ethical guidelines and market conduct rules applied to all physical markets of Nord Pool.

The market conduct rules lay down compliance obligations for all members of Nord Pool Spot's physical markets.[601] Each member must comply with them itself[602] and adopt internal rules for any person involved in trading and/or clearing on its behalf.[603] The market conduct rules are without prejudice to obligations under any applicable law[604] but prevail over other provisions of the Trading Rules. This means that they will influence the interpretation of more specific rules and can be used to fill gaps.[605]

The market conduct rules reflect the contents of REMIT. In addition, they lay down a general obligation to observe good business conduct. The general obligation consists of an open prohibition (members must not "apply unreasonable business methods" when trading on NPS)[606] and a dynamic duty (members must "seek to act in accordance with good business practice").[607] These open duties are complemented by particular dynamic duties and particular prohibitions.

The general good business conduct obligations laid down by the market conduct rules are dynamic also in the sense that members must:

- "seek to promote integrity and efficiency in the Physical Markets"; and
- "take due account to any relevant regulatory or legal obligations, any proper and relevant professional standards of conduct, and the need for the Physical Markets to operate fairly and efficiently for all Members".[608]

In addition, the market conduct rules prohibit certain activities:

- A member must not apply unreasonable business methods.[609]

598 EEX Code of Conduct (24 June 2010).

599 Nord Pool Spot AS, Trading Appendix 7, Ethical Guidelines (29 March 2011).

600 Nord Pool Spot Physical Market, Trading Appendix 5, Market Conduct Rules (7 January 2014).

601 *Ibid*, section 1.1.

602 *Ibid*, section 3.1.

603 *Ibid*, section 1.2.

604 *Ibid*, section 2.6.

605 *Ibid*, section 2.5.

606 *Ibid*, section 3.4.

607 *Ibid*, section 3.4.

608 *Ibid*, section 3.1.

609 *Ibid*, section 3.4.

- Orders and transactions must be genuine.[610]
- A member must not improperly influence the price or price structure in the NPS physical markets.[611]
- A member must not disturb other members' access to or participation in the market.[612]
- The abuse of inside information is prohibited.[613] The market conduct rules also define inside information and related concepts.[614]
- Market manipulation is prohibited.[615]

The market conduct rules require a member to disclose information to the public[616] and to provide information to NPS.[617] The rules on public disclosure are based on REMIT and applied to the Nordic and Baltic electricity markets. A member is required to publicly disclose "information relating to the Nordic or Baltic electricity market" regarding its business or facilities.[618] Public disclosure is limited to certain type of information "relevant to facilities for production, consumption or transmission of electricity". For instance, a member must disclose information about outages.[619]

There are disciplinary sanctions for non-compliance with the market conduct rules.[620] A breach can result in disciplinary sanctions that include a daily charge, a warning, or a violation charge. The choice of sanctions is in the discretion of the board of Nord Pool Spot AS.[621]

Nord Pool Spot used to have Ethical Guidelines. They were removed from the Nord Pool Spot rulebook from 27 October 2014. According to Nord Pool Spot, the Ethical Guidelines were no longer necessary as their subject matter was, to a large extent, covered by other parts of the Nord Pool Spot rulebook. Moreover, the Ethical Guidelines were explicitly stated to be "non-sanctionable" and Nord Pool Spot was of the opinion that the rulebook should only contain legally binding documents.[622] One can also note that there were no ethical guidelines for the N2EX market in the past and that it was necessary to align the regulation of all physical markets of Nord Pool Spot.

---

610 *Ibid*, section 3.2.

611 *Ibid*, section 3.3.

612 *Ibid*, section 3.3.

613 *Ibid*, section 4.1.

614 *Ibid*, section 2.2.

615 *Ibid*, sections 6.1 and 2.3.

616 *Ibid*, section 5.

617 *Ibid*, section 7.

618 *Ibid*, section 5.1.

619 *Ibid*, section 5.2.

620 *Ibid*, section 9.

621 *Ibid*, section 9.3.

622 Nord Pool Spot, Exchange information, No. 37/2014, 13 October 2014.

In any case, the previous Ethical Guidelines can still give information about the general ethical requirements applicable to market participants.

The ethical guidelines for Nord Pool Spot were binding but, unlike market conduct rules, there were no formal sanctions for their breach. Sanctions could be enforced only in case of breach of law, administrative provisions, or the rules of the exchange.[623] The purpose of the ethical guidelines was to increase trust in the market, that is, to make people expect that Nord Pool, its participants, and clearing customers observe good standards of conduct and act in an ethical manner.[624]

The ethical guidelines laid down several general principles that probably still apply. They apply either to categories of parties or transactions.

Many of the principles apply to participants and clearing customers:

- participants and clearing customers must comply with laws and regulations and the rules of the market;
- participants and clearing customers must comply with general standards for good business practice and good professional behaviour[625];
- participants and clearing customers must act "responsibly and seriously",[626] their actions should be justifiable "in a way acceptable to others", their actions should be documented, and they should be open about the purpose of their actions[627]; and
- participants and clearing customers must not compete in an unfair manner.[628]

Moreover, there are general principles applicable to all transactions made in Nord Pool's markets:

- they must be performed "with a genuine and generally acceptable business purpose"[629];
- fictive transactions and mock agreements are prohibited[630];
- it is prohibited to give false or misleading information to the market[631];
- participants and clearing customers must not manipulate markets[632];
- it is prohibited to depart from the pattern of market behaviour unless it is motivated by serious commercial or technical reasons[633]; and

[623] Nord Pool Spot AS, Trading Appendix 7, Ethical Guidelines (29 March 2011), section 1.2.

[624] Nord Pool Spot AS, Trading Appendix 7, Ethical Guidelines (29 March 2011), section 3.1.

[625] Nord Pool Spot AS, Trading Appendix 7, Ethical Guidelines (29 March 2011), section 4.2.

[626] Nord Pool Spot AS, Trading Appendix 7, Ethical Guidelines (29 March 2011), section 4.1.

[627] Nord Pool Spot AS, Trading Appendix 7, Ethical Guidelines (29 March 2011), section 4.4.

[628] Nord Pool Spot AS, Trading Appendix 7, Ethical Guidelines (29 March 2011), section 4.3.

[629] Nord Pool Spot AS, Trading Appendix 7, Ethical Guidelines (29 March 2011), section 6.1.

[630] Nord Pool Spot AS, Trading Appendix 7, Ethical Guidelines (29 March 2011), section 6.2.

[631] Nord Pool Spot AS, Trading Appendix 7, Ethical Guidelines (29 March 2011), sections 6.2 and 6.5.

[632] Nord Pool Spot AS, Trading Appendix 7, Ethical Guidelines (29 March 2011), section 6.3.

[633] Nord Pool Spot AS, Trading Appendix 7, Ethical Guidelines (29 March 2011), section 6.3.

- a participant or clearing customer that is "a leading player in respect to the relevant supply or demand for electricity or electricity derivatives" must assure that it does not "in any inconsiderate way" affect the price development in the relevant market.[634]

Some general principles apply to investment firms dealing with clients. In practice, they must reflect the MiFID II regime.[635] There are also organisational requirements relating to: compliance by the board and the management[636]; the appointment of a compliance officer[637]; and internal ethical guidelines.[638]

N2EX In the N2EX market, the Market Conduct Rules apply to market participants, account holders, and brokers (Market Conduct Parties).[639] They cannot trade in the N2EX market without having to comply with the provisions of the Market Conduct Rules and the applicable law.[640] All contractual obligations are governed by English law.[641]

Where a Market Conduct Party grants trading system access to a third party, it must ensure that the third party complies with the Market Conduct Rules as if they applied to the third party. The third party must sign an adherence form.[642] The Market Conduct Rules are enforced by the Market Surveillance Unit of Nord Pool Spot AS.[643]

In addition to a general obligation to comply with the provisions of the applicable law including information-related duties, the Market Conduct Rules lay down a general prohibition to apply "unreasonable business methods", and a general duty to "seek to act in accordance with good business practice".[644]

Nasdaq Commodities Like N2EX, Nasdaq Commodities requires market participants not to apply "unreasonable business methods" and to "seek to act in accordance with good business conduct" according to its Market Conduct Rules.[645] The

634 Nord Pool Spot AS, Trading Appendix 7, Ethical Guidelines (29 March 2011), section 6.4.

635 Nord Pool Spot AS, Trading Appendix 7, Ethical Guidelines (29 March 2011), sections 5.1 and 5.2. See also Article 24 of Directive 2014/65/EU (MiFID II).

636 Nord Pool Spot AS, Trading Appendix 7, Ethical Guidelines (29 March 2011), section 7.1.

637 Nord Pool Spot AS, Trading Appendix 7, Ethical Guidelines (29 March 2011), section 7.2.

638 Nord Pool Spot AS, Trading Appendix 7, Ethical Guidelines (29 March 2011), section 7.3.

639 N2EX Physical Market, Trading Appendix 5, Market Conduct Rules (1 October 2014), section 1.1.1.

640 N2EX Physical Market, General Trading Terms, Trading Rules (1 October 2014), section 9.1.

641 N2EX Physical Market, General Trading Terms, Trading Rules (1 October 2014), section 18.1.

642 N2EX Physical Market, Trading Appendix 5, Market Conduct Rules (1 October 2014), Annex I.

643 N2EX Physical Market, Trading Appendix 5, Market Conduct Rules (1 October 2014), section 4.1.

644 N2EX Physical Market, Trading Appendix 5, Market Conduct Rules (1 October 2014), section 3.1.

645 NASDAQ OMX, Commodity Derivatives, Trading Appendix 6/Clearing Appendix 6, Market Conduct Rules (7 April 2014), section 6.1.

rules contain detailed disclosure requirements relating to market participants' own business or facilities or the business or facilities of clients.[646]

4.7.3 Market Integrity and Transparency

General Remarks

Traditional ways to increase market integrity include transparency, duties to comply with certain standards, and the prohibition of harmful acts. In particular, there are: (a) rules on registration, reporting, and monitoring; (b) rules laying down duties to other market participants and clients; (c) rules on public disclosure of inside information; and (d) rules that prohibit market abuse.

Approach to Regulation Market integrity is regulated in two main ways. First, it is regulated by transmission system operators and the operators of electricity exchanges. Extensive industry self-regulation is necessary for the functioning of the transmission system and electricity exchanges. TSOs would not be able to fulfil their own obligations such as managing electricity flows on the system[647] without the transparency of market participants' plans and actions. Transparency is facilitated by detailed balance contracts. Moreover, it is necessary for TSOs to require market participants to observe minimum standards. In order for electricity exchanges to work, market participants must even comply with other transparency and disclosure obligations. Second, market integrity is regulated by EU law and the governing law. The regulation of market integrity in European electricity markets follows in the footsteps of the regulation of financial markets.

EU financial markets are largely integrated after the implementation of the Financial Services Action Plan (FSAP).[648] The FSAP was based on the idea that "a genuine Single Market for financial services" is "crucial for economic growth and job creation in the Community".[649] It was assumed that "an integrated and efficient financial market" requires not only freedom to provide investment services across the EU and home-country control but also market integrity.[650] This led to the adoption of legislation that increased transparency and prohibited market abuse.

---

[646] NASDAQ OMX, Commodity Derivatives, Trading Appendix 6/Clearing Appendix 6, Market Conduct Rules (7 April 2014), section 4.

[647] Point (d) of Article 12 of Directive 2009/72/EC (Third Electricity Directive).

[648] Commission Communication, Implementing the framework for financial markets: action plan, COM(1999) 232 final (11 May 1999).

[649] Recital 1 of Directive 2003/6/EC (Directive on market abuse).

[650] Recital 2 of Directive 2003/6/EC (Directive on market abuse).

After the unbundling and integration of EU electricity markets and the emergence of electricity exchanges, it became necessary to adopt similar EU-wide rules on the integrity and transparency of wholesale energy markets.[651]

The regulatory regime for financial markets did not properly address these issues in electricity markets. The gap was addressed by REMIT and by the MAR/MAD II regime. They take into account inter-linkages between spot markets and related derivatives markets.[652]

Integrity REMIT was designed to "foster open and fair competition in wholesale energy markets for the benefit of final consumers of energy" by increasing the integrity and transparency of wholesale energy markets.[653] Their integrity and transparency were expected to benefit final consumers through the price mechanism. Price is influenced by transaction costs and market participants' perceived exposure to risk, among other things. A reduction in these costs and risks means increased liquidity and demand. The question of "integrity" or "confidence in the integrity of electricity and gas markets" is therefore a question of how to reduce transaction costs and perceived risk.[654]

Transparency, Market Abuse, REMIT MAR and REMIT lay down disclosure and reporting obligations and prohibit market abuse. Generally, these Regulations are designed to reflect the connection between disclosure and market abuse issues, and the connection between physical markets and derivatives markets.

The regulation of disclosure obligations should be aligned with the market abuse regime. If the two regimes are not aligned, there is a risk that information that must disclosed can simultaneously be regarded as inside information that must be kept secret.

In electricity wholesale markets, the regulatory regime should also be aligned with the regulation of securities markets, because physical electricity trading is complemented by derivatives trading. The REMIT definitions of inside information, insider trading, and market manipulation under REMIT have therefore been aligned with those applied in securities markets. The alternative would have been to expand the scope of MAR. But although MAR has a broad scope, it was not regarded as appropriate to extend it to "behaviour that does not involve financial instruments, for example, to trading in spot commodity contracts that only affects the spot market".[655]

---

[651] Recitals 1 and 2 of Regulation 1227/2011 (REMIT).

[652] Recitals 5 and 7–9 of Regulation 1227/2011 (REMIT). See also recitals 10 and 20 of Regulation 596/2014 (MAR).

[653] Recital 2 of Regulation 1227/2011 (REMIT).

[654] For securities markets, see Mäntysaari P (2010c), p. 211. Recital 1 of Regulation 1227/2011 (REMIT).

[655] Recital 20 of Regulation 596/2014 (MAR).

The definitions of the regulatory regime should consider the specific characteristics of wholesale energy markets.[656] REMIT provides examples of factors that should be considered.[657] The Commission is empowered to adopt delegated acts for this purpose.[658] Moreover, in the case of wholesale energy products, the competent authorities should consider the REMIT definitions when interpreting the related provisions of MAR.[659]

To sum up, the harmonisation of EU financial markets laws and the adoption of REMIT have contributed to the convergence of electricity exchange operators' market integrity rules as exchange rules must be aligned with mandatory provisions of law.

Registration, Reporting and Monitoring

Registration, reporting, and monitoring rules form an important part of the market integrity regime. Market participants must ensure compliance with overlapping regulatory regimes in this respect. They must comply with: the regulation of the electricity sector; the market abuse regime for trade in financial instruments; and the MiFID regime for investment firms.[660] In the following, we will discuss the regulation of monitoring (by ACER and national regulatory authorities), registration obligations, the duty to disclose market data to regulators or the TSO (Congestion Management Guidelines), the duty to disclose generation or load estimations (CACM Regulation), and data storage before moving on to the market abuse regime.

Monitoring, ACER There is a fundamental monitoring-related difference between electricity markets regulation and securities markets regulation. Electricity market participants must co-operate with many monitors.

While EU financial markets are governed by the principle of home country control,[661] this principle did not extend to electricity markets in the past. Monitoring practices depended on the Member State, and trading activities could be subject

[656] Recital 8 of Regulation 1227/2011 (REMIT).

[657] Article 6(2) of Regulation 1227/2011 (REMIT): "The delegated acts referred to in paragraph 1 shall take into account at least: (a) the specific functioning of wholesale energy markets, including the specificities of electricity and gas markets, and the interaction between commodity markets and derivative markets; (b) the potential for manipulation across borders, between electricity and gas markets and across commodity markets and derivative markets; (c) the potential impact on wholesale energy market prices of actual or planned production, consumption, use of transmission, or use of storage capacity; and (d) network codes and framework guidelines adopted in accordance with Regulations (EC) No 714/2009 and (EC) No 715/2009".

[658] Article 6(1) of Regulation 1227/2011 (REMIT).

[659] Recital 20 of Regulation 596/2014 (MAR).

[660] Article 1(2) of Regulation 1227/2011 (REMIT).

[661] Recitals 1, 2 and 17 of Directive 2004/39/EC (MiFID); Article 5(1) of Directive 2004/39/EC (MiFID); Article 5(1) of Directive 2014/65/EU (MiFID II).

to multiple jurisdictions with monitoring carried out by different authorities located in different Member States.[662] This became a problem because of the increasing integration of wholesale energy markets.[663]

The Third Electricity Directive did not solve the problem. The Directive does require each Member State to designate a single national regulatory authority[664] whose duties include the monitoring of exchanges.[665] However, the Directive does not require many exchange-related duties. Such duties are limited in three respects. First, while the Third Directive requires the regulatory authority to monitor what can be described as competition issues on electricity exchanges,[666] it does not address other exchange-relevant issues. Second, a Member State may provide that the monitoring duties are carried out by other authorities instead of the regulatory authority.[667] Third, TSOs monitor activities to the extent that they relate to physical flows on the system, and exchange-related issues are customarily monitored by securities markets regulators.

Monitoring issues were partly addressed by REMIT. First, REMIT facilitates stronger cross-border market monitoring. Stronger cross-border market monitoring is regarded as "essential for the completion of a fully functioning, interconnected and integrated internal energy market", and "vital for detecting and deterring market abuse on wholesale energy markets".[668] Second, REMIT is also an attempt to increase clarity as to what authority is responsible for monitoring.[669] According to REMIT, ACER is regarded as best placed to carry out such monitoring.

However, there are still many monitors. (a) National regulatory authorities continue to monitor electricity markets at the national level. Close co-operation is therefore necessary between energy regulators.[670] Depending on the Member State, market monitoring duties may be allocated to competition authorities.[671] (b) Moreover, REMIT does not limit the work of securities markets regulators and competition authorities under EU law.[672] Co-operation is therefore required even in this respect to facilitate efficient monitoring of all aspects of trading in wholesale energy products.[673]

---

662 Recital 6 of Regulation 1227/2011 (REMIT).

663 Recital 4 of Regulation 1227/2011 (REMIT).

664 Article 35(1) of Directive 2009/72/EC (Third Electricity Directive).

665 Article 37(1)(j) of Directive 2009/72/EC (Third Electricity Directive).

666 Point (j) of Article 37(1) of Directive 2009/72/EC (Third Electricity Directive).

667 Article 37(2) of Directive 2009/72/EC (Third Electricity Directive).

668 Recitals 4 and 17 of Regulation 1227/2011 (REMIT).

669 Recitals 4 and 6 of Regulation 1227/2011 (REMIT).

670 Article 1(1) of Regulation 1227/2011 (REMIT). See also recital 17 of Regulation 1227/2011 (REMIT).

671 Second subparagraph of Article 7(2) of Regulation 1227/2011 (REMIT).

672 Article 1(2) of Regulation 1227/2011 (REMIT).

673 Article 1(3) and first subparagraph of Article 7(2) of Regulation 1227/2011 (REMIT). See also recital 22.

This leaves the ACER with a relatively weak monitoring role. The Agency collects data and lets other regulatory authorities access the data it has collected.

Registration and Reporting to ACER Under REMIT The REMIT nevertheless requires the disclosure of information to ACER and to national regulatory authorities.[674]

Market participants have to comply with four main reporting obligations that include: a registration duty (REMIT); a duty to report transactions (REMIT); a duty to disclose market data (Congestion Management Guidelines); and a duty to disclose inside information (REMIT).

Registration A market participant must register with one national regulatory authority in the EU[675] prior to entering into a transaction which is required to be reported.[676] REMIT contains a list of market participants and others subject to the registration duty.[677] Generally, they include persons who enter into transactions in one or more wholesale energy markets.[678] Because the "crucial criterion" is the entering into transactions, many entities are regarded as market participants in this respect.[679] A separate legal person must register regardless of the fact that a parent, subsidiary or other related entity is already registered.[680]

The definition of wholesale energy markets is a broad one.[681] Wholesale energy markets are markets within the EU on which wholesale energy products are traded.[682] As it does not matter where and how "wholesale energy products" are traded, even intra-group transactions (OTC contracts entered into with another counterparty which is part of the same group) are regarded as wholesale energy products.[683] On the other hand, contracts for the supply and distribution of electricity or natural gas for the use of final customers are not wholesale energy products unless the final customer has a large consumption capacity.[684]

---

674 Article 7(1) of Regulation 1227/2011 (REMIT). See also recital 18.

675 Second subparagraph of Article 9(1) of Regulation 1227/2011 (REMIT).

676 Article 9(4) of Regulation 1227/2011 (REMIT).

677 Article 8(4) of Regulation 1227/2011 (REMIT).

678 Point 7 of Article 2 of Regulation 1227/2011 (REMIT): "... 'market participant' means any person, including transmission system operators, who enters into transactions, including the placing of orders to trade, in one or more wholesale energy markets; ..."

679 ACER, Guidance on the application of Regulation (EU) No 1227/2011 of the European Parliament and of the Council of 25 October 2011 on wholesale energy market integrity and transparency, 3rd edn (29 October 2013), p. 17.

680 ACER Guidance, p. 19.

681 See also ACER Guidance, p. 16; recital 5 of Regulation 1227/2011 (REMIT).

682 Point 4 of Article 2 of Regulation 1227/2011 (REMIT). See also recital 5 of Regulation 1227/2011 (REMIT); ACER Guidance, p. 16.

683 ACER Guidance, p. 15.

684 Points 4 and 5 of Article 2 of Regulation 1227/2011 (REMIT). For the definition of the term "at full use" and the notion of "single economic entity" in point 5, see ACER Guidance, p. 14.

For an EU firm, the competent national regulatory authority is the regulatory authority in the Member State in which it is "established or resident".[685] In electricity markets, the national regulatory authority is designated in accordance with the Third Electricity Directive.[686]

This registration duty is without prejudice to obligations to comply with the applicable trading and balancing rules that require other kinds of registrations (with the exchange operator, the clearing house/central counterparty, and the TSO).[687]

Transactions The registration obligation is complemented by an ongoing disclosure obligation. Market participants must provide ACER with a record of wholesale energy market transactions, including orders to trade. REMIT contains a list of the data to be reported.[688] The transactions to be reported and the modalities of reporting are defined by the Commission by means of implementing acts.[689] There is a Commission Implementing Regulation setting out the details.[690]

The ongoing duty to report transactions does not apply to the extent that the market participant already has reported the transaction in accordance with MiFID II/MiFIR or EMIR.[691] National regulatory authorities have access to information collected by ACER.[692]

Disclosure of Market Data by the Primary Owner of the Data In addition to general disclosure obligations, electricity firms must disclose market data as set out in the Congestion Management Guidelines, that is, Annex I to Regulation 714/2009[693] and Regulation 543/2013 amending Annex I.[694]

The new disclosure obligations under Regulation 543/2013 are not limited to congestion management in the narrow sense. They are relatively broad and detailed and designed to complement the regulation of the disclosure of inside information

[685] First subparagraph of Article 9(1) of Regulation 1227/2011 (REMIT).

[686] Point 10 of Article 2 of Regulation 1227/2011 (REMIT).

[687] Third subparagraph of Article 9(1) of Regulation 1227/2011 (REMIT).

[688] Article 8(1) of Regulation 1227/2011 (REMIT).

[689] Article 8(2) of Regulation 1227/2011 (REMIT).

[690] Commission Implementing Regulation (EU) No 1348/2014 of 17 December 2014 on data reporting implementing Article 8(2) and Article 8(6) of Regulation (EU) No 1227/2011 of the European Parliament and of the Council on wholesale energy market integrity and transparency.

[691] First subparagraph of Article 8(3) of Regulation 1227/2011 (REMIT). See also Article 58 of Directive 2014/65/EU (MiFID II) and Articles 9 and 10 of Regulation 648/2012 (EMIR).

[692] Article 7(2) of Regulation 1227/2011 (REMIT). In the US, registered swap/SBS dealers and MSPs/MSBSPs are required to disclose swap and other related information with domestic regulators and FSOC. CFTC and SEC shall share information with foreign regulators. 7 USC §6 s (f) and 15 USC §78o-8.

[693] Point 5 of Annex I (Guidelines on the management and allocation of available transfer capacity of interconnections between national systems) to Regulation 714/2009 (on conditions for access to the network for cross-border exchanges in electricity).

[694] Regulation 543/2013 (on submission and publication of data in electricity markets and amending Annex I to Regulation 714/2009).

under REMIT.[695] The liability of the parties is nevertheless limited under Regulation 543/2013.[696]

The disclosure obligations under Regulation 543/2013 apply to data relating to generation, transportation, and consumption of electricity.

The entity subject to the disclosure obligation is "the primary owner of the data" defined as "the entity which creates the data".[697] The primary owner of the data depends on the nature of the data:

- TSOs are regarded as primary owners of data in most cases.[698]
- Generation units and DSOs must provide information on total load.[699]
- Generation units and production units must provide information relating to actual generation.[700]
- Generation units must provide information relating to the unavailability of generation and production units.[701]
- Consumption units must provide information relating to the unavailability of consumption units.[702]
- Production units must provide information relating to the forecast of generation.[703]
- Generation units and DSOs must provide any relevant information required to calculate the year-ahead forecast margin for each bidding zone.[704]
- Power exchanges and transmission capacity allocators must provide information relating to the use of cross zonal capacities.[705]

Information is submitted to TSOs[706] or to the central information transparency platform.[707] In the latter case, parties subject to the disclosure obligation must use a third party acting as data provider on their behalf as agreed by the TSO. Information must be submitted in the required form. It must be "complete, of the required quality and provided in a manner that allows TSOs or data providers to process and deliver the data to the ENTSO for Electricity in sufficient time to allow the ENTSO

[695] Recitals 2 and 3 of Regulation 543/2013.

[696] Article 18 of Regulation 543/2013.

[697] Point 23 of Article 2 of Regulation 543/2013.

[698] Article 4(3) of Regulation 543/2013. See also recital 12.

[699] Article 6 of Regulation 543/2013.

[700] Article 16 of Regulation 543/2013.

[701] Article 15 of Regulation 543/2013.

[702] Article 7 of Regulation 543/2013.

[703] Article 14 of Regulation 543/2013.

[704] Article 8 of Regulation 543/2013.

[705] Article 12 of Regulation 543/2013.

[706] Article 4(1) of Regulation 543/2013.

[707] Article 4(2) of Regulation 543/2013.

for Electricity to meet its obligations".[708] ENTSO-E must develop a manual of procedures.[709]

Generation or Load Estimations The CACM Regulation provides that the individual grid models that each TSO is required to prepare should include information from generation and load units.[710] If a generator or load unit is required to provide information to the TSO responsible for the control area for the purposes of capacity calculation, it must provide information for each capacity calculation timeframe. The data to be provided is specified in the TSO's generation and load data provision methodology.[711]

Data Storage Market integrity is fostered and monitoring made easier by electricity producers' data storage obligations. Large generation undertakings—that is, "generation undertakings which own or operate generation assets, where at least one generation asset has an installed capacity of at least 250 MW"—must store hourly data per plant and keep it at the disposal of the national regulatory authority, the national competition authority, and the Commission for 5 years. The duty applies to data that is "necessary to verify all operational dispatching decisions and the bidding behaviour at power exchanges, interconnection auctions, reserve markets and over-the-counter-markets".[712]

Public Disclosure of Inside Information: General Remarks

Some firms are subject to an ongoing duty to disclose inside information to *the public*. This duty is based either on REMIT or MAR.[713] MiFID II, REMIT, and MAR complement each other. Reporting obligations under REMIT are without prejudice to reporting obligations under the MiFID regime and the market abuse regime.[714]

Market Abuse Regulation MAR is less important than REMIT in electricity wholesale markets, because both MAR and its disclosure obligations have a limited scope.

One of the problems relates to the issuer. According to MAR, the issuer of financial instruments must disclose inside information to the public where the inside information directly concerns the issuer.[715] While it is clear that securities

[708] Article 4(1) of Regulation 543/2013.

[709] Article 5 of Regulation 543/2013.

[710] Recital 9 of Commission Regulation . . ./.. (CACM Regulation).

[711] Articles 15 and 27 of Commission Regulation . . ./.. (CACM Regulation).

[712] Article 12(6) Regulation 714/2009 (on conditions for access to the network for cross-border exchanges in electricity).

[713] Article 17 of Regulation 596/2014 (MAR); Article 4 of Regulation 1227/2011 (REMIT).

[714] Article 1(2) of Regulation 1227/2011 (REMIT).

[715] Article 17(1) of Regulation 596/2014 (MAR). The duty to make a public disclosure is complemented by restrictions on selective disclosures. Article 17(8) Regulation 596/2014 (MAR).

traded on an exchange are issued by a certain issuer and traded on the secondary market between other parties, many contracts traded on electricity exchanges are not issued in any meaningful sense by an issuer other than the exchange operator that decides on the listing of contracts.[716]

Moreover, MAR mainly applies to qualified financial instruments, that is, financial instruments traded on a regulated market, multilateral trading facility (MTF), or organised trading facility (OTF).[717] Many contracts traded on electricity markets are not financial instruments.

In some cases, however, MAR applies to products auctioned on an auction platform whether or not they are financial instruments.[718] In some cases, MAR could even apply to certain spot commodity contracts.[719] Emission allowances are defined as financial instruments[720] (and neither emission allowances nor contracts for green certificates are regarded as wholesale energy products for these purposes).[721]

The inside information rules of MAR apply to different kinds of contracts traded on electricity markets:

- Financial instruments. "Inside information" is defined as qualified information relating to "financial instruments", "commodity derivatives", "emission allowances or auctioned products" or issuers of financial instruments.[722] Because of the broad definition of "financial instruments",[723] some "derivative contracts relating to commodities" such as electricity derivatives can be regarded as "financial instruments".
- Related instruments. Moreover, inside information rules apply to "spot commodity contracts, which are not wholesale energy products"[724] and "emission allowances or auctioned products" that are not financial instruments.[725] Emission allowances under the EU ETS are regarded as "financial instruments".[726]

---

[716] See, for example, Nord Pool Spot's Physical Markets, General Terms, Trading Rules (1 February 2015), section 7.1.1, and NASDAQ OMX, Trading Appendix 2/Clearing Appendix 2, Contract Specifications, Commodity Derivatives (24 November 2014), Part A, section 3.1.2: "The Exchange may admit new Exchange Listed Products by issuing Contract Specifications with standard terms for the relevant Product . . ."

[717] First subparagraph of Article 2(1) of Regulation 596/2014 (MAR).

[718] Second subparagraph of Article 2(1) of Regulation 596/2014 (MAR).

[719] Article 2(2) of Regulation 596/2014 (MAR).

[720] Point 11 of Section C of Annex I to Directive 2014/65/EU (MiFID II).

[721] Article 2(4) of Regulation 1227/2011 (REMIT); ACER, Guidance on the application of Regulation (EU) No 1227/2011 of the European Parliament and of the Council of 25 October 2011 on wholesale energy market integrity and transparency, 3rd edn (29 October 2013), p. 15.

[722] Article 7(1) of Regulation 596/2014 (MAR).

[723] Section C of Annex I to Directive 2014/65/EU (MiFID II).

[724] Article 2(2) of Regulation 596/2014 (MAR).

[725] Second subparagraph of Article 2(1) of Regulation 596/2014 (MAR).

[726] Point 11 of Section C of Annex I to Directive 2014/65/EU (MiFID II).

- Trading. The inside information rules of MAR apply to "financial instruments" and related instruments qualified in relation to trading on a regulated market, an MTF, or an OTF.[727] On the other hand, actions are not qualified. MAR applies to "any transaction, order or behaviour ... irrespective of whether or not such transaction, order or behaviour takes place on a trading venue".
- Exclusions. It is clear that MAR does not apply to trading in spot electricity contracts or physical electricity forward contracts where contracts are settled physically.[728] Generally, some contracts fall outside the scope of the inside information rules of MAR. There are electricity contracts that do not have the characteristics of derivative financial instruments according to the main rule.[729] There are electricity derivatives that are not regarded as "financial instruments" as they are "for commercial purposes". There can be electricity contracts that are regarded as "financial instruments" but not traded on a regulated market, an MTF, or an OTF. Moreover, wholesale energy products that must be physically settled and are traded on an OTF are not financial instruments.[730] Such trading only affects the spot electricity market or the physical electricity forward market.

REMIT Because of the limited scope of MAR, it was thought necessary to extend the scope of this regime while considering the specific characteristics of wholesale electricity markets.[731] According to REMIT, each "market participant" must publicly disclose inside information in respect of its business or facilities.

The scope of the duty to disclose inside information is broad, because duties to disclose inside information under REMIT and MAR are complementary rather than mutually exclusive, because the disclosure duty under REMIT applies to market participants rather than issuers, because the disclosure duty under REMIT applies to wholesale energy products whether or not they are financial instruments,[732] and because the definition of inside information is broad under REMIT.

This raises several questions. What must be disclosed? Who must disclose something? To whom and how must the disclosure be made? When does the disclosure have to be made? Are there exceptions? We will focus on REMIT and physical electricity markets.

---

[727] First subparagraph of Article 2(1) of Regulation 596/2014 (MAR).

[728] Recital 20 and points 15–16 of Article 3(1) of Regulation 596/2014 (MAR).

[729] Point 7 of Section C of Annex I to Directive 2014/65/EU (MiFID II).

[730] Point 6 of Section C of Annex I to Directive 2014/65/EU (MiFID II).

[731] See, for example, recitals 8 and 11 of Regulation 1227/2011 (REMIT).

[732] Articles 1(2) and 4(1) of Regulation 1227/2011 (REMIT).

Inside Information

For the purposes of REMIT, "inside information" is "information of a precise nature which has not been made public, which relates, directly or indirectly, to one or more wholesale energy products and which, if it were made public, would be likely to significantly affect the prices of those wholesale energy products".[733] For the purposes of MAR, "inside information" means similar information that relates to financial instruments or their issuers.[734]

The definition of inside information is thus a broad one. It can be broader than "transparency information" to be published under Regulation 714/2009 or referred to in Regulation 543/2013.[735] However, information is not inside information if it has already been made public. Neither does inside information consist of the market participant's own trading plans or trading strategies.[736]

Like in securities markets, inside information under REMIT consists of many elements.[737] There are nevertheless some differences.

Wholesale Energy Products Information is not inside information under REMIT unless it "relates" to one or more wholesale energy products and, if it were made public, would be "likely to significantly affect" the prices of those "wholesale energy products".[738] For example, inside information in the electricity derivatives market often relates to large production volumes that should be reported to the operator of the exchange but have not yet been disclosed to the market.[739] Changes in production schedules can influence price when the volumes are large. In practice, prices could be influenced even by information from an important electricity producer's board meetings.[740]

---

[733] Point 1 of Article 2 of Regulation 1227/2011 (REMIT).

[734] Article 7(1) of Regulation 596/2014 (MAR).

[735] Article 2(1)(a) of Regulation 1227/2011 (REMIT). ACER, Guidance on the application of Regulation (EU) No 1227/2011 of the European Parliament and of the Council of 25 October 2011 on wholesale energy market integrity and transparency, 3rd edn (29 October 2013), pp. 27–29.

[736] Recital 12 of Regulation 1227/2011 (REMIT); ACER, Guidance on the application of Regulation (EU) No 1227/2011 of the European Parliament and of the Council of 25 October 2011 on wholesale energy market integrity and transparency, 3rd edn (29 October 2013), p. 29.

[737] Case C-19/11, Markus Geltl v Daimler AG, para 25 (on the definition of inside information under the Market Abuse Directive): "The definition of the notion of 'inside information' under point 1 of Article 1 of that directive comprises four essential elements. Firstly, it must be of a precise nature. Secondly, the information must not have been made public. Thirdly, it must relate, directly or indirectly, to one or more financial instruments or their issuers. Fourthly, it must be information which, if it were made public, would be likely to have a significant effect on the prices of those financial instruments or on the price of related derivative financial instruments. The first and fourth elements are defined more specifically in Article 1(1) and (2) respectively of Directive 2003/124".

[738] Point 1 of Article 2 of Regulation 1227/2011 (REMIT).

[739] Godager K (2009), § 18, number 40.

[740] Godager K (2009), § 18, number 41.

Expectations Inside information is qualified by the expectations of market participants. Unlike in securities markets, there are limitations on the information that is regarded as legally relevant.

First, inside information may consist of information that must be disclosed to the public because of legal requirements or market rules.[741]

Second, inside information may consist of "information that a reasonable market participant would be likely to use as part of the basis of its decision to enter into a transaction relating to, or to issue an order to trade in, a wholesale energy product".[742] For instance, this could be "information relating to the capacity and use of facilities for production, storage, consumption or transmission of electricity or natural gas or related to the capacity and use of LNG facilities, including planned or unplanned unavailability of these facilities".[743]

Third, where MAR applies to derivatives on commodities, information is not inside information under that Regulation unless it, "if it were made public, would be likely to have a significant effect on the prices of such derivatives or related spot commodity contracts", and "this is information which is reasonably expected to be disclosed or is required to be disclosed in accordance with legal or regulatory provisions at the Union or national level, market rules, contract, practice or custom, on the relevant commodity derivatives markets or spot markets".[744]

Precise Nature Like in securities markets,[745] information cannot be regarded as inside information unless it is "of a precise nature". The holder of the information bears the risk of assessing the nature of information correctly: "The precise nature of the information is to be assessed by the holder of the information on a case-by-case basis and depends on what the information is and on the surrounding context".[746]

Information is deemed to be of a precise nature if two cumulative conditions are satisfied. The first relates to the existence of a set of circumstances or an event. The second relates to their effect on prices.[747]

According to the wording of REMIT, information is "deemed to be of a precise nature if it indicates a set of circumstances which exists or may reasonably be expected to come into existence, or an event which has occurred or may reasonably be expected to do so, and if it is specific enough to enable a conclusion to be drawn

---

741 Point 1 of Article 2 of Regulation 1227/2011 (REMIT).

742 Point 1(d) of Article 2 of Regulation 1227/2011 (REMIT).

743 Point 1(b) Article 2 of Regulation 1227/2011 (REMIT).

744 Article 7(1)(b) of Regulation 596/2014 (MAR).

745 Article 1(1) of Directive 2003/124 (implementing Directive 2003/6/EC).

746 ACER, Guidance on the application of Regulation (EU) No 1227/2011 of the European Parliament and of the Council of 25 October 2011 on wholesale energy market integrity and transparency, 3rd edn (29 October 2013), p. 29.

747 Case C-19/11, Markus Geltl v Daimler AG, para 29.

as to the possible effect of that set of circumstances or event on the prices of wholesale energy products".[748]

As the existence of information of a precise nature can trigger the disclosure obligation (provided that all the other requirements are met), there is a connection between (a) the existence of such a "set of circumstances" or "event" on one hand and (b) the point in time when the disclosure must be made on the other.

The question of the existence of information of a precise nature is particularly important in protracted processes in which there are intermediate steps (such as negotiations, decisions, or contracts) taken by one body but no final and effective decision without approval by another body. How likely must the occurrence of future events be?

Protracted processes have been discussed in *Markus Geltl v Daimler AG* and addressed in MAR.[749] In *Markus Geltl v Daimler AG*, the CJEU held that information relating to an intermediate step which is part of a protracted process may be regarded as precise information.[750] Moreover, even a future set of circumstances or event may trigger the disclosure obligation, provided that "it appears, on the basis of an overall assessment of the factors existing at the relevant time, that there is a realistic prospect that they will come into existence or occur".[751] In the light of *Markus Geltl v Daimler AG*, the following test must be used to determine whether it is reasonable to think that a set of circumstances will come into existence or that an event will occur:

1. An assessment must be made on a case-by-case basis of the factors existing at the relevant time.[752]
2. High probability is not required.[753]
3. On the other hand, the occurrence of the set of circumstances or events must not be implausible.[754]
4. Therefore, the expression "may reasonably be expected" refers to future circumstances or events from which it appears, based on an overall assessment of the factors existing at the relevant time, that there is a realistic prospect that they will come into existence or occur.[755]

---

[748] Point 1 of Article 2 of Regulation 1227/2011 (REMIT).

[749] Article 7(3) of Regulation 596/2014 (MAR): "An intermediate step in a protracted process shall be deemed to be inside information if, by itself, it satisfies the criteria of inside information as referred to in this Article". See also Article 7(2) of Regulation 596/2014 (MAR) on the "precise nature" of information.

[750] Case C-19/11, Markus Geltl v Daimler AG, para 40.

[751] Case C-19/11, Markus Geltl v Daimler AG, para 56.

[752] Case C-19/11, Markus Geltl v Daimler AG, para 45.

[753] Case C-19/11, Markus Geltl v Daimler AG, para 46.

[754] Case C-19/11, Markus Geltl v Daimler AG, para 48.

[755] Case C-19/11, Markus Geltl v Daimler AG, para 49.

According to MAR, an intermediate step in a protracted process is regarded as inside information "if, by itself, it satisfies the criteria of inside information".[756]

Entities Subject to the Obligation to Disclose Inside Information

The broad scope of the definition of inside information is complemented by the broad scope of entities that are potentially subject to the disclosure obligation under REMIT.

Market Participant A market participant must disclose inside information which it possesses in respect of its own business or facilities.[757]

The number of entities subject to the disclosure obligation is increased, because: (1) the threshold of market connection that triggers the obligation is low; (2) circumstances attributable to the entity can include circumstances of other entities that are sufficiently closely related[758]; (3) the disclosure obligation extends to a larger group of people in the case of selective disclosure[759]; (4) the disclosure obligation applies regardless of whether the wholesale energy product is a financial instrument or not[760]; and (5) some electricity market participants are subject to disclosure obligations under MAR as issuers of financial instruments or emission market participants.[761]

Market Connection We can study the low threshold of market connection first. Each "market participant" in the "wholesale energy market" must disclose inside information under REMIT. The "wholesale energy market" means any market within the EU on which wholesale energy products are traded, and a "market participant" means any person who enters into transactions or places orders to trade in one or more wholesale energy markets. Even transmission system operators are regarded as market participants.[762]

The market connection (that is, entering into transactions, including the placing of orders to trade) is not qualified according to the wording of REMIT.

One might therefore ask (a) whether entering into (at least) one transaction or placing (at least) one order to trade in (at least) one wholesale energy market in the

[756] Article 7(3) of Regulation 596/2014 (MAR). See also Article 7(2) of Regulation 596/2014 (MAR) on the "precise nature" of information.

[757] Article 4(1) of Regulation 1227/2011 (REMIT).

[758] Article 4(1) of Regulation 1227/2011 (REMIT).

[759] Article 4(3) of Regulation 1227/2011 (REMIT).

[760] Article 1(2) of Regulation 1227/2011 (REMIT); ACER, Guidance on the application of Regulation (EU) No 1227/2011 of the European Parliament and of the Council of 25 October 2011 on wholesale energy market integrity and transparency, 3rd edn (29 October 2013), p. 11.

[761] Article 17 of Regulation 596/2014 (MAR).

[762] Points 4–8 of Article 2 of Regulation 1227/2011 (REMIT).

EU can trigger the ongoing disclosure obligation, or (b) whether there must be a greater number of transactions or orders, or a more permanent market connection.

The disclosure obligation seems to be triggered by one transaction for three reasons. First, REMIT provides that a market participant must register with one national regulatory authority in the EU.[763] The registration obligation and the disclosure obligation should apply to the same entities. Second, clear thresholds are to be preferred to make it easier for market participants to comply with the disclosure rules. Third, this would increase: the pool of information that enables market participants "to assess the overall demand and supply situation and identify the reasons for fluctuations in the wholesale price"[764]; and the efficiency of electricity markets.

Attributable Circumstances The second factor increasing the number of entities subject to the disclosure obligation under REMIT is the fact that circumstances attributable to the entity can include circumstances of other legal entities.[765] MAR is narrower in this respect as an issuer's ongoing disclosure duty is limited to "inside information which directly concerns that issuer".[766]

When determining the "market participant" subject to the disclosure obligation under REMIT, the starting point is the legal entity (or natural person) that places an order to trade in the wholesale market.[767] The entity must publicly disclose inside information in respect of its business or facilities.

However, circumstances attributable to the entity are not limited to business directly carried out by the entity or facilities directly owned by the entity.[768] The entities, business, and facilities attributable to the market participant have a broad scope. They include:

- business and facilities that the entity owns;
- business and facilities that the entity controls;
- business and facilities for whose operational matters the entity is responsible in whole or in part; and
- business and facilities of other entities that belong to the same firm by reason of share ownership or control. These entities are the entity's parent undertaking and affiliated undertakings ("related undertakings") as defined in the Seventh Company Law Directive.[769]

[763] Second subparagraph of Article 9(1) of Regulation 1227/2011 (REMIT).

[764] Recital 11 of Regulation 1227/2011 (REMIT).

[765] Article 4(1) of Regulation 1227/2011 (REMIT).

[766] See Articles 5 and 17(1) of Regulation 596/2014 (MAR).

[767] Points 7 and 8 of Article 2 of Regulation 1227/2011 (REMIT).

[768] Article 4(1) of Regulation 1227/2011 (REMIT).

[769] Point 12 of Article 2 of Regulation 1227/2011 (REMIT) on parent undertakings; point 13 of Article 2 of Regulation 1227/2011 (REMIT) on related undertakings; Article 12(1) of Directive 83/349/EEC (Seventh Company Law Directive) on consolidated accounts.

Selective Disclosure The third factor relates to selective disclosure. A larger group of people is subject to the disclosure obligation in the event of selective disclosure.[770] Where a market participant discloses inside information in relation to a wholesale energy product "in the normal exercise of his employment, profession or duties", the market participant must "ensure simultaneous, complete and effective public disclosure of that information". Where a person employed by, or acting on behalf of, a market participant discloses such inside information in that way, either that person or the market participant must ensure public disclosure.[771]

Limitations on the Duty to Disclose Inside Information

Market participants have a duty to disclose some but not all inside information under REMIT. The disclosure duty is limited in four main ways.

No Inside Information Obviously, there is no duty to disclose inside information if there is no inside information in the first place.[772] (a) Information is not inside information to the extent that it has been made public. (b) Moreover, information is not inside information under REMIT unless it "relates" to one or more wholesale energy products. There is no obligation to disclose information about: general corporate matters; securities issued by the entity or related entities; or wholesale energy products as such. There can, nevertheless, be a duty to disclose such information under securities markets laws, market rules, the rules of the transmission system operator, or otherwise. For instance, information can be regarded as inside information according to the provisions of MAR that complement the provisions of REMIT.[773]

Knowledge The second limitation relates to knowledge. A market participant has no duty to disclose inside information unless the information is in its possession.

This limitation can be important in practice because of the broad scope of circumstances attributable to the market participant.[774] For instance, inside information can also relate to a parent or affiliate company's business or facilities. The market participant does not need to disclose circumstances that it is not deemed to be aware of.

MAR lacks a similar general limitation. On the other hand, it also limits disclosure obligations to the circumstances of the issuing legal entity.[775] There is an exception. While emission allowances are regarded as financial instruments that fall within the

[770] Article 4(3) of Regulation 1227/2011 (REMIT).

[771] Article 4(3) of Regulation 1227/2011 (REMIT).

[772] Point 1 of Article 2 of Regulation 1227/2011 (REMIT).

[773] Article 7(1) of Regulation 596/2014 (MAR).

[774] Article 4(1) of Regulation 1227/2011 (REMIT).

[775] Article 17(1) of Regulation 596/2014 (MAR).

scope of MAR, an emission allowance market participant is subject to wider disclosure obligations like commodities market participants under REMIT.[776]

Qualified Inside Information The third limitation relates to the nature of inside information. (a) The duty to disclose inside information under REMIT is limited to inside information "in respect of business or facilities". The disclosure must include "information relevant to the capacity and use of facilities for production, storage, consumption or transmission of electricity ... including planned or unplanned unavailability of these facilities".[777] (b) There is thus no duty under REMIT to disclose information that is not closely enough connected with business or facilities. In contrast, MAR limits the disclosure obligation to inside information that "directly concerns" the issuer.

Delayed Disclosure The fourth limitation is that the disclosure of inside information may be delayed under REMIT[778] and MAR[779] if the conditions are met.

Manner of Disclosure

REMIT sets out the manner of disclosure only in very general terms. The main rule is that market participants must disclose inside information publicly "in an effective and timely manner".[780]

MAR lays down a similar requirement. According to MAR, inside information must be made public "in a manner which enables fast access and complete, correct and timely assessment of the information by the public".[781] MAR refers to the Transparency Directive in this respect.[782] MAR will also be complemented by delegated acts. There are earlier implementing rules on the technical modalities for appropriate public disclosure of inside information for the purposes of the directive that it replaces.[783]

Compliance with Other Disclosure Requirements In practice, this disclosure requirement may be met when the disclosure fulfils simultaneous disclosure requirements based on EU law in the energy sector.[784] Disclosure requirements under REMIT are without prejudice to other disclosure requirements and the disclosure requirements often cover the same events or circumstances. However,

---

[776] Article 17(2) of Regulation 596/2014 (MAR).

[777] Article 4(1) of Regulation 1227/2011 (REMIT).

[778] Article 4(2) of Regulation 1227/2011 (REMIT).

[779] Article 17(4) of Regulation 596/2014 (MAR).

[780] Article 4(1) of Regulation 1227/2011 (REMIT).

[781] Second subparagraph of Article 17(1) of Regulation 596/2014 (MAR).

[782] Second subparagraph of Article 17(1) of Regulation 596/2014 (MAR).

[783] Article 6(10) of Directive 2003/6/EC (Directive on market abuse).

[784] Article 4(4) of Regulation 1227/2011 (REMIT): "The publication of inside information, including in aggregated form, in accordance with Regulation (EC) No 714/2009 or (EC) No 715/2009, or guidelines and network codes adopted pursuant to those Regulations constitutes simultaneous, complete and effective public disclosure".

compliance with one set of rules does not automatically fulfil compliance requirements under another set of rules.[785]

Time of Disclosure The disclosure must be made in a "timely manner".[786] In the event of selective disclosure, there must be simultaneous disclosure to the public. If the selective disclosure was non-intentional, the public disclosure must be made as soon as possible.[787]

REMIT is complemented by ACER Guidance. According to ACER, market participants should develop a clear compliance regime towards real time or close to real time disclosure of inside information and the further REMIT requirements. ACER also gives examples of best practices.[788] For instance, ACER Guidance lays down minimum IT requirements for effective disclosure and requires the use of "Urgent Market Messages" that fulfil certain requirements as to form.[789]

Delayed Disclosure REMIT and MAR set out when the public disclosure of inside information may be delayed. One can distinguish between the right to delay public disclosure in general, the right to delay it following a selective disclosure, and exemptions.

Several conditions are attached to the right to delay public disclosure according to the main rule:

- Exceptional nature. It must be exceptional to delay disclosure. The main rule is disclosure.[790]
- Legitimate interests. The market participant may delay disclosure only in order not to prejudice its legitimate interests.
- Non-misleading. Delayed disclosure is permitted only provided that it is not likely to mislead the public.
- Confidentiality. Delayed disclosure is permitted only provided that the market participant is able to ensure the confidentiality of that information.
- No decisions. Under REMIT, delayed disclosure is permitted only provided that the market participant makes no decisions relating to trading in wholesale energy products based on the information.[791]

Where the market participant delays disclosure, the market participant must provide that information to the competent authority, that is, ACER under REMIT

---

[785] Articles 4(6) and 1(2) of Regulation 1227/2011 (REMIT).

[786] Article 4(1) of Regulation 1227/2011 (REMIT).

[787] Article 4(3) of Regulation 1227/2011 (REMIT).

[788] ACER, Guidance on the application of Regulation (EU) No 1227/2011 of the European Parliament and of the Council of 25 October 2011 on wholesale energy market integrity and transparency, 3rd edn (29 October 2013), pp. 44 and 59.

[789] ACER Guidance, pp. 42–43.

[790] See also Case C-19/11, Markus Geltl v Daimler AG, paras 33–34.

[791] Article 4(2) of Regulation 1227/2011 (REMIT).

and the competent authority under MAR. It must also give them a justification for the delay.[792]

Protracted Processes In securities markets, the question of legitimate interests often arises in the context of negotiations in course and two-stage decision-making processes in which a decision formulated by one corporate body must be approved by another body to be effective (protracted processes).

Directive 2003/124 that implemented the earlier market abuse directive set out a non-exhaustive list of situations in which an issuer may have a legitimate interest to delay disclosure. In the case of negotiations on course or protracted processes, there could be a legitimate interest provided that the act as such was a legitimate act necessary for the issuer (for instance, the conclusion of contracts and internal decision-making are necessary for all firms)[793] and public disclosure would either seriously have jeopardised the act or been likely to mislead the public (jeopardise the correct assessment of the information by the public). In practice, there was room for interpretation meaning that the firm could be exposed to legal risk.[794]

Protracted processes have now been addressed in MAR. An issuer may, under his own responsibility, delay the public disclosure of inside information relating to this process provided that the main requirements are met.[795]

Selective Disclosure Selective disclosure can increase the risk of market abuse and market participants' perceived risk.[796] The main rule, therefore, is the simultaneous disclosure of the same information to the public.

The market participant may delay the public disclosure of inside information even in the event of a selective disclosure, provided that (a) it has a right to delay public disclosure in general and (b) "the person receiving the information has a duty of confidentiality, regardless of whether such duty derives from law, regulation, articles of association or a contract".[797]

There are some rare exemptions. First, a transmission system operator may obtain an exemption from the duty to publish certain data under the Regulation on conditions for access to the network for cross-border exchanges in electricity. If it does obtain an exemption, it is also exempted from the obligation to make that data public under REMIT.[798] Second, a market participant may have a right to delay

[792] Article 4(2) of Regulation 1227/2011 (REMIT).

[793] Article 3(1) of Directive 2003/124 (implementing Directive 2003/6/EC).

[794] See Case C-19/11, Markus Geltl v Daimler AG.

[795] Second subparagraph of Article 17(4) of Regulation 596/2014 (MAR).

[796] Recital 24 of Directive 2003/6/EC (Directive on market abuse). Case C-19/11, Markus Geltl v Daimler AG, para 34.

[797] Article 4(3) of Regulation 1227/2011 (REMIT) and Article 17(8) of Regulation 596/2014 (MAR). See also first subparagraph of Article 17(4) of Regulation 596/2014 (MAR).

[798] Regulation 714/2009 (on conditions for access to the network for cross-border exchanges in electricity); Articles 4(5) and 4(7) of Regulation 1227/2011 (REMIT).

the disclosure of sensitive information relating to the protection of critical infrastructure under some circumstances.[799]

Exchange Rules

The statutory rules are complemented by exchange rules.[800] While some exchange rules merely repeat the contents of the governing law (boilerplate) or leave the disclosure obligation to be regulated by the governing law,[801] others can define the contents of the disclosure obligation in more detail.

Both Nord Pool Spot and Nasdaq Commodities define the modalities of the obligation to disclosure inside information in more detail.

Each member of Nord Pool Spot must publicly disclose information on its business or facilities where the information relates to the Nordic or Baltic electricity market. The disclosure requirements do not apply to information regarding the member's own plans and strategies for trading.[802] Some forms of inside information have been mentioned expressly in a non-exclusive list.[803] Nord Pool Spot's Market Conduct Rules lay down the core minimum technical information of the public disclosure.[804] They address even other modalities of disclosure such as the use of Urgent Market Messages (UMM).[805]

The duties to disclose inside information on Nasdaq Commodities are, to a large extent, a copy of the duties applied on Nord Pool Spot.[806] NASDAQ OMX Market Conduct Rules also provide for exceptions to the disclosure rule.[807] However, the exchange is not in a position to reduce the scope of disclosure rules based on mandatory law. Where an exchange member possesses inside information about its clients, it can be unclear whether it has a duty to disclose it to the exchange.[808]

---

[799] Article 4(7) of Regulation 1227/2011 (REMIT).

[800] See, for example, EPEX Spot Code of Conduct (9 July 2012), section 1(2).

[801] EPEX Spot Code of Conduct (9 July 2012); EEX Code of Conduct (24 June 2010); N2EX Physical Market, Trading Appendix 5, Market Conduct Rules (1 October 2014).

[802] Nord Pool Spot Physical Market, Trading Appendix 5, Market Conduct Rules (7 January 2014), section 5.1.

[803] *Ibid*, section 5.2.

[804] *Ibid*, section 5.3.

[805] *Ibid*, section 5.4.

[806] NASDAQ OMX, Commodity Derivatives, Trading Appendix 6/Clearing Appendix 6, Market Conduct Rules (7 April 2014), section 4.1.

[807] *Ibid*, section 4.2.

[808] *Ibid*, section 4.3: "An Exchange Member is, independent of the disclosure duties of its clients, under an obligation to disclose to the Exchange the information concerning clients as provided for in this Section 4, if and when the Exchange Member possesses such information". Section 4.2: "The disclosure requirements in section 4.1 apply with the following exceptions: . . . c. information that an Exchange Member receives regarding a client, as well as any other information conveyed by a client to an Exchange Member related to the client's pending Orders".

4.7.4 Prohibition of Insider Trading

Market participants' disclosure duties are complemented by the prohibition of insider trading and market manipulation. Insider trading is prohibited both under REMIT (wholesale energy products)[809] and MAR/MAD II (financial instruments).[810] The prohibition applies to a certain category of persons and certain actions. Like MAR, REMIT prohibits three types of actions: use, disclosure, and recommendations. In the following, we will focus on wholesale energy markets and REMIT.

Subjective Scope The prohibitions under REMIT apply to "persons" in possession of inside information in relation to a wholesale energy product. The persons can be natural persons or legal entities.[811] Like MAR, REMIT defines the subjective scope of the prohibition in more detail.[812]

First, the person in possession of inside information in electricity wholesale markets is often a legal person. Information possessed by a legal entity's employees, managers, or organ members can be attributable to the legal entity. For instance, a transmission system operator is in possession of information about market participants' generation facilities, and the owner or operator possesses information about the relevant facilities.

Where the person who possesses inside information is a legal person, the prohibitions apply to the legal person and also to the natural persons who take part in the decision to carry out the transaction for the account of the legal person.[813]

Second, whether the person is a natural person or a legal person, the subjective scope of the prohibitions is quite broad.[814] The categories of persons are defined based on the nature of information or status.

When defined based on the nature of information, the prohibition covers persons because of knowledge, access to information, or criminal activity as follows:

- Knowledge: The prohibition applies to all persons who know, or ought to know, that the information is inside information.
- Access to information: The prohibition applies to persons with access to the information through the exercise of their employment, profession or duties (whether one can prove that they knew or ought to have known that the information was inside information).
- Criminal activity: The prohibition applies to persons who have acquired such information through criminal activity (again, it is not necessary to prove actual or constructive knowledge of the nature of the information).

[809] Article 3(1) of Regulation 1227/2011 (REMIT).

[810] Article 14 of Regulation 596/2014 (MAR).

[811] Point 8 of Article 2 of Regulation 1227/2011 (REMIT).

[812] Article 8 of Regulation 596/2014 (MAR); Article 3 of Regulation 1227/2011 (REMIT).

[813] Article 3(5) of Regulation 1227/2011 (REMIT); Article 8(5) of Regulation 596/2014 (MAR).

[814] Article 3(2) of Regulation 1227/2011 (REMIT); Article 8(4) of Regulation 596/2014 (MAR).

In addition, the subjective scope of the prohibitions covers some persons who are typical insiders of the undertaking:

- Membership of a body: The prohibition applies to "members of the administrative, management or supervisory bodies of an undertaking".
- Holdings: The prohibition applies to "persons with holdings in the capital of an undertaking".

Although the wording of REMIT resembles the wording of MAR, there is an important difference relating to members of a body. The term used in MAR is "the issuer" of the financial instruments to which inside information relates. This is understandable because the issuer's managers and important shareholders can have actual or constructive knowledge of inside information relating to the issuer's own securities. The term used in REMIT is the "undertaking".

The term "undertaking" is not qualified according to the wording of REMIT. It would obviously be unreasonable to apply this term in an unqualified form as there are very many undertakings in the world. It is reasonable to interpret it in one of two ways. It could be limited to mean the market participant whose business or facilities the inside information relates to. This would lead to better alignment of REMIT with MAR—the mutual compatibility of their terms is regarded as important.[815] The alternative would be to interpret it as meaning the market participant, its "parent undertaking", and its "related undertaking" in the sense of Article 4(1) of REMIT.

Prohibitions The actions prohibited by REMIT and MAR are use, disclosure, and recommendations. A person to which the prohibitions apply is prohibited from:

- using inside information by acquiring or disposing of wholesale energy products to which the information relates;
- disclosing inside information to any other person; and
- recommending or inducing another person, based on inside information, to acquire or dispose of wholesale energy products to which that information relates.[816]

Front running is one of the forms of prohibited use of inside information. Front running (or pre-positioning) means a transaction for a person's own benefit, on the basis of and ahead of an order which he is to carry out with or for another, which takes advantage of the anticipated impact of the order on the market or auction clearing price.[817]

Exemptions There are exemptions from the prohibition. They can be of three kinds and relate permitted use and permitted disclosure.

[815] See Recital 8 of Regulation 1227/2011 (REMIT).

[816] Article 3(1) of Regulation 1227/2011 (REMIT); Article 14 of Regulation 596/2014 (MAR).

[817] FCA Handbook, MAR 1.3.2(2) (1 April 2013). Recital 19 of Directive 2003/6/EC (Directive on market abuse) and recital 30 of Regulation 596/2014 (MAR).

First, REMIT does not seem to provide any safe harbour for legal persons that ring-fence possession of inside information and keep it separate from decision-making by applying Chinese walls and compliance programmes.[818]

> MAR provides such a safe harbour. The exception under MAR applies to legal persons that use "adequate and effective internal arrangements and procedures that effectively ensure that neither the natural person who made the decision on its behalf to acquire or dispose of financial instruments to which the information relates, nor any other natural person who may have had any influence on that decision was in possession of the inside information".[819]

Second, some exemptions nevertheless apply to the use of inside information. (a) There is an exemption for transmission system operators that purchase electricity to ensure the safe and secure operation of the system in accordance with their statutory obligations.[820] (b) There is an exemption for prior agreements. It is permitted to conduct transactions for discharging obligations that result from prior agreements.[821] ACER Guidance requires the "hands-off approach" for derivatives contracts.[822] (c) In some cases, it is permitted for electricity producers to enter into transactions to cover the immediate physical loss resulting from unplanned outages.[823] (d) There is also an exception for market participants acting under national emergency rules.[824]

Third, there are exceptions applicable to disclosure. (a) It is permitted to disclose inside information to other persons in the normal course of the exercise of their employment, profession or duties.[825] (b) MAR contains a particular provision on market soundings.[826] (c) Journalists acting in their professional capacity may disseminate information for the purposes of journalism. They must then consider the rules governing the freedom of the press. Journalists must not disseminate inside information unless they act bona fide at least in two ways. They must not derive an advantage or profits, and the disclosure or dissemination must not be made with the intention of misleading the market.[827]

---

[818] See Article 3(5) of Regulation 1227/2011 (REMIT).

[819] Article 9(1) of Regulation 596/2014 (MAR).

[820] Article 3(3) of Regulation 1227/2011 (REMIT).

[821] Article 3(4) of Regulation 1227/2011 (REMIT); Article 9(3) of Regulation 596/2014 (MAR).

[822] ACER, Guidance on the application of Regulation (EU) No 1227/2011 of the European Parliament and of the Council of 25 October 2011 on wholesale energy market integrity and transparency, 3rd edn (29 October 2013), p. 50: "... the Agency considers that the market participant is obliged to refrain from any amendment or selective withdrawal of the order placed ('hands-off approach') in order to comply with the prohibition of insider trading".

[823] Point (b) of Article 3(4) of Regulation 1227/2011 (REMIT).

[824] Article 3(4) of Regulation 1227/2011 (REMIT).

[825] Article 3(1)(b) of Regulation 1227/2011 (REMIT); Article 10(1) of Regulation 596/2014 (MAR).

[826] Article 11(1) of Regulation 596/2014 (MAR).

[827] Recital 15 and Article 3(6) of Regulation 1227/2011 (REMIT); Article 21 of Regulation 596/2014 (MAR).

4.7.5 *Prohibition of Market Manipulation*

Market participants should not manipulate markets. Both cash-settled[828] and delivery-settled contracts are susceptible to manipulation.[829] EU law prohibits market manipulation both on markets in financial instruments (MAR) and on wholesale energy markets (REMIT).[830] Manipulation on wholesale energy markets is defined as "actions undertaken by persons that artificially cause prices to be at a level not justified by market forces of supply and demand, including actual availability of production, storage or transportation capacity, and demand".[831]

It is characteristic of electricity markets that a market participant can have (a) stronger incentives to manipulate markets because of high price volatility and the interaction between commodity markets and derivative markets, and (b) better opportunities to manipulate markets when the market participant controls electricity generation or transmission assets.[832] Moreover, market manipulation may take place (c) within one market or (d) between two or more markets. Manipulation and its effects may occur across borders, between electricity and gas markets and across financial and commodity markets, including the emission allowances markets.[833] Market manipulation can also be (e) actual or (f) attempted.

These characteristic aspects are reflected in the prohibition of market manipulation. On the other hand, prohibitions are not the only way to reduce market manipulation. Opportunities and incentives to manipulate markets depend on the structure and organisation of electricity and transmission markets. Marketplaces can, therefore, be organised in ways that are designed to reduce market manipulation (for US experiences, see Sect. 4.7.6).

Actual Market Manipulation In the EU, REMIT generally prohibits "any engagement in, or attempt to engage in, market manipulation on wholesale energy markets".[834]

According to its wording, REMIT prohibits both actual manipulation and attempted manipulation. The difference is that of effect or intent. While (actual) market manipulation means certain actions or attempted actions that have an effect on the market, attempted market manipulation means similar actions taken with an intent to influence the market.

---

828 Kumar P and Seppi DJ (1992).

829 Pirrong C (2001), pp. 222–223.

830 Article 15 of Regulation 596/2014 (MAR). Article 5 of Regulation 1227/2011 (REMIT). For the definition of market manipulation, see Article 12 of Regulation 596/2014 (MAR). Recital 13 of Regulation 1227/2011 (REMIT).

831 Recital 13 of Regulation 1227/2011 (REMIT).

832 See also Article 6(2) of Regulation 1227/2011 (REMIT). For manipulation in the US markets, see the sources cited in Ledgerwood S and Harris D (2012), footnote 13: Fischel DR and Ross DJ (1991); Kumar P and Seppi DJ (1992); Pirrong C (2001).

833 Recital 13 of Regulation 1227/2011 (REMIT); Godager K (2009), § 18, number 42.

834 Article 5 of Regulation 1227/2011 (REMIT).

REMIT provides a definition of (actual) market manipulation. Market manipulation can consist of (a) entering into any transaction or issuing any order to trade in wholesale energy products under certain circumstances; or (b) disseminating information under certain circumstances.

Transaction or Order A transaction or order may amount to market manipulation in three situations: (1) when a fictitious device or a form of deception is used; (2) when it gives false or misleading signals as to supply, demand, or price; or (3) when it secures the price at an artificial level (unless it is for "legitimate reasons" and in accordance with "accepted market practices").[835]

The interpretation of the open terms of REMIT can be made easier by analogy. (a) There is more legislation and case law about market manipulation in EU securities markets law. It would be reasonable to consider these materials when interpreting the market manipulation provisions of REMIT that are based on them. (b) Directive 2003/124/EC implementing the earlier Directive on market abuse (MAD I) provided for a list of non-exhaustive signals to be considered by market participants and competent authorities. Most of the signals applied to transactions and orders.[836] Some applied to the employment of fictitious devices or other forms of deception.[837] Annex I to MAR now lays down non-exhaustive indicators of manipulative behaviour. They include (1) indicators of manipulative behaviour relating to false or misleading signals and to price securing (in other words, transactions and orders);[838] (2) indicators of manipulative behaviour relating to the employment of a fictitious device or any other form of deception or contrivance.[839] (c) There is also more case-law relating to securities markets. For instance, the CJEU has held that it is not required that the price should maintain an abnormal or artificial level for a certain minimum duration.[840]

The prohibition of market manipulation under REMIT resembles the prohibition of energy market manipulation under US federal law. The US prohibition applies in connection with the purchase or sale of natural gas or electric energy, and in connection with the purchase or sale of transmission services.[841]

Disseminating Information In addition to transactions, market manipulation may also consist of disseminating information under certain circumstances.

This is the case where two conditions are fulfilled: (1) the dissemination of information "gives . . . false or misleading signals as to the supply of, demand for, or price of wholesale energy products", and (2) the disseminating person "knew, or ought to have known, that the information was false or misleading".

"Information" may also consist of rumours or false or misleading news. For example, REMIT prohibits "the deliberate provision of false information to undertakings which provide price assessments or market reports on wholesale energy

---

[835] Point 2 of Article 2 of Regulation 1227/2011 (REMIT).

[836] Article 4 of Directive 2003/124/EC (implementing Directive 2003/6/EC) (on manipulative behaviour related to false or misleading signals and to price securing).

[837] Article 5 of Directive 2003/124/EC.

[838] Section A of Annex I to Regulation 596/2014 (MAR).

[839] Section B of Annex I to Regulation 596/2014 (MAR).

[840] Case C-445/09 IMC Securities BV v Stichting Autoriteit Financiële Markten, paras 29–30.

[841] For the prohibition of electric energy market manipulation, see 18 C.F.R. § 1c.2(a).

products with the effect of misleading market participants acting on the basis of those price assessments or market reports".[842]

It does not matter how information is disseminated. Such dissemination of information may take place "through the media, including the internet, or by any other means".

The prohibition cannot be circumvented by invoking freedom of the press or freedom of expression in other media in cases of self-interest or where the person's intention is to mislead.[843]

Lowering the Threshold The threshold of actual market manipulation has been lowered. For the prohibition to apply, it is not necessary that the transaction or order gives false or misleading signals in fact; it is sufficient that it is "likely to give" them. Moreover, the actual market manipulation provisions of REMIT do not require successful actions to manipulate markets in order for the prohibition to apply; they prohibit even an attempt to employ a form of deception that is likely to give such signals, and an attempt to secure the price at an artificial level.

Attempt to Manipulate the Market In addition to actual manipulation, REMIT prohibits attempts to manipulate the market.

The provisions on attempts to manipulate the market prohibit, under certain circumstances, (a) any action (and not just entering into transactions or issuing orders to trade) relating to a wholesale energy product and (b) disseminating information.[844]

The definition of attempts to manipulate the market is almost a mirror image of the definition of actual market manipulation. What separates the two forms of market manipulation relates to *intent*. While the definition of actual market manipulation requires an effect or attempt, the definition of attempt to manipulate the market lowers the threshold to actions that are deliberate (taken with a certain intent).

One of the forms of attempts to manipulate the market is: "entering into any transaction, issuing any order to trade or *taking any other action* relating to a wholesale energy product *with the intention of* giving false or misleading signals as to the supply of, demand for, or price of wholesale energy products". There are related provisions on securing the price at an artificial level, employing a fictitious device or any other form of deception, and disseminating information.[845]

Examples The recitals of REMIT and the provisions of MAR[846] provide many examples of prohibited ways to manipulate the market or attempt to manipulate

---

[842] Recital 44 of Regulation 596/2014 (MAR).

[843] Point 2(b) of Article 2 of Regulation 1227/2011 (REMIT).

[844] Point 3 of Article 2 of Regulation 1227/2011 (REMIT).

[845] Point 3 of Article 2 of Regulation 1227/2011 (REMIT).

[846] Article 12 of and Annex I to Regulation 596/2014 (MAR).

it. There are further examples in the ACER Guidance on the application of REMIT.[847]

The recitals of REMIT provide the following examples:

- "placing and withdrawal of false orders";
- "spreading of false or misleading information or rumours through the media, including the internet, or by any other means";
- "deliberately providing false information to undertakings which provide price assessments or market reports with the effect of misleading market participants acting on the basis of those price assessments or market reports";
- "deliberately making it appear that the availability of electricity generation capacity or natural gas availability, or the availability of transmission capacity is other than the capacity which is actually technically available where such information affects or is likely to affect the price of wholesale energy products;"[848]
- "conduct by a person, or persons acting in collaboration, to secure a decisive position over the supply of, or demand for, a wholesale energy product which has, or could have, the effect of fixing, directly or indirectly, prices or creating other unfair trading conditions"; and
- "the offering, buying or selling of wholesale energy products with the purpose, intention or effect of misleading market participants acting on the basis of reference prices".[849]

The ACER Guidance gives examples of:

- "false/misleading transactions" (wash trades; improper matched orders; placing orders with no intention of executing them);
- price positioning (marking the close; abusive squeeze, also known as market cornering; cross-market-manipulation; physical withholding, or actions undertaken by persons that artificially cause prices to be at a level not justified by market forces of supply and demand, including actual availability of production, storage or transportation capacity, and demand);
- transactions involving fictitious devices/deception (scalping, or dissemination of false or misleading market information through media, including the internet, or by any other means; pump and dump; circular trading; pre-arranged trading); and
- dissemination of false and misleading information (spreading false/misleading information through the media; other behaviour designed to spread false/misleading information).

---

[847] ACER, Guidance on the application of Regulation (EU) No 1227/2011 of the European Parliament and of the Council of 25 October 2011 on wholesale energy market integrity and transparency, 3rd edn (29 October 2013), pp. 36–38.

[848] Recital 13 of Regulation 1227/2011 (REMIT).

[849] Recital 14 of Regulation 1227/2011 (REMIT).

ACER Guidance also gives examples of signals of possible of market manipulation.[850]

The recitals of REMIT and the ACER Guidance (including the provisions of MAR) thus demonstrate a reliance on examples to define manipulation rather than a cohesive economic theory.[851] The examples are examples of market power manipulations and fraud-based manipulations.[852] REMIT includes both fraud-based anti-manipulation language (like SEC Rule 10b-5 that targets securities fraud) and language prohibiting the creation of an artificial price (like the Commodity Exchange Act that lays down an "artificial price" standard). The creation of an artificial price is often assumed to be the result of a successful exercise of market power.

Safe Harbour There is a safe harbour from market manipulation charges in the case of "accepted market practices" (AMPs). REMIT provides for an exemption from the prohibition to secure (or attempt to secure) prices at an artificial level where "the person who entered into the transaction or issued the order to trade establishes that his reasons for doing so are legitimate and that that transaction or order to trade conforms to accepted market practices on the wholesale energy market concerned".[853] MAR provides for a general safe harbour from the prohibition of market manipulation where "the person entering into a transaction, placing an order to trade or engaging in any other behaviour establishes that such transaction, order or behaviour have been carried out for legitimate reasons, and conform with an accepted market practice".[854]

The question is how a market participant can assess compliance with accepted market practices in advance. (a) In securities markets, there was a procedure for defining AMPs under MAD I. The Commission had power to adopt guidelines. The competent authority could accept AMPs in accordance with the Commission's guidelines. The ESMA (European Securities and Markets Authority) developed draft implementing technical standards in relation to AMPs.[855] (b) Like MAD I, MAR lays down a method to define AMPs. AMPs are specific market practices accepted by the competent authority of a given Member State in accordance with MAR.[856] A practice that is accepted in a particular market is not automatically

[850] ACER, Guidance on the application of Regulation (EU) No 1227/2011 of the European Parliament and of the Council of 25 October 2011 on wholesale energy market integrity and transparency, 3rd edn (29 October 2013), pp. 52–53.

[851] Ledgerwood S and Harris D (2012), p. 23.

[852] Pirrong C (2010), pp. 1–5.

[853] Point 2(a)(ii) of Article 2 of Regulation 1227/2011 (REMIT); point 3(a)(ii) of Article 2 of Regulation 1227/2011 (REMIT). See also recital 14: "... accepted market practices such as those applying in the financial services area ... could be a legitimate way for market participants to secure a favourable price for a wholesale energy product".

[854] Article 13(1) of Regulation 596/2014 (MAR).

[855] Article 1(5) of Directive 2003/6/EC (Directive on market abuse).

[856] Article 13 of Regulation 596/2014 (MAR).

accepted in other markets. The practice is not accepted unless the competent authorities of other markets have officially accepted it.[857] ESMA will publish on its website a list of accepted market practices and in which Member States they are applicable.[858] (c) In energy markets, the Commission is empowered to adopt delegated acts to align definitions in energy and financial markets legislation.[859] Moreover, ACER should publish non-binding guidance on accepted market practices.[860] According to ACER, AMPs accepted by competent authorities according to MAD I may also apply under REMIT, but AMPs under REMIT are not limited to these accepted market practices.[861]

Excursion: Prohibition of Market Manipulation in the US Market manipulation is prohibited in the US as well and one can see convergence of anti-manipulation regulation in the EU and US.[862] However, there is no common standard for defining market manipulation in US and EU legislation.[863]

The two traditional categories of manipulative behaviour are creating an artificial price and fraud. Both are reflected in the statutory definitions of market manipulation.[864]

The Commodity Exchange Act prohibits market manipulation (a) by prohibiting price manipulation,[865] (a) by giving examples of prohibited transactions (such as bucketing an order, fictitious sales, wash sales or accommodation trade)[866] and disruptive practices (such as spoofing),[867] and (c) by prohibiting transactions in contravention of the Commissions' rules.[868]

The CFTC's anti-manipulation regulations are contained in rule 180.1 that also provides examples of prohibited conduct[869] and in rule 180.2 that prohibits price manipulation.[870]

---

[857] Second subparagraph of Article 13(2) of Regulation 596/2014 (MAR).

[858] Article 13(9) of Regulation 596/2014 (MAR).

[859] Article 6(1) of Regulation 1227/2011 (REMIT).

[860] Article 16(1) and recital 27 of Regulation 1227/2011 (REMIT).

[861] ACER, Guidance on the application of Regulation (EU) No 1227/2011 of the European Parliament and of the Council of 25 October 2011 on wholesale energy market integrity and transparency, 3rd edn (29 October 2013), p. 56.

[862] Ledgerwood S and Harris D (2012), p. 19.

[863] Ledgerwood S and Harris D (2012), p. 1.

[864] See Ledgerwood S and Carpenter P (2012), pp. 258–259.

[865] 7 USC § 9(3).

[866] 7 USC § 6c(a)(2).

[867] 7 USC § 6c(a)(5).

[868] 7 USC § 6c(b).

[869] 17 CFR § 180.1(a). See Abrantes-Metz M et al. (2013), p. 392.

[870] 17 CFR § 180.2.

Competing FERC and CFTC jurisdictions can cause problems.[871] The use of examples instead of a clear definition has caused problems in the past.[872]

Several steps have been taken to close regulatory loopholes in recent years.[873] EISA addressed the manipulation of petroleum markets in 2007.[874] Formerly exempt energy derivatives on electronic trading facilities became subject to CFTF regulation in 2008.[875] The Dodd-Frank Act closed the "swaps loophole" in 2010.

The regulation of market manipulation has a long history in the US. The SEC and the CFTC used to be responsible for preventing market manipulation before the turn of the millennium. The authority of the SEC was based on Rule 10b-5 that targets securities fraud,[876] and the authority of the CFTC on the Commodity Exchange Act (CEA).[877] The SEC succeeded in prosecuting cases under a variety of fraud-based theories. The CFTC settled many commodities manipulation cases but it was very difficult for the CFTC to win cases.[878]

There were problems. Rule 10b-5 only applied to securities, and neither commodities nor financial derivatives fell within its scope. The CEA laid down an "artificial price" standard, but it was difficult for the CFTC to successfully prosecute manipulation cases under the "artificial price" standard.[879] Moreover, the authority of the FERC was limited.[880]

For this reason, the FERC was given new powers. (1) In 2003, the FERC issued Market Rule 2 concerning manipulation of wholesale electricity markets. Market Behavior Rule 2 prohibited actions or transactions that: (a) lacked a legitimate business purpose; and (b) were intended to, or foreseeably could, manipulate market prices, conditions, or rules. (2) The Energy Policy Act of 2005 (EPAct 2005) gave the FERC a statutory anti-manipulation mandate tied to the same fraud-based statute that underlies the SEC's Rule 10b-5.[881] (3) In January 2006, the new market manipulation Rule 1c was adopted in Order 670.[882] It gave the FERC the

[871] For the problem of competing FERC and CFTC jurisdictions, see US Senate Committee on Energy and Natural Resources (2010), statement of Vincent P. Duane.

[872] Fischel DR and Ross DJ (1991), pp. 504 and 506. See also p. 507 where the authors recommend the concept of manipulation to be abandoned.

[873] See Spence DB and Prentice R (2012), pp. 172–173.

[874] The Energy Independence and Security Act of 2007.

[875] The Food, Conservation, and Energy Act of 2008.

[876] The SEC's anti-manipulation rule is codified at 17 CFR § 240.10b-5 (2011) (promulgated under the authority granted in 15 USC § 78j(b) (Supp. 2010)).

[877] The CFTC Anti-Manipulation Rule is codified at 7 USC § 13b (Supp. 2010).

[878] Ledgerwood S and Carpenter P (2012), p. 254; Abrantes-Metz M et al. (2013), p. 359: "... the CFTC has won only one case in thirty-seven years".

[879] See Ledgerwood S and Harris D (2012), footnote 6.

[880] Ledgerwood S and Harris D (2012), footnotes 8 and 9.

[881] The authority is based on 15 USC § 78j (2006).

[882] Order No. 670, Prohibition of Energy Market Manipulation, FERC Stats. & Regs. P 31,202, 71 Fed. Reg. 4,244 (2006) (codified at 18 CFR pt. 1c).

ability to prohibit the use of "any device, scheme, or artifice to defraud", the making of "any untrue statement of a material fact or to omit to state a material fact necessary in order to make the statements made ... not misleading", or to "engage in any act, practice, or course of business that operates or would operate as a fraud or deceit upon any entity".[883] (4) In February 2006, the FERC rescinded its earlier Market Behavior Rule 2, because Rule 2 and the new anti-fraud rules shared the same purpose.[884]

The regulatory authority of the CFTC was expanded. In particular, the Dodd-Frank Act eliminated many exemptions from CFTC oversight. Section 753 of the Dodd-Frank Act also provided the authority for the CFTC's new anti-manipulation regulations by amending the Commodity Exchange Act.[885]

4.7.6 Excursion: Market Manipulation Cases in the US

There are cases of market manipulation in Europe. Parties may have manipulated just the derivatives market, or they may have manipulated the price of the underlying product to manipulate the derivatives market. For example in Nord Pool, bids in a local bid market area might be used to influence the system price of the entire Nordic market area which influences the price of physically-settled derivatives and contracts for difference.[886] The number of market manipulation cases detected by the Nord Pool Spot Market Surveillance is low.[887]

There are more published cases about market manipulation in the US. The manipulation practices employed by firms in the US market can illustrate what manipulation practices one can expect to encounter in the EU market. They can also be used to test the application of REMIT to similar facts. Would REMIT have covered similar circumstances?

The Western Energy Crisis and Enron The most notorious case on the effects of the manipulation of electricity markets is the Western Energy Crisis (the Californian electricity crisis). Its causes and the forms of market manipulation that preceded it have been researched in detail. Enron was one of the key participants in the case.[888]

---

[883] 18 CFR § 1c.2.

[884] See Ledgerwood S and Harris D (2012), p. 6.

[885] 7 USC §§ 9, 15 (2012). See Abrantes-Metz M et al. (2013), p. 392.

[886] Godager K (2009), § 18, number 44.

[887] See, for example, Nord Pool Spot, Quarterly report for Market Surveillance 1 July to 30 September 2014. 99 written investigations were initiated in 2013. The number of statements of breach/non-public warnings was 46. Of these, 44 related to disclosure requirements, two to insider trading, and one (also) to good business conduct. There were no cases of market manipulation in 2013. During Q1–Q3 in 2014, no cases of market manipulation were found.

[888] See FERC (2003). See also McLean B and Elkind P (2004), Chapter 17.

Enron and its affiliates manipulated Californian electricity markets by means of various market manipulation schemes between May 1998 and December 2001. Market manipulation was partly made possible by the regulatory framework that encouraged it with additional incentives. Enron "advocated a market that was inefficient and vulnerable to manipulation and then sought out to detect weaknesses in the system that it could exploit".[889]

Enron's schemes are best understood in the specific context of Californian energy markets and the Cal PX and Cal ISO operations and trading rules.

> The California Power Exchange (Cal PX) operated day-ahead and day-of markets in which energy was traded on an hourly basis. The California Independent System Operator Corporation (Cal ISO) operated much of the transmission grid in California and was responsible for balancing generation and load and managing congestion on the system it controlled. Certified scheduling coordinators acted as intermediaries between the Cal ISO and the ultimate customers.[890] Enron Energy Services, Inc., and Enron Power Marketing, Inc. were certified scheduling coordinators on the ISO.
>
> The schemes fell within the scope of the antigaming and/or anomalous market behaviour provisions in the Cal ISO's and Cal PX's Market Monitoring and Information Protocol (MMIP).[891]

An Enron manager explained the firm's trading strategies. They were mainly of two kinds: (1) Some related to *schedules*. Enron filed energy schedules and bids that misrepresented the amount and geographic location of the load Enron intended to serve. Enron did this "for the purpose of increasing the appearance of congestion on transmission lines, increasing the market price for congestion fees for transmission between zones, earning congestion payments that otherwise would not have been available, and increasing the values of [Enron's] FTRs (which only generated revenue when congestion existed)". (2) Some related to *ancillary services*. Enron submitted bids to supply ancillary services that it did not have, or did not intend to supply, in the ISO's day-ahead ancillary services market. The bids contained fabricated information regarding the source and nature of the ancillary services Enron proposed to supply to the ISO. Enron did this to "cancel [its] obligation to supply the ancillary services by purchasing them in the ISO's hour-ahead ancillary services market [and to] profit by capturing the difference in price between the two markets".[892]

False Schedules: The Silver Peak Case Enron's schemes have catching names that are widely used in this context.[893] Many of Enron's trading strategies meant submitting false schedules. This was also done in the Silver Peak case.

---

[889] Enron Power Marketing, Inc., 119 FERC ¶ 63,013 (Initial Decision) (issued 21 June 2007) number 76.

[890] FERC (2003), VI-4.

[891] FERC (2003), VI-1 and VI-8.

[892] FERC (2003), VI-19 and VI-20 (citing the Enron manager's Plea Agreement dated 3 February 2003).

[893] Enron Power Marketing, Inc., 119 FERC ¶ 63,013 (Initial Decision) (issued 21 June 2007) number 76: "... evidence that Enron engaged in Circular Scheduling/Death Star Transactions,

Enron experimented with overscheduling the Silver Peak line in an effort to drive up market prices. Enron scheduled 2,900 MW on a line that only could carry 15 MW. Under the applicable regulations, the system operator was forced to buy the missing amount of power to ensure that the scheduled power could be delivered. Prices in California shot up by more than 70 % because of these late purchases. This enabled Enron to increase its profits from electricity sales.

REMIT would have covered similar actions. According to the wording of REMIT, "any engagement in, or attempt to engage in, market manipulation on wholesale energy markets" is prohibited.[894] The term "any engagement" is open enough to cover a broad range of actions. Because of the way market manipulation and attempted market manipulation have been defined, the question would have been whether the firm entered into a transaction, issued an order to trade, disseminated information by any means, or took any other action with a prohibited intention.

Transactions. The firm would have entered into actual transactions under REMIT when it scheduled power to be delivered, and again when it entered into contracts for the supply of electricity.

> To amount to market manipulation, these transactions must fulfil at least one of three conditions (signaling, securing the price level, or deception). Moreover, the conditions are not fulfilled, unless the transaction has an effect on "the supply of, demand for, or price of wholesale energy products".
>
> The products would have been wholesale energy products in a similar European case.[895] The transactions had the required effect.[896] (a) The firm's scheduling transaction gave false signals both as to the demand for transmission capacity (transmission capacity contracts can be regarded as wholesale energy products) and as to the demand for electricity (electricity supply contracts can also be regarded as wholesale energy products). (b) The firm employed a form of deception which gave false or misleading signals regarding the demand for transmission capacity and, because of congestion on a line, the demand for electricity from alternative sources that did not require the use of the congested line. (c) The scheduling transaction (that related to transmission capacity) was a way to secure the price of electricity supply contracts (other wholesale energy products) at an artificially high level.

Dissemination of information. In the Silver Peak case, a delivery schedule was sent to the transmission system operator (the Cal ISO). One may ask whether the sending of information to just one party could be regarded as dissemination of information under REMIT where the party that receives the information is the TSO.

'Get Shorty' Transactions, Selling Non-Firm Energy as Firm, Load Shifts, Ricochet Transactions/ False Import, Non-Firm Export Transactions and Wheel-Out Transactions in the California electricity markets".

[894] Article 5 of Regulation 1227/2011 (REMIT).

[895] Point 4 of Article 2 of Regulation 1227/2011 (REMIT). See also recital 5 of Regulation 1227/ 2011 (REMIT)

[896] See also Case C-445/09 IMC Securities BV v Stichting Autoriteit Financiële Markten, recital 29.

According to the earlier MAD I and the present MAR, the term dissemination of information seems to mean making information available to the public through the media.[897] The wording of REMIT[898] is based on the wording of the MAD I.

On the other hand, the transmission system operator would be one of the likely targets of manipulators in physical electricity markets. Communications made to the system operator can influence the market because they will influence the behaviour of the system operator and after that the behaviour of other market participants. This is what happened in the Silver Peak case.

Therefore, communications may sometimes influence the market although they are made to just one person and not through media. They may have an effect on the market behaviour of the recipient (use) or after the recipient has made them available to a wider group (spreading).[899] One should not exclude the possibility that the threshold of dissemination of information can be exceeded when communications are made to just one recipient in wholesale electricity markets.

Taking any action. The last alternative is taking any action prohibited as an attempt to manipulate markets. REMIT prohibits "taking any other action" with an intent to cause at least one of the prohibited situations (signaling, securing the price level, or deception). The threshold seems to be lower in this case and the provisions on attempt to manipulate could have been applied to the facts of the Silver Peak case.

Ancillary Services: Fat Boy, Death Star, Load Shift Fat boy, death star, and load shift were trading strategies that related to ancillary services and involved the deliberate submission of false information.

The fat boy trading strategy (also known as the inc-ing load strategy) meant the submission of false information about the load. The strategy had its roots in the regulatory framework. Under the Californian market rules, all schedules submitted to the Cal ISO by the scheduling coordinator had to be balanced. The fat boy trading strategy involved a scheduling coordinator (such as Enron) artificially increasing load on the schedule it submitted to the Cal ISO to correspond with the amount of generation in its schedule. The company then dispatched the generation it scheduled, which was in excess of its actual load. The Cal ISO ended up paying the company for the excess generation at the clearing price established in the real-time market.[900]

The death star and load shift strategies meant artificial counterflows. These strategies were designed to work when congestion was not properly priced. Death star involved the scheduling of energy counterflows but with no energy actually put onto or taken off the grid. The load shift strategy meant creating the appearance of congestion by deliberately overscheduling load in one zone and underscheduling

---

[897] Point (c) of Article 12(1) of Regulation 596/2014 (MAR).

[898] Point 2(b) of Article 2 of Regulation 1227/2011 (REMIT).

[899] For instance, communications can be made to a representative of the media after which the same information is disseminated in the media, and a fabricated rumour can be communicated to one recipient who is likely to disseminate it to a wider group of people.

[900] FERC (2003), VI-20 and VI-24. See also U.S. Energy Information Administration (2002), Chapter 4.

load in another, connected zone, then shifting load from the "congested" zone to the "less congested" zone to earn payments for reducing congestion.[901]

FERC Action for a Better Organisation of the Market Opportunities and incentives to manipulate markets would have been reduced by better organisation of the market and by better congestion management (Chap. 5).

For this reason, the FERC decided to establish a Standard Market Design (SMD) and use a new market model. The FERC modeled its day-ahead and intraday markets after PJM's markets and found the following actions necessary[902]:

- Day-ahead and intraday markets: All day-ahead deals must be binding. Deals must be settled immediately after the bidding period ends, and electricity producers that fail to deliver in real time must pay for the power they do not deliver at real-time market rates. The SMD would thus have prevented the fat boy/incing load strategy. Under the SMD, the generator and the customer would have been paid the previous day at prices that equated overall supplies with demand. There would have been no systematic benefit from overscheduling generation and underscheduling load.
- Congestion management. Congestion must be managed with locational prices. Had locational pricing been in place in California, Enron's various strategies for profiting from anomalies in prices would have failed. Enron's death star and load shift strategies worked only when congestion was not properly priced.

FERC Action Against Banks In recent years, the FERC has investigated several banks and other firms for allegedly manipulating US electricity markets. The following examples can illustrate the FERC's recent actions:

- Deutsche Bank. Deutsche Bank was investigated for the violation of the FERC's Prohibition of Electric Market Manipulation by scheduling and trading energy in California to benefit its Congestion Revenue Rights positions. Deutsche Bank had created schedules in which no power flowed.[903] This case was settled. Deutsche Bank agreed to pay a civil penalty of USD 1.5 million.[904]
- Constellation Energy. The FERC staff alleged that Constellation Energy (CCG) engaged in virtual transactions in the New York Independent System Operator's (NYISO's) Control Area and scheduled day-ahead physical flows between the NYISO and PJM (PJM Interconnection, Inc., Ontario), and/or between the NYISO and ISO-NE (ISO New England, Inc.). According to FERC staff, CCG tried to benefit from its financial positions that settled off the average of the

---

[901] U.S. Energy Information Administration (2002), Chapter 4.

[902] *Ibid.*

[903] FERC, Staff Notice of Alleged Violations (December 15, 2011).

[904] Deutsche Bank Energy Trading, LLC, 142 FERC ¶ 61,056 (January 22, 2013); FERC, News Release, FERC Approves Market Manipulation Settlement with Deutsche Bank, Docket No. IN12-4-000 (January 22, 2013).

day-ahead prices for the settling months in the respective regions of the NYISO and ISO-NE markets.[905] A USD 245 million settlement was agreed.

- Barclays. Barclays Bank was investigated for engaging in a coordinated scheme by trading day-ahead fixed-price physical electricity to benefit Barclays' IntercontinentalExchange (ICE) fixed-for-floating financial swap positions in the same markets. The FERC staff alleged that Barclays assembled substantial physical positions in the opposite direction of Barclays' fixed-for-floating financial swap positions and that Barclays flattened those physical positions in the next-day fixed-price physical markets to move the ICE daily index settlement up if buying and down if selling.[906] For this, Barclays was threatened with fines of USD 470 million.[907] FERC ordered USD 453 million in penalties.[908] Barclays denied wrongdoing and defended the case.[909]

4.7.7 Money Laundering

Money laundering is prohibited.[910] However, money laundering is a smaller problem in electricity wholesale markets. The risk of money laundering is reduced by the physical characteristics of electricity and the nature of transactions on electricity exchanges. Physical electricity flows are controlled by the system operator. Access to trading on an electricity exchange is limited to market participants that manage to fulfil certain requirements, and it is customary to use both a central counterparty and a clearing house. Derivatives in the electricity market are generally utilised to manage the financial risk that results from the volatility of the spot price of electricity. Only a small minority of the electricity derivatives market is made up of speculators trading for a profit, and these speculators must be authorised investment firms under MiFID II.

---

[905] FERC, Staff Notice of Alleged Violations (January 30, 2012).

[906] FERC, Staff Notice of Alleged Violations (April 5, 2012).

[907] BBC, Barclays faces $470 m energy fine from US regulators (1 November 2012).

[908] Barclays Bank PLC, 144 FERC ¶ 61,041 Docket No. IN08-8-000 (July 16, 2013).

[909] Federal Energy Regulatory Commission v. Barclays Bank Plc, 13-01158, U.S. District Court, Eastern District of California (Sacramento).

[910] Article 1(1) of Directive 2005/60/EC (Directive on the prevention of the use of the financial system for the purpose of money laundering and terrorist financing). For conduct regarded as money laundering, see Article 1(2). For the scope of the Money Laundering Regulations 2007 in the UK, see section 3 of the Regulation.

4.8 Particular Obligations and Regulatory Compliance

4.8.1 General Remarks

At a general level, all open and competitive markets are constituted by a set of rules that address the same questions,[911] but exchanges can be organised in many ways. The regulatory compliance regime depends on the context even in electricity markets.

Where the activities of a market participant fall within the scope of the EMIR, MiFID II/MiFIR, or CRD IV/CRR regimes and the market participant cannot benefit from exemptions, it must comply with a long list of regulatory requirements. There is a different set of rules for physical flows. In the following, we will focus on financial flows.

The regulatory regime for physical flows is constrained by physical laws. This reduces convergence with the regulation of financial flows.

In financial markets, related regulatory regimes are likely to converge because it would be difficult for a market operator operating many markets or active in many capacities to ask market participants to comply with different and potentially conflicting sets of rules depending on the context.

An electricity producer participating in electricity wholesale markets will meet the MiFID II regime when trading in financial instruments (or emission rights) on an electricity exchange that is a regulated market, an MTF or an OTF. It meets the EMIR regime when it has large positions in OTC financial contracts subject to the clearing obligation. In practice, however, it faces similar sets of rules in its dealings with the same market operator or clearing house. Market participants can benefit from the convergence of these compliance regimes.[912] It is easier and less costly for them to comply with one set of rules or similar sets of rules.

Regulatory Regime The regulatory regimes for regulated marketplaces address the following main issues (in addition to the general issues[913]):

- Scope. The scope of the regime is a core issue.
- Authorisation. Investment firms or central counterparties need an authorisation (under MiFID II[914] or EMIR[915]).

---

[911] Position rules, boundary rules, authority rules, scope rules, aggregation rules, information rules, and payoff rules. Ostrom E (2005), p. 835.

[912] See, for example, ISDA (2011): "In principle, ISDA supports steps towards more convergence, without duplication, between regulation of physical commodity markets and financial markets and regulatory initiatives designed to improve the safety, soundness and functioning of these markets".

[913] Ostrom E (2005), p. 835.

[914] Article 1(2) of Directive 2014/65/EU (MiFID II).

[915] Article 14 of Regulation 648/2012 (EMIR).

- Capital adequacy and prudential requirements. Authorisation requirements are complemented by capital adequacy and prudential requirements (under CRD IV/CRR[916] or EMIR[917]).
- Clearing. There are mandatory clearing obligations and rules on non-discriminatory access to clearing (under EMIR[918] or MiFIR[919]).
- Market integrity, transparency. Market integrity and transparency is ensured in three main ways. Market participants may have to comply with codes of conduct. Codes of conduct are customarily part of the same regulatory regime that requires an authorisation and lays down organisational requirements (MiFID II).[920] They can also foster compliance with more detailed regulation. There are statutory disclosure obligations (MiFID II,[921] MAR,[922] the Prospectus Directive[923]). There is a market abuse regime (MAR, REMIT). These issues have been discussed earlier in this book (Sect. 4.7)
- Organisation and compliance. If a market participant needs an authorisation, it must comply with organisational requirements (MiFID II[924]). All market participants may need to organise compliance. The organisation of compliance is connected with monitoring and surveillance (see Sect. 4.9).

4.8.2 Scope

General Remarks

MiFID II is at the core of the regulatory regime for financial markets.[925] It is customary to refer to MiFID II/MiFIR definitions when defining the meaning of terms or the scope of other regulatory regimes. For instance, EMIR is necessary because MiFID II does not cover other than organised trading and trading on

[916] Article 28–29 of Directive 2013/36/EU (CRD IV); Articles 92 and 95–96 of Regulation 575/2013 (CRR).

[917] Articles 16 of Regulation 648/2012 (EMIR).

[918] Article 4(1) of Regulation 648/2012 (EMIR).

[919] Article 29(1) of Regulation 600/2014 (MiFIR).

[920] See Article 24 of Directive 2014/65/EU (MiFID II).

[921] See, for example, Article 24(3) of Directive 2014/65/EU (MiFID II).

[922] See, for example, Article 17 of Regulation 596/2014 (MAR).

[923] Articles 3(1) and 7 of Directive 2003/71/EC (Prospectus Directive).

[924] Article 16 of Directive 2014/65/EU (MiFID II). See also Directive 2006/73/EC (implementing Directive 2004/39/EC).

[925] MiFID II is complemented by Regulation 600/2014 (MiFIR). The MiFID regime consisted of a framework Directive (Directive 2004/39/EC), an Implementing Directive (Directive 2006/73/EC) and an Implementing Regulation (Regulation 1287/2006).

regulated trading venues. REMIT is necessary, because MAR only applies to financial instruments as defined in the MiFID regime. The capital adequacy requirements of the CRD IV/CRR regime apply to investment firms as defined in the MiFID II regime. It is, therefore, useful to study the scope of the MiFID II/MiFIR regime in detail. The scope of this regime depends, to a large extent, on the definition of "financial instruments".

MiFID II/MiFIR

The regulatory regime for financial markets has recently been amended for two main reasons. First, it became necessary to align the earlier MiFID regime with the increasingly complex market reality, the regulation of market abuse, and EMIR. Second, developments in commodity markets called for targeted reforms.

"Market reality" means two kinds of concerns. One is that commodity derivatives markets have attracted financial investors. This gave a scapegoat to blame for high commodity prices (although the supply and consumption of the underlying commodity are the more likely culprits). The other was that the integrity of European energy and carbon markets was not as high as it could have been.

The central aim of MiFID II was to ensure that all organised trading is conducted on regulated trading venues: regulated markets, multilateral trading facilities (MTFs), and organised trading facilities (OTFs). There should thus be a level playing field where third-party trading interests are brought together by functionally similar activities.[926]

The reforms addressed exemptions for commodity firms, corporate end-user exemptions from mandatory clearing, and collateral requirements for some OTC derivatives.[927] The new legislation included: (a) reducing the scope of exemptions for commodity derivatives; (b) extending the scope of authorisation and other requirements in relation to commodity derivatives; (c) requirements for certain OTC derivatives to be traded on a regulated market, multilateral trading facility, or organised trading facility; (d) amending the definition of derivatives; and (e) introducing transparency and position limits/management requirements in relation to certain derivatives. The changes influenced even market surveillance.

After the reforms, the scope of the MiFID II regime depends on the nature of the products (what is traded), the nature of the trading venue (where the product is traded), the nature of market participants (who is the trader), and the nature of activities on the trading venue (what is done).

[926] See, for example, recitals 14 and 58 of Directive 2014/65/EU (MiFID II); Proposal for a Directive on markets in financial instruments, COM(2011) 656 final, Explanatory memorandum, section 3.4.1.

[927] For the previous exemptions for commodity firms, see, in particular, Article 2(1)(i) and (k) of Directive 2004/39/EC (MiFID).

Consequently, whether an electricity firm must comply with the regime directly or indirectly depends on the context. Most electricity firms have no duty to comply with the MiFID II regime directly but do need to comply with it indirectly, that is, when the marketplace falls within the scope of the regime.

The Nature of Products, Financial Instruments The nature of products is a core issue, because the MiFID II/MiFIR regime does not apply unless the products are regarded as financial instruments. When defining the scope of this regime, one can thus consider whether the contracts are: commodity contracts; wholesale energy products; contracts that must be settled physically; contracts that can be settled physically or financially; contracts that must be settled financially, contracts that are for commercial purposes; contracts that have the characteristics of derivative financial instruments; or emission allowances.

Contracts not covered by MiFID II have the closest connection to the core business of electricity producers in the wholesale market. MiFID II does not apply to the following contracts:

- Commodity contracts that must be settled physically. Electricity spot contracts, contracts for the physical supply of electricity, or contracts for physical transmission capacity are not financial instruments.[928]
- Contracts for commercial purposes. Contracts that can be settled not only physically but even financially can have the characteristics of derivative financial instruments. However, they are not regarded as financial instruments if they are "for commercial purposes".[929]
- Certain wholesale energy products traded on an OTF. The main rule is that commodity contracts are financial instruments where they are derivative contracts traded on a regulated venue. However, they are not regarded as financial instruments provided that: they are wholesale energy products (REMIT)[930]; they are traded on an OTF; and they must be settled physically.[931]

Physical electricity contracts not traded on a regulated venue are thus not regarded as financial instruments. The meaning of "must be physically settled" is specified in delegated acts. It could mean "at least the creation of an enforceable and binding obligation to physically deliver, which cannot be unwound and with no right to cash settle or offset transactions except in the case of force majeure, default or other bona fide inability to perform".[932]

---

[928] Section C of Annex I to Directive 2014/65/EU (MiFID II).

[929] Point 7 of Section C of Annex I to Directive 2014/65/EU (MiFID II).

[930] Point 4 of Article 2 of Regulation 1227/2011 (REMIT).

[931] Point 6 of Section C of Annex I to Directive 2014/65/EU (MiFID II).

[932] Recital 9 of Directive 2014/65/EU (MiFID II). On the other hand, see recital 10 of Directive 2014/65/EU (MiFID II): "The limitation of the scope concerning commodity derivatives traded on an OTF and physically settled should be limited to avoid a loophole that may lead to regulatory arbitrage. It is therefore necessary to provide for a delegated act to further specify the meaning of the expression 'must be physically settled' taking into account at least the creation of an

Clearing is not relevant for the distinction between financial instruments and other contracts any more. One of the purposes of the MiFID reform was to increase the scope of the MiFID regime by reducing exemptions and by adopting a broader definition of financial instruments. According to the wording of the earlier MiFID Implementing Regulation, physically-settled OTC derivative contracts on commodities fell within the scope of MiFID as "other financial instruments" on certain conditions.[933] One of the conditions was clearing by a CCP or margin requirements. However, clearing by a CCP or margin requirements could not remain as a condition under MiFID II, because EMIR lays down a mandatory clearing obligation for organised trading and all organised trading should be conducted on regulated venues.[934]

There used to be a distinction based on the duration of the contract in the past with different regulatory practices applied in different Member State.[935]

The distinction was based on MiFID Implementing Regulation 1287/2006.[936] It was adopted in the Auctioning Regulation. A two-day spot contract was not regarded as a financial instrument but a five-day forward contract was.[937] The distinction was considered in the preparatory works for MiFID II.[938] It was also included in a draft version of Section C of Annex I to MiFID II.

BaFin has discussed borderline cases in its guidelines for the application of § 32 KWG on electricity business. BaFin does not regard electricity spot contracts, long-term supply contracts, or electricity supply contracts with variable price clauses as financial contracts.[939] However, BaFin can pay attention to the intentions of the parties. The intentions of the parties may be express or implied. BaFin might assume that the parties intended to settle an OTC transaction financially where it is clear to the parties that the seller is not able to supply electricity physically.[940]

Contracts for commercial purposes were defined narrowly in Regulation 1287/2006. A contract is for commercial purposes and not a financial instrument, if "it is

---

enforceable and binding obligation to physically deliver, which cannot be unwound and with no right to cash settle or offset transactions except in the case of force majeure, default or other bona fide inability to perform".

[933] Articles 38 and 39 of Regulation 1287/2006 (MiFID Implementing Regulation).

[934] DG Internal Market and Services, Public Consultation, Review of the Markets in Financial Instruments Directive (MIFID) (8 December 2010), section 5.3.

[935] See also letter of 14 February 2014 from ESMA to Commissioner Michel Barnier (Re: Classification of financial instruments as derivatives), number 12 of ANNEX I: "Differences arise, in particular for FX forwards, depending on the settlement or delivery date, i.e. the frontier between an FX spot and an FX derivative. From the analysis carried out by ESMA, it is not controversial that contracts that settle within two trading days are considered spot contracts and that contracts that settle after seven trading days are FX forwards. In certain countries the contracts that settle up to 7 days are not deemed to be derivatives. Therefore, for contracts with a settlement date between 3 and 7 trading days there are different national laws, in some Member States, determining whether they are or not a derivative. For these FX forwards there is not a common definition and, therefore, they are not clearly identified as derivatives across the Union".

[936] First subparagraph of Article 38(2) of Regulation 1287/2006 (implementing Article 4(1)(2) of Directive 2004/39/EC).

[937] Recital 14 of Regulation 1031/2010 (Auctioning Regulation).

[938] DG Internal Market and Services, Public Consultation, Review of the Markets in Financial Instruments Directive (MIFID) (8 December 2010), section 5.3.

[939] BaFin (2011), sections II.2.b, II.2.c and II.2.d.

[940] BaFin (2011), section II.1.b. See also Hünerwadel A (2007), pp. 59–60.

entered into with or by an operator or administrator of an energy transmission grid, energy balancing mechanism or pipeline network, and it is necessary to keep in balance the supplies and uses of energy at a given time".[941] MiFID II provides for a similar exemption.[942] On the other hand, because electricity spot contracts are not financial instruments, it does not really matter whether they are regarded as contracts for commercial purposes or not.[943]

MiFID II does apply to the following contracts:

- Traded commodity derivatives. Commodity derivatives are regarded as financial instruments when they are traded on a regulated venue (regulated market, an MTF, or an OTF).[944]
- Financial commodity derivatives. Commodity derivatives are regarded as financial instruments where they must be settled in cash or, at the option of one of the parties, may be settled in cash.[945] Commodity contracts are regarded as financial instruments where they have characteristics of other derivative financial instruments and may be settled financially or physically.[946]
- Emission allowances (ETS).[947]

MiFID II can thus apply to some electricity derivatives and emission allowances. For instance, MiFID II regulates position limits and position management controls for commodity derivatives.

> Position limits restrict "the size of a net position which a person can hold at all times in commodity derivatives traded on trading venues and economically equivalent OTC contracts".[948] Position limits shall "specify clear quantitative thresholds for the maximum size of a position in a commodity derivative that persons can hold".[949] However, position limits do not apply to "positions held by or on behalf of a non-financial entity and which are objectively measurable as reducing risks directly relating to the commercial activity of that non-financial entity".[950]

Electricity derivatives are regarded as financial instruments when they may be settled in cash. On the other hand, financial instruments can include even physically settled electricity contracts where they are traded on a regulated venue and are not wholesale energy products.

---

941 Article 38(4) of Regulation 1287/2006 (MiFID Implementing Regulation) (implementing Article 4(1)(2) of MiFID).

942 Article 2(1)(n) of Directive 2014/65/EU (MiFID II).

943 For instance, EPEX Spot defines its electricity spot contracts as commercial contracts. EPEX Spot Exchange Rules (28 November 2014), Article 5.1.

944 Point 6 of Section C of Annex I to Directive 2014/65/EU (MiFID II).

945 Point 5 of Section C of Annex I to Directive 2014/65/EU (MiFID II).

946 Point 7 of Section C of Annex I to Directive 2014/65/EU (MiFID II).

947 Point 11 of Section C of Annex I to Directive 2014/65/EU (MiFID II).

948 First subparagraph of Article 57(1) of Directive 2014/65/EU (MiFID II).

949 Article 57(2) of Directive 2014/65/EU (MiFID II).

950 Second subparagraph of Article 57(1) of Directive 2014/65/EU (MiFID II).

Where energy contracts are not wholesale energy products that fall within the scope of REMIT, they can be regarded as financial instruments not just when they are traded on a regulated market or an MTF but even when they are traded on an OTF.[951] Energy derivatives contracts that can fall within the scope of MiFID II (rather than the scope of REMIT) include, among others, OTF-traded derivatives relating to coal or oil,[952] energy derivatives with non-financial counterparties when the derivatives are traded on a regulated venue (subject to a transitional period),[953] and OTF-traded derivative contracts with retail customers (rather than wholesale customers).[954]

Emission allowances recognised for compliance with the Emissions Trading Scheme (ETS) are regarded as financial instruments that fall within the scope of MiFID II.[955] MiFID II can apply to investment firms whose activities relate to emission allowances.

Emission allowances are an instrument created by the Emissions Trading Scheme Directive.[956] An allowance is a transferable right to emit one tonne of carbon dioxide equivalent during a specified period.[957] The question is whether an allowance should be classified as an intangible asset or as a physical commodity. Before MiFID II, emission allowances themselves were not classified as financial instruments.

> Trading in emission allowances did not fall within the scope of MiFID before it was recast. Neither did the secondary trading of spot emission allowances. On the other hand, derivative contracts on emission allowances (and other environmental credits) were financial instruments under MiFID under the same criteria as derivatives on commodities.[958]

The MiFID II regime does not regulate contract specifications as such. This may change in the future. The Commission services have pointed out that deficiencies in the contract specifications drawn up by the exchange have caused problems of convergence between futures and spot prices in certain US agricultural derivatives. For this reason, the Commission services "consider that a further specification to the MiFID implementing regulation could be added requiring regulated markets, MTFs and organised trading facilities to design commodity derivatives contracts

[951] Recital 9 of Directive 2014/65/EU (MiFID II). See also point 58 of Article 4(1) of Directive 2014/65/EU (MiFID II) and point 4 of Article 2 of Regulation 1227/2011 (REMIT).

[952] Point 16 of Article 4(1) of Directive 2014/65/EU (MiFID II).

[953] Point 6 of Section C of Annex I to Directive 2014/65/EU (MiFID II). See also Article 95 of Directive 2014/65/EU (MiFID II).

[954] Point 6 of Section C of Annex I to Directive 2014/65/EU (MiFID II).

[955] Point 11 of Section C of Annex I to Directive 2014/65/EU (MiFID II).

[956] Article 1 of Directive 2003/87/EC (Emissions Trading Scheme Directive).

[957] Point (a) of Article 3 of Directive 2003/87/EC (Emissions Trading Scheme Directive).

[958] See point 10 of Section C of Annex I to Directive 2004/39/EC (MiFID). See also Articles 38 (3) and 39 of Regulation 1287/2006 (MiFID Implementing Regulation). For the legal aspects of emission allowances, see The Financial Markets Law Committee, Issue 116—Emission Allowances: Creating Legal Certainty (October 2009).

which they admit to trade and which can be physically settled in a way that ensures convergence between futures and spot prices".[959]

The Nature of Marketplaces In addition to the nature of products, the scope of the MiFID II regime depends on the nature of the marketplace. It applies to regulated trading venues. These trading venues are defined as regulated markets, MTFs, and OTFs.[960]

On the other hand, MiFIR lays down an obligation on financial and non-financial counterparties with large positions to trade derivatives on a regulated trading venue when the derivatives are financial instruments.[961] The core issue is therefore the definition of derivatives as financial instruments. The central aim of MiFID II/MiFIR was to create a level playing field and ensure that all organised trading is conducted on regulated trading venues.[962]

The Nature of Market Participants The MiFID II/MiFIR regime applies to investment firms and regulated trading venues.[963] An investment firm is defined as a legal person that performs investment services or activities as a regular occupation or business on a professional basis.[964] There is a long list of investment services and activities in Annex I to MiFID II.

The Nature of Activities on the Trading Venue The MiFID II/MiFIR regime regulates certain activities of regulated trading venues. The obligations that the regime lays down for the regulated trading venues range from *transparency* to *clearing* obligations and the obligation to use a *central counterparty*.

EMIR

EMIR applies to OTC derivative contracts including various market participants.[965] By definition, OTC derivative contracts are not covered by the MiFID II/MiFIR regime.[966]

---

[959] See Article 37(e) of Regulation 1287/2006 (MiFID Implementing Regulation).

[960] Point 24 of Article 4(1) of Directive 2014/65/EU (MiFID).

[961] Article 28 of Regulation 600/2014 (MiFIR); Articles 10(1)(b) and 2(5) of Regulation 648/2012 (EMIR).

[962] Section 3.4.1 of the Explanatory Memorandum, COM(2011) 656 final. Recital 10 of Regulation 600/2014 (MiFIR).

[963] Article 1(1) of Directive 2014/65/EU (MiFID II). For German law, see BaFin (2011).

[964] Point 1 of Article 4(1) of Directive 2014/65/EU (MiFID II).

[965] Article 1 of Regulation 648/2012 (EMIR).

[966] Point 7 of Article 2 of Regulation 648/2012 (EMIR).

4.8.3 Authorisation

Few electricity producers are regarded as investment firms that need an authorisation under MiFID II. An investment firm is defined as a legal person that performs investment services or activities as a regular occupation or business on a professional basis.[967] Exemptions from the authorisation requirement can nevertheless be important for their specialised subsidiaries or TSOs.

There is a long list of investment services and activities in Annex I to MiFID II. For instance, it includes the following services and activities: dealing on own account; reception and transmission of orders in relation to one or more financial instruments; execution of orders on behalf of clients; portfolio management; investment advice; and the operation of MTFs or OTFs.[968]

What dealing on own account means is a question of interpretation. For example, BaFin regards market making as dealing on own account for the benefit of third parties and market making requires an authorisation under German law. Moreover, activities as a general clearer or direct clearer on a derivatives exchange are regarded as dealing on own account. Consequently, an authorisation is required for these activities as well.[969] Bundesbank has issued similar guidance.[970]

A MiFID II authorisation can also bring benefits as it makes it easier for investment firms to do business outside their home Member State. The authorisation works as a "European passport" for the provision of cross-border services or the establishment of a branch.[971]

Because Switzerland is not a Member State of the EU (or the European Economic Area), Swiss investment firms that trade in electricity derivatives must comply with stricter rules in the German market compared with investment firms from other Member States (or the European Economic Area).[972] BaFin thus requires Swiss investment firms that want to provide investment services by means of electricity derivatives in Germany to obtain an authorisation in Germany. To obtain an authorisation a Swiss investment firm must establish a branch that is subject to supervision by the German financial supervision authority.[973] There are some exceptions.[974]

On the other hand, the authorisation requirement is complemented by a very extensive compliance regime and even capital adequacy requirements.

Exemptions Exemptions for particular classes of firms play an important role for electricity market participants. Where the firm can rely on a MiFID II exemption, it

[967] Point 1 of Article 4(1) of Directive 2014/65/EU (MiFID II).

[968] Section A of Annex I to Directive 2014/65/EU (MiFID II).

[969] BaFin (2011), III.5.

[970] Deutsche Bundesbank (2013), section 2.

[971] Article 6(3) of Directive 2014/65/EU (MiFID II).

[972] § 53b(1) KWG. See also Hünerwadel A (2007), pp. 60–61.

[973] § 32(1) KWG. See also Hünerwadel A (2007), p. 61.

[974] § 2(4) KWG. See Hünerwadel A (2007), p. 61.

does not have to comply with the authorisation requirement and capital adequacy requirements. Where the firm is unable to rely on a MiFID II exemption, it must become authorised and regulated to carry on MiFID II business.

The starting point is that the firm is not an investment firm in the first place unless it provides investment services and/or performs investment activities as a regular occupation or business on a professional basis.[975] This will exclude most electricity firms regardless of the existence of any exemptions.

There is an exemption for TSOs. MiFID II does not apply to TSOs when they carry out their statutory duties under EU electricity markets law. Neither does it apply to any persons acting as service providers on their behalf to carry out these tasks. In addition, there is an exemption for any operator or administrator of an energy balancing mechanism.[976]

There is a limited exemption for dealing on own account in financial instruments other than commodity derivatives. Emission allowances and derivatives on emission allowances are regarded as financial instruments in this respect.[977]

There is a limited exemption for two kinds of ancillary activities: dealing on own account in commodity derivatives; and providing other investment services in commodity derivatives, emission allowances, or derivatives thereof to the customers or suppliers of the entity's main business.[978]

For electricity producers, this limited exemption is important, because it may carry on extensive dealing activities itself as an ancillary activity. However, it might prefer to use a specialised entity in the same group for dealing activities on a professional basis. In the latter case, it would have preferred an exemption for commodities dealers.

No Exemption for Commodities Dealers MiFID used to contain a commodities dealer exemption.[979] The exemption was originally introduced on the assumption that commercial and specialist commodity firms neither pose the same systemic risk as their financial counterparts nor interact with investors.[980]

Commodity firms were exempt from MiFID when they dealt on own account in financial instruments or provided investment services in commodity derivatives on an ancillary basis as part of their main business without being subsidiaries of financial groups.[981] For instance, commercial companies active in the oil market were MiFID exempt firms not subject to any MiFID provisions. Consequently, they

---

975 Article 4(1)(1) of Directive 2014/65/EU (MiFID II).

976 Point (n) of Article 2(1) of Directive 2014/65/EU (MiFID II).

977 Point (d) of Article 2(1) of Directive 2014/65/EU (MiFID II).

978 Point (i) of Article 2(1) of Directive 2014/65/EU (MiFID II).

979 Point (k) of Article 2(1) of Directive 2004/39/EC (MiFID).

980 Recital 25 of Directive 2004/39/EC (MiFID).

981 Article 2(1)(i) and (k) of Directive 2004/39/EC (MiFID) exempts the same firms from the Capital Requirements Directive (CRD) as well.

could provide investment services in commodity derivatives as an ancillary activity without having to comply with MiFID's conduct of business rules.[982]

Before the MiFID reform, MiFID exempt firms provided various kinds of ancillary activities. Some of the previously unregulated activities posed very small risks to the financial system. For instance, agricultural cooperatives provide hedging tools to their farmers as an ancillary service. These ancillary services pose very small risks to the financial system. In the past, prudential requirements were not regarded as necessary under MiFID where a party traded on own account only.[983]

However, some national regulators and market participants argued that unsophisticated clients were not adequately protected. Moreover, there was no level playing-field for commodity derivative houses that benefited from a specific exemption under MiFID and commodity firms' incorporated subsidiaries that had obtained an authorisation.

For this reason, exemptions were reduced in MiFID II/MiFIR. According to the Commission services, including securities and prudential regulators, there was a case for reducing the scope of allowed exempt activities in line with the overall purpose of the MiFID regime.[984] The political consensus was to apply exemptions from financial regulation only when necessary.

4.8.4 Capital Adequacy

If the firm is an investment firm under MiFID II/MiFIR or a central counterparty under EMIR, it will also have to comply with capital adequacy requirements. Common standards for investment firms are laid down by CRD IV and CRR. EMIR lays down capital requirements for central counterparties.[985] Capital adequacy and prudential requirements influence even electricity producers and other non-financial market participants. First, the costs of capital adequacy and risk management requirements will ultimately be passed on to non-financial market participants. Costs are increased by collateral requirements. They can give an incentive to use bilateral trading that does not fall within the scope of these regulatory regimes. Second, electricity producers and other non-financial market participants may use entities in the same group for dealing purposes. Capital

[982] See Ministére de l'économie, de l'industrie et de l'emploi (2010), pp. 52–53.

[983] Recital 25 of Directive 2004/39/EC (MiFID). See also points (b), (d), (i), (k) and (l) of Article 2 (1) of Directive 2004/39/EC (MiFID).

[984] CESR-CEBS Technical Advice to the European Commission on the review of commodities business, 15 October 2008, CESR/08-752; DG Internal Market and Services, Public Consultation, Review of the Markets in Financial Instruments Directive (MIFID) (8 December 2010), section 5.2.

[985] Articles 16(1) and 16(2) of Regulation 648/2012 (EMIR).

adequacy and prudential requirements give an incentive to study ways to avoid them or reduce their costs.

The scope of these requirements can therefore matter. Some firms are excluded from the scope of capital adequacy requirements:

- Some firms such as regulated markets and operators of regulated trading venues are not regarded as investment firms. There are also other exemptions.[986]
- Capital adequacy requirements are not applied to "local firms" that deal for their own account for the sole purpose of hedging positions.[987]
- Capital adequacy requirements are not applied to certain firms that cannot be in debt with their clients.[988]
- There is a temporary exemption for commodities dealers.

The temporary exemption for commodities dealers is regarded as necessary on grounds that capital requirements and other prudential rules should be proportionate and should not unduly interfere with the achievement of the goal of the liberalisation of gas and electricity markets.[989] The exemption benefits commodities traders that have carried on their business for a long time.[990] However, the exemption will expire at the end of 2017 at the latest.[991] By end of December 2015, the Commission will propose a regulatory regime to replace it.[992]

4.8.5 Mandatory Clearing

Mandatory clearing is complemented by prudential obligations such as the duty to post collateral to the clearing house. It will influence market participants' costs. Whether there is a clearing obligation for commodity derivatives depends on how they are traded. The clearing obligation can be based on MiFIR or EMIR.

OTC-Derivatives, EMIR EMIR applies to OTC derivatives. There is a clearing obligation for certain classes of OTC derivatives and certain (financial or non-financial) market participants.[993] Access to the central counterparty requires compliance with the clearing obligation in these cases.

[986] Article 2(1) of Directive 2014/65/EU (MiFID II).

[987] Point 2(b) of Article 4(1) of Regulation 575/2013 (CRR). Point 4 of Article 4(1) of Regulation 575/2013 (CRR).

[988] Point 2(c) of Article 4(1) of Regulation 575/2013 (CRR). See already point (b)(iii) of Article 3 (1) of Directive 2006/49/EC (Capital Requirements Directive).

[989] Recital 63 of Regulation 575/2013 (CRR).

[990] First subparagraph of Article 498(1) of Regulation 575/2013 (CRR).

[991] Second subparagraph of Article 498(1) of Regulation 575/2013 (CRR).

[992] Article 498(2) of Regulation 575/2013 (CRR).

[993] Article 4(1) of Regulation 648/2012 (EMIR).

The clearing obligation applies to all derivatives that have been declared subject to the clearing obligation by the competent authority or the regulatory technical standards.[994] Whether a class of derivatives is subject to a clearing obligation under EMIR depends on whether it has been declared subject to clearing by the ESMA.

The clearing obligation does not apply to all market participants. As there is no access to the central counterparty without compliance with the clearing obligation, it was necessary to provide that these market participants can access the central counterparty as clients or indirect clients.[995]

Financial Instruments, MiFIR Clearing rules were included in MiFIR to ensure a level playing field in the light of EMIR.[996] MiFIR lays down a clearing obligation for all transactions in derivatives concluded on a regulated market.[997] In practice, trades on organised trading venues should be cleared one way or another.

Transitional provisions provide for an exemption from the clearing obligation for "C6 energy derivative contracts"[998] until 3 July 2020 in some cases.[999] The exemption is granted by the relevant competent authority.[1000]

Non-discriminatory Access The existence of a clearing obligation, that is, an obligation to have all trades cleared by a central counterparty, could distort the market. It was necessary to adopt rules that reduce competitive distortions. Competitive distortions are reduced by the obligation of CCPs to grant non-discriminatory access to clearing.

> Before EMIR, a derivatives exchange could own a central counterparty that also acted as a clearing institution. EMIR requires mandatory clearing by a CCP.[1001] If the CCP is owned by a derivatives exchange, it has an incentive to refuse to clear transactions executed on competing trading venues. This and the clearing requirement could hamper the business of competing venues that cannot provide low-cost CCP and clearing services.

Non-discriminatory access is based on EMIR or MiFIR. (a) EMIR requires non-discriminatory access to central counterparties (CCPs) in the OTC derivatives market.[1002] A CCP must accept to clear transactions executed on different venues to the extent that those venues comply with the operational and technical requirements established by the CCP. Moreover, as not all market participants that are subject to the clearing obligation are able to become clearing members of the CCP, they must have the possibility to access it as clients or indirect clients.[1003] (b) MiFIR provides

---

[994] Articles 4(1), 5(1) and 5(2) of Regulation 648/2012 (EMIR).

[995] Recital 33 of Regulation 648/2012 (EMIR).

[996] Recital 37 of Regulation 600/2014 (MiFIR).

[997] Article 29 of Regulation 600/2014 (MiFIR).

[998] Point 6 of Section C of Annex I to Directive 2014/65/EU (MiFID II).

[999] Article 95(1) of Directive 2014/65/EU (MiFID II).

[1000] Article 95(2) of Directive 2014/65/EU (MiFID II).

[1001] Article 4(1) of Regulation 648/2012 (EMIR).

[1002] Article 7(1) of Regulation 648/2012 (EMIR).

[1003] Recital 33 and Article 4(3) of Regulation 648/2012 (EMIR).

that financial instruments must be cleared by a CCP on a non-discriminatory and transparent basis regardless of the trading venue.[1004]

The existence of rules on non-discriminatory access to the central counterparty and clearing house can influence competition,[1005] the structure of markets, and merger activity. If a central counterparty owned by a derivatives exchange has an obligation to clear transactions executed on a competing trading venue, the "vertical silo" model of exchanges can be broken up and replaced by competition, and the ownership of clearing institutions and CCPs will cease to be a driver of derivatives exchange mergers. For instance, the attempted merger of the Eurex derivatives exchange of Deutsche Börse with the NYSE Liffe derivatives exchange of NYSE Euronext was designed to create synergies and reduce costs by using a single clearer, Eurex Clearing controlled by Deutsche Börse.

4.9 Market Surveillance

There is a close connection between the obligations of market participants and surveillance. The surveillance mechanism is designed to increase regulatory compliance.

It is characteristic of electricity markets that market surveillance must focus on two main elements: information on trading in the marketplace and information on physical flows in the grid. Moreover, it must consider the cross-border nature of trading.[1006]

Like the regulation of electricity markets in general, the regulation of market surveillance is sector-specific. It is governed by the sector-specific provisions of the governing law, EMIR, and MiFID II. It is also governed by exchange rules. Moreover, it must be aligned with the system operator's rules for physical flows.

EMIR Obligations EMIR lays down uniform requirements covering financial counterparties,[1007] non-financial counterparties (exceeding certain thresholds)[1008] and all categories of OTC derivative contracts[1009] subject to the clearing obligation.[1010] EMIR may thus concern electricity market participants that are financial counterparties or non-financial counterparties with large positions. If the size of the

[1004] Articles 28(1), 29(1), 35(1) 36 and 38 of Regulation 600/2014 (MiFIR).

[1005] Recital 28 of Regulation 600/2014 (MiFIR).

[1006] See ISDA (2011).

[1007] Point 8 of Article 2 of Regulation 648/2012 (EMIR).

[1008] Point 9 of Article 2 of Regulation 648/2012 (EMIR).

[1009] Article 1(1) of Regulation 648/2012 (EMIR).

[1010] Article 4(1) of Regulation 648/2012 (EMIR).

derivatives position of a non-financial entity is regarded as systematically important, the entity must report its trades to the trade repository.[1011]

MiFID II/MiFIR Obligations The obligations that the MiFID II/MiFIR regime lays down for the regulated trading venues range from transparency to clearing obligations and the obligation to use a central counterparty.

Regulated trading venues must even comply with pre-trade and post-trade transparency obligations. Pre-trade obligations apply even to emissions allowances and derivatives that are admitted to trading or traded on a regulated venue.[1012] There are post-trade transparency obligations to make available the price, volume and time of transactions applicable to the same trading venues and the same range of instruments.[1013]

In addition to these transparency obligations, the MiFID II/MiFIR regime lays down several complementary surveillance-related obligations for the competent authorities, markets, investment firms, and the management bodies of investment firms. They will all be reflected in the compliance obligations of participants of financial wholesale electricity markets.

First, Member States' *competent authorities* must monitor the activities of investment firms so as to assess compliance with MiFID II. In addition to (a) compliance with the conditions of initial authorisation[1014] and (b) compliance with operating conditions,[1015] they must monitor (c) compliance with market integrity requirements. They must thus monitor the activities of investment firms to ensure that they act "honestly, fairly and professionally in the best interests" of their clients[1016] and in a manner which promotes "the integrity of the market".[1017] (d) The competent authorities must also obtain the information they need to assess compliance.[1018]

Second, to enable monitoring by the competent authorities, *operators* of regulated markets have certain duties. They must (a) monitor how their members or participants comply with their rules. They must also (b) monitor transactions undertaken under their systems to identify breaches of their rules, disorderly trading conditions, or conduct that may involve market abuse.[1019] Moreover, operators of regulated markets must (c) report significant breaches of their rules or disorderly trading conditions or conduct that may involve market abuse to the competent

[1011] Article 10 of Regulation 648/2012 (EMIR).

[1012] Article 8 of Regulation 600/2014 (MiFIR).

[1013] Article 6 of Regulation 600/2014 (MiFIR).

[1014] Article 21(2) of Directive 2014/65/EU (MiFID II).

[1015] Article 22 of Directive 2014/65/EU (MiFID II).

[1016] Article 24(1) of Directive 2014/65/EU (MiFID II).

[1017] For investment firms, see first subparagraph of Article 9(3) of Directive 2014/65/EU (MiFID II). For market operators, see first subparagraph of Article 45(6) of Directive 2014/65/EU (MiFID II).

[1018] Article 22 of Directive 2014/65/EU (MiFID II).

[1019] Article 56(1) of Directive 2014/65/EU (MiFID II).

authority of the regulated market.[1020] (d) There are similar obligations for operators of MTFs or OTFs.[1021]

Third, all this means that *investment firms* must have broad compliance obligations. An investment firm must (a) comply with the conditions of its initial authorisation[1022] and (b) notify the competent authority of any material changes to the conditions.[1023] It is even more important that an investment firm must (c) report positions in financial instruments to the competent authority.[1024] The scope of transaction reporting has been extended and aligned with the scope of market abuse rules.[1025] An investment firm must also (d) comply with organisational requirements[1026] (such as having "sound administrative and accounting procedures, internal control mechanisms, effective procedures for risk assessment, and effective control and safeguard arrangements for information processing systems"[1027]) and (e) keep records sufficient to enable the competent authority to monitor compliance with the requirements under MiFID.[1028]

Fourth, at the level of the investment firm, several duties under MiFID II are allocated to the *management body*. The management body of an investment firm is responsible for the implementation of governance arrangements that ensure "effective and prudent management . . . and the prevention of conflicts of interest . . . in a manner that promotes the integrity of the market and the interest of clients".[1029] MiFID II lays down detailed obligations to this end.[1030]

The management body must also monitor and periodically assess the effectiveness of the investment firm's organisation and the adequacy of the policies relating to the provision of services to clients and take appropriate steps to address any deficiencies.[1031]

[1020] First subparagraph of Article 54(2) of Directive 2014/65/EU (MiFID II).

[1021] First subparagraph of Article 31(2) of Directive 2014/65/EU (MiFID II).

[1022] Article 21(1) of Directive 2014/65/EU (MiFID II).

[1023] Article 21(2) of Directive 2014/65/EU (MiFID II).

[1024] Article 58 of Directive 2014/65/EU (MiFID II). Complemented by Level 3 Guidelines, MiFID I established a transaction reporting regime. CESR Level 3 Guidelines on MiFID Transaction Reporting (May 2007). See also CESR, Guidance: How to report transactions on OTC derivative instruments (8 October 2010).

[1025] Proposal for a Regulation on markets in financial instruments, COM(2011) 652 final, Explanatory memorandum, section 3.4.7.

[1026] Article 16(1) of Directive 2014/65/EU (MiFID II).

[1027] Second subparagraph of Article 16(5) of Directive 2014/65/EU (MiFID II). See also first subparagraph of Article 16(5) of Directive 2014/65/EU (MiFID II) on restrictions on outsourcing and the use of third parties.

[1028] Article 16(6) of Directive 2014/65/EU (MiFID II).

[1029] First subparagraph of Article 9(3) of Directive 2014/65/EU (MiFID II).

[1030] Article 9(3) of Directive 2014/65/EU (MiFID II).

[1031] Third subparagraph of Article 9(3) of Directive 2014/65/EU (MiFID II). See also fourth subparagraph of Article 9(3) of Directive 2014/65/EU (MiFID II).

Exchange Rules Exchange rules complement the mandatory provisions of law that regulate market surveillance.

MiFID II lays down monitoring obligations. (a) Market operators must establish and maintain effective arrangements and procedures for the regular monitoring of how their members or participants or users comply with their rules. (b) They must monitor transactions to identify breaches of those rules, disorderly trading conditions, or conduct that may involve market abuse. (c) They must also report significant breaches of their rules, disorderly trading conditions, conduct that may involve market abuse to the competent authority.

Nord Pool Spot and Nasdaq Commodities had a joint market surveillance function for the Nordic electricity market from 2002 to 2011. In 2011, the parties discontinued the joint function and established separate market surveillance units.[1032] Following the separation, the Elspot and Elbas markets of Nord Pool Spot and the N2EX market are under the responsibility of Market Surveillance at Nord Pool Spot. The financial markets are monitored by Market Surveillance at Nasdaq Commodities.[1033] These two market surveillance units are a legal requirement under Norwegian law, in particular the Norwegian Stock Exchange Act.

The surveillance responsibility over the Nordic power exchange lies in Norway. Nord Pool Spot operates based on a licence from NVE (the Norwegian energy regulator) and the market supervision is the responsibility of the Norwegian competition authority. NASDAQ OMX Oslo ASA (Nasdaq Commodities) operates based on license from the Norwegian Financial Supervisory Authority.

Members of the Forum of Nordic Energy Regulators (NordREG) have agreed to co-operate despite the fact that the other Nordic regulators have no legal mandate over the Nordic power exchanges.[1034]

4.10 The Balancing Market

4.10.1 General Remarks

As it is not possible to store electricity in large quantities in the wholesale market, there must be a continuous balance between electricity generation and consumption. Balance is achieved by using several complementary mechanisms. (a) Wholesale market participants use bilateral contracts, the day-ahead market (such as Elspot), and the intraday market (such as Elbas) to maintain balance for their own part.[1035] Market participants trade on these markets based on estimates.

[1032] Nord Pool Spot, Exchange Information, No. 24/2011—Separation of the joint Market Surveillance function of Nord Pool Spot and NASDAQ OMX Commodities Europe.

[1033] Nord Pool Spot, Exchange Information, No. 42/2011—Separation of the joint Market Surveillance function of Nord Pool Spot and Nasdaq OMX Commodities Europe.

[1034] See Energy Market Authority, Finland (2013), pp. 39–41.

[1035] See, for example, Lanz M et al. (2011), section 4.4.4, p. 131.

(b) The TSO is responsible for maintaining the system frequency in real time. The TSO procures balancing services to fill the gap closer to real time. These services are called, from the perspective of the TSO, the "ancillary services" of electricity market participants. (c) The costs of imbalances and the costs of the balancing services are retrieved from those market players that are balance responsible.[1036]

Balance Settlement Balance settlement depends on the market structure. (a) A vertically integrated market is cleared virtually real-time. The typical design includes a day-ahead optimisation of generation, transmission and reserves resulting in indicative plans to be re-optimised hour-ahead and in real-time operations. (b) In unbundled markets, the day-ahead market and the intraday market with physical delivery are used to balance the system in advance. Any registered deviations in delivery from the hourly contracted volumes are settled over the balance market.[1037]

There are different national balance settlement rules and practices in the EU, because the European markets are still largely national. The existence of differences can increase transaction costs and entry barriers.

For instance, each of the Nordic TSOs is responsible for balance settlement in its own country.[1038] A report from NordREG, a body that consists of the regulators in these countries, recommended a common end user market and common balance settlement. The NBS (Nordic Balance and Reconciliation Settlement) project is the means to achieve this goal.[1039]

According to the NBS model, a common Nordic body (called the Settlement Responsible, SR) performs the balance settlement and manages invoicing including collateral in dealings with the Balance Responsible Parties (BRPs) on behalf of the Transmission System Operator (TSO) in each country.

Frequency Imbalances affect the frequency of the system. Real-time balancing therefore means maintaining the system frequency, using reserves to contain or restore the frequency, and replacing the reserves.[1040]

Operational security is ensured by load-frequency control (LFC). Effective load-frequency control requires the co-operation of many market participants: TSOs, DSOs, operators of generation installations, and operators of demand facilities.[1041]

[1036] See, for example, NordREG (2008), pp. 9–10; Lanz M et al. (2011), section 4.4.4, pp. 131–132.

[1037] For the Nordic market, see Rud L (2009).

[1038] For reform proposals, see NBS Design (Svenska Kraftnät, Statnett, Energinet.dk, Fingrid, Nordic Balance Settlement (NBS). Common Balance & Reconciliation Settlement Design (26 January 2011).

[1039] NBS Design, p. 10: "The NBS-model is based on the general assumption that a common Nordic body, a so called Settlement Responsible (SR), performs the balance settlement and manages invoicing as well as collaterals towards the Balance Responsible Parties (BRP) on behalf of the Transmission System Operator (TSO) in each country ... The ambition is to create a full Nordic end user market for electricity in the Nordic region".

[1040] For the definition of balancing, see Article 2 of ENTSO-E Network Code on Electricity Balancing (6 August 2014).

[1041] Recitals 4 and 5 of ENTSO-E Network Code on Load-Frequency Control and Reserves (28 June 2013).

Market Conduct and Market Abuse Regime One may ask whether balancing market participants are subject to the same market conduct and market abuse regime as other physical electricity markets (see Sect. 4.7). For instance, TSOs are regarded as "market participants" that must comply with REMIT[1042] and balancing products could fall within the scope of REMIT provided that they are supply contracts regarded as "wholesale energy products".[1043] Moreover, the EFET Principles of Good Conduct have a broad scope (but apply only to EFET member companies).

There are nevertheless broad limitations to the scope of this regime: (a) Clearing and collateral requirements do not apply, because neither MiFID II nor EMIR applies.[1044] TSOs are excluded from the scope of MiFID II when they carry out their tasks under the Third Electricity Directive.[1045] As far as EMIR is concerned, TSOs are not central counterparties,[1046] balancing contracts are not OTC derivative contracts,[1047] there is no mandatory clearing obligation, and there is no duty for balancing market participants to have risk-management procedures.[1048] (b) The prohibition of insider trading (use and recommendations) under REMIT does not apply to the extent that a TSO purchases electricity to ensure the safe and secure operation of the system in accordance with its statutory obligation to manage electricity flows on the system.[1049] (c) Demand management contracts do not fall within the scope of REMIT in the light of the definition of "wholesale energy products" as they are not contracts for the "supply of electricity".[1050] (d) Where an exemption from the obligation to publish certain data has been granted to a TSO in accordance with Regulation 714/2009, the TSO is thereby also exempted from the obligation to disclose inside information under REMIT in respect of that data.[1051]

As balancing is vital for the secure operation of the system, it cannot be compromised by legal requirements applicable to other parts of electricity markets. Instead, the balancing market is regulated in other ways.

About This Section In the following, we will study alternative balancing mechanisms (Sect. 4.10.2), mechanisms used by the TSO/DSO (Sect. 4.10.3), the

---

1042 Recital 18 and point 7 of Article 2 of Regulation 1227/2001 (REMIT)

1043 Point 4 of Article 2 of Regulation 1227/2001 (REMIT).

1044 Article 1(1) of Regulation 648/2012 (EMIR).

1045 Recital 35 and point n of Article 2(1) of Directive 2014/65/EU (MiFID II).
of Directive 2014/65/EU (MiFID II).

1046 Point 1 of Article 2 of Regulation 648/2012 (EMIR).

1047 Point 7 of Article 2 of Regulation 648/2012 (EMIR).

1048 Articles 11(3) and 41(1) of Regulation 648/2012 (EMIR).

1049 Article 3(3) of Regulation 1227/2011 (REMIT).

1050 Point 4 of Article 2 of Regulation 1227/2001 (REMIT): "'wholesale energy products' means the following contracts and derivatives, irrespective of where and how they are traded: (a) contracts for the supply of electricity or natural gas where delivery is in the Union . . ."

1051 Article 4(5) of Regulation 1227/2011 (REMIT).

regulation of "synchronous areas" and "coordinated balancing areas" in the EU (Sect. 4.10.4), and the balancing marketplaces (Sect. 4.10.5).

4.10.2 Introduction to the Mechanisms of Balancing

Globally, countries have used alternative mechanisms to ensure peak generation and facilitate demand response. They can address costs in different ways.

An "energy only" mechanism would mean either very high prices for balance energy or insufficient investment in balance energy generation because of the "missing money problem". The market price of balance energy should be very high to give sufficient investment incentives because of the increased costs of balance energy generation.

First, there are costs for the building and maintenance of capacity that is mostly idle. Because electricity cannot be stored in large quantities in the wholesale market and electricity demand varies widely, sufficient capacity must be built for the few peak hours. Part of the generating capacity should therefore be "in the money" even though it is rarely used and the electricity producers that own the capacity must earn all of the net revenues (revenues net of fuel and other operating costs) required to cover their investment costs during a short period.[1052]

Second, there can be higher operational costs for using the installation only for a short period. Power plant operators require financial compensation for the extra wear and tear caused by fast production ramp up and ramp down.[1053]

Third, the owner of the installation will obviously need to recover its fuel and other operating costs.

Alternative Mechanisms Four main types of solutions have been used to address the missing money problem in the past: strategic reserves detained by the system operator (vertical integration); long-term contracts between the system operator and electricity producers on peak generation (some European countries)[1054]; generation capacity payments (mainly South American countries)[1055]; and a generation capacity market (US regional markets: PJM, New York, New England).

Some of the solutions would not work in the EU because of bad experiences concerning requirements relating to unbundling, or because of requirements relating to the use of use market-based procedures. (a) Strategic reserves detained by the system operator is not a solution for the EU because of the unbundling of the ownership of transmission and generation assets. (b) The use of long-term contracts would have to be in compliance with the Third Electricity Directive that requires

[1052] Joskow PL (2008), pp. 160–161.

[1053] Hotakainen M and Klimstra J (2011), p. 134.

[1054] Rious V et al. (2012), section 4.1.1.

[1055] Finon D and Pignon V (2008); Rious V et al. (2012), Table 4 and section 4.1.2.

the use of market-based procedures.[1056] The long-term contracts are contracts between the TSO and producer in which the producer agrees to make available to the TSO a certain amount of generation capacity at peak time. The producer is paid for the availability of its capacity and for the used energy at prices determined in the contract.[1057] (c) There are mixed results of the use of capacity payments.[1058] On one hand, one might say that the market price of balance energy should be very high to give sufficient investment incentives in the absence of capacity payments (energy only) and that capacity payments (capacity payments and energy price) might help to create sufficient investment incentives at a lower market price.[1059] On the other, capacity payments were used in England and Wales before they were rejected in the 2000 reform known as NETA (New Electricity Trading Arrangements).[1060]

The results of adopting market-based mechanisms in the US suggest that certain kinds of market-based mechanisms could be better than others.[1061] Electricity producers can trade capacity credits on US capacity markets. Capacity markets enable them to be compensated for the capacity they have in addition to the revenue for their output. Capacity markets have proved to be effective and essential for US electricity producers.

> A capacity market works in the following way. The system operator defines the generation reserve criteria for the network and for individual sub-regions. All retail load serving entities (LSEs) have an obligation to pay for their proportionate share of this generating capacity/demand response obligation based on their own LSE load at the time of system peak. LSEs can meet their capacity obligations either by contracting directly with electricity producers for capacity to be available to supply energy at the time of system peak or by purchasing this capacity through an auction process conducted by the system operator. If a producer is paid for the capacity that it has and it turns out that the producer cannot generate electricity accordingly, the producer will face heavy penalties.[1062]

In the EU, market-based methods must be used for the purchase of reserve capacity.[1063] The purchase of reserve capacity means the procurement of Frequency Containment Reserves (FCR or primary control), Frequency Restoration Reserves (FRR or secondary control), and Replacement Reserves (RR).[1064] For this purpose, each TSO must use standard products and specific products when available.[1065]

[1056] Article 15(6) of Directive 2009/72/EC (Third Electricity Directive).

[1057] Rious V et al. (2012), section 4.1.1.

[1058] See Rious V et al. (2012), section 4.1.2; Joskow PL (2008), pp. 168–169.

[1059] Joskow PL (2008), pp. 160–161.

[1060] See Wolfram CD (1998, 1999).

[1061] Joskow PL (2008), p. 168.

[1062] Rious V et al. (2012), section 4.1.3; Joskow PL (2008), p. 168.

[1063] Article 15(6) of Directive 2009/72/EC (Third Electricity Directive).

[1064] See Article 1(1) of ENTSO-E Network Code on Electricity Balancing (6 August 2014). For the definitions of primary control (Primärregelleistung) and secondary control (Sekundärregelleistung), see also BNetzA (the German Federal Network Agency), decision BK6-10-098 of 12 April 2011.

[1065] Article 29(1) of ENTSO-E Network Code on Electricity Balancing (6 August 2014).

ENTSO-E Network Code on Electricity Balancing provides that a TSO must use a market-based method for the procurement of Frequency Restoration Reserves and Replacement Reserves within its responsibility area.[1066] A TSO may contract for the procurement of balancing capacity for a maximum period of 1 year and for a maximum of 1 year in advance of the provision of the balancing capacity. The procurement of balancing capacity for a longer period than 1 year and more than 1 year in advance of the provision of the balancing capacity is subject to regulatory approval. The procurement of upward and downward balancing capacity must be carried out separately. Linking the procurement of upward and downward balancing capacity is allowed for: (a) Frequency Containment Reserves; or (b) Frequency Restoration Reserves and Replacement Reserves upon regulatory approval and when it is demonstrated that it leads to higher efficiency.[1067]

There are related rules for the procurement of balancing capacity within a coordinated balancing area.[1068]

ENTSO-E Network Code on Electricity Balancing also facilitates a secondary market by providing for the transfer of balancing capacity within a responsibility area or scheduling area[1069] or within a coordinated balancing area.[1070]

Increased Demand for Balancing Services The traditional model is that the operation of the power system relies on ancillary services provided by the central generation units. Balance energy would be scarcer without a pricing method that covers even long-term costs and not just the short-term marginal costs.

For many reasons, the value of flexibility and the demand for balancing services are changing.[1071] There is greater demand for balancing services (ancillary services) because of the growing share of electricity generated from renewable sources and the high volatility of wind and solar power.

However, the preferential treatment of electricity generated from renewable sources can hamper investment in conventional balance energy generation capacity and contribute to keeping balance energy scarce.

Therefore, there is room for the generation of balance energy from renewable sources and CHP plants. CHP plants may become more important providers of balance services because of the fact that CHP installations are given preferential treatment in EU energy law and the fact that they are easier to control compared with wind or solar power.[1072] Moreover, virtual power plants could help to generate balance energy from renewable sources.[1073]

There is also reason to create more liquid intraday markets that enable parties to balance their positions closer to real time.[1074]

[1066] Article 34(2) of ENTSO-E Network Code on Electricity Balancing (6 August 2014).

[1067] Article 34 of ENTSO-E Network Code on Electricity Balancing (6 August 2014).

[1068] Article 36 of ENTSO-E Network Code on Electricity Balancing (6 August 2014).

[1069] Article 35 of ENTSO-E Network Code on Electricity Balancing (6 August 2014).

[1070] Article 37 of ENTSO-E Network Code on Electricity Balancing (6 August 2014).

[1071] THEMA Consulting Group (2014), p. 38.

[1072] Madlener R and Kaufmann M (2002).

[1073] See, for example, Lanz M et al. (2011), section 3.1.2.3.

[1074] Recital 16 of Commission Regulation . . ./.. (CACM Regulation).

Allocation of Costs to System Users The costs should be allocated to system users. Generally, a TSO's rules should provide "appropriate incentives" for network users to balance their input and off-takes.[1075] The TSO must adopt rules for charging system users for energy imbalance. The rules must be "objective, transparent and non-discriminatory".[1076]

The TSO incurs costs for actions that it takes to balance the system. Balancing charges are designed to allocate this cost to those parties that are out of balance. They are also designed to give the parties incentives to avoid imbalances. The parties can avoid balancing charges by trading in the day-ahead market or earlier, by fine tuning positions in the intraday market, and by maintaining the reliability of their generation.[1077]

Types of Balancing Services Market participants can provide balancing services to the TSO in two main ways. First, electricity producers can supply balancing energy to the grid. Second, electricity consumers can reduce electricity consumption (demand response). For instance, they can provide interruptible loads.

Balancing services and control reserve products can thus be positive or negative. (a) Positive control reserves mean reserve capacity that can be activated in the event of a shortage of electricity generation. Positive control reserves can be provided by firms that operate flexible generation installations such as hydro, gas, or coal power plants. They can also be provided by thermal power stations (combined heat and power, CHP), emergency power plants, and biogas plants. (b) Negative control reserves mean storage capacity or interruptible load capacity that can be active in the event of a shortage of electricity consumption. These services are provided, among others, by energy intensive industrial installations and pumped-storage hydroelectricity power plants. Demand response can be used to balance power systems provided that there is a real-time metering system to support it. Until recently, this was not the case.[1078]

Demand Response Demand-side management—customer demand response, real-time metering, and real-time pricing schemes—could help to make demand more elastic, reduce price volatility, and increase security of supply. Demand-side management is appealing because of system losses and the fuel efficiency rate. 1 MWh of energy saved is more than 1 MWh of electricity produced.[1079]

In principle, there are three types of flexibility in electricity consumption: energy use can be shut down; one can shift to an alternative type of energy source; energy use can be shifted in time.[1080]

[1075] Article 37(6) of Directive 2009/72/EC (Third Electricity Directive).

[1076] Point (d) of Article 17(2) of Directive 2009/72/EC (Third Electricity Directive). Article 15 (7) of Directive 2009/72/EC (Third Electricity Directive).

[1077] Ofgem (2009), para 3.48.

[1078] Rious V et al. (2012).

[1079] Bhattacharyya SC (2011), p. 138.

[1080] THEMA Consulting Group (2014), p. 19.

Because generation costs are higher when even high-cost generation capacity must be dispatched and electricity prices are most volatile during the on-peak hours of the day, reductions in volatility could be achieved through the use of market mechanisms and demand-side management programs that shift consumption to off-peak hours. "Until customers, especially large ones, are exposed to real-time wholesale price variation, either wholesale electricity prices will remain volatile or the industry will have to maintain significant excess capacity".[1081]

In the EU, the Electricity Efficiency Directive provides that Member States and national energy regulatory authorities must promote the participation of demand side resources in balancing markets.[1082]

> Annex XI to the Energy Efficiency Directive lists three core ways to foster demand response. First, network regulation and tariffs must not prevent network operators or energy retailers from making available system services for demand response measures.[1083] Second, network tariffs must be cost-reflective of cost-savings in networks achieved from demand-side and demand-response measures.[1084] Third, network or retail tariffs may support dynamic pricing for demand response measures by final customers.[1085]

On the other hand, there is more active demand response only provided that (1) there is a demand for flexibility and (2) demand flexibility is able to compete with other flexibility resources. Other flexibility resources include generation, grid investments, and storage.[1086]

There are already mechanisms that contribute to meeting the demand for flexibility. (a) Flexibility is an implicit element of all trading in the physical wholesale market. Changes in forward market prices can change the volumes consumed or generated by some market participants and over time. Electricity producers and end consumers that have flexibility may seek to generate when prices are high and consume when prices are low. For example, they may schedule shut-downs for regular maintenance or decide when to generate from a hydro plant with storage. Short-term flexibility can be sold in the day-ahead or intraday market. (b) The aggregated imbalances in the power system are managed by the TSOs real-time. There is a market for balance energy and reserves.[1087]

Types of Balancing Markets Because of the high cost of balance energy, it would be necessary to design competitive market mechanisms for market participants' balancing services.[1088]

[1081] U.S. Energy Information Administration (2002), Chapter 4.

[1082] Article 15(8) of Directive 2012/27/EU (Energy Efficiency Directive).

[1083] Paragraph 2 of Annex XI to Directive 2012/2/EU (Energy Efficiency Directive).

[1084] Paragraph 1 of Annex XI to Directive 2012/27/EU (Energy Efficiency Directive).

[1085] Paragraph 3 of Annex XI to Directive 2012/27/EU (Energy Efficiency Directive): ". . . such as: (a) time-of-use tariffs; (b) critical peak pricing; (c) real time pricing; and (d) peak time rebates".

[1086] THEMA Consulting Group (2014), pp. 7–8.

[1087] THEMA Consulting Group (2014), pp. 28–31.

[1088] Madlener R and Kaufmann M (2002), section 2.6.3.

There is a regulating power market where producers with adjustable production or end consumers with adjustable demand provide resources to the TSO for up and down regulating.

However, there are in fact many markets for control reserves, because different market participants have different technical capabilities to increase or decrease generation or load.[1089] Peak generators and providers of demand response have different characteristics and are not pure substitutes.[1090]

In the EU, the different competitive markets for balancing services depend on: the area; time of response; the type of load-frequency control and reserves; and product standardisation.

Area One can distinguish between coordinated balancing areas (the area of two or more TSOs) and relevant areas (the area of one TSO). Each coordinated balancing area and each TSO has its own market for balancing services. Moreover, as regards load-frequency control, TSOs must co-operate in "synchronous areas".[1091]

Time of Response One can also distinguish between different kinds of local markets depending on the time of response. First, some installations can provide balancing services within seconds. Such services can only be activated automatically. Balancing services are activated in this way in European balancing markets for coordinated balancing areas. Second, there are installations that can provide balancing services within a few minutes. Even such services can only be activated automatically by the relevant TSO. Third, there are services that can be activated manually according to a schedule-based request.

Type of Control and Reserves There are different kinds of load-frequency control and reserves. In the EU, one can distinguish between the activation and settlement of frequency containment reserves (FCR), frequency restoration reserves (FRR), and replacement reserves (RR). They have been defined in LFCR Network Code[1092] and have different functions: "FCR shall aim at containing the System Frequency deviation after an incident within a pre-defined range. FRR shall aim at restoring the System Frequency to its Nominal Frequency of 50 Hz. RR replace the

[1089] Lanz M et al. (2011), section 4.4.3, p. 128. For the flexibility of generation and demand, see Lanz M et al. (2011), section 5.3.

[1090] Rious V et al. (2012).

[1091] Article 2(1) of ENTSO-E Network Code on Load-Frequency Control and Reserves (28 June 2013): "... Synchronous Area means an area covered by interconnected TSOs with a common System Frequency in a steady operational state such as the Synchronous Areas Continental Europe (CE), Great Britain (GB), Ireland (IRE) and Northern Europe (NE); ..."

[1092] Article 2(2) of ENTSO-E Network Code on Load-Frequency Control and Reserves (28 June 2013).

activated reserves to restore the available reserves in the system or for economic optimisation".[1093]

Product Standardisation The products traded on the market can be standardised or not standardised. The use of market-based methods and auctions requires product standardisation.

4.10.3 Mechanisms Used by the System Operator

Balancing and the operation of load-frequency control belong to the core responsibilities of the TSO as the party responsible for the physical real-time matching of supply and demand.[1094] On the other hand, DSOs may play an increasing role in the future.

Regulation According to the Third Electricity Directive, the TSO must adopt rules for balancing the electricity system. Generally, the rules should provide "appropriate incentives" for network users to balance their input and off-takes.[1095] They must include "rules for charging system users of their networks for energy imbalance". The rules must be "objective, transparent and non-discriminatory".[1096]

Moreover, the Third Electricity Directive requires TSOs to purchase reserve capacity according to "transparent, non-discriminatory and market-based procedures".[1097] Balancing services should be provided "in the most economic manner possible".[1098]

More detailed principles and rules are laid down by: (a) ACER Framework Guidelines on Electricity System Operation[1099] and ENTSO-E Network Code on Load-Frequency Control and Reserves (LFCR Network Code)[1100]; including (b) ACER Framework Guidelines on Electricity Balancing[1101] and ENTSO-E Network Code on Electricity Balancing.[1102]

Legal Mechanisms Used by the TSO In principle, TSOs could use various legal mechanisms in the wholesale balancing market to maintain balance in the system.

1093 Recital 11 of ENTSO-E Network Code on Load-Frequency Control and Reserves (28 June 2013). See also recital 10 of ENTSO-E Network Code on Electricity Balancing (6 August 2014).

1094 Points (c) and (d) of Article 12 of Directive 2009/72/EC (Third Electricity Directive).

1095 Article 37(6) of Directive 2009/72/EC (Third Electricity Directive).

1096 Article 15(7) of Directive 2009/72/EC (Third Electricity Directive).

1097 Article 15(6) of Directive 2009/72/EC (Third Electricity Directive).

1098 Article 37(6) of Directive 2009/72/EC (Third Electricity Directive).

1099 ACER, Framework Guidelines on Electricity System Operation (2 December 2011).

1100 ENTSO-E Network Code on Load-Frequency Control and Reserves (28 June 2013).

1101 ACER, Framework Guidelines on Electricity Balancing (18 September 2012).

1102 ENTSO-E Network Code on Electricity Balancing (6 August 2014).

They range from the obvious ones to more sophisticated mechanisms. They can be listed as follows:

First, there is neither grid access nor access to the spot market without the acceptance of the TSO's contractual framework. The contractual framework applied between market participants and the TSO is often called the balance agreement. Depending on the market, market participants are required to enter into a balance agreement either with the TSO or with a balance responsible party that has entered into a balance agreement with the TSO.

On EPEX Spot, the physical delivery of spot market transactions must be effected according to the clearing conditions and the balance agreements.[1103] Trading on EPEX Spot is not possible without a balance agreement or a balance responsible agreement.[1104] (a) There are multi-party agreements called balance agreements between the TSO, trading participants, the central counterparty/clearing house, and the party responsible for settlement on EPEX Spot. The balance agreement means "all contractual agreements between the transmission system operator ... and the Trading Participant as well as between the transmission system operator ... and ECC and ECC Lux regarding the settlement of power ... deliveries".[1105] (b) Some participants in the EPEX Spot market are balance responsible parties responsible for balance groups. Balance responsibles have a duty to pay for imbalances.[1106]

In the Elspot and Elbas markets of Nord Pool Spot, the trading rules require market participants and clients to have entered into on agreement on balance responsibility with a balance responsible party or the TSO.[1107]

On N2EX, the deliverable electricity contract volumes are delivered in accordance with the terms of the BSC (including the terms of each clearing transaction or ECV Transfer and the clearing rules).[1108] For this reason, the clearing house's counterparties must have established access to an energy account.[1109]

Second, there are important disclosure duties in the wholesale market. Electricity producers must disclose their schedules and large consumers their profiles to the TSO in advance.

Third, the contractual framework of the TSO or the regulatory framework can provide that a market participant must keep electricity inflows and outflows in balance.

According to the Third Electricity Directive, the TSO's rules for balancing the electricity system should provide "appropriate incentives" for network users to balance their input and off-takes.[1110]

[1103] ECC Clearing Conditions (0022a, 30 April 2014), section 5.2.3(1).

[1104] EPEX Spot Exchange Rules (28 November 2014), Article 2.23.

[1105] ECC Clearing Conditions (0022a, 30 April 2014), Chapter 1 Definition of Terms.

[1106] EPEX Spot Rules & Regulations, Appendix, Definitions (28 November 2014).

[1107] Nord Pool Spot's Physical Markets, General Terms, Trading Rules (1 February 2015), section 3.1.4.

[1108] N2EX Physical Market, General Clearing Terms, Clearing Rules (27 November 2014), section 11.1.1.

[1109] N2EX Physical Market, General Clearing Terms, Clearing Rules (27 November 2014), section 3.2.2 and section 5.2.

[1110] Article 37(6) of Directive 2009/72/EC (Third Electricity Directive).

These kinds of requirements can be applied in different ways. (a) In some US power markets, each electricity supplier has particular balance obligations. Each electricity supplier must be able to demonstrate to the Independent System Operator (ISO) that it can withstand all the demands on its customers in case of peak time plus a certain margin. It has three tools to achieve this goal: its own generation capacity; the long-term contracts it has with other producers in the area of its ISO; and additional generation capacity rights that it may acquire or exchange on a dedicated capacity market.[1111] (b) In the EU, each balance group responsible must balance electricity flows between group members (Sect. 9.2).

Fourth, TSOs can increase market participants' incentives to keep supply and demand in balance by requiring market participants to belong to balance groups lead by a balance responsible party (Sect. 9.2).

Fifth, where the TSO has a large control area, imbalances caused by individual market participants or balance groups can to a large extent cancel each other out. When they do, the TSO does not need to procure balancing energy.

Sixth, the TSO can use balancing services, that is, the ancillary services of market participants.[1112] To keep the frequency within acceptable bounds, the TSO may have to call up a generator to increase electricity generation (peak generation to ensure security of supply) or decrease electricity generation.

Where consumption exceeds generation, the frequency of the alternating current will fall below the system frequency 50 Hz (or, in many countries, 60 Hz). In this case, the TSO procures up regulation from a selected group of electricity producers that have excess generation capacity. Where generation exceeds consumption, the frequency will rise to above 50 Hz (or 60 Hz). In this case, the TSO procures down regulation from a selected group of electricity producers by selling power to them so they can reduce their own generation.

Alternatively, the TSO may call up a large industrial end consumer to reduce or increase consumption (demand response).

Seventh, as the TSO must balance the system by procuring balancing energy, the TSO can charge a price for imbalances. The price of imbalances can be positive or negative.

Eighth, TSOs or market regulators can address the problem that pricing mechanisms may fail to give sufficient incentives for investments in peak generation capacity (also known as the missing money problem, see Sect. 4.10.2).

The case of balance energy generation provides an example. (a) In the EU, many legislative reforms have increased investment in the generation of energy from renewable sources. Preferential feed-in tariffs for energy from renewable sources are complemented by priority access to the grid (subject to some security of supply constraints[1113]). Member States must ensure that TSOs and DSOs (1) guarantee the transmission and distribution of electricity produced from renewable energy sources; and (2) provide for either priority access or guaranteed access to the grid-system of electricity produced from renewable energy sources. What applies to electricity from renewable sources applies to (3) electricity

---

[1111] Rious V et al. (2012) and Finon D and Pignon V (2008).

[1112] See point (d) of Article 12 of Directive 2009/72/EC (Third Electricity Directive).

[1113] Article 16(2)(c) of Directive 2009/28/EC (RES Directive).

produced from waste or the production of CHP.[1114] (b) However, wind and solar power must be complemented by balance energy customarily from traditional sources.[1115] The preferential treatment of energy from renewable sources has reduced electricity prices in the wholesale market and limited the access of potential balance energy suppliers to the grid. Consequently, investments in balance energy generation are not as high as they should be and the security of supply may be reduced in the long term.

Balance Responsible Party In the EU, the role of balance responsible parties is regulated by: ACER Framework Guidelines on Electricity Balancing that set out principles for the development of network codes[1116]; and ENTSO-E Network Code on Electricity Balancing.[1117]

According to ACER Framework Guidelines, the function of balance responsible parties is to "support the system's balance in an efficient way and incentivise market participants in keeping and/or helping to restore the system balance".[1118] Moreover, imbalance settlement must be regulated in a way that "supports competition among market participants by creating a level-playing field and does not unduly discriminate against participants without generation or demand inside a control area".[1119]

ACER Framework Guidelines on Electricity Balancing set out the main principles of the role of balance responsible parties.[1120] For example:

- there should be a contract between a balance responsible party and the TSO;
- balance responsible parties should be incentivised to be balanced in real time;
- generation units from intermittent renewable energy sources must not receive special treatment for imbalances and must, therefore have a balance responsible party which is financially responsible for their imbalances;
- TSOs and national regulatory authorities may decide to oblige balance responsible parties to provide balanced programs in the day-ahead timeframe which may be subject to intraday changes; and
- TSOs and national regulatory authorities may also decide to incentivise balance responsible parties to help to restore system balance.

In Germany, the Energy Economy Act (EnWG) provides that electricity traders that supply to delivery points within the control area of a transmission system operator (or trade with electric energy within the control area) must belong to a balance group (the electricity trader's own balance group or another balance group).[1121] A balance group contract regulates the relationship between the balance responsible party and the system operator.

[1114] Article 16(2) of Directive 2009/28/EC (RES Directive). See also Articles 15(3) and 25(4) of Directive 2009/72/EC (Third Electricity Directive).

[1115] There are exceptions. For instance, Next Kraftwerke has interconnected decentralised and flexible renewable energy plants in its virtual power plant (VPP).

[1116] ACER, Framework Guidelines on Electricity Balancing (18 September 2012), section 1.1.

[1117] ENTSO-E Network Code on Electricity Balancing (6 August 2014).

[1118] ACER, Framework Guidelines on Electricity Balancing (18 September 2012), section 5.1.

[1119] ACER, Framework Guidelines on Electricity Balancing (18 September 2012), section 5.1.

[1120] ACER, Framework Guidelines on Electricity Balancing (18 September 2012), section 5.2.

[1121] § 4 StromNZV.

The minimum contents of a balance group contract are based on law.[1122] The core terms of the contract provide for the duty of the balance responsible: (1) to use its best efforts to maintain balance in the balance group; and (2) to settle the cost of remaining imbalances.[1123] A balance group contract thus facilitates financial settlement.[1124]

Moreover, ACER Framework Guidelines set out the principles of the pricing of imbalances. There are harmonised principles for calculating imbalances. All imbalances are subject to compensation via the imbalance pricing. For example, the following principles must be applied[1125]:

- imbalances must be settled in a non-discriminatory, transparent, fair and objective way;
- imbalances must be settled at a price that provides incentives to balance responsible parties to support the system's balance in an efficient way and/or to balance their portfolio before real time actions are necessary from the TSOs;
- imbalances must be settled at a price that reflects the costs of balancing the system in real time;
- imbalance pricing must at least include the costs of activated balancing energy (from frequency restoration reserves and replacement reserves) in the imbalance settlement period;
- imbalance pricing must also consider the cross-border netting of system imbalances and unintentional deviations to avoid distortions of incentives or counter-productive incentives;
- imbalance pricing must not include additional costs linked to possible deviations from the merit order list to alleviate congestions internal to a control area.

Growing Role of the DSO While TSOs play the central role in balancing markets, DSOs will become more and more important in balancing the system when the decentralisation of electricity generation is increased with microgeneration.[1126] At the same time, an increase in decentralisation and microgeneration makes it easier to use such installations for control purposes.[1127]

Denmark is the best example in Europe in this respect. The Danish power system is characterised by very large generation volumes on both the medium and low voltage levels of the distribution system because of large growth in distributed generation such as wind power and dispersed CHP plants. Consequently, there are intermittent bidirectional power flows between all voltage levels.

This led to a paradigm shift in Denmark. It was assumed that the traditional model (with central generation units providing the ancillary services) could be replaced by autonomous "cells" that are self-regulating. Each local distribution grid connected to the transmission

[1122] § 26 StromNZV.

[1123] Neveling S and Schönrock KP (2009), § 29, number 77

[1124] Neveling S and Schönrock KP (2009), § 29, number 76.

[1125] ACER, Framework Guidelines on Electricity Balancing (18 September 2012), section 5.3.

[1126] Lanz M et al. (2011), section 5.4, p. 163.

[1127] Lanz M et al. (2011), section 5.4.1, p. 164.

system could form an active network including all local distribution grid assets and all distribution network operator (DNO) facilities.

This is done in the Cell Controller project that is complemented by the Ecogrid project. The 60 kV distribution grid below each 150/60 kV transformer is defined as an autonomous cell.[1128] It is thus possible to operate the decentralised power system without any central generation or central control.

The Third Electricity Directive leaves room for Member States to allocate more duties to DSOs. DSOs may be required to balance the distribution system and to procure reserve capacity[1129] in addition to their other general obligations.[1130] DSOs, TSOs, and balancing service providers are also required to cooperate to ensure efficient and effective balancing.[1131]

4.10.4 Synchronous Areas, Coordinated Balancing Areas

Each TSO is responsible for procuring balancing services from balancing service providers to safeguard operational security. In the EU, TSOs belong to large "synchronous areas" under the LFCR Network Code and to smaller "coordinated balancing areas" under the Network Code on Electricity Balancing. Such areas are necessary to prevent cascading outages.

There was a cascading outage of the German and European power system on 4 November 2006 when a system operator switched off an extra-high voltage power line across the River Ems without understanding the consequences.[1132]

Synchronous Areas Synchronous areas are areas covered by interconnected TSOs with a common system frequency in a steady operational state. Synchronous areas include Continental Europe (CE), Great Britain (GB), Ireland (IRE), and Northern Europe (NE). The provisions of the LFCR Network Code do not apply to the extent that a transmission system of a Member State is not operating synchronously with a synchronous area.[1133] For instance, the provisions of the LFCR Network Code do not apply to the Åland islands.[1134]

[1128] Lund P (2006); Energinet.dk (2011); Lanz M et al. (2011), section 5.4.2, pp. 164–165.

[1129] Articles 25(6) and 25(5) of Directive 2009/72/EC (Third Electricity Directive). In Germany, the DSO has three main duties relating to balancing the system. Lanz M et al. (2011), section 5.4.1, pp. 163–164: "In Deutschland müssen Verteilnetzbetreiber nach den gültigen Netz-Codes (Transmission, Distribution, Grid) zu folgenden Systemdienstleistungen beitragen: Spannungshaltung ... Versorgungswiederaufbau ... Betriebsführung ..."

[1130] Article 25(1) of Directive 2009/72/EC (Third Electricity Directive). See also Article 25(4).

[1131] Article 23 of ENTSO-E Network Code on Electricity Balancing (6 August 2014).

[1132] Bundesnetzagentur (2007), p. 3.

[1133] Subparagraph 1 of Article 1(4) of ENTSO-E Network Code on Load-Frequency Control and Reserves (28 June 2013). For definitions, see Article 2(1).

[1134] Subparagraph 2 of Article 1(4) of ENTSO-E Network Code on Load-Frequency Control and Reserves (28 June 2013).

The LFCR Network Code[1135] lays down frequency quality parameters and defines the activation time and other technical minimum requirements for each synchronous area.

According to the LFCR Network Code, the activation time is 10–30 s for frequency containment reserves.[1136] There is a different activation time for frequency restoration reserves (with automatic and manual activation)[1137] and replacement reserves.[1138]

The LFCR Network Code provides that load-frequency control must be operated in the form of automatic and manual control.[1139] When load-frequency control is automatic, activation times can be short and measured in seconds.[1140] When the control is manual, activation times must be longer.

Coordinated Balancing Areas Two or more TSOs operating in different Member States must form a coordinated balancing area under the Network Code on Electricity Balancing. A coordinated balancing area will have a common framework.[1141]

Terms of Balancing A TSO is responsible for procuring balancing services from balancing service providers[1142] but may not offer balancing services itself in normal cases.[1143] It must operate either a Self Dispatch system or a Central Dispatch system[1144] and use standard products and specific products to maintain system balance.[1145]

[1135] Article 19 of ENTSO-E Network Code on Load-Frequency Control and Reserves (28 June 2013).

[1136] Article 44(1) of ENTSO-E Network Code on Load-Frequency Control and Reserves (28 June 2013). Article 2(2): "... FCR Full Activation Time means the time period between the occurrence of the Reference Incident and the corresponding full activation of the FCR ..."

[1137] Articles 47(1) and 44(2) of ENTSO-E Network Code on Load-Frequency Control and Reserves (28 June 2013). For definitions, see Article 2(2).

[1138] Article 49(1) of ENTSO-E Network Code on Load-Frequency Control and Reserves (28 June 2013).

[1139] Recital 15 of ENTSO-E Network Code on Load-Frequency Control and Reserves (28 June 2013).

[1140] See Article 44(1) of ENTSO-E Network Code on Load-Frequency Control and Reserves (28 June 2013).

[1141] Article 11 of ENTSO-E Network Code on Electricity Balancing (6 August 2014).

[1142] Article 22(2) of ENTSO-E Network Code on Electricity Balancing (6 August 2014).

[1143] Article 22(4) of ENTSO-E Network Code on Electricity Balancing (6 August 2014).

[1144] Article 2 of ENTSO-E Network Code on Electricity Balancing (6 August 2014): "... Central Dispatch means a scheduling and dispatch arrangement in a Responsibility Area where the TSO performs the Integrated Scheduling Process; and where the TSO issues dispatch instructions directly to the dispatchable Power Generating Facilities and Demand Facilities ... Self Dispatch means a scheduling and dispatch arrangement in a Responsibility Area where the schedule of all generation units and Demand Side Response is determined by the units owners ..."

[1145] Article 29(1) of ENTSO-E Network Code on Electricity Balancing (6 August 2014).

Each TSO must also develop a proposal for the terms and conditions related to balancing for its responsibility area or scheduling area "when appropriate".[1146]

ENTSO-E Network Code on Electricity Balancing lays down the minimum contents of the terms and conditions related to balancing. They include even rules for balancing service providers[1147] and rules for balance responsible parties.[1148]

The terms and conditions must allow the aggregation (pooling) of generation or demand response resources for balancing services.[1149] This is designed to foster decentralised electricity generation, microgeneration, and demand side response. The TSO has these obligations even if it applies a Central Dispatch system.[1150] These terms:

- permit aggregation for offering balancing services (the aggregation of demand side response, the aggregation of generation units, or the aggregation of demand side response and generation units within a responsibility area or scheduling area);
- permit a wider range of market participants to become balance service providers (such as demand facility aggregators, generation units that use conventional or renewable energy sources, storage elements); and
- require each balancing energy bid from a balancing service provider to be assigned to one or more balance responsible parties.

Each coordinated balancing area has its own terms and conditions for balancing. The terms and conditions are developed by all TSOs of the coordinated balancing area.[1151]

The methods used for the procurement of Frequency Containment Reserves (FCR), Frequency Restoration Reserves (FRR), and Replacement Reserves (RR) must be market-based.

Integration Models Moreover, ENTSO-E Network Code on Electricity Balancing facilitates cross-zonal and cross-border trade in balancing services. Cross-zonal trade is a legal requirement, because ENTSO-E Network Code on Electricity Balancing requires each TSO of a coordinated balancing area to "use the Exchange

[1146] Article 27(1) of ENTSO-E Network Code on Electricity Balancing (6 August 2014).

[1147] Articles 27(4) and 27(5) of ENTSO-E Network Code on Electricity Balancing (6 August 2014).

[1148] Article 27(6) of ENTSO-E Network Code on Electricity Balancing (6 August 2014).

[1149] Article 27(4) of ENTSO-E Network Code on Electricity Balancing (6 August 2014).

[1150] Compare Article 26(4) of ENTSO-E Network Code on Electricity Balancing (23 December 2013): "TSOs operating Central Dispatch systems shall not be obliged to allow within the terms and conditions related to Balancing the aggregation of Demand Side Response, the aggregation of generation units, or the aggregation of Demand Side Response and generation units pursuant to paragraph 3".

[1151] Article 11 of ENTSO-E Network Code on Electricity Balancing (6 August 2014).

of Balancing Energy from at least one Standard Product or operate the Imbalance Netting Process".[1152]

There is a "European integration model" or a "regional integration model" for the exchange of balancing energy[1153] for each type of reserves. Each model is based on the (usually multilateral) TSO-TSO model. The (multilateral) TSO-TSO model is the standard model for the exchange of balancing energy.[1154]

The integration models are as follows:

- the European integration model for exchange of balancing energy for RR[1155];
- the European integration model for the exchange of balancing energy for FRR with manual activation[1156];
- the European integration model for the exchange of balancing energy for FRR with automatic activation[1157];
- the European integration model for operating an imbalance netting process[1158];

[1152] Article 11(2) of ENTSO-E Network Code on Electricity Balancing (6 August 2014).

[1153] Article 2 of ENTSO-E Network Code on Electricity Balancing (6 August 2014): "... Exchange of Balancing Energy means the process of instructing the activation of Balancing Energy bids for the delivery of Balancing Energy by a TSO in a different Responsibility Area or Scheduling Area when appropriate, than the one in which the activated Balancing Service Provider is connected ..."

[1154] Article 2 of ENTSO-E Network Code on Electricity Balancing (6 August 2014): "... TSO-BSP Model means a model for the Exchange of Balancing Capacity or the Exchange of Balancing Energy where the Contracting TSO has an agreement with a Balancing Service Provider in another Responsibility Area or Scheduling Area when appropriate. TSO-TSO Model means a model for the Exchange of Balancing Services exclusively by TSOs. The TSO-TSO Model is the standard model for the Exchange of Balancing Services. TSO-TSO Model for FRR and RR means a model for the Exchange of Balancing Capacity of Frequency Restoration Reserves and Replacement Reserves exclusively by TSOs ..."

[1155] Article 14(2) of ENTSO-E Network Code on Electricity Balancing (6 August 2014): "The European integration model for the Replacement Reserves shall consist of a single Coordinated Balancing Area. In this Coordinated Balancing Area all TSOs using Replacement Reserves shall apply a multilateral TSO-TSO model with Common Merit Order List to share and exchange all Balancing Energy bids for Replacement Reserves".

[1156] Article 16(3) of ENTSO-E Network Code on Electricity Balancing (6 August 2014): "The European integration model for the Frequency Restoration Reserves with manual activation shall consist of a single Coordinated Balancing Area. In this Coordinated Balancing Area all TSOs shall apply a multilateral TSO-TSO model with Common Merit Order List to share and exchange all Balancing Energy bids for Frequency Restoration Reserves with manual activation".

[1157] Article 18(3) of ENTSO-E Network Code on Electricity Balancing (6 August 2014): "The European integration model for the Frequency Restoration Reserves with automatic activation shall consist of a single Coordinated Balancing Area. In this Coordinated Balancing Area all TSOs shall apply a multilateral TSO-TSO model to share and exchange all Balancing Energy bids for Frequency Restoration Reserves with automatic activation respecting the principles of Common Merit Order List".

[1158] Article 20(2) of ENTSO-E Network Code on Electricity Balancing (6 August 2014): "The European integration model for the Imbalance Netting Process shall consist of a single Coordinated Balancing Area. In this Coordinated Balancing Area all TSOs shall apply a multilateral TSO-TSO model to operate the Imbalance Netting Process when economically efficient".

- the regional integration model for the exchange of balancing energy for FRR with manual activation[1159];
- the regional integration model for the exchange of balancing energy for FRR with automatic activation[1160]; and
- the regional integration model for operating the imbalance netting process.[1161]

4.10.5 Balancing Marketplaces

General Remarks

The balancing market enables electricity producers and end consumers with flexible generation technology or flexible industrial processes to submit up-regulation or down-regulation bids.

EU law provides for synchronous areas and coordinated balancing areas. Each TSO is responsible for balancing.[1162] Therefore, each TSO must adopt rules for balancing the system. These rules and rules for charging system users for energy imbalance must be objective, transparent and non-discriminatory.[1163] Where the TSO purchases reserve capacity, it must apply "transparent, non-discriminatory and market-based procedures".[1164]

The Balancing Market The balancing market is used after the closure of the spot market. Participants can then submit bids that specify the prices they require (offer)

[1159] Article 15(2) of ENTSO-E Network Code on Electricity Balancing (6 August 2014): "The regional integration model for Frequency Restoration Reserves with manual activation shall consist of one or more Coordinated Balancing Areas. All TSOs involved in such Coordinated Balancing Areas shall apply a multilateral TSO-TSO model with Common Merit Order List to share and exchange all Balancing Energy bids for Frequency Restoration Reserves with manual activation, except unshared bids pursuant to Article 41".

[1160] Article 17(2) of ENTSO-E Network Code on Electricity Balancing (6 August 2014): "The regional integration model for the Frequency Restoration Reserves with automatic activation shall consist of one or more Coordinated Balancing Areas. All TSOs involved in such Coordinated Balancing Areas shall apply a TSO-TSO Model to exchange and optimise the activation of all Balancing Energy bids for Frequency Restoration Reserves with automatic activation, except for unshared bids pursuant to Article 41".

[1161] Article 19(2) of ENTSO-E Network Code on Electricity Balancing (6 August 2014): "The regional integration model for the Imbalance Netting Process shall consist of one or more Coordinated Balancing Areas within the Synchronous Area Continental Europe. All TSOs involved in such Coordinated Balancing Areas shall apply a TSO-TSO Model to perform the Imbalance Netting Process".

[1162] Point (d) of Article 12 of Directive 2009/72/EC (Third Electricity Directive).

[1163] Article 15(7) of Directive 2009/72/EC (Third Electricity Directive).

[1164] Article 15(6) of Directive 2009/72/EC (Third Electricity Directive).

to increase their generation or decrease their consumption (decrease their generation or increase their consumption) for a specific volume immediately.

Some grid operators procure the capacities and energy via published auctions in the intraday market. The intraday market is important even for other market participants because it enables market participants to trade energy close to real-time and to balance or re-balance their position.[1165] According to ACER Framework Guidelines, the CACM Network Codes must support continuous implicit trading with reliable pricing of intraday transmission capacity reflecting congestion.[1166]

The point in time when reserve capacity is cleared is likely to influence the price. (a) If reserve capacity is cleared only after the clearance of the spot market, the last chance to sell the available capacity is in the balancing market. Consequently, prices may be determined based on marginal costs.[1167] (b) If the power exchange has an intraday market in addition to the day-ahead market, electricity producers have more choice and the price can reflect even other costs.[1168]

Example: The Nordic Market In the Nordic and Baltic market, balance is achieved by the combined use of three marketplaces. Elspot is the common Nordic market for trading physical electricity contracts with next-day supply. Elbas is a continuous intraday market for the Nordic and Baltic area and Germany, including the Benelux via the NorNed cable. There is also a market for regulating power. Elbas market participants can trade one-hour-contracts until 1 h or 30 min (Germany) before delivery.[1169] Prices are set based on a first-come, first-served principle where lowest sell price and highest buy price comes first, regardless of when an order is placed.[1170] While Nord Pool Spot is the central counterparty for all trades, the trades are nominated to the local TSO. TSOs allocate transmission capacity every day for Elbas trading.

Deviations from generation and supply in the day-ahead and intraday markets are managed by trading in the regulating market (real-time market) operated by

---

[1165] ACER, Framework Guidelines on Capacity Allocation and Congestion Management for Electricity (29 July 2011), section 5.

[1166] ACER, Framework Guidelines on Capacity Allocation and Congestion Management for Electricity (29 July 2011), section 5: "... The CACM Network Code(s) shall set out all necessary provisions for the implementation of the pan-European intraday target model supporting continuous implicit trading, with reliable pricing of intraday transmission capacity reflecting congestion (i.e. in case of scarce capacity). The method for pricing capacity and the allocation of congestion rents shall be subject to approval by the NRAs concerned. As a transitional measure, direct explicit access to the capacity will also be allowed, subject to the approval by the relevant NRAs and the conditions defined further below".

[1167] Marginal costs include start-up cost, no-load cost, and incremental costs per kWh for actual generation at different levels of output. Hunt S and Shuttleworth G (1996), p. 153.

[1168] Madlener R and Kaufmann M (2002)

[1169] Nord Pool Spot Physical Markets, Trading Appendix 3, Product Specifications (launch of Elbas4), section 3.1.

[1170] Nord Pool Spot Physical Market, Trading Appendix 2b, Elbas Market Regulations (18 February 2013).

each TSO. Participants submit bids to the relevant national TSO for up or down regulation. There is a two-price system with an up-regulation and down-regulation price. There is a common system for the collection of all Nordic bids. The best bid can be activated regardless of the country or area.

Internal Trading and Manipulation Some electricity market participants may need to balance generation capacity and load across different zones. They can use the intraday market for this purpose. However, the lack of liquidity in some areas can make it difficult to cover imbalances by trading with other market participants. Internal trading can help to transfer electricity from one area to another. The question is whether internal trading is permitted by the market operator and whether it is compatible with rules prohibiting market manipulation. Market manipulation has been discussed earlier in this chapter (Sect. 4.7).

The Market Conduct Rules of Elbas do not prohibit internal trading as such. However, market manipulation is prohibited. Because price is not as important in internal trades compared with normal trading, there is a risk that internal trades: give a false or misleading signal as to the supply, demand, or price of a listed product; or secure the price at an abnormal or artificial level. For this reason, it is regarded as important that "all trades are made at prices were the company would also be willing to make trades with other companies at the same price". Nord Pool Spot has indicated that various methods can be used to reduce risk. The firm can: ensure that the prices are justified (for instance, by sales orders that reflect the marginal production costs of the relevant unit); use internal guidelines and routines that tell employees how to handle internal trades in Elbas; avoid placing purchase and sales orders simultaneously (as this hinders other members from reacting to the orders); and disclose internal trades (so other members can see that the trades are in fact internal trades).[1171]

Procurement

The procurement of balancing energy is regulated by ENTSO-E Network Code on Electricity Balancing subject to a transitional period of 2 years.[1172]

ENTSO-E Network Code on Electricity Balancing provides that each balancing service provider must submit its balancing reserve bids to the connecting TSO.[1173] To participate, each service provider must belong to the same relevant area where the imbalance is calculated.[1174] Balancing service providers are allowed to provide these services only to the connecting TSO.[1175] Balancing capacity bids may be updated before the gate closure time of the procurement process.[1176]

[1171] Nord Pool Spot, Internal trading in Elbas.

[1172] Article 70 of ENTSO-E Network Code on Electricity Balancing (6 August 2014).

[1173] Article 24(3) of ENTSO-E Network Code on Electricity Balancing (6 August 2014).

[1174] Article 24(7) of ENTSO-E Network Code on Electricity Balancing (6 August 2014).

[1175] Article 24(6) of ENTSO-E Network Code on Electricity Balancing (6 August 2014).

[1176] Article 24(4) of ENTSO-E Network Code on Electricity Balancing (6 August 2014).

ENTSO-E Network Code on Electricity Balancing requires the use of standard products and specific products.[1177] (a) TSOs are required to develop a proposal for Standard Products for Balancing Capacity and Standard Products for Balancing Energy no later than 1 year after the entry into force of the Network Code.[1178] The Network Code lays down some of the issues that the specifications of the standard products must address,[1179] including general standards for the products.[1180] (b) A TSO may obtain a permission to use Specific Products where Standard Products are not sufficient.[1181]

Procurement of Balancing Capacity Within a Responsibility Area A TSO must use a market-based method for the procurement of Balancing Capacity for at least FRR and RR within its responsibility area.[1182]

It may contract for the procurement of balancing capacity for a maximum period of 1 year and for a maximum of 1 year in advance without regulatory approval, but otherwise not without regulatory approval.[1183]

The procurement of upward and downward balancing capacity must be carried out separately.[1184] On the other hand, it is permitted to link the procurement of upward and downward balancing capacity upon regulatory approval and when it is demonstrated that it leads to higher economics efficiency.

This is because the regulatory authority may grant an exemption when it is demonstrated that the exemption would lead to higher economic efficiency.[1185]

Procurement of Balancing Capacity Within a Coordinated Balancing Area ENTSO-E Network Code on Electricity Balancing facilitates the cross-zonal procurement and exchange of balancing capacity in a coordinated balancing area. A TSO may thus co-operate with another TSO for this purpose. Moreover, TSOs have a duty to submit bids for Standard Products to the common optimisation function.[1186]

There are some regulatory constraints that resemble the constraints that apply to the procurement of balancing capacity within a responsibility area. (a) Again, TSOs

---

[1177] Article 29 of ENTSO-E Network Code on Electricity Balancing (6 August 2014).

[1178] Article 29(2) of ENTSO-E Network Code on Electricity Balancing (6 August 2014).

[1179] Article 29(5) of ENTSO-E Network Code on Electricity Balancing (6 August 2014): "The list of Standard Products for Balancing Capacity and Standard Products for Balancing Energy shall define at least the following standard characteristics of a bid by a fixed value or an appropriate range: (a) Preparation Period; (b) Ramping Period; (c) Full Activation Time; (d) minimum and maximum quantity; (e) Deactivation Period; (f) minimum and maximum duration of Delivery Period; (g) Validity Period; and (h) Mode of Activation".

[1180] Article 29(7) of ENTSO-E Network Code on Electricity Balancing (6 August 2014).

[1181] Article 29(8) of ENTSO-E Network Code on Electricity Balancing (6 August 2014).

[1182] Article 34(2) of ENTSO-E Network Code on Electricity Balancing (6 August 2014).

[1183] Article 34(4) of ENTSO-E Network Code on Electricity Balancing (6 August 2014).

[1184] Article 34(5) of ENTSO-E Network Code on Electricity Balancing (6 August 2014).

[1185] Article 34(6) of ENTSO-E Network Code on Electricity Balancing (6 August 2014).

[1186] Article 36(13) of ENTSO-E Network Code on Electricity Balancing (6 August 2014).

must use market-based methods.[1187] (b) TSOs of a coordinated balancing area may contract for the procurement of balancing capacity for a maximum period of 1 month and a maximum of 1 month in advance without regulatory approval, but for a longer period or more in advance subject to regulatory approval.[1188] (c) The procurement of upward and downward balancing capacity must be done separately.[1189] (d) Linking the procurement of upward and downward balancing capacity is not permitted unless the regulatory authority grants an exemption.[1190]

In this case, TSOs of the coordinated balancing area must define a common pricing method. It must: (a) give correct price signals and right incentives to market participants; and (b) ensure that there are no significant distortions between adjacent coordinated balancing areas.[1191]

Pricing Methods TSOs must harmonise the pricing methods for at least each Standard Product for balancing energy after the entry into force of ENTSO-E Network Code Electricity Balancing.[1192]

The main rule is that the pricing methods must be based on marginal pricing (pay-as-cleared). However, TSOs may show that a different pricing method is better in the light of the general objectives of the balancing market.[1193]

There can be regional variation. TSOs of a coordinated balancing area may propose a different pricing method before the implementation of the European integration model, but they must show that it is "more efficient within this Coordinated Balancing Area in pursuing the general objectives".[1194] Moreover, a TSO may apply a different pricing method for a Standard Product where it does not participate in a coordinated balancing area for this Standard Product.[1195]

Reservation ENTSO-E Network Code on Electricity Balancing permits TSOs to reserve cross-zonal capacity in some cases.[1196] TSOs may also develop a methodology for a market-based reservation process[1197] or propose an economic efficiency analysis.[1198]

[1187] Article 36(7) of ENTSO-E Network Code on Electricity Balancing (6 August 2014).

[1188] Article 36(8) of ENTSO-E Network Code on Electricity Balancing (6 August 2014).

[1189] Article 36(9) of ENTSO-E Network Code on Electricity Balancing (6 August 2014).

[1190] Article 36(10) of ENTSO-E Network Code on Electricity Balancing (6 August 2014).

[1191] Article 36(12) of ENTSO-E Network Code on Electricity Balancing (6 August 2014).

[1192] Article 39(1) of ENTSO-E Network Code on Electricity Balancing (6 August 2014).

[1193] Article 39(2) of ENTSO-E Network Code on Electricity Balancing (6 August 2014).

[1194] Article 39(6) of ENTSO-E Network Code on Electricity Balancing (6 August 2014).

[1195] Article 39(7) of ENTSO-E Network Code on Electricity Balancing (6 August 2014).

[1196] Article 43(1) of ENTSO-E Network Code on Electricity Balancing (6 August 2014): "Each TSO shall have the right to reserve Cross Zonal Capacity for the Exchange of Balancing Capacity or Sharing of Reserves when socio-economic efficiency is proved in accordance with this Section using one of the following approaches: (a) co-optimisation process pursuant to Article 45; (b) market-based reservation process pursuant to Article 46; and (c) reservation based on economic efficiency analysis, pursuant to Article 47".

[1197] Article 46(1) of ENTSO-E Network Code on Electricity Balancing (6 August 2014).

[1198] Article 47(1) of ENTSO-E Network Code on Electricity Balancing (6 August 2014).

Where the TSO-BSP Model is applied,[1199] a balance responsible party may make cross-zonal capacity available to a balancing service provider in the form of a Physical Transmission Right, and this cross-zonal capacity can be reserved for the exchange of balancing capacity.[1200] In this case, the UIOSI or UIOLI principles do not apply.[1201]

Activation ENTSO-E Network Code on Electricity Balancing sets out how balancing electricity bids are activated by each TSO under the TSO-TSO Model.[1202] The Network Code also provides for an activation optimisation function with a common merit order list for Standard Products.[1203]

Germany

In Germany, one can distinguish between primary control reserves (frequency containment reserves), secondary control reserves (frequency restoration reserves), minute control reserves (restoration reserves), and interruptible loads (that belong to demand-side management).[1204]

There is a secondary control market covering the whole country, that is, the control areas of all German TSOs. The nationwide secondary control market was put in place gradually in 2008–2010.[1205]

Primary Control, Secondary Control, Minute Control Primary control reserves are activated within seconds[1206] and secondary control reserves in 5 min.[1207] Both are activated automatically. The purpose of minute control reserves is to replace secondary control reserves.[1208] Since 3 July 2012, even minute control reserves have been activated automatically (according to merit order).

German TSOs must co-operate at different levels. (a) The starting point is that each German TSO is required to maintain a balance between electricity generation and demand in its control area and to provide balancing energy to balancing groups

---

[1199] Article 2 of ENTSO-E Network Code on Electricity Balancing (6 August 2014): "... TSO-BSP Model means a model for the Exchange of Balancing Capacity or the Exchange of Balancing Energy where the Contracting TSO has an agreement with a Balancing Service Provider in another Responsibility Area or Scheduling Area when appropriate ..."

[1200] Article 48 of ENTSO-E Network Code on Electricity Balancing (6 August 2014).

[1201] Article 43(4) and Article 48(4) of ENTSO-E Network Code on Electricity Balancing (6 August 2014).

[1202] Article 40 of ENTSO-E Network Code on Electricity Balancing (6 August 2014).

[1203] Article 42 of ENTSO-E Network Code on Electricity Balancing (6 August 2014).

[1204] § 2 StromNZV (the Electricity Network Access Ordinance).

[1205] Lanz M et al. (2011), section 4.4.3, pp. 129–130.

[1206] Point 8 of § 2 StromNZV (the Electricity Network Access Ordinance); BNetzA (the German Federal Network Agency), decision BK6-10-098 of 12 April 2011.

[1207] Point 10 of § 2 StromNZV; BNetzA, decision BK6-10-098 of 12 April 2011.

[1208] Point 6 of § 2 StromNZV; BNetzA, decision BK6-10-099 of 18 October 2011.

(electricity producers and consumers) from the secondary control and minutes reserve.[1209] (b) Moreover, German TSOs co-operate in the Netzregelverbund. Although each TSO procures secondary control and minutes reserve separately, the TSOs co-ordinate their work. As a result of this co-operation, there is only one price (reBAB, der regelzonenübergreifende einheitliche Bilanzausgleichsenergiepreis) for control reserves in all control areas. (c) Unlike secondary control reserves and minute control reserves, the provision of primary control reserves is facilitated at a European level by ENTSO-E. Primary control reserves are provided by large generation installations that can react automatically to changes in the load.

Platform Since 2001, German TSOs have procured their primary control, secondary control, and minutes reserve in an open, transparent, and non-discriminatory control power market in accordance with the provisions of the Federal Cartel Office (Bundeskartellamt, BKA).[1210]

German law requires TSOs to share an IT-platform (www.regelleistung.net) for tenders.[1211] Since 27 June 2011, there have been weekly tenders for primary and secondary control reserves and since 1 December 2006 daily tenders for minute control reserves.

A precondition for submitting bids in a tender is the conclusion of a framework contract between the supplier and connecting TSO following successful pre-qualification.

In practice, it can be difficult for smaller market participants to fulfil the prequalification conditions for each installation even for minute control reserves.[1212] They might not be able to fulfil requirements as to the response time and the availability of the service.[1213] Smaller installations can nevertheless form pools.[1214] Pools have increased the participation of smaller installations, in particular, decentralised generation of RES-E and microgeneration.[1215]

The connecting TSO is the sole contracting party of the supplier. The connecting TSO is the TSO in whose control area the technical units to be marketed by the supplier are connected to the grid, irrespective of the voltage level. If a supplier markets technical units in several control areas, a framework contract has to be concluded with each connecting TSO.

Calls for tenders for primary control reserves (PCR) are "symmetrical" in the sense that there are no separate calls for tenders for positive PCR (additional power)

[1209] § 13(1) EnWG.

[1210] § 22(2) EnWG.

[1211] § 22(2) EnWG.

[1212] Lanz M et al. (2011), section 4.4.3, p. 130.

[1213] Transmission Code, Anhang D 3 (24 August 2007), section 3.2.

[1214] Transmission Code, Anhang D 3 (24 August 2007), sections 3.2.3 and 3.2.5.

[1215] Lanz M et al. (2011), section 4.4.3, p. 130.

and negative PCR (less power).[1216] Minute control reserves products are positive or negative.[1217]

Interruptible Loads Interruptible loads are a form of demand-side management.[1218] The use of interruptible loads is facilitated by the Energy Industry Act (EnWG)[1219] and the Ordinance on Interruptible Load Agreements (AbLaV). Many large consumption units connected to the high and extra high voltage grid can reduce or interrupt their demand on short notice because of the nature of their production process. They can, therefore, undertake to do this on short notice and for a fixed minimum duration as suppliers of interruptible loads.[1220]

The minimum load must be at least 50 MW,[1221] but it can be shared by up to five installations.[1222] A large industrial installation can thus participate either separately or jointly as part of a virtual power plant.

There are monthly calls for tenders for immediately interruptible loads and quickly interruptible loads. Immediately interruptible loads are activated automatically within the second when the level drops below a predefined grid frequency. Quickly interruptible loads are activated by the TSO by remote control.

The price consists of a fixed and a variable component. A fixed price is payable for the reserved interruptible load (Leistungspreis) regardless of whether the interruptible load is activated or not. The variable component (Arbeitspreis) becomes payable where the interruptible load is activated.[1223]

Northern Europe

The Nordic countries established a common regulation power market in 2002 to handle balancing. Balancing is managed within the Nordic control areas as one system by all four Nordic TSOs. Imbalances are handled and settled according to common rules defined in the System Operation Agreement between the Nordic TSOs. However, imbalances within a country are settled according to principles that vary from one country to another.[1224]

One can distinguish between the following balancing marketplaces in Northern Europe: Nord Pool Spot's Elspot market (the spot market); Nord Pool Spot's Elbas

1216 § 6(3) StromNZV. Rahmenvertrag über die Vergabe von Aufträgen zur Erbringung der Regelenergieart Primärregelleistung, § 3.1(1).

1217 § 6(3) StromNZV; Transmission Code, Anhang D 3 (24 August 2007), section 3.1 and section 3.2.2.

1218 Monopolkommission (2013), numbers 334–335.

1219 § 14a and 14b EnWG.

1220 For definitions, see § 2 AbLaV (the Ordinance on Interruptible Load Agreements).

1221 § 5(1) AbLaV.

1222 § 5(2) AbLaV.

1223 § 4 AbLaV.

1224 Energy Market Authority, Finland (2013), p. 22.

market (the intraday market); and the regulating power market of each TSO with automatic or manual reserves. Each country has its own laws governing TSOs' duties and balance agreements.[1225]

Trading at Nord Pool is voluntary. However, all day-ahead cross-border trading must be done at Nord Pool Spot (NPS).[1226]

Elbas, the Intraday Market The Elspot market of Nord Pool Spot is complemented by Elbas. A member of NPS can trade on both Elspot and Elbas. Each member is granted at least one trading portfolio for the Elspot market and at least one trading portfolio for the Elbas market.[1227]

Elbas is a continuous market. For the Nordic and Baltic areas, trading takes place until one hour before the commencement of delivery. For Germany, it takes place until 30 min before the commencement of delivery.[1228]

Orders are All-or-Nothing Orders, Fill Orders, Fill-or-Kill Orders, Immediate-or-Cancel Orders, or Iceberg Orders.[1229] (a) When the order is an All-or-Nothing Order, matching may only be effected for the full volume. A Block Order is a type of All-or-Nothing Order which combines several consecutive individual hour series. When the order is a Fill Order, matching may be effected either for the full volume or for a part of the volume. Any remaining volume remains valid with the ranking of the original order. (b) Fill-or-Kill is an order that must be immediately matched for the whole order volume or cancelled. Immediate-or-Cancel means an order that must be immediately matched for as much of the order volume as possible and then cancelled. (c) An Iceberg Order has a partly hidden overall volume.

Orders are ranked based on order price and according to the principle first come, first served.[1230] Transactions are matched automatically when concurring orders are registered.[1231]

Nord Pool Spot discloses information on all orders and transactions continuously.[1232]

[1225] NordREG (2008), section 2.2, pp. 16–18.

[1226] NordREG (2012), p. 28.

[1227] Nord Pool Spot Physical Markets, Trading Appendix 4, Clearing Rules (27 November 2014), section 3.1.1; Nord Pool Spot's Physical Markets, General Terms, Trading Rules (1 February 2015), section 3.4.1.

[1228] Nord Pool Spot Physical Markets, Trading Appendix 3, Product Specifications (launch of Elbas4), section 3.1.

[1229] Nord Pool Spot Physical Markets, Trading Appendix 3, Product Specifications (launch of Elbas4), section 3.1.

[1230] Nord Pool Spot Physical Market, Trading Appendix 2b, Elbas Market Regulations (18 February 2013), section 2.2.1.

[1231] Nord Pool Spot Physical Market, Trading Appendix 2b, Elbas Market Regulations (18 February 2013), section 1.1.1 and section 2.3.1.

[1232] Nord Pool Spot Physical Market, Trading Appendix 2b, Elbas Market Regulations (18 February 2013), section 6.1 and section 6.2.

Regulating Power The regulating power is traded by each TSO to keep the frequency at 50 Hz. There is a joint Nordic merit order list. All regulating power orders submitted to the TSOs are ranked based on price.[1233]

The system price (the up-regulation or down-regulation price) is the price of the last regulated MW. It will thus be known only after the end of the specific operating hour. The price of up-regulation is the most expensive up-regulation bid ordered by the TSO during the specific operating hour (and the price of down-regulation is the cheapest down-regulation bid ordered by the TSO during the specific operating hour). All those who have participated in the up regulation (or down regulation) during the specific operating hour receive the same compensation per MWh.[1234] Other suppliers of regulation power (up regulation or down regulation) can thus make a profit that equals the difference between the final regulation price and the offered price.

The participation of electricity producers and others in the maintenance of the reserves as a service provider is voluntary. There is a tendering process of peak load reserve power plants. Companies with controllable capacity can register their resources with the TSO and agree to maintain their reserves. The TSO agrees to pay compensation for the service.

> For instance, the Finnish TSO (Fingrid) has purchased load shedding service as primary and secondary reserve from companies in the pulp and paper, chemical, and metal industries.[1235]
>
> Peak load reserve is a strategic reserve that will be used in the event that the balance has not been achieved in the commercial market (Nord Pool Spot). For this reason, the peak load reserve plants are not allowed to participate and bid on the commercial market. The selected power plants will receive fixed compensation for acting as a reserve. The Finnish TSO is responsible for making agreements with the selected power plants and pays the compensations to the power plants. The peak load reserve system is funded by fees collected from end consumers.[1236]

Imbalances, Nordic Balance Settlement TSOs have participated in two forms of balance settlement in the Nordic area. The first is cross-border balance settlement between different TSOs. Balance power between two countries is priced and settled in the Nordic balancing market (regulation power market). It is a TSO-TSO market with a common merit order. The second is balance settlement inside a country between balance responsible parties and the TSO. This settlement is governed by national balance agreements.[1237] The regime for balance settlement inside a country is about to be replaced by Nordic Balance Settlement (NBS).

1233 Energy Market Authority, Finland (2013), p. 23: "In the Nordic regulation power market all bids are collected in the joint Nordic merit order list and according to this list the production increases and decreases are carried out where they are most advantageous in the price order, however, taking into account congestions between control areas. This leads to the effective utilisation of the Nordic balancing resources".

1234 Energy Market Authority, Finland (2013), p. 23.

1235 Energy Market Authority, Finland (2013), pp. 35–39.

1236 Energy Market Authority, Finland (2013), pp. 49–52.

1237 NordREG (2006), section 3.1, p. 10; NordREG (2012), p. 29.

According to previous national regimes applied before the launch of NBS, an account holder must deliver the open balance according to the national TSO's rules in the main grid in the Elbas area where the account holder is registered.[1238]

A harmonised Nordic model for the calculation and pricing of imbalances was implemented in 2009 with one imbalance price for consumption and two imbalance prices for production.[1239]

However, more harmonisation was deemed necessary to achieve the goal of a common integrated end-user electricity market in the Nordic area. A supplier centric customer interface (model) is the chosen means to reach this goal. A supplier centric model means that most customer contacts are handled by the supplier.[1240]

NBS is an effort to reach common procedures for balance settlement between the TSO and the balance responsible parties in the Nordic area.[1241] The first version of the NBS settlement model was published in a 2011 design report. The design report included the main features of NBS. NBS will go live in the summer of 2015.

Imbalances, Balance Settlement, National Balance Agreements In the wholesale market, market participants (electricity suppliers, retailers, and large end consumers) have a duty to balance agreed flows with actual flows. Market participants may therefore need to purchase or sell electricity not only in the spot market (Elspot) but also in the intraday market (Elbas). Moreover, even market participants may need regulating power in the case of imbalances.

There are two imbalances: (1) production balance power (metered production—planned production—production regulation power); and (2) consumption balance power (metered consumption + planned production + trade—consumption regulation power).[1242]

> Estimates are used in the balance settlement for the profiled consumption (preliminary profiled consumption, PPC) on hourly basis. A new and improved estimate is made on an hourly basis when the metering data becomes available (final profiled consumption, FPC). The settlement of the difference between PPC and FPC is called the reconciliation settlement.[1243]

[1238] Nord Pool Spot Physical Market, Trading Appendix 2b, Elbas Market Regulations (18 February 2013), section 2.3.5.

[1239] NordREG (2012), p. 29: "In Finland generation under 1 MW installed capacity is settled as consumption (against a one-price-settlement), and in Norway generation units under 3 MW are settled as consumption".

[1240] NordREG (2013). See also Bjørnebye H and Alvik I (2012).

[1241] NordREG (2012), p. 29.

[1242] Nordic Balance Settlement (NBS): Common Balance & Reconciliation Settlement Design (22 December 2011), section 2.6. Consumption and sales are regarded as negative, production and purchase are regarded as positive.

[1243] Nordic Balance Settlement (NBS): Common Balance & Reconciliation Settlement Design (22 December 2011), section 2.7.

The two imbalances are priced in different ways. (a) There is a one-price model for the pricing of consumption balance power. Consumption balance power is priced according to the regulation price in the main direction in the price area. (b) On the other hand, a two-price model is used for the pricing of production balance power. Production balance power is priced according to the spot price in the balancing area, but if the imbalance cause regulation in the system the production balance power is priced with the marginal regulation price in the main direction.

In the reconciliation settlement, the difference between FPC and PPC is settled using hourly Elspot prices for the bidding area. What remains uncorrected is the different pricing in the two processes (Elspot prices v balancing power prices).

The Nordic model thus means different things to retailers and electricity producers. On one hand, both must settle balancing power with the TSO. On the other, there is a difference in pricing.

A retailer must settle balancing power with the TSO, if its purchases and sales are imbalanced. Where the TSO sells regulating power to a market participant, the price is set the same way as when the TSO buys regulating power. The TSO thus invoices the up regulation price for up regulation (normally higher than the Nord Pool market price) and the down regulation price for down regulation (normally lower than the Nord Pool market price).

An electricity producer must settle balancing power with the TSO, if it fails to produce according to plan. For instance, this can be the case where the supplier's power plant breaks down 10 min before the agreed hour of operation. The electricity producer cannot buy electricity from any other supplier as the intraday market (Elbas) has closed. However, the retailer must pay the supplier although the supplier has not generated any power. In this case, the TSO sells balancing power to the electricity producer, and the electricity producer resells the power to the retailer.

Where the market participant that buys regulating power from the TSO is an electricity producer, regulating power is priced differently. Electricity producers are given an incentive not to cause up regulation or down regulation in the first place. (a) During an hour with up-regulation, electricity producers producing too little will be invoiced the up-regulating price (normally higher than the market price). Electricity producers producing too much will only be paid the market price (not the up-regulating price). (b) During hours with down regulation, electricity producers producing too much will get paid the down-regulating price (normally lower than the market price). Producers producing too little will be invoiced the market price (not the down-regulating price).

The UK is another example of the use of a dual-price mechanism. While system buy prices (SBP) are charged to parties who are short, system sell prices (SSP) are paid to parties who are long. "Cash-out prices", that is, prices that generators and suppliers pay or are paid for imbalances, are based on the cost of the actions National Grid has had to take. There is also a "main" and "reverse" price. SBP is the main price and SSP the reverse price when the system is short. SSP is the main price and SBP the reverse price when the system is long.[1244]

Ancillary Services One can again distinguish between three categories of balancing services (ancillary services) or reserves provided by market participants[1245]: primary reserves (automatically activated frequency controlled normal operation reserves; automatically activated frequency controlled disturbance reserves); secondary reserves (load frequency control); and tertiary reserves (manually activated fast active disturbance reserves; manually activated regulation bids).

As the provision of tertiary reserves is considered in the balance settlement, it is partly harmonised in the Nordic area. To ensure that the primary and secondary reserves are not treated differently depending on the country,[1246] the Nordic TSOs agreed to harmonise the market rules for primary and secondary reserves as part of NBS.[1247]

NBS At the time of writing, balance control and balance regulation are largely harmonised in the Nordic area. (a) Balance settlement inside a country is a settlement between the system operators and the balance responsible parties. This settlement is governed by national balance agreements. (b) Between two countries, balance power is priced and settled according to the Nordel System Operation Agreement. (c) The Finnish, Norwegian and Swedish TSOs have decided to implement a harmonised balance settlement model at TSO level. They are planning to establish one common operational unit responsible for settlement.[1248]

The national TSOs used to be the national operators of the NBS settlement. In other words, they were regarded as Settlement Responsible (SR) parties responsible for the calculation of market participants' physical and financial obligations.

The Nordic Balance Settlement (NBS) project means that market participants' physical and financial obligations will be calculated by just one entity in the whole Nordic area. The national TSOs will outsource their tasks as national operators of the NBS settlement (that is, their tasks as Settlement Responsible parties) to the common Nordic SR.[1249]

However, the regulation of the electricity market is national in the Nordic area. Each TSO is regulated nationally. The Nordic TSOs cannot outsource their tasks to the Nordic SR unless it is permitted by the applicable national laws and the national laws are harmonised.[1250] Each TSO will continue to be responsible for regulatory

[1244] Ofgem (2009), para 3.49.

[1245] Nordic Balance Settlement (NBS): Common Balance & Reconciliation Settlement Design (22 December 2011), section 2.8.

[1246] For differences between the Nordic countries, see *ibid.*

[1247] *Ibid.*

[1248] Energy Market Authority, Finland (2013), p. 24.

[1249] Nordic Balance Settlement (NBS): Common Balance & Reconciliation Settlement Design (22 December 2011), Terminology: "Settlement Responsible (SR). SR has the responsibility to operate the NBS settlement".

[1250] For the required legislative changes, see *ibid*, section 7.2.

compliance at national level and each TSO will have to agree on the contractual framework the Nordic SR.

Each Balance Responsible Party[1251] will have just one balance settlement agreement, that is, the balance settlement agreement with the Nordic SR. This means that the balance settlement agreement must be in compliance with the applicable laws and regulations regardless of the country in which power is supplied or bought.[1252]

Contractual Framework for Balancing

The provision of ancillary services is facilitated by framework agreements (for master trading agreements generally, see Sect. 8.3). The framework agreements for balancing and the contractual framework for balance groups are discussed later in this book (Chap. 9).

References

Abrantes-Metz M, Rauterberg G, Verstein A (2013) Revolution in manipulation law: the new CFTC rules and the urgent need for economic and empirical analyses. Univ Pa J Bus Law 15 (2):357–418

ACER, Framework guidelines on capacity allocation and congestion management for electricity (29 July 2011)

ACER, Guidance on the application of the definitions set out in Article 2 of Regulation (EU) No 1227/2011 of the European Parliament and of the Council of 25 October 2011 on wholesale energy market integrity and transparency (20 December 2011)

ACER, Guidance on the application of Regulation (EU) No 1227/2011 of the European Parliament and of the Council of 25 October 2011 on wholesale energy market integrity and transparency, 3rd edn (29 October 2013)

BaFin (2011) Merkblatt – Hinweise zur Erlaubnispflicht von Geschäften im Zusammenhang mit Stromhandelsaktivitäten, June

Bhattacharyya SC (2011) Energy economics: concepts, issues, markets and governance. Springer, Heidelberg. doi:10.1007/978-0-85729-268-1

Bjørnebye H, Alvik I (2012) Legal analysis of contract models in a common Nordic electricity retail market: legal advantages and disadvantages with different contract approaches under a supplier centric model. A report commissioned by Nordic Energy Research. NordREG website

Bundesnetzagentur (2007) Report on the disturbance in the German and European power system on the 4th November 2006. Bonn, February

CESR-CEBS (2008) Technical advice to the European Commission on the review of commodities business, CESR/08-752, 15 October

[1251] *Ibid*, Terminology: "Balance Responsible Party (BRP). BRP is a player which has an agreement with the TSO (SR) obliging it to buy/sell balance power from/to TSO to neutralize its imbalances . . ."

[1252] *Ibid*, section 7.1.

Commission Communication, Implementing the framework for financial markets: action plan, COM(1999) 232 final (11 May 1999)
Commission, Draft working document on post-trading (23 May 2006)
Committee on Energy and Natural Resources (2010) Financial derivatives on energy markets. Senate Hearing 111-752. The U.S. Government Printing Office, Washington
Creti A, Fumagalli E, Fumagalli E (2010) Integration of electricity markets in Europe: relevant issues for Italy. Energy Policy 38(11):6966–6976. doi:10.1016/j.enpol.2010.07.013
Däuper O (2009) The oil market (empirical analysis). In: Zenke I, Schäfer R (eds) Energiehandel in Europa. Öl, Gas, Strom, Derivate, Zertifikate, 2nd edn. C.H. Beck, München, § 3
Deutsche Bundesbank (2013) Merkblatt über die Erteilung einer Erlaubnis zum Erbringen von Finanzdienstleistungen gemäß § 32 Abs. 1 KWG, April
DG Internal Market and Services, Public Consultation, Review of the Markets in Financial Instruments Directive (MIFID) (8 December 2010)
Diaz-Rainey I, Siems M, Ashton J (2011) The financial regulation of energy and environmental markets. J Financ Regul Compliance 19(4):355–369. doi:10.1108/13581981111182956
duPont JC (2009) A second chance at legal certainty: AIG collapse provides impetus to regulate credit default swaps. Admin Law Rev 61(4):843–870
EFET (2012) Towards a single European energy market. EFET website
Energinet.dk (2011) Cell controller pilot project: smart grid technology demonstration in Denmark for electric power systems with high penetration of distributed energy resources. 2011 Public Report. Energinet.dk website
Energy Market Authority, Finland (2013) National report 2013 to the agency for the Cooperation of Energy Regulators and to the European Commission, 12 July
Energy Market Authority, Finland (2014) National report 2014 to the agency for the Cooperation of Energy Regulators and to the European Commission, July 10
FERC (2003) Final report on price manipulation in western markets: fact-finding investigation of potential manipulation of electric and natural gas prices. Docket No. PA02-2-000. Prepared by the Staff of the Federal Energy Regulatory Commission, March
Finon D, Pignon V (2008) Electricity and long-term capacity adequacy: the quest for regulatory mechanism compatible with electricity market. Utilities Policy 16(3):143–158. doi:10.1016/j.jup.2008.01.002
Fischel DR, Ross DJ (1991) Should the law prohibit "Manipulation" in financial markets? Harv Law Rev 105(2):503–553
Godager K (2009) Impacts of MiFID on the Nordic electricity derivatives market. In: Zenke I, Schäfer R (eds) Energiehandel in Europa. Öl, Gas, Strom, Derivate, Zertifikate, 2nd edn. C.H. Beck, München, § 18
Green R (2010) Energy regulation in a low-carbon world. In: Moselle B, Padilla J, Schmalensee R (eds) Harnessing renewable energy in electric power systems: theory, practice, policy. Earthscan, Washington, pp 137–158
Härle PA (2010) B. Rechtliche Bewältigung es Handels an der EEX. In: Schwintowski HP (ed) Handbuch Energiehandel, 2nd edn. Erich Schmidt Verlag, Berlin, pp 399–456
Hogan WW (2009) Electricity market structure and infrastructure. In: Gallagher KS (ed) Acting in time on energy policy. Brookings Institution Press, Washington, DC, pp 128–161
Hogan WW (2010) Electricity wholesale market design in a low carbon future. In: Moselle B, Padilla J, Schmalensee R (eds) Harnessing renewable energy in electric power systems: theory, practice, policy. Earthscan, Washington, pp 113–136
Hotakainen M, Klimstra J (2011) Smart power generation, 4th improved edn. Avain, Helsinki
Hünerwadel A (2007) Arten und Formen des Stromhandels, insbesondere Börsen- und Derivathandel. In: Weber RH (ed) Stromhandel. Schulthess, Zürich, pp 49–64
Hunt S, Shuttleworth G (1996) Competition and choice in electricity. Wiley, Chichester
IMF (2013) Global financial stability report: old risks, new challenges. International Monetary Fund, Washington DC, April
ISDA (2003) Restoring confidence in U.S. energy trading markets. ISDA website, April

ISDA (2011) Re: notice of proposed rulemaking – position limits for derivatives. Letter to Commodity Futures Trading Commission, October 3

Joskow PL (2008) Capacity payments in imperfect electricity markets: need and design. Utilities Policy 16(3):161–162. doi:10.1016/j.jup.2008.01.006

Karas J, Sulamaa P (2013) The increasing scope and authority for power exchanges. Elforsk rapport 13:57, June

Kindler J (2008) The future role of power exchanges: a regulator's view. Energy Viewpoints 14:12–13

Krause T (2003) Evaluation of transmission pricing methods for liberalized markets – a literature survey. ETH, EEH power systems laboratory, Zürich, 7 July

Kumar P, Seppi DJ (1992) Futures manipulation with "Cash Settlement". J Finance 47 (4):1485–1502. doi:10.1111/j.1540-6261.1992.tb04666.x

Lanz M, Fricke B, Anthrakidis A et al (2011) CO2-Emissionsminderung durch Ausbau, informationstechnische Vernetzung und Netzoptimierung von Anlagen dezentraler, fluktuierender und erneuerbarer Energienutzung in Deutschland. Umweltbundesamt, Climate Change 20/2011

Ledgerwood S, Carpenter P (2012) A framework for the analysis of market manipulation. Rev Law Econ 8(1):253–295. doi:10.1515/1555-5879.1577

Ledgerwood S, Harris D (2012) A comparison of anti-manipulation rules in U.S. and EU electricity and natural gas markets: a proposal for a common standard. Energy Law J 33 (1):1–40

Lund P, Cherian S, Ackermann T (2006) A cell controller for autonomous operation of a 60 kV distribution area. Int J Distributed Energy Resour 2(2):83–100

Madlener R, Kaufmann M (2002) Power exchange spot market trading in Europe: theoretical considerations and empirical evidence. OSCOGEN, Discussion Paper No. 5, March

Mäntysaari P (2010a) The law of corporate finance. General principles and EU law, vol I: Cash flow, risk, agency, information. Springer, Heidelberg

Mäntysaari P (2010b) The law of corporate finance. General principles and EU law, vol II: Contracts I General. Springer, Heidelberg

Mäntysaari P (2010c) The law of corporate finance. General principles and EU law, vol III: Funding, exit, takeovers. Springer, Heidelberg

Markham JW, Harty DJ (2008) For whom the bell tolls: the demise of exchange trading floors and the growth of ECNs. J Corp Law 33:865–939

McLean B, Elkind P (2004) The smartest guys in the room. The amazing rise and scandalous fall of Enron, updated paperback edn. Penguin, The United States of America

Meeus L (2006) Power exchange – auction trading platform design. Ph.D. Thesis, Katholieke Universiteit Leuven, Belgium

Meller E, Walter B (2009) Die Bedeutung des Energiehandels für die Energieversorgung. In: Zenke I, Schäfer R (eds) Energiehandel in Europa. Öl, Gas, Strom, Derivate, Zertifikate, 2nd edn. C.H. Beck, München, § 9

Midttun A, Handeland J, Henriksen JT et al (2001) Nordic business strategies. In: Midttun A (ed) European energy industry business strategies. Elsevier Global Energy Policy and Economics Series. Elsevier, the Netherlands, pp 23–74

Ministére de l'économie, de l'industrie et de l'emploi (2010) Rapport du groupe de travail sur la volatilité des prix du pétrole, sous la présidence de Jean-Marie Chevalier, février/February

Monopolkommission (2013) Sondergutachten 65. Energie 2013: Wettbewerb in Zeiten der Energiewende. Sondergutachten der Monopolkommission gemäß § 62 Abs. 1 EnWG. Bonn

Monopolkommission (2014) Hauptgutachten XX: Eine Wettbewerbsordnung für die Finanzmärkte. Zwanzigstes Hauptgutachten der Monopolkommission gemäß § 44 Abs. 1 Satz 1 GWB – 2012/2013

Murray JV (2009) The death of copyright protection in individual price valuations, a flawed merger doctrine, and financial market manipulation: New York Mercantile Exchange v. IntercontinentalExchange. Buffalo Law Rev 57(1):279–346

Neveling S, Schönrock KP (2009) Nicht standardisierte Liefer- und Handelsverträge sowie vertragliche Voraussetzungen auf der Netzzugangsseite. In: Zenke I, Schäfer R (eds) Energiehandel in Europa. Öl, Gas, Strom, Derivate, Zertifikate, 2nd edn. C.H. Beck, München, § 29

NordREG (2006) Development of a common Nordic balance settlement. Report 3/2006

NordREG (2008) Towards harmonised Nordic balancing services: common principles for cost allocation and settlement. Report 3/2008

NordREG (2012) Nordic market report 2012. Report 3/2012

NordREG (2013) Road map towards a common harmonised Nordic end-user market. NordREG Report 5/2013

Ofgem (2009) Liquidity in the GB wholesale energy markets, 8 June

Ostrom E (2005) Doing institutional analysis. Digging deeper than markets and hierarchies. In: Ménard C, Shirley MM (eds) Handbook of new institutional economics. Springer, the Netherlands, pp 819–848

Pilgram T (2010) A. Formen des Handels an der EEX. In: Schwintowski HP (ed) Handbuch Energiehandel, 2nd edn. Erich Schmidt Verlag, Berlin, pp 339–398

Pirrong C (2001) Manipulation of cash-settled futures contracts. J Bus 74(2):221–244. doi:10.1086/209671

Pirrong C (2010) Energy market manipulation: definition, diagnosis, and deterrence. Energy Law J 31(1):1–20

Rious V, Roques F, Perez Y (2012) Which electricity market design to encourage the development of demand response? EUI Working Paper RSCAS 2012/12

Rud L (2009) Essays on electricity markets, SNF Report No. 10/09. Online version. Institute for Research in Economics and Business Administration. Available at SNF website. http://www.snf.no/

Sioshansi FP (ed) (2008) Competitive electricity markets: design, implementation, performance. Elsevier, Oxford

Spence DB, Prentice R (2012) The transformation of American energy markets and the problem of market power. B C Law Rev 53(1):131–202

Spicker J (2010) A. Formen des OTC-Handels. In: Schwintowski HP (ed) Handbuch Energiehandel, 2nd edn. Erich Schmidt Verlag, Berlin, pp 31–152

THEMA Consulting Group (2014) Demand response in the Nordic electricity market. TemaNord 2014:553. Nordic Council of Ministers, Copenhagen. doi: 10.6027/TN2014-553

Thomas S (2001) Corporate strategies in the British electricity supply industry. In: Midttun A (ed) European energy industry business strategies. Elsevier Global Energy Policy and Economics Series. Elsevier, the Netherlands, pp 75–150

U.S. Energy Information Administration (2002) Derivatives and risk management in the petroleum, natural gas, and electricity industries, October

Wolfram CD (1998) Strategic bidding in a multiunit auction: an empirical analysis of bids to supply electricity in England and Wales. RAND J Econ 29:703–725. doi:10.2307/2556090

Wolfram CD (1999) Electricity markets: should the rest of the world adopt the United Kingdom's reforms? Regulation 22(4):48–53

Chapter 5
Transmission Marketplaces

5.1 General Remarks

Transmission capacity is allocated in the transmission marketplace. The allocation methods can be market-based (explicit or implicit auctions) or not market-based (bilateral contracting). One can also distinguish between primary and secondary capacity markets.

Producers Electricity producers need a transmission marketplace because electricity cannot be supplied without transmission capacity.[1] Their actions are influenced by the regulation and structure of the transmission marketplace. For example, risk management and investment in both generation and transmission assets can depend on whether electricity producers may use bilateral contracting and long-term contracts in their dealings with transmission service providers. Moreover, investment in generation assets and energy-intensive industrial processes can depend on whether the regulation of transmission costs and prices is designed to give market participants locational signals. The fact that these signals have so far been weak may have helped to increase the distance between electricity generation and consumption.

Monopoly Electricity transmission is a natural monopoly. TSOs are natural sellers of transmission capacity rights and the only players in a position to offer the required firm transmission hedges (see Chap. 12).[2] The regulatory authorities will fix or approve the transmission tariffs or their methodologies, and monitor the TSOs' capacity allocation and congestion management rules.[3] Electricity firms will have to adapt to the relevant TSO's rules.

---

[1] For definitions, see points 3 and 5 of Article 2 of Directive 2009/72/EC (Third Electricity Directive).

[2] EFET (2007).

[3] Article 37 of Directive 2009/72/EC (Third Electricity Directive).

P. Mäntysaari, *EU Electricity Trade Law*, DOI 10.1007/978-3-319-16513-4_5

Operation and Ownership of Transmission Assets In principle, transmission assets could be owned and operated in different ways. (a) They could be owned and operated by one entity or by different entities and (b) the assets could be part of a system operation business (in which case they are owned by the TSO) or a stand-alone business (in which case they are not owned by the TSO).

In the EU, the main rule is that transmission assets must be owned by the TSO. This is one of the cornerstones of ownership unbundling. Ownership unbundling is regarded as necessary to remove "the incentive for vertically integrated undertakings to discriminate against competitors as regards network access and investment".[4]

Ownership unbundling works in three ways in transmission. First, each undertaking which owns a transmission system must also act as a TSO.[5] Cross-border joint-ventures between two or more TSOs are nevertheless permitted.[6] Second, there are restrictions on such an undertaking's right to own a business that performs any of the functions of generation or supply.[7] Third, the same restrictions govern the rights of a firm that performs any of the functions of generation or supply to own a TSO.[8]

In other words, ownership unbundling implies "the appointment of the network owner as the system operator and its independence from any supply and production interests".

In the US, transmission assets are not owned by the system operator. The entities responsible for managing system operations are Regional Transmission Organizations (RTOs) or Independent System Operators (ISOs).

The restructuring of the industry began with the Public Utility Regulatory Policies Act of 1978. Transmission was opened up by the Energy Policy Act of 1992 which was complemented by FERC's Orders No. 888 (in 1996) and No. 2000 (in 1999). Open access to transmission services was designed to foster the independent operation of the power grid. FERC believed that RTOs/ISOs were the best means to implement the open access provisions of the Energy Policy Act of 1992. Neither Congress nor FERC have forced the owners of transmission assets to cede control over the assets to independent operators. Section 219(c) of the Energy Policy Act of 2005 offered rate incentives to owners of transmission assets that joined RTOs/ISOs.[9]

Even in the EU, there are system operators that do not own the transmission system. A Member State may designate an independent system operator (ISO) under certain circumstances.[10] An ISO in the European sense is independent of the owner of transmission assets and owns computing and communication assets.[11] Merchant lines raise the question whether the can be transmission systems that are not owned by a TSO (these issues are not discussed in this book).

---

[4] Recital 11 of Directive 2009/72/EC (Third Electricity Directive).

[5] Article 9(1)(a) of Directive 2009/72/EC (Third Electricity Directive)

[6] Article 9(5) of Directive 2009/72/EC (Third Electricity Directive).

[7] Article 9(2) of Directive 2009/72/EC (Third Electricity Directive).

[8] Articles 9(1)(b) and 9(2) of Directive 2009/72/EC (Third Electricity Directive).

[9] US Senate Committee on Energy and Natural Resources (2010), statement of Vincent P. Duane.

[10] Article 13(1) of Directive 2009/72/EC (Third Electricity Directive).

[11] Article 13(4) of 2009/72/EC (Third Electricity Directive).

Characteristic Problems The TSO faces certain characteristic problems related to capacity and pricing (for characteristic problems inherent in transmission contracts, see Sect. 10.1). First, the TSO must possess enough transmission capacity and prices should cover costs. Capacity costs are the TSO's most important cost factor. Prices should facilitate long-term investment in the transmission grid and cover short-term costs for the use of the system. Second, scarce transmission capacity should be allocated. Capacity cannot be allocated without information about estimated and actual use and congestion. Actual use and congestion can be estimated in advance but become known in real-time or later. Loop flows make it more difficult to predict actual use.[12]

> Actual electricity flows depend on many things ranging from changes in load to the weather. They also depend on loop flows caused by Kirchhoff's laws. Any transaction between two nodes of a meshed network induces some flow in each of its lines.
>
> Loop flows cause two problems. First, loop flow makes it more difficult to determine actual flow-based paths (parallel flows) when multiple users compete on the same transmission system.[13] Second, loop flow can also make it more difficult to forecast the actual use of the transmission system. The more transactions and the more meshed the network, the higher the chance for mismatch between commercial exchanges and physical flows.[14]

Mechanisms for the Allocation of Transmission Capacity Scarce transmission capacity cannot be allocated without information about congestion. One can, therefore, distinguish between: (a) methods used for electricity flows in the more distant future when congestion can only be estimated; and (b) methods that are used when actual congestion is known.

The mechanisms for the allocation of transmission capacity necessarily consist of three components. As the allocation of transmission capacity means bringing together a market participant, a designated electricity flow, and transmission capacity, it is necessary to: allocate transmission capacity to a market participant; allocate transmission capacity to a designated electricity flow; and allocate costs and the price.

When transmission capacity is allocated for electricity flows in the more distant future, it is customary to use a combination of market-based or not market-based mechanisms (Sect. 5.3).

---

[12] Vogelsang I (2006).

[13] The FERC has described the phenomenon of parallel path flow as follows: "In general, utilities transact with one another based on a contract path concept. For pricing purposes, parties assume that power flows are confined to a specified sequence of interconnected utilities that are located on a designated contract path. However, in reality power flows are rarely confined to a designated contract path. Rather, power flows over multiple parallel paths that may be owned by several utilities that are not on the contract path. The actual power flow is controlled by the laws of physics which cause power being transmitted from one utility to another to travel along multiple parallel paths and divide itself along the lines of least resistance. This parallel path flow is sometimes called 'loop flow.'" *Indiana Michigan Power Co. and Ohio Power Co.*, 64 FERC ¶ 61,184, at 62,545 (1993).

[14] Purchala K et al. (2005).

Mechanisms that are not market-based include first-come-first-served (priority list), pro-rata rationing, and retention. The first-come-first-served (priority list) mechanism means here the allocation of capacity according to the order in which the transmission requests have been received by the TSO. Pro-rata rationing means that all requests are partially accepted and partially curtailed in proportion to the requested capacity. Retention means that a proportion of the available capacity is reserved by electricity producers, suppliers, or large end consumers under long-term contracts. There are legal constraints on the use of long-term contracts (Sect. 5.2).

To work properly, the market-based methods would require the existence of competition in the market.[15] The market based-methods include explicit auctions and implicit auctions.

When actual congestion is known inside the control area of the TSO, one can apply particular congestion alleviation methods (Sect. 5.5). Reducing cross-zonal or cross-border flows would be a particular but limited way to manage congestion.[16]

Models for the Allocation of Transmission Capacity Between Designated Flows It is not enough to choose a mechanism for the allocation of transmission capacity between market participants. The transmission capacity must also be allocated between designated electricity flows.

One can choose between different models for this purpose (Sect. 5.4). They can be combined with the chosen mechanism for the allocation of transmission capacity between market participants. The most important factors influencing the choice of the model are the general market model (complete vertical integration or liberalised market) and the structure of the grid. In liberalised electricity markets, one can distinguish between four high-level models for the allocation of transmission capacity: (1) the contract path model; (2) the flow-based model; (3) the point-to-point model with implicit flows; and (4) the entry-exit model.

Pricing Models The mechanism for capacity allocation goes hand in hand with the pricing model (Sect. 5.7).

The pricing model can influence the behaviour of the users of the transmission system by giving locational and temporal signals for electricity supply (feed-in) and extraction (load). (a) Transmission infrastructure is used in a more efficient way when the signals reflect the costs caused by grid users. The existence of such signals contributes to the efficient use of transmission infrastructure in particular where the transmission system is well interconnected and has several alternative sources of supply. (b) The absence of signals that reflect costs implies that costs are socialised. This reduces the efficiency of the use of infrastructure.[17]

[15] Crampes C (2003), p. 115.

[16] Article 16(2) of Regulation 714/2009 2009 on conditions for access to the network for cross-border exchanges in electricity.

[17] This is reflected in Article 14(2) of Regulation 714/2009 on conditions for access to the network for cross-border exchanges in electricity.

Transmission tariffs can have a strong impact on investments in electricity generation and transmission assets.[18]

EU Law and National Practices Some of the many models have been adopted at EU level for the purposes of the allocation (Sect. 5.6) and pricing (Sect. 5.8) of transmission capacity. There is still variation between the practices of different markets and different Member States of the EU although the EU Congestion Management Guidelines[19] have contributed to the convergence of practices.

Disclosure, Market Conduct and Market Abuse Regime Much of the regulation of transmission and transmission marketplaces is sector-specific. This reflects the fact that transmission capacity is allocated by the TSO that has a duty to manage electricity flows on the system.[20]

On the other hand, transmission marketplaces may partly be governed by the same statutory disclosure, market conduct, and market abuse regime as other physical electricity marketplaces (see Sect. 4.7 and 4.10.1): (a) Obviously, this regime must apply where transmission capacity is allocated implicitly. (b) Moreover, TSOs and other primary owners of data relating to transportation have a disclosure duty under Regulation 543/2013 amending Annex I to Regulation 714/2009.[21] (c) REMIT that regulates disclosure and reporting obligations and prohibits market abuse applies to transmission markets in the EU as they are regarded as wholesale energy markets and to transmission contracts as they are regarded as "transportation" contracts. REMIT applies to transportation contracts and related derivatives provided that they are traded but irrespective of where and how they are traded.[22] The definition of wholesale energy products is very broad according to the wording of REMIT[23] and ACER Guidance on the application of REMIT.[24] (d) It is again clear that the MiFID II/MiFIR regime does not apply to pure transmission marketplaces as transmission contracts are not financial instruments. Neither does EMIR that applies to OTC derivatives.

---

[18] Ruester S et al. (2012), Executive Summary.

[19] ACER, Framework Guidelines on Capacity Allocation and Congestion Management for Electricity (29 July 2011).

[20] Point (d) of Article 12 of Directive 2009/72/EC (Third Electricity Directive).

[21] Regulation 543/2013 (on submission and publication of data in electricity markets and amending Annex I to Regulation 714/2009).

[22] Point 4 of Article 4 of Regulation 1227/2011 (REMIT). See also Commission Implementing Regulation 1348/2014 for the details of the data reporting obligation.

[23] Recital 5 of Regulation 1227/2011 (REMIT).

[24] ACER, Guidance on the application of Regulation (EU) No 1227/2011 of the European Parliament and of the Council of 25 October 2011 on wholesale energy market integrity and transparency, 3rd edn (29 October 2013), pp. 15–16.

5.2 Long-Term Contracts

Long-term contracts are a customary way for electricity firms to manage risk. The prohibition of long-term contracts would have a negative impact on long-term investment. For instance, where access to the grid and the use of transmission capacity cannot be secured in advance, investments in new generation capacity are subject to a higher risk. The higher risk exposure of investors could hamper investment and reduce security of supply in the long term.

Even transmission firms may need long-term contracts to reduce investment risk, increase the availability of funding, and reduce funding costs. Long-term contracts help the firm to secure its long-term cash flow in advance.[25]

Long-term contracts for the use of transmission capacity have been a common phenomenon in Europe. For instance, 40–60 % of the capacity on interconnectors was reserved for long-term import contracts in 2001[26] and the Commission pointed out in 2007 that "a significant proportion of existing interconnector capacity" was still allocated based on the priority rights or "pre-liberalisation" contracts. These capacity reservations often related to some of the most congested interconnectors.[27]

Non-discrimination However, bilateral long-term contracts raise the question of non-discrimination. Non-discrimination is regarded as one of the fundamental principles of Community law. The use of long-term transmission contracts is nowadays constrained by the prohibition of discrimination in the electricity sector.

The Third Electricity Directive generally requires TSOs to ensure "non-discrimination as between system users or classes of system users".[28] Regulation 714/2009 requires the coordinated allocation of cross-border capacity through non-discriminatory market-based solutions.[29] Long-term contracts are thus "disqualified as a method for allocating scarce interconnector capacity".[30]

According to ACER's CACM Framework Guidelines, the CACM Network Codes "shall foresee that the options for enabling risk hedging for cross-border trading are Financial Transmission Rights (FTR) or Physical Transmission Rights

---

[25] See, for example, Talus K and Wälde T (2006), point 3.

[26] Commission, Role of interconnectors in the electricity market. A competition perspective. Press release, MEMO/01/76, 12 March 2001.

[27] DG Competition Report on Energy Sector Inquiry, SEC(2006) 1724 (10 January 2007), paras 548–550.

[28] Point (f) of Article 12 of Directive 2009/72/EC (Third Electricity Directive). For connection points, see Article 23. For the duties of regulatory authorities, see point (d) of Article 36.

[29] Article 12(2) of Regulation 714/2009 on conditions for access to the network for cross-border exchanges in electricity.

[30] DG Competition Report on Energy Sector Inquiry, SEC(2006) 1724 (10 January 2007), para 550. For the trend, see, for example, de Hauteclocque A and Talus K (2011).

(PTR) with Use-It-Or-Sell-It (UIOSI), unless appropriate cross-border financial hedging is offered in liquid financial markets on both side of an interconnector". Moreover, the CACM Network Codes "shall require that the TSOs provide a single platform (single point of contact) for the allocation of long-term transmission rights (PTR and FTR) at European level" with regional platforms as a transitional arrangement.[31]

Competition Law In addition to the principle of non-discrimination, the use of long-term transmission contracts is constrained by general competition laws that address the problem of infrastructure foreclosure (Sect. 3.7.3).

In the *Skagerrak cable* case, 60 % of the total capacity of the connecting Western Denmark and Norway was reserved under an agreement with a duration of 20 years and the remaining 40 % under an agreement with a duration of 25 years. The parties agreed to free capacity after the Commission had expressed its doubts.[32]

In *VEMW*, the question was whether priority rights under long-term transmission contracts discriminate other parties that may not use the scarce transmission resources.[33] According to the CJEU, comparable situations must not be treated differently unless the difference in treatment is objectively justified.[34] There was no such justification in *VEMW*.[35] In other words, the CJEU came close to a ban.

With these constraints in mind, we can now study market-based and not market-based capacity allocation mechanisms.

5.3 Mechanisms for Capacity Allocation Between Market Participants

Generally, there are various possible mechanisms for congestion management and the allocation of scarce transmission capacity between market participants (for EU law, see Sect. 5.6). The mechanisms can be used in different contexts. One can distinguish between: (a) *cross-border* or *cross-zonal* congestion management (capacity allocation); and (b) *intra-zonal* congestion management (capacity allocation). One can also distinguish between mechanisms applied to prevent congestion (c) on a *day-ahead* or *intraday* basis or (d) in *real time*.

[31] ACER, Framework Guidelines on Capacity Allocation and Congestion Management for Electricity (29 July 2011), section 4.1.

[32] Commission, Press Release IP/01/30, Increased scope for electricity imports competition in Northern Europe—a step forward towards an internal market for electricity, 11 January 2001. See Cameron PD (2007), p. 341 paras 13.53–54.

[33] C-17/03 VEMW and others [2005] ECR I-4983, para 49.

[34] C-17/03 VEMW and others [2005] ECR I-4983, para 48.

[35] C-17/03 VEMW and others [2005] ECR I-4983, para 71.

Cross-Border or Cross-Zonal Congestion Management (Capacity Allocation) It is characteristic of cross-border congestion management that capacity cannot be allocated before the size of the available cross-border transmission capacity has been estimated. System operators must predict the behaviour of market participants and calculate the available capacity in advance, because traders need time to use the information.[36] The transmission capacity can be different in the two directions.

The European Commission's Sector Inquiry listed the customary mechanisms for the allocation of cross-border transmission capacity.[37] The mechanisms can be market-based or not market-based (Sect. 5.1).

One of the possible alternatives would be to use *priority-based* rules in cross-border capacity allocation. There can be different priority-based methods. The most common method uses chronological ranking of reservations and the first-come-first-served principle. This method favours incumbents at the cost of new market participants and long-term contracts at the cost of short-term trading.

> On EPEX Spot, the intraday capacity service allows for the allocation of cross-border capacity continuously and anonymously under the first-come-first-served rule. That capacity is currently allocated at no cost. The required quantity of cross-border capacity is automatically booked and the remaining capacity is adjusted.[38] The Intraday Capacity Service is not used between the control areas of German TSOs or between the control areas of German and Austrian TSOs.[39]

On the other hand, it is possible to use *market-based* mechanisms—explicit and implicit auctions—instead of priority-based rules. There is a fundamental difference between explicit and implicit auctions in cross-border capacity allocation.

In explicit auctions, transmission capacity is auctioned to the market separately. Transmission capacity is normally auctioned in portions through annual, monthly, or daily auctions.[40] Explicit auctions can thus be for contracts with a relatively long duration. The fact that transmission capacity and electricity are traded separately can reduce transparency. The lack of information about the prices of the other commodity can hamper price convergence.

Implicit auctions can increase price convergence more compared with explicit auctions.[41] They are used in spot markets within one zone. Cross-border implicit auctions are usually referred to as either market coupling (if two or more power exchanges of national electricity markets couple their price zones) or market-

---

[36] The most important components are; Total Transfer Capacity (TTC, the maximal possible power transfer between two adjacent areas); Transmission Reliability Margin (TRM, cross-border capacity withdrawn from the market for security reasons); Net Transfer Capacity (NTC, NTC = TTC – TRM); Already Allocated Capacity (AAC); and Available Transmission Capacity (ATC, cross-border capacity available for commercial trade, ATC = NTC – AAC).

[37] DG Competition Report on Energy Sector Inquiry, SEC(2006) 1724 (10 January 2007), para 545, Table 27.

[38] EPEX Spot Exchange Rules (28 November 2014), Title 4, Chapter 3.

[39] EPEX Spot Exchange Rules (28 November 2014), Title 4, Chapter 3.

[40] CWE Auction Rules, Version 1.0, Article 1.04.

[41] Creti A et al. (2010) citing DG competition report on energy sector inquiry (2007), p. 186.

splitting (if one power exchange splits an area into several price zones in case of congestion between them).[42] In market coupling, the day-ahead transmission capacity is used to integrate the spot markets in different bidding areas. Implicit auctions help to increase electricity flows from surplus areas (low price areas) to deficit areas (high price areas).

Intra-Zonal Capacity Allocation (Congestion Management) Other kinds of congestion management mechanisms are used when congestion is managed within one zone that is treated as a "copper plate"—such as the high-voltage grid in Germany[43]—with no transmission constraints for market participants. These mechanisms will not replace the mechanisms for the allocation of cross-border transmission capacity as it would require overinvestment in the grid to make transmission networks behave like a "copper plate".

The mechanisms include: the socialisation of congestion costs in transmission tariffs (the OTC market model); the socialisation of congestion costs as uplift payments (the exchange model); and locational marginal pricing (nodal pricing). The choice of the mechanism can depend on the structure of the market in the following ways.

Where electricity is mostly traded in the OTC market, market participants have plenty of discretion when negotiating their contracts. On the other hand, grid limitations are not visible to market participants. Consequently, such a market requires a well-developed and strong grid, and the problem of congestion must be solved by the TSO that also has to cover the incurred costs. The costs are customarily socialised, meaning that all users of the grid pay them under a form of transmission tariffs.[44]

Where electricity is traded on an exchange and auctions are used instead of continuous trading, there is a uniform electricity price. During the matching process, the cheapest generation gets priority according to the merit order regardless of grid limitations. If there is congestion, some out-of-merit generators are dispatched at the cost of in-merit generators. The cost of this action constitutes the uplift charge and is added to the electricity price.[45]

Where locational marginal pricing (nodal pricing) is used, pricing is based on the marginal cost of supplying electricity at a specific location in the grid by considering both the marginal cost of generation and the physical aspects of the transmission system. Consequently, congestion costs are not socialised. Each market participant pays for the congestion it causes. The congestion charge is the difference between energy prices at the generation node and the consumption node. Market participants can hedge against this congestion charge by entering into

[42] See Duthaler C and Finger M (2008).

[43] Spicker J (2010), p. 50, number 33.

[44] Purchala K et al. (2005).

[45] Purchala K et al. (2005): "An alternative market organization is a centralized pool model".

financial transmission contracts (FTR). Nodal pricing is regarded as efficient[46] under certain circumstances (Sect. 5.7.6).[47]

Congestion Alleviation Methods One can distinguish between day-ahead capacity allocation and real-time congestion management. Real-time congestion is dealt with by congestion alleviation methods that re-arrange the generation-load pattern. This can be achieved by redispatching production units and/or by shedding load.[48] Congestion alleviation methods are an alternative to building more transmission capacity (Sect. 5.5).

5.4 Models for the Allocation of Transmission Capacity Between Designated Flows

The mechanisms for the allocation of transmission capacity between market participants (Sect. 5.3) are combined with models for the allocation of transmission capacity between designated electricity flows. There are estimated flows in the more distant future and actual flows. We can first study the former (for actual flows and congestion alleviation methods, see Sect. 5.5).

Grid Structure Regulators and TSOs must choose the appropriate model. One of the factors that influence the choice of the model is the structure of the transmission grid.

There are radial and meshed grids. While a radial topology is applied to reduce costs (or to benefit a limited number of firms), a meshed topology is chosen for increasing reliability and security of supply. The choice of a meshed topology depends on the voltage level and the impact of failures.

The traditional system hierarchy is that there is a high voltage transmission level (for example, more than 110 kV) with a meshed grid, a medium voltage distribution level (for example, 6–35 kV or 6–70 kV) with a radial grid, and a low voltage distribution level (for example, less than 1 kV or 0.4 kV) with a radial grid.

In this way, the impact of failures at the distribution level is limited to local outages. As failures at the high voltage transmission level would lead to blackouts that have a large impact, their likelihood is reduced by choosing a meshed topology. For instance, it is then easier to replace the output of a failed generation unit with the output of far away generation units.[49]

Models There are various models for the allocation of transmission capacity between designated electricity flows. One can distinguish between: the contract

[46] See Purchala K et al. (2005).

[47] See OECD/IEA (2005), p. 77.

[48] Purchala K et al. (2005).

[49] Pérez-Arriaga IJ and Smeers Y (2003), p. 178.

path model; the flow-based model; the point-to-point model; and the entry-exit model. (a, b) The contract path model and the flow-based model can be combined with market-based mechanisms (that is, with explicit or implicit auctions). While the contract path model is more likely to be used in radial parts of the transmission grid, the flow-based model can be used even in a meshed grid with loop flows. (c) The allocation mechanism is not market-based under the point-to-point model, because all transmission services are reserved. (d) In contrast, the entry-exit model focuses on pricing rather than the physical allocation of transmission capacity. We can study the models in more detail.

The Contract Path Model Under the contract path model, the parties agree that power flows along a "contract path" consisting of the chain of companies that control the transmission infrastructure between the ultimate receipt and delivery points.

The actual path can be determined by the contract path where the grid is radial (no loop flow). When this is not the case, the contract path is more suitable for the allocation of costs or for pricing rather than for capacity allocation. For instance, it is clear whose transmission assets are used where the transmission infrastructure is owned by just one entity and the flows are not connected to the transmission system of any third-party entity (no loop flow over any third party's lines).

The actual path of electricity that moves through the network is customarily not determined by the contract path fiction in most transmission grids. Most transmission grids are meshed grids. The contract-path model cannot work acceptably in a meshed grid unless cross-zonal electricity trade remains limited and predictable so regional interdependencies and externalities (such as loop-flows) can largely be ignored.[50]

In Europe, the contract path model has been used in some implicit auctions for transmission capacity in radial parts of the grid such as on interconnectors.[51] When the contract path model is used in implicit auctions, the relevant TSO allocates a certain amount of day-ahead transmission rights to the electricity exchange.

In European gas markets, network charges must not be calculated based on contract paths.[52]

"Postage stamp" pricing (Sect. 5.7.5) is an example of the use of the contract path model. Under the postage stamp model, transmission contracts set a single price for energy flow over each TSO's (or, in vertically integrated markets, each utility's) transmission system. The calculation of entry-exit tariffs for each TSO's transmission system results in a "postage stamp" tariff. The terms postage stamp tariff and postage stamp pricing come from the fact that the rate does not depend on how far the electricity moves within one entity's transmission system.

[50] Duthaler C and Finger M (2008).

[51] Duthaler C and Finger M (2008).

[52] Article 13(1) of Regulation 715/2009 on conditions for access to natural gas transmission networks.

The Flow-Based Model The contract path model is not suitable for a meshed grid with loop flows. One solution could be to try to trace the actual flows and include them in the transmission rights. This leads to the flow-based model.[53] Under the flow-based model, electricity is assumed to flow through all parallel paths. The flow-based approach essentially tries to maintain the physical contract-path fiction by accounting for all its implications (such as loop-flows) within a meshed grid.[54] The flow-based model is complemented by flow-based pricing (Sect. 5.8.4).

> In the EU, the flow-based model is applied to cross-border electricity transmission systems. The magnitudes of cross-border flows hosted and of cross-border flows designated as originating and/or ending in national transmission systems are determined based on the physical flows of electricity actually measured during a given period.[55]

It can nevertheless be difficult to measure actual flows when multiple users compete on the same transmission system. Several simplifying assumptions may be necessary to maintain the physical contract-path fiction. The model is unsustainable if the assumptions turn out to be wrong.[56] The flow-based model has in some cases been replaced by the point-to-point model.

The Point-to-Point Model The point-to-point model means that (1) all transmission services are reserved, and the reservations of transmission capacity permit the customer to (2) receive up to a specific amount of power into the grid at specified points of receipt, and to (3) deliver up to a specific amount of power from the grid at specified points of delivery.[57]

> Many of the restructured US electricity markets experimented with the flow-based model in the decade between 1997 and 2007. The experiences of PJM (the RTO for thirteen states and the District of Columbia), CAISO (the California ISO), and ERCOT (Texas) were not satisfying. These three markets abandoned the flow-based zonal model and replaced it by a point-to-point model.[58]
>
> The Federal Energy Regulatory Commission's (FERC) Order No. 888[59] requires public utilities to file "a single open access tariff that offers both network, load-based service and point-to-point, contract-based service".[60]

---

[53] Duthaler C and Finger M (2008).

[54] *Ibid.*

[55] Article 13(5) of Regulation 714/2009 on conditions for access to the network for cross-border exchanges in electricity.

[56] Duthaler C and Finger M (2008).

[57] See Harvey SM et al. (1996), p. 46.

[58] Duthaler C and Finger M (2008). See also CAISO (2006) (submission of CAISO's Market Redesign and Technology Upgrade Tariff or "MRTU Tariff"); ERCOT (2008); Hogan WW (1999).

[59] FERC, Promoting Wholesale Competition Through Open Access Non-discriminatory Transmission Services by Public Utilities; Recovery of Stranded Costs by Public Utilities and Transmitting Utilities, Order No. 888 (10 May 1996).

[60] FERC, Order No. 888, Final Rule. Open Access Transmission Tariff, Section 1.48: "Transmission Service: Point-To-Point Transmission Service provided under Part II of the Tariff on a firm and non-firm basis".

The FERC has "characterized point-to-point service as involving designated points of entry into and exit from the transmitting utility's system, with a designated amount of transfer capability at each point".[61] In Order No. 888 and the Open Access Transmission Tariff, the FERC has defined various qualified point-to-point transmission services.[62] The Open Access Transmission Tariff was amended by Order No. 890.[63]

The minimum term of firm point-to-point transmission service is one day (day-ahead). The maximum term is specified in the service agreement.[64]

As all transmission services are reserved under this model, there should be rules on reservation priority, including rules setting out how the available transmission capacity is calculated.

In the US, both Order No. 888 and Order No. 890 provide for reservation priority. (a) Long-term firm point-to-point transmission service is available on a first-come, first-served basis. (b) Reservations for short-term firm point-to-point transmission service are conditional based upon the length of the requested transaction.[65] (c) There are reservation priorities for some existing firm service customers (wholesale requirements and transmission-only, with a contract term of 5 years or more). These customers have a right to roll over or renew the contract when the contract expires.[66] The required contract term used to be shorter under Order No. 888 (one year or more).[67]

Order No. 888 did not provide for a methodology for calculating the available transmission capacity. This increased the potential for discrimination and made undue discrimination more difficult to detect.[68] Neither did it provide for coordinated, open and transparent transmission planning.

For this reason, the FERC adopted nine planning principles that public utility transmission providers are required to follow.[69] The planning principles relate to: coordination[70]; openness[71]; transparency[72]; information exchange[73]; comparability[74]; dispute resolution[75];

[61] El Paso Electric Company v. Southwestern Public Service Company, 68 FERC _ 61,182 at 61,926 n.9 (1994) (citing Entergy Services, Inc., 58 FERC _ 61,234 at 61,768 (1993), reh'g dismissed, 68 FERC_ 61,399 (1994)). Cited in FERC, Order No. 888, Final Rule, footnote 65.

[62] FERC, Order No. 888, Open Access Transmission Tariff, Section 1.35 (Point To Point Transmission Service); Section 1.13 (Firm Point-To-Point Transmission Service), Section 1.18 (Long-Term Firm Point-To-Point Transmission Service), Section 1.42 (Short-Term Firm Point-To-Point Transmission Service), Section 1.27 (Non-Firm Point-To-Point Transmission Service).

[63] FERC, Preventing Undue Discrimination and Preference in Transmission Service, Order No. 890 (16 February 2007).

[64] FERC, Order No. 888, Open Access Transmission Tariff, Section 13.1.

[65] FERC, Order No. 888, Open Access Transmission Tariff, Section 13.2; FERC, Order No. 890, Open Access Transmission Tariff, Section 13.2.

[66] FERC, Order No. 890, Open Access Transmission Tariff, Section 2.2.

[67] See FERC, Order No. 888, Open Access Transmission Tariff, Section 2.2.

[68] FERC, Order No. 890, para 83.

[69] FERC, Order No. 890, para 84.

[70] FERC, Order No. 890, para 445.

[71] FERC, Order No. 890, para 455.

[72] FERC, Order No. 890, para 461.

[73] FERC, Order No. 890, para 480.

[74] FERC, Order No. 890, para 489.

[75] FERC, Order No. 890, para 496.

regional participation[76]; economic planning studies[77]; and cost allocation for new projects.[78]

The fact that all transmission services must be reserved also means that either market participants themselves or the TSO must be responsible for the scheduling of electricity flows.

In the US, the responsibility for the scheduling of flows is divided between market participants and the system operator (ISO or RTO). (a) The starting point is that each market participant is responsible for the scheduling of its own power plants. A market participant schedules power plants to meet its own load or according to the terms of bilateral trades. (b) In addition, the system operator (ISO or RTO) runs a day-ahead market with central scheduling of generation units.[79]

The Entry-Exit Model Under the entry-exit model, the entry point and the exit point are independent for transmission capacity and tariff purposes. The entry-exit model is regarded as suitable for unbundled and liberalised electricity markets. It is discussed in the context of pricing (Sect. 5.7.4).

5.5 Congestion Alleviation Methods

5.5.1 General Remarks

The mechanisms for the allocation of transmission capacity necessarily consist of three components (Sect. 5.1). One of them is the allocation of transmission capacity for electricity flows (Sect. 5.4). Flows can be flows in the more distant future or actual flows. When actual flows and congestion are known in the control area of a TSO, one can apply particular congestion alleviation methods.

The alleviation of congestion has costs. Some congestion is necessary for reasons of economic efficiency, because there are costs for building new transmission infrastructure. Capacity allocation methods that reduce congestion can also reduce the costs of congestion alleviation.[80] The use of alternative congestion alleviation methods can reduce the need to build new transmission infrastructure.[81]

Transmission system operators are in the best position to manage congestion risks.[82] They use physical and financial congestion alleviation methods.

---

[76] FERC, Order No. 890, para 504.

[77] FERC, Order No. 890, para 529.

[78] FERC, Order No. 890, para 552.

[79] Duthaler C and Finger M (2008).

[80] Twomey P et al. (2006), p. 19.

[81] Monopolkommission (2013), number 514.

[82] EFET (2007).

Physical methods mean changing the level of generation (or demand) at different locations on the grid.[83] They are the primary way to relieve transmission congestion constraints.

Financial methods focus on price differences or volatility caused by congestion. Financial methods tend to be market-based. Physical methods can be market-based or not market-based. We can have a look at financial methods first.

5.5.2 Financial Methods

There are two kinds of financial methods, structural and contractual. The use of structural methods means that the TSO can split its control area in bidding zones. Financial methods mean the use of financial transmission contracts to address the problem of price volatility and regional price differences caused by congestion.

Bidding Zones In most cases, the bidding zone is the control area of the TSO. The TSO may decide to split its control area into two or more bidding zones if there are transmission constraints inside the control area. In this case, there will be a price difference between the zones in the event of congestion.[84]

> There are several examples of bidding zones in Europe: Norway (5), Sweden (4), Denmark (2), the UK (2), and Italy (6 bidding zones for producers, a single price zone for end consumers).[85]

Financial Transmission Contracts The contractual methods mean the use of financial transmission contracts. They include: (a) financial transmission rights (FTRs such as point-to-point FTRs and flowgate FTRs); and (b) contracts for difference (CfDs).

A financial transmission right (FTR) gives its owner a right to a share of congestion rents received by the TSO during transmission congestion. A FTR can be structured as a firm obligation or as an option.[86] The duration of FTRs tends to range from months to years.

FTRs can be obtained in three main ways. FTRs can be allocated at an auction or allocated to transmission service customers who pay the embedded costs of the transmission system.[87] There can also be a secondary market.[88]

One can distinguish between point-to-point FTRs and flowgate FTRs. (a) Point-to-point FTRs give a right to the difference in locational prices times the contractual

[83] FERC (2012), p. 66.

[84] Supponen M (2011), pp. 60–61.

[85] Supponen M (2011), pp. 60–61.

[86] See, for example, Article 2(1) of ENTSO-E Network Code on Forward Capacity Allocation (2 April 2014).

[87] For the allocation of FTRs, see Frontier Economics Pty Ltd (2009), section 2.4.1.

[88] Frontier Economics Pty Ltd (2009), section 4.1.3.

volume. (b) Flowgate FTRs are based on two ideas. The first is that congestion payments should be linked to actual electricity flows. The other is that there are particular transmission constraints called flowgates. Flowgate FTRs give the right to collect payments based on the shadow price associated with a particular transmission constraint (flowgate).

Contracts for difference can be used in various ways (Sect. 12.4). One of them is hedging. They can be used to hedge against the difference between two uncertain spot prices (locational swaps) or against the difference between the spot price and the reference price.[89] They can also be used for basis trading.

5.5.3 Physical Methods

The physical methods inside a zone can be market-based or not market-based. They include: (a) long-term infrastructure solutions like building new lines; (b) locational signals for infrastructure investment; (c) curtailment (transmission loading relief); (d) redispatching and coordinated redispatching; and (e) countertrading.[90] Transmission capacity is regarded as firm when it cannot be curtailed or re-dispatched.

Locational Signals Locational signals matter. For example, peak transmission flows can depend on the location of base-load generators and peak-load generators. Where the base-load generators are located a long way from demand centres and peak-load generators are close to demand, transmission flows are greatest at off-peak times, when the generators close to the load are not running. Where the base-load generators are located close to demand and the peak-load generators further away, the transmission peak will coincide with the demand peak.[91]

Curtailment Curtailment is a physical method that is not market-based. Transactions contributing to congestion can be curtailed. For instance, congestion inside the control area of a TSO could be reduced by limiting flows on an interconnector.[92] The costs of curtailment are allocated to the TSO.

In the US, the procedure used for this purpose is called Transmission Loading Relief. It is based on Reliability Standard IRO-006 3 (as amended)

In the EU, Regulation 714/2009 limits the use of curtailment as far as cross-border transmission capacity is concerned. The permitted use of curtailment is limited to "emergency situations where the transmission system operator must act in an expeditious manner and redispatching or countertrading is not possible". Moreover, any such procedure must be applied in a non-discriminatory manner and market participants who have been allocated capacity must be compensated for any curtailment (except in cases of force majeure).[93]

---

89 Purchala K et al. (2005).

90 NordREG (2007); FERC (2012), p. 66.

91 Green R (2003), p. 140.

92 See, for example, Supponen M (2011), p. 61.

93 Article 16(2) of Regulation 714/2009 on conditions for access to the network for cross-border exchanges in electricity.

> The CACM Network Codes must contain provisions to this effect.[94] There is a common definition of force majeure[95] (see also Sects 8.4.6, 10.7.2 and 10.7.3 in this book). Force majeure events are defined so narrowly that they should be rare.
>
> There are also firmness deadlines after which curtailment is not permitted. The firmness deadlines depend on the duration of the contract (long-term,[96] day-ahead,[97] or single day[98]). There are special rules for force majeure and emergency situations.[99] Generally, TSOs must bear the costs of curtailment or redispatching,[100] but there is a cap.[101] There are also transitional arrangements "until the introduction of price coupling in the day ahead timeframe".[102] Price coupling in the day-ahead timeframe is facilitated by the CACM Regulation.

The use of curtailment is secondary to redispatching and countertrading for legal reasons.[103]

Redispatching Redispatching means the alteration of the initial generation and/or load pattern to relieve congestion by measures activated by the system operator.[104] It is customarily based on the prices that electricity producers communicate to the system operator for up and down regulation. Compared with curtailment, redispatching can be more market-based.

Coordinated redispatching involves two or more system operators that redispatch units on both sides of the congested interconnector. It requires harmonisation of market rules in adjacent areas.

The costs are first allocated to the system operator. Depending on the market, they can be allocated to market participants at a later stage. Where the costs are included in transmission tariffs, they are socialised. Alternatively, they can be charged to specific users that have caused congestion.[105]

Countertrading Countertrading is a simple market-based method. As electricity flows in opposite directions can be set off, the TSO can buy electricity in the control

---

94 ACER, Framework Guidelines on Capacity Allocation and Congestion Management for Electricity (29 July 2011), section 6.4. For the day-ahead market, see section 3.3.

95 *Ibid*, section 6.2. See also point 45 of Article 2 of Commission Regulation .../.. (CACM Regulation).

96 Articles 59(1), 58(1) and 59(2) of ENTSO-E Network Code on Forward Capacity Allocation (2 April 2014).

97 Article 62 of ENTSO-E NC FCA (2 April 2014).

98 Article 71 of Commission Regulation .../.. (CACM Regulation).

99 Article 63 of ENTSO-E NC FCA (2 April 2014); Article 72 of Commission Regulation .../.. (CACM Regulation).

100 Articles 61 and 68 of ENTSO-E NC FCA (2 April 2014).

101 Article 60 of ENTSO-E NC FCA (2 April 2014).

102 Article 72 of ENTSO-E NC FCA (2 April 2014).

103 First subparagraph of Article 16(2) of Regulation 714/2009.

104 Point 26 of Article 2 of Regulation 543/2013 (on submission and publication of data in electricity markets and amending Annex I to Regulation 714/2009).

105 See Purchala K et al. (2005).

zone downstream of congestion and sell it back in the control zone upstream.[106] In other words, the TSO buys additional power from generators in areas that were due to import more than the transmission system could carry, and sells power back to generators in areas that were due to export too much.

As the price of electricity tends to be higher downstream of congestion (in the import-constrained area), the TSO makes a loss buying expensive electricity to sell it back in the low price area (in the export-constrained area). The loss is covered by transmission tariffs.[107]

Electricity producers, on the other hand, can make a profit. In the import-constrained area, where spot prices tend to be high, they can sell electricity to the TSO at a high price and earn more than producers would earn in an unconstrained area. Electricity producers may be given perverse incentives in the export-constrained area, where producers who buy back their power will pay less than the price in the unconstrained market, and thus have the opportunity to earn more than producers in an unconstrained area would earn.[108]

Examples There are various examples of the use of physical congestion alleviation methods in Northern Europe.

In the Nordic electricity market, market splitting is complemented by countertrading. Cross-border congestion is managed by implicit auctions (Sect. 5.3) in the day-ahead market. After day-ahead allocation, the remaining transmission capacity is set for the intraday market and balancing:

- Market splitting and countertrading. It is necessary to manage congestion between the Nordic bidding areas and internal congestion in one area. (a) Congestion between the various bidding areas is managed through market splitting. Market splitting gives participants an opportunity to trade and benefit from the differences between low price areas and high price areas. (b) TSOs manage congestion by countertrading in the real-time balance market. As TSOs have to pay for countertrading, it increases their costs. The costs are normally covered by the grid tariff.[109] Because of the allocation of costs to the TSO, they signal to the TSO that it should reinforce the network.[110]
- Countertrading, adjacent areas. Countertrading can be used where transmission needs to be reduced between two adjacent areas within, say, Sweden. The TSO

---

[106] For a definition, see for example, point 13 of Article 2 of Regulation 543/2013 (on submission and publication of data in electricity markets and amending Annex I to Regulation 714/2009).

[107] Purchala K et al. (2005).

[108] Green R (2003), pp. 148–149.

[109] Energy Market Authority, Finland (2013), p. 32. See also NordREG (2007), Executive summary.

[110] Svenska Kraftnät (2007), p. 6; Green R (2003), p. 149. See also Purchala K et al. (2005): "Counter-trading is also used in Nord Pool. However, its Nordic version is actually a coordinated re-dispatching used to handle intra-zonal constraints and therefore is very much different from the method perceived in continental Europe".

can order an increased level of electricity production in the area with a shortage of production and a decreased level of production in the area with a surplus.

- Countertrading, single area. Countertrading can also be used to manage congestion within a single price area such as Finland or after the closure of the day-ahead market.[111]
- Curtailment. When Sweden still was one bidding zone, intra-zonal congestion was managed by curtailment of cross-border flows and countertrading.[112] Sweden was later divided into four bidding zones.

In Germany, the lack of market splitting has reduced locational signals for generation investments and contributed to congestion. To increase locational signals in the absence of market splitting and nodal pricing, Monopolkommission (the German Monopolies Commission, an expert committee) has proposed the allocation of a greater share of the transmission costs to generation (G-component).[113]

Coordinated Redispatching and Countertrading in the EU ACER Framework Guidelines and the CACM Regulation require coordinated redispatching and coordinated countertrading (Sect. 5.6.3).[114]

5.6 Models for Capacity Allocation in the EU

5.6.1 General Remarks

We have discussed various models available for the allocation of transmission capacity (Sect. 5.3 and 5.4), including models for congestion alleviation (Sect. 5.5). What models have been adopted at EU level? (The related pricing issues are discussed in Sects. 5.7 and 5.8).

EFET Principles EFET has proposed principles for the regulation of transmission capacity allocation at EU level in the interests of European energy traders.[115] The five key principles are as follows: (1) TSOs should auction physical transmission rights or financial rights with equivalent effect; (2) TSOs should auction the maximum of available capacity over appropriate timeframes; (3) transmission rights should be firm; (4) TSOs should not discriminate against holders of trans-

[111] Energy Market Authority, Finland (2013), p. 10.

[112] Statens energimyndighet (2006), p. S-12.

[113] Monopolkommission (2013), number 356.

[114] ACER, Framework Guidelines on Capacity Allocation and Congestion Management for Electricity (29 July 2011), section 6.3.

[115] EFET (2007).

mission rights purchased in advance of day-ahead and intraday timeframes; and (5) transmission rights need to be fungible in a secondary, traded market.[116]

The EFET key principles have largely been implemented in EU electricity markets law (see Sect. 5.6.5). The trend in EU law is the increased use of market-based mechanisms (auctions) for the allocation of transmission capacity. On the other hand, there is still no proper secondary market for physical or financial transmission rights (Chap. 12).

Regulation The allocation of transmission capacity is addressed by the Framework Guidelines on Capacity Allocation and Congestion Management (CACM Guidelines) published by ACER in July 2011. The Framework Guidelines are based on the Third Electricity Directive and Regulation 714/2009.

The CACM Guidelines are implemented by the more detailed CACM Network Codes.[117] (a) The CACM Regulation is such a network code. It "lays down detailed Guidelines on cross-zonal capacity allocation and congestion management in the day-ahead and intraday markets".[118] (b) ENTSO-E Network Code on Forward Capacity Allocation requires the introduction of harmonised allocation rules for PTRs and FTRs according to the principles laid down by the CACM Guidelines.[119] There may be regional specifities in the harmonised allocation rules when it is "appropriate".[120]

Spatial Characteristics The allocation mechanism depends on the nature of transmission capacity. It is necessary to distinguish between the allocation of intra-zonal, cross-zonal, or cross-border transmission capacity. Consequently, various models for the allocation of transmission capacity are used in the EU.

Time Frame The allocation mechanism can also depend on the duration of the contract. One should distinguish between intraday, day-ahead, long-term, and very long-term transmission capacity allocation.

Definition of Zones Before allocating cross-border transmission capacity between zones, it is necessary to define the zones. Bidding zones reflecting supply and demand distribution are regarded as "a cornerstone of market-based electricity trading".[121]

According to the ACER's CACM Guidelines, the CACM Network Codes to be developed must define a zone as "a bidding area". When defining the zones, the TSOs must be guided by the principle of overall market efficiency. In the absence of

---

[116] EFET (2007), Executive summary.

[117] ACER, Framework Guidelines on Capacity Allocation and Congestion Management for Electricity (29 July 2011), section 1.1.

[118] Article 1(1) of Commission Regulation . . ./.. (CACM Regulation).

[119] Article 57 of ENTSO-E NC FCA (2 April 2014). See also CACM Framework Guidelines, section 4.

[120] Article 56(3) of ENTSO-E NC FCA (2 April 2014).

[121] Recital 11 of Commission Regulation . . ./.. (CACM Regulation).

significant internal congestion within or between control areas, one or several control areas may constitute one zone. Zone definitions concern all timeframes (long-term, day-ahead, and intraday) and zone delimitations should be coordinated with balancing zones.[122]

The CACM Regulation enables the review of an existing bidding zone configuration.[123] The CACM Regulation also lays down the criteria to be considered if a review of bidding zone configuration is carried out. They relate to network security, overall market efficiency, and the stability and robustness of bidding zones.[124]

Definition of Available Capacity It is also necessary to define the available capacity. The available capacities have been determined in the same way in the Member States, including in Norway and Switzerland. First, available capacities have depended on ETSO's definitions.[125] ETSO has issued common definitions of cross-border transmission capacities for international exchanges of electricity within the internal electricity market (IEM).[126] Second, the methods to define available capacities have been addressed by the CACM Guidelines. Third, they are regulated by the CACM Regulation.

According to ACER's CACM Guidelines, the principles for the development of the CACM Network Codes include that they must not discriminate between exchanges internal to a zone, cross-zonal exchanges, and cross-border exchanges.[127] Moreover, long-term capacity calculation methodologies must be fully compatible with the adopted short-term capacity calculation.

There has been a move from NTC-based to flow-based market coupling in the EU. The CACM Network Codes must require the use of either a flow-based (FB) method or an available transfer capacity (ATC) method at each zone border for a given timeframe:

- For short-term capacity calculation in highly-meshed networks, the flow-based method is to be preferred to the ATC-method.
- For short-term capacity calculation in less meshed networks (such as the Nordic power system), ATC is the preferred method.

---

[122] ACER, Framework Guidelines on Capacity Allocation and Congestion Management for Electricity (29 July 2011), section 2.2.

[123] Article 32 of Commission Regulation .../.. (CACM Regulation).

[124] Article 33 of Commission Regulation .../.. (CACM Regulation).

[125] ETSO, Procedures for cross-border transmission capacity assessments (October 2001).

[126] The most important components are; Total Transfer Capacity (TTC, the maximal possible power transfer between two adjacent areas); Transmission Reliability Margin (TRM, cross-border capacity withdrawn from the market for security reasons); Net Transfer Capacity (NTC, NTC = TTC – TRM); Already Allocated Capacity (AAC); and Available Transmission Capacity (ATC, cross-border capacity available for commercial trade, ATC = NTC – AAC).

[127] ACER, Framework Guidelines on Capacity Allocation and Congestion Management for Electricity (29 July 2011), section 2.1.2.

- Long-term capacity calculation methodologies must be fully compatible with the adopted short term capacity calculation.[128]
- In contrast, the nodal approach was not chosen as it would have required radical changes.[129]

The CACM Regulation requires the use of a common grid model to implement single day-ahead and intraday coupling. Capacity calculation for the day-ahead and intraday market timeframes should be coordinated at least at the regional level.[130] The two permissible approaches when calculating cross-zonal capacity are the flow-based approach and the coordinated net transmission capacity approach[131]:

- The available capacity should normally be calculated according to the flow-based calculation method.[132] The flow-based approach should be used as a primary approach for day-ahead and intraday capacity calculation where cross-zonal capacity between bidding zones is highly interdependent.[133]
- The coordinated net transmission capacity approach should only be applied in regions where cross-zonal capacity is less interdependent and it can be shown that the flow-based approach would not bring added value.[134]
- Capacity calculation regions applying a flow-based approach shall be merged into one capacity calculation region provided that certain conditions are fulfilled.[135]

5.6.2 Access to Intra-Zonal Transmission Capacity in the EU

A (bidding) zone is the geographical area within which market participants can exchange electrical energy without grid constraints.[136] It is not necessary to allocate

[128] *Ibid*, section 2.1.1.

[129] ERGEG, Draft Framework Guidelines on Capacity Allocation and Congestion Management for Electricity: Initial Impact Assessment. Ref: E10-ENM-20-04 (8 September 2010), pp. 20–31.

[130] Recital 6 and Articles 14–15 of Commission Regulation . . ./.. (CACM Regulation).

[131] Point 8 of Article 2 of Commission Regulation . . ./.. (CACM Regulation): "'coordinated net transmission capacity approach' means the capacity calculation method based on the principle of assessing and defining ex ante a maximum energy exchange between adjacent bidding zones". Point 9: "'flow-based approach' means a capacity calculation method in which energy exchanges between bidding zones are limited with power transfer distribution factors and available margins on critical network elements".

[132] Recital 4 and Article 20(1) of Commission Regulation . . ./.. (CACM Regulation).

[133] Recital 7 of Commission Regulation . . ./.. (CACM Regulation).

[134] Recital 7 of Commission Regulation . . ./.. (CACM Regulation).

[135] Article 15(3) of Commission Regulation . . ./.. (CACM Regulation).

[136] ACER, Framework Guidelines on Capacity Allocation and Congestion Management for Electricity (29 July 2011), section 2.2; point 3 of Article 2 of Regulation 543/2013 (on submission and publication of data in electricity markets and amending Annex I to Regulation 714/2009).

transmission capacity if the grid is regarded as a copper plate. The question therefore is about grid access, dispatching,[137] and curtailment. Intra-zonal allocation models have largely been left to the discretion of Member States.

Grid Access The Third Electricity Directive makes each TSO responsible for ensuring the long-term ability of the system to meet reasonable demands for the transmission of electricity.[138]

For this reason, the main rule is third-party access to transmission and distribution systems. Third party access must be "based on published tariffs, applicable to all eligible customers and applied objectively and without discrimination between system users".[139] Moreover, the power of the TSO to decide on the dispatching of generation installations is "without prejudice to the supply of electricity on the basis of contractual obligations".[140]

The TSO/DSO may refuse access where it lacks the necessary capacity. "Duly substantiated reasons" must be given when access is refused, and they must be based on "objective and technically and economically justified criteria". Where refusal of access takes place, the regulatory authorities must ensure that the TSO or DSO "provides relevant information on measures that would be necessary to reinforce the network".[141]

In Germany, the system operator has far-reaching duties. It must provide access and ensure that there is sufficient capacity to the extent that doing so would not be economically unreasonable. What is regarded as reasonable or unreasonable may depend on the different objectives of the EEG and the EnWG[142] and on whether the customer is a producer of RES-E[143] or generates electricity from other sources.[144] There are sanctions for failure to comply with these obligations.[145]

Special Cases There are special cases. (a) One is direct lines. Member States must take measures necessary to enable the supply of electricity through a direct line.[146] Because of its definition,[147] a direct line can only be used for direct supply contracts between the owner of a certain plant and a certain end customer. (b) The other and more important special case is RES-E. RES-E must enjoy either priority access or guaranteed access to the grid.[148]

---

[137] Article 15 of Directive 2009/72/EC (Third Electricity Directive).

[138] Article 12(a) of Directive 2009/72/EC (Third Electricity Directive).

[139] Article 32(1) of Directive 2009/72/EC (Third Electricity Directive).

[140] Article 15(1) of Directive 2009/72/EC (Third Electricity Directive).

[141] Article 32(2) of Directive 2009/72/EC (Third Electricity Directive).

[142] See Lanz M et al. (2011), section 4.3.2.1, p. 107.

[143] §§ 9(1) and 9(3) EEG 2012; § 8 EEG 2014.

[144] § 11(1) EnWG.

[145] §§ 9 and 12 EEG 2012; § 13 EEG 2014; § 13 EnWG. See also § 32(1) EnWG and Lanz M et al. (2011), section 4.3.2.1, pp. 109–110.

[146] Article 34 of Directive 2009/72/EC (Third Electricity Directive).

[147] Point 15 of Article 2 of Directive 2009/72/EC (Third Electricity Directive).

[148] Article 16(2) of Directive 2009/28/EC (RES Directive).

5.6.3 Allocation of Cross-Zonal Transmission Capacity in the EU

One can distinguish between short-term, long-term, and very long-term allocation of cross-zonal transmission capacity.

Short-Term Cross-Zonal Transmission Capacity The regulation of the allocation of short-term cross-zonal transmission capacity is based on the Target Model with implicit auctions (day-ahead allocation) and continuous trading (intraday allocation).[149]

Generally, TSOs have a duty to foster the allocation of cross-border capacity through non-discriminatory market-based solutions under Regulation 2009/714.[150] Cross-border capacity must therefore be allocated by auctions, but continuous trading may be used for intraday trade.[151] All interconnection capacity may be allocated through implicit auctioning "in regions where forward financial electricity markets are well developed and have shown their efficiency".[152]

The allocation of short-term cross-zonal transmission capacity is regulated by the CACM Regulation. A particular market coupling operator (MCO) function[153] uses a specific algorithm to match bids and offers in an optimal manner. The results of the calculation are made available to power exchanges. Based on the results of the calculation, the power exchanges inform their clients of the successful bids and offers. Energy is then transferred across the network according to the results of the MCO function's calculation. The difference between single day-ahead and single intraday coupling is that intraday coupling uses a continuous process and day-ahead coupling one single calculation.[154]

The main rule under the CACM Regulation is that capacity should be allocated in the day-ahead and intraday market timeframes using implicit allocation methods.[155]

However, there are transitional intraday arrangements: "Where jointly requested by the regulatory authorities of the Member States of each of the bidding zone

---

[149] Recital 13 of Commission Regulation .../.. (CACM Regulation); recital 25 of ENTSO-E Network Code on Capacity Allocation and Congestion Management (27 September 2012). Compare Article 1(1) of ENTSO-E Network Code on Forward Capacity Allocation (2 April 2014) that uses explicit auctions as the default rule.

[150] Article 12(2) of Regulation 714/2009.

[151] Point 2.1 of Annex I to Regulation 714/2009.

[152] Point 2.8 of Annex I to Regulation 714/2009.

[153] Point 30 of Article 2 of Commission Regulation .../.. (CACM Regulation).

[154] Recital 5 of Commission Regulation .../.. (CACM Regulation).

[155] Recital 13 of Commission Regulation .../.. (CACM Regulation).

borders concerned, the TSOs concerned shall also provide explicit allocation, in addition to implicit allocation . . . via the capacity management module on bidding zone borders".[156]

Redispatching and Countertrading In addition to the regulation of short-term capacity allocation, electricity producers are affected by the regulation of grid access, dispatching,[157] and curtailment.[158] According to the CACM Regulation, TSOs should use a common set of remedial actions to deal with both internal and cross-zonal congestion and coordinate the use of remedial actions in capacity calculation to avoid unnecessary curtailments of cross-border capacities. Cross-zonal redispatching or countertrading must thus be coordinated with control area internal redispatching or countertrading. The usual firmness requirements apply.[159]

The CACM Regulation requires TSOs in each capacity calculation region to develop a proposal for a common methodology for coordinated redispatching and countertrading. Each TSO has a duty to abstain from unilateral or uncoordinated redispatching and countertrading measures of cross-border relevance.

The relevant generation units and loads have a duty to give TSOs the prices of redispatching and countertrading before redispatching and countertrading resources are committed. Pricing of redispatching and countertrading must be based on: (a) prices in the relevant electricity markets for the relevant timeframe; or (b) the cost of redispatching and countertrading resources calculated transparently based on the incurred costs.[160]

Long-Term Cross-Zonal Transmission Capacity Long-term means here at least the yearly and monthly timeframes.[161] There have been multiple sets of rules for the allocation of long-term cross-zonal transmission capacity in the Member States. Moreover, there have been different contract practices reflecting freedom of contract.[162] The purpose of the Network Code on Forward Capacity Allocation (NC FCA) is to harmonise these rules at the European level. NC FCA applies to the calculation, allocation, and pricing of long-term transmission capacity.

Long-term cross-zonal transmission capacity must be allocated to market participants by the relevant platforms (a) in the form of physical transmission rights

[156] Article 64 of Commission Regulation . . ./.. (CACM Regulation).

[157] Article 15 of Directive 2009/72/EC (Third Electricity Directive).

[158] For cross-border flows, see Article 16 of Regulation 714/2009 on conditions for access to the network for cross-border exchanges in electricity.

[159] Point 3.1 of Annex I to Regulation 714/2009; ACER, Framework Guidelines on Capacity Allocation and Congestion Management for Electricity (29 July 2011), sections 5, 6.3 and 6.4; Articles 76–80 of ENTSO-E NC CACM (27 September 2012); recitals 10, 12 and 17 of Commission Regulation . . ./.. (CACM Regulation); Article 35 of Commission Regulation . . ./.. (CACM Regulation).

[160] Article 35 of Commission Regulation . . ./.. (CACM Regulation).

[161] Recital 5 of ENTSO-E NC FCA (2 April 2014).

[162] Recitals 16 and 17 of ENTSO-E NC FCA (2 April 2014).

(PTRs) in accordance with the use-it-or-sell-it (UIOSI) principle or (b) in the form of financial transmission rights (FTRs).[163] The main rule is explicit auctions.[164]

The use of PTRs and the UIOSI principle is regarded as relatively uncomplicated for the Member States.[165] The UIOSI principle means that the holder of the right may either use capacity by nominating it or receive an automatic payout for capacity that it has not nominated.[166]

On the other hand, the legal nature of FTRs is regarded as problematic. In addition, they would require the existence of implicit auctions and thus power exchanges.[167]

The use of PTRs (or FTRs), therefore, means explicit auctions. Long-term cross-zonal transmission capacity is auctioned and allocated to market participants based on bids.[168] There will be a single platform for allocation and for secondary trading at the pan-European level. The single platform for allocation is a single point of contact for market participants wanting to participate in explicit auctions to acquire long-term transmission rights.[169]

The calculation of the available long-term capacity must be based on a "coordinated net transmission capacity approach" or a flow-based approach (like the definition of available cross-border transmission capacity). The choice is in the discretion of the TSO.[170] One or more Coordinated Capacity Calculators will determine the cross-zonal transmission capacity.[171]

Very Long-Term Cross-Zonal Transmission Capacity The Network Code on Forward Capacity Allocation (NC FCA) is not really designed for very long-term capacity allocation.[172] For reasons of risk management, it could be necessary for electricity firms to ensure that long-term transmission capacity is reserved for new

---

[163] Article 36(1) of ENTSO-E NC FCA (2 April 2014).

[164] Article 1(1) of ENTSO-E NC FCA (2 April 2014).

[165] ERGEG, Draft Framework Guidelines on Capacity Allocation and Congestion Management for Electricity: Initial Impact Assessment. Ref: E10-ENM-20-04 (8 September 2010), p. 53: "The establishment of this product might . . . be less complicated for most of the Member States than the introduction of a new product, even though it does not deliver the highest optimum and welfare".

[166] Article 2(1) of ENTSO-E NC FCA (2 April 2014).

[167] ERGEG, Draft Framework Guidelines on Capacity Allocation and Congestion Management for Electricity: Initial Impact Assessment. Ref: E10-ENM-20-04 (8 September 2010), p. 55.

[168] Article 2(1) of ENTSO-E NC FCA (2 April 2014): ". . . Auction means the process run by Allocation Platform(s) by which long term Cross Zonal Capacity is offered and allocated to Market Participants who submit bid(s) . . ." ". . . Allocation Platform means the Single Allocation Platform or Regional Platform(s) for the attribution of Long Term Cross Zonal Capacity . . ."

[169] Recitals 13 and 14 of ENTSO-E NC FCA (2 April 2014).

[170] Article 15(4) of ENTSO-E NC FCA (2 April 2014). See also recital 7 of ENTSO-E NC FCA (2 April 2014) and ACER, Framework Guidelines on Capacity Allocation and Congestion Management for Electricity (29 July 2011), section 2.1.1.

[171] Article 29 of ENTSO-E NC FCA (2 April 2014).

[172] See recital 5 of ENTSO-E NC FCA (2 April 2014): ". . . at least at the yearly and monthly timeframes . . ."

installations, and Member States may need to facilitate the reservation of long-term transmission capacity to foster investment in energy generation from renewable sources.[173] For instance, so-called "projects of common interest"[174] may require large long-term investments supported by a long-term contractual framework.

5.6.4 *Allocation of Cross-Border Transmission Capacity in the EU*

Transmission capacity can be allocated between zones or across borders between different countries. (a) Inside the EU, the allocation of cross-border transmission capacity is governed by Regulation 714/2009 and the CACM Network Codes adopted from the CACM Framework Guidelines.[175] It is thus governed by the same regulatory framework as the allocation of cross-zonal transmission capacity. (b) Different rules can apply between a Member State and a third country.

Cross-Border Allocation in the EU Non-market based methods used to be commonplace in the EU.[176] In 2003, the EU emphasised the need for market-based schemes.[177] According to a 2006 decision by the European Commission,[178] transmission capacity must be allocated by means of explicit (capacity) and/or implicit (capacity and energy) auctions. In addition, continuous trading may be used for intraday trade.[179] Each capacity allocation procedure must allocate a prescribed fraction of the available interconnection capacity.[180] Regulation 714/2009 now requires market-based methods for cross-border capacity allocation and emphasises the merits of implicit auctions.[181]

---

[173] Recital 61 of Directive 2009/28/EC (RES Directive): "... In order to accelerate grid connection procedures, Member States may provide for priority connection or reserved connection capacities for new installations producing electricity from renewable energy sources".

[174] Regulation 347/2013 on guidelines for trans-European energy infrastructure.

[175] ACER, Framework Guidelines on Capacity Allocation and Congestion Management for Electricity (29 July 2011), section 1.1.

[176] DG Competition Report on Energy Sector Inquiry, SEC(2006) 1724 (10 January 2007), para 547.

[177] Article 6(1) of Regulation 1228/2003 on conditions for access to the network for cross-border exchanges in electricity. See also Annex to Regulation 1228/2003, General, point 1.

[178] Commission Decision of 9 November 2006 amending the Annex to Regulation (EC) No 1228/2003 on conditions for access to the network for cross-border exchanges in electricity (2006/770/EC).

[179] Paragraph 2.1 of Commission Decision 2006/770/EC.

[180] Paragraph 2.3 of Commission Decision 2006/770/EC.

[181] Articles 12(2) and 16(1) of Regulation 714/2009. Point 2.1 of Annex I to Regulation 714/2009.

Generally, the allocation of long-term cross-border transmission capacity relies on the contract-path model and a physical transmission rights (PTR) framework.[182] It is possible to use the contract-path model, because the number of cross-border interconnectors is limited.

In the past, cross-border interconnections were mostly built for security and back-up purposes rather than for the purposes of the integration of national electricity markets. The limited number and capacity of cross-border interconnectors means congestion. Commercial demand for cross-border transmission capacity can exceed actual network capacity.[183]

Cross-Border Allocation Between a Member State and a Third Country The participation of an adjacent third country in the European single day-ahead coupling and single intra-day coupling would require a bilateral agreement. The coupling of third countries would be decided by the European Commission based on an assessment by ACER.

Issues relating to third countries have been addressed in parts of the EU regulatory framework. For instance, the reporting duties of TSOs may include even cross-border transmission capacity.[184] Third countries have been mentioned in the Third Electricity Directive but only briefly in Regulation 714/2009.

The CACM Regulation addresses the question of Switzerland: "The Union single day-ahead coupling and intraday coupling may be opened to market operators and TSOs operating in Switzerland on the condition that the national law in that country implements the main provisions of Union electricity market legislation and that there is an intergovernmental agreement on electricity cooperation between the Union and Switzerland".[185] Moreover, "participation by Switzerland in day-ahead coupling and single intraday coupling shall be decided by the Commission based on an opinion given by the Agency".[186] The CACM regulation also addresses the question of cost sharing even where a TSO or NEMO is in a third country.[187]

Example: The Nordic Market Congestion is managed by market-based methods in the Nordic market and the main rule is that there are no priority transmission rights for cross-border trade between the Nordic countries.

In the day-ahead market of Nord Pool Spot (Elspot), capacity on interconnectors is allocated by implicit auctions (market splitting).[188] Capacity not used in the Elspot market is offered to the intraday market (Elbas that uses continuous trading) and cross-border balancing in accordance with the ACER Framework Guidelines.

---

[182] Duthaler C and Finger M (2008). For a definition of PTRs, see, for example, Article 2(1) of ENTSO-E NC FCA (2 April 2014).

[183] Duthaler C and Finger M (2008).

[184] See Article 12(1)(h) of Commission Regulation 543/2013.

[185] Article 1(4) of Commission Regulation .../.. (CACM Regulation).

[186] Article 1(5) of Commission Regulation .../.. (CACM Regulation).

[187] Article 80 of Commission Regulation .../.. (CACM Regulation).

[188] Energy Market Authority, Finland (2013), pp. 28–29.

Market participants may use EPADs (Electricity Price Area Differentials, that is, exchange-traded Contracts for Differences) for hedging against price differences between area prices and the system price.[189]

PTRs are used on certain interconnectors. Energinet.dk and TenneT TSO GmbH offer PTRs on the border between DK1 and Germany. Emerginet.dk and 50 Hertz Transmission offer PTRs on the Kontek interconnector between DK2 and Germany. Since 1 July 2014, Energinet.dk has allocated PTRs for capacity on the interconnector between DK1 and DK2. The capacity is allocated in monthly auctions. Auction rules applied on the Danish-German border are applied on the interconnector between DK1 and DK2.[190]

Priority transmission rights are used for the allocation of capacity between Finland and Russia. Market participants can buy rights in auctions arranged by the TSO for one or more years.[191] A new trading scheme called direct exchange trade was adopted in electricity trade between Russia and Finland (the EU) in August 2011. Its volume is limited to 100 MW.[192]

5.6.5 *Summary of Regulation in the Light of EFET Key Principles*

The regulation of transmission capacity allocation can be summed up in the light of EFET key principles. Generally, the principles are reflected in ACER Framework Guidelines on CACM. The CACM Framework Guidelines regulate the contents of CACM Network Codes that apply to cross-zonal transmission services.

Auctions of Physical or Financial Rights The first key principle is that TSOs should auction physical transmission rights or financial rights with equivalent effect.[193] (a) The Third Electricity Directive did not yet address this issue in detail. As regards cross-border transmission capacity, this issue was to be regulated in network codes.[194] (b) Regulation 714/2009 requires the use of market-based methods but—because of its scope[195]—only for the allocation of cross-border

[189] Energy Market Authority, Finland (2013), p. 33; Energy Market Authority, Finland (2014), p. 23.

[190] Nord Pool Spot, Exchange information, No. 22/2014, 14 May 2014.

[191] Energy Market Authority, Finland (2013), pp. 28–29; Energy Market Authority, Finland (2014), p. 23.

[192] Energy Market Authority, Finland (2014), pp. 23–24.

[193] EFET (2007), Executive summary.

[194] Article 38(2) of Directive 2009/72/EC (Third Electricity Directive).

[195] Article 1 of Regulation 714/2009 on conditions for access to the network for cross-border exchanges in electricity.

transmission capacity.[196] (c) EFET key principles are reflected in ACER Framework Guidelines on CACM that apply to cross-zonal transmission services.

The CACM Network Codes must set out: that TSOs provide a single platform (single point of contact) for the allocation of long-term transmission rights (PTR and FTR) at European level (with regional platforms as a transitional arrangement)[197]; that TSOs implement capacity allocation in the day-ahead market from implicit auctions and the marginal pricing principle[198] including necessary provisions for the implementation of the pan-European intraday target model supporting continuous implicit trading (with direct explicit access to the capacity allowed as a transitional measure).[199]

Auction of Maximum Capacity The second principle is that TSOs should auction the maximum of available capacity over appropriate timeframes.[200] ACER Framework Guidelines on CACM address this issue in three ways.

First, there must be a method for the calculation of the available capacity. The CACM Network Codes must require the use of either a flow-based method or an available transfer capacity method for short-term capacity calculation at each zone border, and long-term capacity calculation methods that are fully compatible with the adopted short-term capacity calculation methods.[201] According to NC FCA, the TSO may choose between "coordinated net transmission capacity approach" or a flow-based approach for long-term capacity calculation.[202]

Second, there are particular rules on the volume of long-term or intraday transmission capacity that must be allocated. The CACM Network Codes must

[196] Articles 12(2) and 16(1) of Regulation 714/2009. Point 2.1 of Annex I to Regulation 714/2009. See also DG Competition Report on Energy Sector Inquiry, SEC(2006) 1724 (10 January 2007), para 547.

[197] ACER, Framework Guidelines on Capacity Allocation and Congestion Management for Electricity (29 July 2011), section 4.1. Recital 13 and Article 2(1) of ENTSO-E NC FCA (2 April 2014).

[198] ACER, Framework Guidelines on Capacity Allocation and Congestion Management for Electricity (29 July 2011), section 3.1.

[199] ACER, Framework Guidelines on Capacity Allocation and Congestion Management for Electricity (29 July 2011), section 5.

[200] EFET (2007), Executive summary.

[201] ACER, Framework Guidelines on Capacity Allocation and Congestion Management for Electricity (29 July 2011), section 2.1.1: "The FB method ... is ... to be preferred to the ATC method for short term capacity calculation in cases where transmission networks are highly meshed and interdependencies between the interconnections are high (e.g. the ENTSO-E Continental Europe regional group, or the ACER Central West Europe (CWE) and Central East Europe (CEE) regional initiative groups) ... Provided that it is done in a coordinated way, ATC is considered as an acceptable method for short term capacity calculation in less meshed networks, such as the Nordic power system or possibly the cases of interconnections of or between the large peninsulas or islands in Europe ..."

[202] Article 15(4) of ENTSO-E NC FCA (2 April 2014). See also recital 7 of ENTSO-E NC FCA (2 April 2014); ACER, Framework Guidelines on Capacity Allocation and Congestion Management for Electricity (29 July 2011), section 2.1.1.

require that TSOs determine the volume of long-term capacity rights in accordance with the technical capabilities of the network and for each long-term timeframe.[203] Moreover, all cross-zonal intraday capacity must be allocated via the pan-European platform.[204]

Third, there are particular rules on direct explicit access. There may be direct explicit access (e.g. for bilateral supply OTC contracts) to intraday capacity as a transitional arrangement.[205]

Firmness According to the third EFET principle, transmission rights should be firm.[206] Firmness is regulated in various ways.

When cross-border transmission capacity is allocated on a long-term or medium-term basis, access rights are firm under Regulation 714/2009.[207]

According to ACER Framework Guidelines, physical firmness is the preferred approach, but financial firmness may be accepted in case of explicit auctions. To ensure firmness, TSOs must also ensure that enough redispatching/countertrade means are available.[208] (a) As regards day-ahead capacity allocation, the reduction of allocated capacity must be a last resort measure and a reduction of allocated capacity may only be used "in emergency situations and force majeure, and when all other means are exhausted". Moreover, costs must not be allocated to market participants.[209] (b) As regards intraday capacity allocation, the CACM Network Codes must provide that "the allocated intraday capacity is firm, and that the use of intraday capacity is obligatory when allocated".[210]

The firmness of short-term capacity allocation is now regulated by the CACM Regulation. Orders matched in single day-ahead coupling are considered firm,[211] and there is a day-ahead firmness deadline for cross-zonal capacity allocation.[212] Cross-zonal intraday capacity is firm as soon as soon as it is allocated.[213]

However, firmness is financial firmness under the CACM Regulation. (a) The CACM Regulation defines firmness as "a guarantee that cross-zonal capacity rights will remain unchanged and that a compensation is paid if they are nevertheless

[203] ACER, Framework Guidelines on Capacity Allocation and Congestion Management for Electricity (29 July 2011), section 4.2.

[204] *Ibid*, section 5.

[205] *Ibid*, section 5.

[206] EFET (2007), Executive summary.

[207] Point 2.5 of Annex I to Regulation 714/2009.

[208] ACER, Framework Guidelines on Capacity Allocation and Congestion Management for Electricity (29 July 2011), section 6.4.

[209] ACER, Framework Guidelines on Capacity Allocation and Congestion Management for Electricity (29 July 2011), section 3.3.

[210] *Ibid*, section 5.

[211] Article 47(5) of Commission Regulation .../.. (CACM Regulation).

[212] Articles 69–70 of Commission Regulation .../.. (CACM Regulation).

[213] Article 71 of Commission Regulation .../.. (CACM Regulation).

changed".[214] According to the CACM Regulation, any costs incurred efficiently to guarantee firmness of capacity should be recovered via network tariffs or appropriate mechanisms in a timely manner. NEMOs should be entitled to recover their incurred costs if they are efficiently incurred, reasonable and proportionate.[215] (b) There are particular rules on firmness in the event of force majeure or emergency situations.[216]

Non-discrimination The fourth principle relates to non-discrimination. TSOs should not discriminate against holders of transmission rights purchased in advance of day-ahead and intraday timeframes.[217] (a) Generally, non-discrimination is a general principle of EU law. The non-discrimination of electricity firms is one of the purposes of the Third Electricity Directive.[218] TSOs have a general obligation not to discriminate as between system users.[219] For example, the dispatching of generating installations and the use of interconnectors must be determined based on the criteria which must be "objective, published and applied in a non-discriminatory manner, ensuring the proper functioning of the internal market in electricity",[220] and the tariffs must be non-discriminatory.[221] (b) According to Regulation 714/2009, capacity allocation "shall not discriminate between market participants that wish to use their rights to make use of bilateral supply contracts or to bid into power exchanges". Instead, "[t]he highest value bids, whether implicit or explicit in a given timeframe, shall be successful".[222] (c) These general non-discrimination rules are complemented by the CACM Framework Guidelines. For instance, CACM Network Codes must ensure that there is no "undue discrimination in matching the different types of intraday products"[223] and that TSOs "avoid any discrimination between the different types of commercial exchanges, between the relevant time frames and between exchanges internal to countries and cross-border exchanges" when cross-zonal transactions are curtailed.[224]

---

[214] Point 44 of Article 2 of Commission Regulation . . ./.. (CACM Regulation).

[215] Recital 23 and Article 76 of Commission Regulation . . ./.. (CACM Regulation).

[216] Article 72 of Commission Regulation . . ./.. (CACM Regulation).

[217] EFET (2007), Executive summary.

[218] Article 3(1) of Directive 2009/72/EC (Third Electricity Directive).

[219] Point (f) of Article 12 of Directive 2009/72/EC (Third Electricity Directive).

[220] Article 15(2) of Directive 2009/72/EC (Third Electricity Directive).

[221] Recital 36 and Article 12 of Directive 2009/72/EC (Third Electricity Directive). See also Articles 25, 32(1), 37(1), 37(6)(a), 37(8), and 37(10) of Directive 2009/72/EC (Third Electricity Directive).

[222] Point 2.7 of Annex I to Regulation 714/2009.

[223] ACER, Framework Guidelines on Capacity Allocation and Congestion Management for Electricity (29 July 2011), section 5.

[224] *Ibid*, section 6.4.

Secondary Market The fifth and last EFET key principle is that transmission rights need to be fungible in a secondary, traded market.[225] (a) To start with, there must be a secondary market for the gas market[226] and, under Regulation 714/2009, for contracts for *cross-border* electricity transmission. Cross-border transmission capacity must be freely tradable on a secondary basis, provided that the TSO is sufficiently informed in advance.[227] Rights to cross-border transmission capacity must therefore be firm. In addition, they must be subject to the use-it-or-lose-it or use-it-or-sell-it (UIOSI) principles at the time of nomination.[228] (b) Secondary trading of *cross-zonal* transmission capacity is addressed by the CACM Framework Guidelines. There must be a secondary market for *long-term* transmission rights. The CACM Network Codes must ensure that the TSOs provide "a single platform for anonymous secondary trading at the European level" (with regional platforms as a transitional arrangement).[229]

To facilitate secondary trading, the CACM Network Codes lay down the nature of PTRs and FTRs. (a) PTRs must be defined as options that are subject to the use-it-or-sell-it (UIOSI) principle (unless appropriate cross-border financial hedging is offered in liquid financial markets on both side of the interconnector). Non-nominated capacity rights are thus resold. (b) FTRs must be defined as options or obligations. (c) Hybrid solutions mixing PTR and FTR components are prohibited.[230]

Secondary trading is regulated in greater detail in ENTSO-E Network Code on Forward Capacity Allocation (NC FCA).[231] It is defined as "the trading of Long Term Transmission Rights through which a Market Participant is able to buy or sell Long Term Transmission Rights which were initially allocated by the Allocation Platform(s)".[232] The Network Code requires a Single Allocation Platform responsible for the operation of auction procedures and the performance of other duties relating to Forward Capacity Allocation.[233] Long Term Transmission Rights holders are entitled to "transfer all or part of their Long Term Transmission Rights through Secondary Trading to other Market Participants according to the corresponding Allocation Rules".[234] Market Participants cannot participate unless

[225] EFET (2007), Executive summary.

[226] Article 16(3) of Regulation 715/2009. See also Point 2.2 of Annex I to Regulation 715/2009.

[227] Point 2.12 of Annex I to Regulation 714/2009.

[228] Point 2.5 of Annex I to Regulation 714/2009.

[229] ACER, Framework Guidelines on Capacity Allocation and Congestion Management for Electricity (29 July 2011), sections 4.1 and 4.2.

[230] *Ibid.*

[231] Article 1(1) of Article 2 of ENTSO-E NC FCA (2 April 2014).

[232] Article 2 of ENTSO-E NC FCA (2 April 2014).

[233] Article 53 of Article 2 of ENTSO-E NC FCA (2 April 2014).

[234] Article 49(1) of ENTSO-E NC FCA (2 April 2014).

they are "registered with the Allocation Platforms and meet all eligibility requirements under the corresponding Allocation Rules".[235]

For instance, CASC-CWE is a system that sets out the terms and conditions governing the allocation of available transmission capacities via auctions in both directions on the country borders in the regions Central West Europe (CWE), Central South Europe (CSE), and Switzerland.[236] The auctions are explicit auctions and thus limited to transmission capacity.[237] The available transmission capacities are determined jointly by the concerned TSOs of a country border.[238] Capacity is auctioned via a Joint Auction Office in the form of physical transmission rights on a yearly, monthly, and as the case may be, daily basis.[239] A market participant that has acquired physical transmission rights may exercise them in relation to the relevant TSOs, provided for example that the market participant nominates the capacities according to the terms applicable in each country. The market participant is required to pay the amount resulting from the auction.[240] The valuation amounts of allocated capacities are paid to the Joint Auction Office.[241] There are nevertheless reductions[242] caused by the UIOSI principle for yearly or monthly capacities. Programming authorisations for yearly or monthly capacities that were not nominated by the participant are automatically resold to the relevant daily allocation.[243] The non-nominated programming authorisations for yearly and monthly capacities are financially compensated to the participant depending on the price in the daily allocation.[244]

TSOs must work out harmonised allocation rules for PTRs and FTRs. The rules for PTRs and FTRs should be consistent with each other.[245] NC FCA lays down a list of the minimum contents of the harmonised allocation rules.

The rules must contain at least: (a) harmonised definitions and interpretation; (b) harmonised provisions on eligibility and entitlement, on suspension and renewal, and on costs of participation; (c) a description of the forward capacity allocation process including at least provisions on auction specification, submission of bids, publication of auction results, contestation period and fallback procedures; (d) a description of the types of long-term transmission rights which are offered, including the remuneration principles; (e) harmonised provisions concerning netting policies and financial collaterals

---

[235] Article 42(1) of ENTSO-E NC FCA (2 April 2014).

[236] CWE Auction Rules, Version 1.0, Article 1.01.

[237] CWE Auction Rules, Version 1.0, Article 1.04.

[238] CWE Auction Rules, Version 1.0, Article 2.03.

[239] CWE Auction Rules, Version 1.0, Article 1.01.

[240] CWE Auction Rules, Version 1.0, Article 1.04.

[241] CWE Auction Rules, Version 1.0, Article 9.01.

[242] CWE Auction Rules, Version 1.0, Article 9.01(b). The costs are fully covered by congestion revenues in accordance with Article 16(6) of Regulation 714/2009 or the Swiss Federal Electricity Supply Act, as the case may be.

[243] CWE Auction Rules, Version 1.0, Article 8.01. For a definition of UIOSI, see, for example, Article 2(1) of ENTSO-E NC FCA (2 April 2014).

[244] CWE Auction Rules, Version 1.0, Article 8.02.

[245] Article 56(1) of Article 2 of ENTSO-E NC FCA (2 April 2014).

requirements specific for FTRs; (f) harmonised provisions for secondary trading; (g) harmonised provisions for the return of long-term transmission rights; (h) principle description of the applicable nomination rules[246]; (i) harmonised UIOSI provisions in case of PTRs; (j) firmness provisions and compensation rules; (k) harmonised provisions for financial requirements and settlement; and (l) a contractual framework between the allocation platforms and the market participants including provisions on the applicable law, the applicable language, including confidentiality, dispute resolution, liability and force majeure.[247]

EURELECTRIC and EFET have proposed the use of buy-back schemes.[248] According to EFET, TSOs should buy back capacity in the secondary market instead of curtailing in the event of unexpected operational circumstances. EURELECTRIC would prefer TSOs to arrange a reverse auction when it turns out that they have sold too much capacity.

ENTSO-E believes that capacity buy-back "could only be applied with sufficient lead time and could therefore only address cases where the operational problems become obvious well in advance of real time".[249]

ENTSO-E has also analysed design schemes that could be applied for such a purpose. They include: (a) voluntary buy-back schemes; (b) a compulsory buy-back approach for the total capacity that needs to be curtailed; (c) a compulsory buy-back approach for a partial amount of the capacity; (d) auction buy-back systems, where price formation is left to the market; (e) a fixed price approach with TSOs determining the price and disclosing it in advance; and (f) a reverse auction capacity buy-back approach with TSOs determining the price without disclosing it in advance.

According to ENTSO-E, the current NC FCA formulation does not preclude the possibility of capacity buy-backs taking place. However, ENTSO-E believes that buy-back schemes are not recommended from a TSO perspective.

Secondary Markets and MiFID II A TSO may have to comply with MiFID II where it operates a secondary market for financial instruments such as a platform for secondary trading in financial transmission rights.[250]

[246] For a definition for the purposes of REMIT, see point 8 of second subparagraph of Article 2 of Commission Implementing Regulation 1348/2014: "'nomination' means, – for electricity: the notification of the use of cross zonal capacity by a physical transmission rights holder and its counterparty to the respective transmission system operator(s)(TSOs) ..."

[247] Article 56(2) of Article 2 of ENTSO-E NC FCA (2 April 2014). See also Article 56(3): "The harmonised Allocation Rules shall contain regional specificities, where appropriate".

[248] See ENTSO-E (2013b).

[249] ENTSO-E (2013b).

[250] Point n of Article 2(1) of Directive 2014/65/EU (MiFID II).

5.7 Pricing Models

5.7.1 General Remarks

The model for the pricing of transmission services is connected with the model for capacity allocation (Sect. 5.4). As tarification models are largely unregulated at EU level, transmission tariffs are determined in different ways depending on the Member State[251] but may consist of similar components.[252] In most Member States of the EU, electricity producers generally do not pay the costs for the use of the transmission grid, or pay just a fraction of the costs (the G-component). Costs are mostly allocated to load (the L-component).[253]

Perspective The function of transmission tariffs depends on the perspective. (a) From the perspective of electricity producers, tariffs are a cost for a service. Electricity producers prefer to minimise these costs like any other costs. (b) From the perspective of the TSO, transmission tariffs are designed to cover costs and provide an appropriate return on investment. Costs related to electricity transmission include: infrastructure costs (sunk investment costs, including costs for operation and maintenance); and costs for the use of infrastructure (losses, network constraints, ancillary services).[254] (c) From a welfare perspective, transmission tariffs should also provide adequate long-term investment signals.

Signals The price of transmission can influence the behaviour of electricity producers and end consumers. If prices are low, demand for most goods will be high. If the charges for using the transmission system are low, generation installations and loads can be sited far apart, and the amount of electricity that users wish to transmit between them can be high.[255]

The model for the pricing of transmission services can thus give locational and temporal signals for electricity supply (feed-in) and extraction (load). (a) The signals contribute to efficient use of the transmission infrastructure where they reflect costs caused by grid users, the transmission infrastructure is well interconnected, and the transmission system has several alternative sources of supply.[256] (b) The absence of signals that reflect these costs implies that costs are socialised. The socialisation of costs would reduce the efficiency of the use of

---

[251] Generally, see ENTSO-E Overview of transmission tariffs in Europe: Synthesis 2013 (June 2013). See also Ruester S et al. (2012).

[252] Spicker J (2010), p. 49, number 31.

[253] Monopolkommission (2013), number 347. For Germany, see also Spicker J (2010), p. 52, numbers 34–35.

[254] Ruester S et al. (2012), p. 20.

[255] Green R (2003), p. 137.

[256] This is reflected in Article 14(2) of Regulation 714/2009 on conditions for access to the network for cross-border exchanges in electricity.

infrastructure. It would favour users in high-cost areas at the cost of users in low-cost areas.

Grid connection costs raise similar questions. There are costs for connecting the installation to the grid connection point and costs for upgrades in the distribution network and regional network. There are also network facilities for the provision of services to a single customer (dedicated facilities) and network facilities for the provision of services to multiple customers.[257]

Incentives to invest in generation installations or transmission infrastructure can depend on the allocation of costs for connecting the installation to the grid. The allocation of these costs can give locational and temporal signals. (The allocation of these costs has had an effect on investments in generation assets in the EU, Sect. 5.7.2)

Allocation of Costs It is therefore important how the various kinds of costs are allocated between market participants. It is generally assumed, from the welfare perspective, that cost recovery should, as far as possible, be based on the principle of cost causality.[258]

Provided that there is competition in electricity generation, one might be tempted to argue that residual network costs should be allocated to consumers because they "end up paying the bill anyway".[259] Ultimately, end consumers end up paying all costs.[260] Allocating costs to end consumers (the L-component) could help to create a level playing field for electricity producers and reduce entry barriers.

However, electricity producers would not receive any locational signals regarding the cost of transmission if transmission tariffs were only paid by end consumers. It has turned out that a certain share of the tariff (the G-component) should be allocated to producers from a general welfare perspective.[261]

Transmission Pricing Models Various pricing models have been used in competitive markets for electricity. In addition to the allocation of costs, the models have broader goals from a general welfare perspective.

The pricing of transmission services should: promote economic efficiency; compensate grid companies fairly for providing transmission services; allocate transmission costs reasonably among all transmission users; and maintain the reliability of the transmission grid.[262] According to a working group organised by the Energy Modeling Forum of Stanford University, transmission prices should: (1) promote the efficient day-to-day operation of the bulk power market; (2) signal locational advantages for investment in generation and demand; (3) signal the need

[257] Pérez-Arriaga IJ and Smeers Y (2003), p. 180.

[258] Ruester S et al. (2012), p. 28; Pérez-Arriaga IJ and Smeers Y (2003), p. 176.

[259] Pérez-Arriaga IJ and Smeers Y (2003), p. 194.

[260] Brown MH and Sedano RP (2004), p. 23.

[261] Ruester S et al. (2012), pp. 29–30. See also Monopolkommission (2013), numbers 345–348.

[262] Krause T (2003), p. 10; Cannella MA et al. (1996).

for investment in the transmission system; (4) compensate the owners of existing transmission assets; (5) be simple and transparent; and (6) be politically implementable.[263]

These abstract goals are rarely met. For instance, the models used for the allocation of transmission capacity and for pricing in the national markets of the EU fail to provide sufficient locational signals in many Member States. This is, in particular, the case where transmission tariffs are paid only by end consumers. Moreover, tariffs do not target to recover the same costs in all countries, and tariffs in some cases also include costs not directly related to transmission infrastructure.[264]

Where the pricing of transmission services has several objectives, it is common to use multi-part tariffs.[265] It is also common to use "second-best" solutions in the absence of perfect solutions.[266]

Fixing the Tariffs Transmission tariffs are fixed or their methodology is approved by the market regulator.

There are two customary methods to fix the tariffs in practice. The traditional method is based on costs (rate of return or cost of service regulation). The most common alternative is the use of a fixed price not based on costs (fixed price regulation). (a) Cost of service regulation is relatively easy to apply. However, it is combined with moral hazard (as there are weak incentives to increase efficiency) and adverse selection (as low-cost firms may pretend to be high-cost firms), and figuring out the costs would require high administrative costs. (b) Even fixed price regulation is easy to apply. It solves the problem of moral hazard. However, the problem of adverse selection remains unsolved.

A menu of cost-contingent contracts[267] and simple menus of contracts[268] lie between these two extremes. (a) The menu of contracts regulation could solve both the moral hazard and adverse selection problems. However, it is too complicated to be applied in practice. (b) It would be easier to apply the simple menu of contracts method that is a simplified form of menu of contracts regulation.[269]

Contents In the following, we will discuss the various costs (Sect. 5.7.2) and the various models for the pricing of transmission services (Sect. 5.7.3). We will then discuss pricing models based on the flow (Sect. 5.7.4), distance sensitivity (Sect. 5.7.5), and geographical electricity price differentiation (Sect. 5.7.6). EU law is discussed in Sect. 5.8.

---

[263] Green R (1997), p. 178; Niederprüm M and Pickhardt M (2002). Compare US Senate Committee on Energy and Natural Resources (2008), testimony by Gary Hanson, Chairman South Dakota Public Utilities Commission.

[264] Ruester S et al. (2012).

[265] Pérez-Arriaga IJ and Smeers Y (2003), p. 190.

[266] Pérez-Arriaga IJ and Smeers Y (2003), pp. 190–191.

[267] Laffont JJ and Tirole J (1986).

[268] Rogerson WP (2003).

[269] See Kopsakangas-Savolainen M and Svento R (2010, 2014).

5.7.2 Costs

Transmission costs consist of many components.[270] However, it can be difficult to calculate the costs even where the components are known. One of the reasons is that costs can be defined in different ways. There are different cost concepts, each of them relevant in a particular context. In some cases, the pricing model is not connected with actual costs.

Opportunity Costs To make this character of costs explicit, economists use the concept of opportunity cost. It relates to a decision rather than to an economic good. Opportunity cost is defined as the benefit lost for not having the resources available for an alternative use. When opportunity cost is defined in this way, it is necessary to compare two scenarios. The opportunity cost of a decision depends on the perspective.[271]

Fixed and Variable Costs, Welfare There are also other ways to define costs. One can distinguish between the fixed and variable costs of electricity transmission. Some of these costs are incurred by the TSO. Some costs are costs from a welfare perspective. There are also incremental costs.

First, the TSO will incur high fixed costs for transmission infrastructure. The fixed costs should therefore be allocated between the different categories of grid users.

Second, the TSO will incur some variable costs for the transmission of electricity even though electricity flows by force of nature. In particular, electricity producers must be compensated for the loss of electrical energy during transmission. Like fixed costs, this variable cost should be allocated between different kinds of grid users.

Third, from a welfare perspective, there is a variable cost caused by congestion. (a) Congestion is indirectly caused by the high fixed costs. As transmission infrastructure is costly to maintain and develop, the capacity of lines and nodes is limited and it is reasonable to accept some congestion in parts of the transport grid. (b) The cost caused by congestion is equal to the difference between the maximum welfare obtained without transmission constraints and the welfare that results from the actual dispatch.[272]

Fourth, there are incremental costs, that is, costs for any new facilities.

The pricing model should reflect the TSO's fixed and variable costs, costs caused by congestion, and incremental costs.[273]

---

[270] See, for example, Hsu M (1997), p. 257: "The overall costs for a transmission network can be separated into the following four major components: 1. Returns and depreciation of the capital equipment; 2. operation and maintenance to ensure that the network is robust; 3. losses incurred in transmitting power; and 4. opportunity costs of system constraints".

[271] Curien N (2003), pp. 37–38.

[272] Crampes C (2003), p. 114.

[273] Crampes C (2003), p. 105.

For instance, Regulation 714/2009 provides that tariffs for cross-border transmission services in the EU must "reflect actual costs incurred". Tariff levels must "provide locational signals at Community level, and take into account the amount of network losses and congestion caused, and investment costs for infrastructure".[274]

The pricing model can be designed to achieve this in many ways. For instance, nodal pricing is regarded as the best way to allocate transmission capacity when there is enough competition.[275] When the buyer and the seller of electricity are located at different nodes (node 1 and node 2), there is a difference between the price of electricity at node 1 and node 2. From the perspective of the buyer and the seller, the difference appears as a transport fee. The "merchandising surplus" can therefore be paid to the TSO. By its very definition, the merchandising surplus is not based on the actual costs incurred by the system operator.[276] It can nevertheless indicate willingness to pay for transmission between two nodes.[277]

Ultra Short-Term, Short-Term and Long-Term Costs (Infrastructure and Use) One can also distinguish between long-term costs and two kinds of short-term costs. This means the separation of infrastructure costs and costs incurred for the use of the infrastructure.[278] (1) Long-term costs relate to investment in new transmission infrastructure. The location of supply and demand can depend on tariff components that reflect these long-term costs. (2) Short-term costs relate to the use of the existing transmission infrastructure. They should cover operations and maintenance. The efficient use of existing transmission capacities and congestion management depend on the parts of the tariff aimed at the recovery of these costs.[279] (3) Ultra short-term costs relate to real-time balancing under certainty about electricity supply and demand in the very short run. In this case, the TSO makes dispatch or demand curtailment decisions.[280]

For instance, various cost concepts have been adopted in Regulation 714/2009 and Regulation 838/2010.[281] Regulation 714/2009 identifies long-term costs and the cost of losses. The costs shall be established "on the basis of the forward-looking long-run average incremental costs, taking into account losses, investment in new infrastructure, and an appropriate proportion of the cost of existing infrastructure".[282] Regulation 838/2010

[274] Article 14 of Regulation 714/2009 on conditions for access to the network for cross-border exchanges in electricity.

[275] Crampes C (2003), p. 115.

[276] Crampes C (2003), pp. 116–117.

[277] Green R (2003), p. 138.

[278] Pérez-Arriaga IJ and Smeers Y (2003), p. 180.

[279] Ruester S et al. (2012), p. 20.

[280] Vogelsang I (2006).

[281] Regulation 838/2010 on laying down guidelines relating to the inter-transmission system operator compensation mechanism and a common regulatory approach to transmission charging.

[282] Article 13(6) of Regulation 714/2009 on conditions for access to the network for cross-border exchanges in electricity.

complements Regulation 714/2009 by laying down the concrete methodology and providing for an ITC fund.[283]

Long-Term and Short-Term Marginal Costs Costs can be average costs or marginal costs. There can also be a difference between long-term and short-term marginal costs.[284] From a welfare perspective, optimal prices in the short term reflect the short-term marginal costs of electricity and its transmission. In the long term, however, optimal prices should reflect long-term marginal costs because long-term investments in electricity infrastructure depend on long-term profitability.[285] While short-term marginal costs give correct signals for operations, long-term marginal costs are the appropriate basis for investment decisions.[286]

The short-term marginal cost of transmission could be defined as the sum of the cost of losses and the opportunity cost of congestion. It could also be defined as the difference between nodal prices. The long-term marginal cost of transmission could be defined as the cost of building more capacity to increase the flows that the grid can accept.[287]

Allocation of Costs Between the System Operator Generation and Load One may ask to whom the various transmission costs should be allocated. There are various cost allocation methods (for EU law, see Sect. 5.8).

Obviously, costs cannot be allocated to the TSO as this would not be sustainable in the long term. Even in the short term, the allocation of costs to the TSO would have to be funded. Funding constraints can hamper investment in transmission infrastructure.

In Germany, the TenneT case was an example of funding problems when the TSO was responsible for costs and demand for new transmission capacity was too high.[288]

Costs can be allocated between generation and load (end consumers).[289] In principle, costs could also be allocated to the state in which case transmission services would be subsidised (for state aid, see Sects. 3.7.8 and 8.5.6).

It is necessary to distinguish between transmission costs and costs for grid connection, including between different kinds of costs for grid connection. There are shallow and deep costs for grid connection.

283 Recital 7 of Regulation 838/2010; paragraph 1.1 of Part A of Annex to Regulation 838/2010; paragraph 1.2 of Part A of Annex to Regulation 838/2010.

284 See, for example, Bhattacharyya SC (2011), pp. 308–309.

285 Green R (2003), pp. 137–138.

286 Green R (2003), p. 142.

287 Green R (2003), p. 138.

288 TenneT TSO is a transmission system operator based in Germany and the Netherlands. Bundesnetzagentur, the German regulatory authority was reluctant to grant an authorisation for Tennet TSO because of Tennet's funding. See Bundesnetzagentur, Bundesnetzagentur trifft erste Zertifizierungsentscheidungen, press release (9 November 2012).

289 PJM (2010), p. 23.

The shallow costs of grid connection include the costs for the network facilities needed to connect a single user. The deep costs include the reinforcement of the grid. Whereas it is easy to identify the beneficiary of shallow costs, it is more difficult to identify the beneficiary of deep costs as deep costs may potentially benefit all grid users.

While shallow connections costs should probably be allocated to that particular user to give locational signals, deep connections costs could belong to the "residual network charges" and be treated like system operation costs.[290]

5.7.3 Classification of Pricing Models

Various models have been used for the pricing of transmission services in competitive markets for electricity worldwide. Even in the EU, there is "a wide heterogeneity in the current regulatory practice regarding electricity transmission tarification"[291] (Sect. 5.8). One of the contributing factors is how the electricity industry was organised prior to deregulation.[292]

Different Classifications The models can be classified in many ways. As different classifications focus on different aspects, one and the same model can fall under different classifications.

Cost-Based Transmission Pricing Paradigms To begin with, one can focus on costs and classify the models based on the costs that they are designed to allocate. The cost-based transmission pricing "paradigms" reflect the distinction between costs for existing transmission infrastructure and costs for new facilities. These paradigms include[293]:

- the rolled-in transmission pricing paradigm (all costs are summed up—"rolled-in"—into a single number, all cost components are included, and cost types are not distinguished; these methods include: contract path pricing, postage stamp pricing, the distance-based MW-Mile concept, and the power flow-based MW-Mile concept);
- the incremental transmission pricing paradigm (the customer pays the incremental cost, that is, the full cost for any new facilities that the transaction requires; these methods include: short-run incremental cost pricing, long-run incremental cost pricing, short-run marginal cost pricing, and long-run marginal cost pricing); and

[290] Pérez-Arriaga IJ and Smeers Y (2003), p. 191.

[291] Ruester S et al. (2012), p. 21. For national differences, see ENTSO-E (2013a).

[292] Niederprüm M and Pickhardt M (2002).

[293] Krause T (2003), pp. 11–12; Shirmohammadi D et al. (1991).

- the composite embedded/incremental transmission pricing paradigm (both the existing systems costs and the incremental costs of transmission are included).

Allocation-Based Paradigms Alternatively, one could also study on what basis the models are designed to allocate costs. Costs can be allocated based on different factors from real economy such as:

- generation or consumption (meaning that costs can be socialised by allocating them based on generation/consumption or peak-generation/peak-consumption);
- flow (meaning that the beneficiary pays for the use of transmission facilities based on power flow models);
- monetary gain (meaning that the beneficiary pays for the use of transmission facilities based on the expected monetary gain); or
- a combination of such methods.[294]

Welfare or Efficiency as the Basis of Cost Allocation Another alternative could be to allocate costs based on efficiency. But efficiency can be defined in different ways and studied in different contexts. The models can:

- focus primarily on the efficiency of electricity generation (simple pricing methods such as average cost prices determined by dividing the total annual grid costs by the annual peak load of the grid, the postage stamp method);
- focus primarily on the efficient allocation of transmission services (marginal cost pricing, nodal pricing); or
- seek to use transmission pricing in one way or another as a device to limit full-scale competition in the electricity market (pricing elements that are not based on actual costs, the contract-path method).[295]

Flow Distance-Sensitiveness, Geographical Electricity Price Differentiation, Auctions For the purposes of this book, one could also distinguish between various approaches regarding: (a) the flow; (b) distance-sensitiveness; (c) geographical electricity price differentiation; and (d) auctions. We will thus distinguish between four groups.

First, the models for the allocation of transmission capacity can be classified based on their approach regarding the flow. One can distinguish between:

- the contract path model (the path of the flow is a fictive one);
- the flow-based model (the path is the actual path);
- the point-to-point model (the path is not relevant); and

[294] PJM (2010), Appendix A: Guide of Cost Allocation Methods, and pp. 1–2.

[295] Niederprüm M and Pickhardt M (2002).

- the entry-exit model (the path is not relevant).

Second, the models can be classified based on their approach to distance sensitiveness. One can distinguish between:

- pricing that is not distance sensitive ("license plate" pricing, postage stamp pricing, and the entry-exit model); and
- pricing that is distance sensitive (the contract path model,[296] the point-to-point model, "pancaked rates", the distance-based MW-Mile methodology,[297] and the power-flow based MW-Mile method[298]).

Third, the models can be classified based on their approach regarding geographical electricity price differentiation. One can distinguish between models with[299]:

- uniform marginal pricing;
- a set of nodal or locational marginal prices; or
- only a few zonal marginal prices.

Fourth, costs related to infrastructure use could, to some extent, be recovered by using auctions as the market mechanism. One can therefore distinguish between:

- explicit auctions;
- implicit auctions (that require integrated transmission and electricity markets with zonal pricing, market splitting, or nodal pricing[300]; implicit auctions are applied in radial parts of the grid[301]); and
- other than market-based mechanisms.[302]

Although costs, in principle, could be recovered by auctions, some costs cannot be recovered in practice. Transmission tariffs would therefore need to cover the residual network costs in other ways.[303]

We can now study the various approaches regarding the flow, distance-sensitiveness, and geographical electricity price differentiation.

5.7.4 *Pricing Models: Approach to Flow*

When discussing different pricing models based on their approach to flow (Sect. 5.7.3), one can start with the contract path model.

---

[296] Krause T (2003), p. 13.

[297] Krause T (2003), p. 13.

[298] Krause T (2003), pp. 14–15.

[299] Leuthold FU et al. (2005).

[300] Twomey P et al. (2006).

[301] Duthaler C and Finger M (2008).

[302] Twomey P et al. (2006).

[303] Ruester S et al. (2012), p. 20.

The Contract Path Model Under the contract path model, electricity is assumed to flow according to the contract path fiction. The contract path fiction is not suitable for capacity allocation unless the grid is radial, but it may be used for pricing purposes in both radial and meshed grids.

In the EU, the contract path model has been used in some implicit auctions for transmission capacity in radial parts of the grid such as cross-border interconnectors.[304] When the contract path model is used in implicit auctions, the relevant TSO allocates a certain amount of day-ahead transmission rights to the electricity exchange.

The postage stamp model (Sect. 5.7.5) is an application of the contract path model.

In European gas markets, network charges must not be calculated based on contract paths.[305]

The Flow-Based Model Under the flow-based model, electricity is assumed to flow through all parallel paths. Flow-based pricing establishes a price based on the costs of the various parallel paths actually used when the power flows. Because flow-based pricing can account for all parallel paths used by the transaction, all transmission infrastructure owners with facilities on any of the parallel paths could be compensated for the transaction.[306]

In the EU, the flow-based model is applied to the allocation of costs for the use of cross-border electricity transmission systems. A TSO that hosts cross-border flows of electricity is entitled to compensation. It is paid by the operators of national transmission systems from which cross-border flows originate and the systems where those flows end.[307] The amounts are based on costs incurred[308] and decided on by the Commission.[309] In addition, producers and/or consumers pay the tariffs applied by each TSO. The level of tariffs should provide locational signals at Community level "where appropriate".[310]

In the US, the FERC permits a variety of proposals, including distance-sensitive and flow-based pricing.[311]

The Point-to-Point Model The flow-based model has in some cases been replaced by the point-to-point model. The point-to-point model is based on the use of nodal pricing (Sect. 5.7.6). The actual path of the flow is not relevant. There are examples of the use of the point-to-point model in the US.

---

[304] Duthaler C and Finger M (2008).

[305] Article 13(1) of Regulation 715/2009 on conditions for access to natural gas transmission networks.

[306] FERC, Order No. 888, p. 45, footnote 95.

[307] Articles 13(1) and 13(2) of Regulation 714/2009 on conditions for access to the network for cross-border exchanges in electricity.

[308] Recital 15 and Article 13(6) of Regulation 714/2009.

[309] Article 13(4) of Regulation 714/2009.

[310] Article 14(2) of Regulation 714/2009.

[311] FERC, Order No. 888, p. 45: "The Commission explained that this "[g]reater pricing flexibility is appropriate in light of the significant competitive changes occurring in wholesale generation markets, and in light of our expanded wheeling authority under the Energy Policy Act of 1992", referring to FERC Stats. & Regs. _ 31,005 at 31,136.

The FERC's Order No. 888 requires public utilities to file "a single open access tariff that offers both network, load-based service and point-to-point, contract-based service".[312] The FERC has defined various qualified point-to-point transmission services in Order No. 888 and the Open Access Transmission Tariff.[313] The Open Access Transmission Tariff was amended by Order No. 890.

PJM, CAISO, and ERCOT replaced their previous flow-based zonal models with point-to-point models. Under these models, the system operator (ISO or RTO in the US) computes locational marginal prices for each network node.

The fact that the ISO computes locational marginal prices for each network node exposes market participants to congestion and marginal loss costs. To offset or hedge these costs, market participants can acquire Financial Transmission Rights (FTRs) issued by the ISO (Chap. 12). An FTR entitles its holder to receive the price difference between the two grid nodes specified by the FTR. FTRs are funded by the price differences between grid nodes (the congestion rent) collected by the ISO.[314]

The FERC allows a transmission provider to propose a formula rate that assigns costs consistently to firm point-to-point and network services. The FERC does not require the use of any particular rate methodology.[315]

The Entry-Exit Model Under the entry-exit model, the entry point and the exit point are independent for transmission capacity and tariff purposes (see also Sect. 5.7.5). The tariff paid for transmission is the sum of entry and exit tariffs. Consequently, entry-exit tariffs can give locational and temporal signals. This makes the entry-exit model suitable for unbundled and liberalised electricity markets.

In the EU, there is a difference between electricity and gas markets. (a) The entry-exit model is not mandatory for the electricity market.[316] The choice of the entry-exit model depends on the regulatory authority. The tariffs or the method of calculating them are approved or fixed by the regulatory authority.[317] (b) The entry-exit model is nevertheless mandatory for the EU gas market.[318] The entry-exit model is not constrained by the balance requirement because gas can be stored.[319] In principle, gas can be sold "entry paid" to a

---

[312] FERC, Order No. 888, Final Rule. Open Access Transmission Tariff, Section 1.48: "Transmission Service: Point-To-Point Transmission Service provided under Part II of the Tariff on a firm and non-firm basis".

[313] FERC, Order No. 888, Open Access Transmission Tariff, Section 1.35 (Point-To-Point Transmission Service); Section 1.13 (Firm Point-To-Point Transmission Service), Section 1.18 (Long-Term Firm Point-To-Point Transmission Service), Section 1.42 (Short-Term Firm Point-To-Point Transmission Service), Section 1.27 (Non-Firm Point-To-Point Transmission Service).

[314] Duthaler C and Finger M (2008); Frontier Economics Pty Ltd (2009), section 4.1.3.

[315] FERC, Order No. 888, pp. 301–304.

[316] For electricity, see Article 14(2) of Regulation 714/2009 on conditions for access to the network for cross-border exchanges in electricity.

[317] See recital 36 of Directive 2009/72/EC (Third Electricity Directive). See Articles 15(7), 32(1), 37(1), 37(6), 37(8) and 37(10) of Directive 2009/72/EC (Third Electricity Directive). See also Article 13(4) of Regulation 714/2009 on conditions for access to the network for cross-border exchanges in electricity: "The Commission shall decide on the amounts of compensation payments payable . . ."

[318] Article 13(1) of Regulation 715/2009 on conditions for access to natural gas transmission networks.

[319] See, for example, Articles 15 and 17 of Regulation 715/2009 (on conditions for access to natural gas transmission networks) on storage and LNG facilities.

trading hub such as a central counterparty without any final destination. The development of trading hubs can increase competition between suppliers.

The entry-exit model can reduce congestion problems, if the entry and exit tariffs reflect congestion and give proper locational signals. This depends, first, on the TSO that manages electricity flows and has information about geographical demand/supply imbalances and, second, on its discretion to fix the tariffs.

5.7.5 Pricing Models: Distance Sensitivity

In addition to their approach to flow, pricing models can be classified based on distance sensitivity. (a) The model is distance sensitive where the cost of transmitting power depends on how far the power moves within the entity.[320] (b) The model is not distance sensitive when the rate does not depend on how far the electricity moves within one entity's transmission system.[321]

Distance sensitivity has two sides. On one hand, distance-sensitive rates may discourage unwise investments in long-distance transmission. On the other, distance-sensitive pricing may be a barrier to wholesale power competition and the integration of markets.[322]

In the EU, distance-related tariffs may not be applied by network operators in cross-border electricity trade.[323]

It is customary to distinguish the following models based on distance sensitivity: "pancaked rates" (distance sensitive); "license plate" pricing (not distance sensitive); "postage stamp" pricing (not distance sensitive within one zone); the "highway/byway" rate method (a hybrid); and the entry-exit model (not distance sensitive).

Pancaked Rates Pancaked rates is a term that means a distance-sensitive pricing method for cross-zonal transmission services. The rates are "pancaked" when each system charges its full rate to provide transmission service. This method of pricing is expensive and discourages electricity producers from supplying power over long distances and through several transmission systems.[324]

Before the liberalisation of the European electricity sector, "tariff pancaking" existed in cross-border transmission. An inter-TSO compensation mechanism (ITC) was introduced

[320] FERC, Order No. 888, p. 45, footnote 95.

[321] FERC, Order No. 888, p. 44, footnote 94.

[322] Brown MH and Sedano RP (2004), pp. 24–25.

[323] Article 14(1) of Regulation 714/2009 on conditions for access to the network for cross-border exchanges in electricity.

[324] Brown MH and Sedano RP (2004), pp. 24–25. See also US Senate Committee on Energy and Natural Resources (2008), testimony by Gary Hanson, Chairman South Dakota Public Utilities Commission.

in 2002 to abolish these cross-border tariffs. Pancaking was prohibited.[325] Moreover, there must not be any specific network charge on individual transactions for declared transits of electricity.[326] Consequently, grid charges are paid at the point of generation and/or at the point of consumption in the internal market.[327]

License Plate Pricing License plate pricing is the opposite of pancaked rates. Unlike pancaking, it is not distance sensitive. License plate pricing means that each user of the transmission system pays the tariff applicable in its own area. This approach would favour users in low-cost areas.[328] License plate pricing would not properly allocate costs to grid users.[329]

The Postage Stamp Model or Point Tariffs There is only one postage for mailing a letter anywhere in the same country. "Postage stamp tariffs" could be used even in electricity transmission. Under the postage stamp model, the transmission rate is the same for similar flows in the same zone.

A postage stamp tariff—also known as point tariff—is not distance sensitive within the same zone. As postage stamp pricing is an example of the use of the contract path model, it can be distance-sensitive and result in pancaked tariffs when electricity is transmitted over two or more systems.[330] The calculation of entry-exit tariffs for each TSO's transmission system would result in a postage stamp tariff.

In principle, postage stamp tariffs allow established suppliers and new entrants to compete on an equal cost basis. In practice, however, postage stamp tariffs are average cost tariffs that can distort markets. Without postage stamp tariffs, the more densely populated areas would have lower costs for transmission service compared with rural areas. With postage stamp tariffs, costs are shifted from rural areas to urban areas.[331] Postage stamp tariffs thus cause cross-subsidisation from low cost entry points to high cost entry points, and electricity producers located in less densely populated areas and in higher cost areas should favour postage stamp pricing over "license plate pricing".[332] There would be no cross-subsidisation if postage stamp tariffs reflected costs sufficiently, but locationally differentiated tariffs tend to reflect costs better compared with postage stamp tariffs.

There are many examples of postage stamp pricing worldwide. It has been used in the US, Germany, and the Nordic countries.

---

325 Article 4 of Regulation 1228/2003 and now Article 14 of Regulation 714/2009; Cameron PD (2007), p. 152, para 5.81; Ruester S et al. (2012), p. 25.

326 Article 14(5) of Regulation 714/2009.

327 Cameron PD (2007), p. 152, para 5.82.

328 Brown MH and Sedano RP (2004), pp. 24–25.

329 US Senate Committee on Energy and Natural Resources (2008), testimony by Gary Hanson, Chairman South Dakota Public Utilities Commission.

330 FERC, Order No. 888, p. 44, footnote 94.

331 US Senate Committee on Energy and Natural Resources (2008), testimony by Gary Hanson, Chairman South Dakota Public Utilities Commission.

332 Brown MH and Sedano RP (2004), pp. 24–25.

The Federal Energy Regulatory Commission (FERC) used to allow only postage stamp, contract-path pricing in its Transmission Pricing Policy Statement before its policy change. Under the new policy, the FERC permitted a variety of proposals, including distance-sensitive and flow-based pricing.[333]

Postage stamp pricing was used in Germany under VV II Strom.[334] VV II Strom was the result of the First Electricity Directive that provided for two alternative ways to organise grid access.[335] Member States could choose either the single buyer procedure[336] or negotiated access to the system.[337] Germany was the only Member State that chose negotiated access.[338] VV Strom was a contractual regime negotiated by the associations of German industry. VV I Strom (VV-1 Electricity) failed to obtain Commission support as it envisaged a contract path and distance-based price model and for other reasons.[339] According to VV II Strom, Germany was divided up into the north zone and the south zone. For transmissions within each trade area, there was a transmission charge called the grid utilisation charge (GUC). Within each trade area, the GUC depended on total grid costs and the magnitude of the transacted power. The distance between the supply and demand nodes was irrelevant. An additional charge, the transportation charge, was applied for cross-border trade between the two trade areas or between a trade area and a neighbouring country.[340] According to the Commission, the "T" component was not compatible with competition law.[341] New legislation replaced VV II Strom after the adoption of the Second Electricity Directive.[342]

Postage stamp pricing—also known as the point tariff system—is used in the Nordic countries. An electricity producer pays a fee to the grid operator for each kWh that it supplies to the grid. End users pay a fee for each kWh that they extract from the grid. The energy can be traded freely in the whole area without additional fees.[343] For instance, the point tariff system is a legal requirement in Finland. The point tariff system applies to transmission in the area of Finland but not to cross-border transmission.[344] There are similar legal requirements in Sweden[345] and Norway.[346]

---

[333] FERC, Order No. 888, p. 45.

[334] Verbändevereinbarung über Kriterien zur Bestimmung von Netznutzungsentgelte für elektrische Energie.

[335] Article 16 of Directive 96/92/EC (First Electricity Directive).

[336] Article 18(1) of Directive 96/92/EC (First Electricity Directive).

[337] Article 17(1) of Directive 96/92/EC (First Electricity Directive).

[338] Heuterkes M and Janssen M (2008), pp. 53–54.

[339] Cameron PD (2007), pp. 334–335, para 13.34.

[340] Niederprüm M and Pickhardt M (2002). See also Growitsch C and Wein T (2005).

[341] See Cameron PD (2007), p. 336, para 13.38.

[342] Directive 2003/55/EC (Second Electricity Directive).

[343] Nord Pool Spot, Point tariff system: "This means for example, that a retailer in Southern Sweden may buy power from a producer in Northern Sweden. Of course, such a deal does not cause the producer's power to go all the long way from Northern Sweden to Southern Sweden. The principle is simply that for each hour of operation a producer has to pour an amount of power into the grid that corresponds to the amount that the retailer's customers have tapped off the grid. This system is also referred to as a stamp tariff system".

[344] Subsection 2 of section 15 of the Electricity Markets Act (elmarknadslag/sähkömarkkinalaki 386/1995): "Nätinnehavaren skall för sin del ordna förutsättningar för att en kund genom att betala avgifterna får rätt att använda hela landets elnät utgående från sin anslutningspunkt, med undantag av utlandsförbindelser (punktprissättning)".

[345] Chapter 4, section 2 of the Electricity Act (ellag 1997:857).

[346] Chapter 4, section 1 of the Energy Act (energiloven).

The Highway/Byway Rate Method The highway/byway rate method is a hybrid between the license and postage stamp rates. Under this method higher voltage transmission uses the postage stamp pricing scheme and lower voltage uses the license plate pricing scheme. Consequently, one can avoid some of the cost shift that would be caused by a pure postage stamp model and provide incentives for investment in high voltage transmission and generation.[347]

The Entry-Exit Model The entry-exit model is not distance sensitive. Under the entry-exit model, the entry point and the exit point are independent for transmission capacity and tariff purposes. The tariff paid for transmission is the sum of entry and exit tariffs. In cross-zonal transmission, the calculation of entry-exit tariffs separately for each TSO's system would result in a postage stamp tariff.

5.7.6 Pricing Models: Approach to Geographical Electricity Price Differentiation

The third way to classify pricing models is based on geographical electricity price differentiation. As the transmission of electricity is a service that is differentiated in space and time, cost causality would require network tariffs to have some level of time differentiation and some level of geographical differentiation.[348] As regards geographical electricity price differentiation, it is possible to distinguish between: uniform marginal pricing; zonal marginal pricing; and nodal marginal pricing.

Uniform Marginal Pricing There is no geographical differentiation with uniform marginal pricing. Uniform marginal pricing means that the same price for transmission will be charged for the same volumes regardless of the particular characteristics of the location such as losses and congestion. Uniform marginal pricing typically is pool-based. The absence of price differentiation works efficiently only in the absence of congestion.[349]

Where the market is functioning with a single price, the quality of short-term signals can be improved by considering losses in the financial settlement and by using redispatching.[350]

Zonal Pricing The introduction of zonal pricing is one way to solve problems inherent in uniform marginal pricing.[351] With zonal pricing, the market is divided into two or more zones depending on their respective congestion costs. There is a

[347] US Senate Committee on Energy and Natural Resources (2008), testimony by Gary Hanson, Chairman South Dakota Public Utilities Commission.

[348] Pérez-Arriaga IJ and Smeers Y (2003), p. 179.

[349] Leuthold FU et al. (2005).

[350] Pérez-Arriaga IJ and Smeers Y (2003), pp. 185–186.

[351] Leuthold FU et al. (2005).

reference node for each zone. The price of the respective reference node is applied to the whole zone. Higher prices are paid in zones where demand exceeds system capacity of transmission.[352] Zonal pricing can thus influence competition.

Sweden. The case of *Swedish Interconnectors*[353] shows that the number of bidding zones may influence electricity prices and the utilisation of cross-border interconnectors.[354]

While Norway and Denmark consist of several zones, there used to be just one area for Sweden. At the same time, hydro reservoirs were concentrated in the north of Sweden, while centres for consumption and cross-border interconnectors to Denmark and Germany were in the south.[355]

After complaints filed by Dansk Energi in 2006, the European Commission opened proceedings against Svenska Kraftnät for abuse of a dominant position (Article 102 TFEU) on grounds that the Commission had reason to believe that Svenska Kraftnät was "limiting the amount of export transmission capacity available on electricity interconnectors situated along the Sweden's borders, with the objective of relieving internal congestion on its network".[356]

To address the concerns about the Swedish transmission market, Svenska Kraftnät committed to subdivide the Swedish electricity market into several bidding zones.[357] Since 1 November 2011, Sweden has been divided into four electricity areas.[358] This resulted in structural price differences between northern and southern Sweden and to more effective trading on the power exchange. Electricity prices are expected to remain higher in Southern Sweden because of cross-border flows to Denmark and Germany.[359]

EU. Zonal pricing is the legal requirement for day-ahead markets in the EU. The CACM Network Codes developed by ENTSO-E and applied by TSOs[360] must "foresee that TSOs implement capacity allocation in the day-ahead market on the basis of implicit auctions via a single price coupling algorithm which simultaneously determines volumes and prices in all relevant zones, based on the marginal pricing principle". Calculated zonal prices must differ, if there is insufficient transmission capacity to enable all requested trades.[361] The price of transmission capacity between zones (when congestion occurs) must be defined as "the difference between the corresponding day-ahead zonal electricity prices".[362] The algorithm shall also allow for block bids and other products that are deemed "feasible and appropriate".[363]

---

352 Leuthold FU et al. (2005).

353 Case COMP/B-1/39.351—Swedish Interconnectors.

354 See also Teusch J et al. (2012), p. 23.

355 Teusch J et al. (2012), p. 23.

356 MEMO/09/191.

357 Notice published pursuant to Article 27(4) of Council Regulation (EC) No 1/2003 in Case COMP/B-1/39.351—Swedish Interconnectors (2009/C 239/04).

358 Energimarknadsinspektionen (2012): "Eftersom bakgrunden till att Sverige delades in i fyra elområden den 1 november 2011 var en anmälan från Dansk Energi hos EU:s konkurrensmyndighet som senare resulterat i ett tioårigt åtagande från Svenska kraftnät om en indelning av Sverige i fyra områden med gränser i snitt 1, 2 och 4 så innebär det att elområdena kommer att vara gällande under åtminstone tio år".

359 Energimarknadsinspektionen (2012).

360 ACER, Framework Guidelines on Capacity Allocation and Congestion Management for Electricity (29 July 2011), section 1.1.

361 *Ibid*, section 3.1.

362 *Ibid*, section 3.2.

363 *Ibid*, section 3.1.

However, it is not a legal requirement for the allocation of long-term transmission capacity. According to the ENTSO-E Network Code on Forward Capacity Allocation, "[p] rice determination for Long Term Transmission Rights shall follow the marginal price principle resulting from the corresponding Forward Capacity Allocation".[364] This excludes neither zonal pricing nor nodal pricing.

The limitations of the zonal model have been described in literature and zonal pricing has been criticized. According to theory, it is second-best to nodal pricing. It has been argued that zonal pricing "does not capture the actual state of grid flows and congestion" and that it "fails to provide information ... about the need for transmission reinforcement and investment".[365] Moreover, zonal pricing is regarded as "an effort to treat fundamentally different locations as though they where the same".[366]

On the other hand, a zonal model has also been regarded as an acceptable simplification under certain circumstances.[367] Whereas nodal pricing evolved as a necessity in highly meshed networks (such as in North America), zonal pricing is accepted as a good approximation in more radial networks, where the structure of congestion is less complex. The highly meshed network in continental Europe is developing into a zonal market, often with countries constituting entire zones.[368]

In the future, spatial issues are likely to become more important as an increasing number of relatively small generation installations will be located in areas suitable for electricity generation from renewable sources rather than close to end consumers. The resulting challenges to the grid may increase the differences between nodal and zonal prices.

Nodal Pricing Nodal pricing (locational marginal pricing) is based on nodal valuations.[369] The nodal price of electricity in a certain node of a given network and at a certain time is the marginal cost of supplying electricity at that node and time.[370] The background is that transmission constraints such as congestion and transmission losses can produce different electricity prices at each node. The cumulative effect of such constraints is that the marginal valuation of generation and extraction depends on the node. The marginal cost of transmission can therefore be defined as the difference between nodal valuations.

Marginal valuations vary over time. (a) The transport infrastructure is almost fixed for the medium run. As both electricity generation and electricity

[364] Recital 10 of ENTSO-E NC FCA (2 April 2014), recital 10.

[365] Neuhoff K et al. (2011a), p. 3. See also Neuhoff K et al. (2013).

[366] Hogan WW (1999). See Leuthold FU et al. (2005).

[367] Creti A et al. (2010). See also Pérez-Arriaga IJ and Olmos L (2005); Bjorndal M and Jornsten K (2007); Glachant JM et al. (2006).

[368] OECD/IEA (2005), pp. 19 and 95.

[369] Pérez-Arriaga IJ and Smeers Y (2003), p. 184. See also Schweppe FC et al. (1988).

[370] Pérez-Arriaga IJ and Smeers Y (2003), p. 184.

consumption vary depending on the weather, fuel prices, the availability of generation installations, and other reasons, nodal valuations must vary as well.[371] (b) Marginal valuations vary from node to node depending on the load, that is, the cause of congestion. When the load is low, the difference between nodal valuations is smaller. During peak periods when the load is high, the difference between nodal valuations is greater as there is more congestion.[372]

Nodal prices can provide a good short-term transmission price signal. By definition, nodal prices vary with time and space. They are non-discriminatory, because they are not transaction-based.[373] Nodal pricing is therefore regarded as efficient.[374] Nodal pricing could thus be a way to manage congestion in the short term.[375]

One may ask whether nodal pricing would bring benefits even in the EU as has been claimed.[376] For example, could it help to improve the scheduling of generation and interconnection flows?[377]

Unfortunately, nodal pricing is complicated and likely to increase transaction costs.[378] There would also be problems in the long term,[379] in particular in meshed transmission networks (that is, other than simple linear or radial transmission networks).[380] (a) Nodal prices are incapable of recovering the complete network costs.[381] Neither congestion costs nor transmission losses are directly related to expenditure incurred by the TSO.[382] When transmission prices are determined based on the marginal values of these two costs (nodal prices), they provide a surplus because the prices are, by definition, higher than the energy losses. The surplus can be used to pay for fixed costs, but the surplus is not enough to cover all infrastructure costs.[383] There is a "residual network cost". (b) Specific transmission network charges to the network users would be needed to recover the entire network costs.[384] This leads to multi-part tariffs that even include a charge that is independent of the short-term use of the network.[385]

---

[371] Crampes C (2003), pp. 114–115.

[372] Crampes C (2003), pp. 114–115.

[373] Pérez-Arriaga IJ and Smeers Y (2003), p. 184.

[374] See, for example, Hogan WW (1999); Neuhoff K et al. (2011a), pp. 4–5.

[375] It is also regarded as more efficient than redispatching. See Monopolkommission (2013) number 343.

[376] Neuhoff K et al. (2011), p. 27. See also Monopolkommission (2013), number 342.

[377] Neuhoff K et al. (2011b), p. 11.

[378] OECD/IEA (2005), p. 77.

[379] Pérez-Arriaga IJ and Smeers Y (2003), p. 184.

[380] Oren SS et al. (1995).

[381] Pérez-Arriaga IJ and Smeers Y (2003), p. 177.

[382] Crampes C (2003), p. 114.

[383] Crampes C (2003), p. 105.

[384] Pérez-Arriaga IJ and Smeers Y (2003), pp. 184–185.

[385] Pérez-Arriaga IJ and Smeers Y (2003), p. 189.

> In the US, PJM allocates FTRs principally to utilities that serve retail customers. In other words, FTRs are allocated to "those transmission customers representing consumers that have paid for the fixed investment in the transmission system and are thus entitled to rights to the electricity transfer capability of this system".[386]

Moreover, it is not clear whether the properties of nodal prices might be directly extended to distribution networks.[387]

One can distinguish between full nodal pricing (PJM,[388] New Zealand), generator nodal pricing (New York, New England, Singapore), a hybrid design (Midwest), and markets transitioning to some form of locational marginal pricing (Texas, California). Both full nodal pricing and generator nodal pricing are examples of locational marginal pricing.[389]

5.8 Transmission Pricing Models in the EU

5.8.1 General Remarks

The transmission pricing model should reflect the TSO's fixed and variable costs, costs caused by congestion, and incremental costs. Various cost concepts (Sect. 5.7.2) have been used in EU electricity law depending on the context. This can make it difficult to design transmission tariffs.[390]

Transmission tariffs are determined in different ways depending on the Member State.[391] Tariffs do not target to recover the same costs in all countries, and tariffs in some cases also include costs not directly related to transmission infrastructure.[392]

> For example, Regulation 714/2009 contains the following cost concepts: "costs actually incurred"[393]; "all costs incurred as a result of hosting cross-border flows"[394]; "forward-looking long-run average incremental costs"; "losses"/"network losses"; "congestion"; "investment costs for infrastructure"; "investment in new infrastructure"; "the cost of existing infrastructure"[395]; and "capital or operating costs".[396]

---

[386] US Senate Committee on Energy and Natural Resources (2010), statement of Vincent P. Duane. Citing Pennsylvania-New Jersey-Maryland Interconnection, 81 FERC 61,257 at 62,240–241 (1997).

[387] Pérez-Arriaga IJ and Smeers Y (2003), pp. 186–187. For difficulties, see Box 7–1.

[388] OECD/IEA (2005), pp. 84–86. For the costs and benefits of PJM's model, see Mansur ET and White MW (2012).

[389] Frontier Economics Pty Ltd (2009), Executive summary.

[390] Crampes C (2003), p. 105.

[391] Generally, see ENTSO-E Overview of transmission tariffs in Europe: Synthesis 2013 (June 2013). See also Ruester S et al. (2012).

[392] Ruester S et al. (2012).

[393] Articles 13(3) and 14(1) of Regulation 714/2009.

[394] Article 13(1) of Regulation 714/2009.

[395] Articles 13(6), 14(2) and 14(3) of Regulation 714/2009.

[396] Article 17(1)(e) of Regulation 714/2009.

Regulation 714/2009 defines the main principles for the tarification of cross-border transmission services in the EU. It sets the legal basis for an obligatory inter-TSO compensation mechanism according to which TSOs are compensated for all the costs incurred from hosting cross-border flows of electricity on their networks by those TSOs from whose systems cross-border flows originate or where they end.[397]

Regulation 838/2010 complements Regulation 714/2009 by laying down the concrete methodology and providing for an ITC fund.[398] The ITC fund provides compensation payments for (1) the costs of losses incurred in national transmission systems from hosting cross-border flows of electricity; and (2) the costs of making infrastructure available to host cross-border flows. (1) Losses are estimated by using a "with-and-without-transit" method for 72 defined snapshots a year (opportunity costs). The base scenario refers to the real network flows in the relevant period; the other scenario refers to the flows that would have occurred if no transits of electricity had taken place.[399] (2) As regards the cost for making infrastructure available, ACER shall make a proposal based on a "technical and economic assessment of the forward-looking long-run average incremental costs ... of making such electricity transmission infrastructure available".[400]

The models used for the allocation of transmission capacity and for pricing in the national markets of the EU provide weak or no locational signals in many Member States. This is in particular the case where transmission tariffs are paid only by end consumers (load, the L-component). In the absence of locational signals, electricity generation installations can be located a long way from end consumers.

5.8.2 *Allocation of Costs Between Generation and Load*

General Remarks

One may ask how the various transmission costs should be allocated between generation and load in the light of EU law. The allocation depends on whether the costs are: (a) costs for transmission services; (b) costs for grid connection; or (c) costs for cross-border transmission services.

Transmission Costs

Member States have plenty of discretion. Most Member States tend to allocate transmission costs to load, that is, socialise them among end consumers. The share of end consumers is 100 % in Germany and most other Member States.[401] This reflects the fact that transmission costs were socialised under the previous market

[397] Articles 13(1) and 13(2) of Regulation 714/2009.

[398] Recital 7 of Regulation 838/2010. Paragraphs 1.1 and 1.2 of Part A of Annex to Regulation 838/2010.

[399] Ruester S et al. (2012), p. 26.

[400] Point 5.3 of Part A of Annex to Regulation 838/2010.

[401] See ENTSO-E, Overview of transmission tariffs in Europe: Synthesis 2013 (June 2013).

model when it did not make any sense for a vertically integrated utility to charge itself for transmission.

A few countries allocate a non-negligible component of costs to electricity producers. Many of them (Norway, Sweden, Denmark, Finland, the UK, Ireland) are countries with mature or organised wholesale electricity markets.[402]

In the absence of a cost component allocated to electricity producers (G-component), transmission costs fail to give locational signals to electricity producers.[403] In this case, generation installations can be located a long way from end consumers. To reduce congestion and new infrastructure investment by locational signals, TSOs have an incentive to reduce the L-component and increase the G-component.[404] A high G-component tends to foster electricity generation in locations close to end consumers and locations with a sufficient transmission infrastructure.[405]

Costs for the Grid and Grid Connection

Somebody should pay for the grid. One may ask how costs for the grid and grid connection are allocated. The costs can again be allocated to the TSO, generation, or load.

Main Rule The main rule under the Third Electricity Directive is that the system operator is responsible for the system. The TSO is thus responsible for the connection of electricity producers to the transmission grid[406] and the DSO is responsible for the connection of microgenerators to the distribution grid.[407] System operators have a right to collect tariffs. However, the tariffs must be non-discriminatory, and they will be fixed or approved by the regulatory authority.[408] Consequently, system operators should bear the burden of most costs but allocate them to customers that share the costs in the form of tariffs.

EU law does not require system operators to bear all costs for grid connection. System operators must regulate the allocation of costs in their standard rules.[409]

---

[402] PJM, A Survey of Transmission Cost Allocation Issues, Methods and Practices (10 March 2010), pp. 1–2; Monopolkommission (2013), number 347.

[403] Ruester S et al. (2012), p. 21.

[404] Monopolkommission (2013), number 345. For the need to increase the use of the G-component due to Energiewende, see number 348.

[405] *Ibid*, number 346.

[406] Article 12 of Directive 2009/72/EC (Third Electricity Directive).

[407] Articles 3(3) and 25 of Directive 2009/72/EC (Third Electricity Directive).

[408] Recital 36 and Article 12 of Directive 2009/72/EC (Third Electricity Directive). See also Articles 25, 32(1), 37(1), 37(6)(a), 37(8), and 37(10) of Directive 2009/72/EC (Third Electricity Directive).

[409] First subparagraph of Article 16(3) of Directive 2009/28/EC (RES Directive). See also second subparagraph of Article 16(3) of Directive 2009/28/EC (RES Directive), and Article 14(1) of Regulation 714/2009 on conditions for access to the network for cross-border exchanges.

Member States may require transmission system operators and distribution system operators to bear such costs in full or in part when it is "appropriate" to do so.[410]

In practice, there have been different ways to allocate these costs in the Member States. This can be illustrated with three cases: (1) shallow and deep costs of grid connection; (2) offshore wind farms; and (3) the regulatory practice in Norway.

Example: Shallow and Deep Costs of Grid Connection The shallow costs of grid connection include the costs for the network facilities that are necessary to connect a single user. The deep costs include the reinforcement of the grid. While it is easy to identify the beneficiary of shallow costs, it is more difficult to identify the beneficiary of deep costs as deep costs may potentially benefit all grid users. Deep connection costs could, therefore, belong to "residual network charges" and be treated like system operation costs.[411]

The difference between shallow and deep costs is reflected in the Member States' regulatory practices. In some countries, a new grid user only pays shallow costs. In other countries, the new grid user also has to bear, in whole or in part, costs related to the reinforcement of the core grid. Moreover, there is some variation regarding the allocation of these costs to particular user groups, and renewable generators may be exempted from paying a deep connection charge in some countries.[412]

Example: Offshore Wind Farms Offshore wind farms provide a concrete example of different ways to allocate these shallow and deep costs in the Member States.

To connect an offshore wind farm to the grid, one needs connecting lines. (a) In some Member States of the EU, project developers have to pay for the construction of the line, transformers, and all other necessary installations for the connection to the grid.[413] (b) In Germany, however, costs for connecting offshore wind farms to the grid used to be allocated to the system operator.[414] This rule placed a heavy financial burden on system operators and increases their risk exposure.[415] On the other hand, it also increased investment in wind power. To mitigate the risk exposure of system operators, Germany decided to socialise most of the losses caused by the failure of system operators to connect offshore wind farms to the grid.[416]

---

[410] Article 16(4) of Directive 2009/28/EC (RES Directive).

[411] Pérez-Arriaga IJ and Smeers Y (2003), p. 191.

[412] Ruester S et al. (2012), p. 22.

[413] SOU 2008:13, p. 200, Table 5–3.

[414] § 17 Abs. 2a EnWG. See also Bundesnetzagentur (2009); Tscherning R (2011), p. 83.

[415] In Germany, failure to connect offshore wind farms to the grid can lead to liability for loss sustained by the wind farm operators. See §§ 9 and 10 EEG 2012. Tennet TSO settled one such case. See Windreich AG, Windreich und TenneT einigen sich auf Interimgsanbindung für Offshore-Windpark Deutsche Bucht, press release (25 October 2012).

[416] § 17e and § 17f EnWG.

One may also need upgrades in the grid before the wind farm can be connected to it. (a) In many countries, costs for upgrades in the transmission network are allocated to the system operator (and socialised in the form of tariffs). (b) There are nevertheless exceptions. In Sweden, upgrades that benefit only the wind farm owner have been paid by the wind farm owner. When upgrades benefit others (mainly in the 400 kV grid), the system operator (Svenska Kraftnät, the Swedish national grid) pays part of the costs: "project developers pay the costs if the upgrade refers to a radial line; while costs are shared between the owner of the production plant and Svenska Kraftnät when the upgrade is done in the meshed grid".[417]

In the US, the Pro Forma Open Access Transmission Tariff allocates costs for facilities constructed by the transmission service provider to the service customer where they are constructed for the sole use or benefit of that particular transmission customer.[418]

Example: Investment Contributions in Norway In Norway, a network company may require: (1) an investment contribution to cover the costs of connecting new customers to the network; and (2) an investment contribution for reinforcing the network for existing customers. Investment contributions are fixed independently of the customer's expected energy out-take.

The objective of the investment contribution is to make the customer responsible for the costs related to a new connection or an upgrade of the customer's existing network connection. (a) The network owner may distribute the investment contribution between customers that are connected at the time the installation is brought to completion and customers that will be connected at a later point in time, but no later than 10 years after completion of the installation. (b) In cases where connection requires the reinforcement of installations with several network users, a pro rata share of these costs may be included in the investment contribution. (c) In meshed networks, the network owner can usually not require an investment contribution as it is difficult to attach the need for new investments to one particular customer.[419]

Cross-Border Transmission Costs

From a legal perspective, there is a difference between the allocation of transmission costs and the allocation of cross-border transmission costs in the EU. The main principles for the tarification of cross-border transmission services are based on

[417] SOU 2008:13, pp. 200–203.

[418] FERC Order No. 888, Pro Forma Open Access Transmission Tariff, Appendix D, Section 1.10 Direct Assignment Facilities; FERC Order No. 888, Pro Forma Open Access Transmission Tariff, Appendix D, Section 34 Rates and Charges.

[419] NVE, Annual Report 2009, pp. 30–34.

Regulation 714/2009[420] and Regulation 838/2010[421] as well as Regulation 347/2013.

Although the recovery of costs is not explicitly mentioned in Regulation 714/2009, it is clear that charges must "reflect actual costs incurred" and the level of tariffs must, "where appropriate … provide locational signals at Community level, and take into account the amount of network losses and congestion caused, and investment costs for infrastructure".[422]

Regulation 838/2010 allocates costs for cross-border transmission services in more detail.[423] The Regulation is based on the assumption that the convergence of transmission costs allocated to generators (the G-component) would contribute to a level playing field among electricity producers.[424] On the other hand, it is not regarded as necessary to harmonise costs allocated to load (end consumers, the L-component) in different Member States.[425] Regulation 838/2010 therefore fixes nominal upper levels for the G-component in national tariffs.[426] When monitoring the tariffs, the Agency will consider conflicting objectives.[427]

Regulation 347/2013 that applies to new transmission "projects of common interest" provides "rules and guidance for the cross-border allocation of costs and risk-related incentives" for these projects.[428] The main principle of cost allocation is that "[t]he costs for the development, construction, operation and maintenance … should in general be fully borne by the users of the infrastructure".[429]

Variable Allocation of Costs, Locational Tariffs

There are some examples of the use of variable allocation of costs or locational tariffs in the EU. (a) In the UK, grid access tariffs for electricity producers are area tariffs that depend on the balance of generation and load. In generation surplus areas, grid access tariffs are high. In generation deficit areas, grid access tariffs are

[420] Article 14 of Regulation 714/2009.

[421] Regulation 838/2010 on laying down guidelines relating to the inter-transmission system operator compensation mechanism and a common regulatory approach to transmission charging.

[422] Article 14 of Regulation 714/2009.

[423] Article 1 of Regulation 838/2010.

[424] Point 1 of Part B (Guidelines for A Common Regulatory Approach to Transmission Charging) of Annex to Regulation 838/2010.

[425] Ruester S et al. (2012), p. 25. For national differences, see ENTSO-E, Overview of transmission tariffs in Europe: Synthesis 2013 (June 2013).

[426] Points 1–3 of Part B (Guidelines for A Common Regulatory Approach to Transmission Charging) of Annex to Regulation 838/2010.

[427] Point 4 of Part B (Guidelines for A Common Regulatory Approach to Transmission Charging) of Annex to Regulation 838/2010.

[428] Article 1(1) of Regulation 347/2013 (Regulation on guidelines for trans-European energy infrastructure).

[429] Recital 35 of Regulation 347/2013.

low and can even be negative. The same approach is applied to load. (b) Norway and Sweden have locational access tariffs. Norway applies an hourly modulation of the losses component of the access charge.[430]

5.8.3 *Models for the Pricing of Transmission Services: Main Rules*

Various models have been used for the regulation of the pricing of transmission services worldwide. The pricing model can depend on the transmission capacity allocation model (distance-related, flow-based, the contract path, market-based or not market-based) and the transmission services (cross-border, cross-zonal, intra-zonal).

In the EU, there is "a wide heterogeneity in the current regulatory practice regarding electricity transmission tarification".[431] One of the contributing factors is how the electricity industry was organised prior to deregulation.[432] With increasing market integration, the focus of EU law is moving from the pricing of cross-border transmission services to cross-zonal transmission services.[433]

Moreover, the Third Electricity Directive does not lay down the model for fixing the tariffs in detail. In any case, the tariffs should be cost-reflective and provide system operators appropriate incentives.[434]

The CACM Regulation is more detailed. Several of the provisions of the CACM Regulation relate to the pricing of day-ahead or intraday cross-zonal capacity. The purposes of the CACM Regulation include, among others: promotion of effective competition in the generation, trading and supply of electricity; ensuring optimal use of the transmission infrastructure; ensuring fair and non-discriminatory treatment of market participants; ensuring and enhancing the transparency and reliability of information; respecting the need for a fair and orderly market and fair and orderly price formation; providing non-discriminatory access to cross-zonal capacity[435]; maximising economic surplus for the single intraday coupling per trade[436]; making intraday cross-zonal capacity pricing repeatable and scalable[437]; ensuring

---

[430] Supponen M (2011), p. 66.

[431] Ruester S et al. (2012), p. 21.

[432] Niederprüm M and Pickhardt M (2002).

[433] Point 3 of Article 2 of Regulation 543/2013 (on submission and publication of data in electricity markets and amending Annex I to Regulation 714/2009): "... 'bidding zone' means the largest geographical area within which market participants are able to exchange energy without capacity allocation; ..."

[434] Articles 32(1), 37(1)(a), 37(6)(a) and 37(8) of Directive 2009/72/EC (Third Electricity Directive).

[435] Article 3 of Commission Regulation .../.. (CACM Regulation).

[436] Article 51(1)(a) of Commission Regulation .../.. (CACM Regulation).

[437] Article 51(1)(e) of Commission Regulation .../.. (CACM Regulation).

that intraday cross-zonal capacity is priced in a manner which reflects market congestion and is based on actual orders[438]; and ensuring that capacity traded in the day-ahead and intraday time frames is allocated implicitly.[439]

Prohibition of Discrimination and Distance-Related Tariffs Discrimination is prohibited.[440] In *Essent Netwerk*, the CJEU banned a statutory surcharge to the electricity transmission rate when the proceeds were used to give precedence to domestic electricity producers.[441]

The use of distance-related tariffs is limited in various ways in the EU (but not in the US where the FERC permits a variety of proposals[442]). This can increase the distance between electricity generation and electricity consumption.

First, it is limited in the context of cross-border transmission services. Regulation 714/2009 provides that "charges applied by network operators for access to networks . . . shall not be distance-related".[443] In other words, neither tariffs for cross-border transmission services nor charges for grid connection may be distance-related[444] and it would not normally be appropriate to apply a special tariff to be paid only by exporters or importers (in addition to the general charge for access to the national network).[445]

Second, some limitations apply to tariffs for the transmission of RES-E. Transmission and distribution tariffs must not discriminate against RES-E, including in particular "electricity from renewable energy sources produced in peripheral regions, such as island regions, and in regions of low population density".[446]

Third, there are particular rules on the permitted pricing models (Sect. 5.8.4). In the light of EU electricity law, the available pricing models depend on the nature of the transmission services (cross-border, cross-zonal, intra-zonal). However, these prohibitions say little about the pricing method.

Intra-Zonal Transmission Services The two main rules applicable to the pricing of intra-zonal transmission services leave the pricing method just as open. First, third

---

[438] Article 55(1) of Commission Regulation . . ./.. (CACM Regulation).

[439] Recital 13 of Commission Regulation . . ./.. (CACM Regulation).

[440] Article 32(1) and recital 36 of Directive 2009/72/EC (Third Electricity Directive).

[441] Case C-206/06 Essent Netwerk Noord BV and Others [2008] ECR I-05497; see Gram Mortensen BO (2008).

[442] FERC, Order No. 888, p. 45: ". . . [g]reater pricing flexibility is appropriate in light of the significant competitive changes occurring in wholesale generation markets, and in light of our expanded wheeling authority under the Energy Policy Act of 1992 . . ." FERC referred to FERC Stats. & Regs. _ 31,005 at 31,136.

[443] Article 14(1) of Regulation 714/2009.

[444] The terms charges and tariffs seem to be are used interchangeably. For the use of the term tariffs, see recital 15 of Regulation 714/2009, recital 32 of Directive 2009/72/EC (Third Electricity Directive) and Article 14(2) of Regulation 714/2009. For the use of the term charges, see Article 14(1) of Regulation 714/2009.

[445] Recital 15 of Regulation 714/2009.

[446] Article 16(7) of Directive 2009/28/EC (RES Directive).

party access must be "based on published tariffs, applicable to all eligible customers and applied objectively and without discrimination between system users".[447] Second, the regulatory authority will fix or approve transmission or distribution tariffs or their methodologies.[448]

In practice, there can be great variation depending on the country, the voltage level, and the network company. It is in any case customary to distinguish between: network tariffs for very large-scale industrial consumers (connected to the national grid at the high-voltage level); network tariffs for large-scale industrial consumers (connected to the regional transmission network); network tariffs for the smallest industrial consumers (connected to the distribution network); and local consumers.

> The Swedish Energy Markets Inspectorate described the local network tariffs as follows: "The analysis shows great variation, with some network companies using fixed pricing, while others choose to use a form of pricing using only energy and/or effect-dependent tariff components. However, the result shows that the network companies in general use the same basic principle – 'the customer shall bear the costs it gives rise to' – when allocating costs across the customer collective, and where each cost category (fixed, effect-dependent, energy-dependent) are reflected in a tariff component of equivalent size".[449]

Cross-Zonal Transmission Services For the allocation/pricing of cross-zonal and cross-border transmission capacity, the EU has a target model (Sect. 5.6.1).[450]

Regulation 714/2009 lays down the target model, requires the coordinated allocation of cross-border capacity through non-discriminatory market-based solutions,[451,452] and requires auctions for the allocation of cross-border transmission capacity.[453] There must not be any specific network charge on individual transactions for declared transits of electricity.[454]

For long-term cross-zonal capacity allocation/pricing, the default rule is explicit auctions under ENTSO-E Network Code on Forward Capacity Allocation.[455] Long-term transmission rights (PTR, FTR) must be used for the allocation of long-term

---

[447] Article 32(1) of Directive 2009/72/EC (Third Electricity Directive).

[448] See also Article 37(8) of Directive 2009/72/EC (Third Electricity Directive): "In fixing or approving the tariffs or methodologies and the balancing services, the regulatory authorities shall ensure that transmission and distribution system operators are granted appropriate incentive, over both the short and long term, to increase efficiencies, foster market integration and security of supply and support the related research activities".

[449] Energy Markets Inspectorate (2012), p. 22.

[450] ERGEG, Draft Framework Guidelines on Capacity Allocation and Congestion Management for Electricity: Initial Impact Assessment. Ref: E10-ENM-20-04 (8 September 2010), p. 43 and Annex 4, p. 73; Creti A et al. (2010).

[451] Article 12(2) of Regulation 714/2009.

[452] Points 2.1 and 2.8 of Annex I to Regulation 714/2009.

[453] Point 2.1 of Annex I to Regulation 714/2009.

[454] Article 14(5) of Regulation 714/2009.

[455] Article 1(1) of ENTSO-E NC FCA (2 April 2014).

transmission capacity.[456] TSOs should thus auction physical transmission rights or financial rights with equivalent effect (Sect. 12.1). The Network Code uses the marginal pricing principle for the allocation of forward capacity and for the pricing of long-term transmission rights for each bidding zone border.[457]

The pricing of day-ahead cross-zonal transmission capacity is regulated in another way. The CACM Network Codes must set out that TSOs implement capacity allocation/pricing in the day-ahead market from implicit auctions and the marginal pricing principle.[458] This is reflected in the CACM Regulation.[459] Moreover, the day-ahead cross-zonal capacity charge must "reflect market congestion" and amount to "the difference between the corresponding day-ahead clearing prices of the relevant bidding zones". Other charges are prohibited.[460]

The development of cross-zonal intraday trading would be important for the integration of RES-E. However, it lacks behind. The pricing of intraday cross-zonal capacity is left open in the CACM Regulation. TSOs shall develop a proposal for a single methodology for pricing intraday cross-zonal capacity, including a proposal on harmonised maximum and minimum clearing prices to be applied in all bidding zones which participate in single intraday coupling.[461]

There are several options.[462] (a) For instance, fully implicit trading without congestion prices is applied in ELBAS (the Nordic and Baltic region, Germany, Benelux) and the Flexible Intraday Trading Scheme (FITS, implicit continuous cross-border trading between France, Germany, Austria, and Switzerland). (b) There are also examples of intraday auctions with implicit (or explicit) capacity pricing (Italian and Iberian markets, LMP markets in the US).

While fully implicit trading without congestion prices would increase information efficiency, the choice of intraday auctions with implicit (or explicit) capacity pricing would increase consistency between energy and capacity prices (simultaneous pricing efficiency) and liquidity compared with the other alternative.

5.8.4 *Particular Models for the Pricing of Transmission Services*

The various models for the pricing of transmission services have thus been regulated in different ways in EU electricity law.

---

[456] ACER, Framework Guidelines on Capacity Allocation and Congestion Management for Electricity (29 July 2011), section 4.1.

[457] Recital 10, Article 33(2) and Article 45 of ENTSO-E NC FCA (2 April 2014).

[458] ACER, Framework Guidelines on Capacity Allocation and Congestion Management for Electricity (29 July 2011), section 3.1.

[459] Article 38 of Commission Regulation .../.. (CACM Regulation).

[460] Article 42 of Commission Regulation .../.. (CACM Regulation).

[461] Articles 54–55 of Commission Regulation .../.. (CACM Regulation).

[462] Bellenbaum J et al. (2014).

The Contract Path Model

The contract path model is not generally prohibited in EU electricity law although network charges must not be calculated based on contract paths in European gas markets.[463]

The contract path model has been used in explicit or implicit auctions for transmission capacity in radial parts of the grid.[464] In this case, there is no difference between the contract path and the actual flow.

In a meshed grid, however, contractual flows would not reflect actual physical flows. Neither would they provide efficient locational signals. The contract path model could then distort competition and hamper cross-border trade.

The Flow-Based Model

The flow-based model is being advocated as the target model for highly meshed grids in the EU. It requires a more detailed grid description. If there is sufficient capacity, the flow-based method can increase price convergence. Flow-based pricing is possible even in the US.[465]

The flow-based model must be applied at least to cross-zonal and cross-border electricity transmission in the EU.

First, the flow-based method is a legal requirement for the allocation of cross-zonal transmission capacity. The CASC Framework Guidelines require the use of the flow-based method (or the Available Transfer Capacity Method) for the allocation of transmission capacity at each zone border.[466]

Second, a TSO that hosts cross-border flows of electricity is entitled to compensation under Regulation 714/2009. It is paid by the operators of national transmission systems from which cross-border flows originate and the systems where those flows end.[467]

Because of legal requirements, there are several examples of the use of flow-based pricing in the EU. The flow-based model is used in market coupling projects (Chap. 6).[468]

463 Article 13(1) of Regulation 715/2009 on conditions for access to natural gas transmission networks: "... By 3 September 2011, the Member States shall ensure that, after a transitional period, network charges shall not be calculated on the basis of contract paths ..."

464 Duthaler C and Finger M (2008).

465 See FERC, Order No. 888, p. 45.

466 ACER, Framework Guidelines on Capacity Allocation and Congestion Management for Electricity (29 July 2011), sections 1.1 and 2.1.1.

467 Articles 13(1) and 13(2) of Regulation 714/2009.

468 Point 3.2 of Annex I to Regulation 714/2009.

The Entry-Exit Model, Postage Stamp Pricing

Under the entry-exit model, the tariff paid for transmission is the sum of entry and exit tariffs. As entry-exit tariffs can give locational and temporal signals, the entry-exit model could be suitable for unbundled and liberalised electricity markets.

The entry-exit model is used in different ways in the European electricity and gas markets. It is mandatory for the EU gas market.[469] This has implications for contract practice. As gas can be stored,[470] it would be possible to sell gas "entry paid" to a trading hub such as a central counterparty without any final destination.

The entry-exit model is not mandatory for the electricity market.[471] One can distinguish between (a) cross-border/cross-zonal and (b) intra-zonal transmission services.

As regards cross-border/cross-zonal transmission services, there is no room for the entry-exit model because of legal constraints:

- The choice of the capacity allocation and pricing model is constrained by Regulation 714/2009 that requires explicit or implicit auctions[472] and the flow-based model for cross-border transmission services.
- The choice of the capacity allocation and pricing model is further constrained by network codes under the CACM Framework Guidelines. The CACM network codes must require the use of the flow-based method (or the Available Transfer Capacity Method) for the allocation of transmission capacity at each zone border.[473] The CACM network codes must define the price of transmission capacity between zones (when congestion occurs) as the difference between the corresponding day-ahead zonal electricity prices.[474]

In principle, the entry-exit model can be used even within one bidding zone.[475] Whether the entry-exit model is applied to intra-zonal transmission services (rather than cross-border or cross-zonal transmission services) depends on the regulatory

[469] Article 13(1) of Regulation 715/2009 on conditions for access to natural gas transmission networks: "... Tariffs for network users shall be non-discriminatory and set separately for every entry point into or exit point out of the transmission system. Cost-allocation mechanisms and rate setting methodology regarding entry points and exit points shall be approved by the national regulatory authorities ..."

[470] See, for example, Articles 15 and 17 of Regulation 715/2009 (on conditions for access to natural gas transmission networks) addressing storage and LNG facilities.

[471] See Article 14(2) of Regulation 714/2009.

[472] Point 2.1 of Annex I to Regulation 714/2009.

[473] ACER, Framework Guidelines on Capacity Allocation and Congestion Management for Electricity (29 July 2011), sections 1.1 and 2.1.1.

[474] *Ibid*, section 3.2.

[475] For the definition of bidding zone, see point 3 of Article 2 of Regulation 543/2013 (on submission and publication of data in electricity markets and amending Annex I to Regulation 714/2009): "... 'bidding zone' means the largest geographical area within which market participants are able to exchange energy without capacity allocation ..."

authority and the TSO.[476] Generally, national regulatory authorities "should ensure that transmission and distribution tariffs are non-discriminatory and cost-reflective, and should take account of the long-term, marginal, avoided network costs from distributed generation and demand-side management measures".[477]

Examples of the Use of the Entry-Exit Model There are examples of the use of the entry-exit model in electricity markets. It is used by Nord Pool Spot that calls it a point tariff system or postage stamp pricing.

> Nord Pool Spot has explained its pricing model as follows: "The idea of point tariff system is that the producers are paying a fee to the grid for each kWh that they pour into the grid and the end users pay a fee for each kWh that they draw off the grid. Moreover, the kilowatt-hour can be traded freely in the whole area without additional fees.
>
> This means for example, that a retailer in Southern Sweden may buy power from a producer in Northern Sweden. Of course, such a deal does not cause the producer's power to go all the long way from Northern Sweden to Southern Sweden. The principle is simply that for each hour of operation a producer has to pour an amount of power into the grid that corresponds to the amount that the retailer's customers have tapped off the grid. This system is also referred to as a stamp tariff system".[478]
>
> In Finland, transmission pricing is based on the entry-exit model and postage stamp tariffs. Unlike in Sweden, there is only one area. The tariffs are the same in the whole country independent of location.[479]

The Point-to-Point Model and Nodal Pricing in the EU

One may ask whether it would be permitted to use the point-to-point model and nodal pricing in the EU. It seems that the regulation of capacity allocation and pricing models does not leave much room for nodal pricing in EU electricity law.

First, there are constraints on the choice of the pricing model: distance-related tariffs may not be applied by network operators in cross-border transmission services[480] (and point-to-point tariffs might be regarded as distance-related)[481]; explicit or implicit auctions must be used to allocate cross-border transmission capacity[482]; and the flow-based method (or the ATC method) must be used for the allocation of transmission capacity at each zone border.[483]

---

[476] See Articles 15(7), 32(1), 37(1), 37(6), 37(8) and 37(10) of Directive 2009/72/EC (Third Electricity Directive). See also Article 13(4) of Regulation 714/2009: "The Commission shall decide on the amounts of compensation payments . . ."

[477] Recital 36 of Directive 2009/72/EC (Third Electricity Directive).

[478] Nord Pool Spot (2014). See also Hammer U (2009), p. 273.

[479] Energy Market Authority, Finland (2012), section 3.1.3.

[480] Article 14(1) of Regulation 714/2009.

[481] CEER (2002).

[482] Point 2.1 of Annex I to Regulation 714/2009.

[483] ACER, Framework Guidelines on Capacity Allocation and Congestion Management for Electricity (29 July 2011), sections 1.1 and 2.1.1.

Second, there are constraints on the use of congestion income necessary to pay for the system operators' costs in cross-border transmission. The constraints apply, in particular, to existing interconnectors.[484] There is an exemption for new direct current interconnectors.[485] The constraints make it more difficult for system operators to cover their fixed costs under this model.[486]

Excursion: The Point-to-Point Model and Nodal Pricing in the US

The point-to-point model based on nodal pricing is regarded as efficient in electricity markets theory[487]—at least in the short term (Sect. 5.7.6). The flow-based model has in some cases been replaced by the point-to-point model in the US.

To start with, the Federal Energy Regulatory Commission's (FERC) Order No. 888[488] requires public utilities to file "a single open access tariff that offers both network, load-based service and point-to-point, contract-based service".[489] The FERC has defined various qualified point-to-point transmission services in its Order No. 888 and the Open Access Transmission Tariff.[490] The Open Access Transmission Tariff was amended by Order No. 890.[491]

PJM, CAISO, and ERCOT replaced the previous flow-based zonal model with a point-to-point model. According to this model, the system operator (ISO or RTO in the US) computes locational marginal prices for each network node.

---

484 Article 16(6) of Regulation 714/2009. See also point 6 of Annex I to Regulation 714/2009. For example, Article 16(6) of Regulation 714/2009 was considered in CWE Auction Rules, Version 1.0, Article 9.01(b): "For the avoidance of any doubt, all costs which arise by guaranteeing the compensations to Participants for Reductions of Held Capacities are fully covered by the congestion revenues used as described in article 16.6 of Regulation (EC) No 714/2009 . . ."

485 Article 17(1) of Regulation 714/2009.

486 Crampes C (2003), p. 105.

487 Hogan WW (1999).

488 FERC, Promoting Wholesale Competition Through Open Access Non-discriminatory Transmission Services by Public Utilities; Recovery of Stranded Costs by Public Utilities and Transmitting Utilities, Order No. 888 (10 May 1996).

489 FERC, Order No. 888, Final Rule, Open Access. See also FERC, Order No. 888, Open Access Transmission Tariff, Section 1.48: "Transmission Service [means]: Point-To-Point Transmission Service provided under Part II of the Tariff on a firm and non-firm basis".

490 FERC, Order No. 888, Open Access Transmission Tariff, Section 1.35 (Point-To-Point Transmission Service); Section 1.13 (Firm Point-To-Point Transmission Service), Section 1.18 (Long-Term Firm Point-To-Point Transmission Service), Section 1.42 (Short-Term Firm Point-To-Point Transmission Service), Section 1.27 (Non-Firm Point-To-Point Transmission Service).

491 FERC, Preventing Undue Discrimination and Preference in Transmission Service, Order No. 890 (16 February 2007).

The FERC allows a transmission service provider to propose a formula rate that assigns costs consistently to firm point-to-point and network services. The FERC does not require the use of any particular rate methodology.[492]

The fact that the ISO computes locational marginal prices for each network node exposes market participants to congestion and marginal loss costs. To offset or hedge these costs, market participants can acquire Financial Transmission Rights (FTRs) issued by the ISO (see Chap. 8). An FTR entitles its holder to receive the price difference between the two grid nodes specified by the FTR. FTRs are funded by the price differences between grid nodes (the congestion rent) collected by the ISO.[493]

In the US, PJM allocates FTRs principally to utilities that serve retail customers: "These rights in total reflect the physical capability of the transmission system to deliver electricity; they are finite and their number is determined through analyses conducted by the RTO/ISO. The allocation of these finite rights is made to those transmission customers representing consumers that have paid for the fixed investment in the transmission system and are thus entitled to rights to the electricity transfer capability of this system".[494]

References

Bellenbaum J, Bucksteeg M, Kallabis T et al (2014) Intra-day cross-zonal capacity pricing. Study on behalf of OFGEM. University of Duisburg-Essen, Chair for Management Science and Energy Economics Prof. Dr. Christoph Weber

Bhattacharyya SC (2011) Energy economics: concepts, issues, markets and governance. Springer, Heidelberg. doi:10.1007/978-0-85729-268-1

Bjorndal M, Jornsten K (2007) Benefits from coordinating congestion management—the Nordic power market. Energy Policy 35(3):1978–1991. doi:10.1016/j.enpol.2006.06.014

Brown MH, Sedano RP (2004) Electricity transmission: a primer. National Council on Electricity Policy, Washington, DC

CAISO (2006) California independent system operator corporation electric tariff filing to reflect market redesign and technology upgrade, February 9. Available at CAISO website. http://www.caiso.com/Documents/TransmittalLetter_09-Feb-06.pdf

Cameron PD (2007) Competition in energy markets: law and regulation in the European Union, 2nd edn. Oxford University Press, Oxford

Cannella MA, Disher EO, Gagliardi RT (1996) Beyond the contract path: a realistic approach to transmission pricing. Electr J 9(9):26–33. doi:10.1016/S1040-6190(96)80455-6

CEER (2002) Guidelines for tariff structure pertaining to intrastate and cross border transport and transit. Position Paper of the CEER for the Madrid V Regulatory Forum, Madrid, 7/8 February 2002. Version 2.0, 28 January

Crampes C (2003) Cost recovery and short-run efficiency. In: Lévêque F (ed) Transport pricing of electricity networks. Kluwer, Boston, pp 105–154. doi:10.1007/978-1-4757-3756-1_4

---

[492] FERC, Order No. 888, p. 301: "... we will allow a transmission provider to propose a formula rate that assigns costs consistently to firm point-to-point and network services. While not requiring the use of any particular rate methodology, we will no longer summarily reject a firm point-to-point transmission rate developed by using the average of the 12 monthly system peaks".

[493] Duthaler C and Finger M (2008).

[494] US Senate Committee on Energy and Natural Resources (2010), statement of Vincent P. Duane.

Creti A, Fumagalli E, Fumagalli E (2010) Integration of electricity markets in Europe: relevant issues for Italy. Energy Policy 38(11):6966–6976. doi:10.1016/j.enpol.2010.07.013

Curien N (2003) Cost calculation. In: Lévêque F (ed) Transport pricing of electricity networks. Kluwer, Boston, pp 35–72. doi:10.1007/978-1-4757-3756-1_2

de Hauteclocque A, Talus K (2011) Capacity to compete: recent trends in access regimes in electricity and natural gas networks. In: Delvaux B, Hunt M, Talus K (eds) EU energy law and policy, vol 3. Intersentia, Cambridge, pp 234–235

DG Competition Report on Energy Sector Inquiry, SEC(2006) 1724 (10 January 2007)

Duthaler C, Finger M (2008) Financial transmission rights in Europe's electricity market. Ecole Polytechnique Fédérale de Lausanne and Delft University of Technology, Discussion paper series on the coherence between institutions and technologies in infrastructures, WP0803, November. http://mir.epfl.ch/webdav/site/mir/users/181931/public/wp0803.pdf

EFET (2007) Key principles in the treatment of electricity transmission capacity rights and their linkage to day ahead allocation mechanisms, June

Energimarknadsinspektionen (2012) Elområden i Sverige. Analys av utveckling och konsekvenserna på marknaden. EI R2012:06. Eskilstuna

Energy Market Authority, Finland (2012) National report 2012 to the agency for the Cooperation of Energy Regulators and to the European Commission Finland, 13 July

Energy Market Authority, Finland (2014) National report 2014 to the agency for the Cooperation of Energy Regulators and to the European Commission, 10 July

Energy Markets Inspectorate (2012) The Swedish electricity and natural gas markets 2011. EI R2012:11. Eskilstuna

ENTSO-E (2013a) Overview of transmission tariffs in Europe: synthesis 2013. June

ENTSO-E (2013b) Policy note on TSO capacity buy-back schemes. Market Integration Working Group, November

ERCOT (2008) Understanding: Texas Nodal Market Implementation. Available at ERCOT website

FERC (2012) Energy primer: a handbook of energy market basics. July. Available at FERC website

Frontier Economics Pty Ltd (2009) Generator Nodal pricing – a review of theory and practical application: a report prepared for the Australian Energy Market Commission, Melbourne, February

Glachant JM, Belmans R, Meeus L (2006) Implementing the European internal energy market in 2005–2009. Eur Rev Energy Mark 1(3):51–85

Gram Mortensen BO (2008) The European Court of Justice decision in Case C-206/06, Essent Netwerk Noord BV. Eur Energy Environ Law Rev 17(6):389–393

Green R (1997) Electricity transmission pricing: an international comparison. Utilities Policy 6 (3):177–187. doi:10.1016/S0957-1787(97)00022-2

Green R (2003) Cost recovery and the efficient development of the grid. In: Lévêque F (ed) Transport pricing of electricity networks. Kluwer, Boston, pp 137–153. doi:10.1007/978-1-4757-3756-1_5

Growitsch C, Wein T (2005) Negotiated third party access—an industrial organisation perspective. Eur J Law Econ 20:2165–2183. doi:10.1007/s10657-005-1735-0

Hammer U (2009) Norwegian regulation of wind turbines. In: Anker HT, Egelund Olsen B, Rønne A (eds) Legal systems and wind energy: a comparative perspective. DJØF Publishing, Copenhagen, pp 269–275

Harvey SM, Hogan WW, Pope SL (1996) Transmission capacity reservations implemented through a spot market with transmission congestion contracts. Electr J 9(9):42–55. doi:10.1016/S1040-6190(96)80457-X

Heuterkes M, Janssen M (eds) (2008) Die Regulierung von Gas- und Strommärkten in Deutschland. Beiträge aus der angewandten Wirtschaftsforschung Nr. 29. Westfälische Wilhelms-Universität Münster, Münster

Hogan WW (1999) Transmission congestion: the Nodal-Zonal debate revisited. http://www.hks.harvard.edu/fs/whogan/nezn0227.pdf

Hsu M (1997) An introduction to the pricing of electric power transmission. Utilities Policy 6 (3):257–270. doi:10.1016/S0957-1787(97)00013-1

Kopsakangas-Savolainen M, Svento R (2010) Comparing welfare effects of different regulation schemes: an application to the electricity distribution industry. Energy Policy 38 (11):7370–7399. doi:10.1016/j.enpol.2010.08.013

Kopsakangas-Savolainen M, Svento R (2014) Sähkömarkkinoiden sääntelystä ja sääntelymuotojen hyvinvointivaikutuksista. Kansantaloudellinen aikakauskirja 110(2):151–161

Krause T (2003) Evaluation of transmission pricing methods for liberalized markets – a literature survey. ETH, EEH power systems laboratory, Zürich, 7 July

Laffont JJ, Tirole J (1986) Using cost observation to regulate firms. J Polit Econ 94(3):614–641. doi:10.1086/261392

Lanz M, Fricke B, Anthrakidis A et al (2011) CO2-Emissionsminderung durch Ausbau, informationstechnische Vernetzung und Netzoptimierung von Anlagen dezentraler, fluktuierender und erneuerbarer Energienutzung in Deutschland. Umweltbundesamt, Climate Change 20/2011

Leuthold FU, Rumiantseva I, Weigt H et al (2005) Nodal pricing in the German electricity sector – a welfare economics analysis, with particular reference to implementing offshore wind capacities. http://dx.doi.org/10.2139/ssrn.1137382

Mansur ET, White MW (2012) Market organization and efficiency in electricity markets. Working Paper, January

Monopolkommission (2013) Sondergutachten 65. Energie 2013: Wettbewerb in Zeiten der Energiewende. Sondergutachten der Monopolkommission gemäß § 62 Abs. 1 EnWG. Bonn

Neuhoff K, Boyd R, Grau J et al (2011a) Renewable electric energy integration: quantifying the value of design of markets for international transmission capacity. DIW Discussion Papers No. 1166, Berlin

Neuhoff K, Hobbs BF, Newbery D (2011b) Congestion management in European power networks: criteria to assess the available options. Deutsches Institut für Wirtschaftsforschung, DIW Discussion Papers 1161, Berlin

Neuhoff K, Barquin J, Bialek JW et al (2013) Renewable electric energy integration: quantifying the value of design of markets for international transmission capacity. Energy Econ 40:760–772. doi:10.1016/j.eneco.2013.09.004

Niederprüm M, Pickhardt M (2002) Electricity transmission pricing: the German case. Atlantic Econ J 30(2):136–147. doi:10.1007/BF02299158

Nord Pool Spot (2014) The Nordic electricity exchange and the Nordic model for a liberalized electricity

NordREG (2007) Congestion management in the Nordic region: a common regulatory opinion on congestion management. Report 2/2007, June. NordREG, Copenhagen

OECD/IEA (2005) Lessons from liberalised electricity markets. IEA, Paris

Oren SS, Spiller PT, Varaiya P, Wu F (1995) Nodal prices and transmission rights: a critical appraisal. Electr J 8(3):24–35. doi:10.1016/1040-6190(95)90198-1

Pérez-Arriaga IJ, Olmos L (2005) A plausible congestion management scheme for the internal electricity market of the European Union. Utilities Policy 13(2):117–134. doi:10.1016/j.jup.2004.12.003

Pérez-Arriaga IJ, Smeers Y (2003) Guidelines on tariff setting. In: Lévêque F (ed) Transport pricing of electricity networks. Kluwer, Boston, pp 175–203. doi:10.1007/978-1-4757-3756-1_7

PJM (2010) A survey of transmission cost allocation issues, methods and practices, 10 March

Purchala K, Meeus L, Belmans R (2005) Congestion management in a market environment. In: Mielczarski W (ed) The European power supply industry. Elecktroenergetyki Politechniki Lodzkiej, pp 169–192

Rogerson WP (2003) Simple menus of contracts in cost-based procurement and regulation. Am Econ Rev 93(3):919–926. doi:10.1257/000282803322157160

Ruester S, von Hirschhausen C, Marcantonini C et al (2012) Topic 6. EU involvement in electricity and natural gas transmission grid tarification. Final Report. European University Institute, January. doi:10.2870/35561, doi:10.2870/35676

Schweppe FC, Caramanis MC, Tabors RD, Bohn RE (1988) Spot pricing of electricity. Kluwer, Boston

Shirmohammadi D, Rajagopalan C, Alward ER, Thomas CL (1991) Cost of transmission transactions: an introduction. IEEE Trans Power Syst 6(3):1006–1016. doi:10.1109/59.117002

SOU 2008:13. See Ackermann T, Centeno-Lopez E (2008)

Spicker J (2010) A. Formen des OTC-Handels. In: Schwintowski HP (ed) Handbuch Energiehandel, 2nd edn. Erich Schmidt Verlag, Berlin, pp 31–152

Statens energimyndighet (2006) Prisbildning och konkurrens på elmarknaden. ER 2006:13

Supponen M (2011) The influence of national and company interests on European electricity transmission investments. Dissertation, Aalto University

Svenska Kraftnät (2007) The Swedish electricity market and the role of Svenska Kraftnät. January

Talus K, Wälde T (2006) Electricity interconnectors: a serious challenge for EC competition law. Competition Regul Netw Indus 7(3):355–391

Teusch J, Behrens A, Egenhofer C (2012) The benefits of investing in electricity transmission: lessons from Northern Europe. CEPS Special Report, January

Tscherning R (2011) The European offshore supergrid and the expansion of offshore wind energy in Germany, Ireland and the United Kingdom – legal, political and practical challenges. Part 1. Eur Energy Environ Law Rev 20(3):76–87

Twomey P, Neuhoff K, Newbery D (2006) Incentives for an adequate, economic and reliable Swiss transmission grid. Final version. Swiss Federal Office of Energy (SFOE), Bern

US Senate Committee on Energy and Natural Resources (2008) Challenges and regional solutions to developing transmission for renewable electricity resources, 17 June

Vogelsang I (2006) Electricity transmission pricing and performance-based regulation. Energy J 27(4):97–126. doi:10.5547/ISSN0195-6574-EJ-Vol27-No4-5

Chapter 6
Market Coupling

6.1 General Remarks

Because of physical constraints, electricity markets have been national or regional. Electricity firms can nevertheless benefit from a larger market. Market coupling is a way to integrate neighbouring physical markets. Market coupling increases the market's size and liquidity and makes it attractive to participants. Market coupling belongs to the cornerstones of efforts to create the single (or internal) electricity market and has been estimated to bring large benefits.[1]

Benefits to Electricity Producers Market coupling can bring benefits to electricity producers. Obviously, electricity producers can benefit from a larger market for their generation capacity and different generation technologies. Increased use of implicit auctions (day-ahead markets) and continuous trading (intraday markets) across borders can increase liquidity and reduce volatility.[2] Moreover, access to cross-zonal trade in balancing services (Sect. 4.10.4) can help electricity producers to make better use of their flexible generation technologies.[3]

Market coupling can influence the bidding strategies of firms. It can increase the use of derivatives by reducing the cost of financial derivatives: market coupling increases liquidity and reduces spreads between the participating markets (Sect. 6.5). Financial instruments can also be used to replace physical flows (Chap. 12).

Market coupling can increase arbitrage. (a) Before market coupling, EU cross-border trade was mainly short-term arbitrage.[4] (b) After market coupling, arbitrage is not limited to the day-ahead or intraday market. This is because access rights for

[1] Booz & Company (2013), pp. 3–4.

[2] Article 1(1) of ENTSO-E NC CACM (27 September 2012). See also recitals 25 and 31.

[3] Article 11(2) of ENTSO-E Network Code on Electricity Balancing (6 August 2014).

[4] Booz & Company (2013), p. 74.

P. Mäntysaari, *EU Electricity Trade Law*, DOI 10.1007/978-3-319-16513-4_6

long- and medium-term capacity allocations must be firm transmission capacity rights subject to the use-it-or-lose-it (UIOLI) principle or the use-it-or-sell-it (UIOSI) principle.[5] Where transmission capacity rights sold in an explicit auction are subject to the UIOSI principle, the capacity is placed into an implicit auction should the holder fail to nominate any physical flows. The holder then receives the spread between the two markets (similar to the holder of financial transmission rights in the US). The fact that the holder can benefit from congestion financially can reduce the need for physical nominations and increase arbitrage.

Regardless of market coupling, balancing will still be carried out by TSOs within national transmission systems.[6]

Interconnectors The integration of national electricity markets would not be possible without cross-border interconnectors.[7] The building of new interconnectors can give investment signals to electricity producers as price differences in the two price zones are likely to be reduced. In the higher price zone (with possibly too little generation capacity), prices are reduced and electricity producers have worse incentives to invest in generation installations. In the lower price zone (with possibly greater generation capacity), prices are increased and electricity producers are given better incentives to invest in generation installations. The building of interconnectors can thus increase both market integration and the generation imbalance between zones.[8]

Third Electricity Directive One of the objectives of the Third Electricity Directive is to increase cross-border interconnection capacity. First, Member States are required to provide adequate economic incentives for the maintenance and construction of the necessary interconnection capacity.[9] Second, transmission system operators must be required to comply with minimum standards for the maintenance and development of interconnection capacity.[10] Third, transmission system operators must manage electricity flows on the system by considering exchanges with other interconnected systems.[11]

Transmission Capacity On the other hand, the mere existence of interconnectors between two markets does not in itself mean market integration.

---

[5] Annex I to Regulation 714/2009, point 2.5.

[6] Booz & Company (2013), p. 74.

[7] For definitions, see points 13–14 of Article 2 of Directive 2009/72/EC (Third Electricity Directive) and Article 2(1) of Regulation 714/2009 (on conditions for access to the network for cross-border exchanges in electricity). See also recitals 5 and 59–60 of Directive 2009/72/EC (Third Electricity Directive).

[8] Supponen M (2011), p. 81: "There is no natural end to the development of this generation imbalance if there is a permanent advantage in investing in one price zone compared to the other".

[9] Article 3(10) of Directive 2009/72/EC (Third Electricity Directive). See also Article 6(1).

[10] Article 15(5) of Directive 2009/72/EC (Third Electricity Directive).

[11] Point (d) of Article 12 of Directive 2009/72/EC (Third Electricity Directive).

There is no cross-border trade without the co-operation of TSOs, that is, unless the TSO in the exporting control area allows a generation surplus and the TSO in the importing control area allows a corresponding generation deficit. TSOs manage cross-border flows by first calculating in a network model how big this surplus and deficit can be considering the technical constraints. The result of the calculation is a cross-border transmission capacity that can be offered to the market (for the methods, see Sects. 5.3 and 5.7).[12]

Transmission Rights A cross-border trader needs transmission rights on the interconnector. In the past, cross-border trade was not possible unless traders bought transmission rights on the relevant interconnector directly from the capacity holder or on a transmission capacity auction. This did not ensure the optimal use of transmission capacity as congestion problems remained.

Market Coupling The purpose of market coupling is to allocate capacity by optimising the total economic surplus of the different coupled spot markets' order books, while ensuring that the physical limits of the grid are respected. Particular market coupling mechanisms can thus be used to manage congestion problems and to determine the optimal direction, volume, and price of electricity flows between the markets.

In market coupling, co-operation between TSOs and power exchanges ensures, during every hour of operation, that all the available trading capacity is utilised with power flowing from the low-price area to the high-price area. Coupling can help to increase security of supply and reduce regional price differences without full integration of the markets. Existing electricity exchanges and TSOs have an incentive to promote market coupling as it does not require any structural changes in the market but enables the exchanges and TSOs to stay independent and continue their business.

Target Model There are various models for market coupling (Sect. 6.2). The agreed target design for day-ahead markets in Europe is price coupling (Sect. 6.3). The key rules are based on Regulation 714/2009, which replaced Regulation 1228/2003.[13]

The EU also has a target model for the allocation of transmission capacity. When the European Council set the target of 2014 for the completion of the internal electricity market in February 2011, the European Council asked regulators to contribute to a "European Energy Work Plan 2011–2014". In July 2011, ACER therefore issued Draft Framework Guidelines on Capacity Allocation and Congestion Management for Electricity (CACM Framework Guidelines). The CACM Framework Guidelines identify four key elements for the design of the target

[12] See, for example, Supponen M (2011), pp. 11–12.

[13] Regulation 714/2009 on conditions for access to the network for cross-border exchanges in electricity and repealing Regulation (EC) No 1228/2003.

model, namely: methods for calculating capacity and zone definition (either flow-based or available transfer capacity)[14]; forward markets for capacity allocation (a single platform for the allocation of long-term transmission rights—PTR and FTR—at European level)[15]; day-ahead capacity allocation (implicit auctions)[16]; and intraday capacity allocation (continuous implicit trading, direct explicit access as a transitional measure).[17]

Market Coupling Projects The target model can only be implemented stepwise, "as the regulatory framework for electricity trade and the physical structure of the transmission grid are characterised by significant differences between Member States and regions". Market coupling at the regional level may therefore be used as an intermediate step.[18]

The North-Western Europe (NWE) market coupling went live on 4 February 2014. NWE coupled the day-ahead markets across Central Western Europe (CWE), the UK, the Nordic countries, the Baltic countries, and the SwePol link between Sweden and Poland. NWE market coupling was therefore a significant achievement in the integration of European electricity markets (Sect. 6.4). NWE day-ahead market coupling uses the Price Coupling of Regions (PCR) solution. The full price coupling of the South-Western Europe (SWE) and NWE day-ahead electricity markets went live on 13 May 2014. On 19 November 2014, the 4M Market Coupling (4M MC) was launched. It prepares the way for the integration of the CEE region and the rest of Europe.

Nominated Electricity Market Operators The CACM Regulation requires the designation of entities as NEMOs. The function of a NEMO is to perform the single day-ahead and/or intraday coupling. They are thus electricity exchanges.[19]

Subject to certain exceptions, a NEMO designated in one Member State has the right to offer day-ahead and intraday trading services with delivery in another Member State.[20] This means that the CACM Regulation increases competition by allowing power exchanges to compete within the same countries or bidding areas.

---

[14] ACER, Framework Guidelines on Capacity Allocation and Congestion Management for Electricity (29 July 2011), section 2.1.1.

[15] *Ibid*, section 4.1.

[16] *Ibid*, section 3.1.

[17] *Ibid*, section 5.

[18] Recital 28 of Commission Regulation . . ./.. (CACM Regulation).

[19] First subparagraph of Article 7(1) of Commission Regulation . . ./.. (CACM Regulation): "NEMOs shall act as market operators in national or regional markets to perform in cooperation with TSOs single day-ahead and intraday coupling. Their tasks shall include receiving orders from market participants, having overall responsibility for matching and allocating orders in accordance with the single day-ahead coupling and single intraday coupling results, publishing prices and settling and clearing the contracts resulting from the trades according to relevant participant agreements and regulations".

[20] Article 4(5) of Commission Regulation . . ./.. (CACM Regulation).

Table 6.1 MCO, NEMO, and TSO

<table>
<tr><td colspan="2">European level, MCO functions[a]:
• carried out by NEMOs jointly with other NEMOs;
• matching orders from the day-ahead and intraday markets for different bidding zones in an optimal manner;
• making the results of the calculation available to all power exchanges;
• simultaneous allocation of cross-zonal capacities.</td></tr>
<tr><td>National level, NEMO[b]:
• performs tasks related to single day-ahead or single intraday coupling;
• carries out MCO functions jointly with other NEMOs.</td><td>National level, TSO[c]:
• is responsible for the calculation of available capacities and scheduling;
• notifies NEMO and MCO of available capacities for implicit auctions.</td></tr>
</table>

[a]Recital 5, point 30 of Article 2, and Article 7(2) of Commission Regulation …/.. (CACM Regulation)
[b]Point 23 of Article 2 of Commission Regulation …/.. (CACM Regulation)
[c]Article 8 of Commission Regulation …/.. (CACM Regulation)

Each Member State and Norway must designate at least one NEMO within 4 months of the entry into force of the CACM Regulation. NEMOs shall be designated for an initial term of 4 years.[21] The CACM Regulation also creates a governance framework for NEMOs.

Market Coupling Operator Functions The CACM Regulation defines MCO functions.[22] However, there does not have to be any particular MCO (at least not in the short term). MCO functions are carried out by NEMOs jointly with other NEMOs. NEMOs must submit a plan that sets out how to jointly set up and perform the MCO functions not later than 8 months after the entry into force of the CACM Regulation.[23]

According to the CACM Regulation, the joint performance of MCO functions "shall be based on the principle of non-discrimination and ensure that no NEMO can benefit from unjustified economic advantages through participation in MCO functions".[24]

If the co-operation between NEMOs fails, it is possible that the MCO functions will be taken over by ENTSO-E or another entity.[25]

Table 6.1 shows the relationship between MCO functions (at the the European level), NEMOs (at the national level), and TSOs (at the national level).

[21] Articles 4–6 of Commission Regulation …/.. (CACM Regulation). For the application of the NEMO designation criteria, see, for example, Ofgem, Implementing the Electricity EU Network Codes (18 December 2014).

[22] Point 30 of Article 2 and Article 7(2) of Commission Regulation …/.. (CACM Regulation).

[23] Article 7(3) of Commission Regulation …/.. (CACM Regulation).

[24] Article 7(4) of Commission Regulation …/.. (CACM Regulation).

[25] Article 7(6) of Commission Regulation …/.. (CACM Regulation).

6.2 Models for Market Coupling

Market coupling can take many forms. On one hand, one can distinguish between explicit and implicit auctions for the allocation of transmission capacity on the interconnector. On the other, one can distinguish between market splitting and market coupling.

Explicit Auction A transmission capacity auction is "explicit" when transmission capacity and electricity are traded at two separate auctions.[26] Transmission capacity is normally auctioned in portions through annual, monthly and daily auctions.

In principle, explicit auctions are a simple method. In practice, however, there is a problem caused by lack of information. If transmission capacity and electricity are traded at two separate auctions, the price of one commodity cannot reflect the price of the other as closely as it could. This can lead to an inefficient utilisation of interconnectors.[27]

Implicit Auction An implicit auction provides a way to integrate electricity spot markets in two regions connected by an interconnector. A transmission capacity auction is "implicit" when the auctioning of transmission capacity is included in an electricity auction "implicitly". Electricity buyers bid for electricity supplied by electricity generators from the other side of the interconnector and transmission capacity is included in the price. In other words, implicit auctioning reduces cross-border trade inefficiencies by internalising the arbitrage into the auction procedures of the power exchanges that are organising trade nationally.[28]

First you need market data from the marketplaces in the connected markets. The flow on the interconnector is estimated on the basis of differences in bids. Electricity is expected to flow from the surplus area (low price area) to the deficit area (high price area). This flow is included in the market offering and made available to bidders. Implicit auctions can thus increase price convergence. The resulting prices reflect both the cost of electricity in each bidding area and the cost of congestion.

In practice, the coupling of markets that use implicit auctions means that market participants do not actually need to receive any cross-border capacity allocations. Instead, market participants can bid for generation or consumption in their own areas.[29]

The existence of implicit auctions does not exclude the use of explicit auctions. Implicit auctions would not be possible, unless owners of interconnectors allocated

---

[26] ERGEG, Draft Framework Guidelines on Capacity Allocation and Congestion Management for Electricity: Initial Impact Assessment. Ref: E10-ENM-20-04 (8 September 2010), p. 45: "... this was and still is the allocation method used at most of the European continental borders (e.g. Northern borders of Italy, France-Spain, France-England, CEE Region) for day-ahead capacity allocations".

[27] Meeus L (2011), p. 413.

[28] *Ibid.*

[29] ACER/CEER (2012), p. 51.

transmission capacity to market participants. Transmission capacity can be allocated in explicit auctions before the implicit auctions.

Market Splitting Implicit auctions can be used either for market coupling or for market splitting. In market splitting, the implicit auction of transmission capacity is organised within the day-ahead electricity auction by one single power exchange.

Market splitting is caused by limited transmission capacity between the power exchange's internal bidding areas. Because of limited transmission capacity, there can sometimes be different prices in different bidding areas. In other words, price convergence is not perfect, and there is a "split" between the markets.

However, market splitting is not the same thing as the separation of markets. Market splitting is a form of congestion management. It is used to level out price differences.[30] It increases the price in the low-price area and decrease the price in the high-price area. Market splitting is applied in the Nordic market[31] and in the Iberian market between Portugal and Spain.[32]

Market Coupling In market coupling, the implicit auction is organised in cooperation between two or more power exchanges. The exchanges are thus "coupled".

Market coupling requires plenty of information. The necessary market information is provided by the participating exchanges. TSOs provide information about transmission capacity between the market areas. A central coupling algorithm delivers information about flows and prices in all market areas. This information can then be used in different ways depending on the way market coupling is implemented.

Market coupling can be implemented in various ways. One can distinguish between price market coupling, tight volume market coupling, and loose volume market coupling:

- Price market coupling means a high level of market integration. In this case, the central algorithm determines the prices in the underlying bidding areas, a list of selected block orders for each bidding area, and the net positions (or flows) between the bidding areas. This information is adapted by each power exchange. Price coupling can be ATC-based (based on available transmission capacities)[33] or flow-based.

---

[30] ACER/CEER (2012), p. 51.

[31] ACER/CEER (2012), p. 51, para 85.

[32] ACER/CEER (2012), p. 51, para 86: "Market Coupling also operates between Slovenia and Italy (2011), and between the Czech Republic and Slovakia (2010), while Market Splitting is applied in the Iberian market MIBEL between Portugal and Spain (2007)".

[33] Daily capacities at the French–Belgian and Dutch–Belgian borders were implicitly allocated via price coupling in 2006–2010 (Trilateral Coupling, TLC). ERGEG, Draft Framework Guidelines on Capacity Allocation and Congestion Management for Electricity: Initial Impact Assessment. Ref: E10-ENM-20-04 (8 September 2010) p. 47: "Price coupling is performed in the TLC (Trilateral Coupling between France, Belgium and The Netherlands), in the Nordic area (by . . . Nord Pool), in MIBEL (by . . . OMEL in Portugal and Spain), and in Italy . . ."

- Tight volume coupling means a lower level of market integration. Only the determined flows between each exchange area are adapted by each power exchange. Prices are calculated by each power exchange separately for its own area in a second step. Volume coupling may thus result in small adverse flows or price discrepancies. It is used for practical reasons, because it might not be possible to include all markets in price market coupling at the same time.
- Loose volume coupling resembles tight volume coupling. The difference is a matter of degree. Each power exchange adapts only the determined flows between the exchange areas. Prices are calculated separately. Volume coupling is the looser; the differences there are between the matching algorithms, the less market rules that are implemented in the central algorithm, and the less completeness of market data delivered from the power exchanges.

6.3 EU Law

European market coupling is derived from a European legal framework. While the general principles and guidelines can be derived from EU law, it would not be possible to provide a fully harmonised and sufficiently detailed legal framework for market coupling at Community level. A lot can be regulated better by exchange operators and market participants themselves.[34]

Regulation 714/2009 Regulation 714/2009 sets out the key rules at Community level. The purpose of Regulation 714/2009 is to: (a) provide directly applicable rules and principles; (b) set fair rules for cross-border exchanges in electricity; (c) establish a compensation mechanism for cross-border flows of electricity; and (d) set harmonised principles on cross-border transmission charges and the allocation of available capacities of interconnections between national transmission systems.[35]

Fairness must be ensured by addressing network congestion problems with non-discriminatory market-based solutions.[36] The maximum capacity of the interconnections and/or the transmission networks affecting cross-border flows must be made available to market participants.[37] Congestion problems must "preferentially" be addressed by methods that do not involve a selection between the contracts of individual market participants ("non transaction-based methods").[38] Capacity must be allocated to market participants for an operational period in an open, transparent,

[34] For the principle of subsidiarity, see, for example, recitals 30 and 13 of Regulation 714/2009 on conditions for access to the network for cross-border exchanges in electricity.

[35] Recital 10 and Article 1 of Regulation 714/2009.

[36] Article 16(1) of Regulation 714/2009.

[37] Article 16(3) of Regulation 714/2009.

[38] Article 16(1) of Regulation 714/2009.

and non-discriminatory manner.[39] On the other hand, transactions that relieve congestion must never be denied.[40]

The compensation mechanism is based on a number of rules. First, TSOs must receive compensation for costs incurred as a result of hosting cross-border flows of electricity on their networks,[41] but revenues resulting from the allocation of interconnection must be used for certain purposes[42] and the Commission decides on the amounts of compensation payments payable. Exemptions may be granted upon request for new interconnectors under certain circumstances.[43] Second, the compensation must be paid by the operators of national transmission systems from which cross-border flows originate and the systems where those flows end.[44] Third, the charges must not be distance-related, but the level of tariffs applied to producers and/or consumers should provide locational signals.[45] For this reason, there must not be any specific network charge on individual transactions for declared transits of electricity.[46] The level of the tariffs should nevertheless take into account the amount of network losses and congestion, including investment costs for infrastructure.[47] Fourth, compensation payments must be made on a regular basis with regard to a given period of time in the past.[48] Fifth, the Commission must adopt guidelines according to the principle of subsidiarity.[49] The Regulation and the guidelines are without prejudice to the rights of Member States to adopt detailed provisions.[50]

Commission Guidelines The Commission's guidelines are annexed to Regulation 1228/2003 and Regulation 714/2009.[51] For purposes of market coupling, its most important provisions relate to congestion management methods. They must be market-based. Transmission capacity on an interconnector must be allocated by means of explicit (capacity) or implicit (capacity and energy) auctions, or a

[39] Article 16(4) of Regulation 714/2009.

[40] Article 16(5) of Regulation 714/2009.

[41] Article 13(1) of Regulation 714/2009.

[42] Article 16(6) of Regulation 714/2009.

[43] Article 17 of Regulation 714/2009. See Talus K (2005); Cameron PD (2007), pp. 158–160, para 5.100.

The first formal decision was made with respect to the Estlink project between the Finnish and Estonian grids.

[44] Article 13(2) of Regulation 714/2009.

[45] Article 14(1), recital 15, Article 14(2) and recital 14 of Regulation 714/2009.

[46] Article 14(5) of Regulation 714/2009.

[47] Article 14(2) of Regulation 714/2009.

[48] Article 13(3) of Regulation 714/2009.

[49] Article 18 of Regulation 714/2009.

[50] Article 19 of Regulation 714/2009.

[51] Annex I to Regulation 714/2009, Guidelines on the management and allocation of available transfer capacity of interconnections between national systems.

combination of explicit and implicit auctions. Continuous trading may be used for intraday trade.[52]

Implicit Auctions: Day-Ahead and Intraday Capacity Allocation The use of implicit allocation is the main rule cross-zonal capacity allocation in the day-ahead and intraday market timeframes according to the CACM Regulation.[53] Unless transitional arrangements apply, the method is implicit auctions on day-ahead markets and continuous implicit allocation on intraday markets.

Explicit allocation could be used as a transitional arrangement under the ENTSO-E Network Code that preceded the CACM Regulation.[54] The Network Code permitted system operators to use explicit allocation on those bidding zone borders where they are requested to do so by national regulatory authorities.[55] Explicit requests were not permitted for interconnections in other cases.[56]

The CACM Regulation limits the use of explicit auctions as a transitional arrangement to intraday markets.[57]

Explicit Auctions: Long-Term Capacity Allocation Explicit allocation is the main rule for long-term cross-zonal capacity allocation under ENTSO-E Network Code on Forward Capacity Allocation.[58]

Congestion management mechanisms may need to allow for both short- and long-term transmission capacity allocation depending on competition conditions.[59] There are two permissible approaches for the calculation and allocation of long-term capacity: the coordinated net transmission capacity based approach and the flow-based approach.[60] Moreover, long-term capacity should be calculated and allocated at least for yearly and monthly timeframes.[61]

Each capacity allocation procedure must allocate a prescribed fraction of the available interconnection capacity plus any remaining capacity not previously allocated and any capacity released by capacity holders from previous allocations.[62] The access rights for long- and medium-term allocations must be firm transmission capacity rights. They must be subject to the use-it-or-lose-it (UIOLI) or use-it-or-sell-it (UIOSI) principles at the time of nomination.[63]

---

[52] Point 2.1 of Annex I to Regulation 714/2009.

[53] Recital 13 of Commission Regulation .../.. (CACM Regulation).

[54] Article 91 of ENTSO-E NC CACM (27 September 2012).

[55] Article 92 of ENTSO-E NC CACM (27 September 2012).

[56] Article 95 of ENTSO-E NC CACM (27 September 2012).

[57] Article 61 of Commission Regulation .../.. (CACM Regulation).

[58] Article 1(1) of ENTSO-E NC FCA (2 April 2014).

[59] Annex I to Regulation 714/2009, point 2.2.

[60] Recital 7 of ENTSO-E NC FCA (2 April 2014).

[61] Recital 5 of ENTSO-E NC FCA (2 April 2014).

[62] Annex I to Regulation 714/2009, point 2.3.

[63] Annex I to Regulation 714/2009, point 2.5.

The main rule is that the highest value bids shall prevail. Capacity allocation may not discriminate between market participants that wish to use their rights to make use of bilateral supply contracts or to bid into power exchanges.[64] In principle, all potential market participants should be permitted to participate in the allocation process without restriction. However, the participation of some market players may be limited because of competition concerns.[65]

In regions where forward financial electricity markets are well developed and have shown their efficiency, all interconnection capacity may be allocated through implicit auctioning.[66] Moreover, such regions may allocate all interconnection capacity through day-ahead allocation.[67]

Although the starting point was that different congestion management methods have been used depending on the market, the ultimate goal of the Commission's guidelines is forming "a truly integrated Internal European Electricity Market". For this reason, the guidelines require "compatible congestion management procedures" and "compatible regional systems" in all existing regions.[68]

6.4 Examples of Market Coupling

6.4.1 European Initiatives

There are different market coupling solutions for the European regions. The agreed target design for day-ahead markets in Europe is price coupling.[69] Some market coupling solutions are already in place. There are several initiatives to link two or more regions or to enlarge existing ones. Market coupling is a work in progress in the EU.

Earlier Solutions MIBEL, the Nordic market, Kontek, and TLC are examples of early market coupling solutions.

The Kontek Cable between Denmark and Germany provides an example of the move from explicit auctions to implicit auctions. Explicit auctions were replaced by implicit auctions in 2005 when the Nordic market was increased with the German bidding area Kontek in Nord Pool Spot's Elspot market.[70] The Kontek day-ahead bidding area was closed down in November 2009 because of the launch of the EMCC market coupling between Denmark and Germany.

[64] Annex I to Regulation 714/2009, point 2.7.

[65] Annex I to Regulation 714/2009, point 2.10.

[66] Annex I to Regulation 714/2009, point 2.8.

[67] Annex I to Regulation 714/2009, point 3.3.

[68] Annex I to Regulation 714/2009, point 3.4.

[69] See, for example, recital 18 of Commission Regulation .../.. (CACM Regulation).

[70] See Meeus L (2011); Energimarknadsinspektionen (2010), p. 16.

MIBEL and the Nordic market use *market splitting*. Operador del Mercado Iberico de Energía—Polo Español, S.A. (OMEL) is the spot market operator responsible for market splitting in MIBEL according to the terms of the MIBEL agreement between Portugal and Spain.[71] In the Nordic and Baltic market, Nord Pool Spot AS is responsible for market splitting as the spot market operator.

Trilateral Market Coupling (TLC) between Belgium, France, and the Netherlands was an example of *price coupling*. TLC was also the first decentralised market coupling initiative implemented in Europe. As its name implies, this coupling solution involved three spot exchanges in three regions: APX in the Netherlands, BELPEX in Belgium, and EPEX Spot in France. In TLC, the exchanges implicitly made available the daily cross-border capacity between the Netherlands, Belgium and France. This capacity was provided by three TSOs.[72] TLC was replaced by the CWE market coupling in November 2010.

Initiatives The European market coupling initiatives include the PCR, the CWE, the NWE, and the ITVC (EMCC) projects. The initiatives relate to different regions.[73]

CWE The purpose of the CWE Flow-Based Market Coupling project was to design a continuous implicit market for the Central Western Europe region by 2014 with day-ahead and intraday market coupling. The CWE region consists of Belgium, France, Germany, Luxemburg, and the Netherlands. Price market coupling in the CWE region was launched in November 2010.

ITVC Interim Tight Volume Coupling (ITVC) was an interim solution. ITVC concerned the coupling of day-ahead markets between the CWE region and the Nordic region. The interim volume coupling services on the interconnectors between the CWE and the Nordic market were provided by EMCC. The same with price market coupling in the CWE region, ITVC was launched in November 2010. ITVC and EMCC became obsolete after the NWE Price Coupling went live in February 2014.

[71] "Agreement between the Portuguese Republic and the Kingdom of Spain relative to the constitution of an Iberian Electrical Energy Market" signed on 1 October 2004.

[72] Elia, RTE, and TenneT.

[73] Annex I to Regulation 714/2009, point 3.2: "A common coordinated congestion-management method and procedure for the allocation of capacity to the market at least annually, monthly and day-ahead shall be applied by 1 January 2007 between countries in the following regions: (a) Northern Europe (i.e. Denmark, Sweden, Finland, Germany and Poland), (b) North-West Europe (i.e. Benelux, Germany and France), (c) Italy (i.e. Italy, France, Germany, Austria, Slovenia and Greece), (d) Central Eastern Europe (i.e. Germany, Poland, Czech Republic, Slovakia, Hungary, Austria and Slovenia), (e) South-West Europe (i.e. Spain, Portugal and France), (f) UK, Ireland and France, (g) Baltic states (i.e. Estonia, Latvia and Lithuania) . . .".

NWE NWE Price Coupling replaced ITVC with full price coupling of the day-ahead wholesale electricity markets in the North-Western Europe (NWE) region. The NWE day-ahead price coupling was launched on in February 2014.

NWE covers 75 % of the European electricity market. The NWE region consists of 15 countries: the CWE region (Belgium, France, Luxemburg, Netherlands, Germany, and Austria that belongs to a single bidding area with Germany); Great Britain (N2EX operates an open access platform, the so-called "GB virtual hub"); the Nordic region (Denmark, Sweden, Norway, Finland); and countries in the Baltic region coupled to the Nordic market via Nord Pool Spot (the Baltic countries and Poland).

The NWE day-ahead project was initiated by the Regional Group North West Europe of ENTSO-E.

PCR The Price Coupling of Regions (PCR) is the first EU-wide coupling project. All EU electricity exchanges that operate spot markets are full or associate members of the project.

The PCR is the initiative of seven power exchanges to develop an infrastructure for European Price Coupling. The PCR parties signed the PCR Cooperation Agreement and PCR Co-ownership Agreement in June 2012. European Price Coupling was preceded by other projects initiated by TSOs and power exchanges.

The PCR is based on three main principles: one single algorithm; decentralised governance; and decentralised operation. The three principles address the conflict between path dependency and the objective of market integration. On one hand, the PCR initiative is focused on the delivery of a common European price coupling solution. On the other, the solution must be implemented in a variety of local regulatory and governance settings. Therefore, the PCR is designed to build on the existing contractual, regulatory, and operational solutions, setting the needed harmonisation and governance principles at the European level.

NWE Price Coupling was the first to implement the Price Coupling of Regions (PCR) with the SWE region (Spain and Portugal) next in line.

SWE South-Western Europe (SWE) Price Coupling Project is a joint project between the French, Spanish and Portuguese TSOs (RTE, REE, REN) and the power exchanges OMIE (Spain and Portugal) and EPEX Spot (France). The purpose of the project is to enable the implementation of price coupling between the NWE region and the Iberian day-ahead markets in accordance with the PCR solution.

The full coupling of the SWE day-ahead market was launched in May 2014. As a result, day-ahead markets of the NWE region and the SWE region are fully coupled. The daily explicit auctions for transmission capacity on the French-Spanish border have ceased. Capacity is allocated implicitly through PCR in the day-ahead markets.[74]

---

[74] Nord Pool Spot, Exchange information, 18/2014, 24 April 2014.

Switzerland The Commission will decide whether market operators (NEMOs) and TSOs operating in Switzerland may participate in the Union single day-ahead coupling and intraday coupling. The Commission's decision depends on the contents of Swiss law and the existence of an intergovernmental agreement on electricity cooperation between the Union and Switzerland.[75]

6.4.2 CWE

Price coupling is recognised as the target day-ahead market coupling solution for Europe.[76] In Northern Europe, the price coupling project for Central Western Europe (CWE) was the most important price coupling project before the NWE project.

CWE was launched in 2009 for the purpose of improving the management of transmission system bottlenecks in the Central Western Europe Region (Belgium, the Netherlands, France, Germany and Luxembourg). CWE price coupling was launched in 2010. The TSOs of the Central South East Region (CSE) and Switzerland joined the cooperation.[77]

CWE price coupling paved the way for the coupling of the CWE market with the Nordic market and was followed by, first, the CWE-Nordic tight volume coupling operated by EMCC and, second, by the NWE initiative.

On CWE market coupling borders, CWE Shadow Auctions are organised as a backup solution in the event that the NWE market coupling cannot take place.[78]

CWE Auction Rules CWE Auction Rules set out the terms and conditions that govern the allocation of available capacity in both directions on country borders within the CWE region.[79] To participate, firms must accept a large contractual framework.[80]

Capacity is auctioned in the form of physical transmission rights of electrical energy on a yearly, monthly, or daily basis.[81]

[75] Article 1 of Commission Regulation . . ./.. (CACM Regulation).

[76] The Florence Regulatory Forum of 4–5 June 2009.

[77] On 1 October 2013, CASC had 14 TSOs as shareholders: Creos, Elia, TransnetBW GmbH, TenneT TSO GmbH, TenneT TSO B.V, RTE, Amprion, Austrian Power Grid AG, Elektro—Slovenija, Independent Power Transmission Operator S.A., Swissgrid, Terna, Energinet.dk, and Statnett.

[78] CWE Auction Rules, Version 1.0, Article 4.02.

[79] CASC, Rules for Capacity Allocation by Explicit Auctions within Central West Europe Region (CWE), Central South Europe Region (CSE) and Switzerland (CWE Auction Rules), Version 1.0, Article 1.01.

[80] CWE Auction Rules, Version 1.0, Article 3.03.

[81] CWE Auction Rules, Version 1.0, Article 1.01.

The auctions are explicit closed auctions. In other words, the auctions are limited to the available transmission capacity. The price is the marginal price.[82]

Bids The individual electricity exchanges collect bids and offers from their participants. The exchanges then submit their aggregated and anonymous order books to the market coupling system.

After the market coupling has been performed and the price has been set, the individual electricity exchanges are responsible for executing all orders placed by their participants that are within the calculated price, and to conclude contracts with them.[83]

A bid that is selected following an auction is binding on the TSO and the market participant. The TSOs are required to provide the participant with allocated transmission capacity and the participant must pay the amount resulting from the auction.[84]

Capacity Allocation, Joint Auction Office The TSOs have outsourced their task of capacity allocation to a Joint Auction Office.[85] The Joint Auction office is CASC.EU SA,[86] a company having its seat in Luxembourg. CASC means the Capacity Allocation Service Company. CASC.EU is designed to increase liquidity and competition within the participating markets in two main ways. First, CASC.EU acts as a single point to implement and operate services related to the auctioning of power transmission capacity on the common borders between the participating countries. Second, this leads to the standardisation of systems and rules.

6.4.3 CWE-Nordic (ITVC)

The Nordic region (Nord Pool Spot) used to be connected to the CWE region (EPEX Spot) through Interim Tight Volume Coupling (ITVC). The ITVC solution was based on the previous EMCC tight volume coupling model on the German borders with Denmark and Sweden. The ITVC was an interim solution replaced by NWE price coupling. European Market Coupling Company GmbH (EMCC), the operator of ITVC, was closed down after the go-live of NWE price coupling on 4 February 2014. One can nevertheless study ITVC as an example of tight volume coupling.

---

[82] CWE Auction Rules, Version 1.0, Articles 1.01 and 1.04.

[83] The CWE MC Project, Project Document: A report for the regulators of the Central West European (CWE) region on the final design of the market coupling solution in the region (January 2010), section 10.2.2.

[84] CWE Auction Rules, Version 1.0, Article 1.04.

[85] CWE Auction Rules, Version 1.0, Article 1.03.

[86] CASC-CWE S.A. was renamed CASC.EU S.A. on 10 November 2010.

The tight volume coupling of Nord Pool Spot and EPEX Spot consisted of many steps: (1) submission of information about the the available transmission capacity; (2) submission of information about aggregated bids; (3) calculation of the optimal flow (market coupling flows); (4) submission of additional bids/offers to the electricity exchanges; and (5) calculation of prices by considering bids from EMCC.

First, owners of transmission capacity on interconnectors between the market areas put all or part of their capacity at the disposal of EMCC the morning day-ahead. Second, each exchange received bids from participants in its market area. Bid information for each bidding area was aggregated by the relevant electricity exchange and submitted to the coupling algorithm of EMCC. Third, EMCC carried out the day-ahead calculation for each interconnector to find out the low price (surplus) and the high price (deficit) area. EMCC calculated the day-ahead prices and day-ahead plans for the energy flows between bidding areas on the basis of what was optimal flow between the market areas (the economic welfare criterion). Fourth, EMCC submitted additional price-independent bids/offers to the power exchanges reflecting the calculated market coupling flow. Fifth, the exchanges took the bids from EMCC into account when calculating their own day-ahead prices, day-ahead plans for the energy flows between the bidding areas, and the traded volumes per participant (volume coupling). Sixth, EMCC also nominated the market coupling flow on the interconnectors by sending it to the TSOs.

If there was no congestion, the prices in the two areas were the same. If there was congestion, the prices were different. For example, different prices could be caused by constraints on the change in the flow direction from hour to hour ("ramping") or grid loss on the interconnector.

If the prices were different on the two power exchanges, EMCC collected a congestion rent. The congestion rent was subsequently paid to the owners of the interconnectors, but it must be used to enhance grid quality or extend the transmission network. This was a legal requirement.[87]

EMCC's obtained most of its revenue from the capacity owners that paid its operational costs and a service fee for day-ahead congestion management services. Nord Pool Spot AS and EPEX Spot AG were responsible for its operations.

6.4.4 NWE

NWE Price Coupling replaced ITVC with full price coupling of the day-ahead wholesale electricity markets in the North-Western Europe (NWE) region.[88]

---

[87] Article 16(6) Regulation 714/2009 (on conditions for access to the network for cross-border exchanges in electricity).

[88] Nord Pool Spot Market, Trading Appendix 1, Definitions (27 November 2014): "NWE Price Coupling [means] Price Coupling by and between certain power exchanges (including Nord Pool Spot) and transmission system operators of, respectively, the CWE region, the Nordic/Baltic Region and the UK pursuant to the terms of the NWE Day Ahead Operations Agreement".

The NWE day-ahead project was initiated by the Regional Group North West Europe of ENTSO-E. NWE price coupling is based on the European Day-Ahead Target Model and the Price Coupling of Regions (PCR) solution.

One Algorithm There is a fundamental difference between NWE price coupling and ITVC. Under the ITVC solution, the participating exchanges (Nord Pool Spot, EPEX Spot, APX, Belpex) submitted bidding information to EMCC. EMCC submitted additional bids. After this, the exchanges took EMCC's bids into account when calculating their own prices. (b) The NWE solution simplifies market coupling, because the exchanges can use a single algorithm to calculate all market prices, net positions, and cross-border flows at the same time.

Coordinated Matching In practice, NWE means the coordinated matching of orders on a spot electricity market (Nord Pool Spot, EPEX Spot, APX, N2EX) with orders on the markets of other power exchanges according to the terms of the NWE Day-Ahead Operations Agreement. A participating power exchange forwards aggregated and anonymised order information to the other participating power exchanges for the purpose of daily price coupling.[89] For example, EPEX Spot can then coordinate its day-ahead auctions for Austria/Germany and France with the Nordic area, the UK and the Benelux. Nord Pool Spot, APX, and N2EX coordinate their day-ahead auctions in a similar way.[90] NWE price coupling is thus a "mechanism whereby, with the goal of maximising social welfare, the market clearing prices and net positions for different day-ahead electricity markets are determined in a single step by reference to physical hourly ATC and/or flow-based capacities".[91]

Curtailment, Second Auction Curtailment influences the price. A second auction procedure is used in the event that the market is curtailed or the price reaches a pre-defined maximum or minimum threshold. The timing of the second auction procedure enables the activation of reserves (production or load, see Sect. 4.10).[92] Generally, the second auction can also be triggered by exceptional circumstances[93] or unforeseen uncoupling.[94]

---

[89] See, for example, Nord Pool Spot's Physical Markets, General Terms, Trading Rules (1 February 2015), section 14.2.4.

[90] EPEX Spot Exchange Rules (28 November 2014), Title 1, Preamble. APX Power NL Market Rules, Version 3.0 (20 January 2014), section 1.3.

[91] Nord Pool Spot Market, Trading Appendix 1, Definitions (27 November 2014), see the definition of Price Coupling.

[92] See, for example, EPEX Spot Operational Rules (28 November 2014), Article 1.7.

[93] See, for example, APX Power NL Market Rules, Version 3.0 (20 January 2014), para 25.1.

[94] See, for example, Nord Pool Spot Physical Market, Trading Appendix 2a, Elspot Market Regulations (18 November 2014), section 2.3.1 (setting a price range), section 4.3.1 (procedure in case of non-matching), section 5 (reopening in case of unforeseen decoupling), section 9.1 (roll-back or fall-back from NWE price coupling).

Decoupling, Fall Back Algorithm, Roll-Back Solution There must be a procedure for the matching of bids when NWE price coupling is not available. A situation in which the process of price coupling is suspended and/or cancelled is called decoupling or market decoupling.[95] Exchanges then need a fall-back algorithm.[96] Exchanges also have a roll-back solution and can "roll back" to the regime before NWE and reactivate the previous systems.[97]

6.4.5 France, Germany, Austria and Switzerland (EPEX Spot)

The Nordic and Baltic region (Nord Pool Spot) and the CWE region (EPEX SPOT and APX) are the most important blocks in NWE Price Coupling, together in the EU-wide PCR. Each region has its own internal market coupling solution.

The EPEX Spot area consists of France, Germany, Austria, and Switzerland. There is no common market coupling for the EPEX Spot area as a whole.

The key aspects of market coupling and the management of transmission capacity constraints in the EPEX Spot area can be summed up as follows: (1) EPEX Spot is the common spot exchange based in Paris. (2) Market coupling is implemented in day-ahead auctions. (3) The goal is to use transparent mechanisms for pricing and coordination.[98] Both price coupling and volume coupling have been used on EPEX Spot,[99] but only *price coupling* remains after the go-live of NWE price coupling.[100] Two types of contacts can be admitted to trading on EPEX Spot: physical power contracts and market coupling contracts that are listed for the purpose of price coupling. The commodity underlying market coupling contracts is physical transmission rights (PTRs).[101] (4) There are five market areas on EPEX Spot: the French Market Area (a day-ahead auction); the German Market Area (a continuous intraday market and an intraday auction); the Austrian Market Area (a continuous intraday market); the German/Austrian Market Area (a day-ahead auction); and the Swiss Market Area (a day-ahead auction and a

---

[95] See Nord Pool Spot Market, Trading Appendix 1, Definitions (27 November 2014).

[96] See Nord Pool Spot Market, Trading Appendix 1, Definitions (27 November 2014).

[97] See Nord Pool Spot Market, Trading Appendix 1, Definitions (27 November 2014).

[98] EPEX Spot Exchange Rules (28 November 2014), Title 1, Preamble.

[99] See, for example, EPEX Spot Exchange Rules (6 June 2013), Title 1, Preamble: "The purpose of the merger is . . . to create the largest possible zone where the prices of different electrical areas are set and coordinated via transparent mechanisms, including a tight price-coupling (market splitting) wherever possible". See also EPEX Spot Exchange Rules (6 June 2013), Title 4.

[100] See EPEX Spot Exchange Rules (28 November 2014), Title 1, Preamble; EPEX Spot Exchange Rules (28 November 2014), Article 4.2.

[101] EPEX Spot Exchange Rules (28 November 2014), Article 5.3 and Article 5.4.

continuous intraday auction).[102] Each has its own place of delivery (delivery zone). (5) The day-ahead auctions on the French and the German/Austrian market areas are coupled via *price coupling* with the day-ahead markets of the Netherlands, Belgium, Great Britain and Nordic/Baltic region.[103] Before NWE price coupling, the day-ahead auction on the German/Austrian market area was coupled by EMCC GmbH via *volume coupling* with the Nord Pool day-ahead market.[104] (6) In the absence of a market coupling solution, a *second auction* procedure can be used to cure the imbalance. The second auction procedure means that EPEX Spot SE asks exchange members to submit further bids that reduce the imbalance.[105]

Exchange Rules of EPEX Spot The market coupling initiatives required the adaptation of the Exchange Rules of EPEX Spot. Market Coupling Facilitators have been included as a new category of members[106] and Market Coupling Contracts as a new type of product.[107]

This was necessary for two reasons. The first was compliance. Market Coupling Facilitators are TSOs in EPEX Spot's market areas. They must meet the national and EU law requirements applicable to TSOs.[108] For example, the contractual relationship between EPEX Spot and the Market Coupling Facilitators must comply with the legal requirements applicable to TSOs' contracts and with unbundling requirements. A TSO must not perform any of the functions of generation or supply.[109] It is therefore necessary to distinguish between two kinds of exchange members and two kinds of contracts: exchange members that sign a Trading Agreement and exchange members that sign a Market Coupling Facilitator Agreement.[110]

The second reason for the adoption of new rules was the existence of several providers of transmission rights on interconnectors. The interconnectors should be used in an integrated manner to ensure welfare maximisation and maximum price

[102] EPEX Spot Exchange Rules (28 November 2014), Article 5.10.

[103] EPEX Spot may extend price coupling to other market areas. EPEX Spot Exchange Rules (28 November 2014), Article 5.8.

[104] EPEX Spot Exchange Rules (6 June 2013), Article 4.10.

[105] EPEX Spot Operational Rules (28 November 2014), Article 1.7.

[106] According to the older version of the Rules, they were called Implicit Participants. EPEX Spot Exchange Rules (21.7.2010), Article 2.7: "An Implicit Participant is a Transmission System Operator (TSO), or any other entity appointed by a TSO, which can have transmission rights or capacity on one or more electrical interconnections linking transmission networks to an interconnected power transmission system. The intervention of Implicit Participants on EPEX Spot SE is restricted to the activities required for the purpose of Market Coupling as Price Coupling within TLC". See also EPEX Spot Exchange Rules (21.7.2010), Article 2.28.

[107] For earlier rules, see EPEX Spot Exchange Rules (6 June 2013), Article 2.26. For present rules, see EPEX Spot Exchange Rules (28 November 2014), Article 5.3.

[108] Articles 13 and 15 of Directive 2009/72/EC (Third Electricity Directive); Regulation 714/2009 on conditions for access to the network for cross-border exchanges in electricity.

[109] Article 9(1) of Directive 2009/72/EC (Third Electricity Directive).

[110] EPEX Spot Exchange Rules (28 November 2014), Article 2.1.

convergence. For this reason, transmission capacity rights are separated from Market Coupling Contracts. Market Coupling Contracts are derivatives with physical transmission rights on interconnectors as the underlying commodity.[111] The physical transmission rights are made available to EPEX Spot when Market Coupling Facilitators give sell orders on Market Coupling Contracts.[112] Orders on Market Coupling Contracts can only be sell orders sent by the relevant Market Coupling Facilitator.[113] The Market Coupling Contracts are considered to be sold by the Market Coupling Facilitator to ECC.[114] The price is the price difference—positive or negative—between the two market areas.[115] ECC uses the physical transmission rights to nominate energy flows on the relevant electrical borders.[116]

While the Market Coupling Contracts enable TSOs to sell transmission capacity rights in an optimal way, the transmission capacity rights for the interconnectors are allocated implicitly.

6.4.6 The Nordic and Baltic Countries (Nord Pool Spot)

The Nordic and Baltic market uses *market splitting*. Physical day-ahead and intraday trading takes place on Nord Pool Spot that has many bidding areas because of grid bottlenecks. Implicit auctions are used for the formulation of area prices, the allocation of cross-border capacity, and congestion management in the day-ahead market. The price differentials emerge as a function of insufficient transfer capacity between the bidding areas.[117]

For each country, the local TSO decides which bidding areas the country is divided into. In 2014, the number of Norwegian bidding areas was five. Denmark had two bidding areas (Eastern Denmark and Western Denmark). Finland, Estonia, Lithuania, and Latvia constituted one bidding area each. The Swedish TSO (Svenska Kraftnät) divided Sweden into four bidding areas on 1 November 2011 as part of its competition law commitments to the European Commission (Sect. 3.6.3).[118]

[111] EPEX Spot Exchange Rules (28 November 2014), Article 5.3.

[112] EPEX Spot Exchange Rules (28 November 2014), Article 4.1.

[113] EPEX Spot Exchange Rules (28 November 2014), Article 6.7.

[114] EPEX Spot Exchange Rules (28 November 2014), Article 4.1.

[115] EPEX Spot Exchange Rules (28 November 2014), Article 4.1.

[116] EPEX Spot Exchange Rules (28 November 2014), Article 4.1.

[117] Energy Market Authority, Finland (2013), p. 9.

[118] Moreover, congestion used to be moved the borders of control areas. This practice was not in compliance with points 1.7 and 1.8 of Annex I to Regulation 714/2009. ERGEG, Draft Framework Guidelines on Capacity Allocation and Congestion Management for Electricity: Initial Impact Assessment. Ref: E10-ENM-20-04 (8 September 2010), p. 35.

The transmission capacity between the Nordic and Baltic bidding areas is handled implicitly in the price and bid matching calculation performed by the operator of the electricity exchange (Nord Pool Spot AS). Sometimes the price calculated for the whole market (the system price) can be applied in the whole area.[119] However, Nord Pool Spot must calculate two or more area prices[120] when limited transmission capacity causes a "split" in the markets. In 2012, market splitting in the Nordic electricity market was forced 75 % of the time.[121]

In the Nordic and Baltic countries, the TSOs that own the high-voltage transmission grid are mostly non-commercial monopolies.[122] Inside the Nordic area, only Nord Pool Spot may trade on the transmission capacity on the interconnectors between the different bidding areas. This applies both to cross-border electricity trading and to cross-zonal capacity on the interconnectors connecting national bidding areas.[123]

6.5 Excursion: Germany—Denmark East (Kontek)

There are interconnectors between the Nordic region and the CWE region. There are two interconnectors between Germany and Denmark. Germany—DK West is operated by Energinet.dk and TenneT TSO. Germany—DK East is operated by Energinet.dk and 50Hertz. Germany—DK East is also known as Kontek. The interconnector between Denmark West and Denmark East (the Great Belt cable) is operated by Energinet.dk alone. There is one interconnector between Sweden and Germany (the Baltic cable).

Germany—Denmark East (Kontek) Kontek is a HVDC interconnection cable between Eastern Denmark and Eastern Germany.

KONTEK is also the name of a former bidding area in Nord Pool Spot's Elspot market. Nord Pool introduced it in October 2005. The capacities of the Kontek cable were then handled by Nord Pool Spot based on an implicit capacity auction mechanism that replaced the previous explicit auctions.[124] This Elspot bidding area

[119] Nord Pool Spot, Elspot Market Regulations (1 July 2014), sections 4.1.3, 4.1.1 and 6.1.1.

[120] For the definition of area and area price, see also NASDAQ OMX, Trading Appendix 2/Clearing Appendix 2, Contract Specifications, Commodity Derivatives (24 November 2014), Part B, section 1.2.1.

[121] NordREG (2013), p. 5.

[122] The Nordic shareholders include Statnett (Norway), Energinet.dk (Denmark), Svenska Kraftnät (Sweden), and Fingrid (Finland). Fingrid is owned partly by the Finnish State but has even other shareholders. The Baltic transmission system operators that are shareholders of Nord Pool Spot include Elering (Estonia), Litgrid (Lithuania), and Augstsprieguma tīkls (AST, Latvia).

[123] Nord Pool Spot, Elspot Market Regulations (1 July 2014), section 2.2.4: "The Participant can only quote Orders in Bidding Areas where the Participant or Client undertakes production, consumption or is party to contracts relating to physical delivery or purchase".

[124] Energimarknadsinspektionen (2010), p. 16.

was closed down in November 2009 because of the launch of the EMCC market coupling between Denmark and Germany.[125]

Ownership of the Interconnector Unlike the Baltic cable, Kontek is not owned by a special-purpose company. It is owned by the two TSOs whose transmission grids it connects. Energinet.dk is a TSO existing under Danish public law.[126] 50Hertz Transmission GmbH is a TSO incorporated in Germany (and formerly known as Vattenfall Europe Transmission).[127]

Ownership of Transmission Capacity One must distinguish between ownership of the cable and ownership of transmission capacity rights. This is also for legal reasons as Danish law requires large-scale infrastructure to remain in public ownership.[128] The cable's owners hold 1/3 of the capacity rights each with the remaining 1/3 or 200 MW of the capacity held by Vattenfall. Vattenfall holds capacity rights under a long-term contract in exchange for financial guarantee obligations.[129]

All three electricity undertakings trade on Elspot, EPEX Spot, or both. 50Hertz Transmission GmbH is designated as a TSO under German law (Berlin).[130] It is a trading member on EPEX Spot[131] but not a participant on Nord Pool Spot's Elspot market. Energinet.dk is a participant on Nord Pool Spot's Elspot market but not a trading member on EPEX Spot. Vattenfall AB is a large energy company, and its subsidiaries trade on both markets.

Allocation of Transmission Capacity In the past, the capacity on Kontek used to be sold by EMCC on behalf of the capacity owners. EMCC applied the ITVC market coupling mechanism (implicit auctions) by trading on Nord Pool Spot and EPEX Spot. ITVC market coupling was volume coupling. It also meant a change from the use-it-or-lose-it principle to the use-it-or-sell-it principle (UIOSI).[132]

---

[125] See also Meeus L (2011).

[126] Lov nr. 1384 af 20. december 2004 om Energinet.dk, § 1 stk. 1: "Klima- og energiministeren kan oprette Energinet.dk som en selvstændig offentlig virksomhed".

[127] 50Hertz Transmission GmbH was formerly known as Vattenfall Europe Transmission. 50Hertz Transmission GmbH is a wholly-owned subsidiary of Eurogrid GmbH, a German limited-liability company, which is a wholly-owned subsidiary of Eurogrid International CVBA/SCRL, a cooperative limited-liability company incorporated under Belgian law. 60 % of the shares of this company are owned or controlled by Elia, a Belgian TSO, and 40 % by Industry Funds Management (IFM) through Luxembourg No. 2 S.à.r.l., a private limited liability company incorporated under the laws of the Grand Duchy of Luxembourg.

[128] Lov nr. 1384 af 20. december 2004 om Energinet.dk, § 1 stk. 2: "Den overordnede infrastruktur på el- og gasområdet, som varetages af Energinet.dk, skal forblive i offentligt eje".

[129] Energimarknadsinspektionen (2010), p. 14.

[130] § 4(1) EmWG: "Die Aufnahme des Betriebs eines Energieversorgungsnetzes bedarf der Genehmigung durch die nach Landesrecht zuständige Behörde".

[131] EPEX Spot Exchange Rules (28 November 2014), Article 2.4.

[132] Energitilsynet, Sekretariatsafgørelse 24. oktober 2013 (13/09342), Metodeanmeldelse Energinet.dk—PTR på Kontek og nye auktionsregler for PTR gældende for begge grænser til Tyskland, paras 23–26.

There were explicit auctions for transmission capacity on Germany—DK West. In this case, transmission capacity was auctioned in the form of PTRs.[133]

Now that ITVC and EMCC have been replaced by the NWE market coupling (that is, price coupling with better expected results),[134] the same procedure and the same rules (Long-term Auction Rules) are applied on all three interconnectors in Denmark (Germany—DK West, Germany—DK East, DK West—DK East) and in both directions. The Long-term Auction Rules[135] have been accepted by the competent regulators.[136]

There are explicit, implicit, and shadow auctions. The allocation methods are regulated by Regulation 714/2009 (see Sect. 5.6).

There are explicit auctions for physical transmission rights (PTRs) on a yearly and monthly basis. The use-it-or-sell-it (UIOSI) principle applies. Where the owner of PTRs does not nominate physical flows, the transmission rights go to the day-ahead allocation. They will thus be sold in the spot market and the owners of PTRs will receive the congestion revenue.[137]

There are no FTRs on the German–Danish interconnectors.[138] FTRs were not chosen for legal reasons as it was deemed possible that FTRs fall within the scope of MiFID. To reduce the risk that TSOs would have to comply with the MiFID regime, the participating electricity regulators and TSOs chose not to introduce FTRs on German–Danish interconnectors. After this, the Danish and German regulators sent a letter to Energinet.dk and 50 Hertz Transmission asking them to introduce PTRs on Kontek from 1 January 2014.[139]

---

[133] Energitilsynet, Sekretariatsafgørelse 24. oktober 2013 (13/09342), Metodeanmeldelse Energinet.dk—PTR på Kontek og nye auktionsregler for PTR gældende for begge grænser til Tyskland, para 23.

[134] Energitilsynet, Sekretariatsafgørelse 24. oktober 2013 (13/09342), Metodeanmeldelse Energinet.dk—PTR på Kontek og nye auktionsregler for PTR gældende for begge grænser til Tyskland, para 24.

[135] Energinet.dk, TenneT, 50Hertz, Rules for the Long-Term Capacity Allocation by Explicit Auctions on the German–Danish borders and the interconnector between Denmark West and Denmark East (Great Belt) for the year 2014 (1 October 2013) (Long-Term Auction Rules), Article 4.3.

[136] For Energinet.dk. see Energitilsynet, Sekretariatsafgørelse 24. oktober 2013 (13/09342), Metodeanmeldelse Energinet.dk—PTR på Kontek og nye auktionsregler for PTR gældende for begge grænser til Tyskland.

[137] Energinet.dk, TenneT, 50Hertz, Rules for the Long-Term Capacity Allocation by Explicit Auctions on the German–Danish borders and the interconnector between Denmark West and Denmark East (Great Belt) for the year 2014 (1 October 2013) (Long-Term Auction Rules), Article 6.

[138] Regulation 714/2009 requires the use of market-based methods for the allocation of cross-border transmission capacity, that is, implicit or explicit auctions and FTRs or PTRs for the allocation of long-term transmission capacity.

[139] Energitilsynet, Sekretariatsafgørelse 24. oktober 2013 (13/09342), Metodeanmeldelse Energinet.dk—PTR på Kontek og nye auktionsregler for PTR gældende for begge grænser til Tyskland, para 18: "Som konsekvens sendte SET og Bundesnetzagentur den 4. juli 2013 et fælles

There are implicit auctions for day-ahead market coupling. Where the NWE day-ahead market coupling cannot be performed, the Joint Auction Office organises explicit daily auctions in the form of shadow auctions for the German–Danish borders.[140]

Electricity Producers Electricity producers need transmission capacity on an interconnector to supply electricity across the Nordic-CWE border.

Generally, electricity producers can buy long-term transmission capacity or day-ahead transmission capacity on an interconnector.

Market participants must first accept the relevant TSO's legal framework. A market player in Energinet.dk's area must be registered with Energinet.dk as a "partner", a market player in the TenneT TSO area must be registered with Tennet TSO as a "partner", and a market player in the 50Hertz area must be registered with 50Hertz as a "partner". There can thus be trade on DK-West—DK-East provided that both market players have been registered with Energinet.dk as "partners".[141]

Now, markets for long-term transmission capacity have been organised in different ways in different European countries. (a) In most countries, long-term transmission capacity is sold as PTRs. Market participants can thus use PTRs to manage risk. (b) There are no PTRs inside the Nordic market. Risk is therefore managed in the financial market as far as electricity is transmitted inside the Nordic area. (c) There are nevertheless PTRs on the German–Danish interconnectors. PTRs are the commodity underlying the Market Coupling Contracts. The delivery of the underlying asset means then delivery of PTRs.[142]

This influences the way electricity producers manage risk. Inside the Nordic market, market participants can manage risk by using futures with the Nord Pool Spot system price as the reference price.[143] They can also use contracts for

brev til Energinet.dk og 50 Hertz Transmission, hvor de to selskaber anmodes om at indføre PTR på Kontek fra den 1. januar 2014".

[140] Energinet.dk, TenneT, 50Hertz, Rules for the Long-Term Capacity Allocation by Explicit Auctions on the German–Danish borders and the interconnector between Denmark West and Denmark East (Great Belt) for the year 2014 (1 October 2013) (Long-Term Auction Rules), Article 3.2.

[141] Energinet.dk, TenneT, 50Hertz, Rules for the Long-Term Capacity Allocation by Explicit Auctions on the German–Danish borders and the interconnector between Denmark West and Denmark East (Great Belt) for the year 2014 (1 October 2013) (Long-Term Auction Rules), Article 4.3.

[142] EPEX Spot Exchange Rules (28 November 2014), Article 1.2. See also EPEX Spot Exchange Rules (28 November 2014), Article 5.3. The delivery procedure for these Market Coupling Contracts is nomination by ECC to TSOs (that is, Tennet TSO GmbH-Energinet for EPEX SPOT Germany to Denmark and Energinet-Tennet TSO GmbH for Denmark to EPEX SPOT Germany)

[143] For the different futures, see NASDAQ OMX, Trading Appendix 2/Clearing Appendix 2, Contract Specifications, Commodity Derivatives (24 November 2014).

difference (CfD) to hedge against the difference between an area price and the system price.[144]

Example: An electricity supplier supplies electricity to its customers at a fixed price. The supplier must purchase electricity in the spot market. It is therefore exposed to a price risk. In principle, the supplier has alternatives. It can use financial derivatives. It can buy futures at the system price. It can also hedge against differences between the area prices and the system price by using contracts for difference (CfD) and exchange-traded CfDs called Electricity Price Area Differentials (EPAD).

In trade across the Danish–German border, PTRs are an alternative way to manage risk.[145] PTRs can be functional equivalents of CfDs. A PTR can be used to fix an area price.

Example. A supplier in Eastern Denmark can buy a PTR on Kontek and a futures contract on the German spot price. The PTR is a functional equivalent of a CfD, because the price difference can be paid to the owner of the PTR in the event the owner does not notify flows.[146]

References

ACER/CEER (2012) Annual report on the results of monitoring the internal electricity and natural gas markets in 2011, 29 November

Booz & Company (2013) Benefits of an integrated European energy market: revised final report. Prepared for European Commission Directorate-General – Energy, 20 July

Cameron PD (2007) Competition in energy markets: law and regulation in the European Union, 2nd edn. Oxford University Press, Oxford

Energimarknadsinspektionen (2010) Marknadsöppning av Baltic Cable och SwePol Link. EI R2010:10. Eskilstuna

Energy Market Authority, Finland (2013) National Report 2013 to the Agency for the Cooperation of Energy Regulatory and to the European Commission, 12 July 2013

ENTSO-E Network Code on Capacity Allocation and Congestion Management (27 September 2012)

ENTSO-E Network Code on Electricity Balancing (6 August 2014)

ENTSO-E Network Code on Forward Capacity Allocation (2 April 2014)

Meeus L (2011) Implicit auctioning on the Kontek Cable: third time lucky? Energy Econ 33(3): 413–418. doi:10.1016/j.eneco.2010.10.008

NordREG (2013) Nordic Market report 2013: development in the Nordic electricity market. Report 6/2013

Supponen M (2011) The influence of national and company interests on European electricity transmission investments. Dissertation, Aalto University

Talus K (2005) First experience under the exemption regime of EC Regulation 1228/2003 on conditions for access to the network of cross-border exchanges in electricity. J Energy Nat Resourc Law 25(3):266–281

[144] Energitilsynet, Sekretariatsafgørelse 24. oktober 2013 (13/09342), Metodeanmeldelse Energinet.dk—PTR på Kontek og nye auktionsregler for PTR gældende for begge grænser til Tyskland, paras 10–11.

[145] *Ibid*, para 26.

[146] *Ibid*, Boks 1.

Chapter 7
Electricity Generated from Renewable Sources and Emission Marketplaces

7.1 General Remarks

EU law has increased investment in the generation of electricity from renewable sources (RES-E). There are different kinds of promotion strategies for renewables. They can be (1) regulatory or voluntary and (2) direct or indirect. Moreover, they can address (3) price or quantity. They can also foster (4) investment or generation.[1]

Investments in RES-E are regulation-driven rather than market-driven. The most important regulatory drivers include: authorisations; feed-in tariffs and alternative systems; priority access and dispatching; allocation of costs for grid connection; duties of the TSO/DSO; net metering; and guarantees of origin. The EU Emission Trading Scheme (ETS)[2] is thus not the most important driver.

The EU ETS is a regulated system for the auctioning of emission allowances and emissions trading. It means cap-and-trade.[3] Emissions trading is potentially important for electricity producers, because electricity generation belongs to the biggest sources of greenhouse gas emissions. Electricity producers no longer receive free allowances and have to buy them.

[1] Haas R et al. (2011), section 5.1.

[2] See NASDAQ OMX, Trading Appendix 2/Clearing Appendix 2, Contract Specifications, Commodity Derivatives (24 November 2014), Part B, section 3.2.1.

[3] Directive 2003/87/EC (EU Emissions Trading Scheme Directive). The second-largest cap-and-trade scheme in the world is California's AB32. See, for example, Lo Schiavo G (2012) and Poncelet C (2011).

P. Mäntysaari, *EU Electricity Trade Law*, DOI 10.1007/978-3-319-16513-4_7

7.2 The Preferential Treatment of RES-E

7.2.1 *Regulation*

General Remarks

The combined effect of priority authorisation, grid access, dispatching, and feed-in tariffs is to: reduce the wholesale market price for electricity; reduce incentives to invest in electricity generation from non-renewable sources; reduce the scope of the free electricity market that works on a competitive basis; and increase subventions. Current regulation is expensive but does not seem to result in any major reduction in greenhouse gas emissions.[4]

Germany provides an example. Wind power and solar power capacity have been increased in Germany by very high feed-in tariffs under the German Renewable Energy Act (EEG, now EEG 2014). At the same time, it would not make much commercial sense to invest in new conventional installations. Conventional installations are not competitive, because wholesale electricity prices are kept low by the very low marginal production costs of wind and solar power. Emissions have been increased, because old coal-powered installations have the lowest marginal production costs.

EEG has not contributed to a reduction of emissions at the European level either. Because there is more wind power and solar power capacity, there is less demand for emission rights. The available emission rights have been used in other parts of the EU.[5]

Dependence on the current favourable regulation and high levels of future subventions is combined with exposure to legal risk as laws may change.

This can again be illustrated with German experiences. As the EEG 2012 regime was neither economically nor environmentally sustainable and the Commission had opened an in-depth investigation that focused on the reductions for energy-intensive users in December 2013, the Bundesregierung submitted a proposal for a reform. EEG 2014 was adopted in July 2014. Under the new rules, the renewables sector will be subject to competition from 2017 onwards.

Authorisations

The 20 % target will influence the *authorisation procedure* for the construction of new generating capacity. When Member States lay down the criteria for the granting of an authorisation, Member States must consider, for example: the nature of the primary sources; the contribution of the generating capacity to meeting the overall Community target of at least a 20 % share of energy from renewable sources; and the contribution of generating capacity to reducing emissions.[6]

---

[4] See, for example, Ollikka K (2013). For the Kyoto Protocol, see Korhola ER (2014), p. 91.

[5] Sinn HW (2009); Ollikka K (2013), p. 290.

[6] Article 7(2) of Directive 2009/72/EC (Third Electricity Directive). See points c, f, g, j, and k.

Guarantees of Origin

Guarantees of origin are designed to *increase demand* for electricity from renewable sources or from high-efficiency cogeneration plants.

Guarantees of origin are regulated by the Directive on the promotion of the use of energy from renewable sources (RES Directive) (energy from renewable sources),[7] the Directive on the promotion of cogeneration, and the Energy Efficiency Directive (electricity produced from high-efficiency cogeneration plants).[8]

A guarantee of origin can be transferred, independently of the energy to which it relates, from one holder to another.[9] There is thus an electricity market and a market for the environmental benefit derived from the way the electricity was generated. While guarantees of origin is the term used in EU law, green certificates or electricity certificates traded under national systems are basically the same thing.

There is a joint Swedish and Norwegian electricity certificate (El-Cert) system.[10] Each state gives electricity certificates to the owners of electricity generation installations for every produced MWh of RES-E provided that they fulfil certain standards. The standards are technology neutral. The certificates can be sold. The price is decided by supply and demand.[11] Demand is secured by a quota obligation. In Sweden, electricity suppliers, some wholesale market participants, large self-generators, and electricity-intensive industries must own a certain amount of certificates.[12] However, energy intensive industries are largely exempted from the requirement.[13]

There is also a joint market for contracts with El-Certs as the contract base.[14]

Feed-in Tariffs and Alternative Systems

The choice between feed-in tariffs and alternative systems such as government tendering systems and quota-based trading systems has a major impact on investment.

[7] Article 15 of Directive 2009/28/EC (RES Directive).

[8] Recital 39 and Article 14(10) of Directive 2012/27/EU (Energy Efficiency Directive).

[9] Recital 52 of Directive 2009/28/EC (RES Directive).

[10] The joint Swedish and Norwegian Electricity Certificate System came into force on 1 January 2012. It is based on: lag om elcertifikat (2011:1200) (the Swedish Electricity Certificates Act) and the Swedish Energy Agency's regulations and general guidelines for certificates (STEMFS 2011:4); and lov om elsertifikater 24.06.2011 nr. 39 (Norwegian law on electricity certificates).

[11] See Inwinkl P and Rosenberg J (2011) who discuss sanctions for fraud.

[12] Chapter 4, section 1 of the Swedish Electricity Certificates Act.

[13] Chapter 4, section 5 of the Swedish Electricity Certificates Act.

[14] NASDAQ OMX, Trading Appendix 2/Clearing Appendix 2, Contract Specifications, Commodity Derivatives (24 November 2014), Part B, section 4.2.1: "... El-Cert or Electricity Certificates means any Electricity Certificate unit representing one (1) Electricity certificate issued for each (1) MWh of electricity produced from renewable energy sources".

Feed-in Tariffs Feed-in tariffs—in combination with priority access to the grid and priority dispatching—are the main mechanism for the Member States of the EU to give support to generators of RES-E. Feed-in tariffs attract plenty of investment where they are set above the generation level and sufficiently generous.

The Member States use many different feed-in tariff systems. Feed-in tariffs can be fixed (such as EEG 2012 in Germany) or variable. One example of variable feed-in tariffs is guarantee prices (such as in Denmark).[15]

In Germany, the biggest market in Europe, TSOs were required to purchase renewable power at fixed feed-in tariffs under EEG 2012.[16] They were compensated by electricity undertakings further down the chain.[17] Final consumers ended up paying the difference between market prices and the fixed feed-in tariffs.[18] When market prices were negative, final consumers (who were not paid the negative prices for consuming more electricity) ended up paying even more.[19]

EEG 2014 distinguishes between two supported ways to market RES-E, that is, direct marketing (Direktvermarktung)[20] and the sale of RES-E to the TSO.[21] In the former case, the buyer pays the market price and the TSO a variable monthly premium on top of the market price.[22] In the latter case, the TSO pays a fixed feed-in tariff. The fixed feed-in tariff is designed for small installations.[23] A RES-E producer may choose the support system monthly in advance.[24]

Quota-Based Systems Quota-based systems are used in some Member States (Sweden, Poland, Belgium, the UK, Italy, and Romania), in about 20 US states and the District of Columbia, and in Japan.[25] The duty to comply with the quota can be allocated to suppliers (the UK, Belgium, Poland, Romania), generators (Italy), end-users (Sweden until the end of 2006), or a combination such as the combination of suppliers and end-users (Sweden since 2007). In any case, a market participant can comply with these obligations in three alternative ways. It can (1) produce tradable green certificates (TGSs) by generating electricity at an eligible renewable plant; (2) purchase TGCs from other eligible generators, other suppliers or traders, or exchanges; or (3) pay the penalty or "Buy-Out Price" set by the regulatory authority.[26]

---

[15] Kitzing L et al. (2012); Haas R et al. (2011), section 6; Ollikka K (2013).

[16] § 2 and § 5(1) EEG 2012.

[17] §§ 34–37 EEG 2012.

[18] § 34 EEG 2012.

[19] For example, Mihm A (2009).

[20] Point 1 of § 19(1) EEG 2014 and § 2(2) EEG 2014.

[21] Point 2 of § 19(1) EEG 2014.

[22] § 34 EEG 2014; Annex 1 to EEG 2014.

[23] §§ 37–38 EEG 2014.

[24] § 20 EEG 2014.

[25] See Haas R et al. (2011), section 6.3.

[26] Haas R et al. (2011), section 6.3.

The Swedish model with El-Certs has attracted interest in Germany that woke up to the cost of EEG 2012.[27] (a) In Sweden, the capacity that qualifies for certificates is mainly new. Originally, some old capacity was allowed. This led to "free riding" capacities and "windfall profits" for plants that preceded the TGC system. (b) In 2007, the compliance obligation was moved from end-users to suppliers. Originally, there were tax incentives and investment subsidies especially for wind power plants.[28]

Government Tendering The same with quota-based trading systems, government tendering systems are an alternative to feed-in tariff systems.[29] They have been used in many states in the US and, in the past, in some European countries. However, European countries tend to replace government tendering systems with other systems, that is, a feed-in tariff system or a renewables obligation.[30]

Priority Access, Dispatching

Preferential feed-in tariffs are complemented by priority access to the grid (subject to some security of supply constraints[31]). Member States must ensure that TSOs and DSOs (a) guarantee the transmission and distribution of electricity produced from renewable energy sources and (b) provide for either priority access or guaranteed access to the grid-system of electricity produced from renewable energy sources. What applies to electricity from renewable sources applies to (c) electricity produced from waste or the production of CHP.[32]

For reasons of security of supply, Member States may also choose that priority must be given to the dispatch of generating installations using "indigenous primary energy fuel sources". There is a cap of 15 % of the overall primary energy necessary to produce the electricity consumed in the Member State.[33]

One may ask whether such measures can amount to quantitative restrictions on imports under the TFEU.[34] In *PreussenElektra v Schleswag* the CJEU found that they can.[35] However, the CJEU held that there is a justification for such measures.[36]

[27] Monopolkommission (2013), section 3.3.3 and number 514. For a comparison of the UK model and the German model before EEG 2014, see Toke D (2010), p. 29.

[28] See Haas R et al. (2011), section 6.3.4.

[29] For auction mechanisms, see Ausubel LM and Cramton P (2011).

[30] Haas R et al. (2011), section 6.2. For renewables obligations in the UK, see Otitoju A et al. (2010).

[31] Article 16(2)(c) of Directive 2009/28/EC (RES Directive).

[32] Article 16(2) of Directive 2009/28/EC (RES Directive). See also Articles 15(3) and 25(4) of Directive 2009/72/EC (Third Electricity Directive).

[33] Article 15(4) of Directive 2009/72/EC (Third Electricity Directive).

[34] Article 34 TFEU.

[35] Case C-379/98 PreussenElektra v Schleswag [2001] ECR I-2099, paras 69–71.

[36] Case C-379/98 PreussenElektra v Schleswag [2001] ECR I-2099, paras 72–73.

Allocation of Costs for Grid Connection and Other Investment Incentives

Member States provide various investment incentives and investment-based tax incentives for electricity generation from renewable sources.[37] The allocation of costs for grid connection can play a big role.

Allocation of Costs for Grid Connection As major grid investments are necessary, incentives to invest in generation installations can also depend on the allocation of costs for connecting the installation to the grid. There will be: costs for connecting the installation to the grid connection point; and costs for upgrades in the distribution network and regional network.

The position of EU law is to allocate most costs to the system operators and to socialise them. (a) The main rule under the Third Electricity Directive is that the system operator is responsible for the system. The TSO is thus responsible for the connection of electricity producers to the transmission grid[38] and the DSO is responsible for the connection of microgenerators to the distribution grid.[39] (b) System operators have a right to collect tariffs. However, the tariffs must be non-discriminatory, and they will be fixed or approved by the regulatory authority.[40] (c) As a result, system operators should bear the burden of most costs but allocate them to customers that share the costs in the form of tariffs.

EU law does not require system operators to bear all such costs. System operators must regulate the allocation of costs in their standard rules.[41] Member States may nevertheless require transmission system operators and distribution system operators to bear such costs in full or in part when it is "appropriate" to do so.[42]

In practice, there have been different ways to allocate these costs in the Member States.

> This can be illustrated with offshore wind farms. (a) In some countries, project developers have to pay for the construction of the line, transformers, and all other necessary installations for grid connection.[43] (b) In Germany, the biggest market, costs for connecting offshore wind farms to the grid are allocated to the system operator.[44] This rule has placed

[37] See Haas R et al. (2011), sections 6.4 and 6.5.

[38] Article 12 of Directive 2009/72/EC (Third Electricity Directive).

[39] Articles 3(3) and 25 of Directive 2009/72/EC (Third Electricity Directive).

[40] Recital 36 and Article 12 of Directive 2009/72/EC (Third Electricity Directive). See also Articles 25, 32(1), 37(1), 37(6)(a), 37(8), and 37(10) of Directive 2009/72/EC (Third Electricity Directive).

[41] First subparagraph of Article 16(3) of Directive 2009/28/EC (RES Directive). See also second subparagraph of Article 16(3) of Directive 2009/28/EC (RES Directive), and Article 14(1) of Regulation 714/2009 on conditions for access to the network for cross-border exchanges.

[42] Article 16(4) of Directive 2009/28/EC (RES Directive).

[43] SOU 2008:13, p. 200, Table 5-3.

[44] § 17e EnWG. See also Bundesnetzagentur (2009).

a heavy financial burden on system operators and increased their risk exposure. However, it has also increased investment in wind power.[45] In order to mitigate the risk exposure of system operators, Germany decided to socialise part of the losses caused by the failure of system operators to connect offshore wind farms to the grid.[46] (c) In many countries, costs for upgrades in the transmission network are allocated to the system operator (and socialised in the form of tariffs). (d) There are nevertheless exceptions. In Sweden, as an illustration, upgrades that benefit only the wind farm owner have been paid by the wind farm owner. When upgrades benefit others (mainly in the 400 kV grid), the system operator (Svenska Kraftnät, the Swedish national grid) pays part of the costs.[47]

The Duties of the TSO/DSO

The duties of the system operator are designed to *increase the supply* of electricity produced from renewable sources. A system operator has a general duty to act with due regard to the environment.[48] In particular, the duties relate to:

- grid access (the duty to grant electricity produced from renewable energy sources priority or guaranteed access to the grid)[49];
- transmission and distribution (the duty to guarantee the transmission or distribution of electricity produced from renewable energy sources)[50];
- dispatching (the duty to give priority to generating installations using renewable energy sources[51] when the TSO is responsible for dispatching the generating installations in its area)[52];
- combined heat and power (a Member State may require TSOs to give priority to generating installations producing CHP when they dispatch generating installations)[53]; and

[45] What the heavy costs can mean in the worst case can be illustrated with the problems faced by TenneT TSO, a transmission system operator based in Germany and the Netherlands. Bundesnetzagentur, the German regulatory authority was reluctant to grant an authorization for Tennet TSO in the light of Tennet's funding. See Bundesnetzagentur (2012). Failure to connect offshore wind farms to the grid can lead to liability for loss sustained by the wind farm operators. Tennet TSO settled one such case. See Windreich AG, Windreich und TenneT einigen sich auf Interimsanbindung für Offshore-Windpark Deutsche Bucht, press release (25 October 2012).

[46] Frankfurter Allgemeine Zeitung, Stromverbraucher sollen für Netze vor der Küste haften, 25 August 2012, p. 9.

[47] SOU 2008:13, pp. 200–203.

[48] Point a of Article 12 of Directive 2009/72/EC (Third Electricity Directive).

[49] Point b of Article 16(2) of Directive 2009/28/EC (RES Directive).

[50] Point a of Article 16(2) of Directive 2009/28/EC (RES Directive).

[51] In so far as the secure operation of the national electricity system permits. Point c of Article 16 (2) of Directive 2009/28/EC (RES Directive).

[52] Article 15(1) of Directive 2009/72/EC (Third Electricity Directive).

[53] Article 15(3) of Directive 2009/72/EC (Third Electricity Directive). See also Article 16(11) of Directive 2009/28/EC (RES Directive).

- tariffs (there is a particular duty not to charge discriminatory tariffs for the transmission or distribution of electricity from renewable energy sources).[54]

Metering

Net metering, net billing, and two-way metering can change the nature of the market.

Net Metering The introduction of net metering and net billing can increase microgeneration that is distributed generation and often generation from renewable sources. In the US, all public electric utilities are required, upon request, to make net metering available to their customers.[55] Europe uses two-way metering instead.

Two-Way Metering In the EU, the Commission has recommended "import/export and reactive metering" as one of the common minimum functional requirements for smart metering systems to promote distributed generation.[56] Current tax rules are regarded as a barrier to full net billing.[57]

The new Energy Efficiency Directive provides for two-way metering at the request of final customers to the extent that Member States implement intelligent metering systems and roll out smart meters as set out in the Third Electricity Directive. According to the new Energy Efficiency Directive, Member States shall, at the request of the final customer, "require meter operators to ensure that the meter or meters can account for electricity put into the grid from the final customer's premises".[58]

Two-way metering may enable microgenerators to (a) sell electricity when it is generated and buy it when there is no generation, or to (b) buy electricity when prices are low and sell electricity when prices are higher. Moreover, an end consumer that puts RES-E into the grid may be entitled to (c) obtain guarantees of origin or green certificates that it can sell in the market.[59]

Two-way metering will obviously increase costs because it facilitates electricity flows in two directions. It will increase metering costs and—even more importantly—costs for grid security.

---

[54] Articles 16(7) and 16(8) of Directive 2009/28/EC (RES Directive).

[55] Section 1251 of the Energy Policy Act of 2005.

[56] Commission Recommendation of 9 March 2012 on preparations for the roll-out of smart metering systems (2012/148/EU), para 42. See also Thomas S (2001), p. 120: "The DGES, a strong advocate of metering as a way of allocating costs appropriately, reluctantly came to the conclusion in 1995 that 'smart' meters were not viable and that 'profiling', at that time being introduced in Norway, was the only viable solution".

[57] See, for example, Energy Markets Inspectorate (2011), section 7.3.10.

[58] Point c of Article 9(2) of Directive 2012/27/EU (Electricity Efficiency Directive). See also point d.

[59] Hedström L and Stridh B (2006). See, for example, recital 52 of Directive 2009/28/EC (RES Directive) and para 135 of Guidelines on State aid 2014–2020.

As a microgenerator can only sell small volumes, the allocation of metering costs—and the costs of grid access—can have a major impact on volumes put into the grid. (a) If the costs are allocated to microgenerators, the costs may in many cases exceed the income they would generate. This could reduce supply.[60] (b) Allocation of these costs to the system operator would reduce the system operator's incentives to provide services to microgenerators. (c) This leaves the socialisation of costs.

7.2.2 Signalling the Use of RES-E

For commercial reasons, suppliers may want to sell RES-E to end consumers and non-energy firms may want to signal that they use RES-E. They have alternative ways to signal that the electricity is from renewable sources. These alternatives can have an impact on the business models and operations of electricity producers.

The main options are procuring certificates, procuring RES-E, power purchase agreements, and ownership of RES-E generation assets. (a) According to Global Corporate Renewable Index 2002,[61] purchasing credits or green certificates is the most popular option as it leaves much to the parties' discretion. (b) Instead of procuring certificates, an end consumer can purchase RES-E under a supply contract. In this case, it can agree with its supplier that the contract electricity is RES-E. Electricity suppliers can "make or buy" RES-E. Electricity producers react by investing more in RES-E generation assets. (c) A power purchase agreement means that electricity is supplied from a certain plant under a long-term agreement. (d) An end consumer can generate the electricity itself, such as by investing in wind power or solar panels. This can increase demand for operation and maintenance services. (e) An end consumer can purchase carbon offsets. However, carbon offsets are not necessarily generated by renewable energy projects.

7.3 Emissions Trading

7.3.1 General Remarks

The EU introduced its own trading system for greenhouse gas emission allowances on 1 January 2005. The purpose of this market-based approach is to provide economic incentives for achieving reductions in greenhouse gas emissions. It is

[60] Hedström L and Stridh B (2006).

[61] Bloomberg New Energy Finance, Vestas Wind Systems A/S, Global Corporate Renewable Index (CREX) 2012, section 2.2.

also designed to influence investment. Because an increased price of greenhouse emission permits would spill over into wholesale electricity prices, it could, in principle, have an impact on the choice of technology, fuel, and other cost factors.[62] In practice, the system has been a disappointment.

The system is established by Directive 2003/87/EC (the ETS Directive).[63] As a rule, these allowances are transferable[64] and recognised by the competent authorities of other Member States.[65] A Central Administrator designated by the Commission maintains an independent transaction log recording the issue, transfer and cancellation of allowances.[66]

The allowances are transferable between operators within the EU[67] and to some extent even across the EU's border.[68] International trading is organised by the UN through the Green Development Mechanism.

International Emissions Trading The Linking Directive[69] facilitates a connection between Member States' emission targets, trading in emission allowances, and international emissions trading.[70]

Under the Kyoto Protocol, industrialised countries can achieve part of their emission reduction commitments by investing in emission-saving projects in developing countries through the Clean Development Mechanism (CDM).[71] The mechanism allows projects that reduce greenhouse-gas emissions in poor countries to earn a carbon credit (a "certified emission reduction", CER) for each tonne of carbon dioxide avoided.[72] The credits can be sold to firms in rich countries which

---

[62] International Energy Agency (2007).

[63] Directive 2003/87/EC (ETS Directive). See Roberts R and Staples C (2008).

[64] Article 12(1) of Directive 2003/87/EC (ETS Directive).

[65] Article 12(2) of Directive 2003/87/EC (ETS Directive).

[66] Article 20(1) of Directive 2003/87/EC (ETS Directive).

[67] Point a of Article 12(1) of Directive 2003/87/EC (ETS Directive).

[68] Point b of Article 12(1) as well as Articles 25(1) and 25(2) of Directive 2003/87/EC (ETS Directive).

[69] Directive 2004/101/EC amending Directive 2003/87/EC establishing a scheme for greenhouse gas emission allowance trading within the Community, in respect of the Kyoto Protocol's project mechanisms.

[70] Article 30(3) of Decision 406/2009/EC of the European Parliament and of the Council on the effort of Member States to reduce their greenhouse gas emissions to meet the Community's greenhouse gas emission reduction commitments up to 2020.

[71] Communication from the Commission, 20 20 by 2020 – Europe's climate change opportunity, COM(2008) 13 final, COM(2008) 16 final, COM(2008) 17 final, COM(2008) 18 final, COM (2008) 19 final, COM(2008) 30 final. For the Kyoto Protocol, see, for example, Korhola ER (2014).

[72] See NASDAQ OMX, Trading Appendix 2/Clearing Appendix 2, Contract Specifications, Commodity Derivatives (24 November 2014), Part B, section 3.2.1.

are obliged under Kyoto to cut their emissions. Emission credits are thus recognised even where a Member State obtains them from another country.[73]

7.3.2 *Allocation of Emission Allowances*

Emissions trading must be complemented by a mechanism for the allocation of emission allowances by the Member States.[74]

Some installations are exempted and do not require any emission allowances because of their small size. The ETS Directive applies to "combustion of fuels in installations with a total rated thermal input exceeding 20 MW".[75] As a result, the ETS Directive does not apply to a large number of small installations that produce heat only but does apply to more effective CHP installations that are larger. Investments in new large CHP installations would thus be hampered if emission allowances were expensive.[76]

In any case, large installations need these emission allowances.

Phase III During Phase I (2005–2007), most emission allowances were allocated free of charge.[77] The supply of credits exceeded demand and prices collapsed.[78] The market-based mechanism did not work properly. The problems were made worse by the preferential treatment of RES-E and the existence of parallel incentive systems.[79]

Phase III[80] changed this starting 2013.[81] While 10 % of emission allowances were auctioned in Phase II, 60 % are auctioned in Phase III. The allocation of allowances depends on the sector. The electricity sector and CCS installations are auctioned from 2013.[82] In the industrial sector, 20 % of allowances were auctioned and 80 % allocated for free in 2013. Thereafter, the free allocation decreases each

[73] Article 5 of Decision 406/2009/EC of the European Parliament and of the Council on the effort of Member States to reduce their greenhouse gas emissions to meet the Community's greenhouse gas emission reduction commitments up to 2020.

[74] For an introduction, see, for example, Okinczyc S (2011) and Lo Schiavo G (2012).

[75] Annex I to Directive 2003/87/EC (as amended by Directive 2009/29/EC).

[76] Lanz M et al. (2011), section 4.2.1, pp. 88–89.

[77] Articles 9–11 of Directive 2003/87/EC (ETS Directive).

[78] The Economist, Complete Disaster in the Making. The world's only global carbon market is in need of a radical overhaul (13 September 2012).

[79] See, for example, Aatola P et al. (2013), p. 279.

[80] See Lo Schiavo G (2012) and Okinczyc S (2011).

[81] Phase III commenced on 1 January 2013 after the adoption of a revised EU ETS Directive (Directive 2009/29/EC). The Aviation Directive (Directive 2008/101/EC) had already added aviation as an additional sector to the EU ETS.

[82] Recital 19 of Directive 2009/29/EC.

year by equal amounts. In 2020, 70 % of allowances will be auctioned and the free allocation reduced to 30 %. There should be no free allocation in 2027.[83]

Platforms The Auctioning Regulation[84] tells you how emission allowances are auctioned in Phase III. For auctioning one needs one or more auction platforms and a selection procedure for platforms.

There are two kinds of platforms. On one hand, there is a common auction platform.[85] The Commission appointed European Energy Exchange AG (EEX) as the first common platform. On the other, a Member State may decide not to participate in the joint action.[86] Germany, Poland, and the UK have decided to opt out of the common platform and to appoint their own auction platforms. Germany has selected EEX as its opt-out auction platform.[87] The UK appointed ICE Futures Europe as its opt-out auction platform.[88]

Auctions The Auctioning Regulation lays down the modalities of the auction process[89] according to the principles of the ETS Directive.[90] Allowances are offered for sale on an auction platform by means of standardised electronic contracts[91] and an electronic interface that can be accessed remotely.[92]

Each Member State auctions allowances in the form of two-day spot contracts or five-day futures.[93]

> In the past, two-day spot contracts were not regarded as financial instruments in EU securities markets law, but five-day futures were financial instruments (see Sect. 4.8.2).[94] This distinction was based on Regulation 1287/2006 implementing MiFID.[95] A distinction

---

[83] Recital 21 of Directive 2009/29/EC and Article 10a (11) of Directive 2003/87/EC (as amended by Directive 2009/29/EC).

[84] Regulation 1031/2010 (Auctioning Regulation).

[85] Article 26 of Regulation 1031/2010 (Auctioning Regulation). See also recital 7.

[86] Article 30 of Regulation 1031/2010 (Auctioning Regulation). See also recital 8.

[87] Regulation 784/2012.

[88] Regulation 1042/2012. ICE Futures Europe is a Recognised Investment Exchange (RIE) and Recognised Auction Platform (RAP). It is regulated by the FSA.

[89] See point 16 of Article 3 of Regulation 1031/2010 (Auctioning Regulation).

[90] For the objectives of the process, see recital 3 of Regulation 1031/2010 (Auctioning Regulation) referring to the ETS Directive.

[91] Article 4(1) of Regulation 1031/2010 (Auctioning Regulation).

[92] Article 16 of Regulation 1031/2010 (Auctioning Regulation).

[93] Article 4(2) of Regulation 1031/2010 (Auctioning Regulation). For definitions, see points 1–4 of Article 3 of Regulation 1031/2010 (Auctioning Regulation).

[94] Recital 14 of Regulation 1031/2010 (Auctioning Regulation).

[95] First subparagraph of Article 38(2) of Regulation 1287/2006 (implementing Article 4(1)(2) of Directive 2004/39/EC): "A spot contract for the purposes of paragraph 1 means a contract for the sale of a commodity, asset or right, under the terms of which delivery is scheduled to be made within the longer of the following periods: (a) two trading days; (b) the period generally accepted in the market for that commodity, asset or right as the standard delivery period".

based on the duration of the contract was not regarded as controversial in practice.[96] However, emission allowances and derivatives are now defined as financial instruments under MiFID II regardless of the duration of the contract.[97]

Bids are submitted by bidders. A bidder can bid on its own account or on behalf of a client.[98] Only persons admitted to bid may submit bids directly in an auction,[99] and only certain persons are eligible to apply for admission to bid directly in auctions. They include: compliance buyers (bidding on own account); business groupings of compliance buyers (bidding on own account and acting as an agent on behalf of their members); members or participants of the auction platform (where the auction platform organises a secondary market); investment firms and credit institutions authorised under the MiFID (Directive 2004/39/EC) or the Credit Institutions Directive (Directive 2006/48/EC) (bidding on own account or on behalf of clients); and other intermediaries specifically authorised by the home Member State (bidding on own account or on behalf of clients).[100]

An electricity producer may apply for admission to bid: on its own account fur the purpose of complying with its own obligations; and on its own account for the benefit of entities that belong to the same group.

A bidder must be represented by the bidder's representative who is: a natural person established in the Union; appointed by the bidder to bind the bidder for all purposes relating to the auctions; and authorised.[101]

Bids may only be submitted during a given bidding window. The main rule is that each bid is binding once submitted and may not be withdrawn.[102]

Each successful bidder pays the same auction clearing price for each allowance regardless of the price bid.[103]

There is a clearing system, a settlement system, a central counterparty, and margining.[104] The auction platform should be connected to at least one clearing system and at least one settlement system, and more than one system may be connected to the platform. The Auctioning Regulation is designed to foster competition between different potential auction platforms.[105]

The Auctioning Regulation lays down market conduct rules for persons authorised to bid on behalf of others.[106]

---

[96] See ESMA (2014) number 12 of ANNEX I.

[97] Point 11 of section C of Annex to Directive 2014/65/EU (MiFID II).

[98] Article 6 of Regulation 1031/2010 (Auctioning Regulation).

[99] Article 15 of Regulation 1031/2010 (Auctioning Regulation).

[100] Articles 18 and 19 of Regulation 1031/2010 (Auctioning Regulation).

[101] Articles 6(3) and 19(2)(d) of Regulation 1031/2010 (Auctioning Regulation).

[102] Articles 5 and 6 of Regulation 1031/2010 (Auctioning Regulation).

[103] Article 5 and 7 of Regulation 1031/2010 (Auctioning Regulation).

[104] For definitions, see Article 3 of Regulation 1031/2010 (Auctioning Regulation).

[105] See recital 32 of Regulation 1031/2010 (Auctioning Regulation).

[106] Article 59 of Regulation 1031/2010 (Auctioning Regulation).

Moreover, the market abuse regime has been adapted to emissions trading. Both the two-day spot contracts and the five-day futures are regarded as financial instruments for this purpose meaning that the market abuse regime is applicable.[107]

7.3.3 *Secondary Trading*

Emission allowances are issued into the secondary market[108] rather than allocated directly to the operators of installations or to aircraft operators. This influences the obligations of the auctioneer and the obligations of clearing or settlement systems: they are not responsible for the delivery of allowances.[109] OTC-trading is possible. The International Emissions Trading Association (IETA) has drafted a master agreement for EU ETS.[110] The market can also develop allowance derivatives.[111]

> EEX carries out so-called primary market auctions for emission allowances in the Spot Market. The Spot Market is also the secondary market in which EEX offers EU Allowances (EUA) and Certified Emission Reductions (CER). In the Derivatives Market, trading participants can trade EUA (EU Allowances), EUAA (EU Aviation Allowances), CER (Certified Emission Reductions) and ERU (Emission Reduction Units) futures.

References

Aatola P, Marjamaa E, Ollikainen M, Ollikka K (2013) Euroopan unionin päästöoikeuskauppa ja ilmastopolitiikka. Kansantaloudellinen aikakauskirja 109(3):275–288

Ackermann T, Centeno-Lopez E (2008) SOU 2008:13. Grid Issues for electricity production based on renewable energy sources in Spain, Portugal, Germany, and United Kingdom. Annex to report of the grid connection inquiry. Stockholm

Ausubel LM, Cramton P (2011) Comparison of auction formats for auctioning wind rights. Report to Bureau of Ocean Energy Management, Regulation and Enforcement

Bundesnetzagentur (2009) Positionspapier zur Netzanbindungsverpflichtung gemäß § 17 Abs. 2a EnWG. Available at Bundesnetzgentur website. http://www.bundesnetzagentur.de/

Bundesnetzagentur (2012) Bundesnetzagentur trifft erste Zertifizierungsentscheidungen. Press release, 9 November. Available at Bundesnetzgentur website. http://www.bundesnetzagentur.de/

[107] Articles 36–43 of Regulation 1031/2010 (Auctioning Regulation).

[108] Article 4 of Regulation 1031/2010 (Auctioning Regulation). For a definition, see point 11 of Article 3 of Regulation 1031/2010 (Auctioning Regulation).

[109] Recital 27 of Regulation 1031/2010 (Auctioning Regulation): "...The auction platform should be responsible solely for conducting the auctions ..." Recital 38 of Regulation 1031/2010 (Auctioning Regulation): "... it is inappropriate for the clearing system(s) or settlement system (s) to be bound by any obligations of specific performance of the delivery of allowances ..."

[110] Emissions Trading Master Agreement for the EU Scheme (Version 3.0, 2008).

[111] Recital 14 of Regulation 1031/2010 (Auctioning Regulation).

Communication from the Commission, 20 20 by 2020 – Europe's climate change opportunity, COM(2008) 13 final, COM(2008) 16 final, COM(2008) 17 final, COM(2008) 18 final, COM (2008) 19 final, COM(2008) 30 final

Energy Markets Inspectorate (2011) Adapting electricity networks to a sustainable energy system – smart metering and smart grids. EI R2011:03. Eskilstuna

ESMA (2014) Letter from ESMA to Commissioner Michel Barnier (Re: Classification of financial instruments as derivatives), 14 February

Haas R, Panzer C, Resch G et al (2011) A historical review of promotion strategies for electricity from renewable energy sources in EU countries. Renewable Sustainable Energy Rev 15(2): 1003–1034. doi:10.1016/j.rser.2010.11.015

Hedström L, Stridh B (2006) Villkor för försäljning av el från nätanslutna solcellanläggningar – nuläge och förbättringsförslag. Elforsk rapport 06:48

International Energy Agency (2007) Tackling investment challenges in power generation in IEA countries. OECD/IEA, Paris

Inwinkl P, Rosenberg J (2011) The Swedish Certificates Act and its compatibility with the European convention on human rights. Eur Energy Environ Law Rev 20(2):45–57

Kitzing L, Mitchell C, Morthorst PE (2012) Renewable energy policies in Europe: converging or diverging? Energy Policy 51:192–201. doi:10.1016/j.enpol.2012.08.064

Korhola ER (2014) Climate change as a political process: the rise and fall of the Kyoto protocol. Dissertation, University of Helsinki

Lanz M, Fricke B, Anthrakidis A et al (2011) CO2-Emissionsminderung durch Ausbau, informationstechnische Vernetzung und Netzoptimierung von Anlagen dezentraler, fluktuierender und erneuerbarer Energienutzung in Deutschland. Umweltbundesamt, Climate Change 20/2011

Lo Schiavo G (2012) The EU emissions trading scheme in Phase III and the new Californian cap-and-trade system: a comparative assessment. Eur Energy Environ Law Rev 21(3):106–122

Mihm A (2009) Wenn der Strompreis negativ wird, zahlt der Verbraucher doppelt. Frankfurter Allgemeine Zeitung, 10 December, p 17

Monopolkommission (2013) Sondergutachten 65. Energie 2013: Wettbewerb in Zeiten der Energiewende. Sondergutachten der Monopolkommission gemäß § 62 Abs. 1 EnWG. Bonn

Okinczyc S (2011) European Union emissions trading scheme: Phase III. Eur Energy Environ Law Rev 20(4):164–173

Ollikka K (2013) Uusiutuvien energiamuotojen tukeminen. Kansantaloudellinen aikakauskirja 109(3):289–310

Otitoju A, Strachan PA, Toke D (2010) Assessing the performance of the UK renewables obligation: Cinderella or an ugly sister? In: Strachan PA, Toke D, Lal D (eds) Wind power and power politics: international perspectives. Routledge studies in science, technology, and society 9. Routledge, New York, pp 140–167

Poncelet C (2011) The emission trading scheme directive: analysis of some contentious points. Eur Energy Environ Law Rev 20(6):245–254

Roberts R, Staples C (2008) Emissions trading in the European Union. Capital Mark Law J 3(1): 5–17. doi:10.1093/cmlj/kmm036

Sinn HW (2009) Warum die Umweltpolitik neu definiert werden muss. Frankfurter Allgemeine Zeitung, 4 December, p 12

SOU 2008:13. See Ackermann T, Centeno-Lopez E (2008)

Thomas S (2001) Corporate strategies in the British electricity supply industry. In: Midttun A (ed) European energy industry business strategies. Elsevier Global Energy Policy and Economics Series. Elsevier, the Netherlands, pp 75–150

Toke D (2010) Wind-power outcomes: myths and reality. In: Strachan PA, Toke D, Lal D (eds) Wind power and power politics: international perspectives. Routledge studies in science, technology, and society 9. Routledge, New York, pp 18–36

Part III
Physical Contracts

Chapter 8
Long-Term Electricity Supply Contracts

8.1 General Remarks

Electricity supply contracts can be (1) standardised, mainly short-term, and traded in an organised way; or (2) not standardised, rather long-term, and agreed bilaterally. Standardised contracts are more likely to be traded on an exchange or a regulated marketplace. They can be simple contracts traded in the spot market (Sect. 4.5). Standardised contracts are used even in the market for balance energy and control reserves (Sect. 4.10). In this case, trading or auctions are organised by the TSO. Contracts that are not standardised can have a longer duration. OTC contracts can be relatively simple bilateral long-term contracts or more complex structured contracts.[1]

This chapter focuses on long-term electricity supply contracts in the OTC market. Spot contracts and contracts for the provision of control reserves are discussed in Chap. 4. Balancing contracts are discussed even in Chap. 9.

The topics discussed in this chapter include: the use of long-term supply contracts as part of the business model of the firm (Sect. 8.2); the role of physical electricity derivatives governed by master trading agreements (Sect. 8.3); the general provisions of the EFET General Agreement (Sect. 8.4); the particular objectives of the firm in long-term electricity supply contracts and the ways to reach them (Sect. 8.5); and reliance on the preferential treatment of electricity generation from renewable sources (RES-E) as an alternative to long-term supply contracts (Sect. 8.6). In this section, we will briefly discuss the nature of long-term electricity supply contracts, the reasons for their use, the ways to regulate them, and other general issues.

The Nature of Long-Term Electricity Supply Contracts The liberalisation of markets and the emergence of physical and financial exchanges brought electricity

[1] See, for example, Ofgem (2009), paras 1.15–1.18.

P. Mäntysaari, *EU Electricity Trade Law*, DOI 10.1007/978-3-319-16513-4_8

contracts closer to traditional commodity contracts.[2] However, electricity supply contracts are really contracts for the provision of services (Sect. 2.7). Their services nature is clearer to see when the duration of the contract is long, because the customary complexity of long-term contracts makes it necessary for the parties to regulate the modalities of their respective obligations in greater detail.

Long-term bilateral contracts for the physical supply of electricity are commonplace regardless of the progress of liberalisation.[3] Their functions can partly be explained by: market structure in general and unbundling in particular[4]; risk mitigation; and funding issues.

Many Reasons to Use Long-Term Contracts The business model of the electricity producer and the choice between long-term and short-term contracts depend on the structure of the market.[5] Unbundling therefore plays a particularly important role. The purpose of long-term contracts depends on the prevailing competition model.

Their purpose is not limited to security of supply in unbundled and liberalised markets. Security of supply can be ensured even by other means. Structurally, security of supply is increased by the existence of a competitive wholesale market, the existence of efficient marketplaces, market coupling, the entry of new suppliers, the integration of new power plants to the electricity network, and so forth. At transaction level, parties can use various products to increase security of supply.

There can, therefore, be even other reasons to use long-term contracts: (1) All long-term contracts provide a way to manage risks. (2) Electricity producers can use long-term supply contracts to ensure security of consumption, that is, the existence of buyers for their generation. One may call this locking in consumers. The preferential treatment of RES-E means that some electricity producers may enjoy security of consumption under mandatory provisions of law without long-term supply contracts (Sect. 8.6). The preferential treatment of RES-E is having a major impact on the business model of electricity producers. (3) Long-term supply contracts can be used to reduce the price risk. Because of unbundling, previously integrated electricity firms and new market entrants must now rely more on electricity supply contracts for their profits.[6] While spot prices tend to be volatile,[7] long-term contracts can help to reduce dependence on electricity exchanges and

---

[2] Varholy J and Fuhr T (2009), § 28, number 6 on the deregulation of the North American gas market.

[3] DG Competition report on energy sector inquiry, SEC(2006) 1724 (2007), pp. 232–244 and 283–294. See Glachant JM and de Hauteclocque A (2009).

[4] Article 9(1) of Directive 2009/72/EC (Third Electricity Directive).

[5] Industrial organisation theories focus on such issues. For an example of this type of approach, see Aghion P and Bolton P (1987).

[6] Putzka F (2009), p. 26.

[7] See, for example, The Economist, Tilting at the windmills (16 June 2011). In June 2011, the Bonneville Power Administration (BPA) had to produce lots of hydropower because of melting snows. For this reason, it had to take all its regions wind turbines offline for a few hours daily, give electricity away for free, and pay the transmission costs of utilities willing to take it.

spot markets and to fix a sufficient profit margin. (4) Long-term contracts can be used by distributors to increase their own security of supply. The unbundling of electricity generation and distribution has also increased the number of distributors that compete for upstream contracts in the wholesale market. Electricity distributors need an optimal portfolio of purchase contracts to ensure security of supply.—Like electricity producers, distributors also need to manage price volatility. Sometimes they complement long-term supply contracts with the ownership of shares in electricity generating companies.[8] (5) Particular long-term supply contract structures can be created to accommodate the diverging needs of electricity producers and their customers.[9] (6) Particular long-term supply contracts can facilitate the provision of control reserves (Sect. 4.10) and balance energy (Chap. 9).

Risk Mitigation There are thus many reasons for electricity producers to use long-term supply contracts. One of the traditional reasons is risk mitigation.

First, the use of long-term contracts enables electricity firms to hedge price and quantity.[10] It is a way to mitigate risks caused by the extreme price volatility of spot markets[11] and helps large electricity consumers and distributors to ensure security of supply in a relatively simple way.[12]

Second, long-term contracts help to manage opportunistic behaviour[13] in electricity markets. The risk of opportunistic behaviour can be high because of the high sunk costs and asset specificity of energy investments.[14] For instance, an electricity producer can face a hold-up problem where its power plant is dependent on one large end consumer.

Funding There are also funding reasons. Long-term contracts are customarily used in corporate finance. Long-term supply contracts are an essential part of the contractual structure of many large-scale energy investments.[15] They can be necessary, because the risk exposure of investors influences the access of the electricity firm to funding and the firm's funding costs. Long-term contracts are a means to reduce exposure to various risks.

Long-term supply contracts are particularly important in project finance in which the project is "ring-fenced" and the project company's cash flow is used as collateral.[16] A long pay-back period can be supported by long-term take-or-pay

---

[8] Putzka F (2009), p. 26.

[9] See, for example, de Hauteclocque (2009a).

[10] Finon D and Perez Y (2008) and Glachant JM and de Hauteclocque A (2009). For gas, see Talus K (2010), p. 128.

[11] Putzka F (2009), p. 19.

[12] Putzka F (2009), p. 26.

[13] Opportunistic behaviour is studied in new institutional economics.

[14] Neuhoff K and von Hirschhausen C (2005).

[15] For an example of the economic literature on long-term contracts, see Neuhoff K and von Hirschhausen C (2005).

[16] See, for example, Wurmnest W (2008). For gas, see Talus K (2010), p. 15.

contracts. Generally, project finance can be a suitable way to finance energy projects because of high up-front financing costs, the long operational phase, the long-term duration of the supply contracts, and the take-or-pay provisions used in the contracts.[17]

The availability of long-term supply contracts makes it easier to invest in high fixed-cost generation technology that customarily is employed in the generation of base load and balance energy. Therefore, they can increase the mix of generation technologies and contribute to a reduction in marginal costs.[18]

Regulation For many reasons, long-term supply contracts are less regulated compared with many other contracts in the wholesale electricity market.

Bilateral and long-term supply contracts are not contracts traded on an exchange or in a multilateral system.[19] They do not require the participation of intermediaries for the matching of bids or the participation of a central counterparty.

These contracts are not based on external rules adopted by the operator of a trading venue.[20] Consequently, these contracts are not subject to mandatory clearing. In contrast, some simple OTC supply contracts that are based on the rules of a multilateral system can be subject to mandatory clearing because of the broad definition of "regulated markets" for the purposes of MiFID II.[21] In principle, simple OTC supply contracts could also fall within the scope of the clearing obligation under EMIR provided that they are declared subject to the clearing obligation.[22]

Bilateral supply contracts do not fall within the scope of the MiFID regime as they are neither traded on a regulated market nor regarded as "financial instruments" (Sect. 4.8.2).

However, there are competition law constraints on the use of long-term contracts and take-or-pay clauses (Sect. 8.2.5).

Standardisation Although bilateral supply contracts are not standardised under the rules of the market, other factors have contributed to the convergence of their terms.

Obviously, bilateral supply contracts fall within the scope of the regulatory regime for physical electricity markets. The parties must comply with the rules of the TSO for access to the grid and the use of transmission capacity. The rules of the TSO should be non-discriminatory under the Third Electricity Directive.

Moreover, it is customary to use master agreements that lay down the terms of many supply contracts. In principle, a master agreement can be negotiated bilaterally between the parties. In practice, however, it is customary to use model

[17] Arowolo O (2005). For gas, see Talus K (2010), p. 16.

[18] Green (2006) and Finon D and Perez Y (2008).

[19] See already recital 6 of Directive 2004/39/EC (MiFID). See, for example, Hünerwadel A (2007), p. 62.

[20] Recital 112 of Directive 2014/65/EU (MiFID II).

[21] Point 21 of Article 4(1) of Directive 2014/65/EU (MiFID II).

[22] Article 4(1) of Regulation 648/2012 (EMIR).

agreements such as the EFET General Agreement Concerning the Delivery and Acceptance of Electricity. Such model agreements are also known as master trading agreements. They have become the preferred and customary documentary support for the vast majority of wholesale trading of energy products in Europe's electricity and natural gas markets.[23]

Contract Terms The contract terms must necessarily address the issues that are characteristic of electricity supply contracts (Sect. 2.5). The EFET General Agreement gives many examples of how the characteristic issues can be regulated in the supply contract. Other contract terms depend on the particular contract type and the circumstances of the case. The long-term nature of the contract relationship is reflected in the contract terms.

Contract Types Long-term bilateral contracts for the physical supply of electricity in the wholesale market can be divided into particular contract types.

One can broadly distinguish between electricity futures/forwards (Sects. 8.2.3 and 11.2), individually negotiated long-term contracts, and more complex structured contracts. Structured contracts range from tolling contracts to load-serving total supply contracts (load-serving full-requirement contracts).[24]

The contract can also cover one transaction or many similar transactions that the parties repeat during a long contract period (repeat transactions). In repeat transactions, the parties can use a master agreement that lays down the detailed terms of all transactions, and shorter contracts that confirm the core commercial terms of each transaction.

Risks Structured contracts and other long-term contracts enable electricity producers and other wholesale market participants to transfer risks over a long contract period. On the other hand, this increases exposure to other risks because of the very nature of long-term contracts[25] and the particular characteristics of long-term electricity supply contracts.

The exposure of the electricity producer to counterparty risk can be increased by the high upfront investment in generation installations (and sometimes even in transmission installations). It is also increased by limitations on the transferability of the contract. There must be limitations on the transferability of the contract because of: physical constraints (electricity cannot be supplied without grid access and transmission capacity); the fact that the contract requires timely compliance with detailed modalities of a technical nature; and the high upfront investment.

Transparency and Liquidity Bilateral and individually negotiated long-term contracts are not as transparent as exchange-traded contracts. Neither are they designed to increase the liquidity of the market. On the other hand, volumes sold using these

---

[23] Varholy J and Fuhr T (2009), § 28, number 1.

[24] Deng SJ and Oren SS (2006), pp. 946–948.

[25] For counterparty corporate risk and counterparty commercial risk, see Mäntysaari P (2010b), sections 6.2 and 6.3.

is a major shareholder of the buyer, the exposure of the electricity producer to counterparty risk is reduced.

8.2.2 Excursion: Block-Ownership

Ownership of shares can influence price and risk. For instance, industrial firms may transfer their generation assets to specialised electricity producers in return for shares and rights to purchase electricity at special prices.[32] Alternatively, large suppliers or end consumers can participate in a consortium that invests in new generation capacity to ensure security of supply and special prices.

The share ownership structure of the electricity producer can influence the price. The price of electricity is likely to be the lowest when the buyer is a major shareholder (or a similar stakeholder) of the electricity producer.[33] This is likely to be in the interests of that particular shareholder, but it can also be in the interests of the electricity producer.

From the perspective of the firm, shareholders have a function.[34] Selling electricity to a shareholder at a lower price is neither good nor bad as such. Depending on the circumstances of the firm, it may be in the long-term interests of the firm to sell electricity at a low price to a major shareholder or any shareholder.

Block-ownership can influence the relationship between the electricity producer and the customer in two main ways. Block-ownership can be used for aligning interests indirectly or directly.

Indirectly, a shareholder/customer may be entitled to a share of the electricity producers profits as a residual claimant. Although block-ownership can align interests indirectly, mere block-ownership is not sufficient to align the interests of the parties.

Generally, a shareholder does not want to pay overprice for electricity as the company's profits would be shared by other shareholders. A major shareholder is more likely to pay less for electricity as these private benefits are not shared by other shareholders. A shareholder may try to use its legal or de facto rights to ensure that the price is low.

On one hand, the customer has an investment risk where the customer is a shareholder of the electricity producer. A shareholder will bear its indirect share of the risk of production shortfalls and the commercial success of the electricity producer in general, although its risk is limited by the limited liability of shareholders. If the customer has paid a large enough sum for the electricity producer's shares, the customer may have an incentive to

[32] For the Finnish market, see Midttun A et al. (2001), p. 31.

[33] Putzka F (2009), p. 32.

[34] For the function of shareholders, see Mäntysaari P (2010a), section 8.7.2; Mäntysaari P (2012), section 7.9.

purchase electricity supplied by the electricity producer and to pay a sufficient price for electricity supplies.

On the other hand, the customer's direct benefits in the form of lower prices can outweigh its indirect share, in its capacity as shareholder, of the electricity producer's direct loss.[35] Fortunately for the electricity producer, a single block-holder may not be able to force the electricity producer to offer better terms because of constraints on shareholders' powers under the applicable provisions of company law and the allocation of power in the company. The firm is protected by the company's board that has a legal duty to act in the interests of the company (the firm).[36]

More fundamentally, block-ownership can change the whole business model of the electricity producer. Where the electricity producer is a closed company whose shares are held by a small number of customers, the rates are customarily based on the production costs of the electricity producer rather than on market prices. The electricity producer is dependent on its few shareholders, and its shareholders rely on the electricity producer for security of supply and low prices.

The Finnish Mankala model provides an example. The Mankala model is based on two decisions of the Finnish Supreme Administrative Court.[37] The Mankala model means that the production is purchased by a small number of wholesale customers that are shareholders. The purpose of the Mankala company is to produce electricity for the joint shareholders at the lowest possible cost.[38]

8.2.3 The Business Models of the Electricity Producer: Basic Business Models

The electricity producer can choose from a pool of six basic business models for the power plant: (1) a merchant power plant[39]; (2) long-term supply contracts; (3) a PPA power plant (based on a Power Purchase Agreement); (4) a tolling contract[40]; (5) a share of production[41]; and (6) a virtual share of capacity.[42]

---

[35] Mäntysaari P (2010a), p. 275.

[36] For the function of the board, see Mäntysaari P (2010a), sections 8.3 and 9.2.11; Mäntysaari P (2012), section 7.8.

[37] KHO 1963 I 5 and KHO 1968 B II 521. A company called Oy Mankala Ab was party to one of the cases.

[38] See, for example, OECD/IEA (2005), pp. 129–130.

[39] In German: Handelskraftwerk.

[40] In German: Lohnverstromung.

[41] In German: Kraftwerksscheibe.

[42] In German: Virtuelle Kraftwerksscheibe.

Merchant Power Plant

A merchant power plant is a stand-alone generator which sells all its production on short-term markets at a fixed price and without long-term contracts. Merchant generators are the canonical business model in economics,[43] but they were rare in the EU when the basic market model was complete vertical integration and "virtually unheard of prior to 1980" in the US.[44]

Two things are characteristic of merchant power plants: the mechanism for finding electricity consumers and the mechanism for raising funds.

When an electricity producer owns a merchant power plant, it relies on the spot or futures marketplace for its income. A merchant power plant does not have pre-identified customers.

As the electricity generated by a merchant power plant is not reserved for any pre-identified customers, customers will not participate in the construction, operation, or maintenance of the plant. Investment in a merchant power plant is funded by other parties.

The electricity producer is exposed to increased market risk. A merchant power plant cannot make a profit (and survive) unless the market price is higher than the merchant plant's indirect and direct production costs. Because electricity generation is capital intensive and investments are made up front, funding costs and investors' perceived risk exposure are an issue. Variation in the price of fuel is important as a factor influencing direct production costs. Moreover, the electricity producer is exposed to the risk that its power plant is not dispatched.

Investments in merchant power plants are heavily influenced by EU law. On one hand, the unbundling of electricity markets is designed to increase the number of merchant power plants. On the other, the 2020 targets of the EU influence market prices, dispatching, and the allocation of investment.

EU law fosters investment in RES-E and distributed generation. Installations that use renewable energy sources or waste or produce combined heat and power have priority access to the grid.[45] Moreover, the market price depends on the regulation of feed-in tariffs. Feed-in tariffs are the main support mechanism applied by the EU Member States to increase the share of energy generated from renewable energy sources.

Futures

Physical electricity futures lead to the physical supply of electricity. Physical electricity futures are relatively simple contracts and can thus be exchange-traded.

[43] For the basic assumptions behind this model economics, see Finon D and Perez Y (2008).

[44] Spence DB and Prentice R (2012), p. 146.

[45] Articles 15(3) and 25(4) of Directive 2009/72/EC (Third Electricity Directive).

ICE Endex. For instance, "Dutch Power Baseload Futures" can be traded on ICE Endex in continuous trading. These futures are contracts for "physical delivery of power to/from the Dutch high voltage grid".

The trading period is "up to 59 consecutive month contracts", "up to 9 consecutive quarters", or "up to 4 consecutive years".

ICE Clear Europe (ICEU) acts as central counterparty to all trades. There is an Initial Margin. There are Daily Margins and there can be Variation Margins. Open contracts are marked-to-market daily.

Delivery is made "equally each hour throughout the delivery period from 00:00 (CET) on the first day of the month until 24:00 (CET) on the last day of the month". Matching nominations must be made by the buyer and the seller and ICEU to TenneT before 13:00 (CET) on each day prior to the commencement of the delivery period.

"German Power Base Load Futures" are a similar product of ICE Endex. They are contracts for "physical delivery of power to and from the high voltage grid in the TSO zones where ICE Clear Europe is a [balance responsible party] and specified by the trading participant by means of the relevant designation form". Again, matching nominations must be made to TenneT before the delivery of power.

EEX. Futures traded on EEX provide a further example. The maturities of these contracts can vary depending on the area. The manner of settlement depends on the contract. There is "physical delivery" for Dutch or Belgian Power Futures, "cash settlement or physical fulfilment" for French Power Futures, and "cash settlement" for Italian Power Futures.

Physical futures can be distinguished from financial electricity futures. The difference in terminology is discussed more closely in the context of financial contracts (Sect. 11.2).

Long-Term Supply Contracts

The opposite of the business model of a merchant power plants is the use of long-term supply contracts. They can be used to hedge price and volumetric risks and to reduce transaction costs. Long-term supply contracts can be bulk power contracts not limited to any power plant or contracts limited to a certain plant (such as PPA power plants). Of the two, bulk contracts provide more flexibility to the electricity producer that may select the lowest cost source of supply.[46]

Types There are various kinds of long-term supply contracts that are bulk contracts. (a) The most basic form is an electricity forward contract with a fixed volume. Electricity forward contracts are contracts for the supply and off-take of a fixed amount of electricity at a pre-specified contract price (the forward price) at certain time in the future (maturity or expiration time).[47] (b) Alternatively, the contracts can be load-serving contracts or schedules designed to match the pre-estimated load. (c) The electricity producer and the customer can even use more complex long-term supply contracts with a flexible volume. (d) The duration of the contract and exit can be regulated in various ways. Like in forward contracts,

[46] Hunt S and Shuttleworth G (1996), p. 119.

[47] Deng SJ and Oren SS (2006), pp. 942–943.

the duration of the contract can be limited in time and expire on a certain date. Alternatively, the contract can provide for termination on notice (see Sect. 8.4.6). (e) Like in all long-term contracts, it is particularly important to regulate the price (Sect. 8.5.6) because circumstances are bound to change over time.

Terms Long-term supply contracts must address the issues that are characteristic of all physical electricity supply contracts (Sect. 2.5) and the flexibility, price, and exit issues that are customarily addressed in all long-term contracts.[48] These issues are discussed collectively for all electricity supply contracts (Sects. 8.4.8 and 8.5).

The EFET General Agreement Concerning the Delivery and Acceptance of Electricity is an example of how these issues can be regulated by the parties (see Sect. 8.4). Moreover, where more complex long-term contracts are negotiated individually because of customer requirements, their terms must reflect the commercial objectives of the customer.

The main rule in contract practice is that a long-term contract for the physical supply of electricity is not freely transferable because of physical constraints and high exposure to counterparty risk. This is regardless of the fact that the transferability of claims belongs to the basic ways to manage both the agency relationship between two contract parties and risk and is the legal default rule.

A major difference between contracts traded on regulated markets (exchange-traded contracts) and contracts traded outside regulated markets relates to collateral and margining. Each exchange has rules on collateral and margining and there are also daily margin calls (Sect. 4.6.2). Outside regulated markets, parties agree on collateral requirements bilaterally[49] and do not need to apply daily margin calls (see Sects. 8.4 and 8.5).

PPA Power Plant

Long-term supply contracts can be bulk contracts without any designated power plant or, like power purchase agreements, limited to a certain power plant (PPA power plant).[50] Power purchase agreements are particular kinds of contracts used in long-term projects.[51] The business model of the electricity producer is then the PPA power plant.

[48] Mäntysaari P (2010b), section 5.5.

[49] See Fried J (2010), p. 290, point 512.

[50] Hunt S and Shuttleworth G (1996), p. 119.

[51] In the UK, the term power purchase agreement refers to other kinds of contracts. Section 50 (3) of the Energy Bill: "For the purposes of this section and section 51—(a) a power purchase agreement scheme is a scheme established by supply licence conditions and regulations under section 51 for promoting the availability to electricity generators of power purchase agreements, and (b) 'power purchase agreement' means an arrangement under which a licensed supplier agrees to purchase electricity generated by an electricity generator at a discount to a prevailing market price".

PPA power plants raise the same two core issues as merchant power plants. Electricity consumers are found in a particular way, and there is a particular way for raising funds. A PPA power plant has just one or a small number of pre-identified customers whose purchases ensure the commercial viability of the project.

A power purchase agreement means a long-term contract between (a) an electricity producer that generates electricity in a certain new facility for sale (the seller) and (b) an electricity consumer that intends to purchase electricity generated in that facility for balancing its electricity consumption (the buyer).

The buyer is customarily a distributor (a utility or a wholesaler). The buyer may want to combine purchases under a number of PPAs with spot purchases and sales to achieve a close match with the volume of electricity required to service wholesale or retail contracts.[52] The purchase of electricity generated in a certain facility rather than any electricity supplied by the electricity producer can be a way to increase security of supply, meet renewable-energy portfolio standards, or obtain tax credits.[53]

A power purchase agreement regulates two main issues: action that is necessary before the reliable commercial operation of the facility can be started (there can be a construction period, a testing period, and an agreed completion date); and the supply of electricity from the facility.

These two issues can be illustrated with a sample power purchase agreement used by the United States Department of Energy represented by Bonneville Power Administration (BPA).

The two parties to the contract are BPA and the seller. The characteristic terms of the contract reflect the intentions of the parties set out in the preamble of the contract: (a) BPA is authorised to acquire sufficient capacity and energy from power production facilities to meet the electric power requirements placed on BPA by its regional customers; (b) the seller desires to construct, own, and operate a power generation plant; (c) the seller desires to sell to BPA all (or a portion) of the energy output generated by the facility; and (d) BPA desires to buy it from the seller.

The seller undertakes to "construct, operate, and maintain the Facility".[54] The Completion Date plays an important role. The production facilities must be operational by the Completion Date.[55] Beginning on the Completion Date, the seller undertakes to supply to BPA the entire energy output from the Facility, and BPA undertakes to buy it.[56]

It is characteristic of power purchase agreements that the buyer undertakes to purchase all or most of the electricity generated in the facility.

When Electricité de France (EDF) and Zweckverband Oberschwäbische Elektrizitätswerke (OEW) acquired joint control of Energie Baden-Württemberg AG (EnBW), power

---

[52] Hunt S and Shuttleworth G (1996), p. 109.

[53] In Joined Cases T-80/06 and T-182/09 Budapesti Erőmű Zrt v Commission, ECLI:EU:T:2012:65, the buyer was a Hungarian State-owned public undertaking that undertook, as a single buyer, to buy a fixed quantity of electricity at a fixed price. This raised questions of state aid.

[54] Section 4(a) of the sample Power Purchase Agreement developed by United States Department of Energy and Bonneville Power Administration.

[55] *Ibid*, Sections 1(h) and 6(a).

[56] *Ibid*, Sections 6(b) and 1(c).

purchase agreements were mentioned in the competition law commitments undertaken by EDF.[57] EDF had already signed Power Purchase Agreements with French co-generators promising to buy all their electricity production over a 12-year-period. EDF undertook to make available to competitors access to in total 6,000 MW generation capacities located in France, 5,000 MW in the form of virtual power plants (VPP) and 1,000 MW in the form of back to back agreements to existing co-generation power purchase agreements.

Power purchase contracts can be relevant even when the basic market model is complete vertical integration. In this case, the owner of the transmission system may have weak incentives to build transmission infrastructure to be used mainly by other electricity producers. It may have better incentives to build the necessary transmission infrastructure and connect the plant to the grid if the whole output is sold to it. These kinds of "output contracts" were used in the gas market before the liberalisation of the market.[58]

The power purchase agreement also sets out the price. Combined with the long duration of the contract, these terms can reduce the electricity producer's market risk and give it incentives to invest.

Because of the long-term nature of power purchase agreements, the parties need to regulate what will happen on termination of the contract. There are several alternatives: the parties may renew the contract with different terms; the contract may expire and the electricity producer may be free to sell electricity to any buyer; the buyer may have an option to purchase the generating equipment; or the buyer may request that the equipment be removed.

Power purchase agreement can influence the availability and cost of funding. Generally, the existence of a long-term power purchase agreement can make it easier for the plant's owner to raise external funding for the construction project. If project finance is used, the assets and revenue streams of the project company will be "ring-fenced". Cash flow from the power purchase agreement ensures that project finance debt can be repaid. The power purchase agreement will then be the core component of the legal framework of the asset-backed funding transaction.

A Tolling Contract

Like a power purchase agreement, a tolling contract is a contract between the owner of a power plant and an electricity buyer. The most characteristic difference between power purchase agreements and tolling contracts relates to control of the plant.

The term tolling means the control of an asset without ownership and the associated development or operation costs. According to the terms of a tolling contract, the customer determines when electricity is to be produced and how much electricity should be produced at any given time. A tolling contract thus gives the buyer the right either (a) to operate and control the scheduling of the power plant or (b) to simply take the output electricity.

[57] Case COMP/M.1853—EDF/EnBW.

[58] Varholy J and Fuhr T (2009), § 28, number 4.

A tolling contract transfers electricity price risk from the owner of the plant to the customer. The owner of the plant retains the operational risk.

The owner of the plant could be remunerated in alternative ways. (a) The plant's owner should in any case be paid enough to cover its fixed costs regardless of the production level. The buyer therefore agrees to pay an upfront fee for the right to operate and control the scheduling of the power plant. The size of the fixed fee depends even on the other terms of the contract. (b) Where the buyer pays a price for the electricity that it takes, the amount of the fixed fee could be reduced if the customer undertakes to purchase minimum volumes. The customer may therefore be prepared to accept a take-or-pay clause.[59] (c) Alternatively, the customer could pay a fixed fee over the life of the contract in exchange for the right to supply fuel and market the power output from the plant.

> The Commission has used the term "drawing rights contract".[60] These contracts involve the payment of a capacity fee to the plant operator. Drawing rights contracts customarily are not coupled with any minimum off-take obligation (*Budapesti Erőmű*).[61] They are thus tolling contracts.

As a tolling contract gives the customer the right to control the plant's output, tolling contracts are sometimes initiated by the customer. (a) For instance, tolling contracts could be used by an energy merchant with strong marketing skills and little interest in the operation of the plant (Sect. 2.3.4). (b) A tolling contract could be the result of financial engineering and outsourcing where an industrial firm sells its electricity generation assets to an electricity company but wants to retain control. (c) Tolling contracts may also interest fuel suppliers. For instance, a fuel supplier may prefer to pay a fee for the option to convert fuel into electricity rather than sell the fuel. Converting fuel into electricity might yield a higher return at some point in time.

There are often contractual limitations on how the buyer may operate the power plant or take the output electricity. For instance, the buyer may have a right to take the output electricity during pre-specified time periods only and subject to other constraints.[62]

Tolling-type agreements tend to be relatively short in duration (i.e., months).[63]

A Share of Production

The owner of a power plant can grant the buyer rights to a share of the production of the power plant (Kraftwerksscheibe). Contracts for a share of production, or a virtual share of capacity, are customarily long-term contracts for the physical

---

[59] Putzka F (2009), pp. 29–30.

[60] DG Competition Report on Energy Sector inquiry, 10 January 2007, SEC(2006) 1724, para 431.

[61] Joined Cases T-80/06 and T-182/09 Budapesti Erőmű Zrt v Commission, ECLI:EU:T:2012:65, paras 75 and 78.

[62] Deng SJ and Oren SS (2006), p. 946.

[63] Hsu M (1998), pp. 35–36.

delivery of electricity combined with a take-or-pay clause.[64] A contract for a share of production can also be cemented by the ownership of a block of shares.

A contract for a share of production, or a virtual share of capacity, can be used in two ways. It can be used for balancing the customer's own electricity consumption. Alternatively, the customer can sell the electricity to a third party.[65]

The parties are free to agree on the allocation of risks and costs. (a) As the volume is expressed as a share of electricity production, the starting point is that the buyer bears the risk of production shortfalls. The owner of the power plant may nevertheless guarantee the supply of electricity up to a certain fixed maximum volume in the event of unplanned production shortfalls. (b) As the buyer of a share of production is a separate legal entity that is not the owner of the power plant, the buyer is not responsible for the costs of the power plant. However, the buyer may assume responsibility for part of the costs. This can reduce the price.[66] (c) Moreover, the buyer undertakes take-or-pay obligations.

These contracts enable the buyer to reduce its funding needs. From the perspective of the buyer, the owner of the power plant is its "asset investor" in the sense that the buyer of a share of production can use the assets of the plant owner without having to invest in the assets itself and without having to raise funding from debt investors or shareholders for the plant.[67] On the other hand, it is particularly important to manage exit in these kinds of contracts, because the buyer may still need to use the assets or similar assets in its operations after the expiry of the contract.

There are various ways to regulate the rights of the buyer on termination of the contract. The duration of the contract can be limited in time and expire on a certain date. Alternatively, the contract can be valid for an indefinite period (golden end clause), or the contract can give the buyer an option for a longer contract period after the first expiry date (optional golden end clause).[68]

A Virtual Power Plant

Instead of a share of production, the electricity producer may offer to sell a virtual share of capacity (virtuelle Kraftwerksscheibe). In Europe, it is known as the virtual power plant (VPP).

A VPP contract gives a right to part of the producer's generation capacity. It can give a right to draw electricity from a plant or a pool of plants under the terms of the

---

[64] Putzka F (2009), pp. 29–30.

[65] Borchert J and Hasenbeck M (2009), p. 115.

[66] Putzka F (2009), pp. 29–30.

[67] For the concept of asset investors in the context of corporate finance law, see Mäntysaari P (2010c), pp. 23 and 325–327.

[68] Putzka F (2009), pp. 29–30.

contract. The capacity can also relate to base load or peak load. There are thus base-load virtual power plants and peak-load virtual power plants.[69]

A VPP contract can resemble financial market option contracts.[70] A VPP contract is then sold or auctioned at a price that gives the right to draw energy at the predetermined energy price. These prices can be regarded as the option premium and the predetermined strike price.[71] Where VPPs are auctioned, the set period is customarily a month, a quarter, or a year.[72]

A VPP contract can also contain a take-or-pay clause. The buyer may then consume its share of the production capacity or sell it on the market.

A VPP contract customarily provides that buyers must give one day's advance notice if they wish to exercise the VPP. In effect, such a clause means that the contract cannot be used in the real-time market for balancing power.

A VPP contract brings benefits to both parties. (a) For the buyer, the VPP contract increases security of supply. The buyer does not bear the risk of production shortfalls in VPP contracts (whereas the buyer would bear this risk in a contract for a share of production). The allocation of this risk to the electricity producer can increase the price that the buyer is prepared to pay.[73] (b) The seller benefits from flexibility because the contract is not tied to any particular plant. The volumes are not constrained by actual plant configuration. (c) Moreover, a virtual power plant can also consist of the microinstallations of a group of end consumers that use smart metering. Smart metering and a VPP help microgenerators to sell their production in the market, and the operator of the VPP to buy that surplus generation for resale in the wholesale market.

Generally, the use of virtual power plants is likely to increase in the future. This trend is connected with the increased decentralisation of power generation, in particular the increased generation of electricity from wind and other renewable sources, microgeneration by small end consumers, and major own generation by large industrial end consumers. On one hand, electricity suppliers can use virtual power plants as a mechanism to buy this new supply of energy and sell it in the market. On the other, electricity suppliers will be exposed to increasing competition by their own customers that have an incentive to increase the share of their own electricity generation when electricity costs are high (because of high retail electricity prices and the size of the L-component of transmission costs).[74] Customers' incentives to compete with their electricity suppliers are even greater if they have a chance to benefit from high feed-in tariffs for RES-E[75] or energy prices are high.

---

[69] Case COMP/M.1853—EDF/EnBW, para 98.

[70] OECD/IEA (2005), pp. 64–65.

[71] OECD/IEA (2005), p. 64.

[72] OECD/IEA (2005), p. 64.

[73] Putzka F (2009), p. 30.

[74] Frankfurter Allgemeine Zeitung, Die Stromrechnung zahlen andere, 16 October 2013, p. 12.

[75] For instance, the sawmill industry is a consumer of electricity. However, it can also generate electricity by using its raw material as fuel. A high feed-in tariff increases electricity generation's

Next Kraftwerke has created a virtual power plant which interconnects different types of RES-E units. A biogas plant or a CHP unit can generate power when the wind is not blowing or the sun is not shining.

The establishment of virtual power plants can increase competition and improve the functioning of the market.[76] Virtual capacity auctions have been used in European markets to increase the liquidity of the forward market. There are cases of the use of virtual capacity auctions as part of the competition law commitments undertaken by electricity producers such as EDF and DONG Energy.

EDF. In *EDF/EnBW*, EDF undertook to make available to competitors access to in total 6,000 MW generation capacities located in France, 5,000 MW in the form of virtual power plants (VPP) and 1,000 MW in the form of back-to-back agreements to existing co-generation power purchase agreements.[77]

The VPP contracts were awarded through an open, non-discriminatory public auction.[78] Both base-load and peak-load VPP were offered simultaneously, but separately. The VPP contracts were concluded with the successful bidders.

The VPP contracts were for 3 months, 6 months, 1 year, 2 years, and 3 years.[79] Over the duration of the contract, the buyer had the right to call upon EDF at any time to request delivery up to the agreed generation capacity (x MW).[80]

The price consisted of two components, the capacity price and the energy price. The successful bidder paid the capacity price for x MW of generation capacity.[81] The buyer also paid the energy price for the electricity consumed.[82]

DONG Energy. The VPP auctions of DONG Energy A/S, a Danish company, were based on competition law commitments given by the parties to the Danish Competition Council when it approved the merger between Elsam A/S (now DONG Energy) and NESA A/S on 24 March 2004. An important condition for the approval of the merger was that Elsam sells by action 600 MW electricity generation capacity in an infinite period through Virtual Power Plants. Generation capacity was sold at 35 VPP auctions from 22 November 2005 until 6 May 2014. On 28 May 2014, the Danish Competition Council abolished the commitment as market conditions had improved significantly and there was strong competitive pressure on DONG Energy.

DONG Energy auctioned the rights to a portion of its production capacity. It offered capacity options of three different durations (3 months, 12 months, and 36 months). The VPP auctions took place on a quarterly basis.

VPP power was physically delivered to the high voltage grid in the Danish DK1 price area. The price consisted of the option price and the energy price. Whereas the option price and the allocation of capacity were determined by auction, the energy price of exercising the option to produce electricity was set in advance. It was based on DONG Energy's most

share of the turnover of sawmills. There are major differences in the feed-in tariffs for electricity generated by sawmills in Finland, Sweden, and Germany according to a study commissioned by the Finnish Ministry for Employment and the Economy. Pöyry Management Consulting Oy (2013).

[76] Recital 37 of Directive 2009/72/EC (Third Electricity Directive).

[77] Case COMP/M.1853—EDF/EnBW, para 93.

[78] Case COMP/M.1853—EDF/EnBW, para 95.

[79] Case COMP/M.1853—EDF/EnBW, para 94.

[80] Case COMP/M.1853—EDF/EnBW, para 97.

[81] Case COMP/M.1853—EDF/EnBW, para 97.

[82] Case COMP/M.1853—EDF/EnBW, para 98.

effective central power plant in the DK1 price area and remained fixed throughout the duration of each individual product.

DONG Energy cooperated with a number of parties to facilitate the auctions. There was a party that was responsible for the implementation of the VPP auctions and acted as the auction administrator (Deloitte). The technical infrastructure for the auctions was provided by Nord Pool. Where the winning bidder wanted to exercise the option, it must nominate deliveries to a nomination aggregator that also informed DONG Energy of the aggregated hourly deliveries of power. The entity responsible for the physical delivery of electricity was DONG Energy Power A/S, a company in the DONG Energy group.

Access to the auctions was restricted. To participate in the auctions, a party: must have in place all agreements required by the relevant TSO; must have been approved by the Danish Competition Authority; and must comply with the eligibility criteria set out in the Auction and Credit Rules.

Bidders were also required to establish three types of credit support at different stages of the auctions: bid security (all bidders prior to each quarterly auction); option security (winning bidders following each quarterly auction); and energy security (winning bidders prior to the delivery of power).

Load-Serving Contracts

Load-serving contracts are customary supply contracts designed to match the changing consumption needs of the buyer. There are various kinds of load-serving contracts.

Contracts for the Supply of Base Load or Peak Load In the wholesale market, individually negotiated load-serving contracts customarily are contracts for the supply of base load, peak load, or weekend base load. For instance, energy intensive industries need access to base load at a low cost.

Peak-load-serving contracts can be categorised based on the delivery period during a day. One can distinguish between forwards on peak electricity, off-peak electricity (the remaining period during a day), and "around-the-clock" electricity (24 h/day).[83]

While the basic form of a standardised traded contract is a contract limited to electricity supply during a certain hour, block orders can be used to aggregate bids for several hours (Sect. 4.5.4).[84]

Load-Serving Total Supply Contracts Load-serving contracts with final customers can also be total supply contracts (load-serving full-requirement contracts). Total supply contracts belong to structured contracts. All contracts between the utility and

---

[83] See, for example, EEX Contract Specifications (0041a, 22 November 2014), section 2.1.3. "Base" is defined as "00:00 until 24:00 for all days of the week". "Peak" is defined as "08:00 until 20:00 for all days Monday through Friday (Peak) and 08:00 until 20:00 for the days Saturday and Sunday (Peak Weekend) respectively". "Off-Peak" is defined as "00:00 until 08:00 and 20:00 until 24:00 Uhr for all days Monday through Friday as well as the hours between 00:00 and 24:00 at weekends (Off-Peak)". For US terminology, see Deng SJ and Oren SS (2006), p. 943.

[84] Hünerwadel A (2007), p. 57.

the end consumer used to be total supply contracts under the vertically integrated market model.[85]

In wholesale markets, load-serving total supply contracts reflect the customary preferences of large electricity consumers that may want to: maximise the flexibility of the volume term so it matches their actual consumption; and pay a fixed rate per unit of energy for the actual consumption quantity regardless of the quantity being high or low.[86]

Load-serving total supply contracts are contracts for the supply of the actual consumption quantity. They could also be defined as call options with the fixed price for each billing period as the strike price of the option.[87]

Load-serving total supply contracts can be complemented by elements of forward contracts, in particular where an industrial customer has a predictable load or a load that can be up- or down-regulated with relative ease. For instance, the supply contract could lay down an exact load profile at a fixed energy price. The contract could also set another price for the difference between the agreed volume and the actual volume. In effect, the load-serving total supply contract would then consist of (a) a forward contract for volumes that match the agreed load profile (the energy price paid by the buyer); (b) a call option for the difference when actual consumption exceeds the agreed volume (the energy price paid by the buyer); and (c) a put option for the difference when the agreed volume exceeds the actual volume (the energy price paid by the seller).[88]

Load-serving total supply contracts can also be limited to a certain percentage of the buyer's total demand, or cover the buyer's residual needs.[89] The free quota not covered by the contract can be defined in relative terms or fixed as a certain amount of power (MW) or energy (MWh).[90] The buyer pays the market price for volumes not covered by the total supply contract.[91]

The parties customarily agree that the buyer may purchase certain standard products from a third party or the supplier. The contract could give the buyer the right to purchase forwards covering, say, 30 % or 50 % of the load.[92] In this case, the buyer agrees to inform the supplier of purchases from a third party within a certain period.[93]

Another alternative is to use the spot market price for part of the volume covered by the load-serving total supply contract. This can also be an option.[94]

---

[85] Spicker J (2010), p. 93, number 132, and p. 102, point 158.

[86] Deng SJ and Oren SS (2006), p. 947.

[87] Spicker J (2010), p. 103, number 159.

[88] Spicker J (2010), p. 103, numbers 160–161.

[89] Neveling S and Schönrock KP (2009), § 29, number 56.

[90] Neveling S and Schönrock KP (2009), § 29, number 64.

[91] Spicker J (2010), p. 93, number 134.

[92] Spicker J (2010), pp. 93–94, number 135.

[93] Neveling S and Schönrock KP (2009), § 29, number 64.

[94] Spicker J (2010), p. 94, number 136.

Functional Equivalents

There can be functional equivalents of long-term contracts for the supply of electricity. For instance, instead of burning fuel and turning steam to electricity, the owner of the plant may prefer to sell the steam to a buyer that either turns it into electricity or uses it in its own production process. These kinds of functional equivalents are discussed in the following section.

8.2.4 End Consumer's Alternatives to Vertical Integration

Like all firms, an end consumer takes "make or buy" decisions. (a) It may prefer to generate its own electricity ("make") for various reasons. For instance, an end consumer whose production process is energy-intensive may need to increase security of supply and reduce its exposure to price risk by self-generation. (b) There are alternatives to such vertical integration. The end consumer may purchase electricity ("buy"). (c) As there are various degrees of control of the plant, an end consumer may achieve some of the advantages of vertical integration through block-ownership (Sect. 8.2.2) or contracting (Sect. 8.2.3). From a legal perspective, vertical integration is less complicated than its functional alternatives (such as business outsourcing).[95]

The German market provides examples of models designed to replace the purchase of electricity with the customer's own generation or the purchase of other goods or services.

In Germany, EEG 2012 required end consumers to pay a fee for RES-E (EEG-Umlage, EEG surcharge)[96] but exempted industrial firms to the extent that they consumed electricity from their own generation (industrieller Eigenverbrauch, Eigenverbrauchsprivileg).[97]

Like EEG 2012 that it replaces, EEG 2014 provides for an EEG surcharge[98] and reductions from the EEG-surcharge. The reductions apply to energy-intensive users in certain sectors[99] and to certain self-generators (Eigenerzeuger).[100] The consumption of electricity from self-generation is fostered even by other regulation.[101]

To circumvent the EEG 2012 rules, some consumers tried to use purchase models that replaced the purchase of electricity with: (a) self-generation; (b) the

[95] See Mäntysaari P (2010a), section 9.7. See also Ofgem (2009), para 3.14.

[96] § 37(2) EEG 2012.

[97] § 37(3) EEG 2012.

[98] § 60(1) EEG 2014 and § 61 EEG 2014.

[99] See § 64 EEG 2014 and Annex 4 to EEG 2014.

[100] § 61(2) EEG 2014 and § 61(3) EEG 2014.

[101] They include, for example, § 1 StromNEV, § 9(3) KWKG, § 19(2) StromNEV, § 18 AbLaV, § 17f(5) EnWG, and § 9(1) StromStG. See Bardt H et al. (2014a), pp. 5–19; Bardt H et al. (2014b).

purchase of products used for energy storage; or (c) the purchase of services. These models (which might not be recognised under the EEG but show what could be done) include the following[102]:

- Tolling, rental, PPA (das Pachtmodell). In this two-party contract, the generation installation is owned by one party but operated by another party. There are two main alternatives. (a) The installation can be owned by a third party and operated by the consumer that bears the commercial risk (tolling contract). (b) The installation could also be owned by the consumer and operated by a third party that bears the commercial risk (rental). Such rental contracts resemble power purchase agreements (PPA) but are rarely used in Germany.[103]
- Co-ownership (das Betreibergemeinschafts-/Betriebsführungsmodell). This contract means that the generation installation is owned by many consumers but operated by a third party. Each consumer takes its share of production and bears its share of the commercial risk.
- Co-rental, a share of production (das Scheibenpachtmodell). Alternatively, the installation can be owned by a third party but operated by many consumers. Each consumer takes its share of production and bears its share of the commercial risk.
- Steam or compressed air contracts (Dampf-/Druckluftcontracting). The generation installation is in this case both owned and operated by a third party that supplies steam or compressed air to the customer.
- Service contracts or "light contracts" (Lichtcontracting). The generation installation is again owned and operated by a third party. In addition, that party undertakes to supply and to take care of the operation and maintenance (O&M) of technical facilities (such as lightning, air conditioning, elevators, escalators) that typically consume plenty of energy. The customer pays for the services provided by the third party.
- Outsourcing (Lohncontracting). The generation installation is owned by a third party that operates it according to the instructions of the customer. The customer supplies fuel free of charge. The owner/operator turns the fuel into power or heat. The customer pays the owner/operator for this service rather than for electricity or heat.[104]

8.2.5 Long-Term Supply Contracts and Competition Law

There is a large variety of long-term supply contracts and they can have different effects on the market.[105] Some long-term supply contracts are deemed to restrict

[102] Mikešić I et al. (2012), section 1.

[103] Mikešić I et al. (2012), footnote 6.

[104] Ofgem (2009), para 3.13.

[105] See, for example, de Hauteclocque A (2009b), pp. 93 and 96.

competition under Article 101(1) TFEU (Sects. 3.6.3 and 5.2).[106] On the other hand, long-term supply contracts can also produce efficiency gains. In particular, they enable both parties to manage risks.[107] The question is where to draw the line.

Legal risk is reduced by the Block Exemption Regulation for vertical agreements and the Commission's Guidelines on Vertical Restraints.[108] The main rule is that vertical agreements do not restrict competition as such.

Under some circumstances, however, long-term downstream contracts with a high commitment level can lock in consumers, increase barriers of entry, and reduce competition.[109] As the purpose of long-term contracts and their effect on competition depend on the prevailing market model (Sect. 8.1), the answer may depend on (a) the market model, (b) the market share of the supplier or the buyer, and (c) other contract terms.

For instance, off-take obligations are often made stronger by a take-or-pay clause or an excess charge applied when the customer's actual consumption differs from the forecast.[110] Moreover, the existence of long-term contracts with a high commitment level can limit market access and reduce competition more where the electricity producer has a dominant position in the market.

Long-term contracts can be regarded as more restrictive in unbundled and liberalised markets and in the light of the competition-enhancing goals of the electricity directives.[111] This could increase legal risk for firms. Long-term contracts might not be assessed according to the old doctrines, and traditional rules might be applied in new ways in markets that are in the process of being liberalised.[112]

Eighty Percent, Single Branding According to existing competition law, any long-term electricity supply contract can give rise to de facto exclusivity of supply where the customer's off-take obligation is fixed at values close to the customer's estimated total consumption. An obligation to purchase more than 80 % of the buyer's total purchases from only one supplier is regarded as a non-compete obligation.[113] Such long-term agreements are regarded as single branding agreements.[114]

---

[106] For entry barriers generally, see Aghion P and Bolton P (1987).

[107] For an analysis of the economics of long-term supply contracts, see Glachant JM and de Hauteclocque A (2009).

[108] Regulation 330/2010 (Block Exemption Regulation for vertical agreements); Guidelines on Vertical Restraints, Official Journal C 130, 19.05.2010, pp. 1–46.

[109] Communication from the Commission, Inquiry pursuant to Article 17 of Regulation (EC) No 1/2003 into the European gas and electricity sectors, 10.1.2007, COM(2006) 851 final, para 20.

[110] DG Competition report on energy sector inquiry, SEC(2006)1724 (10 January 2007), pp. 284–285, para 989.

[111] See also Case C-17/03 VEMW and others [2005] ECR I-4983.

[112] See Bellantuono G (2008).

[113] Point (d) of Article 1(1) of Regulation 330/2010 (Block Exemption Regulation for vertical agreements).

[114] Commission, Guidelines on Vertical Restraints (2010/C 130/01), para 129.

Block Exemption On the other hand, vertical restraints contained in vertical agreements are exempted under the Block Exemption Regulation for vertical agreements.[115] The block exemption applies provided that neither the supplier nor the buyer has a market share that exceeds 30 % of the relevant market.[116]

The main rule is that the exemption covers even non-compete obligations. The exemption does not apply to "any direct or indirect non-compete obligation, the duration of which is indefinite or exceeds five years".[117]

Single branding is thus exempted by the Block Exemption Regulation where the supplier's and buyer's market shares do not exceed 30 % and the duration of the non-compete obligation is 5 years or less.[118]

Test The parties may be able to obtain an individual exemption under Article 101 (3) TFEU for clauses that do not benefit from the Block Exemption Regulation. There is a test.

In the past, hardly any distinction was made between electricity and gas related cases in Commission practice.[119] The maximum duration of permitted long-term supply contracts was some 15 years.[120] Why the Commission drew the line here was unclear.

The Commission permitted such contract periods in the *Electricidade de Portugal/Pego project* case[121] (the Commission regarded 15 years as a legitimate maximum duration for both financing and investment), in the *REN/Turbogas* case[122] (the Commission accepted a 15-year duration while it also insisted on removal of the right of first refusal by the Portuguese transmission operator and inclusion of third-party access as condition for supporting this duration),[123] and in the *Electrabel* case (the Commission accepted a duration of 14 years, reduced from the original 20–30 year duration and with a gradual fade-out for the volume of power supplied).[124]

The earlier lack of sufficient reasoning changed after the judgment of the CJEU in *European Night Services*.[125] According to the CJEU, the duration of an exemption granted under Article 101(3) TFEU must be sufficient to enable the beneficiaries to achieve the benefits justifying the exemption.

In *European Night Services*, the benefits could not be achieved without considerable investment. For this reason, the CJEU stated that "the length of time required to ensure a

---

[115] Article 2(1) of Regulation 330/2010 (Block Exemption Regulation for vertical agreements).

[116] Article 3(1) of Regulation 330/2010 (Block Exemption Regulation for vertical agreements).

[117] Article 5(1)(a) of Regulation 330/2010 (Block Exemption Regulation for vertical agreements).

[118] Commission, Guidelines on Vertical Restraints (2010/C 130/01), para 131.

[119] Talus K (2010), p. 154.

[120] See, for example, de Hauteclocque A (2009b), p. 95.

[121] Electricidade de Portugal/Pego Project [1993] OJ C265/3.

[122] REN/Turbogas [1996] OJ C118/7.

[123] Commission Decision REN/Turbogas, OJ C 118/7, 1996.

[124] Talus K (2010), p. 154.

[125] Joined Cases T-374/94, T-375/94, T-384/94 and T-388/94, European Night Services Ltd (ENS) and Others v Commission [1998] ECR II-3141.

proper return on that investment is necessarily an essential factor to be taken into account when determining the duration of an exemption".[126] In other words, proper return on investment should be the starting-point in assessing the acceptable duration where the long contract term is motivated by investment reasons.

The present test was developed in cases *Distrigaz*,[127] *EDF*,[128] *Electrabel*,[129] and *E.On/Ruhrgas*.[130]

In 2007, the Commission opened proceedings against *EDF* (France)[131] and *Electrabel* (Belgium)[132] because of concerns that, by virtue of their scope of application, duration and nature, the use of long-term electricity supply contracts significantly limited the possibilities of other undertakings to conclude contracts for the supply of electricity to large industrial customers as the main or secondary supplier.[133] The Commission applied the same principles as in the *Distrigaz* case (Belgium).[134]

The Commission identified five elements to be considered when determining whether long-term contracts are to be considered illegal under competition rules: the market position of the supplier; the share of the customer's demand tied under the contracts; the duration of the contracts; the overall share of the market covered by contracts containing such ties; and efficiencies.

The Commission thus did not primarily focus on imposing any fixed maximum contract duration. Instead, it introduced a model according to which a certain part of the overall demand in the market must be subject to competition.[135]

In the *E.On/Ruhrgas* case,[136] the German Bundeskartellamt (BKA) ordered the dominant German gas operator to stop writing long-term supply contracts with distributors that: (a) cover more than 80 % of total annual demand for more than 2 years; or (b) cover more than 50 % of its customers' total annual demand for more

[126] *Ibid*, para 230. See also Talus K (2010), pp. 155–156.

[127] Case COMP/37.966—Distrigaz.

[128] Case COMP/39.386—Long Term Electricity Contracts France.

[129] Case COMP/39.387—Long Term Electricity Contracts Belgium.

[130] BKartA v E.ON Ruhrgas, decision of 13 January 2006 (B8-113/03), upheld by BGH, judgment of 10 February 2009—KVR 67/07.

[131] Case COMP/39.386—Long Term Electricity Contracts France.

[132] Case COMP/39.387—Long Term Electricity Contracts Belgium.

[133] Summary of Commission Decision of 17 March 2010 relating to a proceeding under Article 102 of the Treaty on the Functioning of the European Union and Article 54 of the EEA Agreement (Case COMP/39.386—Long Term Electricity Contracts France).

[134] See also Commission, Competition: Commission confirms sending Statement of Objections to Distrigaz concerning Belgian gas supply market, MEMO/06/197, 16 May 2006; Commission, Notice published pursuant to Article 27(4) of Council Regulation (EC) No 1/2003 in Case COMP/B-1/37966—Distrigaz [2007] OJ C77/14; Commission, Antitrust: Commission increases competition in the Belgian gas market—frequently asked questions, MEMO/07/407, 11 October 2007; Scholz U and Purps S (2010).

[135] See Scholz U and Purps S (2010).

[136] BKartA v E.ON Ruhrgas, decision of 13 January 2006 (B8-113/03), upheld by BGH, judgment of 10 February 2009—KVR 67/07.

than 4 years. The BKA gave some long-term supply contracts the green light: (a) For contracts covering more than 80 % of the requirements, a maximum term of up to 2 years was accepted. (b) Where the gas supply contracts covered 50 to 80 % of total customer requirements, the contracts could not exceed a term of 4 years.[137]

The nature of the customer is one of the factors that may play a role. For example, different maximum contract durations were allowed for contracts with different customers such as resellers, large industrial users, and electricity producers in *E.ON Ruhrgas* and *Distrigaz*.[138]

Take-or-Pay Clauses There are particular competition law constraints on the use of take-or-pay clauses (Sect. 8.5.3).

8.3 Introduction to Master Trading Agreements

Bilateral long-term electricity supply contracts and other OTC contracts are often governed by master trading agreements. The use of master trading agreements can reduce transaction costs (as parties share the same legal platform) and operational costs (as the firm may use the same platform other market participants use, the same platform for many transactions of the same kind, and the same platform for different kinds of transactions).[139]

In Europe, the most important master trading agreement for electricity supply contracts is the EFET General Agreement Concerning the Delivery and Acceptance of Electricity (the EFET General Agreement). The UK power market has its own Grid Trade Master Agreement (GTMA). For the EU ETS, the International Emissions Trading Association (IETA) has published the Emissions Trading Master Agreement (that provides an alternative to the use of modified versions of the EFET General Agreement or the ISDA Master Agreement).[140] In the US, the most important master trading agreement is the Master Power Purchase and Sale Agreement of Edison Electric Institute (the EEI Agreement).

The most important master trading agreement for OTC trading in derivatives is the ISDA Master Agreement. It has served as a model even for electricity master trading agreements.

History The roots of master trading agreements for the European gas and electricity markets lie in the US gas market of the late 1980s and early 1990s.[141]

---

[137] See Talus K (2010), pp. 160–161.

[138] Talus K (2010), p. 163.

[139] For platforms generally, see Mäntysaari P (2010b), section 2.2. For an example, see Fried J (2010), pp. 182–183, point 296.

[140] EFET Allowances Appendix (Power); Form of Part [7] to the Schedule to an ISDA Master Agreement for EU Emissions Allowance Transactions (incorporating options) (Version 5: May 2012) (Modified for Phase 3 delivery). See Fried J (2010), pp. 265–267, points 448–449.

[141] Varholy J and Fuhr T (2009), § 28, number 3.

Before the liberalisation of the US gas market, US contract documents were long and detailed because of large contract volumes, long contract periods, and the customary drafting practices applied in common law countries.[142]

The gradual liberalisation of the gas market meant that smaller and smaller volumes could be sold and resold. Trades in the new market were being transacted principally by telephone, and mark-to-market accounting was applied to trading positions. The liberalisation of the gas market gave rise to new risks such as: credit risk; performance or settlement risk; carrier default risk; price risk; contract risk; and new categories of regulatory risk. Consequently, the traditional individually negotiated sales contracts had to be replaced by standardised general terms and conditions.[143]

The general terms and conditions used by market participants tended to be fairly similar.[144] However, each transaction was still regarded as a separate transaction and the parties had to agree on the use of general terms and conditions separately for each transaction.

This led to the emergence of master trading agreements.[145] Each company used its own master trading agreements first. Consequently, the first agreements were biased. A party could use one master trading agreement as a seller and another when it was a buyer.

These agreements were replaced by a single master trading agreement to be used by sellers and buyers.[146]

The early master trading agreements were not very sophisticated. The vast majority of them contained little or no language intended to mitigate counterparty insolvency and related credit risk. The first standardised natural gas trading agreement, the Gas Industry Standards Board Agreement, contained no early termination, close-out netting or similar clauses for the mitigation of credit-based risks.[147]

The EEI Agreement When the US electricity market was liberalised, the benefits of an industry standard were recognised.[148] The master trading agreements employed in the electricity market were similar to the master trading agreements for gas but more sophisticated.

The dominant master trading agreement in the US electricity wholesale market is the EEI Agreement.[149] In addition, the master trading agreements of Western Systems Power Pool (WSPP) and the Electric Reliability Council of Texas

[142] Varholy J and Fuhr T (2009), § 28, number 5.
[143] Varholy J and Fuhr T (2009), § 28, numbers 7 and 9.
[144] Varholy J and Fuhr T (2009), § 28, number 10.
[145] Varholy J and Fuhr T (2009), § 28, number 11.
[146] Varholy J and Fuhr T (2009), § 28, number 12.
[147] Varholy J and Fuhr T (2009), § 28, number 13.
[148] Varholy J and Fuhr T (2009), § 28, number 15.
[149] Varholy J and Fuhr T (2009), § 28, number 17.

(ERCOT) are used in particular geographic markets (the Western System Power Pool and Texas, respectively).[150]

The EFET General Agreement US experiences influenced and speeded up the process of developing standardised master trading agreements for the European electricity market.[151]

In the UK power market, GTMA is the standard set of terms for the majority of electricity forward trades.[152] The cross-border nature of the European power markets required a contractual platform that could be used in cross-border transactions.[153] In 2000, the European Federation of Energy Traders (EFET) released the first version of the EFET General Agreement. The EFET General Agreement is drafted with the German market and cross-border transactions in mind. The EFET General Agreement is the most important contractual platform for trading physical electricity across Continental Europe.[154]

The EFET General Agreement was developed with the intention of facilitating cross-border trade in wholesale power in Europe's interconnected electricity markets. For this reason, the rights and obligations of electricity buyers and sellers under the EFET General Agreement must be sufficiently general and generic, and the EFET General Agreement must be enforceable in different European countries.[155]

8.4 The EFET General Agreement

8.4.1 General Remarks

The EFET General Agreement, the GTMA, and the EEI Agreement resemble the ISDA Master Agreement in many respects. The ISDA Master Agreement has served as a model even for electricity master trading agreements.

There are nevertheless some fundamental differences between the ISDA Master Agreement and the other agreements. While master agreements for derivatives or swap contracts provide for financial settlement, master trading agreements for electricity supply contacts must even regulate issues that are characteristic of all electricity supply agreements that are settled physically (Sects. 2.5, 8.4.8 and 8.5). Moreover, the Emissions Trading Master Agreement is designed for the EU ETS.

[150] Varholy J and Fuhr T (2009), § 28, number 17.

[151] Varholy J and Fuhr T (2009), § 28, number 18.

[152] Ofgem (2009), para 3.74.

[153] Varholy J and Fuhr T (2009), § 28, number 19.

[154] Varholy J and Fuhr T (2009), § 28, number 20.

[155] Varholy J and Fuhr T (2009), § 28, number 21.

There are also some differences between the EFET General Agreement and the EEI Agreement. The most fundamental differences relate to the nature of the contract and the governing law. While the EFET General Agreement is an agreement designed for cross-border trading and governed by the law of a civil law country, the EEI Agreement is designed to be used inside the US that is a common law country.[156]

In the following, we will study the contents of the EFET General Agreement and compare it with the EEI Agreement and the ISDA Master Agreement.

8.4.2 Scope

The scope of the EFET General Agreement is defined in relation to transactions—future or present—and in relation to the governing law.

Future Transactions Like all master trading agreements, the EFET General Agreement applies to all future transactions between the parties[157] (and may even be applied to existing transactions depending on the Election Sheet[158]). The terms of the EFET General Agreement are thus incorporated into the contracts that the parties will enter into.[159] The EEI Agreement works in the same way.[160]

As the parties have agreed on the unchanging terms in advance, it is enough for them to focus on the key commercial terms of each transaction. This reduces transaction costs and saves time. There would be increased transaction costs if the parties derogated from the terms of the EFET General Agreement.[161]

Governing Law The agreed terms are complemented by the governing law. The terms of the contractual relationship consist of the mandatory provisions of the governing law, the agreed terms, and the dispositive provisions of the governing law. One can also distinguish between the law governing the master trading agreement and the law that governs the individual contracts made under it.

It would bring benefits to choose the law of one country as a platform for many similar contracts.[162] Interpretation risk would be reduced if all contract law disputes were resolved in the same manner irrespective of the location of the parties.

[156] The IETA Emissions Trading Master Agreement for the EU Scheme is governed by English law unless the parties agree otherwise. Section 14.7 of the IETA Master Agreement (Version 3.0, 2008).

[157] EFET General Agreement (Version 2.1(a)), § 1.1.

[158] EFET General Agreement (Version 2.1(a)), § 1.2.

[159] Varholy J and Fuhr T (2009), § 28, number 28.

[160] The EEI Agreement (Version 2.1), Section 2.2.

[161] See also Varholy J and Fuhr T (2009), § 28, number 28.

[162] Generally, see Mäntysaari P (2010b), section 2.2.

Moreover, it would reduce transaction costs and facilitate international (global, European-wide) contract management.[163]

The EFET General Agreement is governed by German law according to its default choice of law clause. The application of the CISG is expressly excluded reflecting the fact that the sale of electricity falls within the scope of sale of goods law in Germany (Sect. 2.7.2).[164] The choice of law clause can only cover contractual matters.[165] For instance, it does not cover insolvency.[166]

Whether individual contracts made under the EFET General Agreement are governed by German law is a matter of interpretation. The wording of the choice of law clause does not explicitly cover individual contracts. On the other hand, the terms of the EFET General Agreement are incorporated into each individual contract ("single agreement", Sect. 8.4.4).[167]

The EEI Agreement is governed by the law of New York.[168] The choice of law clause does not address the issue of the law governing individual agreements.

Terms, Appendices The terms of the EFET General Agreement are general in nature. They may need to be adapted to consider legal requirements in the different countries in which the terms are applied. For this reason, the EFET General Agreement is complemented by appendices developed by the EFET.[169] The same technique is used in the EEI Agreement.[170]

8.4.3 Conclusion of Individual Contracts

The purpose of standard trading agreements is to make it easier to conclude individual contracts and to reduce transaction costs. The basic documentation for an individual transaction consists of the EFET General Agreement, an Election Sheet (known as the Schedule in the ISDA Master Agreement) adapting the EFET General Agreement to the particular circumstances of the parties (with standardised terms for the customisation of the EFET General Agreement and additional provisions), and a confirmation.

[163] Varholy J and Fuhr T (2009), § 28, number 23.

[164] EFET General Agreement (Version 2.1(a)), § 22.1. The exclusion of the CISG is not necessary, because the CISG does not apply to the sale of electricity. CISG Article 2(f).

[165] Article 1 of Regulation 593/2008 (Rome I).

[166] For the governing law, see Article 4(1) of Regulation 1346/2000 (Insolvency Regulation).

[167] EFET General Agreement (Version 2.1(a)), § 1.1.

[168] The EEI Agreement (Version 2.1), Section 10.6.

[169] Varholy J and Fuhr T (2009), § 28, number 25.

[170] The EEI Agreement (Version 2.1), Section 1.2 and Cover Sheet.

Short Confirmation Because of the existence of the EFET General Agreement and the Election Sheet that set out the largest part of the legal framework, the confirmation can be short and limited to the core commercial terms of the transaction.

There are also Long Form Confirmations, also known as Single Trade Agreements. They repeat all terms customarily found in the master trading agreement and confirmations. Long Form Confirmations are used where a party trades with a counterparty before a master trading agreement is signed or in the rare circumstances where a transaction is not to be subject to any master trading agreement.[171] Long Form Confirmations are coupled with higher legal risk.[172]

Form and Representation According to the governing law, the default rule is that contracts can be concluded in any form of communication. This main rule is applied even in the EFET General Agreement.[173]

As contracts can be deemed to have been concluded even orally, it is important for the parties to limit the number of people that may represent them and identify the authorised representatives. The EFET General Agreement permits the parties to list the persons that may represent them.[174]

Interpretation The contractual relationship consists of many documents. One may ask what their mutual ranking is in the event of inconsistencies. The main rule is that the specific prevails over the general (generalia specialibus non derogant). There is a particular term in the EFET General Agreement to this effect. The terms of the individual contract prevail for the purposes of the individual contract, and the provisions of the Election Sheet prevail over the other provisions of the EFET General Agreement.[175]

8.4.4 The Single Agreement Concept

The EFET General Agreement is not just an "umbrella" agreement. Like other master trading agreements, the EFET General Agreement defines itself and the multiple transactions covered by it as a single agreement.[176] They are thus intended to be part of a single and legally inseparable contractual relationship.[177] The same concept is used in the EEI Agreement.[178]

[171] Harding PC (2010), pp. 12–13 and 23.

[172] Fried J (2010), pp. 184–185, point 301.

[173] EFET General Agreement (Version 2.1(a)), § 3.1.

[174] EFET General Agreement (Version 2.1(a)), § 3.4.

[175] EFET General Agreement (Version 2.1(a)), § 3.2.

[176] EFET General Agreement (Version 2.1(a)), § 1.1.

[177] Varholy J and Fuhr T (2009), § 28, number 30.

[178] The EEI Agreement (Version 2.1), Section 2.2.

The single agreement concept is important in the event of default and in the insolvency of a party. In combination with close-out netting, it is designed to reduce the risk of cherry-picking.[179]

8.4.5 Payments, Netting, Tax, Collateral

As regards payments, the main rule under the EFET General Agreement is monthly invoicing[180] and monthly payments.[181] Invoicing and payments are based on scheduled contract quantities in accordance with all applicable delivery schedules for the respective month.[182]

Option premiums are an exception to the main rule. They are invoiced as agreed between the parties and due and payable on the agreed premium payment date.[183]

The EFET General Agreement regulates questions of default interest and disputed amounts. The interest rate is specified in the Election Sheet.[184] There is a provision on disputed amounts. The parties may choose one of two alternatives in the Election Sheet: (a) pay now, litigate later; or (b) pay the undisputed sum.[185]

Netting The parties may also agree to use payment netting in the Election Sheet. Payment netting means that the party owing the greater aggregate amount pays the net amount where each of two parties is required to pay one or more amounts in the same currency under one or more individual contracts on any day.[186]

The parties can extend the scope of netting by the EFET Cross Product Payment Netting Agreement. In this case, netting applies to individual contracts based on different master agreements. The EFET Cross Product Payment Netting Agreement is drafted with the EFET Power Agreement, the EFET Gas Agreement, the GTMA, the ZBT Terms (Zeebrugge Hub Natural Gas Trading Terms and Conditions 2004), and the NBP Master (the Short Term Flat NBP Trading Terms and Conditions 1997) in mind but could in principle be chosen to cover even other master agreements such as the 2002 ISDA Master Agreement.[187]

---

[179] Varholy J and Fuhr T (2009), § 28, number 31.

[180] EFET General Agreement (Version 2.1(a)), § 13.1.

[181] EFET General Agreement (Version 2.1(a)), § 13.2. See also EFET General Agreement (Version 2.1(a)), § 8.3.

[182] EFET General Agreement (Version 2.1(a)), § 13.4.

[183] EFET General Agreement (Version 2.1(a)), § 13.1, § 13.2 and § 5.2.

[184] EFET General Agreement (Version 2.1(a)), § 13.5.

[185] EFET General Agreement (Version 2.1(a)), § 13.6.

[186] EFET General Agreement (Version 2.1(a)), § 13.1 and § 13.3.

[187] See Principal Agreement Annex. See also Fried J (2010), p. 239, point 385a.

Tax Both parties have a qualified contractual duty to minimise taxes.[188] In addition, the EFET General Agreement lays down other duties relating to tax. (a) The EFET General Agreement is neutral as far as value added tax (VAT) is concerned. Where VAT is payable, the buyer must pay to the seller an amount equal to the VAT.[189] (b) Generally, the delivery point is used to divide tax liability between the buyer and the seller.[190] (c) The parties may elect to use a tax grossing-up clause that supports the duty to make payments free of any withholding of or deduction for tax.[191]

Collateral and Other Credit Enhancements The parties are free to agree on collateral and other credit enhancements[192] in bilateral trading and customarily do so. In electricity trading, collateral often consists of guarantees (parent company guarantees, bank guarantees, or demand guarantees).[193]

The EFET General Agreement addresses the question of collateral and other credit enhancements in various ways. While the parties are free to agree on credit enhancements in advance, the EFET General Agreement gives a party the right to ask for better collateral in the event of material adverse change:

- The parties may agree on "guarantees and credit support".[194]
- Whether they have agreed or not, a party may require "performance assurance" when it believes that a material adverse change has occurred.[195]
- To illustrate, there is a material adverse change: when the agreed credit rating is downgraded[196]; when a performance assurance or an agreed credit support document expires or fails[197]; or when "in the reasonable and good faith opinion" of the party the ability of the other party to perform its obligations is materially impaired.[198]

[188] EFET General Agreement (Version 2.1(a)), § 14.4.

[189] EFET General Agreement (Version 2.1(a)), § 14.1.

[190] EFET General Agreement (Version 2.1(a)), § 14.2.

[191] EFET General Agreement (Version 2.1(a)), § 14.3.

[192] For credit enhancements in general, see Mäntysaari P (2010b), section 11.6. For electricity trading, see Fried J (2010), pp. 290–307, points 512–551.

[193] Fried J (2010), p. 291, point 516.

[194] EFET General Agreement (Version 2.1(a)), § 16.

[195] EFET General Agreement (Version 2.1(a)), § 17.1.

[196] EFET General Agreement (Version 2.1(a)), § 17.2(a).

[197] EFET General Agreement (Version 2.1(a)), § 17.2.

[198] EFET General Agreement (Version 2.1(a)), § 17.2.

8.4.6 *Contract Period, Assignment, Changed Circumstances, Termination, Close-Out Netting*

The long-term nature of the EFET General Agreement and the electricity supply contracts that fall within its scope is reflected in the contents of the EFET General Agreement in many ways. It has influenced clauses on: the contract period; changed circumstances; the termination of individual supply contracts and/or the EFET General Agreement; and close-out netting. In spite of the single agreement principle, one can distinguish between the EFET General Agreement and individual contracts for these purposes.

The Contract Period The EFET General Agreement is in force for an indefinite period. It may be terminated in two ways: by notice to expire after a termination period (Ordinary Termination); or for a material reason to expire immediately (Termination for Material Reason).[199]

As regards individual contracts, the contract period (total supply period) is chosen by the parties. The total supply period is part of the schedule.[200]

In case of Ordinary Termination, the notice period is 30 days. The expiry of the EFET General Agreement will not affect individual contracts concluded before the expiry date. The General Agreement remains binding on the parties until the parties have performed their obligations under the terms of individual contracts concluded before the expiry date.[201]

In the event of termination for a material reason, all individual contracts will likewise be terminated. A lump sum (Termination Amount) will replace the original obligations as the sum of all settlement amounts.[202] The parties may also agree on payment netting in the Election Sheet.[203]

Assignment Transferability is one of the customary ways to mitigate counterparty risk in long-term contracts. However, transferability is limited in long-term electricity supply contracts (Sect. 8.2.3).

The EFET General Agreement addresses transferability in several ways. (a) The main rule is a prohibition. A party may not assign its "rights and obligations" to a third party without the prior written consent of the other party. A prohibition is necessary in the light of the fact that the trading relationship requires the ability to settle individual contracts physically and is based on mutual assessment of counterparty risk. A party's counterparty risk could be increased by the assignment. The assignee's creditworthiness could be worse, and there could be less room for netting after an assignment because netting requires the existence of mutual claims.

[199] EFET General Agreement (Version 2.1(a)), § 10.1.
[200] EFET General Agreement (Version 2.1(a)), § 4.2.
[201] EFET General Agreement (Version 2.1(a)), § 10.2.
[202] EFET General Agreement (Version 2.1(a)), § 11.1.
[203] EFET General Agreement (Version 2.1(a)), § 13.3.

(b) However, the prohibition does not apply with its full force. It is diluted because a party must not unreasonably delay, refuse, or withhold its consent.[204] (c) Moreover, the parties may agree in the Election Sheet that a party may assign its rights and obligations to an affiliate with the same or better creditworthiness.[205] One may ask whether the parties should choose this alternative in the light of the problems.[206] (d) Whether the assignment is permitted depends, among others, on the representations and warranties that a party must comply with.[207]

While the EFET General Agreement regulates the assignment of "rights and obligations", it remains open whether the EFET General Agreement addresses the assignment of individual rights or obligations and not just the assignment of the whole agreement. According to German law (the governing law), a party may not assign its obligations without the consent of the other party but may assign its rights. The EFET General Agreement for gas regulated the assignment and transfer of the whole agreement.

Changed Circumstances All long-term contracts tend to address the problem of changed circumstances. The EFET General Agreement provides for various mechanisms for this purpose.

In the event of a material adverse change[208] in respect of one party, the other party is entitled to require a "performance assurance", that is, a form of credit enhancement.[209]

Where the contract price is based on a variable reference price (and is a floating price rather than a fixed price),[210] the market disruption clause provides for an alternative settlement price as a fallback mechanism in the event of market disruption.[211]

There is also an optional tax crossing-up clause.[212]

The EFET General Agreement contains the customary force majeure clause. The particular characteristics of electricity supply agreements have been addressed in three ways.

First, a party is released from its duty to perform its obligations for so long as and to the extent that the force majeure event prevents their performance. In other words, the duty to perform is not just suspended.[213] As there is no breach of contract in this case, the other party has no right to compensation for damage. On the other

[204] EFET General Agreement (Version 2.1(a)), § 19.1.

[205] EFET General Agreement (Version 2.1(a)), § 19.2.

[206] Fried J (2010), p. 247, point 402.

[207] For representations and warranties, see EFET General Agreement (Version 2.1(a)), § 21.

[208] EFET General Agreement (Version 2.1(a)), § 17.2.

[209] EFET General Agreement (Version 2.1(a)), § 17.1.

[210] EFET General Agreement (Version 2.1(a)), § 15.1.

[211] EFET General Agreement (Version 2.1(a)), § 15.2, § 15.3, and § 15.4.

[212] EFET General Agreement (Version 2.1(a)), § 14.3(b).

[213] EFET General Agreement (Version 2.1(a)), § 7.2.

hand, the other party is released from its corresponding acceptance and payment or delivery obligations.[214] The EEI Agreement contains similar force majeure provisions.[215]

Second, it is not required in the EFET General Agreement that the impediment was unforeseeable or that the party would not have been able to consider the occurrence of the impediment at the time of the conclusion of the contract.[216] In electricity markets, the impediments tend to be foreseeable. Force majeure is therefore defined as "an occurrence beyond the reasonable control" of a party "which it could not reasonably have avoided or overcome" and "which makes it impossible" for the party to perform its delivery or acceptance obligations.

There is a difference between the broader definition of force majeure events under the EFET General Agreement and the slightly narrower definition used in the EEI Agreement. According to the wording of the EEI Agreement, an event or circumstance that was anticipated when the transaction was agreed on by the parties cannot be invoked as a force majeure event.[217]

Third, some important examples of force majeure events have been expressly mentioned in the EFET General Agreement. They relate to the system operator.[218]

In contrast, the EEI Agreement is more restrictive as curtailment may only to a limited extent be invoked as a force majeure event.[219]

In the light of ACER's CACM Framework Guidelines, the CACM Network Codes must contain a narrow definition of force majeure events. The force majeure clause is designed with the TSOs' duties in mind.

The CACM Network Codes must also set out the effects of force majeure. While customary force majeure clauses used in electricity markets tend to release the party from fulfilling its obligations (because of the balance requirement), the Framework Guidelines only provide that the party's obligations are "suspended from the beginning of force majeure".[220]

A party invoking the force majeure clause must notify the other party of the occurrence of the force majeure event. The wording leaves open whether notification is a precondition of invoking the clause and whether the clause can be applied to facts before a notification was made. (The fact that obligations are "suspended from the beginning of force majeure" implies that the force majeure clause can be applied to earlier facts.)

Ordinary Termination The EFET General Agreement and the EEI Agreement regulate the termination of the master trading agreement. Whether the individual contracts are terminated at the same time in accordance with the single agreement

[214] EFET General Agreement (Version 2.1(a)), § 7.4.

[215] The EEI Agreement (Version 2.1), Section 3.3.

[216] EFET General Agreement (Version 2.1(a)), § 7.1.

[217] The EEI Agreement (Version 2.1), section 1.23.

[218] EFET General Agreement (Version 2.1(a)), § 7.1.

[219] The EEI Agreement (Version 2.1), section 1.23.

[220] ACER, Framework Guidelines on Capacity Allocation and Congestion Management for Electricity (29 July 2011), section 6.2.

principle depends on the master trading agreement and the reason why the master trading agreement is terminated.

One can distinguish between ordinary termination and early termination. Ordinary termination means here termination by written notice and the expiry of the contract after a notice period. Both master trading agreements provide for a notice period of 30 days. If the expiration date is fixed in advance, the contract will expire on that date without notice according to the EFET General Agreement.[221]

In the event of ordinary termination, the termination of the master trading agreement does not influence the individual contracts that are still in force. The terms of the master trading agreement continue to apply to these contracts.[222] The EEI Agreement contains a similar provision.[223]

Early Termination According to the EFET General Agreement, early termination means (a) termination for a material reason or (b) automatic termination. In this case, termination will influence the individual contracts. They will be terminated as well and the obligations will be replaced by the payment of a lump sum.

The fact that the EFET General Agreement provides for termination for a material reason can partly be explained by the governing law. German law provides that long-term contracts may be terminated for a material reason.[224] Termination for a material reason under the EFET General Agreement requires the giving of notice specifying the material reason and the designation of an early termination date. With effect from the early termination date, all further payments and performance in respect of all individual contracts will be released and existing duties and obligations of the parties replaced by the obligation of one party to pay a lump sum (the termination amount).

The EEI Agreement provides for early termination upon the occurrence of an event of default. (a) The EEI Agreement therefore lists events of default. They include, among others: any breach of a material covenant or obligation after a short grace period (of 3 business days after written notice); failure to make a payment; misrepresentation; bankruptcy; breach of credit enhancement obligations; merger-related issues; guarantor-related issues; and (if elected) cross-default.[225] (b) However, termination is not automatic. The non-defaulting party may designate an early termination date.[226] (c) On the early termination date, all transactions between the parties will be terminated and all amounts owing between the parties will become due. A settlement amount will be calculated for each terminated transaction. All settlement amounts will be aggregated into a single amount

---

[221] EFET General Agreement (Version 2.1(a)), § 10.2.

[222] EFET General Agreement (Version 2.1(a)), § 10.2.

[223] The EEI Agreement (Version 2.1), section 10.1.

[224] § 314(1) BGB.

[225] The EEI Agreement (Version 2.1), section 5.1.

[226] The EEI Agreement (Version 2.1), section 5.2.

- The non-defaulting party may cease further deliveries of electricity until all outstanding amounts have been paid in full. Deliveries are not suspended.[262] The non-defaulting party is released from its delivery obligations. Moreover, this right is not limited to the relevant individual contract or contracts. It covers all deliveries under all individual contracts in line with the single agreement concept.[263]

A party may terminate the contract—that is, the single agreement—for a material reason. Although the material reasons have been defined as "the exclusive reasons for Early Termination" under the early termination provision of the EFET General Agreement, the EFET General Agreement does not seem to exclude other causes of action under the governing law. In any case, early termination for a material reason under the EFET General Agreement is limited to the following reasons[264]: non-performance; failure to make a payment; qualified cross-default; winding up, insolvency, or certain related situations; long duration of force majeure events; or misrepresentation or breach of warranty.

8.4.8 Terms Characteristic of Electricity Supply Contracts

Certain issues are characteristic of physical electricity supply contracts and addressed in all of them (Sect. 2.5). On the other hand, the modalities of electricity transmission depend on the system operator. It would be difficult to apply the EFET General Agreement or the EEI Agreement to a wide range of transactions, unless their terms were very generic and the characteristic issues were regulated in detail by the parties themselves. The parties address many of the characteristic issues in the schedule (the schedule of physical electricity supply is not to be mixed with the Schedule of the ISDA Master Agreement) and the provisions laying down the primary obligations of the parties.

Schedule Compared with the EEI Agreement, the EFET General Agreement directs more issues to be regulated by the parties in the schedule. This can reflect the fact that the EFET General Agreement is designed to apply to a broader range of contracts and to cross-border contracts between different European countries. It would more difficult to fix the modalities of the parties' obligations in a master trading agreement.

Both definitions are broader than the ENTSO-E definition that focuses on information rather than actions and defines the schedule as a reference set of values

[262] Compare CISG Article 71.

[263] EFET General Agreement (Version 2.1(a)), § 9.

[264] EFET General Agreement (Version 2.1(a)), § 10.5.

representing the generation, consumption or exchange of electricity between the parties for a given time period.[265]

In the EEI Agreement, the schedule is limited to the parties' actions of "notifying, requesting and confirming to each other the quantity and type of Product to be delivered on any given day or days during the Delivery Period at a specified Delivery Point".[266]

In the EFET General Agreement, the schedule basically means all actions necessary for a party to effect its delivery or acceptance obligations.[267]

Primary Obligations The primary obligations of the parties consist of the scheduling of electricity flows, the supply of electricity to the grid at a certain point (delivery), the extraction of electricity from the grid (acceptance or receipt), and the payment of the price. The modalities depend on the system operator's requirements.

The EFET General Agreement and the EEI General Agreement lay down the following primary obligations:

> The EFET General Agreement: "In accordance with each Individual Contract, the Seller shall Schedule, sell and deliver, or cause to be delivered, and the Buyer shall Schedule, purchase and accept, or cause to be accepted, the Contract Quantity at the Delivery Point; and the Buyer shall pay to the Seller the relevant Contract Price".[268]
>
> The EFET General Agreement: "Electricity shall be delivered in the current, frequency and voltage applicable at the relevant Delivery Point agreed in the Individual Contract and in accordance with the standards of the Network Operator responsible for the Delivery Point".[269]
>
> The EEI General Agreement: "With respect to each Transaction, Seller shall sell and deliver, or cause to be delivered, and Buyer shall purchase and receive, or cause to be received, the Quantity of the Product at the Delivery Point, and Buyer shall pay Seller the Contract Price; provided, however, with respect to Options, the obligations set forth in the preceding sentence shall only arise if the Option Buyer exercises its Option in accordance with its terms. Seller shall be responsible for any costs or charges imposed on or associated with the Product or its delivery of the Product up to the Delivery Point. Buyer shall be responsible for any costs or charges imposed on or associated with the Product or its receipt at and from the Delivery Point".[270]

The parties must also ensure that there is available transmission capacity. The responsibility for arranging transmission capacity is divided by the delivery point which also allocates risk between the parties. The EEI General Agreement and the EFET General Agreement contain terms to this effect:

> The EEI General Agreement: The seller is responsible for transmission service to the delivery point. The buyer is responsible for transmission service at and from the delivery

[265] Article 2(2) of ENTSO-E Network Code on Operational Planning and Scheduling (24 September 2013).

[266] The EEI Agreement (Version 2.1), section 1.54.

[267] EFET General Agreement (Version 2.1(a)), § 4.2.

[268] EFET General Agreement (Version 2.1(a)), § 4.1.

[269] EFET General Agreement (Version 2.1(a)), § 6.1.

[270] The EEI Agreement (Version 2.1), section 3.1.

point. Each party arranges the transmission service with its own transmission service provider.[271]

The EFET General Agreement: The seller is responsible for all costs and bears all risks associated with scheduling, transmission and scheduling up to the delivery point. The buyer is responsible and bears all risks at and from the delivery point.[272]

8.4.9 *Physical Electricity Options*

The EFET General Agreement can apply to contracts for the purchase and sale of physical options to buy electricity (call) or sell electricity (put).[273] Unlike the ISDA Master Agreement, the EFET General Agreement contains particular provisions on options.[274]

Premium and Contract Price There are particular provisions on payment of the premium. In this case, neither the main rule of monthly invoicing[275] nor monthly payments will apply.[276] The premium will become due and payable on the 5th business day following the conclusion of the contract. The parties will agree on invoicing. The contract price will become due and payable according to the main rule.[277]

Exercise The holder of an option may exercise its rights by giving the writer irrevocable notice during the exercise period.[278] Options are thus not exercised automatically.

Notice of Exercise A notice of exercise is effective upon receipt by the writer. The holder therefore bears the risk for communication problems. While a notice of exercise may be given in writing or verbally, it may not be effected by e-mail or by leaving a message on a voice mail or similar verbal electronic messaging system. In the case of verbal exercise, the holder must promptly confirm the exercise in writing, for instance, by fax. The written confirmation is for information reasons and does not affect the validity of the notice of exercise.[279]

---

[271] The EEI Agreement (Version 2.1), section 3.2.

[272] EFET General Agreement (Version 2.1(a)), § 6.7.

[273] EFET General Agreement (Version 2.1(a)), § 5.1.

[274] See Fried J (2010), p. 198, point 327.

[275] For options, EFET General Agreement (Version 2.1(a)), § 13.1.

[276] For options, EFET General Agreement (Version 2.1(a)), § 13.2. See also EFET General Agreement (Version 2.1(a)), § 8.3.

[277] EFET General Agreement (Version 2.1(a)), § 5.2.

[278] EFET General Agreement (Version 2.1(a)), § 5.3.

[279] EFET General Agreement (Version 2.1(a)), § 5.4.

8.5 The Objectives of the Parties

8.5.1 General Remarks

In addition to the general terms applicable to a large number of transactions, the parties must agree on the attainment of their commercial objectives in each transaction. One may ask what the commercial objectives are.

One can distinguish between three kinds of objectives. (1) Regardless of the business model, the parties have similar commercial and legal objectives at a high level of generality. In fact, the firm manages certain generic issues by legal tools and practices in all transactions. (2) In addition, the firm manages particular issues by legal tools and practices in the context of long-term contracts. (3) It has even particular objectives in the context of electricity supply contracts. You can see these distinctions even in electricity supply contracts.

All Transactions In all transactions, all firms try to manage, in one way or another: (1) cash-flow and the exchange of goods or services; (2) risk; (3) principal-agency relationships; and (4) information. The tools and practices used by firms for managing such issues include: (a) the choice of a business form; (b) contracts; (c) compliance and organisational measures; (d) generic ways to manage agency relationships; and (e) generic ways to manage information.[280]

Electricity Supply Contracts In addition, there are particular issues that are characteristic of all electricity supply contracts. Parties to physical electricity trading have particular objectives because of physical laws and economic efficiency.

In the physical market, the parties must manage: (1) grid access, delivery point, and voltage level; (2) volume; (3) transmission and distribution capacity; (4) balance; (5) measurement; (6) separation of physical rights, service rights, and financial rights; (7) settlement; and (8) price volatility (Sect. 11.1). Because of physical laws and economic efficiency, all issues apart from price volatility must be addressed at the time of contracting and settlement.

We can first study the contract terms designed to address these issues in the light of the long-term nature of the contract.

8.5.2 Grid Access, Delivery Point, Voltage Level

The issues relating to grid access, delivery point, and voltage level are connected (Sect. 2.5.2). Parties to an electricity supply contract must: (a) ensure grid access; (b) agree on the place where the supply of electricity should match electricity extraction; and (c) ensure rights to use transmission or distribution capacity. In

[280] Generally, see Mäntysaari P (2010a, 2012).

addition, the parties will agree on the allocation of costs and risk between the parties.

Grid Access First, each party must agree on grid access with the system operator (TSO or DSO). The delivery point is used to allocate these responsibilities between the parties.[281] For this reason, neither the EFET General Agreement nor the EEI Agreement needs to regulate grid access in detail.

There are various types of agreements regulating grid access (Chap. 10). They depend on the parties (end consumer, supplier, system operator) and the grid level (end consumption, distribution, transmission). Moreover, the contract can be limited to one transaction or be a master agreement that applies to many transactions.[282]

Place Second, one must determine a place where the supply of electricity should match electricity extraction. Electricity flows are not matching unless they are electricity flows in the same grid and at the same grid/voltage level. It is, therefore, necessary to specify the grid and the grid/voltage level.

There can be plenty of variation in the wholesale market, because electricity can be extracted at any grid level.[283] Depending on the grid level or the switching gear in the point where the customer extracts electricity, the lines employed to supply electricity to the customer operate at different voltage levels.[284]

The entry and exit points can be identical, where the buyer is the system operator itself (for the balancing market and reserves, see Sect. 4.10; for the duty of the system operator to buy RES-E, see Sect. 7.2). Where the buyer is the system operator, the parties must therefore specify the point of entry.

The entry and exit points are not identical in unbundled electricity markets, where the buyer is not the system operator. Electricity is supplied to the grid and extracted from the grid. It is, therefore, necessary to specify the grid and the grid/voltage level in each individual contract.

The modalities of organising physical flows can make it necessary to specify the place of the performance in greater detail. The parties may specify the place for allocating responsibilities, costs, and risk. To illustrate, the parties may need to allocate technical compliance obligations, transmission costs, and risks relating to the availability of transmission capacity. There are examples of these practices in the EFET General Agreement and the EEI Agreement. Both the EFET General Agreement and the EEI Agreement provide for a delivery point and delivery schedules to organise the modalities[285]:

---

281 See, for example, EFET General Agreement (Version 2.1(a)), § 6(1) on the current, frequency and voltage.

282 See Neveling S and Schönrock KP (2009), § 29, number 73.

283 See, for example, Balthasar M (2007), pp. 34–35.

284 Neveling S and Schönrock KP (2009), § 29, number 65.

285 EFET General Agreement (Version 2.1(a)), § 6.7; The EEI Agreement (Version 2.1), section 3.2.

The EFET General Agreement: "Electricity shall be delivered in the current, frequency and voltage applicable at the relevant Delivery Point agreed in the Individual Contract and in accordance with the standards of the Network Operator responsible for the Delivery Point".[286]

The EFET General Agreement: "Electricity shall be delivered according to the Delivery Schedules specified in each Individual Contract".[287]

The EFET General Agreement: "In accordance with each Individual Contract, the Seller shall Schedule, sell and deliver, or cause to be delivered, and the Buyer shall Schedule, purchase and accept, or cause to be accepted, the Contract Quantity at the Delivery Point; and the Buyer shall pay to the Seller the relevant Contract Price".[288]

The EFET General Agreement: "Seller shall bear all risks associated with, and shall be responsible for any costs or charges imposed on or associated with Scheduling, transmission and delivery of the Contract Quantity up to the Delivery Point. Buyer shall bear all risks associated with, and shall be responsible for any costs or charges imposed on or associated with acceptance and transmission of, the Contract Quantity at and from the Delivery Point".[289]

The EFET General Agreement: "'Schedule' shall mean, as applicable, those actions necessary for a Party to effect its respective delivery or acceptance obligations, which may include nominating, scheduling, notifying, requesting and confirming with the other Party, their respective designated agents and authorised representatives, and the Network Operator, as applicable, the Contract Quantity, Contract Capacity, Delivery Point, Delivery Schedule, Total Supply Period, and any other relevant terms of the Individual Contract in accordance with all applicable rules of the Network Operator and other customary industry practices and procedures".[290]

The EEI Agreement: "Seller shall arrange and be responsible for transmission service to the Delivery Point and shall Schedule or arrange for Scheduling services with its Transmission Providers, as specified by the Parties in the Transaction, or in the absence thereof, in accordance with the practice of the Transmission Providers, to deliver the Product to the Delivery Point. Buyer shall arrange and be responsible for transmission service at and from the Delivery Point and shall Schedule or arrange for Scheduling services with its Transmission Providers to receive the Product at the Delivery Point".[291]

Transmission Capacity Third, the parties must ensure rights to the use of transmission or distribution capacity. The supplier and the buyer can allocate this task in two main ways. (a) Each party may purchase such rights for its own use. (b) Alternatively, the parties may agree on a delivery point.

The agreed delivery point is the point where the obligation of the supplier to ensure the availability of sufficient and functioning transmission or distribution capacity ends.

---

[286] EFET General Agreement (Version 2.1(a)), § 6.1.

[287] EFET General Agreement (Version 2.1(a)), § 6.2.

[288] EFET General Agreement (Version 2.1(a)), § 4.1.

[289] EFET General Agreement (Version 2.1(a)), § 6.7.

[290] EFET General Agreement (Version 2.1(a)), § 4.2.

[291] The EEI Agreement (Version 2.1), section 3.2.

The agreed delivery point can also be used to allocate responsibility for risks inherent in the physical flow of energy.[292] Unlike oil or gas, however, electricity can neither be handed over nor stored at the agreed delivery point.[293]

All-Inclusive Contracts There is a particular delivery point in all-inclusive contracts. All-inclusive contracts are used in trade with end consumers. In this case, the delivery point is the exit point, that is, the end consumer's point of access to the grid at a certain grid level. The supplier is responsible for the cost of rights to use transmission or distribution capacity. These costs will be charged from the end consumer. For example, the end consumer may reimburse the supplier for the supplier's actual payments to the TSO, or pay a lump sum regardless of the amount of the supplier's actual costs.[294]

8.5.3 Volume

General Remarks

In addition to issues relating to grid access, delivery point, and voltage level, the parties must regulate the volume of electricity. The parties can use fixed or variable terms. For instance, the volume clause is variable in load-serving contracts and fixed in delivery schedules. The parties may also agree on the availability of generation capacity. When the volume is fixed, the buyer's obligations can be made stronger by a take-or-pay clause.

Freedom of Contract To start with, the parties are free to specify the volume (the contract quantity) according to their own preferences.[295]

Management of Volumetric Risks and the Market Model The volume clause is a way to manage quantity risks (volumetric risks). The market model plays a role. In vertically integrated electricity markets, the management of volumetric risks is less important, because the generation, transfer, and distribution of electricity are in the hands of the same undertaking. It is more important to manage volumetric risks in unbundled electricity markets.

---

[292] EFET General Agreement (Version 2.1(a)), § 6.7.

[293] For the role of the delivery point of oil, see, for example, The Economist, Wide-spread confusion. What exactly, is the price of oil? (16 June 2011): "The contracts for WTI stipulate 'for delivery' to windswept Cushing, Oklahoma ... which is strategically situated to serve the refineries of the Gulf of Mexico ... This gave oil firms lots of incentive to build pipelines to Cushing: in recent months oil has poured into Cushing's growing and labyrinthine storage facilities".

[294] Neveling S and Schönrock KP (2009), § 29, number 66.

[295] Annex 1 to the EFET General Agreement (Version 2.1(a)) for the definition of "Contract Quantity". The EEI Agreement (Version 2.1), section 1.49.

The contents of the volume clause are connected with the balance requirement. An electricity supply agreement facilitates the balancing of electricity generation with electricity extraction and vice versa. The volume clause is a way to allocate risk between the parties. In addition to the volume clause, the management of volumetric risks may require two kinds of contracts with third parties. Electricity derivatives can be employed to transfer volumetric risks, and both parties must enter into a balance agreement with the system operator.[296]

Management of Availability Risk A related risk is the unavailability of generation capacity. Electricity producers are in a better position to manage this risk. They tend to use three different techniques for this purpose.[297] First, an electricity producer can invest in a portfolio of power plants to spread the risk (like an energy merchant, Sect. 2.3.4).[298] Second, the electricity producer could dilute its supply obligations by using "as available" provisions that allow it to restrict the volume to the level of availability of a particular power plant. In this case, the parties would try to design appropriate contract bonuses and penalties for availability. Third, the electricity producer can buy option contracts to limit exposure to price risk in the event that it must purchase electricity in the spot market to cover its supply obligations.

Volume Fixed or Variable The supplier can transfer volumetric risk to the buyer when the volume is fixed in advance and the volume term is combined with a take-or-pay clause. The buyer can transfer volumetric risk to the supplier by load-serving contracts.

On the other hand, fixed and variable components can be complementary because of the balance requirement and depend on the point in time. Estimates about consumption may become more reliable over time. With variable components, the exact volume must be determined more exactly the closer one gets to the point in time when electricity is supplied.

The parties may therefore regulate the legal relevance of information about the volume gradually starting with non-binding indicative estimates about the volume and ending with very detailed information binding as a contract term close to the actual time electricity is supplied.[299] This is also a way to transfer volumetric risk to the supplier.

Load-Serving Contracts and Delivery Schedules The distinction between fixed and variable volume terms is reflected in the distinction between load-serving contracts, availability contracts, and delivery schedules.

[296] See, for example, Neveling S and Schönrock KP (2009), § 29, number 4.

[297] Hunt S and Shuttleworth G (1996), pp. 128–129.

[298] Hunt S and Shuttleworth G (1996), p. 129.

[299] Neveling S and Schönrock KP (2009), § 29, number 62.

Load-Serving Contracts

Types of Load-Serving Contracts The volume is variable in load-serving contracts. In principle, the supplier could undertake to supply the volume that matches the buyer's actual consumption. For reasons of risk management, such an obligation would be complemented by a cap and/or a floor and other limitations.[300] There are, therefore, various kinds of load-serving contracts.

First, there are load-serving full-requirement contracts. Load-serving full-requirement contracts are contracts for the supply of the actual consumption quantity, regardless of the quantity being high or low.

Such contracts can also be limited to a certain percentage of the buyer's total demand, or cover the buyer's residual needs. The "free" quota can thus be defined in relative terms or fixed as a certain amount of power (MW) or energy (MWh).[301]

The parties customarily agree that the buyer may purchase certain standard products from a third party. The buyer agrees to inform the supplier of purchases from a third party within a certain period.[302]

Second, there are contracts for the supply of base load or peak load. Peak-load-serving contracts can be categorised based on the delivery period during a day. For instance, one can distinguish between forwards on peak electricity, off-peak electricity (the remaining period during a day), and "around-the-clock" electricity (24 h/day).[303]

Load-Serving Contracts and Metering Load-serving contracts give rise to a metering problem. As the exact volume of electricity supplied under the contract depends on the volume extracted by the buyer, the volume can be determined only afterwards. The parties often use ¼-h measurement periods.[304] Metering can also be facilitated by balance groups (Chap. 9).[305]

Load-Serving Contracts and Risk Management Risks caused by the openness of the volume term in load-serving contracts can be mitigated in various ways.

First, the supplier may prefer a contractual cap on the scope of its obligations. The supplier may limit the power or energy to be supplied to the buyer.

Second, the parties may mitigate risk by the price term. The relatively open volume can be combined with a fixed or variable price.

> A large end consumer with a load-serving full-requirement contract may prefer to reduce the price risk and pay a fixed rate per unit of energy for the actual consumption quantity. The supplier could then use futures contracts to lock in a fixed quantity of electricity supply

[300] Neveling S and Schönrock KP (2009), § 29, number 61.

[301] Neveling S and Schönrock KP (2009), § 29, number 64.

[302] Neveling S and Schönrock KP (2009), § 29, number 64.

[303] See, for example, EEX Contract Specifications (0041a, 22 November 2014), section 2.1.3. For US terminology, see Deng SJ and Oren SS (2006), p. 943.

[304] Neveling S and Schönrock KP (2009), § 29, number 56.

[305] For German law, see § 4 StromNZV. See also Neveling S and Schönrock KP (2009), § 29, number 57.

at a fixed cost. However, the supplier would still be exposed to the risk of under- or over-hedging, as the consumption quantity of the customer is likely to deviate from the amount hedged by the futures contracts.[306] To hedge this volumetric risk, the supplier can do two things. It can buy an electricity option on the consumption quantity of its customers. However, such an option is usually unavailable in the marketplace. Alternatively, it can exploit the correlation between load and temperature and buy weather derivatives.[307]

Third, the supplier can also mitigate risk by limiting the load and increasing the reliability of information about the load.

In a forward contract with a distributor, the supplier may prefer to limit not only the power or energy to be supplied to the distributor but also the consumers that the distributor supplies with electricity, or their delivery points. The customers that the distributor is allowed to supply with electricity may be limited to: existing customers (or include even new customers); customers within a certain geographical area (or include even customers outside the area); or customers with other particular characteristics (or any customers).[308] This could nevertheless give rise to competition law concerns (Article 101 TFEU).[309]

Availability Contracts Actual volumes are very variable in contracts whose main purpose is to ensure the availability of capacity rather the actual supply of a certain volume. (a) For instance, system operators must ensure the availability of generation capacity to balance system. For this reason, electricity producers provide balancing services (the ancillary services of market participants, Chap. 9). (b) Electricity distributors may need to ensure that there is enough peak generation capacity available at specific times of the year.

Electricity producers are given an incentive to keep generation capacity available by availability payments. Availability payments can provide extra revenue to the electricity producer as they can help to cover the capital and other fixed costs which are not covered by the energy price per MWh.[310]

Delivery Schedules

The volume is fixed in a delivery schedule. The supplier is then not responsible for differences between the agreed volumes and the volumes that the buyer extracts from the grid. Volumetric risk is transferred to the buyer.[311]

A delivery schedule must set out the core terms and even the modalities of performance. The detailed contents of the delivery schedule must be notified to the system operator as the delivery schedule cannot be performed without the system operator's participation.[312] The parties must choose the party who is responsible for

---

[306] Deng SJ and Oren SS (2006), p. 947.

[307] *Ibid.*

[308] Neveling S and Schönrock KP (2009), § 29, number 63.

[309] See, for example, Wegerich C and Seiferth C (2009).

[310] Hunt S and Shuttleworth G (1996), p. 111.

[311] Neveling S and Schönrock KP (2009), § 29, number 54.

[312] For the definition of (delivery) schedule, see EFET General Agreement (Version 2.1(a)), § 4.2.

making the necessary notifications. It is important to regulate notifications carefully.[313] Notifications to the system operator are governed by the system operator's legal framework that the parties must comply with (Chap. 10). Physical settlement of electricity supply contracts in the wholesale market is not possible without notifications to the system operator (Sect. 8.5.7).

The fixed volume term can be complemented by a take-or-pay clause.

Excursion: Take-or-Pay Clauses

In electricity wholesale markets, suppliers' standard contracts include a take-or-pay clause. Take-or-pay clauses have three main functions. First, take-or-pay clauses are a customary risk management tool relating to core services in electricity supply contracts (Sect. 2.5.8). Volumetric risk can be hedged and changed into a price risk in liquid markets. Take-or-pay clauses are designed to transfer volumetric risk to the buyer. Second, they are a way to manage the agency relationship between the parties. The electricity producer may use take-or-pay clauses for increasing the end consumer's commitment level. Third, take-or-pay clauses can be used for funding reasons.

Risk Management and Pricing As a take-or-pay clause allocates risk between the parties, it influences pricing and belongs to the core terms of the contract in combination with the price term. This explains, among others, why it is regarded as a price term that does not fall within the scope of the mandatory regulation of the contents of general contract terms under German law (AGB-Recht).[314]

Funding Take-or-pay clauses can be important for funding reasons especially in ring-fenced projects in which the repayment of project loans depends on payments made by the offtaker and the project company's cash flow is used as collateral.[315] A long pay-back period is thus supported by long-term take-or-pay contracts.

Take-or-pay clauses are designed to increase the predictability of project cash flow and to reduce lenders' credit risk. However, take-or-pay clauses do not provide full protection. A take-or-pay clause customarily does not require the offtaker to

---

[313] See also Neveling S and Schönrock KP (2009), § 29, number 55.

[314] BGH, judgment of 24 March 2010—VIII ZR 178/08. The BGH argued: "Da die Vertragsparteien nach dem im bürgerlichen Recht geltenden Grundsatz der Vertragsfreiheit Leistung und Gegenleistung grundsätzlich frei regeln können, sind allerdings formularmäßige Abreden, die Art und Umfang der Hauptleistung oder der hierfür zu erbringenden Vergütung unmittelbar bestimmen, von der gesetzlichen Inhaltskontrolle nach §§ 307 ff. BGB ausgenommen . . . Ihre Festlegung ist grundsätzlich Sache der Vertragsparteien, denn es gibt vielfach keine gesetzliche Preisreglung, die bei Unwirksamkeit der vertraglichen Abrede gemäß § 306 Abs. 2 BGB an deren Stelle treten könnte . . . Zu den einer richterlichen Inhaltskontrolle nach §§ 307 ff. BGB entzogenen Preisbestimmungen zählen auch solche Klauseln, die den Preis bei Vertragsschluss zwar nicht unmittelbar beziffern, jedoch die für die Ermittlung des Preises maßgeblichen Bewertungsfaktoren und das hierbei einzuhaltende Verfahren festlegen . . . Denn auch die vertragliche Festlegung preisbildender Faktoren gehört zum Kernbereich privatautonomer Vertragsgestaltung . . ."

[315] For gas, see Talus K (2010), p. 15.

pay if the project company is unable to deliver. Consequently, the clause does not protect lenders in the event of a serious supply disruption.[316]

Project finance generally can be a suitable way to finance energy projects because of high up-front financing costs, the long operational phase, the long-term duration of supply contracts, and the use of take-or-pay provisions.[317]

Discretion of the Buyer The buyer gets more discretion as there is no obligation to take delivery. The buyer may prefer just to pay. On the other hand, the buyer may want to use the generation capacity when it needs electricity for its own consumption, supplies electricity to a third party (such as distributors or end consumers), or trades electricity on an exchange or in the OTC-market. It is often used in structured contracts (Sect. 8.2).[318]

A take-or-pay clause can be complemented by a clause limiting the use of electricity to the buyer's own consumption (and restricting the transfer of the right to take delivery and the right of the buyer to supply electricity to a third party). In such a case, the supplier may be able to find a new buyer.

Such a clause raises two kinds of questions. Is the original buyer entitled to the price paid buy the new buyer? Would the clause be compatible with competition law?

The parties may of course agree that the price belongs to the original buyer. For example, the original buyer may be the TSO/DSO and the take-or-pay clause may permit the TSO/DSO not to extract the energy. In this case, the seller resells the energy on the spot market, receives the contractual price from the TSO/DSO, and pays the spot market price back to the latter. Whether the original buyer would have a similar right under the default provisions of the governing law is another matter.

In Germany, the rights of the supplier to receive payment are regarded as a primary claim (Primäranspruch) rather than as a secondary claim to compensation for loss or damage (Sekundäranspruch). Consequently, the supplier does not have a duty to reduce its loss by supplying electricity to a third party. As the supply of electricity to a third party falls outside the scope of the original contract, the original buyer is not entitled to the price paid by the new buyer.

Electricity Market Law and Competition Law Take-or-pay clauses raise regulatory and competition law issues.[319]

Of course, there can be competition law issues even in the absence of take-or-pay clauses. Any long-term electricity supply contract can give rise to de facto exclusivity of supply where the customer's off-take obligation is fixed at values close to the customer's estimated total consumption. But such an off-take obligation is often made stronger by a take-or-pay clause or an excess charge applied when the customer's actual consumption differs from the forecast.[320]

---

[316] Finnerty J (1996), pp. 59–60.

[317] Arowolo O (2005). For gas, see Talus K (2010), p. 16.

[318] Putzka F (2009), pp. 31–32.

[319] Generally, see Cameron P (2007).

[320] DG Competition report on energy sector inquiry, SEC(2006)1724 (10 January 2007), pp. 284–285, para 989.

Take-or-pay clauses are treated in slightly different ways in electricity and gas markets. In the electricity market, the use of take-or-pay clauses is subject to more constraints. There are two kinds of constraints.

First, take-or-pay clauses can have the effect of increasing exclusivity, but there are constraints on the use of exclusivity clauses under the Third Electricity Directive.

According to the Directive, large non-household customers "should be protected against exclusivity clauses the effect of which is to exclude competing or complementary offers".[321] Moreover, the duties of the regulatory authority include "monitoring the occurrence of restrictive contractual practices, including exclusivity clauses which may prevent large non-household customers from contracting simultaneously with more than one supplier or restrict their choice to do so".[322]

Second, take-or-pay clauses are used in long-term contracts, but the terms of long-term contracts are generally constrained by competition law.

In the light of the CJEU's judgment in *European Night Services*, the duration of a take-or-pay obligation must not exceed what is sufficient to enable the beneficiaries to achieve the benefits justifying the exemption from Article 101(1) TFEU.

In this case, the benefits could not be achieved without considerable investment. For this reason, the CJEU stated that "the length of time required to ensure a proper return on that investment is necessarily an essential factor to be taken into account when determining the duration of an exemption".[323]

In the early *Scottish Nuclear* case,[324] the Commission required the duration of certain exclusive take-or-pay agreements relating to nuclear energy to be reduced from 30 years to 15 years. The Commission said that "this period seems necessary to allow Scottish Nuclear to attain full profitability and become competitive" without explaining how this figure was reached. The UK Government had argued in detail that the longer period was linked with the expected lifetime of the power stations.[325] In *Transgas/Turbogas*,[326] the Commission approved a 25-year take-or-pay agreement for an Algerian company to supply gas to a Spanish power station. This much longer contract period was balanced by an increase in security of supply.[327]

Take-or-Pay Clauses in the Gas Wholesale Market Take-or-pay clauses are viewed a bit differently in the gas wholesale market.

In the gas wholesale market, long-term contracts generally are regarded as a good thing. Upstream long-term gas supply contracts were regarded as beneficial for the EU in the First and Second Gas Market Directives.[328] According to the Third

---

[321] Recital 20 of Directive 2009/72/EC (Third Electricity Directive).

[322] Article 37(1)(k) of Directive 2009/72/EC (Third Electricity Directive).

[323] Joined Cases T-374/94, T-375/94, T-384/94 and T-388/94, European Night Services Ltd (ENS) and Others v Commission [1998] ECR II-3141, para 230. See also Talus K (2010), pp. 155–156.

[324] Scottish Nuclear, Nuclear Energy Agreement (Case IV/33.473) Commission Decision 91/329/EEC [1991] OJ L178/31.

[325] Talus K (2010), p. 154.

[326] Transgás/Turbogás, XXVIth Report on Competition Policy (1996), pp. 133–135.

[327] Talus K (2010), p. 155.

[328] Recital 13 of the First Gas Market Directive; recitals 7–8 and recital 25 of the Second Gas Market Directive; Talus K (2010), p. 121.

Gas Market Directive,[329] long-term contracts "will continue to be an important part of the gas supply of Member States and should be maintained as an option for gas supply undertakings in so far as they do not undermine the objective of this Directive and are compatible with the Treaty, including the competition rules".[330] This is caused by the physical characteristics of gas.[331] The Directive on the security of natural gas supply recognises that long-term gas supply contracts have played a crucial role in the upstream market in securing gas supplies for the EU.[332]

In the gas market, take-or-pay obligations are a characteristic feature of upstream long-term contracts. (a) They may be in the interests of the supplier where the supplier must enter into long-term agreements as a buyer to hedge its supply obligations. (b) They can be in the interests of the buyer as an alternative source of flexibility.[333] (c) They can also constitute a de facto exclusive off-take obligation where the take-or-pay clause is close to the customer's foreseeable total demand.[334]

The Gas Directives recognise take-or-pay provisions. For instance, the Third Gas Directive provides that economic difficulties in connection with take-or-pay provisions in import contracts (that is, the refusal of the buyer to take delivery) can be a justification for denying network access to third parties (that is, parties who would like to supply gas).[335] The derogation for these take-or-pay agreements is then further specified in the Directive.[336] There were similar exceptions in the Second Gas Directive.[337]

On the other hand, the positive remarks about long-term supply contracts are conditioned by references to competition law compliance in the Gas Directives.[338]

8.5.4 Balance

The question of volume is connected with the balance issue. Obviously, the whole point of electricity supply contracts is to balance electricity consumption with electricity generation. Electricity flows must be balanced at every moment of the

[329] Directive 2009/73/EC (Third Gas Market Directive).

[330] Recital 42 of Directive 2009/73/EC (Third Gas Market Directive).

[331] See, for example, recital 37 of Directive 2009/73/EC (Third Gas Market Directive).

[332] Recital 37 of Directive 2004/67/EC.

[333] DG Competition report on energy sector inquiry, SEC(2006)1724 (10 January 2007), p. 209, para 639.

[334] *Ibid*, p. 236, para 775.

[335] Article 35(1) of Directive 2009/73/EC (Third Gas Directive). See also Article 48(1) on temporary derogations from Article 32 in the event of serious economic and financial difficulties because of take-or-pay commitments.

[336] Article 48(3) of Directive 2009/73/EC (Third Gas Directive).

[337] See Articles 21(1), 27(1), and 27(3) of Directive 2003/55/EC (Second Gas Directive). See also Talus K (2010), pp. 122–125.

[338] Talus K (2010), p. 122.

contract period. In practice, however, extraction volumes may vary. Consequently, the parties must manage the risk that supply and extraction volumes are not perfectly balanced. This risk is customarily managed in three ways.

First, the balance requirement is managed between the supplier and the buyer. Generally, the balance requirement must be considered when regulating the volume term, the modalities, and the effects of non-performance.

While the buyer can mitigate risk by choosing a load serving contract, the supplier can mitigate risk by using fixed volume terms in delivery schedules. The supplier can also use fixed maximum and minimum consumption limits combined with financial incentives not to exceed the limits.

For example, the parties may agree that the buyer must pay the spot price or a higher contract price for consumption that exceeds the maximum limit.[339] Such excess charges are not unusual. Moreover, both parties may benefit from take-or-pay clauses.[340]

The balance requirement is considered when regulating the effects of non-performance.

This can be illustrated with the force majeure clause. A customary force majeure clause postpones performance for so long as the impediment subsists. In an electricity forward contract, however, a force majeure clause releases a party from the performance of its obligations rather than just postpone their performance.[341] As the other party will have to balance its consumption or generation at any point in time, it will not need performance after the agreed point in time.

Second, the balance requirement must be managed by the system operator. Differences cancel each other out to some extent, but a net difference remains. The parties therefore need a balance agreement with the TSO, and the TSO must procure balancing power (Sects. 4.10 and 9.3). The TSO charges system users for energy imbalance according to its rules.[342]

Third, the duty to balance differences can partly be delegated by the TSO to balance responsible parties (Sect. 9.2). Electricity users can be required to form groups with one of the members responsible for balancing the difference for the whole group.

The German Energy Economy Act (EnWG) provides that electricity traders that supply to delivery points within the control area of a TSO (or trade with electric energy within the control area) must belong to a balance group (the electricity trader's own balance group or another balance group). There is also a balance group contract that regulates the relationship between the balance responsible party and the system operator.

---

[339] Neveling S and Schönrock KP (2009), § 29, number 69.

[340] DG Competition report on energy sector inquiry, SEC(2006)1724 (10 January 2007), pp. 284–285, para 929.

[341] EFET General Agreement (Version 2.1(a)), § 7.2 and § 7.4.

[342] See Articles 16(7) and 37(6) of Directive 2009/72/EC (Third Electricity Directive).

8.5.5 Metering

It would not be possible to balance electricity flows without metering. What makes metering particularly challenging is the need to balance electricity flows at every moment of the contract period. In full-requirement contracts, for instance, the volumes will become known only after the buyer's meter has been read.[343]

This means two things. First, it is necessary to use electricity demand models to forecast the demand. There are also end-use models that represent a bottom-up demand modelling approach.[344] Second, supply and consumption should be measured at least as frequently as the price changes.[345]

> German law provides that the balance responsible party must ensure that there is a balance in each ¼-hour measurement period. Consequently, somebody must make estimates about consumption in each ¼-hour period, and the parties must both allocate the duty to make the estimates and determine its modalities (when, how detailed, how binding, based on what information, does the other party have a duty to provide information, and so forth).[346]

8.5.6 Price

General Remarks

Virtually all contracts lay down payment obligations,[347] and long-term electricity supply contracts are no exception. The price term reflects the characteristic performances of the contract, that is, the core services that the buyer pays for. In a contract for the physical supply of electricity, the characteristic performances can relate to volume and transmission or distribution capacity.

Electricity Volume The volatility of market prices makes it necessary to manage the price risk in electricity supply contracts.

Price risk can be allocated between the parties or transferred to a third party. Price terms are an important part of risk management for both parties[348] and they can be very complicated.[349] In addition to fixed or variable price terms, the primary instruments used in the management of price risk are electricity forwards and electricity futures.

A party can combine electricity forwards and futures in different ways depending on its position in the electricity distribution chain (electricity producer,

---

[343] Hunt S and Shuttleworth G (1996), p. 142.

[344] Generally, see Gross G and Galiana FD (1987) and Alfares HK and Nazeeruddin M (2002).

[345] Hunt S and Shuttleworth G (1996), p. 148.

[346] Neveling S and Schönrock KP (2009), § 29, number 58.

[347] See, for example, Mäntysaari P (2010b), Chapters 8–11.

[348] Neveling S and Schönrock KP (2009), § 29, number 72.

[349] See, for example, Neveling S and Schönrock KP (2009), § 29, number 67.

distributor, end consumer). The preferred allocation of price risk can require the use of a large number of contracts.

A distributor that purchases electricity in the wholesale market and sells electricity to consumers in the retail market can combine several months of forward/futures contracts in the wholesale market to form a close match to the long-term load shape of its customers in the retail market.[350]

A party that transfers price risk achieves price certainty but loses the opportunity to make additional profits.[351] A party can lock in its profits by hedging its supply and purchase obligations and locking in the price.

Electricity Transmission Depending on the contract, the price may include transmission costs in addition to the price of the electricity volume. While pure supply contracts do not include payments for transmission, they are included in all-inclusive contracts. In the latter case, the contract can provide that the buyer will reimburse the supplier for its actual transmission costs payable to the transmission system operator, or that the buyer will pay a lump sum.[352]

Information About Market Price Pricing would be made easier by access to useful information about the market price. While the prices of standardised base or peak contracts are relatively transparent, the prices of individually negotiated delivery schedules are not. An hourly price forward curve is necessary for the valuation of delivery schedules. Delivery schedules can nevertheless be divided into a set of standardised contracts that are transparent.[353]

Fixed Price

Fixed price terms are used in standardised products traded on an electricity exchange and even in some bilateral agreements.[354]

There is some variation. (a) The simple form is a single price per MWh. (b) Alternatively, the parties can specify different prices for the different stages of operation (for instance, per start-up) and a different price for different levels of output. (c) Fixed prices can also be set by a formula which includes separate terms for the cost of fuel and the assumed rate of conversion into electricity (thermal efficiency).[355]

A fixed price term can be combined with (a) a variable volume term, (b) a fixed volume term, or (c) an availability term.

[350] Deng SJ and Oren SS (2006), p. 943.

[351] Kristiansen T (2004).

[352] Neveling S and Schönrock KP (2009), § 29, number 71.

[353] See Lokau B and Ritzau M (2009), § 5, number 22.

[354] For gas, see Däuper O and Lokau B (2009), § 4, number 7.

[355] Hunt S and Shuttleworth G (1996), p. 110.

Variable Volume Term For example, a large electricity consumer may prefer to pay a fixed rate per unit of energy for the actual consumption quantity, regardless of the quantity being high or low. In this case, a fixed price would be combined with a variable quantity term in a load-serving total supply contract (a load-serving full-requirement contract).[356]

If this is the case, the supplier can mitigate its risk exposure in various ways. The supplier can mitigate the volumetric (balance) risk, the market risk, or both.

First, the supplier may mitigate the balance risk: by giving financial incentives in the form of reduced price if the buyer meets its estimated consumption targets; and/or by charging an increased price according to the supplier's own price list or the price list of the TSO for consumption that exceeds the consumption estimates. This could be combined with a tolerance zone.[357]

Second, the supplier may use futures to lock in a fixed quantity of electricity supply at a fixed cost for hedging the expected energy consumption of the customer. However, the supplier would still be exposed to the risks of under- and over-hedging because of the volumetric uncertainty in its customers' load and the positive price-load correlation.[358] To hedge the volumetric risk, the supplier would need to buy an electricity option on the consumption quantity of its customers.

Fixed Volume Term The same methods (the methods mentioned in the first group) can be used when the parties have agreed on a fixed volume term. A fixed volume term may be combined with financial incentives not to deviate from the agreed volumes or not to exceed minimum and maximum limits. For instance, the use of a take or pay clause (minimum limit) or spot prices (maximum limit) for consumption that exceeds the limits can provide financial incentives to comply with the agreed volumes.[359]

Availability Term Payments for availability can be used to provide incentives for electricity producers to keep generation capacity available at times when the system needs generation capacity. In this case, the parties agree on: a target level of availability; a fixed payment for a certain period to be paid of the electricity producer achieves the target level of availability; and availability bonuses and penalties for availability above or below the target level. The fixed payment would normally be expected to cover the non-variable costs of the electricity producer, including a normal rate of profit.[360]

---

[356] Deng SJ and Oren SS (2006), p. 947.

[357] Neveling S and Schönrock KP (2009), § 29, numbers 68 and 71.

[358] Deng SJ and Oren SS (2006), p. 947.

[359] Neveling S and Schönrock KP (2009), § 29, number 69.

[360] Hunt S and Shuttleworth G (1996), pp. 111–112.

Variable Price

The price can also be variable. The variability of the price, or price adjustment, can be achieved in different ways. In particular, the parties can: (a) link it to a reference price; or (b) apply a mechanism to agree on the price adjustment.

Linking The parties can link the price to a reference price in two main ways. First, the price can be linked to the price of electricity contracts that are *standardised*. Spot prices or futures prices can thus be used as the basis for automatic price adjustment.[361] Second, the price can be linked to *fuel* prices, actual thermal *efficiency*, the price of a *commodity*, or an *index*.

The cost of fuel can vary. It can be important for the electricity producer to transfer the fuel price risk.

If the electricity producer mitigates this risk by including the actual fuel costs in the price, the buyer would need to consider that this would reduce the producer's incentives to seek out lower cost fuels. Linking the price to the electricity producer's actual thermal efficiency would reduce the producer's incentives to increase efficiency of operation.

For these reasons, the buyer may prefer to link the price to external indices which are not influenced by the decisions of the plant's operator.[362]

It is possible to design complex electricity forwards by linking their price to an index in another field (such as the price of aluminium).[363] Such prices can be binding directly (by virtue of an express price term linking the price to such an index), or influence the price indirectly (when the price is linked to the market price of standardised electricity products whose supply and demand are influenced by the price of competing energy products).[364]

Linking the price to the price of a commodity can cause legal concerns. For instance, a clause linking the price of gas to the price of oil in the general contract terms of the supplier was held invalid by the German Federal Court (BGH) under § 307(1) BGB.[365] According to the BGH, the supplier has only one legitimate interest to use price adjustment clauses: the passing of cost increases on to the buyer. There was no causal connection between changes in oil prices and the gas supplier's costs. The fact that such contract terms were customarily used in similar contracts lacked legal relevance in this case.

On the other hand, prices in the electricity wholesale market are influenced by the price of fuel as the market price is based on marginal production costs. The

[361] Neveling S and Schönrock KP (2009), § 29, number 70.

[362] Hunt S and Shuttleworth G (1996), p. 110.

[363] Lokau B and Ritzau M (2009), § 5, number 36; Fried J (2010), p. 285, point 500.

[364] Däuper O and Lokau B (2009), § 4, number 7.

[365] BGH, judgment of 24 March 2010—VIII ZR 178/08.

correlation between the price of a certain fuel and electricity wholesale prices depends on the market (country).

> Prices in the German wholesale market are low when there is wind and daylight because of the low marginal production costs of wind power and solar power. In the UK wholesale energy market, however, there is a high degree of correlation between electricity and gas prices, because "almost 40 % of installed generation capacity is gas-fired and such plant is frequently at the margin hence setting the price"[366] (for spark spreads, see Sect. 11.4).

Consensus Linking is one of the ways to achieve the variability of the price. Alternatively, the parties could agree on a particular price adjustment mechanism that requires consensus. The use of such a price adjustment mechanism can be in the interests of both parties as it can help to maintain or restore the balance of their mutual performances. In the absence of a price adjustment mechanism, the buyer would pay a premium for the price risk assumed by the seller (see also Sect. 8.5.3 for take-or-pay clauses).[367]

The Customary Choice The choice between a fixed or variable price and, in the latter case, the choice of the price adaptation mechanism, depend on the contract type. Long-term contracts customarily contain a variable price term.[368]

The agreed price adaptation mechanism belongs to the most important terms in complex long-term contracts for the physical delivery of electricity. The price can be adapted in various ways.[369] There are examples of relatively simple mechanisms:

- Many electricity supply contracts contain a price adjustment clause that links the price to the level of *wholesale prices*. The final price does not have to be identical to the wholesale price.[370]
- The price clause can consist of a *fixed* component and a *variable* component. For instance, this combination is used in tolling contracts (Sect. 8.2.3).[371]
- It is easier for the parties to agree on a variable price where the buyers are the electricity producer's only shareholders. In this case, share ownership tends to be complemented by long-term supply contracts that contain take-or-pay clauses.

---

[366] Ofgem (2009), para 3.81.

[367] BGH, judgment of 24 March 2010—VIII ZR 178/08. The BGH argued: "Daher hat die höchstrichterliche Rechtsprechung Preisänderungsklauseln nicht generell für unwirksam erachtet. Sie stellen vielmehr ein geeignetes und anerkanntes Instrument zur Bewahrung des Gleichgewichts von Preis und Leistung bei langfristigen Verträgen dar. Denn sie dienen dazu, einerseits dem Verwender das Risiko langfristiger Kalkulation abzunehmen und ihm seine Gewinnspanne trotz nachträglicher ihn belastender Kostensteigerungen zu sichern, und andererseits den Vertragspartner davor zu bewahren, dass der Verwender mögliche künftige Kostenerhöhungen vorsorglich schon bei Vertragsschluss durch Risikozuschläge aufzufangen versucht …"

[368] For variable terms in long-term contracts in general, see Mäntysaari P (2010b), section 5.5.4.

[369] Putzka F (2009), p. 133.

[370] See, for example, Commission decision (2004/271/EC) in Case COMP/M.2947—Verbund/ EnergieAllianz, para 86.

[371] Putzka F (2009), p. 133.

The price can depend on the production costs of the electricity producer rather than the market price in these cases.[372]

Excursion: Price Terms in the Wholesale Gas Market Similar legal tools and practices are used in the gas market. Long-term contracts facilitate the amortisation of capital investment and enable large gas distributors to secure the supply of gas.[373] Customarily, the volumetric risk is borne by the distributor.[374] It can be addressed by take-or-pay clauses.[375] The price risk is borne by the gas producer. The distributor's exposure to price risk can be mitigated by linking the price to the market price of competing products such as oil.[376] The parties customarily agree to adjust the volume and the price on a regular basis (for instance, every 2–5 years).[377]

Excursion: Preferential Prices as State Aid Price terms used by state-controlled electricity undertakings are constrained by state aid rules. State aid is prohibited in the EU.[378] The prohibition covers both advantages granted directly by a Member State and advantages granted by a public or private body designated or established by a Member State.[379]

State-controlled electricity undertakings are not prohibited from using preferential electricity tariffs when the tariffs reflect ordinary business practice. The test is that of a private operator in a market economy (*Budapesti Erőmű*).[380] Was the market operator acting on purely commercial grounds? The point of reference is "a market operator who is subject to the same obligations and who has the same opportunities" and "who is faced with the same legal and economic conditions". For the Commission, the test involves a complex economic appraisal. To carry out that analysis, it is necessary to identify the main practices of commercial operators on European electricity markets and assess whether the actions were in line with those practices.

Economic advantages granted by a state-controlled electricity undertaking can be regarded as prohibited state aid where the state-controlled undertaking would not have granted them had it acted in accordance with the rules of a competitive market.

---

[372] Putzka F (2009), p. 28.

[373] Däuper O and Lokau B (2009), § 4, number 4:

[374] Däuper O and Lokau B (2009), § 4, number 4.

[375] Däuper O and Lokau B (2009), § 4, number 5.

[376] Däuper O and Lokau B (2009), § 4, number 4.

[377] Däuper O and Lokau B (2009), § 4, number 5.

[378] Article 107(1) TFEU.

[379] See Case C-379/98 PreussenElektra [2001] ECR I-2099, para 58.

[380] Joined Cases T-80/06 and T-182/09 Budapesti Erőmű Zrt v Commission, ECLI:EU:T:2012:65, paras 65–69.

The Commission decided that electricity prices fixed by contracts that EDF had negotiated with large industrial users reflected a commercial price set according to economic considerations which would have been acceptable to a private electricity producer facing a situation similar to that of EDF.[381]

In the *Alumix* decision,[382] the Commission concluded that ENEL had behaved like a rational market operator in the circumstances although the price only covered variable production costs and a small contribution to fixed costs. In this case, ENEL sold electricity to Alcoa, its best customer. There was overcapacity in electricity generation and ENEL would not have been able to find alternative outlets for electricity generated in the region. The Commission regarded the deal as an ordinary business transaction.

The Alumix mechanism was later modified. Italy started to make direct payments to Alcoa to ensure that Alcoa could continue to pay the historical tariff that was less than half the market price. The Commission prohibited the modified practice in the *Alcoa* decision[383] according to the same principles as in *Terni*.[384]

Futures, Derivatives and Swaps

In addition to fixed price or variable price clauses, the parties can use financial instruments to manage the price risk. Financial instruments can offer both future price discovery and price certainty, and they can also be used for arbitrage. In physical electricity markets, such financial instruments include electricity futures, derivatives, and swaps (Sect. 11.1).

8.5.7 Settlement

Contracts for the physical supply of electricity must be settled both financially and physically. There is also balance settlement.

Financial Settlement The financial settlement of long-term supply contracts means the settlement of the parties' payment obligations.

Financial settlement should be influenced by (a) the increased counterparty risk in long-term contracts,[385] as well as (b) the absence of a central counterparty and margin payments in long-term contracts for the physical supply of electricity.[386]

---

[381] Commission, press release IP/91/642, 3 July 1991. The companies were Allied Signal, EKA Nobel, and Stracel/UPM. The Commission also referred to previous contracts with Pechiney, Usinor Sacilor, and Exxon Chemicals.

[382] Case C 38/1992 Alumix, Decision of 4 December 2006, OJ C 288, 1.10.1996, p. 4.

[383] Cases Nos C 38/a/2004 and 36/b/2006 Alcoa, OJ L 227, 28.8.2010, pp. 62–94.

[384] Case No C36/A/2006 Terni, OJ L 144, 4.6.2008, pp. 37–54. Appeals dismissed in Joined cases C-448/10 P to C-450/10 P ThyssenKrupp Acciai Speciali Terni and Others v Commission [2011] ECR I-00147.

[385] For counterparty risk generally, see Mäntysaari P (2010b), Chapter 6.

[386] See Lokau B and Ritzau M (2009), § 5, number 23.

To reduce exposure to counterparty credit risk, financial settlement customarily takes place at regular intervals after electricity has been supplied. The seller may require collateral and use other customary credit enhancement methods[387] to mitigate credit risk further. Financial settlement is complemented by agreed terms on payment netting and close-out netting.

Physical Settlement Whether a contract is settled even physically and not just financially depends on the contract terms. Because of physical constraints, the physical settlement of electricity supply contracts is more difficult compared with the settlement of pure financial transactions or the delivery of physical goods. It is not possible without the participation of the relevant TSO/DSO,[388] grid access, and transmission capacity. Moreover, the modalities of physical settlement include addressing all issues that are characteristic of electricity supply contracts (apart from financial issues).[389]

Settlement of Each Individual Contract One can distinguish between the settlement of each individual contract and balance settlement. The settlement of each individual contract means the discharging of supply and off-take obligations. It requires: (a) a delivery schedule (specified in each individual contract)[390]; (b) the supply of electricity according to the delivery schedule; (c) the extraction of electricity according to the schedule; (d) notifications; and (e) measurement.[391]

Generally, parties to the supply contract must comply with the rules adopted by the TSO/DSO that is responsible for managing electricity flows on the system. Each TSO/DSO has rules on notifications that must be made to the TSO/DSO by system users, and on notifications that the TSO/DSO makes to system users.[392]

Both supply and extraction must be measured or verified in accordance with the requirements of the TSO/DSO.[393] Measurement and notifications are important because of the balance requirement and because the TSO/DSO must reconcile inconsistencies between scheduled and actual flows. The parties must ensure that actual deliveries and actual extraction are documented.[394]

---

[387] For credit enhancement methods generally, see Mäntysaari P (2010b), section 11.6.

[388] Articles 12 and 15 of Directive 2009/72/EC (Third Electricity Directive).

[389] The parties must manage: (1) grid access, delivery point, and voltage level; (2) volume; (3) transmission and distribution capacity; (4) balance; (5) measurement; (6) separation of physical rights, service rights, and financial rights; (7) settlement; and (8) price volatility.

[390] See, for example, EFET General Agreement (Version 2.1(a)), § 6.2 (according to which electricity shall be delivered according to the delivery schedules specified in each individual contract) and § 4.2 (defining the schedule).

[391] See, for example, EFET General Agreement (Version 2.1(a)), § 4.1 (referring to the contract quantity at the delivery point).

[392] Article 12(d, g) of Directive 2009/72/EC (Third Electricity Directive). For DSOs, see Articles 25(1) and 25(3).

[393] See also EFET General Agreement (Version 2.1(a)), § 6.4.

[394] EFET General Agreement (Version 2.1(a)), § 6.5.

Balance Settlement The TSO is responsible both for operating the system and for balance settlement. Balance settlement is a natural monopoly (see Sect. 4.10.1).

8.6 Excursion: The Preferential Treatment of RES-E as an Alternative

The regulation of energy generation from renewable sources (RES-E) can influence the use of long-term supply contracts, because the regulatory regime enables producers of RES-E to enjoy some of the benefits traditionally associated with long-term supply contracts.

Generally, long-term supply contracts help to (a) ensure security of consumption by locking in buyers, (b) manage price risk, and (c) facilitate long-term investments in generation installations. Depending on the Member State, the regulation of RES-E can provide similar protection for owners of generation installations.[395]

There is a difference between market-based and fixed-price systems. Owners of RES-E generation installations may prefer secure contracts and accept a potentially lower price in market-based systems. This would not be necessary in fixed-price systems in which the TSO has an obligation to purchase RES-E.[396]

Regardless of the system, electricity firms might use upstream or downstream structured contracts for commercial reasons. Upstream structured contracts with producers of RES-E enable a larger electricity firm to increase the RES-E generation capacity that it can offer to its own end consumers. Downstream contracts with a larger electricity firm can enable a producer of RES-E to obtain a better price in some cases. For instance, an energy merchant could buy the distributed production of many RES-E microgenerators or producers of CHP under long-term agreements and sell it as balance energy or control reserves.

References

Aghion P, Bolton P (1987) Contracts as a barrier to entry. Am Econ Rev 77(3):388–401. http://www.jstor.org/stable/1804102

Alfares HK, Nazeeruddin M (2002) Electric load forecasting: literature survey and classification of methods. Int J Syst Sci 33(1):23–34. doi:10.1080/00207720110067421

Arowolo O (2005) Abolition of long-term contracts: what are the implications and options for bankability in energy projects financing? CAR (CEPMLP Annual Review) 8. Available at CEPMLP website. http://www.dundee.ac.uk/cepmlp/

[395] For the German model, see Monopolkommission (2013).

[396] See Toke D (2010), pp. 29–30.

Balthasar M (2007) Elektrizitätslieferungsverträge im Hinblick auf die Strommarktöffnung unter besonderer Berücksichtigung des schweizerischen und europäischen Wettbewerbsrechts. Schulthess, Zürich

Bardt H, Chrischilles E, Growitsch C et al (2014a) Gutachten. Eigenerzeugung und Selbstverbrauch von Strom. Stand, Potentiale und Trends. Im Auftrag des BDEW Bundesverband der Energie- und Wasserwirtschaft e. V. Institut der deutschen Wirtschaft Köln (IW), Energiewirtschaftliches Institut an der Universität zu Köln (EWI), Cologne, 4 April

Bardt H, Chrischilles E, Growitsch C et al (2014b) Eigenerzeugung und Selbstverbrauch von Strom – Stand, Potentiale und Trends. Zeitschrift für Energiewirtschaft 38(2):83–99. doi:10.1007/s12398-014-0133-0

Bellantuono G (2008) Long term contracts in US and EU: where are we going? EU Energy Policy Blog

Borchert J, Hasenbeck M (2009) Bewertung und Steuerung von Kraftwerksscheiben. Zeitschrift für Energiewirtschaft 33(2):115–126. doi:10.1007/s12398-009-0014-0

Cameron P (2007) Competition in the energy markets: law and regulation in the European Union. OUP, Oxford

Commission, Guidelines on Vertical Restraints (2010/C 130/01)

Däuper O, Lokau B (2009) Der Markt für Gas (empirische Darstellung). In: Zenke I, Schäfer R (eds) Energiehandel in Europa. Öl, Gas, Strom, Derivate, Zertifikate, 2nd edn. C.H. Beck, München, § 4, pp 37–59

de Hauteclocque A (2009a) Efficiency, competition and long term contracts in electricity markets. Summary and conclusions. Presented at the workshop organized by the Loyola de Palacio Program of the European University Institute and Gis Larsen, Florence, 15–16 January 2009

de Hauteclocque A (2009b) Legal uncertainty and competition policy in European deregulated electricity markets: the case of long-term exclusive supply contracts. World Competition 32 (1):91–112

Deng SJ, Oren SS (2006) Electricity derivatives and risk management. Energy 31(6–7):940–953. doi:10.1016/j.energy.2005.02.015

DG Competition Report on Energy Sector inquiry, 10 January 2007, SEC(2006) 1724

Finnerty J (1996) Project financing: assets-based financial engineering. Wiley, New York

Finon D, Perez Y (2008) Investment risk allocation in restructured electricity markets. The need of vertical arrangements. LARSEN Working Paper no 12

Fried J (2010) B. Rechtliche Bewältigung des OTC-Handels. In: Schwintowski HP (ed) Handbuch Energiehandel, 2nd edn. Erich Schmidt Verlag, Berlin, pp 153–336

Glachant JM, de Hauteclocque A (2009) Long-term energy supply contracts in European competition policy: Fuzzy not crazy. Energy Policy 37(12):5399–5407. doi:10.1016/j.enpol.2009.07.054

Green R (2006) Investment and generation capacity. In: Lévêque F (ed) Competitive electricity markets and sustainability. Edward Elgar, Cheltenham, pp 21–53. doi:10.4337/9781847204356.00011

Gross G, Galiana FD (1987) Short-term load forecasting. Proc IEEE 75(12):1558–1573. doi:10.1109/PROC.1987.13927

Harding PC (2010) Mastering the ISDA master agreements: a practical guide for negotiation, 3rd edn. Pearson Education Limited, Harlow

Hsu M (1998) Spark spread options are hot. Electr J 11(2):28–39

Hünerwadel A (2007) Arten und Formen des Stromhandels, insbesondere Börsen- und Derivathandel. In: Weber RH (ed) Stromhandel. Schulthess, Zürich, pp 49–64

Hunt S, Shuttleworth G (1996) Competition and choice in electricity. Wiley, Chichester

Kristiansen T (2004) Pricing of contracts for difference in the Nordic market. Energy Policy 32 (9):1075–1085

Lokau B, Ritzau M (2009) Der Markt für Strom (empirische Darstellung). In: Zenke I, Schäfer R (eds) Energiehandel in Europa. Öl, Gas, Strom, Derivate, Zertifikate, 2nd edn. C.H. Beck, München, § 5

Mäntysaari P (2010a) The law of corporate finance. General principles and EU law, vol I: Cash flow, risk, agency, information. Springer, Heidelberg

Mäntysaari P (2010b) The law of corporate finance. General principles and EU law, vol II: Contracts I General. Springer, Heidelberg

Mäntysaari P (2010c) The law of corporate finance. General principles and EU law, vol III: Funding, exit, takeovers. Springer, Heidelberg

Mäntysaari P (2012) Organising the firm: theories of commercial law, corporate governance and corporate law. Springer, Heidelberg

Midttun A, Handeland J, Henriksen JT et al (2001) Nordic business strategies. In: Midttun A (ed) European energy industry business strategies. Elsevier Global Energy Policy and Economics Series. Elsevier, the Netherlands, pp 23–74

Mikešić I, Thieme H, Strauch B (Salans LLP) (2012) Juristische Prüfung der Befreiung der Eigenerzeugung von der EEG-Umlage nach § 37 Absatz 1 und 3 EEG – Kurzgutachten – Bundesministerium für Umwelt, Naturschutz und Reaktorsicherheit, 27 August

Monopolkommission (2013) Sondergutachten 65. Energie 2013: Wettbewerb in Zeiten der Energiewende. Sondergutachten der Monopolkommission gemäß § 62 Abs. 1 EnWG. Bonn

Neuhoff K, von Hirschhaussen C (2005) Long-term vs. short-term contracts: a European perspective on natural gas. CWPE 0539 and EPRG 0505. Available at EPRG website. http://www.eprg.group.cam.ac.uk/

Neveling S, Schönrock KP (2009) Nicht standardisierte Liefer- und Handelsverträge sowie vertragliche Voraussetzungen auf der Netzzugangsseite. In: Zenke I, Schäfer R (eds) Energiehandel in Europa. Öl, Gas, Strom, Derivate, Zertifikate, 2nd edn. C.H. Beck, München, § 29

OECD/IEA (2005) Lessons from liberalised electricity markets. IEA, Paris

Ofgem (2009) Liquidity in the GB wholesale energy markets, 8 June 2009

Pöyry Management Consulting Oy (2013) Suomalaisen saha- ja puutuoteteollisuuden toimiympäristön vertailu keskeisimpiin kilpailijamaihin nähden. Loppuraportti. Työ- ja elinkeinoministeriö, 3 September

Putzka F (2009) Die Anwendbarkeit der AGB-rechtlichen Inhaltskontrolle auf Leistungsvorhaltungs- und Stromlieferverträge zwischen Erzeuger und Weiterverkäufer. Veröffentlichungen des Instituts für Energierecht an der Universität zu Köln, Band 151. Nomos, Baden-Baden

Scholz U, Purps S (2010) The application of EC competition law in the energy sector. J Eur Competition Law Pract 1(1):37–51

Spence DB, Prentice R (2012) The transformation of American energy markets and the problem of market power. B C Law Rev 53(1):131–202

Spicker J (2010) A. Formen des OTC-Handels. In: Schwintowski HP (ed) Handbuch Energiehandel, 2nd edn. Erich Schmidt Verlag, Berlin, pp 31–152

Toke D (2010) Wind-power outcomes: myths and reality. In: Strachan PA, Toke D, Lal D (eds) Wind power and power politics: international perspectives. Routledge studies in science, technology, and society 9. Routledge, New York, pp 18–36

Talus K (2010) Vertical natural gas transportation capacity, upstream commodity contracts and EU competition law. Dissertation, University of Helsinki

Varholy J, Fuhr T (2009) The evolution of master agreements for the forward trading of wholesale, physical energy commodities in Europe. In: Zenke I, Schäfer R (eds) Energiehandel in Europa. Öl, Gas, Strom, Derivate, Zertifikate, 2nd edn. C.H. Beck, München, § 28

Wegerich C, Seiferth C (2009) Zur kartell- und zivilrechtlichen Zulässigkeit von Take-or-Pay-Klauseln in Gaslieferverträgen mit Weiterverteilern. Recht der Energiewirtschaft 2/2009, pp 48–54

Wurmnest W (2008) Windige Geschäfte? Zur Bestellung von Sicherungsrechten an Offshore-Windkraftanlagen. Rabels Zeitschrift für ausländisches und internationales Privatrecht 72 (2):236–263

Chapter 9
Balancing Contracts and Balance Group Contracts

9.1 General Remarks

The TSO uses contracts to facilitate the maintenance of the system frequency, that is, balance in the system. One can roughly distinguish between two kinds of contracts.

First, there are contracts designed to reduce imbalances in advance. For instance, a supplier cannot have access to the grid without undertaking a duty to balance electricity inflows and outflows, and a balance responsible party must undertake to balance electricity flows in a group.

The use of balance groups and the partial delegation of monitoring to a balance responsible party can increase both the proximity and quality of monitoring and market participants' incentives to keep supply and demand in balance.

Second, there are balancing contracts that facilitate real-time balancing (the ancillary services of market participants) after the closing of the spot market. Such contracts could include bilaterally negotiated long-term reserves, which are framework contracts combined with an allocation mechanism for the use of capacity real-time. Electricity suppliers or large end consumers can provide demand-side management services under long-term demand management contracts.[1]

In this chapter, we can briefly study three particular contract types: balance responsible and balance group contracts (Sect. 9.2); balancing contracts (Sect. 9.3); and demand management contracts (Sect. 9.4). The balancing market and auctions for reserves were discussed in Sect. 4.10.

[1] See also Finon D and Pignon V (2008) distinguishing between four main types of solutions to compensate for the "missing money problem": strategic reserves detained by the system operator (vertical integration), long-term contracts, capacity payments, and the capacity market.

P. Mäntysaari, *EU Electricity Trade Law*, DOI 10.1007/978-3-319-16513-4_9

9.2 Balance Responsible Party and Balance Group Contracts

In the EU, electricity grid users must form groups with one of the group members responsible for balancing the difference between electricity inflows and outflows for the whole group. This requirement applies even to balancing service providers.[2] Balance group requirements would be reflected in the rules of a spot market. For instance, some participants in EPEX Spot are balance responsible parties responsible for balance groups.[3]

Regulation The role of balance responsible parties is regulated by ACER Framework Guidelines on Electricity Balancing that set out principles for the development of network codes[4] and ENTSO-E Network Code on Electricity Balancing.[5] While ACER Framework Guidelines define the function of balance responsible parties[6] and set out the main principles that govern the role of balance responsible parties[7] and imbalance pricing (Sect. 4.10.3),[8] ENTSO-E Network Code on Electricity Balancing lays down the duties of balance responsible parties.

Rules of the TSO The TSO must have rules for balance responsible parties. Their minimum contents have been set out in ENTSO-E Network Code on Electricity Balancing.

The rules must contain at least: (a) the requirements for becoming a balance responsible party; (b) the requirement that a balance responsible party is financially responsible for the imbalance to be settled with the connecting TSO; (c) the data and information required by the connecting TSO to calculate imbalance; (d) the rules for changing the position; (e) the settlement procedures; and (f) the consequences for non-compliance.[9]

Imbalances are calculated on the basis of the volumes allocated to the balance responsible party.[10] Imbalances are defined as the difference, within a given imbalance settlement period, between: (a) the allocated volume attributed to the balance responsible party; and (b) its final position and any imbalance adjustment applied to the balance responsible party.

---

[2] Point (c) of Article 27(4) of ENTSO-E Network Code on Electricity Balancing (6 August 2014).

[3] EPEX Spot Rules & Regulations, Appendix, Definitions (28 November 2014).

[4] ACER, Framework Guidelines on Electricity Balancing (18 September 2012), section 1.1.

[5] ENTSO-E Network Code on Electricity Balancing (6 August 2014).

[6] ACER, Framework Guidelines on Electricity Balancing (18 September 2012), section 5.1.

[7] ACER, Framework Guidelines on Electricity Balancing (18 September 2012), section 5.2.

[8] ACER, Framework Guidelines on Electricity Balancing (18 September 2012), section 5.3.

[9] Article 27(8) of ENTSO-E Network Code on Electricity Balancing (6 August 2014).

[10] For definitions, see Article 2 of ENTSO-E Network Code on Electricity Balancing (6 August 2014).

Contract There must be a contract between a balance responsible party and the TSO. The contract provides that the balance responsible party is responsible for imbalances.[11]

A balance responsible party has several duties according to the Network Code.[12] Each balance responsible party:

- must be balanced or help the power system to be balanced in accordance with the TSO's terms and conditions related to balancing;
- must provide a balanced position in the day ahead timeframe on the request of its connecting TSO[13];
- may change its position prior to Intraday Cross Zonal Gate Closure Time pursuant to the TSO's terms and conditions related to balancing;
- must not change its position after the Intraday Cross Zonal Gate Closure Time without the consent of its connecting TSO;
- must submit any change of the position to the connecting TSO; and
- is financially responsible for the imbalance to be settled with the connecting TSO.

In addition, each connecting TSO may include certain additional terms in its terms and conditions according to the Network Code.[14]

Particular Aspects The core duties of the balance responsible party are thus laid down in the Network Code on Electricity Balancing.

One may ask whether an obligation to take reasonable measures to keep imbalances to a minimum (a duty to use skill and care) would comply with the requirements under the Network Code. The answer seems to be no. Although the balance responsible party might prefer to dilute its obligations in this way, the wording of the Network Code requires an obligation to achieve a balanced position and pay for imbalances. This obligation is a duty to achieve a result.

In Germany, the duty has been limited to the use of best efforts. (a) The Energy Economy Act (EnWG) requires electricity traders that supply to delivery points within the control area of a transmission system operator (or trade with electric energy within the control area) to belong to a balance group (the electricity trader's own balance group or another balance group).[15] The conclusion of balance group contracts is thus a legal

[11] Article 2 of ENTSO-E Network Code on Electricity Balancing (6 August 2014).

[12] Article 25 of ENTSO-E Network Code on Electricity Balancing (6 August 2014).

[13] Article 2 of ENTSO-E Network Code on Electricity Balancing (6 August 2014): "... Position means an energy volume representing the sum of scheduled commercial transactions of a Balance Responsible Party, on organised electricity markets or between Balance Responsible Parties, for the calculation of the Imbalance, or, where appropriate, means an energy volume representing scheduled injections, scheduled withdrawals or the sum of scheduled injections and withdrawals of a Balance Responsible Party, for the calculation of the Imbalance of that Balance Responsible Party ..."

[14] Article 27 of ENTSO-E Network Code on Electricity Balancing (6 August 2014).

[15] § 4 StromNZV (Verordnung über den Zugang zu Elektrizitätsversorgungsnetzen).

requirement.[16] A balance group contract regulates the relationship between the balance responsible party and the system operator. (b) The minimum contents of the contract have been regulated in an ordinance (the Electricity Grid Access Ordinance, Stromnetzzugangsverordnung, StromNZV).[17] The core terms of the contract lay down the duty of the balance responsible (1) to use its best efforts to maintain balance in the balance group and (2) to settle the cost of remaining imbalances.[18] A balance group contract thus facilitates financial settlement.[19] (c) The terms have been standardised by the Federal Network Agency (BNetzA) that has issued a model contract.[20]

The core duties are complemented by other terms, (a) The TSO can reduce imbalances in advance by requiring the balance responsible party to balance flows in the day-ahead market and limiting the use of the balance market. The use of the balance market can be limited to unforeseen differences. (b) The TSO may interrupt unauthorised flows according to its own rules.[21] The TSO should have a corresponding duty in the light of its general obligations under the Third Electricity Directive.[22] (c) Both parties know that there will be unplanned outages. The balance responsible party needs a grace period to balance the group to the extent that differences are caused by unplanned outages. The parties should also regulate the effect of congestion. (d) The contract must contain an imbalance pricing term.[23]

The contract must even regulate necessary modalities that reflect the mandatory duties of the TSO. Generally, the TSO is responsible for the operation of the system and balancing it.[24] Where balance groups are used, the TSO will remain responsible for modalities such as disclosure of information, maintaining accounts, and billing. Moreover, the contract may need to address further issues characteristic of balance responsible agreements such as the use of sub-balance groups.

---

[16] § 26(1) StromNZV.

[17] § 26(2) StromNZV: "Der Vertrag muss unter Berücksichtigung der Vorschriften des Energiewirtschaftsgesetzes und dieser Verordnung mindestens Regelungen zu folgenden Gegenständen enthalten: 1. Vertragsgegenstand; 2. Rechte, Pflichten und Leistungen des Betreibers von Übertragungsnetzen; 3. Rechte und Pflichten des Bilanzkreisverantwortlichen; 4. Datenaustausch zwischen dem Betreiber von Übertragungsnetzen und dem Bilanzkreisverantwortlichen; 5. Haftungsbestimmungen; 6. Voraussetzungen für die Erhebung einer Sicherheitsleistung in begründeten Fällen; 7. Kündigungsrechte der Vertragsparteien". § 26(3) StromNZV: "In den Bilanzkreisverträgen ist sicherzustellen, dass die Bilanzkreisverantwortlichen gegen angemessenes Entgelt ihren Bilanzkreis für Fahrplangeschäfte öffnen, die der Bereitstellung von Minutenreserve dienen, die ein Bereitsteller des eigenen Bilanzkreises über einen anderen Bilanzkreis abwickeln will".

[18] See Neveling S and Schönrock KP (2009), § 29, number 77.

[19] Neveling S and Schönrock KP (2009), § 29, number 76.

[20] Zuordnungsvereinbarung zwischen Verteilnetzbetreiber (VNB) und Bilanzkreisverantwortlicher (BKV), Version 1.0, 9 June 2011. See Neveling S and Schönrock KP (2009), § 29, number 76.

[21] See, for example, Zuordnungsvereinbarung zwischen Verteilnetzbetreiber (VNB) und Bilanzkreisverantwortlicher (BKV), Version 1.0, 9 June 2011, Chapter 15.1.

[22] Article 12 Directive 2009/72/EC (Third Electricity Directive).

[23] See Article 61 of Network Code on Electricity Balancing (6 August 2014).

[24] Articles 12 and 15 of Directive 2009/72/EC (Third Electricity Directive).

There are also contract terms that are customary in long-term contracts in electricity markets. For instance, the parties may need to regulate the question of collateral, including the term and termination of the contract and sanctions for breach of contract.[25]

9.3 Balancing Contracts

9.3.1 General Remarks

There are differences between the scheduled and actual volumes. The parties can reduce the differences by trading in the day-ahead and the intraday market. Where the operator of the spot market increases the trading of contracts in the intraday market close to delivery, the TSO may need to trade less in the balancing market.[26]

The TSO is responsible for the real-time balancing of the system. The TSO uses balancing contracts to facilitate real-time balancing and to allocate the costs of real-time balancing to the market participant that caused them (imbalance settlement, see also Sect. 4.5.8). Parties may not trade in the physical wholesale market without a balancing contract with the TSO.[27]

In principle, the contracts that facilitate real-time balancing can be (1) bilaterally negotiated long-term reserve capacity contracts and long-term demand response contracts or (2) auctioned reserves.

Long-Term Contracts for Peak Generation or Demand Response Bilaterally negotiated contracts are long-term framework agreements. They facilitate peak generation or demand response.

In principle, the contracts could be (a) between the TSO and a party that owns the designated installations itself, or (b) between the TSO and a middleman (an energy merchant or a control center) that aggregates small individual capacities of third parties into volumes that a big enough to be tradable.

In the latter case, the available capacity varies as the portfolio of third parties and their installations changes over time. However, the TSO needs a fixed capacity. The parties would manage this inherent problem in the contract.[28] The TSO could, alternatively, limit the use of aggregators and rely on more reliable service providers.[29] An alternative for the

[25] Neveling S and Schönrock KP (2009), § 29, numbers 78–80.

[26] Pilgram T (2010), p. 343, point 631.

[27] See also Hunt S and Shuttleworth G (1996), p. 141.

[28] See Rious V et al. (2012).

[29] *Ibid.*

aggregator would be to transfer this risk upstream and agree on fixed capacity with the third parties that own the installations.[30]

Comparison with EFET, EEI, ISDA The framework agreements for the provision of balancing services facilitate simple physical transactions. They lack some of the core clauses customarily used in master trading agreements such as the EFET General Agreement, the EEI Agreement (Sects. 8.4 and 8.5), and the ISDA Master Agreement (Sect. 11.6).

While these master trading agreements are based on the single agreement principle and provide for close-out netting for the purpose of managing counterparty and systemic risk, such provisions are not necessary in balancing contracts. Neither are there any provisions on margining.

This is because the exposure of market participants to counterparty and systemic risk is minimal. Market participants supply ancillary services to the TSO. Whether the TSO activates the reserves is in the discretion of the TSO. The ability of the TSO to fulfil its obligations to the supplier of ancillary services under the framework agreement or individual contracts is not dependent on the behaviour of any other supplier of ancillary services.

These bilateral contracts nevertheless need to address the same characteristic issues as standard products used for the same purpose in the EU.

Standard Products in the EU The Third Electricity Directive requires the TSO to purchase reserve capacity according to "transparent, non-discriminatory and market-based procedures".[31] Market-based methods must be used for the procurement of Frequency Containment Reserves (FCR), Frequency Restoration Reserves (FRR), and Replacement Reserves (RR). Moreover, each TSO must use standard products and specific products for this purpose.[32]

ENTSO-E Network Code on Electricity Balancing lays down the issues that are characteristic of the standard products without defining their contents. The characteristic issues include the following[33]:

- the preparation period (period of time between the TSO's request and start of the energy delivery);
- the ramping period;
- the full activation time (period of time between the TSO's activation request and the full activation of the product);
- minimum and maximum quantity;
- the deactivation period (period of time for ramping, from full delivery or withdrawal back to a set point);
- the price of the bid;

[30] *Ibid*, footnote 25.

[31] Article 15(6) of Directive 2009/72/EC (Third Electricity Directive).

[32] Article 29(1) of ENTSO-E Network Code on Electricity Balancing (6 August 2014).

[33] Article 29 of ENTSO-E Network Code on Electricity Balancing (6 August 2014). For definitions, see Article 2 of ENTSO-E Network Code on Electricity Balancing (6 August 2014).

- divisibility (the possibility for the TSO to use only part of the balancing energy bids or balancing capacity bids offered by the balancing service provider, either in terms of power activation or duration);
- minimum and maximum duration of the delivery period;
- location;
- validity period (period of time when the balancing energy bid can be activated);
- mode of activation (manual or automatic activation of balancing energy bids; balancing energy is triggered manually by an operator or automatically by means of a closed-loop regulator); and
- the minimum duration between the end of the deactivation period and the following activation.

The terms of the standard products must facilitate the participation of load entities, energy storage facilities, RES-E generation installations, and aggregation facilities.[34]

Modalities In addition to these terms, it is necessary to set out the terms for modalities. In the following, the modalities will be studied in the light of the model framework agreements used in Germany for the purpose of purchasing reserve capacity according to market-based procedures.[35] There are model framework agreements for primary control reserves, secondary control reserves, minute reserves, and interruptible loads. Because the framework agreements are fairly similar, we can focus on the framework agreements for the provision of primary control reserves and those for interruptible loads.

9.3.2 *Example: Germany*

Prospective participants must complete a prequalification procedure. In Germany, the prequalification requirements are contained in the Transmission Code 2007 (Netz- und Systemregeln der deutschen Übertragungsnetzbetreiber) issued by the German TSOs. For instance, one of the prequalification requirements for primary control reserves is that the participating technical unit can provide at least 2 % of its nominal capacity and no less than 2 MW.[36]

Firms cannot participate in tenders for primary control reserves without a framework agreement in place.[37]

[34] Article 29(7)(b) of ENTSO-E Network Code on Electricity Balancing (6 August 2014).

[35] For the balance energy market, see also Lanz M et al. (2011), section 4.4.

[36] Section 3.2.3 of Appendix D1 to the Transmission Code; Lanz M et al. (2011), section 4.4.3, pp. 128–129.

[37] Rahmenvertrag über die Vergabe von Aufträgen zur Erbringung der Regelenergieart Primärregelleistung, § 1.1(1) and § 3.1(2).

The acceptance of a bid means the conclusion of an individual contract for the provision of ancillary services (the supply of balancing energy).[38]

The framework agreement and contracts for individual trades must be distinguished from contracts for grid access and transmission capacity.[39] All of them are necessary before a party can participate in physical wholesale markets.

The provider of ancillary services must comply with the prequalification requirements and agrees to comply with them during the term of the framework agreement. Because of its own duties, the TSO needs to retain the right to change the prequalification requirements.[40]

The framework agreement lays down the modalities of offers.[41] It also sets out on what basis offers are accepted. In Germany, offers for primary control reserves are ranked on the basis of price.[42] Because of the general obligations of the TSO, this must be subject to the requirements of network security.[43]

After the acceptance of the offer, the supplier must cease to market the reserved capacity.[44] The core duty of the supplier is to keep the reserved capacity available for the agreed purpose in accordance with the applicable activation times.[45]

The supplier must supply the services at the agreed grid points. The place of delivery is the transmission grid of the connection TSO.[46] The supplier must use designated installations for this purpose.[47]

The control reserves are activated automatically.[48] The supplier must take all reasonable action to supply the services from the designated installation or another prequalified installation.

There is an exception for force majeure that postpones the fulfilment of contractual duties.[49] Generally, failure to take all reasonable action to provide the service is regarded as a breach of contract.[50]

The connection TSO reduces the price to the extent that the agreed services are not provided.[51] Liquidated damages may be used to give the supplier an incentive to

---

[38] *Ibid*, § 1.1(2), § 5.3(1) and § 5.3(3).

[39] *Ibid*, § 1.2.

[40] *Ibid*, § 2.3(1).

[41] *Ibid*, § 4.1.

[42] *Ibid*, § 5.2(2): "Die Annahme der Angebote (Zuschlag) erfolgt in einem Vergabeprozess nach folgenden Kriterien: – Niedrigster Leistungspreis. – Bei Gleichheit der Leistungspreise: Frühester Eingangszeitstempel".

[43] *Ibid*, § 5.2(3): "Die Belange des sicheren Netzbetriebes, z. B. im Falle von Netzengpässen, werden vorrangig berücksichtigt".

[44] *Ibid*, § 5.2(4).

[45] *Ibid*, § 6.1(1).

[46] *Ibid*, § 6.3.

[47] *Ibid*, § 6.2(2) and § 6.4(1).

[48] *Ibid*, § 7.1(1).

[49] *Ibid*, § 6.1(2) and § 12(1).

[50] *Ibid*, § 12(2).

[51] *Ibid*, § 13(1) and § 13(2).

fulfill its obligations.[52] Moreover, the supplier can be made liable for loss or damage caused by the breach of contract.[53] The ultimate sanction for non-compliance is withdrawing the suppliers pre-qualification.[54]

The framework agreement may have to be amended in the event of changed circumstances. Changed circumstances can also be addressed with a "salvatorian clause".[55]

Moreover, the framework agreement can be terminated in two ways. One can distinguish between regular termination (termination by notice and the expiry of the agreement after the expiry of a notice period) and termination upon the occurrence of a termination event (fault-based termination, termination for a material reason, termination in the event of insolvency).[56]

Individual contracts concluded under the framework agreement may be terminated for a material reason. In the absence of the single agreement principle and close-out netting, the termination of the framework agreement does not mean the automatic termination of individual contracts.[57]

9.4 Demand Management

The contractual framework is similar for interruptible loads. In Germany, the framework is facilitated by the Energy Industry Act (EnWG) and by means of the Ordinance on Interruptible Load Agreements (AbLaV).

It is again necessary to distinguish between the framework agreement, individual contracts facilitated by the framework agreement, and contracts for the transmission of electricity.

A party may not participate in bidding unless a framework agreement is in place.[58] Electricity transmission does not fall within the scope of the framework agreement.[59]

The acceptance of a bid means that an individual contract is concluded between the TSO and the bidder. Although the individual contract is concluded on terms set out in the framework agreement, the two do not form a single agreement.[60]

---

[52] *Ibid*, § 13(3).

[53] *Ibid*, § 13(4).

[54] *Ibid*, § 13(5).

[55] *Ibid*, § 16 and § 18.

[56] *Ibid*, § 19(1), § 19(2) and § 19(6).

[57] *Ibid*, § 19(4).

[58] Rahmenvertrag über die Vergabe von Aufträgen zur Erbringung von Abschaltleistung aus abschaltbaren Lasten, § 2.1(7).

[59] *Ibid*, § 1.2(1).

[60] *Ibid*, § 1.1 and § 5.3(4).

There are prequalification requirements for the ancillary service provider and its installations. The prequalification documents signed by the service provider are part of the contract.[61]

As the service provider is an electricity consumer, it must have agreed on the balancing of electricity consumption with electricity generation with an electricity supplier and a party responsible for balancing. The contractual framework that facilitates electricity consumption by the electricity consumer should also enable the electricity consumer to reduce consumption on short notice in its capacity as provider of ancillary services.[62]

Individual contracts are concluded on the basis of accepted bids. The framework agreement regulates the acceptance of bids. In Germany, bids are ranked according to a merit order rather than the lowest price.[63]

After the bid has been accepted, the service provider must neither market nor sell the interruptible load to any third party.[64]

The framework contract lays down the core obligations of the supplier of the interruptible load (the electricity consumer, the provider of the ancillary service). The supplier of the interruptible load must: (1) keep the interruptible load available during the term of the individual contract; and (2) interrupt the load when the interruptible load is activated.[65] There is an in the event of force majeure (höhere Gewalt).[66]

The framework agreement regulates the activation of the interruptible load.[67]

References

ACER, Framework Guidelines on Electricity Balancing (18 September 2012)

ENTSO-E Network Code on Electricity Balancing (6 August 2014)

Finon D, Pignon V (2008) Electricity and long-term capacity adequacy: the quest for regulatory mechanism compatible with electricity market. Utilities Policy 16(3):143–158

Hunt S, Shuttleworth G (1996) Competition and choice in electricity. Wiley, Chichester

Lanz M, Fricke B, Anthrakidis A et al (2011) CO2-Emissionsminderung durch Ausbau, informationstechnische Vernetzung und Netzoptimierung von Anlagen dezentraler, fluktuierender und erneuerbarer Energienutzung in Deutschland. Umweltbundesamt, Climate Change 20/2011

Neveling S, Schönrock KP (2009) Nicht standardisierte Liefer- und Handelsverträge sowie vertragliche Voraussetzungen auf der Netzzugangsseite. In: Zenke I, Schäfer R (eds)

[61] *Ibid*, § 2.1(1) and § 2.1(5).

[62] *Ibid*, § 2.2(1).

[63] *Ibid*, § 5.2.

[64] *Ibid*, § 5.3(5).

[65] *Ibid*, § 6.1(1).

[66] *Ibid*, § 6.1(2) and § 12.

[67] *Ibid*, § 7.1.

Energiehandel in Europa. Öl, Gas, Strom, Derivate, Zertifikate, 2nd edn. C.H. Beck, München, § 29

Pilgram T (2010) A. Formen des Handels an der EEX. In: Schwintowski HP (ed) Handbuch Energiehandel, 2nd edn. Erich Schmidt Verlag, Berlin, pp 339–398

Rious V, Roques F, Perez Y (2012) Which electricity market design to encourage the development of demand response? EUI Working Paper RSCAS 2012/12

Chapter 10
Transmission Contracts

10.1 General Remarks

Electricity cannot be supplied without connecting wires and transmission capacity. Physical transmission contracts are contracts for the supply of transmission capacity.

A bilateral transmission contract is a contract between (a) a transmission service provider (usually the TSO that manages the grid or the operator of a merchant cable in countries that permit such business[1]) and (b) a transmission service customer (a distributor, an electricity producer that is directly connected to the grid, or a direct consumer that has a point of connection to the grid).

Mutual Rights and Obligations, Ancillary Services A bilateral transmission contract lays down the parties' mutual rights and obligations. (1) The transmission service provider: (a) undertakes to facilitate the transmission service customer's grid connection (the connection of the customer's equipment or plant used for the consumption, conveyance, or generation of electricity through lines at the point of connection); (b) undertakes to keep a certain amount of transmission capacity available for the service buyer for the transport of electricity between two locations according to the agreed schedule or schedules; and (c) provides ancillary services that facilitate the transport of electricity. For these services, the transmission service provider (d) collects payments (charges, tariffs, the price).[2] (2) The service buyer (a) obtains the right to supply or extract electricity according to particular schedules; (b) undertakes to pay the price; (c) undertakes to supply or extract electricity according to the schedules; (d) undertakes to purchase the necessary ancillary

[1] Article 17(4) of Regulation 714/2009. For Regulation 1228/2003, see de Hauteclocque A and Rious V (2010).

[2] See Articles 12(h) and 13(4) of Directive 2009/72/EC (Third Electricity Directive).

P. Mäntysaari, *EU Electricity Trade Law*, DOI 10.1007/978-3-319-16513-4_10

services from the transmission service provider; and (e) undertakes to provide its own ancillary services.

In the US, the transmission service provider's ancillary services are defined in the Pro Forma Open Access Transmission Tariff. Ancillary services are defined as "services that are necessary to support the transmission of capacity and energy from resources to loads while maintaining reliable operation of the Transmission Provider's Transmission System in accordance with Good Utility Practice".[3] The transmission provider is required to provide and the transmission customer to purchase the services. The ancillary services are defined as (1) Scheduling, System Control and Dispatch Service; (2) Reactive Supply and Voltage Control from Generation Sources Service; (3) Regulation and Frequency Response Service; (4) Energy Imbalance Service; (5) Operating Reserve—Spinning Reserve Service; and (6) Operating Reserve—Supplemental Reserve Service.[4]

To fulfil its own obligations in liberalised markets, the transmission service provider/system operator needs to purchase services from balancing service providers (Sect. 4.10). These services can be called the ancillary services of grid users.

ACER defines the transmission customer's ancillary services as "services necessary to support transmission of electric power between generation and load, maintaining a satisfactory level of operational security and with a satisfactory quality of supply. The main elements of ancillary services include active and reactive power reserves for balancing power and voltage control. Active power reserves include automatically and manually activated reserves and are used to achieve instantaneous physical balance between generation and demand. Further elements of ancillary services may include black start, inertial response, trip to houseload, spinning reserve and islanding capability".[5]

In the EU, the TSO must use market-based methods used for the procurement of Frequency Containment Reserves (FCR), Frequency Restoration Reserves (FRR), and Replacement Reserves (RR). Moreover, each TSO must use standard products and specific products for this purpose.[6]

Characteristic Issues There are characteristic issues managed in transmission contracts in addition to the generic issues, which are managed in all transactions and the issues managed in all long-term contracts.

The characteristic issues include: (a) connecting the customer's assets to the transmission assets at the point of connection so the flow of electricity is possible (subject to energisation) (Sect. 10.2); (b) energising the point of connection to enable electricity to flow (Sect. 10.3); (c) scheduling the flow (Sect. 10.4); (d) exchange of information and metering (Sect. 10.5); (e) compliance with technical requirements (Sect. 10.6); (f) prevention of the flow (Sect. 10.7); (g) firmness and transferability (Sect. 10.8); (h) the allocation of the cost of losses (Sect. 10.9); (i) the setting of grid charges (Sect. 10.9); (j) the choice of sanctions for unauthorised use (Sect. 10.10); and (k) allocation of liability (Sect. 10.11).[7]

---

[3] FERC Order No. 888, Pro Forma Open Access Transmission Tariff, Appendix D, Section 1.1.

[4] FERC Order No. 888, Pro Forma Open Access Transmission Tariff, Appendix D, Section 3.

[5] ACER, Framework Guidelines on Electricity Grid Connections (20 July 2011), section 1.3.

[6] Article 29(1) of ENTSO-E Network Code on Electricity Balancing (6 August 2014).

[7] Compare Knops HPA et al. (2009) who "decompose" the function of "transport adequacy" by means of "function-based legal design and analysis" (FULDA) method.

These issues are only partly regulated in Articles 32, 12, and 15 of the Third Electricity Directive. The purpose of the Third Electricity Directive is not to regulate transmission contracts as such.

Contract Types The characteristic issues are addressed one way or another in all such contract relationships. The way they are addressed can depend on the particular type of transmission contract, and the contract types can depend on the model for the allocation of transmission capacity.

Generally, it can be distinguished between three conceptual models for the allocation of transmission capacity: the contract path model, the flow-based model, and the point-to-point model with implicit flows.

Of the three models, the contract path model is simple but problematic. Its starting point is the fiction that electricity moves over the contracted path of transmission lines. Of course, electricity does not really move over the contract path. The exception is a direct line, that is, a single transmission line connecting the power plant to the load. A direct line can also be a direct current (DC) or high-voltage direct current (HDVC) line.[8]

One can therefore distinguish between three main contract types for independent transactions for the supply of transmission capacity: (1) contracts for the use of a direct line or a closed circuit system (the contract path); (2) other explicit bilateral transmission contracts (the flow-based model); and (3) implicit transmission contracts (the point-to-point model with implicit flows).

System Operator's Rules, Balance Contracts For technical reasons, system operators must either adopt or apply rules setting out operational requirements for connection to the system.[9] Because system operators are responsible for maintaining balance in the grid, they must also adopt balancing rules (Sect. 9.2).[10]

For reasons of risk management, system operators make sure that these rules are incorporated into the transmission contract by reference. Acceptance of the TSO's rules is often called the "balance agreement" (Sect. 4.5.7). There are also particular balancing contracts or control reserve contracts that facilitate real-time balancing (Sects. 4.10 and 9.3).

The terms of transmission contracts are constrained by the system operator's rules (which influence actual flows).

Open Terms Some of the customer's contractual obligations must be relatively open because of the system operator's own compliance obligations. In particular, the customer must comply with the detailed operational requirements for connection to the system as applied from time to time. These detailed requirements can be

---

[8] Brown MH and Sedano RP (2004), pp. 29–30.

[9] See Article 5 of Directive 2009/72/EC (Third Electricity Directive); Case C-17/03 VEMW and others [2005] ECR I-4983.

[10] See Articles 15(6) and 15(7) of Directive 2009/72/EC (Third Electricity Directive).

complemented by an open term such as the customer's duty to observe due skill and care or good electricity industry practice.[11]

Firm or Non-firm Transmission Services Firmness is a related question. Electricity transmission services can be firm or non-firm. The difference relates to reservation priority and priority when the flow is interrupted. (a) Depending on the agreed terms of the contract and the governing law, firm transmission services could be defined as transmission services that "may not be interrupted for any reason except during an emergency when continued delivery of power is not possible".[12] In EU law, one can distinguish between physical and financial firmness. Capacity holders must be compensated for any curtailment.[13] (b) In contrast, non-firm transmission services may be interrupted for the benefit of firm transmission schedules or for other reasons.

> When its services are firm, the system operator should of course be able to manage the risk that it cannot fulfil the contract. The TSO can do it in many alternative ways. EFET has given the following examples: (1) rescheduling or re-dispatching (either domestic or cross-border); (2) countertrading; (3) coordinating dispatch or re-dispatch of power plants and transmission asset management with neighbouring TSOs; (4) repurchasing transmission rights (either on its auction platform or on the secondary capacity market); (5) purchasing energy calls or selling energy puts; (6) curtailment (payments financed by revenues from prior sale of firm transmission rights); (7) creating additional price areas; and (8) conducting physical improvements to the transmission system.[14]

Transferable or Non-transferable The question of firmness is connected with transferability. Long-term transmission contracts are a way to reduce risk, but it is possible that the transmission capacity becomes surplus to requirements. One may ask whether electricity transmission contracts are transferable or non-transferable. If contracts are not transferable, greater transmission capacity may need to be built to reduce congestion and transmission prices.[15] If the contracts are firm and transferable, they have a higher market value.[16]

Fixed or Variable Obligations In principle, all obligations can be fixed or variable.[17] There are core obligations that necessarily have to be fixed because of the nature of electricity transmission, core obligations that are fixed because of benefits

[11] See, for example, section 1.3 of the Electricity Industry Customer Transfer Code 2004 of Act of the State of Western Australia: "... 'good electricity industry practice' means the exercise of that degree of skill, diligence, prudence and foresight that a skilled and experienced person would reasonably and ordinarily exercise under comparable conditions and circumstances consistent with applicable laws and applicable recognised codes, standards and guidelines ..."

[12] Brown MH and Sedano RP (2004).

[13] ACER, Framework Guidelines on Capacity Allocation and Congestion Management for Electricity (29 July 2011), section 6.4.

[14] EFET (2008), p. 3.

[15] Hunt S and Shuttleworth G (1996), p. 212.

[16] OECD/IEA (2005), p. 149.

[17] For flexibility generally, see Mäntysaari P (2010), section 5.5.4.

to both parties, and core obligations that are fixed because of the bargaining power of a party.

Both parties can benefit if some of the core obligations are fixed. (a) Disclosure of information belongs to the core fixed obligations because of the nature of electricity transmission. (b) Moreover, the system operator can make more effective use of the transmission network where the transmission service buyer has an obligation to supply electricity to the grid (or an obligation to extract electricity from the grid) rather than a mere option to do so. A fixed obligation makes it easier for the system operator to schedule other flows, in particular counter flows.[18] (c) Investors in power plants can prefer firm transmission rights rather than a mere promise of being allowed to participate in a short-term spot market for transmission services.[19]

The obligations of sellers and buyers are fixed on electricity spot markets such as Nord Pool Spot[20] and EPEX Spot.[21]

Microgeneration There are particular aspects relating to the regulation of the connection of microinstallations (microgeneration) to the grid (Sect. 10.2.3).

10.2 Connecting the Customer's Assets to the Transmission Network

10.2.1 General Remarks

There are no electricity flows from or to the transmission service buyer's assets, unless its relevant assets are connected to the transmission service provider's transmission assets. The customer thus needs a contract facilitating grid connection. The contract on grid connection can be part of the transmission contract or a separate contract preceding the transmission contract. An agreement on grid connection does not yet give the customer any right to supply electricity, extract electricity, or use the grid for the purposes of the transmission of electricity.

There are two kinds of assets that will be connected under the contract on grid connection, namely the customer's relevant assets and the transmission assets. (1) The customer's relevant assets are assets that are: (a) used for the consumption,

[18] Twomey P et al. (2006).

[19] Hogan WW (1992).

[20] Nord Pool Spot Physical Markets, Trading Appendix 4, Clearing Rules (27 November 2014), sections 4.1.3 and 4.1.4.

[21] EPEX Spot Exchange Rules (28 November 2014), Article 5.2.

conveyance, or generation of electricity; and (b) connected to the agreed point of connection. The assets may consist of lines, equipment, or a plant. They may be owned or managed by the customer. (2) The transmission assets consist of the grid (or the direct line) and assets that form part of the grid (or the direct line).

In the EU, the connection of generation assets to the grid (that is, a transmission, distribution, or closed distribution network) is regulated in detail by ENTSO-E Network Code on Requirements for Grid Connection applicable to all Generators (NC RfG). Each owner of a power generating facility must ensure that it complies with the requirements under the Network Code throughout the lifetime of the facility.[22] NC RfG is complemented by ENTSO-E Network Code on Demand Connection. The latter sets up a common framework for network connection agreements between network operators and demand facility owners or distribution network operators.[23] In situations where generation and demand co-exist in a demand facility or closed distribution network, the one Network Code applies to pure generation and the other to pure demand.[24]

10.2.2 Contract Terms

The transmission service provider (the TSO) and the customer must agree on a number of things to connect the assets:[25] the characteristics of assets; the allocation of costs the right to connect assets; TSO approvals; compliance with technical requirements; product safety; compliance with general standards; and land rights.

Existence of Assets First, the necessary assets must exist and fulfill the technical requirements. These requirements can be derived from the regulatory framework or contract. Technical requirements are partly based on regulation. The technical requirements must be "objective and non-discriminatory" in the EU.[26] They are partly harmonised by the Network Code on Requirements for Generators (NC RfG).[27]

---

[22] Article 34(1) of ENTSO-E Network Code for Requirements for Grid Connection Applicable to all Generators (8 March 2013). For planned modifications, see Article 34(2). For operational incidents or failures, see Article 34(3).

[23] Articles 1 and 2(2) of ENTSO-E Network Code on Demand Connection (21 December 2012).

[24] Article 1 of ENTSO-E Network Code on Demand Connection (21 December 2012).

[25] See, for example, the definitions of Connection Agreement and Connection Point in Article 2 of ENTSO-E Network Code for Requirements for Grid Connection Applicable to all Generators (8 March 2013).

[26] Article 5 of Directive 2009/72/EC (Third Electricity Directive).

[27] ACER, Framework Guidelines on Electricity Grid Connections (20 July 2011), section 2.1: "... the network code(s) shall define the requirements on significant grid users in relation to the relevant system parameters contributing to secure system operation, including: – Frequency and voltage parameters; – Requirements for reactive power; – Load-frequency control related issues; – Short-circuit current; – Requirements for protection devices and settings; – Fault-ride-through

If the necessary assets do not yet exist or do not yet fulfill the technical requirements, the assets must be built and installed or improved. It is necessary to regulate the allocation of responsibilities and the distribution of these costs.

One may ask whether the TSO has a duty to connect the customer's relevant assets to the grid where the transmission assets do not yet exist. Obviously, it would be impossible to connect the assets in this case. It would be possible to lay down a duty to ensure that the relevant transmission assets are in place and allocate costs caused by the delay.

The allocation of responsibilities and costs can also be from mandatory law. The Third Electricity Directive provides that each TSO is responsible for "ensuring the long-term ability of the system to meet reasonable demands for the transmission of electricity"[28] and for "contributing to security of supply through adequate transmission capacity".[29]

Allocation of Costs Second, there is thus the question of allocation of costs. The Third Electricity Directive does not state exactly how these costs should be allocated, but it is clear that the method of allocating them must be objective and non-discriminatory.[30]

In Germany, the existence of both a duty to connect assets and a duty to pay for the costs[31] have placed a heavy financial burden on system operators in the case of offshore wind farms (Sect. 5.8.2).

In the US, the Pro Forma Open Access Tariff gives the transmission provider a right to defer providing service until it completes construction of new transmission facilities or upgrades whenever it determines that providing the requested service would, without such new facilities or upgrades, impair or degrade reliability to any existing firm services.[32] Moreover, the obligation to provide the requested transmission service can be terminated in the event that the facility additions remain unfinished.[33]

The allocation of costs can depend on whether the costs are related to the upgrade of the transmission grid, the distribution grid, or a radial line. Upgrades in the transmission grid and in the distribution/regional grid are treated differently in different countries. (a) Costs related to the upgrade of the transmission grid are generally socialised. In other words, the costs are borne by network companies that can recover them via network tariffs. (b) The costs of upgrades of the distribution network are often allocated to the customer that caused the upgrade. (c) However, there are different ways to regulate this issue. Costs are allocated in different ways in Germany, Sweden, and the US.

capability; and – Provision of ancillary services ..." See also ENTSO-E Network Code for Requirements for Grid Connection Applicable to all Generators (8 March 2013).

[28] Article 12(a) of Directive 2009/72/EC (Third Electricity Directive).

[29] Article 12(c) of Directive 2009/72/EC (Third Electricity Directive).

[30] Article 32(1) of Directive 2009/72/EC (Third Electricity Directive).

[31] § 17 Abs. 2a EnWG. See also Bundesnetzagentur (2009).

[32] FERC Order No. 888, Pro Forma Open Access Transmission Tariff, Appendix D, Section 15.5.

[33] FERC Order No. 888, Pro Forma Open Access Transmission Tariff, Appendix D, Section 20.3.

In Germany, the costs of upgrades of the distribution network are socialised. In Sweden, project developers pay the costs for the upgrade of a radial line while costs for upgrades in the meshed grid are shared between the owner of the production plant and Svenska Kraftnät. Project developers in Sweden have to pay most network investment costs.[34] In the US, the Pro Forma Open Access Tariff provides that the transmission provider will use due diligence to expand or modify its transmission system to provide the requested firm transmission service, but only provided the customer agrees to pay the costs.[35]

The grid connection assets may need to be changed for capacity, security, or other reasons. In the absence of mandatory legislation, the parties may agree on the allocation of these costs and that changes in the connection assets are considered in the tariffs or the transmission pricing methodology (for the regulation of transmission pricing, see Sects. 5.7.3 and 5.8.3).

Right to Connect Assets Third, the TSO permits the customer to: (a) connect particular customer assets to the grid at the points of connection; and to (b) remain connected for the purpose of the transfer of electricity between the grid and the customer's assets.

No Connection Without Prior Approval Fourth, the customer must not connect any equipment to the grid without the prior approval of the TSO. The TSO needs to control the design and specifications of equipment connected to the grid. The TSO may also require prior testing according to a testing plan, which it has approved in advance. Moreover, the TSO may require the replacement of equipment.

Compliance with Technical Requirements Fifth, both parties agree to comply with the relevant technical requirements. They include the technical requirements of: connection; the operation of the connection; and the maintenance of the connection.

Because the technical requirements are vital for safety and reliability, the agreed obligations of the customer to comply with the technical requirements have a relatively broad scope. According to the agreed terms, the customer is responsible for any equipment that can affect the security or operation of the grid. The customer is thus made responsible both for assets physically connected to the grid and for assets that are not physically connected to the grid but can affect the security, management, operation, or performance characteristics of the grid.

The contract lays down the most important requirements. However, the TSO needs to reserve the right to change the requirements because of its own general duties. The customer wants to limit the changes to what is necessary. The contract may thus provide, for instance, that the TSO may unilaterally impose any reasonable technical requirements in accordance with good electricity industry practice.

The technical requirements that the parties must regulate relate to, for instance: the connection of instrumentation and control circuits; the grid interface (the provision of grid interface switchgear; the insulation of equipment at the grid interface; earthing

[34] See, for example, SOU 2008:13, p. 203.

[35] FERC Order No. 888, Pro Forma Open Access Transmission Tariff, Appendix D, Section 13.5 Transmission Customer Obligations for Facility Additions or Redispatch Costs, Section 15.4 Obligation to Provide Transmission Service that Requires Expansion or Modification of the Transmission System, and Section 27 Compensation for New Facilities and Redispatch Costs.

arrangements for the grid interface); the control of voltage levels and imbalances (the equipment must be designed and maintained so voltage levels and imbalances can be controlled); and the clearance of faults.

In addition to such technical requirements relating to connection, the parties must regulate maintenance obligations. They undertake a general duty to maintain equipment so it always complies with the applicable standards.

There are also several operating requirements. Each party must ensure that its equipment: (a) has no adverse effect on the grid or the ability of the TSO to manage the grid; (b) can be operated within the minimum and maximum system voltages; (c) has no adverse effect on other customers or their ability to manage their equipment; (d) is designed and installed so maintenance can be carried out; (e) does not present a safety hazard to the other party or other customers (or their respective employees and agents) or the general public; (f) does not cause a contract party to breach any legislation; (g) performs its intended function to the required standard; (h) does not cause the maximum short circuit power and current limits specified in the contract to be exceeded on or nearby to the grid; (i) is capable of being operated and operates within the limits that the customer has disclosed to the transmission service provider; and (j) meets any other requirements imposed by the transmission service provider in writing acting reasonably and in accordance with good electricity industry practice.[36]

Product Safety Sixth, each party agrees to ensure product safety. The customer ensures that the connection, operation, and maintenance of the customer's assets will not adversely affect the grid or the management of the grid. The transmission service provider ensures that the grid connection and the maintenance and operation of the grid do not adversely affect the customer's assets or the use or management of the customer's assets.

General Standards Seventh, each party agrees to comply with other applicable general standards.

Land Rights Eighth, the parties must agree on land rights. There must be a physical place for the point of connection and the necessary equipment and structures.

10.2.3 Microgeneration

Microgeneration (distributed generation)[37] is connected to the low voltage distribution level or the medium voltage distribution level (for grid levels, see Sect. 5.4).[38] The DSO is responsible for the connection of microgenerators to the

[36] Transpower, Transmission Agreement (4 November 2010), clause 5.1.

[37] Point 31 of Article 2 of Directive 2009/72/EC (Third Electricity Directive): "'distributed generation' means generation plants connected to the distribution system".

[38] See, for example, Pöyry Energy Oy (2006), section 2.1, p. 14.

distribution grid.[39] The introduction of net metering and net billing is designed to increase microgeneration.

Preferential Treatment As microgeneration is often generated from renewable sources or waste or CHP, it benefits from preferential treatment than electricity generated from conventional sources.

Each DSO has a general obligation to operate and develop the distribution system in its area,[40] including an obligation to connect customers to its network.[41] Microgeneration must therefore be connected to the grid (for the allocation of costs, see Sect. 5.8.2). Even microgeneration must comply with the terms of NC RfG.[42]

Discrimination is prohibited,[43] but a Member State may "require the distribution system operator, when dispatching generating installations, to give priority to generating installations using renewable energy sources or waste or producing combined heat and power".[44] These installations can also benefit from preferential feed-in tariffs and other preferential treatment (Sect. 3.7.7 and Chap. 7).

It is nevertheless to be noted that there is no exemption from the regulation of grid connection,[45] there is no exemption from the regulation of imbalances and the duty to have a balance responsible party,[46] and there is no preferential treatment for the provision of balancing services (although EU law facilitates wider participation in this respect).[47]

Closed Distribution Systems and Power Generating Facilities In practice, it is possible that a microgeneration unit is integrated with other microgeneration units or electrical appliances. One may ask whether they form a distribution system or a closed distribution system, that is, a person's own network that serves the owner itself.[48] Depending on the Member State, closed distribution systems may partly be exempted from some of a DSO's obligations.[49] Can a microgenerator that uses its

---

[39] Articles 3(3) and 25 of Directive 2009/72/EC (Third Electricity Directive).

[40] Point 6 of Article 2 of Directive 2009/72/EC (Third Electricity Directive).

[41] Articles 3(3) and 37(6) of Directive 2009/72/EC (Third Electricity Directive).

[42] Article 1 of ENTSO-E Network Code for Requirements for Grid Connection Applicable to all Generators (8 March 2013).

[43] Article 25(2) of Directive 2009/72/EC (Third Electricity Directive).

[44] Article 25(4) of Directive 2009/72/EC (Third Electricity Directive).

[45] ENTSO-E Network Code for Requirements for Grid Connection Applicable to all Generators (8 March 2013).

[46] ACER, Framework Guidelines on Electricity Balancing (18 September 2012), section 5.1.

[47] ACER, Framework Guidelines on Electricity Balancing (18 September 2012), section 2.1. See Articles 10(1) and 29(7) of ENTSO-E Network Code on Electricity Balancing (6 August 2014).

[48] Article 28(1) of Directive 2009/72/EC (Third Electricity Directive).

[49] See Article 28(2) of Directive 2009/72/EC (Third Electricity Directive): "Member States may provide for national regulatory authorities to exempt the operator of a closed distribution system from: (a) the requirement under Article 25(5) to procure the energy it uses to cover energy losses and reserve capacity in its system according to transparent, non-discriminatory and market based procedures ..."

own network be regarded as a DSO[50] or as an operator of a closed distribution system (CDSO)?[51]

According to the wording of the Third Electricity Directive, regulated distribution requires the existence of a "customer" to whom electricity is distributed.[52] This seems to: (a) exclude systems that do not supply any person other the undertaking itself; but (b) include systems that serve even one or more outsiders.

This leaves the definition of closed distribution systems. A closed distribution system is a qualified distribution system. It is "a system which distributes electricity within a geographically confined industrial, commercial or shared services site … if: (a) for specific technical or safety reasons, the operations or the production process of the users of that system are integrated; or (b) that system distributes electricity primarily to the owner or operator of the system or their related undertakings".[53] Such sites include, for instance, "train station buildings, airports, hospitals, large camping sites with integrated facilities or chemical industry sites … because of the specialised nature of their operations".[54]

The system can also be regarded as a power generating facility. A power generating facility is neither a distribution system nor a closed distribution system. A microgenerator can customarily be regarded as a power generating facility owner rather than as a DSO or CDSO in the light of definitions in NC RfG:

- A power generating facility owner is defined as a natural or legal entity owning a power generating facility.
- A power generating facility is defined as a facility to convert primary energy to electrical energy which consists of one or more power generating modules connected to a network at one or more connection points.
- A power generating module is either a synchronous power generating module[55] or a power park module.[56]

[50] Article 24 of Directive 2009/72/EC (Third Electricity Directive): "Member States shall designate or shall require undertakings that own or are responsible for distribution systems to designate, for a period of time to be determined by Member States having regard to considerations of efficiency and economic balance, one or more distribution system operators. Member States shall ensure that distribution system operators act in accordance with Articles 25, 26 and 27".

[51] Article 2 of ENTSO-E Network Code for Requirements for Grid Connection Applicable to all Generators (8 March 2013): "… Closed Distribution System Operator (CDSO) – is a natural or legal person operating, ensuring the maintenance of and, if necessary, developing a closed distribution Network according to Article 28 of Directive 2009/72/EC …"

[52] Point 5 of Article 2 of Directive 2009/72/EC (Third Electricity Directive).

[53] The system is not a closed distribution system if it supplies household customers, unless the use is "incidental". Articles 28(1) and Article 28(4) of Directive 2009/72/EC (Third Electricity Directive).

[54] Recital 30 of Directive 2009/72/EC (Third Electricity Directive).

[55] For a definition, see Article 2 of ENTSO-E Network Code for Requirements for Grid Connection Applicable to all Generators (8 March 2013).

[56] For a definition, see *ibid*, Article 2.

10.3 Energising the Point of Connection

One can distinguish between connection and energisation. On one hand, electricity cannot flow across the connection point between the system of the transmission service provider and the customer's system unless the systems are connected. On the other, there will be no electricity flows unless the connection point is energised. A connection point is energised by moving a switch or adding a fuse. A metering point or a metering system is energised by adding a meter.

NC RfG provides that the operational notification procedure for connection for each new Type D Power Generating Module consists of: an Energisation Operational Notification (EON); an Interim Operational Notification (ION); and a Final Operational Notification (FON).[57] An Energisation Operational Notification is issued by the relevant network operator.[58] It will entitle the power generating facility owner to energise its internal network and auxiliaries for the power generating modules by using the grid connection that is defined by the connection point.[59]

10.4 Allocation of Transmission Capacity and Scheduling

The customer uses the transmission capacity allotted to it. Because of the balance requirement and scarce transmission resources, the transmission system operator must ensure that there is a mechanism for the allocation of transmission capacity and for the scheduling of electricity flows. It is necessary to agree on the flows in advance.

The allocation of transmission capacity depends on the market (Chap. 5). (a) The use of implicit auction mechanisms means that transmission capacity is allocated implicitly and the customer does not need to agree on the allocation of transmission capacity separately. (b) On the other hand, there are also explicit bilateral transmission contracts (the flow-based model). In this case, the parties must agree on the allocation of transmission capacity explicitly.

According to the CACM Regulation, implicit allocation is the main rule for cross-zonal capacity allocation in the day-ahead and intraday timeframes.[60]

Explicit allocation could be used as a transitional arrangement under ENTSO-E Network Code for Capacity Allocation and Congestion Management (NC CACM) that preceded the CACM Regulation.[61] The CACM Regulation limits the use of explicit auctions as a transitional arrangement to intraday markets.[62]

NC CACM contained a particular rule on explicit requests for capacity: "The explicit request for capacity can only be submitted by a Market Participant for an interconnection where the Explicit Allocation is applicable. For each explicit request for capacity the

[57] *Ibid*, Article 28.

[58] *Ibid*, Article 29(2).

[59] *Ibid*, Article 29(1).

[60] Recital 13 of Commission Regulation . . ./.. (CACM Regulation).

[61] Article 91 of ENTSO-E NC CACM (27 September 2012).

[62] Article 64 of Commission Regulation . . ./.. (CACM Regulation).

Market Participant shall submit the volume and the price to the Capacity Management Module. The price and volume of Explicit Allocated Capacity shall be made publicly available".[63]

Explicit auctions are the main rule for long-term cross-zonal capacity allocation according to ENTSO-E Network Code on Forward Capacity Allocation.[64]

In principle, the allocation of transmission capacity and the obligations of the TSO can be firm or non-firm (Sect. 5.6.5).

ENTSO-E Network Code on Forward Capacity Allocation and the CACM Regulation lay down firmness deadlines. The firmness deadlines depend on the duration of the contract (long-term,[65] day-ahead,[66] or intraday[67]). There are special rules for force majeure and emergency situations.[68]

Characteristic Terms We can focus on explicit contracts. In bilateral transmission contracts, the transmission service provider agrees to make transmission capacity available. The availability of transmission capacity is limited to: the agreed circuit (s) of transmission lines; the agreed points of supply (injection, delivery) and extraction (off-take, receipt); and the agreed schedule.

The customer agrees to submit schedules in advance. In other words, it must notify the TSO of the flows.

In the EU, ENTSO-E Network Code on Operational Planning and Scheduling requires the use of a scheduling agent. Schedules are submitted to the TSO by the scheduling agent.[69]

In the US, the Pro Forma Open Access Transmission Tariff provides that schedules for the transmission customer's firm point-to-point transmission service must be submitted to the transmission provider no later than 10 a.m. on the day before the commencement of the transmission service—or a reasonable time that is generally accepted in the region and is consistently adhered to by the transmission provider.[70]

10.5 Exchange of Information and Metering

There are extensive disclosure duties because of the nature of electricity transmission and the balance requirement. The transmission contract will lay down obligations to provide information about: the relevant assets; the operation of the relevant

[63] Article 95 of ENTSO-E NC CACM (27 September 2012).

[64] Article 1(1) of ENTSO-E NC FCA (2 April 2014).

[65] *Ibid*, Articles 58(1), 59(1) and 59(2).

[66] Article 62 of ENTSO-E NC FCA (2 April 2014) and Article 69 of Commission Regulation . . ./.. (CACM Regulation).

[67] Article 70 of Commission Regulation . . ./.. (CACM Regulation).

[68] Article 63 of ENTSO-E NC FCA (2 April 2014) and Article 72 of Commission Regulation . . ./.. (CACM Regulation).

[69] Articles 53(1) and 52(1) of ENTSO-E Network Code on Operational Planning and Scheduling (24 September 2013).

[70] FERC Order No. 888, Pro Forma Open Access Transmission Tariff, Appendix D, Section 13.8.

assets; demand or supply (the anticipated supply of electricity or the anticipated demand for electricity); and conveyed electricity (metered quantities).

For metering and disclosure of information, the transmission customer needs metering and communications equipment, which is compatible with transmission service provider's equipment. The equipment must be installed and maintained.[71]

10.6 Compliance with Technical Requirements

Compliance with the system operator's technical requirements and the applicable technical standards belongs to the customer's core obligations. The parties agree on this obligation in various ways. (a) Compliance with the agreed technical requirements is a precondition for grid access and permitted flows. (b) The transmission agreement lays down specific technical requirements. (c) Moreover, the specific agreed requirements are complemented by open clauses such as the duty to comply with the system operator's technical requirements as they are applied from time to time and the duty to comply with good industry practice.

The supplier has a duty under the EFET General Agreement to deliver electricity "in the current, frequency and voltage applicable at the relevant Delivery Point agreed in the Individual Contract and in accordance with the standards of the Network Operator responsible for the Delivery Point".[72]

In the US, the Pro Forma Open Access Transmission Tariff refers to good utility practice. Both the transmission provider[73] and the transmission customer must comply with good utility practice.[74] For instance, ancillary services are defined as services "that are necessary to support the transmission of capacity and energy from resources to loads while maintaining reliable operation of the Transmission Provider's Transmission System in accordance with Good Utility Practice".[75] The transmission customer is also required to maintain a power factor within the same range as the transmission provider pursuant to good utility practice.[76] Good utility practice has been defined in the Pro Forma Open Access Transmission Tariff.[77]

---

[71] See, for example, FERC Order No. 888, Pro Forma Open Access Transmission Tariff, Appendix D, Section 24.1 Transmission Customer Obligations and Section 24.2 Transmission Provider Access to Metering Data.

[72] EFET General Agreement (Version 2.1(a)), § 6.1.

[73] FERC Order No. 888, Pro Forma Open Access Transmission Tariff, Appendix D, Section 28.2 Transmission Provider Responsibilities.

[74] FERC Order No. 888, Pro Forma Open Access Transmission Tariff, Appendix D, Section 35.1 Operation under The Network Operating Agreement.

[75] FERC Order No. 888, Pro Forma Open Access Transmission Tariff, Appendix D, Section 1.1 Ancillary Services.

[76] FERC Order No. 888, Pro Forma Open Access Transmission Tariff, Appendix D, Section 24.3 Power Factor.

[77] FERC Order No. 888, Pro Forma Open Access Transmission Tariff, Appendix D, Section 1.14 Good Utility Practice.

10.7 Preventing the Flow, De-energisation, Disconnection, Termination, Curtailment

10.7.1 General Remarks

The flow may need to be prevented for various reasons such as safety concerns, non-compliance with operational requirements, default, force majeure, and the expiry of the transmission contract (Sect. 10.7.2). The flow may also need to be curtailed (Sect. 10.7.3).

10.7.2 Preventing the Flow

Mechanisms

The flow can be prevented in three main ways. One can distinguish between interruption, de-energisation, and disconnection. What do they mean?

Interruption Under normal conditions, there should not be any interruptions. However, interruptions are caused by grid bottlenecks and outages.

There are planned interruptions caused by scheduled outages. The parties can thus agree that there should be no outages having a material effect on the capability of the grid to provide the agreed service apart from scheduled outages.

There are unplanned interruptions caused by grid bottlenecks. The TSO has an obligation to ensure that transmission capacity is "adequate",[78] but it is customary to have some congestion for reasons of economic efficiency. The TSO may also have to comply with a statutory obligation to give priority access to energy generation from renewable sources.[79]

Moreover, unplanned interruptions can be caused by unplanned outages. Unplanned outages are forced outages or cascading outages. Forced outage means the shutdown of a generating installation, transmission line, or other facility for emergency reasons.[80] Cascading outages are worse. Cascading outage means the uncontrolled, successive loss of system elements triggered by an incident at any location.[81]

[78] Points (a)–(c) of Article 12 of Directive 2009/72/EC (Third Electricity Directive).

[79] Article 16(2) of Directive 2009/28/EC (RES Directive).

[80] Brown MH and Sedano RP (2004), Glossary.

[81] Brown MH and Sedano RP (2004), Glossary.

De-energisation De-energisation is a deliberate act to prevent the flow of electricity between the transmission system and the customer's installation through the connection point.[82] A connection point is de-energised by moving a switch or removing a fuse.[83]

Unlike disconnection, de-energisation is of a more temporary nature. Where premises are to be unused for a period, they may be de-energised by removing the main cut-out fuse. Where the premises are to be re-occupied, they may be re-energised.

Disconnection Disconnection can be permanent or temporary. (a) Permanent disconnection means the permanent removal of the equipment that was installed for the purposes of providing a connection at the connection point. After the disconnection of a connection point, it is not possible to energise it. (b) Temporary disconnection means in effect de-energisation. It can be manual or automatic.[84]

Contract Terms

The purpose of the transmission contract is to make the grid available for the transmission of electricity. It is contrary to the purpose of the contract to prevent the flow. It is therefore important for the parties to regulate interruptions (reliability), de-energisation, and disconnection, including their effect on the parties' mutual obligations.

Reliability As outages cannot be excluded in the normal course of a TSO's business, it is in the interests of the TSO to ensure that it is responsible only after a certain threshold is exceeded. On the other hand, the customer does not want to pay to the extent that the service has not been available. It is in the interests of the TSO to ensure that the transmission contract sets out to what extent the obligations of the customer are affected. Moreover, the TSO wants to limit the customer's contractual remedies as there may be remedies for the customer under the dispositive provisions of the governing law.

First, the parties may regulate the required level of availability. They may do this by defining the maximum level of unavailability because of (a) planned outages, (b) unplanned outages, and (c) momentary outages.

This can be illustrated with three examples. (a) The level of unavailability because of planned outages can be limited to a percentage of hours over a period that the TSO's relevant assets are unavailable at a customer point of service because of a planned outage of one minute or longer (unavailable for no more than __%). (b) The level of unavailability because of unplanned outages can be limited in the same way to a percentage of hours over a period that the TSO relevant assets are unavailable at a customer point of service because

---

[82] For the definition of "de-energise", see DCUSA, section 1.1.

[83] For the definition of "de-energisation works", see DCUSA, section 1.1.

[84] The term disconnection was used in this sense in ENTSO-E Network Code for Requirements for Grid Connection Applicable to all Generators (8 March 2013).

of an unplanned outage of one minute or longer (unavailable for no more than __%). (c) The level of unavailability because of momentary outages can be limited to the number of times over a certain period that the TSO's relevant assets are unavailable because of outages that are shorter than one minute.

Second, the parties may agree on the required level of reliability measured as (a) the maximum number of interruptions, (b) the maximum duration of interruptions, and (c) the maximum amount of unserved energy. Again, the TSO ensures that it is not responsible for interruptions unless a certain threshold is exceeded.

For example, the parties can limit (a) the number of planned or unplanned interruptions of any length, (b) the loss of connection minutes caused by planned or unplanned outages of one minute or longer, and (c) the amount of unserved energy because of planned or unplanned interruptions of one minute or longer (MWh).

There are no reliability standards at EU level for transmission services as such, but there are reliability standards for TSOs. The network codes must establish minimum standards and requirements related to system operation.[85]

In the US, transmission reliability standards are based on agreements between NERC (the North American Electric Reliability Council) and electric utilities. There are sanctions for utilities that do not comply with the standards. However, FERC (the Federal Energy Regulatory Commission, the regulator of wholesale power markets) has no legal authority to enforce NERC's reliability standards.[86]

De-energisation De-energisation can be voluntary or involuntary for the customer depending on the agreed terms.

First, the parties may agree that a point of connection will be de-energised at the customer's request.

Second, the TSO reserves the right to de-energise the point of connection in the event of customer default, in particular non-payment or technical non-compliance. It is important to reserve the de-energisation right even in the latter case, because failure to comply with the minimum technical and operational requirements can prejudice safety and security of supply. For instance, the TSO may retain the right to de-energise the point of connection for so long as it reasonably considers that the non-compliance is likely to have a material adverse effect on: the power quality or security of the grid; the performance characteristics and/or management of the grid; or any third party.

In the US, the right to terminate transmission services because of a payment default is constrained in two ways under the Pro Forma Open Access Transmission Tariff. There is a 30-day grace period and transmission services may not be terminated without the consent of the FERC.[87] In Germany, the grace period is 4 weeks after notification.[88]

---

[85] ACER, Framework Guidelines on Electricity System Operation (2 December 2011), section 1.5.

[86] For the basics of transmission, see Brown MH and Sedano RP (2004).

[87] FERC Order No. 888, Pro Forma Open Access Transmission Tariff, Appendix D, Section 7.3 Customer Default.

[88] See § 19(2) StromGVV. See also BGH, judgment of 11 December 2013—VIII ZR 41/13.

Third, the TSO may reserve a general catch-all right to de-energise a point of connection for important reasons. In particular, the transmission service provider should have the right to de-energise a point of connection where it reasonably considers it necessary to do so for safety or system security reasons. This right should reflect the TSO's own obligations as the TSO is responsible for the technical safety of the system.[89]

Fourth, de-energisation can be triggered by an agreed force majeure event. One of the agreed force majeure events can relate to government action in the broad sense. This is necessary, because there is high exposure to legal and regulatory risk. Electricity transmission is highly regulated and it is monitored and supervised by the regulatory authorities.[90]

> The FERC definition of force majeure includes a list of the most important forms of force majeure events in addition to the catch-all clause "any other cause beyond a Party's control". There is a reference to government action.[91] In contrast, the ACER definition of force majeure relies on open wording and contains no similar list.[92]

The TSO should probably ensure that the de-energisation of one point of connection will not relieve the customer from any obligation to pay any continuing charges in relation to the remaining points of connection, and that the customer indemnifies the TSO for its direct costs resulting from de-energisation where the reason for de-energisation is customer request or customer default.

Disconnection Disconnection can be constrained by laws. In the EU, it is constrained by the Third Electricity Directive.

On one hand, system operators have a duty to connect customers and keep them connected. (a) Some electricity consumers are protected by the existence of public service obligations. A distribution company must connect electricity consumers to its network, and all customers are entitled to have their electricity provided by a supplier.[93] (b) As regards transmission, there are rules on the connection of power plants to the transmission system. The TSO must have transparent and efficient procedures for non-discriminatory connection of new power plants to the transmission system.[94]

---

[89] See, for example, Articles 5, 7(2)(a) and 12(a) of Directive 2009/72/EC (Third Electricity Directive). See also Article 8(4) of ENTSO-E Network Code on Operational Security (24 September 2013) and Article 2(1) of ENTSO-E Network Code on Operational Security (24 September 2013).

[90] See, for example, Article 37 of Directive 2009/72/EC (Third Electricity Directive).

[91] FERC Order No. 888, Pro Forma Open Access Transmission Tariff, Appendix D, Section 10.1 Force Majeure.

[92] ACER, Framework Guidelines on Capacity Allocation and Congestion Management for Electricity (29 July 2011), section 6.2. See also point 45 of Article 2 of Commission Regulation .../.. (CACM Regulation).

[93] First subparagraph of Article 3(3) and Article 3(4) of Directive 2009/72/EC (Third Electricity Directive).

[94] Article 23(1) of Directive 2009/72/EC (Third Electricity Directive).

The TSO must not refuse the connection of a new power plant on the grounds of possible future limitations to available network capacities,[95] and the TSO must not refuse a new connection point, on the ground that it will lead to additional costs linked with necessary capacity increase of system elements in the close-up range to the connection point.[96]

On the other hand, the TSO is responsible for operational security.[97] The TSO may have a duty to disconnect demand in the event of low frequency.[98]

Now, the Third Electricity Directive lays down rules on the connection of consumers and new power plants. While it does not expressly regulate disconnecting them, the possible right to be and remain connected does not include the right to be and remain energised.[99]

Whether the customer is or remains energised is subject to the TSOs right to de-energise a connection point. Moreover, the right to be and remain energised can depend on whether: the customer has the necessary permits (such as the permit for the generation installation); the customer is able to perform and comply with its contractual obligations[100]; and there is no emergency situation.

According to the agreed terms of the transmission contract, disconnection may be triggered by the same events as de-energisation. The TSO may have a legal duty to disconnect installations in the event of emergency.

In addition, disconnection is connected with the termination or expiry of the contract. The contract can be terminated in whole or in respect of a point of connection.

Effect on Other Rights and Obligations It is in the interests of the TSO to ensure that the transmission contract sets out to what extent the obligations of the customer will be affected. In the absence of agreed terms, the customer might have a right to suspend the performance of its own obligations.[101]

In particular, the TSO may prefer to ensure: (1) that the prevention of the flow in one point of connection will not relieve the customer of any obligation to pay any continuing tariffs in relation to the remaining points of connection; and (2) that the customer has a duty to indemnify the TSO for all direct costs resulting from the prevention of the flow where it is caused by the customer breaching its contractual obligations (default), effected because of the customer's default, or at the customer's request.

It is in the interests of the customer that tariffs will be recalculated for the relevant connections with effect from the date of the interruption, de-energisation, or disconnection.

---

[95] Article 23(2) of Directive 2009/72/EC (Third Electricity Directive).

[96] Article 23(3) of Directive 2009/72/EC (Third Electricity Directive).

[97] Article 12 of Directive 2009/72/EC (Third Electricity Directive).

[98] See ENTSO-E Working Draft Network Code on Emergency and Restoration (22 January 2015).

[99] DCUSA, Schedule 2B (National Terms of Connection), Section 3, Clause 3.3: "The right to be (and remain) Connected does not include the right to be (and remain) Energised".

[100] See DCUSA, Schedule 2B (National Terms of Connection), Section 3, Clause 4.1.

[101] Compare Articles 71 and 73 of the CISG.

Moreover, it is in the interests of both parties that they have a right to disclose the reason for the interruption, de-energisation, or disconnection. The parties can have extensive disclosure obligations in electricity markets and financial markets and on contractual grounds.

Termination There are issues relating to termination in general, to the termination of a point of connection, and to disconnection.

While many other contracts can be terminated when a party fails to fulfill its core obligations, this remedy is less relevant for the transmission service customer that cannot choose an alternative supplier but must rely on the same TSO for transmission capacity. And because transmission is a natural monopoly, the TSO is not free to choose its customers.[102] This does not prevent the parties from regulating damages.

Depending on the case, the contract can distinguish between the termination of the whole contract and the termination of a point of connection. The transmission contract provides for the transmission of electricity between different locations and may provide for multiple points of connection to the grid. If this is the case, the contract can set out whether the contract may be terminated in respect of a particular point of connection.

In any case, it is in the interests of the transmission service provider to ensure that the contract will not expire in respect of a point of connection before the customer causes its assets to be disconnected from the grid at that point of connection.

10.7.3 Curtailment

It is rarely possible for the transmission service provider to guarantee that a specific level of capacity will always be available. Random fluctuations in the pattern of flows over the network and occasional forced outages of generation and transmission can all affect the amount of capacity available on any part of the network.[103] The capacity may need to be curtailed.

Curtailment could be defined as "a reduction in firm or non-firm transmission service in response to a transmission capacity shortage as a result of system reliability conditions".[104]

---

[102] See, for example, Articles 17(2)(c) and 12 of Directive 2009/72/EC (Third Electricity Directive).

[103] Hunt S and Shuttleworth G (1996), pp. 213–214.

[104] FERC Order No. 888, Pro Forma Open Access Transmission Tariff, Appendix D, Section 1.7 Curtailment.

Curtailment is regarded as the exception in the EU. It should only be used when redispatching or countertrading are not sufficient,[105] and its use must be non-discriminatory.[106] In the US, FERC has left system operators more discretion in this respect.[107]

Legal Duty In cases of emergency, the system operator has a legal duty to curtail transmission services as the party responsible for the security and reliability of the system.[108]

Terms of Curtailment and Allocation of Costs As curtailment terms are constrained by mandatory laws, one may ask to what extent transmission service providers and transmission customers may define the terms of curtailment and the responsibility for its costs in the transmission contract.

The parties could agree on the circumstances that can trigger curtailment and the form of curtailment. However, this could be extremely complicated.[109] One might ask whether the network of transmission service provider's contracts is non-discriminatory and whether it permits curtailment in prohibited cases. Contracts that restrict curtailment are designed to transfer the risk of curtailment to other transmission customers.[110]

One alternative would be to define transmission capacity as "as-available" or "curtailable" capacity. In this case, the transmission service provider is permitted to curtail capacity rights according to the agreed terms of the contract. Again, one may ask whether the right to curtail capacity is constrained by mandatory provisions of law.

Regulation 714/2009 provides that network congestion problems should "preferentially be solved with non-transaction based methods, i.e. methods that do not involve a selection between the contracts of individual market participants".[111] Market participants who have been allocated capacity must be compensated for any curtailment except in cases of force majeure.[112]

One could therefore ask whether "as-available" or "curtailable" capacity has been allocated or not yet allocated, and whether selection of contracts ex post and ex ante can be treated differently. The answer is provided by the regulation of

[105] First subparagraph of Article 16(2) of Regulation 714/2009 on conditions for access to the network for cross-border exchanges in electricity. Compare FERC Order No. 888, Pro Forma Open Access Transmission Tariff, Appendix D, Section 33.2 Transmission Constraints as well as Section 33.7 System Reliability.

[106] Point (f) of Article 12 of Directive 2009/72/EC (Third Electricity Directive). First subparagraph of Article 16(2) of Regulation 714/2009. Compare FERC Order No. 888, Pro Forma Open Access Transmission Tariff, Appendix D, Section 33.5 Allocation of Curtailments.

[107] See also Hunt S and Shuttleworth G (1996), pp. 213–214.

[108] Article 12 of Directive 2009/72/EC (Third Electricity Directive).

[109] See Hunt S and Shuttleworth G (1996), pp. 213–214.

[110] Compare Hunt S and Shuttleworth G (1996), pp. 213–214 on "limited interruptibility and compensation".

[111] Article 16(1) of Regulation 714/2009.

[112] See also second subparagraph of Article 16(2) of Regulation 714/2009.

firmness (Sect. 5.6.5). The main rule is that transmission rights must be firm. They must be firm in intraday capacity allocation,[113] in cross-zonal capacity allocation,[114] and when cross-border transmission capacity is allocated on a long-term or medium term basis.[115]

EU law does not require any compensation for curtailment in cases of force majeure. According to CACM Framework Guidelines, CACM Network Codes must provide for a common definition of force majeure.[116] Force majeure events are defined so narrowly in CACM Framework Guidelines that they should be rare.

> For instance, there is usually some congestion, and each TSO is required to "publish information on where congestion usually occurs and how, where and when it is physically relieved".
>
> Ensuring that there is enough transmission capacity in most cases is not "beyond the reasonable control" of the TSO. Congestion can be a "sudden" event, but it is seldom a "sudden unforeseeable event". Congestion can often be solved by various kinds of measures, and it may be "reasonably possible" for the TSO to take these measures "from a technical, financial and/or economic point of view".

In any case, a supplier needs to consider the risk of curtailment in downstream contracts. For instance, it can define curtailment as a force majeure event in the electricity supply contract.

Contract or Market-Based Measures as an Alternative One may ask whether parties to the transmission contract could agree on load shedding as an alternative to curtailment. (a) In the US, load shedding has been mentioned in the Pro Forma Open Access Transmission Tariff. The transmission service provider and the customer must establish load shedding procedures in advance.[117] Load is shedded in the event of a system contingency when the transmission service provider determines that it is necessary for the parties to shed load.[118] (b) In the EU, however, Regulation 714/2009 provides that network congestion problems should "preferentially be solved with non-transaction based methods, i.e. methods that do not involve a selection between the contracts of individual market participants".[119]

---

[113] ACER, Framework Guidelines on Capacity Allocation and Congestion Management for Electricity (29 July 2011), section 5; Article 71 of Commission Regulation …/.. (CACM Regulation).

[114] ACER, Framework Guidelines on Capacity Allocation and Congestion Management for Electricity (29 July 2011), section 6.4.

[115] Point 2.5 of Annex I to Regulation 714/2009: "The access rights for long and medium-term allocations shall be firm transmission capacity rights. They shall be subject to the use-it-or-lose-it or use-it-or-sell-it principles at the time of nomination".

[116] ACER, Framework Guidelines on Capacity Allocation and Congestion Management for Electricity (29 July 2011), section 6.2.

[117] FERC Order No. 888, Pro Forma Open Access Transmission Tariff, Appendix D, Section 33.1 Procedures.

[118] FERC Order No. 888, Pro Forma Open Access Transmission Tariff, Appendix D, Section 33.6 Load Shedding.

[119] Article 16(1) of Regulation 714/2009.

10.8 Firmness and Transferability

Electricity transmission services can be firm or non-firm with firmness as the mandatory main rule in the EU (Sects. 5.6.5 and 10.7). The difference relates to reservation priority and priority when the flow is interrupted. Depending on the agreed terms of the contract, firm transmission services could be defined as transmission services that "may not be interrupted for any reason except during an emergency when continued delivery of power is not possible". In contrast, non-firm transmission services may be interrupted for the benefit of firm transmission schedules or for other reasons.[120] One can also distinguish between physical and financial firmness.[121] Firmness could, therefore, even be defined as "arrangements to guarantee that capacity rights remain unchanged or are compensated".[122]

There is a connection between firmness and transferability as non-firm transmission contracts are subject to higher risk. Where an electricity producer's long-term transmission contracts are transferable, it can benefit in three ways. First, long-term contracts can provide security against price changes. Second, widespread use of transferable contracts can reduce transmission prices because of efficient allocation of existing capacity.[123] Third, the use of long-term and transferable contracts can make it easier for the transmission service provider to recover sunk costs and to invest in new transmission capacity. This can again reduce transmission prices.[124]

Use Both firm and non-firm transmission services are used worldwide. (a) Transmission services tend to be firm where supply contracts are exchange traded and an implicit auction mechanism is used for the allocation of transmission capacity. (b) On the other hand, the preferential treatment of energy generation from renewable sources (Sect. 7.2) would give the TSO reason to use non-firm obligations for the transmission of electricity generated from other sources.[125] (c) Investors in power plants can prefer firm transmission rights rather than a mere promise of being allowed to participate in a short-term spot market for transmission services.[126]

Terms of Non-firmness In any case, it is important not only for the customer but even for the TSO to define the circumstances in which non-firm transmission services may be interrupted. It is important for the TSO, because it does not want

[120] For the definition of firm transmission and non-firm transmission, see also Brown MH and Sedano RP (2004).

[121] ACER, Framework Guidelines on Capacity Allocation and Congestion Management for Electricity (29 July 2011), section 6.4.

[122] Article 2 of ENTSO-E Network Code on Electricity Balancing (23 December 2013).

[123] Hunt S and Shuttleworth G (1996), p. 212.

[124] See Hunt S and Shuttleworth G (1996), pp. 211–212.

[125] Article 16(2) of Directive 2009/28/EC (RES Directive).

[126] Hogan WW (1992).

to risk breach of contract when complying with its general statutory obligations as TSO.

In the US, the Open Access Transmission Tariff Original distinguishes between firm transmission services and non-firm transmission services. Non-firm transmission services are subordinate to firm transmission services in the sense that non-firm transmission services are curtailed before firm transmission services are curtailed.[127] The Open Access Transmission Tariff lays down the reservation priority in detail.[128]

10.9 Losses and Transmission Pricing

System operators must address the question of losses for various reasons. First, the fact that part of energy is lost as heat influences balance. Second, system operators must comply with legal requirements relating to losses. Third, these legal compliance requirements are reflected in the contractual framework for transmission services. Fourth, the way losses are dealt with depends also on the method of transmission pricing. The pricing models used in the EU have already been discussed in Sects. 5.7.3 and 5.8.3 in this book.

Compliance Requirements In the EU, system operators must comply with obligations to (a) procure the energy they use to cover energy losses, (b) procure the energy according to transparent, non-discriminatory, and market-based procedures,[129] and (c) collect balancing charges to cover costs for such ancillary services (balancing costs, energy for losses).[130]

There is a difference between the EU and the US. In the US, the customer is responsible for replacing real power losses as calculated by the transmission provider.[131]

10.10 Sanctions for Unauthorised Use

Unauthorised flows can destabilise the system. The flow is unauthorised when parties to an electricity supply contract schedule a transmission flow without a corresponding physical transmission contract. Unauthorised flows can also be from

[127] FERC Order No. 888, Pro Forma Open Access Transmission Tariff, Appendix D, Section 13.6 Curtailment of Firm Transmission Service.

[128] FERC Order No. 888, Pro Forma Open Access Transmission Tariff, Appendix D, Section 14.2 Reservation Priority.

[129] Articles 15(6) and 25(5) of Directive 2009/72/EC (Third Electricity Directive).

[130] Point (d) of Article 17(2) of Directive 2009/72/EC (Third Electricity Directive).

[131] FERC Order No. 888, Pro Forma Open Access Transmission Tariff, Appendix D, Section 15.7 Real Power Losses.

unilateral action (for manipulation, see Sect. 4.7.5). System operators try to reduce unauthorised use of the system.

First, the TSO's rules or the transmission agreement specify the rate payable, including other terms and conditions applicable in the event that a customer exceeds its reserved capacity.[132]

Second, the TSO may impose sanctions in the form of penalty payments according to its rules or the terms of the transmission agreement.[133]

Third, the TSO may intervene by interrupting the unauthorised flow.

For instance, the model balance group contract issued by the Federal Network Agency (BNetzA) in Germany provides that the TSO may intervene, at any time, in energy supplies and the grid operation "to prevent the endangerment of the stable grid operation by an unauthorized use of the TSO's transmission grid". In the case of pending danger, the TSO may do this even without prior notice to the balance responsible party.[134]

10.11 Allocation of Liability

Generally, the TSO is exposed to the legal risk of liability for death, personal injury, or damage to property (for product liability, see Sect. 2.7.4). It is in the interests of the TSO to try to channel this risk to the customer to the extent that these events are caused by actions attributable to the customer.

In the US, the Pro Forma Open Access Transmission Tariff contains a hold harmless clause to this effect: "The Transmission Customer shall at all times indemnify, defend, and save the Transmission Provider harmless from, any and all damages, losses, claims, including claims and actions relating to injury to or death of any person or damage to property, demands, suits, recoveries, costs and expenses, court costs, attorney fees, and all other obligations by or to third parties, arising out of or resulting from the Transmission Provider's performance of its obligations under this Tariff on behalf of the Transmission Customer, except in cases of negligence or intentional wrongdoing by the Transmission Provider".[135]

In EU law, the focus is not on these risks. Instead, Regulation 714/2009 allocates "the financial consequences of failure to honour obligations associated with the allocation of [cross-border] capacity" to the party responsible for the failure.[136]

---

[132] For US practices, see FERC Order No. 888, Pro Forma Open Access Transmission Tariff, Appendix D, Section 13.7.

[133] Twomey P et al. (2006).

[134] Zuordnungsvereinbarung zwischen Verteilnetzbetreiber (VNB) und Bilanzkreisverantwortlicher (BKV), Version 1.0, 9 June 2011, Chapter 15.1.

[135] FERC Order No. 888, Pro Forma Open Access Transmission Tariff, Appendix D, Section 10.2 Indemnification.

[136] Point 2.13 of Annex I to Regulation 714/2009.

References

ACER, Framework Guidelines on Capacity Allocation and Congestion Management for Electricity (29 July 2011)
ACER, Framework Guidelines on Electricity Balancing (18 September 2012)
ACER, Framework Guidelines on Electricity Grid Connections (20 July 2011)
ACER, Framework Guidelines on Electricity System Operation (2 December 2011)
Ackermann T, Centeno-Lopez E (2008) SOU 2008:13. Grid issues for electricity production based on renewable energy sources in Spain, Portugal, Germany, and United Kingdom. Annex to Report of the Grid Connection Inquiry. Stockholm
Brown MH, Sedano RP (2004) Electricity transmission: a primer. National Council on Electricity Policy, Washington, DC
Bundesnetzagentur (2009) Positionspapier zur. Netzanbindungsverpflichtung gemäß § 17 Abs. 2a EnWG. Available at Bundesnetzagentur website. http://www.bundesnetzagentur.de/
de Hauteclocque A, Rious V (2010) Regulatory risk for European merchant transmission investors. Netw Ind Q 12(3):13–16
EFET (2008) Electricity transmission capacity rights: making firmness a reality. November
ENTSO-E Network Code for Requirements for Grid Connection Applicable to all Generators (8 March 2013)
ENTSO-E Network Code on Capacity Allocation and Congestion Management (27 September 2012)
ENTSO-E Network Code on Demand Connection (21 December 2012)
ENTSO-E Network Code on Electricity Balancing (23 December 2013)
ENTSO-E Network Code on Forward Capacity Allocation (2 April 2014)
ENTSO-E Network Code on Operational Planning and Scheduling (24 September 2013)
ENTSO-E Network Code on Operational Security (24 September 2013)
Hogan WW (1992) Contract networks for electric power transmission. J Regul Econ 4(3):211–242
Hunt S, Shuttleworth G (1996) Competition and choice in electricity. Wiley, Chichester
Knops HPA, de Jong HM, de Vries LJ (2009) How will the new EU energy legislation affect investments in infrastructure? In: Proceedings of the 32nd IAEE international conference energy, economy, environment: the global view. IAEE, San Francisco, pp 1–18
Mäntysaari P (2010) The law of corporate finance. General principles and EU law, vol II: Contracts I General. Springer, Heidelberg
OECD/IEA (2005) Lessons from liberalised electricity markets. IEA, Paris
Pöyry Energy Oy (2006) Sähkön pientuotannon liittäminen verkkoon. Helsinki
SOU 2008:13. See Ackermann T, Centeno-Lopez E (2008)
Twomey P, Neuhoff K, Newbery D (2006) Incentives for an adequate, economic and reliable Swiss transmission grid. Final version. Swiss Federal Office of Energy (SFOE), Bern

Part IV
Financial Contracts

Chapter 11
Financial Contracts

11.1 General Remarks

This chapter focuses on the characteristic legal aspects of financial electricity contracts (derivatives). Financial electricity contracts do not result in the physical supply of electricity. Financial contracts are traded either on electricity exchanges or over the counter (OTC). The majority of counterparties are electricity firms. Other counterparties include investment firms and banks.[1]

The customary forms of financial electricity contracts are futures, options, and swaps. Futures and options are the most common forms of financial electricity contracts.

The financial contracts discussed in this chapter include both exchange-traded electricity futures (Sect. 11.2) and options (Sect. 11.3) as well as OTC-traded derivatives. Exchange-traded derivatives are governed by the rules of the exchange. OTC-traded derivatives are often governed (a) by the ISDA Master Agreement (Sect. 11.6) that applies to derivatives that are settled in cash or (b) by the EFET General Agreement that applies to electricity forwards or options that are settled physically (and is discussed in that context in Sect. 8.4). Particular OTC-traded financial contracts include spark-spread options (Sect. 11.4) and electricity swaps (Sect. 11.5).

Electricity Futures Electricity futures are often financial contracts unlike electricity forwards that are more likely to be regarded as contracts for the physical supply of electricity (the terminology can be vague in business practice, see Sect. 11.2). The party that buys security and sells risk under a futures transaction (the risk shredder) is primarily motivated by security rather than the profit derived from the transaction. The party that buys risk and sells security (the speculator)

[1] Hünerwadel A (2007), p. 58.

P. Mäntysaari, *EU Electricity Trade Law*, DOI 10.1007/978-3-319-16513-4_11

under a futures transaction is motivated by the profits that are achieved by the successful prediction of price movements.[2]

Electricity Swaps Electricity swaps (Sect. 11.5) are an application of futures contracts. Their function is to change the commercial result of the underlying contract without changing its terms as such. This can be illustrated with a forward contract for the physical supply of electricity. If the parties have agreed on a fixed price, an electricity swap can enable the buyer to pay a variable price for the underlying electricity over the contracted time period. If the price of electricity is variable, an electricity swap can enable the buyer to pay a fixed price.

Electricity swaps are typically established for a fixed quantity of power referenced to a variable spot price at either a generator's or a consumer's location. Electricity swaps are widely used in providing short- to medium-term price certainty up to a couple of years.[3] There are also electricity locational basis swaps (Sect. 11.5.3).

Other Derivatives There is a large number of other electricity derivatives such as callable forwards and putable forwards.[4] Very exotic instruments can resemble betting contracts that may be legally unenforceable in some jurisdictions.[5]

Underlying Asset In this chapter, we will focus on electricity derivatives with electricity supply contracts or related assets as the underlying asset. In principle, the underlying could be a spot contract or a futures contract or their auction price. In futures, the underlying can also be an index, such as the "Phelix Base index" or the "APX Power NL index". The underlying can also be a system price, such as the Elspot system price for the Nordic region. In options, the contract base can be a future that can be assigned. As illustration, there are options on "Phelix Base® Month Futures" (EEX) and "German Electricity Base Year Futures" (Nasdaq Commodities).

There are also financial contracts based on contracts for transmission capacity (Chap. 12), emission allowances, or green certificates (such as Swedish and Norwegian El-Certs).[6] In addition, electricity firms can use weather derivatives and insurance contracts.[7]

Most electricity derivatives relate to a delivery period during a day. Moreover, the contracts can be contracts for the supply of base load or peak load.

[2] Pure arbitrage involves zero risk and no commitment of capital. Kristiansen T (2004), citing Khoury SJ (1984).

[3] Deng SJ and Oren SS (2006), p. 944.

[4] See Deng SJ and Oren SS (2006), p. 946.

[5] For German law, see § 762(1). See Fried J (2010), p. 285, point 502.

[6] See, for example, NASDAQ OMX, Trading Appendix 2/Clearing Appendix 2, Contract Specifications, Commodity Derivatives (24 November 2014).

[7] U.S. Energy Information Administration (2002), Chapter 4.

Purpose of Financial Electricity Contracts Financial electricity contracts—derivatives—are long-term contracts in the sense that there is a gap of weeks, months, or years between the conclusion of the contract and final settlement.[8] Generally, they can be used for three purposes. The first is *hedging*. Financial electricity contracts enable market participants to obtain protection against price volatility—provided that price volatility can be kept within reasonable limits as extreme volatility would make the cost of financial electricity contracts prohibitive.[9] Financial electricity contracts can also enable electricity producers to stabilise their cash flows. The stability of cash flows can be important for funding reasons as electricity generation is capital intensive. The second purpose is *arbitrage* (speculating). In addition, financial electricity contracts can be used for *basis trading*.

Hedging

In electricity markets, it is particularly important to manage price volatility.[10] It is important for electricity producers, suppliers/distributors, and end consumers alike. (a) Obviously, electricity producers rely on the price of electricity for their profits. (b) An electricity producer may also need to manage price volatility for funding reasons. For instance, it may need debt funding for a new installation. Because price volatility affects its ability to service the debt, banks might not provide the necessary funding unless the firm is able to sell its production at a fixed price. (c) Many industrial production processes require plenty of power. If electricity prices rise too much, the end consumer will not be able to make a profit. For this reason, the end consumer needs to fix the price that it will pay in the future.

The price risk can be transferred to a party that is better placed to manage it.[11] A market participant can manage price risk in various ways. (a) An end consumer can transfer the price risk to the retailer by a fixed-price retail contract. The retailer can pass the price risk to the supplier by a fixed-price supply contract. (b) Alternatively, both can buy electricity under variable-price contracts and combine the variable-price contracts with financial hedges. (c) They can also buy electricity in the spot market and combine the spot purchases with separate financial hedges. (d) An electricity producer can transfer price risk to its customer by fixed-price bilateral contracts. Alternatively, it can sell electricity in the spot market or under variable-price contracts and combine the sales with financial hedges.[12]

In addition to price volatility, electricity firms can be exposed to other financial risks because of the fact that exchange-traded physical products are relatively

[8] Fried J (2010), p. 167, point 270.

[9] U.S. Energy Information Administration (2002), Chapter 4.

[10] All firms manage cash flow and risk. Generally, Mäntysaari P (2010a), p. 1; Mäntysaari P (2012).

[11] ISDA (2003), p. 3.

[12] NordREG (2010), p. 12.

simple and standardised.[13] Standardised contracts might not match their needs perfectly.

Hedging Alternatives There are three ways to use derivatives for hedging: one-on-one hedging; portfolio hedging; and anticipatory hedging.[14]

One-on-one hedging means that a market participant merely hedges its existing position in the underlying security or contract.

Portfolio hedging means that firms aggregate their internal exposures and hedge the net exposures as a portfolio.

> According to the ISDA, "[h]edges of physical production, physical supply, pricing exposure to movements of benchmarks, arbitrage from one region versus the other and time period hedges form a matrix of positions that are best hedged on a portfolio basis".[15]

Electricity market participants may also need to hedge anticipatory exposures. Anticipatory hedging means hedging prior to the execution of the actual position. To illustrate, they may need to hedge unsold commercial production or anticipated commercial requirements. Generally, electricity producers and suppliers invest in a portfolio of assets to meet anticipated demand, but actual demand depends on many things. Many electricity firms will therefore decide whether financial instruments are needed to mitigate all or a portion of the risk exposure.

Inherent Problems in Hedging The use of derivatives to manage electricity price risk can be difficult for several reasons.

First, the existence of products that are traded in the financial electricity market depends on the existence of underlying physical electricity products traded in the physical electricity market. The quality of the financial electricity market depends on the quality and liquidity of the underlying physical electricity market. Second, the simple pricing models used to value derivatives in other industries or other energy industries do not work well in the electricity sector because of the physical characteristics of electricity.[16] Third, problems in price transparency can make it difficult to develop accurate models for pricing derivatives.[17] Pricing transparency would also require information about operational matters relating to production, consumption, transmission, and storage as well as relevant information about other areas.[18]

This can give an incentive to use even other instruments. (a) There may be demand for derivatives that are based on something other than the underlying electricity spot price. Such derivatives may include weather derivatives and

[13] Kristiansen T (2004).

[14] See, for example, ISDA (2011).

[15] ISDA (2011).

[16] Deng SJ and Oren SS (2006), p. 948.

[17] For past experiences in the US, see U.S. Energy Information Administration (2002), Chapter 4.

[18] See Article 4(1) of Regulation 1227/2011 (REMIT).

specialty insurance contracts. (b) For the same reasons, there can be more use of physically-settled forward contracts using increasingly standardised terms as a replacement for futures contracts that are settled financially.[19]

Arbitrage

In arbitrage, a party (the arbitrageur) capitalises on unjustifiable price differences over space or time.[20] Financial electricity contracts can be used on a naked basis without an offsetting position in the underlying reference assets. This reflects an opinion about the outlook of the reference asset. Similar mechanisms are generally used in financial markets regardless of the reference asset.[21]

One may ask whether speculation by index funds and other financial investors has an effect on the price of physical electricity. This does not seem to be the case. The fundamental cause of price volatility is not speculation but the physical characteristics of electricity, increased use of intermittent generation technologies, and the limited price elasticity of consumer demand. Even very small changes in electricity supply and electricity consumption can lead to large price shifts. Index funds and financial investors influence neither supply nor load. No market participant can hoard electricity, and no market participant can be party to physical electricity forwards or futures without grid access.[22]

Basis Trading

The third way to use electricity derivatives is basis trading. Financial electricity contracts can be used to replicate the cash flows of underlying physical contracts. Market participants can thus profit from pricing differences between financial electricity contracts and the underlying physical contracts by taking offsetting positions in the two.[23]

Standardisation

Financial electricity derivatives are based on relatively standardised terms regardless of whether they are exchange-traded or OTC-traded. Standardisation increases trading liquidity and price transparency and reduces transaction and monitoring costs.

Exchange-traded contracts must be highly standardised. Because of lower transaction costs, the delivery quantity specified in financial electricity contracts can be significantly smaller than in physically-settled electricity contracts. On the other hand, the high level of standardisation means that the specifications and the transaction quantities specified in the contracts are rigid.[24]

---

[19] *Ibid.*

[20] Pure arbitrage involves zero risk and no commitment of capital. Kristiansen T (2004), citing Khoury SJ (1984).

[21] For example, see IMF (2013), Chapter 2 for arbitrage in the context of SCDS contracts.

[22] For commodities in general, see OECD Trade and Agriculture Directorate (2010).

[23] For basis trading in the context of SCDS contracts, IMF (2013), Chapter 2.

[24] Deng SJ and Oren SS (2006), pp. 943–944 and 951.

The high level of standardisation of exchange-traded contracts means that market participants may not be able to hedge their risks perfectly. There is demand for custom-made financial electricity instruments regardless of the higher transactions costs.[25]

This can be illustrated with the area prices and system price used by Nord Pool Spot. (a) While an electricity producer is paid the area price in its area of production, an electricity consumer pays the area price for the consumption area. If electricity producers and consumers are located in different areas, there can be a difference between the area price and the system price of Nord Pool Spot because of congestion. (b) Where the reference price for financial futures contracts is the Nordic system price, a perfect hedge using these instruments would require the absence of congestion. (c) Market participants can thus need financial instruments to hedge against the difference between the area price and the system price.[26] There are also listed instruments for this purpose. In particular, they may use Electricity Price Area Differentials (EPAD).[27] These products allow exchange members to hedge against the area price risk. EPADs are exchange-traded CfDs.[28]

While the terms of exchange-traded contracts are standardised for obvious reasons, even OTC contracts tend to be standardised. It is customary to use a legal platform in OTC derivatives transactions.[29] The ISDA Master Agreement[30] has provided a way to reduce risk, in particular legal risks (general legal risks, transaction-specific legal risks, and contributory legal risks),[31] counterparty risks (counterparty corporate risk,[32] counterparty commercial risk,[33] and counterparty credit risk[34]), and systemic risk. In the EU, the EFET General Agreement is used as a legal platform for electricity forwards settled physically. The EFET General Agreement applies even to contracts for the purchase and sale of a physical option to buy electricity (call) or to sell electricity (put).[35]

Central Counterparty, Margins, Daily Settlement Central counterparties, margin requirements, and daily settlement are common practice for exchange-traded derivatives. There can be more variation in the OTC market, in particular to the extent

[25] Deng SJ and Oren SS (2006), p. 951.

[26] Kristiansen T (2004).

[27] For German and Nordic EPADs, see NASDAQ OMX, Trading Appendix 2/Clearing Appendix 2, Contract Specifications, Commodity Derivatives (24 November 2014).

[28] Energy Market Authority, Finland (2014), p. 23.

[29] For legal platforms, see Mäntysaari P (2010b), pp. 11–12.

[30] See, for example, duPont JC (2009), pp. 865–866.

[31] For legal risk, see Mäntysaari P (2010b), section 3.1.

[32] For counterparty corporate risk, see Mäntysaari P (2010b), section 6.2.

[33] For counterparty commercial risk, see Mäntysaari P (2010b), section 6.3.

[34] For counterparty credit risk, see Mäntysaari P (2010b), section 11.1.

[35] EFET General Agreement (Version 2.1(a)), § 1.1 and § 5.1.

that the products do not fall within the scope of EMIR and the mandatory clearing obligation.[36]

11.2 Exchange-Traded Electricity Futures

Electricity futures are contracts for the sale of a certain volume of electricity (the underlying asset) at a pre-defined price at a given time in the future.[37]

In the futures market, financial settlement links the futures price to the spot price. Futures prices and spot prices tend to converge where a party, at maturity, may choose between physical delivery (that is, the registration of underlying contract positions) or cash settlement.[38]

Trading Electricity futures are traded on organised venues. They can be exchange-traded or available for clearing as OTC products. The clearing of OTC electricity derivatives is regulated by EMIR.[39] Central counterparties can therefore offer to clear OTC-traded futures in addition to exchange-traded futures. We will focus on exchange-traded electricity futures.

Purpose Like derivatives in general, electricity futures can be used in various ways. (a) They can be used for risk management (hedging). The risk of falling power prices can be managed by the sale of futures contracts (short hedge) and the risk of increasing power prices by the purchase of futures contracts (long hedge). (b) Electricity futures can also be used for arbitrage or speculation. For instance, there can be price differences between exchange-traded futures and similar contracts traded over-the-counter. In this case, a market participant can buy the cheaper derivatives and sell the expensive derivatives. A speculator may assume risks with a contrary view of the market.[40]

Terminology In the following, we will call all financially-settled contracts of this type electricity *futures*.[41] This reflects European practices. Financially-settled contracts are likely to be called futures in Europe.

[36] Article 4(1) of Regulation 648/2012 (EMIR).

[37] EEX Product Brochure Power (7 August 2012), section 3.1.1. NASDAQ OMX, Trading Appendix 1/Clearing Appendix 1, Definitions, Commodity Derivatives (27 April 2014).

[38] Rud L (2009).

[39] Articles 1(1) and 4(1) of Regulation 648/2012 (EMIR).

[40] EEX Product Brochure Power (7 August 2012), section 3.1.2.

[41] For the terminology of the General Court, see Joined Cases T-80/06 and T-182/09 Budapesti Erőmű Zrt v Commission, ECLI:EU:T:2012:65, para 72: "... In 'forward' markets, power is traded for delivery further ahead in time ..." See, for example, Hünerwadel A (2007), pp. 57–58: "Bei finanziellen Stromfutures vereinbaren die Parteien, die Preisdifferenz zwischen dem vereinbarten Preis und dem zukünftigen Marktpreis für eine definierte Stromlieferung in bar auszugleichen".

The difference seems to be a matter of convention rather than law and depend on the market. Both futures and forwards are contracts for the sale of a certain volume of electricity (the underlying asset) at a pre-defined price at a given time in the future.[42] Both can be settled physically or financially depending on the contract and the market. Both can be traded in the physical market or in the financial market. In practice, futures and forward contracts can also be regarded as equivalents as far as the hedging result is concerned.

US. In the US, the terminology is connected to the division of authority between the CFTC and the SEC. One of the two traditional ways to allocate authority over new financial products is to look at the product and ask whether it meets the definition of a security or a future.[43] The Commodity Exchange Act of 1936 (CEA) does not define the term futures contract. Futures are simply customised, exchange-traded forwards. In forwards, the buyer agrees to pay a specified price at a future date, while the seller agrees to deliver an asset.[44]

The terminology is also based on convention. Contracts called futures contracts are often regarded as standardised exchange-traded products that are market-to-marked on a daily basis via a margin account. Contracts called forward contracts are traded over-the-counter and settled at expiration. However, most commodity futures contracts are settled by delivery of the underlying asset.[45]

Auctioning Regulation. The difference between futures and forwards under the EU Auctioning Regulation is that futures are subject to cash variation margining but forwards are variation margined through non-cash collateral.[46]

EEX. On EEX, the main distinction is between futures and options. All unconditional contracts traded on EEX are called futures contracts. Electricity futures are settled either physically or financially depending on the contract terms.[47]

Nasdaq Commodities. In the past, both futures and forwards were defined in the Commodity Derivatives Definitions of NASDAQ OMX Commodities. Both were settled in cash. Electricity forwards could have a longer maturity. The main difference between electricity forwards and electricity futures was that electricity futures were subject to daily market settlement.[48] On the other hand, allowance contracts traded on NASDAQ OMX Commodities were settled physically. Such contracts included CER forwards (standardised forward contracts for Certified Emission Reduction units)

---

[42] See EEX Product Brochure Power (7 August 2012), section 3.1.1; NASDAQ OMX, Trading Appendix 1/Clearing Appendix 1, Definitions, Commodity Derivatives (7 April 2014).

[43] duPont JC (2009), p. 861.

[44] duPont JC (2009), pp. 861–862.

[45] Pirrong C (2001), p. 221.

[46] Recital 16 and Article 3 of Regulation 1031/2010 (Auctioning Regulation).

[47] See EEX Product Brochure Power (17 August 2012), section 3.1.1; EEX Products 2014, p. 1: "On the EEX Power Derivatives Market financially settled futures for Germany/Austria (Phelix Futures), France (French Futures) and Italy (Italian Futures) and Phelix Options can be traded. In addition, physical French, Dutch and Belgian Power Futures can be traded".

[48] NASDAQ OMX, Trading Appendix 1/Clearing Appendix 1, Definitions, Commodity Derivatives (26 November 2012): "Forward Contract or Forward means a Contract specified as such in the Contract Specifications for the purchase and sale of a particular quantity of an asset or the cash equivalent of the asset's value against a Contract Base or Fix, at a predetermined price at a future time or time period ..."

and EUA forwards (standardised forward contracts for European Union Allowance units).

The contract types mentioned in the 2014 NASDAQ OMX Contract Specifications are futures and options.[49] Forwards are not defined in the NASDAQ OMX Definitions.[50] On the other hand, the legal framework distinguishes between Futures and DS Futures. Like before, Futures are subject to daily market settlement.[51] Like the earlier Forwards, DS Futures (Deferred Settlement Futures) are not subject to daily market settlement.[52] Futures, DS Futures, and Options relate to various product types. The offered product types are electricity contracts, natural gas contracts, allowance contracts, Swedish and Norwegian electricity certificates (El-Certs) contracts, and freight and fuel oil contracts. Electricity contracts and allowance contracts are Futures, DS Futures, or Options. El-Certs Contracts are Futures or DS Futures. Natural gas contracts are Futures.

Contracts for Difference Electricity futures that are settled financially are contracts for difference. What is settled is the difference between the contract price and the market price. Payment obligations under such contracts are unconditional but variable.

In contrast, payment obligations are unconditional and fixed where electricity forwards are settled physically.[53]

It is, therefore, necessary to define the method of calculating the difference. The market price of the underlying physical electricity contracts cannot be defined without choosing the attributes that are characteristic to electricity supply agreements. These attributes include the delivery period, the load profile, the place of delivery, and the contract volume.[54]

---

[49] See NASDAQ OMX, Trading Appendix 2/Clearing Appendix 2, Contract Specifications, Commodity Derivatives (24 November 2014).

[50] NASDAQ OMX, Trading Appendix 1/Clearing Appendix 1, Definitions, Commodity Derivatives (7 April 2014).

[51] NASDAQ OMX, Trading Appendix 1/Clearing Appendix 1, Definitions, Commodity Derivatives (7 April 2014): "... Futures Contract or Future means a Contract specified as such in the Contract Specifications, and which is subject to Daily Market Settlement, for the purchase and sale of a particular quantity of an asset, or the cash equivalent of the asset against a Contract Base or Fix, at a predetermined price at a specified future time or time period ..."

[52] NASDAQ OMX, Trading Appendix 1/Clearing Appendix 1, Definitions, Commodity Derivatives (7 April 2014): "... DS Futures Contract or DS Future means a Contract specified as such in the Contract Specifications for the purchase and sale of a particular quantity of an asset or the cash equivalent of the asset's value against a Contract Base or Fix, at a predetermined price at a future time or time period ..."

[53] EEX Product Brochure Power (13 April 2011), section 3.2 (as it then was): "In the case of futures with physical settlement, the seller and the buyer agree to deliver or pay power with a certain quantity, a certain load profile and place of delivery at the price agreed on during a given period of time in the future upon the conclusion of the transaction".

[54] EEX Product Brochure Power (7 August 2012), section 3.2.

In the EEX Derivatives Market, for instance, the *delivery periods* that can be traded are weeks (Week Futures), months (Month Futures), quarters (Quarter Futures), and years (Year Futures).[55] The *load profiles* which can be traded on EEX are base load, peak load and off-peak load.[56] The *place of delivery* depends on the futures product. Depending on the product, the place of delivery can mean the admissible balancing zones of the EEX Spot Market, the balancing zone of the German RWE Transportnetz Strom GmbH, or the balancing zone of the French RTE.[57] The *contract volume* means the quantity of power on which the futures contract is based. It is the product of "delivery rate × delivery days × delivery hours/ day". The delivery rate (power volume per hour) of the futures contract is 1 MW.[58]

Margins and Settlement As both the seller (that has a short position) and the buyer (that has a long position) have obligations that must be settled, both the holder of the long position and the holder of the short position are required to furnish collateral (margins).

Financial electricity futures are customarily settled daily during the term of the contract before final settlement. This means that contract parties either receive payments of money or have to effect payments throughout the entire period until the end of the delivery period or until the position is closed. There are daily margin calls in addition to daily cash settlement.

The customary daily margin calls and daily cash settlement are used on Nasdaq Commodities[59] and EEX.[60] There are even other margin calls (Sect. 4.6.2).

The amount payable by a party during the term of the contract depends on the change in the value of the position. The change in the value is calculated based on the difference in the daily settlement prices of the current and of the preceding business day. Only net payments will be invoiced.

This principle is shared by Nasdaq Commodities[61] and EEX.[62]

The amount of collateral calls is reduced by the fact that the futures position is assessed on a "mark-to-market" basis every day and the generated profits and losses are balanced in terms of liquidity. What matters is just the possible price change during the next exchange trading day. The clearing house demands collateral covering the maximum closing-out costs to be expected in the event of the most unfavourable price development during the next exchange trading day.

[55] EEX Product Brochure Power (7 August 2012), section 3.2.1.

[56] EEX Product Brochure Power (7 August 2012), section 3.2.2.

[57] EEX Product Brochure Power (7 August 2012), section 3.2.3.

[58] EEX Product Brochure Power (7 August 2012), section 3.2.4.

[59] NASDAQ OMX Clearing AB, General Terms, Clearing Rules, Commodity Derivatives (9 June 2014), sections 5.3.1 and 6.2.1.

[60] ECC Clearing Conditions (0022a, 30 April 2014), section 4.2.1.2.

[61] NASDAQ OMX, Trading Appendix 2/Clearing Appendix 2, Contract Specifications, Commodity Derivatives (24 November 2014), Part A, section 5.1.2; NASDAQ OMX Clearing AB, General Terms, Clearing Rules, Commodity Derivatives (9 June 2014), section 6.2.1.

[62] ECC Clearing Conditions (0022a, 30 April 2014), section 3.4.7(1).

The settlement method can be complemented by cascading when the delivery period is long, such as a year or a quarter. Cascading means that the contract is replaced with equivalent futures contracts with shorter delivery periods on the last day of trading.

In the EEX Derivatives Market, year futures and quarter futures are fulfilled by cascading. To illustrate, three exchange trading days before the beginning of the delivery period, every position in year futures is replaced by equivalent positions in month futures for January, February and March and quarter futures for the second, third and fourth quarter, whose delivery periods taken together correspond to the year.[63]

Cascading is also used on Nasdaq Commodities. There is mandatory cascading for open positions in some series. Cascaded series normally spans the same delivery period as the original series. For instance, a year series are transformed to four quarter series spanning the same year.[64]

The final settlement price is the settlement price upon expiry. In the case of futures subject to cascading, the final settlement price defines the value of the position to be cascaded. In the case of futures not subject to cascading because of their shorter delivery period (a week or a month), the final settlement price constitutes the basis for the calculation of the cash settlement.

11.3 Exchange-Traded Electricity Options

Electricity options are used by electricity suppliers and buyers to protect themselves against price changes in the physical market. Electricity producers can use electricity options even to increase revenue.

Option An option gives a right to buy (call options) or sell (put options) the underlying asset at a fixed price in the future. Depending on the marketplace, the buyer may also be called the purchaser or the option holder, and the seller may also be called the option issuer or option writer.[65]

Electricity call options offer the purchaser the right, but not the obligation, to buy physically settled electricity contracts at a pre-specified price by the option expiration time. Put options offer a similar right to sell physically settled electricity contracts.

In return, the seller of the option (buy/call option or sell/put option) receives the option price (premium) paid by the buyer of the option. Table 11.1 shows the different option rights and duties.

---

[63] EEX Product Brochure Power (7 August 2012), section 4.2.2.

[64] NASDAQ OMX, Trading Appendix 1/Clearing Appendix 1, Definitions, Commodity Derivatives (7 April 2014). NASDAQ OMX, Trading Appendix 2/Clearing Appendix 2, Contract Specifications, Commodity Derivatives (24 November 2014), Part, A, section 5.7.

[65] NASDAQ OMX, Trading Appendix 2/Clearing Appendix 2, Contract Specifications, Commodity Derivatives (24 November 2014), Part A, section 2.2.1.

Table 11.1 Option rights and duties[a]

Buyer of a call option	Seller of a call option	Buyer of a put option	Seller of a put option
Has the right to buy the underlying asset at the agreed exercise price but has no duty to do so.	Has the duty to sell the underlying asset at the agreed exercise price if the buy option (call) is exercised.	Has the right to sell the underlying asset at the agreed exercise price but has no duty to do so.	Has the duty to buy the underlying asset at the agreed exercise price if the sell option (put) is exercised.

[a]EEX Product Brochure Power (7 August 2012), section 3.4.1, Table 3.1

When the option is not in the money on the expiry day, the buyer will not exercise the option but lets it expire. The losses of the buyer are thus limited to the premium. The seller of the option is exposed to the risk that an option which is in the money is exercised by the buyer on the expiry day. In this case, the difference between the exercise price and the market price for the underlying contract means that the seller will make a loss. The option premium is the price of this risk.[66]

These four basic derivatives transactions—buy of a call option, sell of a call option, buy of a put option, sell of a put option—can be combined in various ways.[67] For example, a market participant may use volatility or investment strategies such as “straddles” and “strangles”.

Intrinsic Value and Fair Value An option has an intrinsic value and a fair value. (a) An option has intrinsic value when it permits buying or selling of the underlying asset at a favourable price than on the market at the time of the assessment. An option that has an intrinsic value of more than zero is in-the-money. An option without intrinsic value is out-of-the-money. At-the-money means that the exercise price corresponds to the market price of the underlying asset.[68] (b) Its fair value relates to opportunity and risk. It comprises the possibility that the buyer’s expectations regarding the development of the underlying asset might be fulfilled during the remaining term to maturity.[69] The fair value therefore depends on the volatility of the price of the underlying asset (the higher the volatility, the higher the fair value). It will also depend on the remaining term (the closer the last day of trading,

[66] See EEX Product Brochure Power (7 August 2012), section 3.5.

[67] Spicker J (2010), p. 101, points 155–156.

[68] EEX Product Brochure Power (7 August 2012), section 3.4.10.

[69] EEX Product Brochure Power (7 August 2012), section 3.4.10.

Table 11.2 Option prices[a]

The price of a buy option (call)	
The price of a call option is *higher*, when • the price of the underlying asset is higher • the exercise price is lower • the remaining term to expiry is longer • the volatility is higher • the interest rate is lower	The price of a call option is *lower*, when • the price of the underlying asset is lower • the exercise price is higher • the remaining term to expiry is shorter • the volatility is lower • the interest rate is higher
The price of a sell option (put)	
The price of a put option is *higher*, when • the price of the underlying asset is lower • the exercise price is higher • the remaining term to expiry is longer • the volatility is higher • the interest rate is lower	The price of a put option is *lower*, when • the price of the underlying asset is higher • the exercise price is lower • the remaining term to expiry is shorter • the volatility is lower • the interest rate is higher

[a]EEX Product Brochure Power (7 August 2012), 3.4.10, Tables 3.4 and 3.5

the lower the fair value). The fair value amounts to zero on the last date the option may be exercised.[70]

Option Price (Premium) The option price (the premium) depends on many things. Generally, the option price (the premium) consists of the option's intrinsic value (positive or zero) and fair value (positive or zero). Table 11.2 shows the customary factors that increase or reduce the price of a buy (call) option and the customary factors that increase or reduce the price of a sell (put) option.

Purpose Electricity options are used for hedging purposes (a) by electricity suppliers and consumers as well as (b) by electricity producers.

Electricity suppliers and end consumers can use them to protect themselves against price changes in the physical market. The option buyer can replace its exposure to price risk by the price that it pays for the option (the premium). (a) Call options enable a party to buy protection against rising electricity prices. Where the price of the electricity future exceeds the contract price and the premium on maturity, the party exercises the option and realises the difference as profit. (b) Put options enable a party to buy protection against falling electricity prices. Where the price of the electricity future falls below the contract price less the premium, the buyer may again want to exercise the option and realise the difference as profit.[71]

The use of call options can be illustrated with the following example.[72] An industrial firm with a base load of 25 MW needs to purchase power for the month of May. To be competitive, the firm cannot pay more than €X/MWh and prefers to pay as little as possible.

[70] EEX Product Brochure Power (7 August 2012), section 3.4.10.

[71] Lokau B and Ritzau M (2009), § 5, number 31.

[72] EEX Product Brochure Power (7 August 2012), section 3.6.2, Industrial enterprise buys a buy option (call).

The firm assumes that the futures price will fall, but its internal risk management guidelines require the firm to cover its energy needs now. By buying a buy option (call), the firm secures both supply and a maximum purchase price (the premium and the exercise price, €X/MWh or less).

Electricity producers may use electricity options even to optimise production and increase revenue. Where the production costs at a plant exceed the physical market price, the generator does not use the plant. However, it can increase revenue by selling a buy option (call) with its generation costs as the exercise price. The buy option (call) will not be exercised, if the exercise price is higher than physical market prices. But the firm has already received the premium and may still sell power in the physical market due. The buy option will be exercised, if physical market prices are higher than the exercise price. In this case, the firm's profit is limited to the premium.[73]

Electricity suppliers may need options even because of customer preferences. Many customers prefer supply contracts that include a flexible volume term and a fixed rate per kWh/MWh regardless of actual consumption. However, a supplier must try to balance the load in advance. Where the supplier uses forward contracts (or physically settled futures contracts) with fixed volume terms, there can be a difference between the volume purchased by the supplier and the customer's actual load. The supplier can mitigate risk by buying an option to purchase additional electricity at a fixed price.[74]

The Underlying Asset, the Spread The underlying asset customarily consists of exchange-traded electricity futures or physical electricity.[75] One can distinguish between electricity options that are contracts for difference and electricity options that are settled physically. This section focuses on financial electricity options that are contracts for difference. There are also particular spread options (Sect. 11.4).

There are different kinds of spreads and spread traders in the energy markets. One can distinguish between temporal spread traders (that try to take advantage of the differences in prices of the same commodity at two different dates in the future), locational spread traders (that try to hedge transportation/transmission risk exposure from futures contracts on the same commodity with physical deliveries at two different locations), and particular spread traders that deal with at least two different physical commodities.[76]

Trading and Clearing Financial electricity options can be traded on an electricity exchange or OTC. In Europe, cash-settled options on futures are traded on

---

[73] EEX Product Brochure Power (7 August 2012), section 3.6.1, Power plant operator sells a buy option (call).

[74] U.S. Energy Information Administration (2002), Chapter 4.

[75] Deng SJ and Oren SS (2006), p. 945.

[76] Carmona R and Durrleman V (2003), p. 634.

electricity exchanges. Other kinds of cash-settled electricity options can be OTC traded.

Exchange-traded financial electricity options can be created by using exchange-traded electricity futures as the underlying asset. Trading participants hold positions on the option market by buying and selling options. Positions in options can be "long" (buyer) or "short" (seller). They can be closed out by means of a matching transaction in the same option contract. A buy position is thus closed out by a corresponding sell position.[77] Closing out is not the same thing as fulfilment. Exchange-traded options are fulfilled by booking in the corresponding futures position at the exercise price when the option is exercised.[78]

Both exchange-traded and OTC-traded options can be cleared in the same way. Clearing is mandatory under EMIR for all standardised options.[79]

The power options that could be traded in the EEX Power Derivatives Market in 2014 were options on Phelix base-load futures with a maturity of 1 month, 3 months, or 1 year.[80] OTC transactions in these option contracts and/or in similar contracts can be submitted to ECC for clearing. Exchange-traded and OTC-traded options are cleared in the same way. Consequently, an option position can be opened on the exchange and closed out over the counter, or vice versa.[81]

On Nasdaq Commodities, Nordic Electricity Base DS Future Year Options are based on the Nordic Electricity Base Year DS Future contract,[82] and Nordic Electricity Base DS Future Quarter Options are based on the Nordic Electricity Base Quarterly Electricity DS Future contract.[83] NASDAQ OMX Clearing AB, the clearing house of Nasdaq Commodities, provides even OTC clearing.[84]

Margins The duty to make margin payments is one sided in option contracts. The buyer has no duty to furnish margins, because the buyer has already fulfilled its side of the deal by paying the premium. On the other hand, the seller of the option must furnish margins, because the seller has to make payments in the event that the buyer chooses to exercise the option.[85]

[77] EEX Product Brochure Power (7 August 2012), section 3.4.1.

[78] EEX Contract Specifications (0041a, 22 November 2014), section 5.7.1; Hünerwadel A (2007), pp. 57–58.

[79] Article 4(1) of Regulation 648/2012 (EMIR).

[80] EEX Contract Specifications (0041a, 22 November 2014), section 2.6.5.

[81] EEX Product Brochure Power (7 August 2012), section 3.4.2.

[82] NASDAQ OMX, Trading Appendix 2/Clearing Appendix 2, Contract Specifications, Commodity Derivatives (24 November 2014), Part D, section 1.41.

[83] NASDAQ OMX, Trading Appendix 2/Clearing Appendix 2, Contract Specifications, Commodity Derivatives (24 November 2014), Part D, section 1.42.

[84] NASDAQ OMX, Clearing Appendix 4, Non Exchange Clearing Procedures, Commodity Derivatives (16 June 2014), section 1.1.

[85] EEX Product Brochure Power (7 August 2012), sections 4.4 and 3.5.

The ECC Clearing Conditions set out in detail how margins are established. Margins are based on net positions in all option series and futures contracts.[86] There is a premium margin (for the costs of potential closing out at the settlement price)[87] and an additional margin (which covers the changes in the close-out costs for all option positions in case the most unfavourable price development until the next calculation of margins established by ECC occurs).[88]

Similar principles are applied on Nasdaq Commodities. There are daily margin calls[89] according to the general terms of the clearing rules.[90]

Settlement The settlement of financial electricity options has its particular characteristics. (a) One can distinguish between the settlement of the premium and the settlement of other aspects of the financial electricity option. (b) One can also distinguish between the financial and physical settlement of financial electricity options. (c) Settlement depends on whether the option is exercised or expires. (d) Moreover, there is a difference between American-style settlement and European-style settlement.

The premium is payable after closing. The option is settled later.[91]

In the EEX Derivatives Market, the premium is payable on the first trading day after closing.[92]

On Nasdaq Commodities, the premium settlement is included in the daily cash settlement amount on the first bank day following the day on which the option is registered as a clearing transaction.[93]

There is no daily settlement of the value of the option. However, there may be daily margin payments.

There is no daily settlement of the change in the value of the option on EEX.[94] There are nevertheless margin payments that depend on the costs of potential closing out at the settlement price.[95]

---

86 ECC Clearing Conditions (0022a, 30 April 2014), section 4.1.

87 ECC Clearing Conditions (0022a, 30 April 2014), section 4.2.3.3(1).

88 ECC Clearing Conditions (0022a, 30 April 2014), section 4.2.3.3(2).

89 NASDAQ OMX, Trading Appendix 1/Clearing Appendix 1, Definitions, Commodity Derivatives (7 April 2014). NASDAQ OMX Clearing AB, General Terms, Clearing Rules, Commodity Derivatives (9 June 2014), section 5.3.1.

90 NASDAQ OMX Clearing AB, General Terms, Clearing Rules, Commodity Derivatives (9 June 2014), section 5.1.1.

91 Lokau B and Ritzau M (2009), § 5, number 29.

92 ECC Clearing Conditions (0022a, 30 April 2014), section 4.2.3.2(1).

93 NASDAQ OMX, Trading Appendix 2/Clearing Appendix 2, Contract Specifications, Commodity Derivatives (24 November 2014), Part A, sections 5.4.1 and 5.4.2.

94 ECC Clearing Conditions (0022a, 30 April 2014), section 4.2.3.2(2).

95 ECC Clearing Conditions (0022a, 30 April 2014), section 4.2.3.3(1) on the Premium Margin and section 4.2.3.3(2) on the Additional Margin.

On Nasdaq Commodities, open positions in options will be settled at the option exercise time.[96] There are margin calls according to the general terms of the clearing rules.[97]

In principle, financial electricity options could be settled in three different ways depending on the terms of the option. (a) They could be settled in cash through the payment of the difference between the agreed price and value of the underlying futures contract (contracts for difference). (b) Where the options are exchange-traded, one could open futures positions for the parties (a long position and a short position). (c) The futures positions could lead to the physical delivery of power when the futures positions are settled, or be settled in cash.[98]

One can therefore distinguish between financial electricity options settled: (a) in cash; (b) by registering underlying contract positions and settling the underlying position in cash; or (c) by registering underlying contract positions and settling the underlying position by physical delivery.

On Nasdaq Commodities, financial electricity options are settled by registering new clearing transactions. The exercise price of the option is registered as the contract price for the underlying forward contract.[99] The financial electricity options are nevertheless contracts settled "financially", because the forward positions are settled in cash only.[100]

On EEX, the clearing house opens futures positions for the parties. The futures positions can lead to the physical delivery of power when the Phelix Futures are settled physically.[101] The trading participant can combine the financial fulfilment of its positions in Phelix Futures with a physical delivery or partial delivery.[102]

Exercising An electricity option expires unless it is exercised. Whether the option is exercised in fact depends on its intrinsic value.

The fact that electricity options can have intrinsic value influences the way electricity options are exercised. The exercising of options can be organised in various ways depending on the marketplace. In principle, options could be exercised on every trading day or the last trading day, and the exercising of electricity options could be automatic or explicit.

---

[96] NASDAQ OMX, Trading Appendix 2/Clearing Appendix 2, Contract Specifications, Commodity Derivatives (24 November 2014), Part A, section 5.5.1.

[97] NASDAQ OMX, Trading Appendix 2/Clearing Appendix 2, Contract Specifications, Commodity Derivatives (24 November 2014), Part B, section 1.4. NASDAQ OMX Clearing AB, General Terms, Clearing Rules, Commodity Derivatives (9 June 2014), section 5.1.1.

[98] Hünerwadel A (2007), pp. 57–58.

[99] NASDAQ OMX, Trading Appendix 2/Clearing Appendix 2, Contract Specifications, Commodity Derivatives (24 November 2014), Part B, section 5.6.1.

[100] NASDAQ OMX, Trading Appendix 2/Clearing Appendix 2, Contract Specifications, Com modity Derivatives (24 November 2014), Part D, section 1.41, Nordic Electricity Base DS Future Year Option. Part D, section 1.32 Nordic Electricity Base Year DS Future.

[101] EEX Product Brochure Power (7 August 2012), section 3.4.4.

[102] EEX Product Brochure Power (7 August 2012), section 4.2.3.

There is a difference between American-style options and European-style options as regards the point in time when the option may be exercised. If the option is an American-style option, the buyer can exercise the option right on every exchange trading day until the last trading day. Such options can thus be exercised in a flexible way according to price changes in the wholesale market.[103] If the option is a European-style option, the buyer can exercise it only on the last trading day.[104]

Options traded on the EEX Derivatives Market are European-style options exercised on the last day of trading.[105] Options traded on Nasdaq Commodities are exercised on the expiration day.[106] Physically-settled American-style electricity options can be traded in the OTC market.[107]

Moreover, electricity options could be exercised expressly or automatically. (a) One alternative would thus be to require express notification of the exercise of the option. (b) On the other hand, the exercising of options could also be automatic as the clearing house can determine their value. If the rules of the marketplace provide for automatic exercising, the default rule is that the clearing house exercises the option on behalf of the buyer where the option has positive intrinsic value. (c) Automatic exercising can be combined with an opt-out rule. In this case, the buyer may choose not to exercise the option whether it has value or not.

On Nasdaq Commodities, option exercise takes place either by Standard Exercise or by Manual Exercise. (a) Standard Exercise is the default rule.[108] It means that the clearing house exercises the option automatically on behalf of the account holder.[109] The default rule is complemented by rules on the Option Fix, that is, rules on how the price is calculated for the purposes of the automatic exercise of options.[110] Automatic Exercise depends on the value of the option.[111] (b) Manual Exercise is the opt-out mechanism. It means that the

[103] Lokau B and Ritzau M (2009), § 5, number 32; Fried J (2010), p. 282, point 493.

[104] EEX Product Brochure Power (7 August 2012), section 3.4.1.

[105] See, for example, EEX Contract Specifications (0041a, 22 November 2014), sections 2.6.3 and 2.6.8.

[106] NASDAQ OMX, Trading Appendix 2/Clearing Appendix 2, Contract Specifications, Commodity Derivatives (24 November 2014), Part A, section 5.5.2.

[107] Lokau B and Ritzau M (2009), § 5, number 32.

[108] NASDAQ OMX, Trading Appendix 2/Clearing Appendix 2, Contract Specifications, Commodity Derivatives (24 November 2014), Part A, section 5.5.2(c).

[109] NASDAQ OMX, Trading Appendix 2/Clearing Appendix 2, Contract Specifications, Commodity Derivatives (24 November 2014), Part A, section 5.5.2(a).

[110] NASDAQ OMX, Trading Appendix 1/Clearing Appendix 1, Definitions, Commodity Derivatives (7 April 2014). NASDAQ OMX, Trading Appendix 2/Clearing Appendix 2, Contract Specifications, Commodity Derivatives (24 November 2014), Part A, section 4.6.1.

[111] See, for example, NASDAQ OMX, Trading Appendix 2/Clearing Appendix 2, Contract Specifications, Commodity Derivatives (24 November 2014), Part D, section 1.41 Nordic Electricity Base DS Future Year Option.

account holder can send an exercise order to the clearing house. The option will be exercised or not exercised according to the exercise order.[112]

In the EEX Derivatives Market, the default form is automatic exercising. Manual exercising is the opt-out mechanism.[113]

Registration of Contract Positions If the option is not settled in cash, the exercising of financial electricity options on futures means that corresponding and opposite futures positions are opened for the buyer and the seller. Where a buy (call) option on a certain future is exercised, a long position in the future is opened for the buyer of the option, and a short position is opened for the seller of the option. Where a sell (put) option on the future is exercised, a short position is opened for the option buyer and a long position for the option seller.[114] In other words:

- Exercise of a call option leads to a long position in futures.
- Assignment of a call option leads to a short position in futures.
- Assignment of a put option leads to a long position in futures.
- Exercise of a put option leads to a short position in futures.[115]

On Nasdaq Commodities, the procedure is explained as follows: "… a new Clearing Transaction reflecting the Contract Base of the Option Contract is automatically and immediately registered to the Option Holders and the Option Writer's applicable Clearing Accounts. The Option Holder will be registered as buyer of the Contract Base in respect of a call Option, and as seller in respect of a put Option. The Option Writer will be registered with the opposite position. The Exercise Price of the Option Contract will be registered as the Contract Price for the Contract Base ('delivery to strike')".[116] Similar rules apply on EEX.[117]

Obviously, the central counterparty cannot register the opposite futures positions, unless the futures exist. On an exchange, the central counterparty allocates the necessary futures to the parties.

On Nasdaq Commodities, the clearing house randomly selects corresponding contracts.[118] On EEX, the clearing house (ECC AG) applies "a procedure maintaining the neutrality of the assignment process".[119]

---

[112] NASDAQ OMX, Trading Appendix 2/Clearing Appendix 2, Contract Specifications, Commodity Derivatives (24 November 2014), Part A, section 5.5.2(b).

[113] EEX Product Brochure Power (7 August 2012), section 3.4.3. See, for example, EEX Contract Specifications (0041a, 22 November 2014), section 2.6.8.

[114] EEX Product Brochure Power (7 August 2012), section 3.4.4.

[115] EEX Product Brochure Power (7 August 2012), section 3.4.1, table 3.3.

[116] NASDAQ OMX, Trading Appendix 2/Clearing Appendix 2, Contract Specifications, Commodity Derivatives (24 November 2014), Part A, section 5.5.3. See also Part A, section 5.5.4.

[117] EEX Contract Specifications (0041a, 22 November 2014), sections 5.7.1 and 2.6.1.

[118] NASDAQ OMX, Trading Appendix 2/Clearing Appendix 2, Contract Specifications, Commodity Derivatives (24 November 2014), Part A, section 5.5.4.

[119] EEX Contract Specifications (0041a, 22 November 2014), section 5.7.2.

11.4 Spark-Spread Options

Natural gas and oil-fired plants are customarily used for peak production. When there is a strong correlation between electricity prices and fuel prices, market participants may use the fuel market as an alternative means to hedge their exposure to electricity prices.[120] On the other hand, they can also use spark-spread options.[121]

Spark-spread options are cross-commodity options designed to minimise differences between the price of electricity and the price of fuels that electricity producers use to generate the electricity.[122] They are typically OTC-traded (for the contractual framework and the ISDA Master Agreement, see Sect. 11.6).

Spark Spread The key concepts here are spread options and the spark spread. (a) The spark spread is the margin that can be earned by buying fuels, using them to produce power, and then selling the power. In other words, the spark spread is the electricity price less the fuel cost of generating a unit of electricity at given power plant efficiency. (b) A spread option is an option written on the difference of two underlying assets.[123] In the energy markets, the most frequently quoted spread options are crack-spread options and spark-spread options.[124] (c) There are various kinds of spark spreads and spark-spread options. By definition, spark spreads do not include operation, maintenance, or transport costs.[125] There are also dark spreads,[126] clean spark spreads,[127] and clean dark spreads.[128] In addition to spark-spread options, the spark-spread hedging instruments include spark-spread swaps and spark-spread swaptions. Clean spark-spread options are spark-spread options that take into account the price of emission allowances.[129]

Relevance Spark-spread options enable generators to hedge effectively. A power plant is unhedged if it sells electricity on the spot market (at variable prices) and purchases fuel on the spot market (at variable prices). For example, the operator of a natural gas power plant that buys gas and sells electricity in this way may need to manage the risk of changes in the difference between gas and electricity prices. Spark-spread options can help to fix the price difference.[130]

In addition to hedging, spark-spread options increase liquidity through speculation by fuel producers and other market participants.

---

[120] Ofgem (2009), para 3.83.

[121] See, for example, Carmona R and Durrleman V (2003).

[122] U.S. Energy Information Administration (2002), Chapter 4.

[123] Carmona R and Durrleman V (2003), p. 628.

[124] Carmona R and Durrleman V (2003), pp. 634–635.

[125] DG Energy, Market Observatory for Energy (2013), Glossary.

[126] *Ibid.*

[127] *Ibid.*

[128] *Ibid.*

[129] Maribu KM et al. (2007), p. 176.

[130] Fried J (2010), p. 285, point 500.

Rights In a spark spread option, you must first define the spark spread. The spark spread depends on technology. The amount of fuel that a power plant burns to produce one unit of electricity depends on the power plant's fuel efficiency or heat rate. Heat rate is the ratio of energy input required to produce one unit of power output. The standard unit for heat rate is expressed in Btu/kWh.[131]

The holder of a spark-spread call option written on fuel X at a fixed heat rate Y has the right, but not the obligation, to pay at the option's maturity Y times the fuel price at maturity time, and receive the price of one unit of electricity.[132] Spark-spread options thus pay out the difference between the price of electricity sold by electricity producers and the price of the fuels used to generate it.

Users Spark-spread options can be used by the owners of power plants, producers of fuel (in particular, natural gas), and electricity suppliers.

For example, the owner of a natural gas power plant with operational flexibility can hedge profits by buying spark-spread options for future delivery. Spark-spread options would not prevent it from adjusting later generation according to the development of energy prices.[133]

Gas producers are natural buyers of spark-spread call options. They enable gas producers to obtain "virtual generation" capacity (Sect. 8.2.3) and participate in the electricity market. (a) Although a gas producer might be interested in investing in power plants, it could be unwilling to lock up additional capital into these fixed assets because of funding constraints. Moreover, many gas producers do not possess expertise in electricity generation. (b) Spark-spread call options enable a gas producer to replace power plants with virtual generation capacity. By paying an up-front premium, it obtains a chance to benefit when electricity is very expensive compared to gas. The gas producer can then exercise the option and earn more profit. However, a net loss may occur where the option expires out of the money because of a low gas price.[134]

For electricity suppliers, spark-spread call options are closely related to tolling agreements (Sect. 8.2.3). A spark-spread call option is equivalent to owning a power plant with operational flexibility if one disregards operational costs and operational constraints.[135] (a) In a tolling arrangement, the buyer supplies the fuel and obtains the right to use generation assets to produce power. The owner of the power plant receives a payment that can be fixed or variable or a combination thereof. (b) In a reverse tolling arrangement, the power marketer arranges to exchange power for fuel based on the conversion heat rate. The reverse tolling

[131] Hsu M (1998), p. 29.

[132] Deng SJ and Oren SS (2006), p. 945.

[133] Maribu KM et al. (2007), p. 173.

[134] Hsu M (1998), p. 37. See also Ofgem (2009), para 3.83, footnote 56.

[135] Maribu KM et al. (2007), p. 176; Deng SJ and Oren SS (2006), p. 945.

arrangement means in effect the unwinding of fixed-price contracts when the market heat rate is below the unit's operating heat rate.[136]

Spark-spread options can also be used for valuing operationally flexible electricity generation assets that can quickly be taken into use when prices are high.[137]

11.5 Electricity Swaps

11.5.1 General Remarks

A swap means a contract for the exchange of financial flows. A swap contract thus has two "legs". In financial markets, the most basic OTC swap transaction is the "plain vanilla interest rate swap" in which a debtor with fixed-rate liabilities agrees to swap interest payments with a debtor who has floating-rate liabilities (fix-for-floating-swaps).[138]

Now, electricity prices can be fixed or variable. Whether fixed or variable, the price term in long-term contracts is combined with exposure to risk. (a) Prices are often referenced to a variable spot price at either a generator's or a consumer's location. Fixed prices would provide price certainty in the short term. Fixed prices would bring price certainty even in the long term but increase exposure to other risks. In particular, future market prices could be lower or higher than the fixed price. (b) The parties can be exposed to risks also because of the fact that there can be two (or more) relevant prices. This is not unusual in the light of the fact that electricity is generated in one location and consumed in another.

Electricity swaps can be used as a means to change the nature of financial flows. Electricity swaps are traded in the OTC-market.

Terminology The concept of swap contracts is well-known in the financial community. For this reason, there was no need to define swap contracts in MiFID. It is clear that swaps belong to the category of financial contracts according to MiFID[139] and MiFID II.[140] In the US, however, the definition of "swaps" is important because it is used as a normative concept in various ways (Sect. 11.7).

[136] Hsu M (1998), pp. 35–36.

[137] Maribu KM et al. (2007), p. 173; Deng SJ and Oren SS (2006), p. 945.

[138] Waldman AR (1994), pp. 1028–1029.

[139] Section C of Annex I to Directive 2004/39/EC (MiFID).

[140] Section C of Annex I to Directive 2014/65/EU (MiFID II).

11.5.2 Price Swaps

One can distinguish between price swaps and locational basis swaps. A price swap is a contract under which the parties swap price risk exposures over a predetermined period. Price swaps enable the holder to change fixed financial flows into variable ones or variable financial flows into fixed ones. In particular, price swaps enable the holder to pay a fixed price for underlying electricity over the contracted time period where the price of underlying electricity is variable, or to pay a variable price for underlying electricity where its price is fixed.

The two legs of the price swap are thus a fixed payment stream and a variable payment stream. By convention, the party regarded as the buyer of the price swap is the party making the fixed payment. The seller of the swap makes the variable payment. Consequently, the buyer benefits when prices increase and exceed the fixed payment level, and loses when prices decrease and fall below the fixed payment level.

Price Swaps and Futures Price swaps can serve the same economic function as futures contracts. However, there are important differences between price swaps and futures for market participants.

Price swaps are OTC transactions. Unlike electricity futures, the terms of price swaps are *negotiable* rather than standardised. Consequently, swaps can be tailored to meet the needs of the buyer and seller. For instance, the parties may agree on a longer contract term or a larger volume.

Compared with electricity futures, price swaps are *less liquid* and there is *less transparency*. The lack of transparency might enable market participants to hedge large exposures without affecting the market.

For the same reasons, price swaps give rise to a *higher counterparty risk* (credit risk). Market participants can prefer the higher liquidity and transparency of electricity futures when hedging short-term risks.[141]

Use of Price Swaps Price swaps can be used by many physical market participants. They can be used by electricity producers, suppliers, and end customers.

An electricity producer can sell a swap and agree on a fixed price. The producer can then sell electricity in the spot market. The producer receives the spot market price for the electricity that it supplies. The producer pays the spot price to the price swap counterparty and the price swap counterparty—the buyer—pays the agreed fixed price in return. If the variable spot price is lower than the agreed fixed price, the electricity producer is protected against the decrease in price. If the variable spot price is higher than the agreed fixed price, the producer cannot benefit from price increases.

Even an end customer can benefit from a price swap. The end customer can buy a swap and agree on a fixed price. The end customer can then pay a variable price for electricity in the spot market. The end customer receives the variable price from the

[141] For the reasons to use swaps, see Stoft S et al. (1998), section 4.1.

price swap counterparty and pays the fixed price in return. If the variable spot price is higher than the agreed fixed price, the end customer is protected against price increase. If the variable spot price is lower than the agreed fixed price, the end customer cannot benefit from the price decrease.

A supplier can purchase electricity from producers and sell it to end customers. Price swaps can enable it to buy electricity from producers at a fixed price, sell electricity to end customers at a fixed price, and to lock in a profit. The supplier can achieve this in the following way. (a) The supplier sells electricity at a variable price referenced to the spot market price. To transfer the price risk, it buys a price swap. The price swap counterparty pays the agreed fixed price to the supplier, and the supplier pays the variable price to the counterparty. (b) The supplier buys electricity at the variable spot market price. To transfer the price risk, it buys a price swap. The price swap counterparty pays the variable price to the supplier. The supplier pays the agreed fixed price to the counterparty.

The parties must agree on: the fixed price; the determinant of the variable price; the time period covered by the swap; and the notional size of the swap.[142]

Index Swaps The underlying reference entity can also be a commodity index.[143]

11.5.3 Locational Basis Swaps

The other main form of financial electricity swaps is the locational basis swap. Locational basis swaps can also be physical transactions.

Basis swaps are customarily used to lock in a fixed price at a location other than the delivery point of the futures contract. That is, the holder of an electricity basis swap has agreed to either pay or receive the difference between the specified contract price and the locational spot price at the time of the transaction.[144]

Locational Basis Swaps and Futures Like price swaps, locational basis swaps can be used as an alternative to futures contracts. In this case, what is exchanged is not a fixed payment stream and a variable payment stream. Instead, a locational basis swap enables a party to lock in a fixed price at a location other than the delivery point of the futures contract. This may be necessary for risk management purposes where the party is exposed to a price risk in one location but the delivery point of the (standardised) futures contracts is in another location.[145] Electricity locational swaps have also been described as "a strip of electricity forwards with multiple settlement dates and identical forward price for each settlement".[146]

[142] Stoft S et al. (1998), section 4.1.

[143] Fried J (2010), p. 284, point 498.

[144] U.S. Energy Information Administration (2002), Chapter 4.

[145] Stoft S et al. (1998), section 4.2.

[146] Deng SJ and Oren SS (2006), p. 944.

Use of Locational Basis Swaps Like price swaps, locational basis swaps can be used by electricity producers, end customers, suppliers, and middlemen.[147] They are customarily: established for a fixed quantity of power referenced to a variable spot price at either the producer's or the end consumer's location; and used to provide short- to medium-term price certainty up to a couple of years.[148]

When used by the electricity producer for such purposes, the producer enters into three kinds of contracts: (1) futures contracts in location A; (2) spot contracts in location B; (3) locational basis swap contracts with the locational basis swap counterparty. The producer will enter into transactions that will cancel each other out financially with the exception of receiving a fixed price for the supply of electricity in location B.[149]

For instance, both an area price and a system price are used in the Elspot market. The prices may not be identical. CfDs or exchange-traded CfDs (EPADs) could be used in the Nordic market because of the possible difference between the area price and the system price: "To create a perfect hedge against the price differential, a three-step process using CfDs must be used: (1) Hedge the specified volume by using forward contracts. (2) Hedge against the price differential—for the same period and volume—by using CfDs. (3) Accomplish physical procurement by trading in the Elspot area of the holder of the contract".[150] Locational swaps are an alternative.

An end consumer can use the same mechanism. While an electricity producer would sell a futures contracts and sell a basis swap to lock in a fixed price and receive the premium, an end consumer would buy a futures contract and buy a basis swap.[151]

11.5.4 Trading, Clearing, Margins

In principle, highly standardised financial electricity swap contracts could be exchange-traded. In practice, electricity swaps are customarily OTC transactions.

Even OTC-traded electricity swaps can be standardised. When this is the case, they can be subject to clearing and there can be both a central counterparty and margin requirements (see Sects. 4.4.5 and 4.6.2).

In the EU, there is an obligation to trade on regulated markets, MTFs or OTFs where derivatives belong to a class of derivatives that has been declared subject to the trading obligation.[152] There are also mandatory clearing obligations for some OTC derivatives under EMIR.[153]

---

[147] Stoft S et al. (1998), section 4.2.

[148] Deng SJ and Oren SS (2006), p. 944.

[149] Stoft S et al. (1998), section 4.2.

[150] Kristiansen T (2004).

[151] Stoft S et al. (1998), section 4.2.

[152] Article 28 of Regulation 600/2014 (MiFIR).

[153] Article 4(1) of Regulation 648/2012 (EMIR).

In the US, swaps subject to mandatory clearing must also be traded through a board of trade designated as a contract market or on a registered or exempt swap execution facility.[154] However, many swap agreements are exempt transactions.[155]

When electricity swap contracts are not standardised, they can only be OTC transactions. The participation of a central counterparty and a clearing house that requires margins is not necessary for such transactions. Such electricity swaps are customarily governed by the ISDA Master Agreement.

11.6 ISDA Master Agreement

11.6.1 General Remarks

There are bilateral contracts for a single transaction and contracts designed to facilitate multiple transactions. The latter are customarily called master trading agreements. They have become the customary documentary support for OTC transactions in European electricity and gas wholesale markets.[156]

Electricity derivatives that are not standardised are OTC transactions customarily governed by the ISDA Master Agreement that can be applied to a wide range of OTC derivatives.[157]

ISDA[158] is an international organisation founded in 1985 and incorporated in the US. Its mission is to make OTC derivatives markets safe and efficient. According to its mission statement, "ISDA fosters safe and efficient derivatives markets to facilitate effective risk management for all users of derivative products". ISDA's members include a broad range of OTC derivatives market participants. Some of them are energy and commodities firms.

ISDA has helped to reduce credit and legal risk by developing the ISDA Master Agreement and related documentation materials. The first was the 1992 ISDA Master Agreement for parties entering into multiple OTC derivative transactions. There were several 1992 Master Agreements. They were updated by the 2002 ISDA Master Agreement. The several ISDA Master Agreements are here collectively referred to as the ISDA Master Agreement.

There are even other master trading agreements for OTC derivatives. For instance, the German Master Agreement for Financial Derivatives Transactions (Deutscher Rahmenvertrag für Finanztermingeschäfte) was adopted by the Association of German Banks (Bundesverband Deutscher Banken) in 1993.[159] The Master Agreement for

---

154 7 USC §2(h)(8). See also 15 USC §78c-3(h) on clearing for security-based swaps.

155 17 CFR § 35.2 (exempting swap agreements from regulation under the CEA provided they are entered into by eligible swap participants, are customized agreements, the creditworthiness of a party subject to the contract was a material consideration in determining the terms of the agreement, and the agreement was not entered into and traded on or through a multilateral transaction facility).

156 Varholy J and Fuhr T (2009), § 28, number 1.

157 Harding PC (2010), pp. 24–25.

158 International Swaps and Derivatives Association, Inc. See, for example, Mertens CJ (2006), p. 236.

159 Fried J (2010), p. 177, point 287.

Financial Transactions (the European Master Agreement, EMA) is a multi-language, multi-jurisdictional, and multi-product agreement sponsored by the European Banking Federation (EBF) in cooperation with the European Savings Bank Group and the European Association of Cooperative Banks.

Documentation and Incorporation The ISDA contractual framework consists of many documents. First, the parties agree to the ISDA Master Agreement. Second, the ISDA Master Agreement is complemented by a "schedule". The schedule contains terms made necessary by the applicable laws and the party-specific terms of the framework agreement. Third, the core commercial terms are agreed in a "confirmation". Any OTC derivative transaction defined as a transaction in an ISDA-style confirmation is automatically covered by the ISDA Master Agreement.[160] Fourth, ISDA definitions are incorporated by reference. This core documentation is complemented by other documentation.[161]

Risk and Transaction Costs The ISDA Master Agreement is used as a platform to reduce legal risk, counterparty risk, and transaction costs, and to increase liquidity. (a) The ISDA Master Agreement sets forth other than the core commercial terms of the transaction. The parties may thus trade by merely agreeing on the core commercial terms.[162] (b) Moreover, the characteristic core terms of the ISDA Master Agreement are designed to reduce legal risk, counterparty risk, and transaction costs. (c) The law governing the ISDA Master Agreement and the individual transactions is either New York law or English law. The parties may specify the governing law in the Schedule.

A market participant can complement the use of the ISDA Master Agreement with limits such as (a) limits based on the market participant's own generation portfolio or consumption portfolio; (b) term, volume, and value limits for each trader; and (c) pre-approved credit limits for each counterparty.

Core Terms The characteristic core terms of the ISDA Master Agreement relate to close-out netting, termination, and the single agreement principle. We can have a closer look at the key provisions.

11.6.2 Single Agreement

The ISDA Master Agreement lays down the single agreement principle as follows: "[a]ll Transactions are entered into in reliance on the fact that this Master Agreement and all Confirmations form a single agreement between the parties (collectively referred to as this 'Agreement'), and the parties would not otherwise enter

[160] Harding PC (2010), p. 5.

[161] See Harding PC (2010).

[162] Mertens CJ (2006), p. 236.

into any Transactions".[163] There is a similar provision in the EFET General Agreement.[164]

The single agreement principle reduces counterparty risk by increasing incentives to comply with the terms of each individual transaction and the ISDA Master Agreement. If all confirmations and the Master Agreement form a single agreement, the breach of the terms of an individual transaction are regarded as the breach of the terms of the Master Agreement and the terms of all other individual transactions. The single agreement principle could thus be regarded as a functional equivalent of a cross-default clause limited to transactions covered by the ISDA Master Agreement.[165]

The single agreement principle can be used regardless of whether a central counterparty is party to all contracts between market participants.

However, the single agreement principle would not be feasible when contracts are traded on a regulated market. In this case, all transactions are governed by the rules of the market.

The rules adopted by the market operator are designed to reduce both counterparty risk and systemic risk. Systemic risk and counterparty risk are reduced by rules on access to the market (a screening mechanism) as well as by the use of a central counterparty and margin requirements. Although the single agreement principle could increase an individual counterparty's incentives to comply with its obligations, the single agreement principle could also increase systemic risk by increasing the impact of a default rather than reducing it. When the single agreement principle is used, default under one individual transaction is not limited to that particular transaction but will be regarded as default under all transactions that belong to the same contractual relationship.

11.6.3 Default, Early Termination, Close-Out Netting

The clauses of the 2002 ISDA Master Agreement on default, early termination, and close-out netting are designed to mitigate counterparty credit risk.

Termination The 2002 ISDA Master Agreement provides for early termination. Early termination applies to the obligation to make normal payments or deliveries. Early termination does not mean the termination of the "Agreement"—that is, the contractual relationship consisting of the 2002 ISDA Master Agreement framework and the individual transactions.[166] Many obligations survive the early termination.[167]

---

[163] Section 1(c) of the 2002 ISDA Master Agreement.

[164] EFET General Agreement (Version 2.1(a)), § 1.1.

[165] Section 5(a)(vi) of the 2002 ISDA Master Agreement contains an express cross-default clause.

[166] See Harding PC (2010), p. 263.

[167] Section 9(c) of the 2002 ISDA Master Agreement.

The ISDA Master Agreement distinguishes between two forms of early termination. A party may have a right to terminate all outstanding transactions (a) upon the occurrence of a termination event or (b) upon the occurrence of an event of default. The ISDA Master Agreement thus distinguishes between (a) termination events and (b) events of default.[168]

The mechanism of termination depends on whether the event is a termination event or an event of default.

Termination Events The purpose of the list of termination events is to allow a party to close out where the event substantially alters the transaction economics or the risk profile of its counterparty.[169] If a termination event occurs, a party may terminate all outstanding transactions by giving notice of the termination event.

Events of Default If en event of default occurs, a party may give notice of termination, but the parties may also have chosen automatic early termination to govern their contractual relationship.

The 2002 ISDA Master Agreement lists eight events of default.[170] For reasons of risk management, they are not limited to events that traditionally would trigger breaches of contract. For instance, a bankruptcy event is an event of default.[171]

Closing Out The method of calculating payments upon the occurrence of an event of default or termination is closing out. Other methods—the market quotation method and the loss calculation method—were used under the 1992 Agreement.

Close-Out Netting When counterparties use close-out netting, only a small fraction of the notional amount is actually at risk. Close-out netting has contributed to the stability of financial markets.[172]

Close-out netting means the combination of three things. First, all outstanding transactions are terminated immediately (closed out). Second, the obligations of a party are quantified as a close-out amount. Third, the obligations of each party are netted into one payment payable by one party.

Close-out netting is designed to address the risk of "cherry-picking" when one of the parties has become insolvent. Market participants are often engaged in a web of interrelated swap and derivative agreements. An insolvent counterparty is unable to fulfill its part of a transaction. On the other hand, an insolvent counterparty wants to collect the amount owed to it by the non-defaulting party under the same or other transactions. Insolvency administrators may have a right to choose between the performance and non-performance of transactions. Consequently, non-defaulting parties could start defaulting on their own obligations and the market could

[168] See, for example, Mertens CJ (2006), pp. 239–242.

[169] Harding PC (2010), p. 225.

[170] Section 5(a) of the 2002 ISDA Master Agreement. See Harding PC (2010), p. 201.

[171] For financial institutions in Germany, see also § 46 a I KWG. Fried J (2010), pp. 219–221, point 365 and point 365a.

[172] Waldman AR (1994), p. 1032.

collapse. This will not happen when close-out netting clauses are valid and enforceable.

The ISDA Master Agreement would have little practical effect as a useful risk management tool unless the close-out netting provisions were recognised in the relevant jurisdiction.[173] In the EU, this is facilitated by the Settlement Finality Directive[174] and the Collateral Directive.[175]

11.6.4 Settlement

OTC derivatives are settled in many ways. As the ISDA Master Agreement is designed to be used in a large number of different kinds of derivative transactions, it does not regulate settlement in detail.[176]

The ISDA Master Agreement allows counterparties to select from a number of elective settlement and payment procedures. The ISDA Master Agreement contains a netting clause designed to reduce settlement risk.[177] Only the net amount will be payable on the scheduled payment date. Netting means that smaller sums are at risk.[178]

The parties may elect to extend the scope of netting to multiple transactions (Multiple Transaction Payment Netting).[179]

11.7 Excursion: The Definition of "Swaps" in the US

For reasons of clarity, it is necessary to study the definition of "swaps" in the US. There are many statutory definitions. They are defined in detail in the Commodity Exchange Act.[180] "Security-based swaps" are defined in the Securities Exchange Act.[181] For instance, the definitions include even master agreements for swaps. The concept of swap is also used in other statutes such as the Commodity Futures Modernization Act (CFMA), the Dodd-Frank Act (Dodd-Frank Wall Street Reform and Consumer Protection Act), and the US Bankruptcy Code.

---

173 See, for example, Waldman AR (1994), pp. 1058–1062.

174 Articles 3(1) and 10(1) of Directive 98/26/EC (Directive on settlement finality).

175 Directive 2002/47/EC (Directive on financial collateral arrangements).

176 For payments, see section 2(a)(ii) of the 2002 ISDA Master Agreement.

177 Section 2(c) of the 2002 ISDA Master Agreement.

178 See Harding PC (2010), pp. 12 and 181; duPont JC (2009), p. 847.

179 Section 2(c) of the 2002 ISDA Master Agreement.

180 The Commodity Exchange Act—7 U.S.C. §1a(47).

181 For "security-based swaps" (SBS), see the Securities Exchange Act of 1934—15 U.S.C. §78c (a)(68).

CFMA The purpose of the CFMA was to provide legal certainty for swap agreements. The CFMA prohibited the SEC (the Securities and Exchange Commission) and the CFTC (the Commodity Futures Trading Commission) from regulating OTC swaps markets. The SEC got some anti-fraud authority over "security-based swap agreements" such as credit default swaps. However, the authority of the SEC was limited. This also limited the SEC's ability to detect and deter fraud in the swap markets.

Dodd-Frank Act The Dodd-Frank Act addresses the gap in the regulation of OTC swaps. The Dodd-Frank Act divides regulatory authority over swap agreements between the CFTC and the SEC in four ways. First, the SEC has regulatory authority over "security-based swaps". Security-based swaps are included within the definition of "security" under the Securities Exchange Act of 1934 and the Securities Act of 1933. Second, the CFTC has regulatory authority over all other swaps. It has therefore authority over energy swaps. Third, the CFTC and SEC share authority over "mixed swaps". They are security-based swaps that also have a commodity component. Fourth, the SEC has anti-fraud enforcement authority also over "security-based swap agreements". They are swaps that are related to securities but that do not come within the definition of "security-based swap".

The Dodd-Frank Act defines the terms "swap", "security-based swap", "mixed-swap", and "security-based swap agreements".[182] The CTFC and the SEC may further define them.[183]

However, the existence of these normative concepts made it necessary to define even related concepts. For instance, are futures swaps for the purposes of law? The CTFC declined to adopt a rule to distinguish between swaps and futures. Instead of a transparent test, the CTFC applies a case-by-case approach.[184] One can also point out that the CFTC extended the scope of the Brent Interpretation[185] and withdraw its 1993 Energy Exemption.[186]

US Bankruptcy Code Swaps are used as a normative concept even in the US Bankruptcy Code. Certain transfers from the debtor that otherwise would be subject to preference or constructive fraudulent transfer liability are exempted from avoidance under sections 546(e) and (g) of the Bankruptcy Code. "Swap agreements" belong to the contracts that can be exempted.[187] There is a detailed definition of swap agreements in the Bankruptcy Code.[188]

---

[182] Sections 721(a) and 761(a) of the Dodd-Frank Act.

[183] 77 FR 48208 (August 13, 2012). CFTC and SEC, Further Definition of "Swap", "Security-Based Swap", and "Security-Based Swap Agreement"; Mixed Swaps; Security-Based Swap Agreement Recordkeeping.

[184] *Supra*, VIII.A.

[185] Statutory Interpretation Concerning Forward Transactions, 55 FR 39188 (September 25, 1990) (Brent Interpretation).

[186] Exemption for Certain Contracts Involving Energy Products, 58 FR 21286-02 (April 20, 1993) (Energy Exemption).

[187] 11 U.S.C. § 546(e) and 11 U.S.C. § 546(g).

[188] 11 U.S.C. § 101(53B).

"Commodity forward agreements" are regarded as "swap agreements" under the Bankruptcy Code.[189] (a) For this reason, a commodity forward contract might contain the following clause in the US: "Your commodity supply agreement with the debtor is a swap agreement and therefore the transfers you received cannot be avoided".[190] (b) In the case *In re National Gas Distributors, Inc.*, the Bankruptcy Court had held that contracts that related to the purchase and sale of physical gas were not "commodity forward agreements" under the Code because they were not sufficiently tied to financial markets. However, the US Court of Appeals for the Fourth Circuit reversed the ruling and found that a natural gas supply agreement could be regarded as a "commodity forward agreement" and, for the purposes of the Bankruptcy Code, an exempted "swap agreement", although it was individually negotiated, physically settled, and not traded on any exchange or in a market. (c) The Court did not provide a definition of "commodity forward agreement" in its decision. However, the Court identified four characteristics of a "commodity forward agreement" that the Bankruptcy Court may find influential in reaching its determination on remand.

References

Cahill CM (2011) Commodity supply agreements are swap agreements: a counterintuitive but quite real safe harbour from preference avoidance. Int Corporate Rescue 8(4):268–277

Carmona R, Durrleman V (2003) Pricing and hedging spread options. SIAM Rev 45(4):627–685

Deng SJ, Oren SS (2006) Electricity derivatives and risk management. Energy 31(6–7):940–953. doi:10.1016/j.energy.2005.02.015

DG Energy, Market Observatory for Energy (2013) Quarterly Report on European Electricity Markets 6(2)

duPont JC (2009) A second chance at legal certainty: AIG collapse provides impetus to regulate credit default swaps. Admin Law Rev 61(4):843–870

Energy Market Authority, Finland (2014) National report 2014 to the agency for the Cooperation of Energy Regulators and to the European Commission, 10 July

Fried J (2010) B. Rechtliche Bewältigung des OTC-Handels. In: Schwintowski HP (ed) Handbuch Energiehandel, 2nd edn. Erich Schmidt Verlag, Berlin, pp 153–336

Harding PC (2010) Mastering the ISDA master agreements: a practical guide for negotiation, 3rd edn. Pearson Education Limited, Harlow

Hsu M (1998) Spark spread options are hot. Electr J 11(2):28–39. doi:10.1016/S1040-6190(98)00004-9

Hünerwadel A (2007) Arten und Formen des Stromhandels, insbesondere Börsen- und Derivathandel. In: Weber RH (ed) Stromhandel. Schulthess, Zürich, pp 49–64

IMF (2013) Global financial stability report: old risks, new challenges. International Monetary Fund, Washington DC, April

ISDA (2003) Restoring confidence in U.S. energy trading markets. ISDA website, April

ISDA (2011) Re: notice of proposed rulemaking – position limits for derivatives. Letter to Commodity Futures Trading Commission, October 3

Khoury SJ (1984) Speculative markets. Macmillan Publishing Co., New York

---

[189] 11 U.S.C. § 101(53B).

[190] Cahill CM (2011), p. 268.

Kristiansen T (2004) Pricing of contracts for difference in the Nordic market. Energy Policy 32(9): 1075–1085. doi:10.1016/S0301-4215(03)00065-X
Lokau B, Ritzau M (2009) Der Markt für Strom (empirische Darstellung). In: Zenke I, Schäfer R (eds) Energiehandel in Europa. Öl, Gas, Strom, Derivate, Zertifikate, 2nd edn. C.H. Beck, München, § 5
Mäntysaari P (2010a) The law of corporate finance. General principles and EU law, vol I: Cash flow, risk, agency, information. Springer, Heidelberg
Mäntysaari P (2010b) The law of corporate finance. General principles and EU law, vol II: Contracts I General. Springer, Heidelberg
Mäntysaari P (2012) Organising the firm: theories of commercial law, corporate governance and corporate law. Springer, Heidelberg
Maribu KM, Galli A, Armstrong M (2007) Valuation of spark-spread options with mean reversion and stochastic volatility. Int J Electr Bus Manag 5(3):173–181
Mertens CJ (2006) Australian insolvency law and the 1992 ISDA master agreement – catalyst, reaction, and solution. Pac Rim Law Policy J 15(1):232–264
NordREG (2010) The Nordic financial electricity market. Report 8/2010
OECD Trade and Agriculture Directorate (2010) Speculation and Financial Fund Activity, Draft Report, April 27
Ofgem (2009) Liquidity in the GB wholesale energy markets, 8 June
Pirrong C (2001) Manipulation of cash-settled futures contracts. J Bus 74(2):221–244. doi:10.1086/209671
Rud L (2009) Essays on electricity markets, SNF Report No. 10/09. Online version. Institute for Research in Economics and Business Administration. Available at SNF website. http://www.snf.no/
Spicker J (2010) A. Formen des OTC-Handels. In: Schwintowski HP (ed) Handbuch Energiehandel, 2nd edn. Erich Schmidt Verlag, Berlin, pp 31–152
Stoft S, Belden TN, Goldman CA, Pickle SJ (1998) Primer on electricity futures and other derivatives. Environmental Energy Technologies Division, Ernest Orlando Lawrence Berkeley National Laboratory, University of California, Berkeley
U.S. Energy Information Administration (2002) Derivatives and risk management in the petroleum, Natural Gas, and Electricity Industries, October
Varholy J, Fuhr T (2009) The evolution of master agreements for the forward trading of wholesale, physical energy commodities in Europe. In: Zenke I, Schäfer R (eds) Energiehandel in Europa. Öl, Gas, Strom, Derivate, Zertifikate, 2nd edn. C.H. Beck, München, § 28
Waldman AR (1994) OTC derivatives & systemic risk: innovative finance or the dance into the abyss? Am Univ Law Rev 43(3):1023–1090

Chapter 12
Financial Derivatives on Transmission Capacity

12.1 General Remarks

The choice of products for hedging transmission risk depends on how transmission capacity is allocated.

Market-Based Allocation Methods In the EU, the Target Model is the use of market-based methods for the short-term or long-term allocation of cross-border or cross-zonal transmission capacity (Sect. 5.6). Market-based methods mean the use of explicit auctions, implicit auctions, or both. Continuous trading may be used for intraday trade.[1] Long-term cross-zonal transmission capacity must be allocated to market participants in the form of physical transmission rights (PTRs) or financial transmission rights (FTRs).[2]

Not Market-Based Allocation Methods Methods that are not market-based include, for instance, the reservation of transmission capacity under long-term contracts, the first-come-first-serve mechanism, and pro-rata allocation.

When transmission capacity is allocated for electricity flows in the more distant future, it is customary to use a combination of market-based and not market-based mechanisms (for very long-term capacity allocation, see Sect. 5.6.3).

Products Wholesale electricity market participants can use various kinds of financial contracts to hedge transmission price risk. They may use financial products for congestion alleviation, that is, FTRs and contracts for difference (CfDs). A US alternative would be to use particular transmission congestion contracts (TCCs).

Many products can be functional equivalents depending on the case. It may be possible to achieve the same commercial result with FTRs, CfDs and PTRs. While

---

[1] Article 12(2) of Regulation 714/2009 on conditions for access to the network for cross-border exchanges in electricity. See also Articles 2.1 and 2.8 of Annex I Guidelines on the management and allocation of available transfer capacity of interconnections between national systems.

[2] Article 36(1) of ENTSO-E NC FCA (2 April 2014).

P. Mäntysaari, *EU Electricity Trade Law*, DOI 10.1007/978-3-319-16513-4_12

PTRs may allow market participants deliver electricity power across borders for a fixed price, FTRs may provide a pay out to the holder of the right representing the price difference across the border. Therefore, capacity rights do not absolutely need to be physical.[3]

Market Imperfections In financial markets, many parties are both buyers and sellers of derivatives. Derivatives on electricity transmission capacity are different. The market is one-sided, because most market participants need to by protection. TSOs are natural sellers of transmission capacity rights and the only players in a position to offer the required firm transmission hedges.[4] Moreover, the development of a liquid market for financial transmission contracts would require the existence of a sound underlying physical market. In the absence of such a physical market, the seller would have to accept a speculative risk. As a result, the risk premiums would be high and unacceptable for market participants.[5]

In the following, we will study the use of physical transmission rights (PTRs, Sect. 12.2), financial transmission rights (FTRs, Sect. 12.3), contracts for difference (CfDs, Sect. 12.4), and transmission congestion contracts (TCCs, Sect. 12.6).

12.2 Physical Transmission Rights

Physical transmission rights (PTRs) are option contracts. They provide the option to transport a certain volume of electricity in a certain period between two areas in a specific direction.[6] In principle, the holder of PTRs might prefer to withhold these rights from the market and reduce the capacity of the congested interface.[7] To prevent this, PTRs are complemented by the use-it-or-sell-it principle (UIOSI, see Sect. 5.6.3). According to the UIOSI principle, the holder of the PTR may either use capacity by nominating it or receive an automatic payout for capacity that it has not nominated.[8] The UIOSI mechanism thus means that not nominated capacities will automatically be sold in the day-ahead market.

Explicit Auctions PTRs can be used both in explicit as well as in implicit auctions but in different ways.

[3] EFET (2007), Executive summary. See also ACER, Framework Guidelines on Capacity Allocation and Congestion Management for Electricity (29 July 2011), section 4.1.

[4] EFET (2006, 2007).

[5] EFET (2006) explains how Nord Pool failed to make contracts for location price differences work in 2006.

[6] Generally, see Duthaler C and Finger M (2008), section 1.1.

[7] Joskow PL and Tirole J (1999b); Joskow PL and Tirole J (2000), p. 453,

[8] See point 2.5 of Annex I to Regulation 714/2009; Articles 36(1) and 2(1) of ENTSO-E Network Code on Forward Capacity Allocation (2 April 2014).

In an explicit auction, a TSO auctions off available cross-border or cross-zonal transmission capacity to market participants through PTRs. Regulation 714/2009 provides that rights to transmission capacity must be firm and subject to the use-it-or-lose-it (UIOLI) or use-it-or-sell-it (UIOSI) principle at the time of nomination.[9]

> The available transmission capacity is allocated in the form of PTRs with UIOSI in explicit closed auctions for the purpose of allocating cross-border transmission capacity in an area that consists of CWE (the Central Western Europe Region), the CSE (the Central Southern Europe Region), and Switzerland. Capacity is auctioned on a yearly, monthly, and daily basis.[10] Not nominated capacities are automatically resold to the relevant daily allocation.[11] The available transmission capacity is auctioned by a Joint Auction Office. In practice, the TSOs have outsourced parts of their tasks to CASC.EU S.A. acting as the Joint Auction Office.[12]

Implicit Auctions The use of implicit auction mechanisms means that the market participant does not need to purchase transmission capacity separately. Implicit auctions are based on the use of different electricity price areas (market splitting) with electricity prices that depend on the amount of congestion. Electricity prices are equal between two areas when there is no congestion but different in the event of congestion.

Implicit auctions for the allocation of cross-border transmission capacity have been used in radial parts of the grid (such as EMCC) or between radially aligned countries (such as MIBEL and TLC) in the past. Transmission capacity was first allocated by TSOs to power exchanges in the form of PTRs. The power exchanges matched the PTRs to trades implicitly.[13] NWE price coupling is based on the use of such implicit auctions.[14]

12.3 Financial Transmission Rights

Financial transmission rights (FTRs) are connected with the electricity price difference between different locations of the network (different nodes). (a) Electricity buyers and sellers submit bids to the system operator to buy and sell power at

[9] Point 2.5 of Annex I to Regulation 714/2009.

[10] CWE Auction Rules, Version 1.0, Articles 1.04 and 8.01. See also ENTSO-E (2012), section 2.1.

[11] CWE Auction Rules, Version 1.0, Article 8.01. See ENTSO-E (2012), section 2.1.

[12] CWE Auction Rules, Version 1.0, Article 1.03.

[13] Duthaler C and Finger M (2008), section 1.1.

[14] See EPEX Spot Exchange Rules (28 November 2014), Title 1, Preamble. APX Power NL Market Rules, Version 3.0 (20 January 2014), section 1.3, Nord Pool Spot Market, Trading Appendix 1, Definitions (27 November 2014).

different nodes. The system operator chooses the lowest cost bids to balance electricity supply and demand subject to physical laws and the available transmission capacity. The bid price at a node becomes the market clearing price at the node. An upstream supplier that supplies power to customers downstream of the congested interface receives a lower net price than do suppliers located downstream in proximity to consumers. The difference between the downstream price and the upstream price is the congestion price.[15] (b) Holders of financial rights over the congested interface receive a share of the congestion revenues.[16]

Financial transmission rights (FTRs) are either option contracts or obligations. In both cases, they are settled financially. FTR options entitle their holder to receive a financial compensation equal to the positive (if any) market price differential between two areas during a specified time period in a specific direction. In addition, FTR obligations even oblige their holder to pay for a negative market price differential.[17] Flowgate FTRs or flowgate rights (FGR) are a particular form of FTRs (see Sect. 5.5).[18]

A market participant can benefit from FTRs in different ways. (a) Where an electricity producer upstream of the congested interface has covered all of its deliveries by acquiring FTRs, it is in the same position as an electricity producer that has acquired enough physical transmission rights to cover its deliveries. (b) Where an electricity producer has market power in the importing area, holding FTRs can increase its market power. If an electricity producer has market power in the exporting area, holding FTRs does not enhance its market power or affect prices paid by consumers.[19]

Italian Market FTRs have been used in the Italian electricity market.[20] While consumers pay the same spot market price (the Single National Price, SNP) for electricity throughout Italy, producers are grouped into geographical zones. Producers can hedge the difference between the zonal price and the SNP by acquiring FTRs auctioned by Terna. Such a FTR is called CCC (Contract Covering the Risk of Volatility of the Fee for Assignment of Rights of Use of Transmission Capacity).[21]

Excursion: PJM and the Use of FTRs in the US There is nevertheless more experience in the US. FTRs are widely used in the US as an integral part of the provision of firm transmission service. They can only be created by RTOs/ISOs. PJM is one of the RTOs that use FTRs (Sect. 5.7.4). Other RTOs or ISOs make

---

[15] Joskow PL and Tirole J (1999a).

[16] Joskow PL and Tirole J (1999a).

[17] ENTSO-E (2012) Executive Summary.

[18] Deng SJ and Oren SS (2006), section 2.4.2.

[19] Joskow PL and Tirole J (2000), pp. 452–453; Joskow PL and Tirole J (1999a)

[20] See ENTSO-E (2012), section 2.2.

[21] Duthaler C and Finger M (2008), section 2.1.

available similar products although the products may have different names depending on the RTO or ISO.[22]

In the past, PJM, CAISO (in California), and ERCOT (in Texas) used to apply a flow-based model that was based on the contract-path fiction. The system operator (RTO or ISO) allocated path-dependent PTRs. However, it was not possible to maintain the contract-path fiction in a meshed grid without several simplifying assumptions. The assumptions turned out to be unsustainable.

The three markets therefore replaced the flow-based model with a point-to-point model. The system operator computes locational marginal prices for each network node. To offset or hedge congestion costs, the market participants can acquire FTRs issued by the system operator. FTR auctions are governed by tariff rules set by FERC. FTRs are funded by the congestion rent (i.e., the price differences between grid nodes) collected by the system operator.[23]

The use of FTRs is based on FERC regulation and the Energy Policy Act of 2005. FTRs help to facilitate equitable access to the transmission grid. (a) Section 217 of the Energy Policy Act of 2005 (the "native load" provision) provides that FERC must exercise its authority in a manner that "enables load-serving entities to secure firm transmission rights (or equivalent tradable or financial transmission rights) on a long term basis for long term power supply arrangements made, or planned, to meet such needs". (b) These "firm transmission rights, or equivalent tradable or financial transmission rights" are designed to be used by load-serving entities "to the extent required to meet the service obligation of the load serving entity", that is, "to deliver the output or purchased energy, or the output of other generating facilities or purchased energy".[24] (c) They are also transferable to the extent that the service obligation is transferred to another load-serving entity.[25]

Because of transferability, FTRs can be used by various kinds of transmission customers. Both electricity suppliers and consumers can use them to hedge their congestion costs.[26]

First, they are designed to be used by electricity suppliers, that is, load-serving entities that are transmission customers. Utilities (also known as local distribution companies or LDCs) have preferential access to FTRs.

> In *Pennsylvania-New Jersey-Maryland Interconnection*,[27] FERC found that FTRs "provide an effective method of protecting against incurrence of congestion costs when suppliers engage in transactions that use their firm transmission service reservations".[28]

---

[22] US Senate Committee on Energy and Natural Resources (2010), statement of Vincent P. Duane.

[23] Duthaler C and Finger M (2008), section 1.1.

[24] Section 217(b)(2) of the Energy Policy Act of 2005.

[25] Section 217(b)(3)(A) and section 217(b)(3)(B) of the Energy Policy Act of 2005.

[26] US Senate Committee on Energy and Natural Resources (2010), statement of Joseph T. Kelliher.

[27] 81 FERC 61,257 (1997).

[28] 81 FERC 61,257 (1997) at 62,257, 62,260. FERC also concluded that PJM's allocation of FTRs to transmission providers "to meet native load requirements (i.e. the customers for whom the transmission grid was planned and constructed in the first instance)" was appropriate. Id. 62,260.

Second, excess FTRs can also be bought by other transmission customers. The FTRs auctioned by the RTOs are those that have not already been claimed by the LDCs.[29]

> In *Pennsylvania-New Jersey-Maryland Interconnection*,[30] FERC found that there needed to be "a process for auctioning FTRs beyond those retained by ... transmission customers".[31] For example, FERC has accepted PJM's design of an FTR auction process that would both (i) provide a means to distribute excess FTRs, and (ii) allow FTR holders the choice to sell those FTRs which they had been allocated and buy FTRs on different pathways that might more effectively hedge their power supply procurements.[32]

These FTRs are not like customary derivatives in the financial market. (a) These FTRs are both constrained by physical flows and finite. They reflect the physical capability of the transmission system to deliver electricity. In contrast to derivatives in the financial market, the underlying physical transactions must be physically feasible.[33] In a nutshell, these FTRs "provide the holder a right to deliver power from point A to point B with protection against the risk that prices at point B might be higher than at point A".[34] (b) They can only be created by RTOs/ISOs and their number is determined by the relevant RTO/ISO.[35] (c) They are based on the point-to-point model. A point-to-point FTR is specified over any two locations in the power transmission grid.[36] The FTR is the means by which PJM as a transmission provider discharges its obligation to provide firm transmission service under FERC's open access regime.[37] (d) In the absence of congestion, no FTRs would be necessary as there would not be any price difference between different grid points. Unlike financial institutions that try to expand the market for the instruments they sell, RTOs/ISOs try to reduce the need for FTRs by enhancing the physical capability of the grid.[38] (e) Buyers of FTRs are not matched with sellers. FTRs are allocated by RTOs/ISOs. (f) There is no material exposure to systemic risk. For this reason, positions are not marked-to-market by the RTO/ISO and there is no method for variation margining. (g) FTRs are neither cleared nor settled according to the

---

[29] US Senate Committee on Energy and Natural Resources (2010), statement of Joseph T. Kelliher.

[30] 81 FERC 61,257 (1997).

[31] Id. 62,260.

[32] PJM Interconnection, L.L.C., 87 FERC 61,054 (1999). See US Senate Committee on Energy and Natural Resources (2010), statement of Vincent P. Duane.

[33] US Senate Committee on Energy and Natural Resources (2010), statement of Joseph T. Kelliher.

[34] US Senate Committee on Energy and Natural Resources (2010), statement of Vincent P. Duane. Citing Pennsylvania—New Jersey—Maryland Interconnection, 81 FERC 61,257 at 62,240–241 (1997).

[35] US Senate Committee on Energy and Natural Resources (2010), statement of Vincent P. Duane.

[36] Deng SJ, Oren SS (2006) section 2.4.1; ENTSO-E (2012), section 2.3.1.

[37] US Senate Committee on Energy and Natural Resources (2010), statement of Vincent P. Duane.

[38] US Senate Committee on Energy and Natural Resources (2010), statement of Vincent P. Duane.

core principles for "derivatives clearing organizations" under the Commodity Exchange Act.[39] There is no CFTC-registered clearinghouse.[40]

12.4 Contracts for Difference

In contracts for difference (CfDs), the underlying value is the price difference between two reference prices. The buyer of the contract will receive money from the seller where the price difference is positive and pay the difference to the seller where the difference is negative.[41]

The Nordic Market The use of CfDs can be illustrated with the Nordic market. The Nordic spot market consists of several bidding areas each with its own area price and a system price. The system price represents the common Nordic price that would have been achieved in the spot market had there been just one bidding area for the whole Nordic area. There can be a difference between area prices and the system price because of congestion. Market participants are thus exposed to a system price risk and an area price risk.

Market participants have several alternatives. (a) One alternative could be to keep the local area price risk and only hedge the system price risk with system price derivatives. (b) On the other hand, CfDs can be used for hedging the area price against the system price.

The value of Nordic CfDs is determined by the difference between a certain area price and the system price. (c) Market participants can manage both the area price risk and the system price risk and get a perfect hedge by using a combination of CfDs and forward contracts with the system price as the reference price.[42]

Exchange-traded CfDs are called Electricity Price Area Differentials (EPAD).[43] The clearing house (NASDAQ OMX Stockholm AB) acts as the counterparty to both the buyer and the seller once a trade is done on the exchange or once an OTC trade is registered for clearing.[44]

The Spanish–Portuguese Border There are CfDs also for the price difference between Spain and Portugal.[45]

---

[39] CEA Sec. 5b(c)(2), 7 U.S.C. § 7a-1(c)(2).

[40] US Senate Committee on Energy and Natural Resources (2010), statement of Vincent P. Duane.

[41] ENTSO-E (2012), Executive Summary.

[42] *Ibid*, section 2.4.1.

[43] NASDAQ OMX, Trading Appendix 1/Clearing Appendix 1, Definitions, Commodity Derivatives (7 April 2014): "... Electricity Price Area Differential or EPAD means a contract specified as such in the Contract Specifications, and is the price difference, in the currency of the contract, for 1 MWh of electricity between the daily Elspot System Price for the Nordic region or the Phelix German System price for the German-Austrian region and the applicable Area Price (as specified in the Series Designation) ..."

[44] Generally, see NordREG (2010), p. 18.

[45] ENTSO-E (2012), section 2.5.1.

12.5 Hedging

Products for the hedging of transmission risk have different characteristics. One can distinguish between two categories of products: (a) products used for hedging purposes; and (b) products used for speculation purposes.[46]

Complete Hedge For hedging purposes, a market participant that is active in two areas could use FTR obligations or CfDs. Both can provide a perfect hedge but prevent their holder from benefiting from price differences.[47]

On one hand, the market participant could make itself insensitive to price differences between two zones by using FTR obligations. The profits and losses would cancel each other out.

On the other, the market participant could use a combination of system price derivatives and CfDs in a given area. For instance, where the market participant generates in one area and sells or consumes in another, the market participant can hedge its positions in both areas. It can sell CfDs in the area where it generates. It can buy CfDs in the area where it sells or consumes.

Hedge and Options For hedging purposes, a market participant could also use physical transmission contracts with the use-it-or-sell-it mechanism (PTRs with UIOSI) and financial transmission rights as options (FTR options). Both can enable the market participant to benefit from price differences.[48]

First, the market participant can purchase PTRs to perform its obligations under a physical electricity supply contract. PTRs entitle their holder to carry out electricity transfers in one direction between two market areas. The market participant has price certainty in this case.

Second, the market participant can cover price differences between the two market areas by using PTRs with UIOSI in the opposite direction without nominating the PTRs. In this case, PTRs with UIOSI are functional equivalents of FTR options.

Speculation The same products can be used for the purpose of speculation. (a) PTRs with UIOSI and FTR options provide the same potential benefits. (b) FTR obligations and CfDs are combined with a higher risk exposure as holders bear the risk of having to pay negative price differences.[49]

Counterparty Risk Exposure to counterparty risk depends on the product. (a) The seller's exposure to counterparty risk is higher in CfD transactions and FTR obligation transactions as the holder not only pays the premium but may have to pay the negative difference to the seller. (b) The seller's exposure to counterparty

---

[46] ENTSO-E (2012), section 3.2.

[47] ENTSO-E (2012), section 3.2.

[48] ENTSO-E (2012), section 3.2.

[49] ENTSO-E (2012), section 3.2.

risk is lower in PTR or FTR option transactions. The seller is nevertheless exposed to the risk that the holder does not pay the price of the acquired transmission rights.

Counterparty risk can be mitigated by the use of margining, collateral (cash deposits or bank guarantees), and a central counterparty. It would be particularly important for CfD and FTR obligation transactions.[50]

12.6 Transmission Congestion Contracts

Transmission Congestion Contracts (TCCs) enable energy sellers and buyers to hedge transmission price fluctuations. TCCs are used by the New York Independent System Operator (NYISO) in the US. The NYISO TCC system has been operating since the spring of 2000.

NYISO TCCs are financial derivatives that can be freely traded both by market participants and by speculators. TCCs can be created when locational marginal cost pricing is the pricing model for the use of short-term transmission capacity. In the US, an independent system operator (ISO) determines the locational prices.[51]

A TCC holder has either the right to collect or the obligation to pay the difference between the spot price of electricity at two specified locations, the point of injection and the point of withdrawal. The difference between the spot prices is the transmission charge between these two points. The holder of a TCC thus has either the right to collect congestion rents or the duty to pay them. System operators are in the best position to issue TCCs.

Because TCCs can be long-term contracts, they enable a market participant to lock in part of its transmission costs.[52]

12.7 Secondary Market

The role of the secondary market depends on the product. (a) CfDs are sold and re-sold continuously. There is just one market and no distinction between a primary and secondary market for CfDs. (b) A secondary market for long-term rights would give market participants a chance to adjust their position.[53] PTRs with UIOSI are a move towards a secondary market as not nominated capacities will be sold. The existence of a working secondary market would require the use of FTRs. (c) Both FTRs and TCCs are used in the US. NYISO TCCs are financial derivatives that can be freely traded both by market participants and by speculators. FERC requires

[50] ENTSO-E (2012), section 3.5.

[51] Hogan WW (1999), pp. 33–45.

[52] Green R (2003), pp. 145 and 147.

[53] ENTSO-E (2012), section 3.6.

ISOs to operate a secondary market for rights, but does not recommend a structure for this market.[54]

References

Bartholomew ES, Siddiqui AS, Marnay C, Oren SS (2003) The New York transmission congestion contract market: is it truly working efficiently? Electr J 16(9):14–24. doi:10.1016/j.tej.2003.09.006

Deng SJ, Oren SS (2006) Electricity derivatives and risk management. Energy 31(6–7):940–953. doi:10.1016/j.energy.2005.02.015

Duthaler C, Finger M (2008) Financial transmission rights in Europe's electricity market. Ecole Polytechnique Fédérale de Lausanne and Delft University of Technology, Discussion paper series on the coherence between institutions and technologies in infrastructures, WP0803. http://mir.epfl.ch/webdav/site/mir/users/181931/public/wp0803.pdf

EFET (2006) More transmission capacity for European cross border electricity transactions without building new infrastructure: Improving firmness of capacity rights and maximizing capacity allocation using new Regulatory incentives for transmission system operators. May

EFET (2007) Key principles in the treatment of electricity transmission capacity rights and their linkage to day ahead allocation mechanisms. June

ENTSO-E (2012) Transmission risk hedging products – an ENTSO-E educational paper. Updated Version, 20 June

ENTSO-E Network Code on Forward Capacity Allocation (2 April 2014)

Green R (2003) Cost recovery and the efficient development of the grid. In: Lévêque F (ed) Transport pricing of electricity networks. Kluwer, Boston, pp 137–153. doi:10.1007/978-1-4757-3756-1_5

Hogan WW (1999) A concurrent auction model for transmission congestion contracts. In: Weyant J (ed) Energy and environmental policy modeling. International Series in Operations Research & Management Science, vol 18. Kluwer, Boston

Joskow PL, Tirole J (1999a) Transmission rights and market power on electric power networks I: financial rights. Centre for Economic Policy Research, Discussion Paper No. 2093

Joskow PL, Tirole J (1999b) Transmission rights and market power on electric power networks II: physical rights. Centre for Economic Policy Research, Discussion Paper No. 2087

Joskow PL, Tirole J (2000) Transmission rights and market power on electric power networks. RAND J Econ 31(3):450–487

NordREG (2010) The Nordic financial electricity market. Report 8/2010

US Senate Committee on Energy and Natural Resources (2010) Financial Derivatives on Energy Markets. Senate Hearing 111-752. The U.S. Government Printing Office, Washington

[54] Bartholomew ES et al. (2003).

MIX
Papier aus verantwortungsvollen Quellen
Paper from responsible sources
FSC® C105338
FSC
www.fsc.org

If you have any concerns about our products,
you can contact us on
ProductSafety@springernature.com

In case Publisher is established outside the EU,
the EU authorized representative is:
Springer Nature Customer Service Center GmbH
Europaplatz 3, 69115 Heidelberg, Germany

Printed by Libri Plureos GmbH
in Hamburg, Germany